PENGUIN MODERN CLASSICS

Mahatma Gandhi: The Great Indian Way

RAJA RAO, a path-breaker of Indian writing in English, was born in Hassan, Mysore. He was awarded the Padma Vibhushan, the Sahitya Akademi Award and the Neustadt International Prize for Literature.

Select Acclaim for Raja Rao's Books

KANTHAPURA
'Perhaps the best novel in English to come from India.'

E.M. Forster

'Perhaps the most brilliant—and certainly the most interesting—writer of modern India . . . It has all the content of an ancient Indian classic.'
The New York Times Book Review

THE SERPENT AND THE ROPE
'Magnificent . . . Packed with the real magic of poetry . . . A truly contemporary work—one by which an age can measure itself, its values.'
Lawrence Durrell

'Defies the reviewer's word limits . . . A book to read and re-read.'
The Times, London

THE CAT AND SHAKESPEARE
'The most mature of his novels . . . a profound vision of life for our entire fragmentary civilisation.'

C.D. Narasimhaiah

COMRADE KIRILLOV
'An unforgettable character for whom Marxism is a metaphysics . . . an interesting incursion into the mind of a great writer.'
World Literature Today, USA

THE CHESSMASTER AND HIS MOVES
'*Chessmaster* is an *ouevre* which evaluates, situates, a period on many levels—a major work.'

Kathleen Raine in *Temenos*, London

'It is to masters like Proust and Joyce that we must turn for a writer of comparable stature . . . a metaphysical novel without equal in our time.'
R. Parathasarathy

ON THE GANGA GHAT
'The work of a master.'

Khushwant Singh

THE MEANING OF INDIA
'A wonderfully engaging and stimulating book . . . most important . . . a portent for our age.'

Indian Review of Books

RAJA RAO

Mahatma Gandhi
THE GREAT INDIAN WAY

With a new Introduction
by Makarand R. Paranjape

PENGUIN BOOKS
An imprint of Penguin Random House

PENGUIN BOOKS

USA | Canada | UK | Ireland | Australia
New Zealand | India | South Africa | China

Penguin Books is part of the Penguin Random House group of companies
whose addresses can be found at global.penguinrandomhouse.com

Published by Penguin Random House India Pvt. Ltd
7th Floor, Infinity Tower C, DLF Cyber City,
Gurgaon 122 002, Haryana, India

Published in Penguin Books by Penguin Random House India 2020

ISBN 9780143448594

Typeset in Adobe Garamond Pro by Manipal Technologies Limited, Manipal
Printed at Replika Press Pvt. Ltd, India

www.penguin.co.in

Contents

Introduction to the New Edition

1

The twenty-fourth of March 1997. I am sitting on the floor in front of Raja Rao in his small apartment on Pearl Street, Austin. He is reclining comfortably in his bed, which somehow seems too large for him. Rao is a small, distinguished-looking man, with fine features, aquiline nose, and longish, unkempt white hair.

He is just a year short of ninety, but his eyes are full of sparkle. He seems the very embodiment of life and light. He speaks softly, almost in a whisper, yet his mind is razor-sharp, capable of the most abstruse ideas and complex conversations.

I am a part of a small group of admirers and scholars who are here to felicitate him on being conferred the Fellowship of the Sahitya Akademi, India's national academy of letters. The Fellowship is its highest form of recognition, usually given to our most eminent writers for a lifetime's contribution to literature. Rao's award was announced the previous year, in 1996, but he was unable to travel to India to receive it.

Now, the president of the Sahitya Akademi, himself one of India's great writers, U.R. Ananthamurthy, has come all the way to Austin to bestow it upon Rao. The ceremony has already taken place earlier in the day at the Center for Asian Studies, University of Texas, Austin, along with a symposium in Rao's honour.[1]

It's evening. It has been a busy day, with several papers and presentations. I have to leave early next morning, so this is my last opportunity to talk to Rao.

I imagine he will be tired, but I am delighted to discover that he is alert and quite willing to have a conversation.

After talking about the symposium for some time, he suddenly asks, 'Who are some of the interesting writers in India these days?'

I mention a few, one of whom, Ananthamurthy, has just conferred the Fellowship on Rao.

'He writes in Kannada, my mother tongue, but I haven't read him yet. Tell me, what does he write about?'

I feel uncomfortable. The sheer directness of the question, if not its bluntness, is disconcerting.

If the question were asked somewhat differently, I should have preferred to take refuge behind some vague generalizations or platitudes rather than risk any value judgements.

But that escape route is not available with Raja Rao. If I may be forgiven a somewhat colloquial expression, I know that I can't bullshit him.

So, I take a deep breath and plunge ahead.

---

[1] 'Seeing with Three Eyes: Raja Rao and the Gandhian Way' at 'Word as Mantra: The Art of Raja Rao', symposium in honour of Raja Rao, University of Texas at Austin, USA, 24 March 1997. An earlier account of this conversation with Rao appeared in '"Clip Joint" by U.R. Ananthamurthy: A Response', *Indian Literature*, 179 (May–June 1997): 124–35.

'Ananthamurthy's fiction is about the tussle between tradition and modernity—or, rather, between traditions and modernities.

'What is interesting is that he seems to be on the side of modernity, but it is only after a careful reading that one realizes that neither wins.

'In fact, one might even argue that in the later works, there is a move towards respecting a certain kind of tradition more than the available modernities . . .'

Rao seems interested. His lips are set, his eyes flash. At length he says, 'Very correct. Modernity cannot satisfy us.'

'But,' I add, 'most of Ananthamurthy's energies have gone in documenting the corruptions of tradition.

'Look at *Smaskara*, his most celebrated work. Tradition is represented by Praneshacharya's crippled wife and the orthodox Brahmins in the *agrahara*. The former can satisfy him neither physically nor intellectually. The latter tie themselves up in knots but cannot deal with the force of the outside world, symbolized by the plague that has killed Naranappa and brought their community into a crisis.

'On the other hand, Praneshacharya, the protagonist, like the knight in Bergman's *The Seventh Seal*, is a transitional being. He begins as a traditionalist, but discovers that tradition is totally incapable of handling the problem caused by modernity—the rotting corpse of Naranappa.

'It is only after his second birth through Naranappa's "low-caste" mistress, Chandri, that he finds the strength to face the harsh realities of the world outside the fenced-off *agrahara*.'

Rao: 'What happens at the end of the novel? Where does Ananthamurthy leave you?'

'Well, that's where I have a problem with him. He leaves you with an ambiguity, an uncertainty. It's a sort of existentialist dilemma.

'The real world outside the *agrahara*, too, is in a real mess. Praneshacharya cannot find any lasting happiness there. He returns to his village, sadder, more puzzled.

'Life, it would seem, has no inherent purpose or meaning; then, how is one to make one's existence meaningful? This, I think, is the central question in Ananthamurthy's fiction.'

I guess what Raja Rao is thinking. The gaping hole is the absence of the guru. Without the guru, how could life be meaningful?

'In one of his short stories, however, there is a village simpleton, who with a mere touch banishes the doubts of his modernized childhood friend. The latter is visiting the village after spending most of his life in cities.

'In this story, the simpleton, if I remember correctly, wants to wrestle with a tiger. The modern city-bred man is that tiger, whom he wrestles with and overcomes.'

It is getting late. I have to leave. My conversation with Rao is left incomplete.

2

In the symposium on Raja Rao on 24 March 1997, I had spoken on his forthcoming book *The Great Indian Way: A Life of Mahatma Gandhi*. This was a marvellous retelling of Bapu's life in the form of a modern purana. Rao had called it 'an experiment in honesty', adding that the 'Pauranic style, therefore, is the only style an Indian can use'.

The publisher was Kapil Malhotra of Vision Books, who in 1996 had published *The Meaning of India*. Malhotra had inherited one-half of what used to be Dina Nath Malhotra's Hind Pocket Books, India's first paperback imprint. Malhotra, believing in Rao's genius, had also published *The Chessmaster and His Moves* in 1988. That book had won Rao the coveted Neustadt Prize. The manuscript was part of a veritable treasure trove of unpublished material that some of us, who were close to Rao, had been fortunate to be able to see. But there were many more such unpublished works, which I had seen at the Harry Ransom Humanities Research Center, where Rao's papers now rested.

After the *Chessmaster*, Malhotra published *On the Ganga Ghat* (1989) too. It was a unique collection of short stories with the common theme and location of Varanasi. It was clear that we were in the midst of a quiet Raja Rao efflorescence. It would culminate in his being posthumously awarded India's second-highest civilian honour, the Padma Vibhushan, in 2007, ten years after the prestigious Sahitya Akademi Fellowship mentioned earlier.

What was so special about Rao's book, yet another of the hundreds written on Gandhi? Why had Mulk Raj Anand called it 'Among the most authentic accounts of the Mahatma's life and work'? It was this question that I had tried to answer in my presentation on Rao in the symposium in 1997.

The clue came from Rao himself. 'Facts of course are there,' he says in the preface, 'but facts are shrill.' Facts, in other words, do not tell the whole truth: 'They have a way of saying more than they mean, and disbelievingly so. The silences and the symbols are omitted, and meaning taken out of breath and performance.'

What else do we have other than facts? It is, as Rao says, the 'rasa, flavour, to makes facts melt into life'. The Indian experience is complex and multi-layered, requiring a special style to express it, even in modern times: 'the Indian experience is such a palimpsest, layer behind layer of tradition and myth and custom go to make such an existence: gesture is ritual, and each act a statement in terms of philosophy, superstition, historical or linguistic provincialism, caste originality, or merely a personal one, and yet it's all a whole, it's India.'

Rao, next, makes a very bold statement: 'Thus to face honesty against an Indian event, an Indian life, one's expression has to be epic in style or to lie.' Facts alone cannot tell the Indian story, nor can myths, rituals, or fables by themselves. The two must be combined in a unique manner. That was Rao's reinvented pauranic style. Not in the manner of the old puranas which, from the point of modern history, are hobbled by their unverifiable material. Nor the contemporary accounts which are slaves to facts. But a unique combination of both.

This is what I called 'seeing with three eyes'. The first eye sees only facts. The second espies the fable behind and around the fact. It is only the third eye, the eye of wisdom, that can combine both to see into the depths of things, their secret significance and meaning.

This special way of seeing is what Rao calls 'fact against custom, history against time . . . geography against space'. In his book on the Mahatma, this is precisely what Rao accomplishes, making 'life larger than it seems, and its small impurities and accidents and parts, must perforce be transmuted into equations where the mighty becomes normal, and the normal in its turn becoming myth. Prose and poetry thus flow into one another, the personal and the impersonal, making the drama altogether noble and simple.'

An important feature of traditional Indian society, which persists to this very day, is its enormously rich and varied method of chronicling and celebrating life. In rural society, for instance, even humble craftspersons like weavers, potters, blacksmiths and wood workers have a specially designated *bhiksha vritti jati*, a group of mendicant performers, to record and disseminate their deeds. Thus, all our communities have their own jati puranas or community histories. Likewise, each village, each region, each state has its own legends, songs and stories. All these go into making up our rich narrative traditions.

Raja Rao, as he himself has often reiterated, belongs very much to this pauranic tradition. He has performed his duty as a writer as faithfully and sincerely as our ancient poets, who have told the stories of gods and demons, heroes and villains, apsaras and princesses, sages and mendicants with such zealous relish. A key and recurring figure in Raja Rao's works is one of the greatest men of our times, Mahatma Gandhi. This book is Rao's retelling of and tribute to Gandhi's extraordinary life.

3

Raja Rao was born in an ancient and respected Brahmin family in Hassan, Karnataka. He was the eldest son in a family of two brothers and seven sisters. His father taught Kannada at Nizam's College in the neighbouring princely state of Hyderabad. When he was only four, his mother died. This was a defining, if tragic, loss. Indeed, the absence of his mother and the sense of being an orphan recur in his fiction. Perhaps the earliest influence on Raja was his grandfather, with whom he stayed both in Hassan and in Harihalli, in Karnataka, while his father was in Hyderabad. He seems to have imbued a spiritual orientation from his grandfather, a preoccupation that stayed with him throughout his life and is evident in all his works.

Raja joined his father in Hyderabad, going there to attend high school. He studied at the Madrasa-i-Aliya, then the most prestigious school in the state, where the aristocracy of Hyderabad sent their children. Raja was the only Hindu in his class. He was then sent to Aligarh Muslim University. His Aligarh days proved to be crucial in shaping his intellectual growth. Influenced by Eric Dickinson, Rao's literary sensibilities were awakened. As a visiting professor from Oxford, Dickinson, though a minor poet in Britain, greatly inspired students in India. Rao's fellow student friend, Ahmed Ali, went on to become a famous novelist; another peer, Chetan Anand, an influential film producer–director. Rao also began learning French at Aligarh, which contributed to his decision to go to France a couple of years later. After matriculating in 1927, he returned to Hyderabad to enrol in a BA course at Nizam's College. Two years later, he graduated, having majored in English and history.

In 1929, Rao won the Asiatic Scholarship of the Government of Hyderabad. He went out of India for the first time in his life. In a sense, he never quite returned home again. His scholarship took him to the University of Montpellier in France. He was researching the missing link in India's impact on Europe, particularly the Cathars, who he believed had been influenced by Buddhism, and whether they could provide the vital clue.

At Montpellier, he also met Camille Mouly, a French teacher. They married later that same year. As Rao told me, 'We had a very simple arrangement. I would write and she would support me.' Camille was the most important person in his life till the marriage broke up some ten years after. She features, thinly disguised as a fictional character, in his major works such as *The Serpent and the Rope* and *The Chessmaster and His Moves*.

Rao's first efforts as a writer were in Kannada, his mother tongue. Between 1931 and 1933, he published three essays and a poem in Kannada in a journal called *Jaya Karnataka*. For the next two years, he researched the influence of India on Irish literature at the Sorbonne. His first short stories were published in journals such as *Asia* (New York) and *Les Cahiers du Sud* (Paris). In 1933, Rao abandoned research to devote himself to writing.

Rao, however, soon shifted to English from Kannada. As he recalled to me, 'I realized that the time was not ripe to become a global writer in Kannada. Though I was proudly nationalistic, I thought writing in English would make a greater impact on the world.' His early short stories were published in a collection called *The Cow of the Barricades and Other Stories* in 1947. Another volume, *The Policeman and the Rose* (1978), came out much later. It retained the seven earlier published stories, with three new ones written in the 1960s.

In addition to novels and short stories, Rao published essays, travelogues and biographical sketches in various journals and popular magazines. Some of these have been collected in *The Meaning of India*. But much earlier, he co-edited, with Iqbal Singh, two collections of essays, *Changing India* (1939) and *Whither India* (1948). He was also the editor of Jawaharlal Nehru's *Soviet Russia: Some Random Sketches and Impressions* (1949).

Although Rao lived abroad, he never ceased to be an Indian in temperament and sensibility. In fact, his awareness of Indian culture grew, even though he could not settle down permanently in India. He became a compulsive visitor, returning to India again and again for spiritual and cultural nourishment. In that sense, Rao never completely left India. In 1933, he visited Pandit

Taranath's ashram in his quest for self-realization. In 1938, his small masterpiece, *Kanthapura*, although written earlier, was published from London.

One year later, Rao's marriage disintegrated; he found himself back in India, his spiritual search renewed. He even appeared to give up writing to seek the truth. In the next few years, Rao visited a number of ashrams and religious teachers, notably Ramana Maharshi of Tiruvannamalai and Narayana Maharaj of Kedgaon. He also called on Mahatma Gandhi at Sevagram, an account of which is in *The Meaning of India*. Around this time, Rao also became a public figure in India, active in several social and political causes.

In 1942, when most of India's major leaders were imprisoned during the Quit India movement, he participated in the underground agitation, along with several Congress socialists such as Aruna Asaf Ali and Achyut Patwardhan. During this period, Rao also started a journal called *Tomorrow*, to be published from Bombay (now Mumbai), co-edited with his friend and fellow-writer Ahmed Ali. Rao was also associated with the cultural-spiritual organization Chetana, which still exists. Another of Rao's dream projects during this period was to start Sri Vidya Samiti, with the help of his then friend and patron Raja J. Rameshwar Rao of Wanaparthy. However, his plans failed to take off and he also parted ways with Rameshwar Rao.

Around the same time, in 1943, Rao's life, however, took a decisive turn from politics back to spirituality. He found his preceptor at last in Krishna Menon, better known as Sri Atmananda Guru. Menon had been a police officer before being shown his true vocation by a mysterious wandering spiritual master from north India. Rao's life underwent a great change after meeting his master. He shifted to Trivandrum (now Thiruvananthapuram), living there on and off for several years. After India became independent, Rao returned to France in 1948, finding it difficult to settle down permanently in India. He visited the United States in 1953. The same year, his fable, 'India—A Story', appeared in *Encounter* (London) and was reprinted in *The Meaning of India* with a slightly altered title. He came back to India in 1958 with André Malraux, Charles de Gaulle's emissary to Nehru. Rao's account of that important visit is also included in *The Meaning of India*.

In 1959, he published 'The Cat' in *The Chelsea Review* (New York). This story would later be expanded into his novel, *The Cat and Shakespeare* (1965). In 1960, twenty-two years after *Kanthapura*, Rao's masterpiece, *The Serpent and the Rope*, was published. About ten years later, *Comrade Kirillov* (1970) came out in English, although it had appeared earlier in a French translation, *Le Comrade Kirillov* (1965). That year, Rao moved permanently to the United States, when he was invited to be a professor of philosophy at the University of Texas at Austin (UT-A). Also in 1965, he married Katherine Jones, an American stage actress. They had a son, Christopher Rama. Rao divided his time between the United States, France and India until his retirement from the University of Texas in 1980.

At UT-A, Rao was a legendary teacher, lecturing to very large classes. His pedagogy was most unusual. He was known to come to class and announce, 'Ask me a question, any question you like.' The class took off from such a challenge. I asked him once, 'What if you didn't know the answer?' He replied, 'I meditated on my guru; the answer would come.' He also cultivated, over the years, friendships with writers, scholars, poets and a variety of influential people. These included the great proto-Indo-

European linguist and machine translation pioneer Winfred P. Lehmann, who had invited him to UT-A; physical scientist and Nobel laureate Ilya Prigogine; and theoretical physicist E.C. George Sudarshan. All of them worked on the same campus, as did other famous novelists from the subcontinent, including G.V. Desani and Zulfikar Ghose. Rao was also acquainted with a number of extraordinary personalities, including E.M. Forster, Albert Camus, J. Krishnamurti, Czeslaw Milosz, Octavio Paz, Woodrow Wilson and Indira Gandhi, all of whom he corresponded with and wrote about.

In 1986, after his divorce with Katherine, Rao married Susan, who is today the custodian of his incredible legacy. His third wife, Susan, many years younger, served and tended to him more devotedly than any Hindu wife I know. Her kitchen in their small apartment always smelt of herbs. Everything served at her table was organically grown and, of course, vegetarian. The only exceptions were some rich desserts specially ordered from a shop nearby or some south Indian food brought from a restaurant.

Rao's widely awaited magnum opus, *The Chessmaster and His Moves*, was finally released in June 1988. The story of its publication is, by no means, commonplace. The book is part of a trilogy that is more than 1500 pages long. Written, in most part, over three or four years, 1980–83, the manuscript had been ready at least five years before its actual publication. More than one major American publisher had shown interest in the manuscript, but considered the book too long. Viking suggested a reduction to a third of its present size of 735 pages. What was even more amazing is that the manuscript being shown around was merely the first part of a projected trilogy! Rao refused to omit a single page of his book.

Subsequently, Vision Books of Delhi, the pioneers of the paperback business in India, whose earlier imprints, Hind Pocket Books and Orient Paperbacks, had published nearly every major contemporary Indian author either in original English or in English translation, accepted the book as it was. The publisher took more than three years to release it. As it happened, when the proofs were ready, Rao became one of the contenders for the prestigious Neustadt International Prize for Literature awarded by the University of Oklahoma. The photocopies of the proofs, corrected by R. Parthasarathy, poet-professor and former flatmate of Rao, were circulated among members of the jury. Professor and poet Edwin Thumboo from the National University of Singapore, a member of the jury, played a key role in promoting and championing Rao's cause. Rao went on to win the prestigious prize, which was awarded to him on 4 June 1988. Shortly thereafter, the book was formally released in India.

Chessmaster appeared twenty-eight years after Rao's last major book, *The Serpent and the Rope*. It was certainly a major literary event in the world of Indian English literature. Much anticipation had been built up by the long years of silence, and the Neustadt award only added to the excitement of those waiting for the book's release. To say the least, everybody expected something big—at last, the great Indian English novel!

On the morning of 8 July 2006, Rao passed away at the age of ninety-seven in Austin, Texas, far away from his beloved India. In an obituary that I wrote, I had said that he was truly one of the great writers of the twentieth century.[2] His life not

---

[2]   Makarand Paranjape, 'First Philosopher-Novelist of Indian Fiction in English, Raja Rao, Dies', *India Today*, 24 July 2006, https://www.

only spanned almost the entire century, but his works engaged with all its major events and intellectual cross-currents. More than 100 million people died unnatural deaths owing to manmade wars, conflicts, famines and ideological misadventures in this bloodiest of centuries. It would be no exaggeration to say that more than any other contemporary Indian writer, it was Rao who engaged most seriously with the problem of human suffering and its solution.

The urgency behind this recollection of Rao's extraordinary life and oeuvre is the astonishing Raja Rao archive, bequeathed to the Harry Ransom Humanities Research Center, UT-A, by his wife Susan. The Raja Rao papers are spread across forty-two cartons and five document boxes. I am fortunate to be the first scholar to take a comprehensive look at the whole collection. Before these papers were given to the Harry Ransom Center, they were stored in many boxes. The most important of these were lodged in the basement of Rao's Pearl Street apartment, not too far from the university where he taught philosophy for twenty years.

My personal connection with Rao was nurtured from my very first contact with him in 1981 as a graduate student at the University of Illinois at Urbana-Champaign. Rao, then in his early seventies, had come to lecture in a class taught by the famous professor of linguistics and authority on world Englishes, Braj B. Kachru. Great writer though he was, Rao was not only unbelievably gracious to me but fostered a bond, which only grew deeper with the years. I was one of the few in the wide

---

indiatoday.in/magazine/obituary/story/20060724-first-philosopher-novelist-of-indian-fiction-in-english-raja-rao-dies-782701-2006-07-24 (accessed on 21 February 2020).

circle of Rao's admirers, scholars, students and friends who not only saw some of these unpublished works when he was alive but also had an idea of what he meant to do with them. One of his strongest wishes was the publication of the two remaining volumes of his beloved *Chessmaster* trilogy.

Rao was working on the remaining unpublished volumes, 'Daughter of the Mountain' and 'Myrobalan in the Palm of the Hand', until practically his last days, stopping only when his health deteriorated. While I read the unedited typescripts, with squiggles of the author's handwritten corrections, I was astounded at just how significant the unpublished works were. I am convinced that when the trilogy is finally published, it will be one of the longest and most distinguished works of fiction in the English language.

Rao, who considered writing a sadhana, a spiritual discipline, himself called the trilogy an extended dialogue between the Brahmin and the rabbi, or between zero and infinity. Reading and studying him, I felt his words, like Bhartrihari's notion of *vac*, were meant to lead us from the mundane–material to the transcendental–sublime. Rao's writings have the capacity to lift up our consciousness from the lowest depths of the horrors of human experience to the heights of wholeness, integrity and liberation.

What has overwhelmed me even more since I started examining the papers at the Harry Ransom Center is the huge quantum of material waiting to be resurrected and brought to light—not only the above two volumes of the *Chessmaster* trilogy, but other novels, plays, essays and translations, besides several older and occasional pieces. For instance, I came across two unpublished essays, one on the Watergate scandal in the United States and another intriguingly titled 'How to

Defeat Communism'. Rao, I know now more than ever, was an outstanding thinker, philosopher and champion of Indic civilization, in addition to being one of the greatest writers of the twentieth century. That is why we must not only commemorate him, but also endeavour to do justice to his unfinished projects.

4

Raja Rao is regarded as one of the most important Indian English novelists.[3] The reasons for his pre-eminence are both historical and artistic. Rao is important historically because his first novel, *Kanthapura*, was published during the 1930s, when Indian English fiction first began to gain recognition. Although Bankim Chandra Chatterjee's incomplete romance, *Rajmohan's Wife* (1864), is considered to be the first Indian English novel, it was only in the 1930s that this genre began to demonstrate the maturity and accomplishment of a major literary mode. This coming of age was heralded by the publication of Mulk Raj Anand's *Untouchable* (1935), R.K. Narayan's *Swamy and Friends* (1935) and Rao's *Kanthapura* (1938). Hence, the historic significance of Rao.

Artistically, Rao is important because of his unique formal and thematic accomplishments. Although his published output of five novels seems modest in comparison to Anand's or Narayan's more prolific output, Rao's achievement is probably more impressive. Formally and stylistically, he is the most

---

[3]   Portions of this Introduction have appeared in my Introduction to *The Best of Raja Rao* (New Delhi: Katha, 1998) and my earliest essay on Raja Rao, an entry on the author published in *The Survey of Long Fiction* (Englewood Cliffs, N.J.: Salem Press, 1983), edited by Frank N. Magill.

adventurous of the three. As M.K. Naik has elaborated in his monograph *Raja Rao* (1972), Rao consistently tried to modify the Western form of the novel to suit his Indian subject matter.

In fact, it would not be incorrect to say that he reinvents and Indianizes the novel as no one else has. He accomplishes this feat by using traditional Indian genres such as the Purana, the *sthalakatha* and the beast fable to structure his works. Thus, formally, his novels are based on Indian models. Furthermore, they are written in an English that is uniquely Indian in style, tone, mood and rhythm. The Indianness of style is achieved by relying heavily on translation, quotation and the use of Indian proverbs, idioms and colloquial patterns. Rao adroitly manipulates vocabulary and syntax to enhance the Indian flavouring of his English.

The result is a style that, although distinctly Indian, is evocative and perfectly intelligible to Western readers as well. This language is unique to Rao, a highly refined medium of expression that suggests truths beyond those normally available in our everyday speech. To put it somewhat dramatically, Rao has restored sacredness to the word.

Thematically, too, Rao is somewhat different from the other two major Indian English novelists, Anand and Narayan. Rao is a metaphysical novelist whose concerns are primarily religious and philosophical. *Kanthapura*, for example, shows a strong Gandhian influence as it documents the progress of a non-violent agitation against the British in a remote south Indian village. *The Serpent and the Rope* and *The Cat and Shakespeare* are expositions of the ancient Indian philosophical outlook, Vedanta. *Comrade Kirillov* is an evaluation of the efficacy of communism.

The Chessmaster and His Moves, the first novel in a trilogy, in fact, surpasses all his earlier works in its sweep. It is nothing less than an examination into the entirety of the modern human condition. Its highlight is an intense and revelatory dialogue between the Brahmin and the rabbi, not only as individuals but as representatives of two ancient and contrasting civilizational perspectives. Even his short fiction and non-fictional prose is imbued with this spirit of inquiry into the meaning of things. It is both playful and serious, creating and not merely discussing philosophy. Thus, in Rao's works, there is an ongoing discussion of major systems of thought, chiefly of India but also of the West. Both stylistically and thematically, then, Rao succeeds in capturing the spirit of India in his works. His formal and stylistic innovations have expanded the expressive range of English and have influenced other writers who share Rao's predicament: the task of writing about a culture in a language that is not native to it. Although Rao's oeuvre seems limited, his reputation is secure. Indeed, despite the appearance of dozens of talented new writers in the last few decades, it would be safe to assert that there is no one else who has even attempted to do what Rao has accomplished: to portray and justify the wisdom of traditional India to the modern world. No one, moreover, has even approached, let alone reached, his heights of spiritual illumination. The aesthetic delight that obtains in his works is as rare as it is authentic. All told, C.D. Narasimhaiah's claim that Raja Rao is the greatest Indian English novelist is as true today as when it was first made, some fifty years ago.

An understanding of Raja Rao's art is enhanced by contextualizing his novels. Although Rao admits to several Western influences, his work is best understood as part of the Indian tradition. Rao regards literature as sadhana; for him, writing is a consequence of his metaphysical life. His novels, hence, essentially represent a quest for the Absolute. From

Kanthapura to *Comrade Kirillov*, Rao's protagonists grapple with the same concern: 'What is Truth? How is one to find it?' Their methods vary, as do their results, but they share the same preoccupations. The novels thus become chronicles of this archetypal search. Formally, too, all four novels share certain features. The plot is de-emphasized; the narrative, generally subjective, is not linear, but circular, in the Puranic manner of storytelling, which Rao adapts to the form of the Western novel. There are digressions, detours, stories within stories, songs, philosophical disquisitions, debates and essays. Characters, too, are frequently symbolic figures; often, the motivations for their actions might seem puzzling or insufficient. Finally, because the narration is subjective, the language of the narrator, too, tends to be unique, reflecting his or her social, regional and philosophical make-up and peculiarities.

Raja Rao's stories were first collected in the book *The Cow of the Barricades* (1947). Later, these and three others were published in *The Policeman and the Rose* (1978). Rao is thus not a very prolific writer of short stories. Most of these stories, moreover, can be divided into two groups. The first are stories written chiefly in the 1930s and reflect his interest in social and political problems. 'Javni' and 'Akkayya' are good examples. Both comment not only on the caste system and on the position of women in Indian society, but also show the heroism, courage, wisdom and loyalty of the common folk of India. The second set of stories uses a great deal of symbolism and is essentially metaphysical in its orientation.

A good example is 'India—A Fable'. Here, Pierre, the European child, is at first fascinated by the camel of the desert and but later switches his loyalty to the majestic elephant of India. What is suggested is that India offers non-duality, which is preferable to the monotheism of Semitic religions. There are, of course, other ways of reading the story. 'The Policeman and the Rose' is the story of a beautiful woman who cannot find release until she meets the guru in the form of the policeman. It is, as its subtitle 'A True Story' suggests, a deeply personal tale, narrated in an elliptical, allegorical manner. Another story, 'Companions', hasn't been discussed or appreciated much. However, I think it is a powerful allegory about Hindu–Muslim unity. Only when Islam gets truly Indianized does its spiritual force manifest itself fully. In this story, this is illustrated in the transformation of an ordinary snake charmer into a Sufi with healing powers, all because of the advice of his serpent, who is the reincarnation of a fallen Brahmin.

Published twenty-two years after *Kanthapura*, *The Serpent and the Rope* is Rao's most appreciated work. If the former is modelled on an *upapurana* (minor Purana), the latter is a kind of *mahapurana* (major Purana) or epic. Geographically, historically, philosophically and formally, its sweep is truly epical. The novel includes a variety of settings, ranging from metropolitan Paris to Ramaswamy's ancestral home in a south Indian village, from European locales such as Aix-en-Provence, Montpellier, Pau, Provence, Cambridge and London, to Indian cities such as Hyderabad, Delhi, Lucknow, Bombay, Bangalore and Benares. Even historically, its sweep is truly staggering. Rao delves into almost the whole of Indian history, from the invasion of the Aryans to the advent of British rule; he also explores European history, chiefly the Albigensian heresy, and Chinese history. These and many other topics are explored as the protagonist, Rama, a historian by training, expounds his theories in conversations with the leading characters. Philosophically, too, the novel's range is formidable. Rao discusses Hinduism,

Buddhism, Catholicism, Islam, Taoism, Marxism, Darwinism and Nazism.

Its content is so varied, it is not surprising to find *The Serpent and the Rope* extremely diverse in form as well. Rao quotes from an array of languages, including Sanskrit, Hindi, French, Italian, Latin and Provencal; only the Sanskrit quotations are translated. There are long interludes and stories, such as Grandmother Lakshamma's story of a princess who becomes a pumpkin and Ishwara Bhatta's 'Story of Rama'. In addition, the novel contains songs, myths, legends and philosophical discussions in the manner of the Puranas. The main narrative, the gradual disintegration of Rama's marriage with his French wife, Madeleine, is thus only a single strand holding a voluminous and diverse book together.

The Serpent and the Rope is an extremely challenging work thematically as well. Savithri's words in the novel sum it up well. It is 'a sacred text, a cryptogram, with different meanings at different hierarchies of awareness' (235).[4] It may be approached on at least two levels, the literal and the symbolic, although the two usually operate simultaneously.

At the literal level of plot, the novel may appear puzzling and unsatisfying. The crux is: Why does the marriage of Rama and Madeleine disintegrate? Critics have attempted various answers, ranging from incompatibility between the Indian Rama and the French Madeleine, to Rama's infidelity. Although such answers are plausible, they do not satisfy completely because these reasons are not perceived by the characters themselves. Rama and Madeleine are both aware of the growing rift between them, but they do not attempt to bridge it on a practical level.

---

[4]   Published first by John Murray in 1960, it was reprinted by Penguin Books India in 2014. Quotations are from the latter edition.

Instead, both watch the dissolution of the union with an almost fatalistic helplessness. Similarly, it is hard to understand why Rama seeks fulfilment in other women while averring his love for Madeleine at the same time, or why he never tells her of his affairs in spite of his claim that he keeps no secrets from her. Rama, the narrator, does not answer such questions; he only chronicles the breakdown of the relationship almost impersonally, as if there were little he could do to save it. He also does not feel himself responsible for having affairs with other women, one of which involves a ritual second marriage, while being married to Madeleine at the same time.

What is lacking, then, is adequate motivation for the actions of the characters, something that most readers are conditioned to expect from a novel. Instead of asking of the novel something that it did not intend to give, perhaps a better approach is to consider what it does clearly provide; indeed, questions that appear unresolved on the literal level are resolved more satisfactorily on the symbolic level.

Rama, the Brahmin hero, is a seeker of Truth both by birth and by vocation (a Brahmin is one who seeks Brahman, or the Absolute). As an Indian scholar in France, Rama is seeking Truth in the form of the missing link in the puzzle of India's influence on the West. According to Rama, this missing link is the Albigensian heresy; he thinks that the Cathars were driven to heresy by the influence of Buddhism, which had left India. Rama's quest for Truth is also manifested in his search for the ideal woman, because, in the Hindu tradition, the union of man and wife is symbolic of the union of man and God. The marriage of Shiva and Parvati is one such paradigmatic union, in which Shiva, the Absolute, the abstract, the ascetic, is wedded to Parvati, the human, the concrete, the possessor of the Earth.

Another such union is that between the mythical Savithri and her husband, Satyavan ('satya' means 'truth'). Savithri, through her devotion, restores her dead husband to life.

In keeping with these paradigms, Rama—the thinker, the meditator, the seeker of Truth—can only find fulfilment in a Parvati or a Savithri who can bring him back to Earth by her devotion. Madeleine, however, who has given up her Catholicism for Buddhism, becomes an ascetic, renouncing the Earth, denying her body through abstinence and penance. Significantly, her union with Rama is barren; both their children are stillborn. Madeleine also regards Truth as something outside of herself, something that has to be striven for in order to be realized. Her dualism is the philosophical opposite of Rama's non-dualism.

Rama believes, following the Advaita Vedanta, that the self is part of Truth, as the wave is part of the sea, and that all separateness is illusion, like the illusion in which a rope is mistaken for a serpent. Rama's true mate is an Indian undergraduate at Cambridge named, interestingly, Savithri. Savithri, despite her modishness—she dances to jazz music, smokes, wears Western clothes and so on—is essentially an Indian. Unlike Madeleine, Savithri does not seek Truth, but instinctively and unselfconsciously is Truth. Her union with Rama is thus a natural and fulfilling one. Savithri, however, like Rama's sister, Saroja, opts for an arranged marriage in the traditional Indian manner with someone else; hence, her relationship with Rama is never consummated. At the end of the book, Rama, divorced from Madeleine, sees a vision of his guru in Travancore and plans to leave France for India.

Rama's path to Truth, unlike Moorthy's karma yoga, is jnana yoga (the path of knowledge), also enunciated in the Bhagavad

Gita. Rama is not a man of action but an intellectual. Although he has accumulated knowledge, he does not apprehend Truth clearly; like the deluded seeker in the fable, he mistakes the rope for the serpent, failing to see himself already united with Truth as Savithri is. Traditionally, a guru is necessary for the jnana yogi, because only a guru can cure his delusion by showing him that what appears to be a serpent is really a rope. Thus, in the end, Rama resolves to seek his guru to be cured of his delusion.

The Cat and Shakespeare, Rao's next novel, which he described as 'a metaphysical comedy', clearly shows a strong Upanishadic influence in its form. The spiritual experiences of its narrator, Ramakrishna Pai, are reminiscent of the illuminative passages in the *Chandogya Upanishad*, which describe the experience of the Infinite. The dialogues in the novel are also Upanishadic in their question-and-answer patterns; the best example is the conversation between Govindan Nair and Lakshmi in the brothel.

Nair's metaphysical speculations, such as 'Is there seeing first or the object first?', seem to be modelled on philosophical queries in the Upanishads. Though the cat links the novel to the Indian beast fable and Nair's comic roguery shows similarities to the rogue fable in the *Panchatantra*, the story, really, illustrates the *marjara nyaya* (the path of the cat) of *vishistadvaita*, not the practical and crafty animals of the *Panchatantra*.

The major Western debt is to William Shakespeare, who is acknowledged in the title. Shakespeare is a symbol for the universal; according to Rao, Shakespeare's vision transcends duality and arrives at a unified view of the world. There are numerous allusions to *Hamlet* in the novel, culminating in the 'rat-trap episode', in which a cat is trapped in a large rat-trap; this prompts Nair to deliver a parody of *Hamlet*, which begins, 'A kitten sans cat, that is the question.'

The Cat and Shakespeare is Rao's sequel to *The Serpent and the Rope* in that it shows what happens after a seeker's veil of illusion has been removed by the guru. Its theme may be summed up in Hamlet's words to Horatio towards the end of the play: 'There is a divinity that shapes our ends. / Rough-hew them how we will.' A similar view of grace is embodied in the novel in what Nair, the man who is united to Truth, calls 'the way of the Cat'. The 'way of the Cat', simply, is the notion that just as the kitten is carried by the scruff of its neck by the mother cat, man is completely at the mercy of the Divine; consequently, the only way to live is to surrender oneself to divine grace, as the helpless kitten surrenders itself to the mother cat. Nair lives this philosophy and is responsible for teaching it to his ignorant neighbour, the narrator Pai. Pai is like the innocent hunter in the story who unknowingly heaped leaves on a Shivalingam and was rewarded with a vision.

Between Pai's house and Nair's is a wall over which Nair leaps every time he visits Pai. The wall is an important symbol because it represents the division between illusion and Truth, or duality and non-duality, or the relative and the Absolute. Nair crosses it easily, but Pai has never gone across. Towards the end of the novel, following Nair's cat, Pai accidentally crosses the wall. Like the lucky hunter, he, too, is vouchsafed a divine vision: For the first time, Pai sees the whole universe as a unity of sense, meaning and existence.

The novel ends with Pai's spiritual as well as material fulfilment, having partially realized his lifelong ambition of owning a three-storey house. *The Cat and Shakespeare*, although not as ambitious as *Kanthapura*, is as successful on its own terms. The novel is an elaborate puzzle, which the author challenges the reader to solve; a solution is not only possible at all levels, but is completely satisfying as well. The way to the Absolute here is not karma yoga or jnana yoga of the two previous novels, but bhakti yoga, or the path of devotion. The seeker recognizes himself as dependent on divine grace for his salvation and surrenders himself to the Benevolent Mother like a trusting kitten.

Comrade Kirillov, published in English in 1976, is generally recognized as Rao's least ambitious novel; it is clearly a minor work compared to its three illustrious predecessors. Formally, it is an extended *vyakti-chitra*, or character sketch, a popular genre in Indian regional literature. The main story, narrated by one 'R.', standing perhaps for Rao himself, is a mere ninety-three pages in large type, to which are appended twenty-seven pages of the diary of Kirillov's wife, Irene, and a concluding seven pages by the narrator; the effect is of a slight, sketchy novella. Kirillov, alias Padmanabha Iyer, leaves India for California to propagate theosophy but, after a period of disillusionment, becomes a communist.

From California, he moves to London, where, marrying a Czech immigrant, Irene, he settles down to the life of an expatriate intellectual. Like Rao's other protagonists, Kirillov starts as a seeker of Truth, but after becoming a communist, he is increasingly revealed by the narrator to be caught in a system that curtails his access to Truth. Thus, Kirillov continuously rationalizes the major events in the world to suit his perspective. Nevertheless, following a visit to India several years after he has left, he realizes that his communism is only a thin upper layer in an essentially Indian psyche. Irene also recognizes in her diary that he is almost biologically an Indian Brahmin, and only intellectually a Marxist. By the end of the book, Kirillov is shown to be a man of contradictions: attacking and worshipping Gandhi simultaneously, deeply loving traditional India but campaigning for a communist revolution, reciting Sanskrit shlokas but professing communism.

The narrator is Kirillov's intellectual opposite, an adherent of Advaita Vedanta. There are numerous interesting discussions on communism in the book, which add to its value as a social document, capturing the life of Indian expatriate intellectuals between 1920 and 1950. Also of interest is Kirillov's relationship with Irene, which recalls Rama's relationship with Madeleine. Numerous similarities aside, this relationship is more successful; this marriage lasts, and the couple have a child, Kamal. Soon after Kirillov's return from India, however, Irene dies in childbirth, followed by her newborn daughter. Kirillov leaves for Moscow and is last heard of in Peking. The novel ends with the narrator taking Kamal, now in India, to Kanyakumari. Despite its humour, pathos and realism, *Comrade Kirillov* falls short of Rao's three previous novels.

There has been a great deal of speculation as to the identity of Kirillov. Critics have wondered if the character is based on V.K. Krishna Menon or M.N. Roy. I myself have argued that Kirillov might have been inspired by Virendranath Chattopadhyaya, Sarojini Naidu's younger brother, who wrote a thesis on India and imperialism, which was presented at the Third Congress of the Communist International. Chatto, as he was called, was killed in the Stalinist purges.

When I asked Rao himself, he said the original was a man called K.S. (Krishnarao Shivarao) Shelvankar (1906–96), author of *The Problem of India* (1940), one of the first books by an Indian published by Penguin. He was born in Chennai, and educated at the Theosophical School, Adyar. He later attended the University of Madison-Wisconsin, the United States, and the London School of Economics. He was also a correspondent for

The Hindu from 1942 to 1968. Shelvankar eventually became the Indian ambassador to the USSR. Before Independence, he was working for the communists in Europe. He had married a European woman named Mary. Like Kirillov, he had written an anti-Gandhian tract.

The other important thing about this neglected novel is that it predicts the downfall of communism. The paradox of history, however, is that though this ideology has collapsed the world over, it persists in India. In the novel, on the other hand, it is seen as inappropriate for India, whatever be its use to the rest of the world.

It is interesting to note that *Comrade Kirillov*, first published in a French translation in 1965, was written earlier. Thematically, it represents the stage of negation before the spiritual fulfilment of *The Cat and Shakespeare*. Kirillov, as a communist and atheist, has negated the karma yoga of *Kanthapura* and the jnana yoga of *The Serpent and the Rope* by denying the existence of the Absolute; thus, his quest results in failure. The bhakti yoga of *The Cat and Shakespeare*, especially in the character of Nair, is the culmination of the various stages of spiritual realization in the earlier novels. Nair is the first character in Rao's novels who does not merely seek Truth, but who has found it, who actually practises it.

The Chessmaster and His Moves, as we have already seen, was the last novel Rao published. When it came out in 1988, it practically polarized the Indian English critical community into those who couldn't stand Rao and those who loved him. I am going to argue that *Chessmaster*, by being such an extreme example of a Raja Rao text, highlighted certain problems for its readers as never before. Not that these problems were absent in his earlier works, but while *The Serpent and the Rope* was praised and hailed as a classic, *Chessmaster* seems to have been viewed as an embarrassment. Even faithful Raja Rao fans do not seem to have wanted him to go so far. It would appear that even subversion of the Western novel, after all, has its limits. Rao seems to have delivered an impossible sort of book, a novel that is really an anti-novel, a novel to end novels, a book that not only challenges, but actually resists reading in the normal sense of the word. In short, a book that makes impossible demands on its readers, strains their patience and almost forces them to reject it.

In *Chessmaster*, we have a particular version of Advaita that has, as I see it, the following major sources. One is the philosophical practice of Sri Ramana Maharshi and the other is the *sunyavada* of the Buddhist philosopher Nagarjuna. Allied to the former is, of course, the philosophy of Rao's guru, Sri Atmananda, and Nagarjuna's thought, equally obviously, is derived from the Buddha. What is sought here is not the realization of self as in the earlier works, but a *dissolution*. While Moorthy through right action illustrates karma yoga, Rama, jnana yoga or the path of knowledge, and Govindan Nair, a type of bhakti yoga, of complete self-surrender to the Divine, Sivarama Sastri represents the power of negative dialectics, the attempt not to achieve something, but to vaporize one's self into nothing.

Here the familiar dichotomies between the male and the female, vowels and consonants, India and the West, the Brahmin and the Kshatriya, the sage and the saint, logic and devotion, truth and the world, all hinge on the opposition between zero and infinity. The Judeo-Christian tradition is shown to represent the quest for perfect society here on earth, while India is seen as denying the validity of the world itself. The way out, for Rao, is not to improve things as the saint-soldier does, but to dissolve contradictions completely. For him, all numbers dissolve into zero as they emerge out of it. Infinity is merely cumulative, while zero is total negation that cuts the root of illusion. One can never become perfect in time, but attain perfection only by negating time.

The only meaningful dialogue, for Rao, is between the Brahmin (zero, dissolution, negation) and the rabbi (infinity, completion, affirmation). The former is vertical, denying time; the latter is horizontal, finding fulfilment through time. It is such a framework that provides the skeleton of the plot of the novel. The first part, 'The Turk and the Tiger Hunt', shows the incompatibility of Siva and Suzanne like that of Rama and Madeleine in the earlier novel; the second part is dominated by Siva's affair with Mireille; and the third with the dialogue with Michel, the Jewish Holocaust survivor. Rao said in an interview that the book is a tribute to and acknowledgment of the great suffering of the Jews on behalf of humankind; this is elaborated at length in the story of Michel. But the suffering of Michel does not make the world any more real for Siva; his solution to the world's problems still lies in self-extinction—not suicide, but an undoing of the self.

The steadfastness of the Siva–Jayalakshmi relationship and the impossibility of its consummation, and Siva's relationship with his stepsister, Uma, and her inability to bear a child— these two relationships provide the glue that keeps the novel together. In addition, there are the usual asides, departures, stories within stories, letters, diary extracts and long speculative internal monologues that characterize Rao's narrative technique. A certain degree of novelty is offered in two or three characters whose role in the lot is minimal, but who are important—Abd'l Krim, the exiled Algerian leader, and Ratilal, the French Jain diamond merchant.

Chessmaster is an ambiguous book in which neither zero nor infinity wins. It accommodates not just the Brahmin and the rabbi, but the Jain and the revolutionary—though the violent ways of the latter are viewed unfavourably through Gandhian eyes. *Chessmaster* moves beyond these positions to a kind of indeterminacy. Siva, Rao's spokesman, is no longer always right. Nor does he pretend to be in full control of his metaphysical project. There is always the more powerful presence of the 'Chessmaster' behind the movements of the characters in the book. Of course, any notion of a personalized chessmaster or prime mover is just another version of the God that Siva, the rationalist mathematician, would deny till he realizes that it is the guru in human form who is the real agent of transformation rather than some abstract or distant God. But this is one of the apparent contradictions of the book, which will only be resolved in the later volumes of the trilogy, only when Siva encounters the guru.

Chessmaster is almost a rewriting to *The Serpent and the Rope*. In the earlier novel, Rama tells Savithri:

Zero makes all numbers, so zero begins everything. All numbers are possible when they are in and of zero. Similarly all philosophies are possible in and around Vedanta. But you can no more improve on Vedanta than improve on zero. The zero, you see, the *sunya*, is impersonal; whereas one, two, three and so on are all dualistic. (226)

Chessmaster picks up this opposition, between zero and infinity, the impersonal and the personal, the monistic and the dualistic:

Either you accept the world, and build a human empire, accepting death and, therefore, the pyramids (whether you called it a mausoleum for Mao or for Tutankhamen), or you transcend the world and as such death itself, and find the Truth of Sankara's 'Sivoham, Sivoham'. (145)[5]

Or as Siva puts it cryptically in his dialogue with Michel: 'The quarrel of man is between zero and infinity, between Truth—and God.' (670) But what is important to realize is that the philosophical positions in *Chessmaster* are more clearly defined and more neatly expressed. Thus, not only are the thematic preoccupations similar, they are carried out by similar characters in both novels.

Hence, we can propose the following schema; the → indicates how the former leads to or evolves into the latter:

The Serpent and the Rope	→	*Chessmaster*
Ramaswamy	→	Sivarama Sastri
Madeleine	→	Suzanne
Savithri	→	Jayalakshmi
Savithri's husband, Pratap	→	Jaya's husband, Surrendar Anand (Savithri's brother) Raja Ashok
Saroja	→	Uma
Subramanya Sastri	→	Ramachandra Iyer
Catherine	→	Mireille
Lakshmi	→	Rati
Grandfather	→	Father
Tante Zoubie	→	Madame X
Georgias	→	Michel
Lezo	→	Jean Pierre

---

5   Quotations are from the Vision Books edition of 1988.

The arrow mark indicates that the latter character has evolved from the former. Sometimes the resemblances are so pronounced as to make them almost identical. At the other end of the spectrum of similarity, the former is merely a hint of the latter, as with Anand turning into Ashok. In all cases, there is a strong relationship, either in the traits of the two that make up the set or in their functions in the narrative. Not just the central characters, but incidents, events, discussions and locations, and even the quotations, are common to both books. It would require a more detailed analysis to discuss the implications of these resemblances.

It is almost as if *Chessmaster* were written by an older Raja Rao, revisiting the terrain of the earlier novel. This movement is seen in the shift from the early fascination with the philosophy of history to the fulfilling discovery of an Indian way of doing mathematics. This discovery of a unified Indian method is crucial. From such a perspective, the *Chessmaster*'s resemblance to *The Serpent and the Rope* does not pose a problem at all, but illustrates a rather audacious example of intertextuality.

The second interpretive tool has to do with Rao's method of reasoning in *Chessmaster*. Most readers have not been able to figure out whether or not there is a system to Sivarama Sastri's philosophical disquisitions. Is his erudition simply impressionistic badinage or does he work from some logical principles? Often, we are baffled by the numerous discussions in the book, which seem vaporous, incoherent and directionless. We are challenged to unravel his method of reasoning and philosophizing.

Some clues are provided by the text. Siva is shown to be a mathematician in the book, but he hardly does any mathematics. True, there are references to Poincaré, Pascal, Einstein and, above all, to Ramanujan, and his Goddess Namakkal, and a sprinkling of mathematical terminology throughout the book, but the fact is that Siva spends most of his time discussing philosophy with lovers, friends and acquaintances. Rao would imply that he is a mathematician not because he does mathematics, but because he uses a mathematical method to do philosophy. Siva explains his method somewhat like this:

> The fact is, like in any mathematical equation, you make a series of statements, and you reduce one to the other, till you get one clear class. As I was telling Michel ... the only equation that now remains and remains to be solved, is the hindu-hebraic [sic] one, the vertical or the horizontal, I repeat, the zero or the infinity, historylessness or Krishna or Moses. (260)

This method is in its early stage in *The Serpent and the Rope*, where Rama, the historian, spends most of his time in the same kind of discussions. As Savithri says of him, 'History for him is a vast algebra, and he draws in unknowns from everywhere to explain it.' (183) Or as Rama says to himself: 'And thus I tried to formulate myself to myself. I like these equations about myself or others, or about ideas: I feed on them.' (195)

Similarly, Siva tries to find the equation or formula of ideas:

> [I]n mathematics when you have a certain method to the solution of a problem ... you apply the same method to all sets of problems in the same series. Similarly, when you understand one fundamental principle in indian [sic] philosophy, you apply the same method of interpretation to every other problem in the same system, the same series. And

I treat all indian [sic] mythology as a set of equations, and I apply my technique to it, and the results are astounding. (271)

This is Siva's 'new doctrine of mathematics or philosophy'—'words are numbers and numbers words...' (318)

Siva's method is therefore a kind of reduction. The Latin root of 'reduce' is *reducere*, 'to lead back'—*re* (back) + *ducere* (to lead)—whose past participle is *ductus* (a leading, conducting), which gives us the modern word, 'duct', hence 'conduce' and 'conduct'. Among the meanings of 'reduce', these apply to Rao's method: 'to put into a simpler or more concentrated form'; 'to bring into a certain order; systematize'; and 'to break up into constituent elements by analysis' (Webster's *New World Dictionary*). Rao rightly calls his method 'a doctrine' because we realize, when we read his books, that his method is far from 'scientific' or 'logical'. This logic is all his own; everything must have 'instantaneous meaning'; that is why Swanston, the Cambridge leftist intellectual, tells Rama, 'There are too many incomprehensible factors in your statement, sir.' (200)

Rao's method of reduction is, therefore, more poetic than philosophical in the traditional sense of the word. The knowledge that this method produces is not knowledge in the strict sense of the term; it is more like a totalized realization. It is by employing this type of personalized, intuitional reduction that Siva comes to the conclusion that India represents the quest for zero, the vertical, the ahistorical and the abhuman, while the Judeo-Christian, Chinese and communist civilizations represent the quest for the infinite, the horizontal, the historical, the human. Moreover, it is by this system that each character comes to represent some sort of abstraction, a formula, and relationships become equations—to be solved and resolved.

Chessmaster, as I see it, is the most powerful attempt in contemporary English literature to temporize and legitimize an ideology that denies the reality of the phenomenal world. In doing this, Rao is going against the dominant culture not only of the West, where he has spent most of his life, but of today's India. This book defies the dominant culture not only in its content, but also in its form. It goes against the practices of the Western book trade with its cynical consumerism, cheap sales gimmicks and corrupting system of incentives and threats. This is not the kind of book that will be promoted at black-tie cocktail parties or expensive publishers' bashes. This is an embarrassing book to have been written in the present world. Certainly, no 'mainstream' author could have written such a book and found a publisher for it. It has no relevance to contemporary issues or to current publishing trends. It does not fit into any slot, not even into the slot of the great Indian English novel. It has not been written merely for the here and now, but for the hereafter. Mulk Raj Anand once said to me about Raja Rao, 'It's not enough to go on and on about Atman and Brahman, about the reality of Brahman and the illusion of the world; it won't do to cling blindly to Sankara's Advaita of the ninth century. Our problems are different. How do we solve them? Can Sankara's answers serve us today?' These were challenging questions for an admirer of Rao to answer, so I kept quiet. But on reading *Chessmaster*, I think I have found at least one way of answering them. Rao does not deny the world or its suffering, brutality and violence. His book is imbued with the very real problem of dukkha, the cosmic sorrow that the Buddha sought to eliminate from the world.

Rao does not turn a blind eye to history or its record of cruelty, to Birkenau and Buchenwald. He does not neglect politics, economics or history. But to challenges that the human being faces anywhere—whether in Paris, London or Calcutta—Rao's answers point inward, from the exterior to the interior, from the outside to the inside, from the world to the self. Each one of us, he seems to say, must perform this little operation on ourselves—to dissolve ourselves into the nothing from which the whole world was created. To put an end to ourselves and thus to solve, once and for all, the problem of humanity. Deny yourself to become *That*. To me it is not only this philosophy or its viability that are important, but the enormous energy and artistic integrity with which it is mediated through 700 pages of *The Chessmaster and His Moves*. It would be unfair to accuse this philosophy of being unreal, because the characters are real, their suffering is real and their concern with the human problem is real.

After *Chessmaster*, Rao published an extraordinary little book, *On the Ganga Ghat* (1989). It is a collection of eleven stories, all of which are set in Benares. In an opening note to the reader, Rao says, 'These stories are so structured that the whole book should be read as a single novel.' Once again, we see how he pushes the form of the novel into a new direction. Indeed, the question arises, how do these seemingly different stories make one novel? After all, each story seems complete in itself, with its characters confined to its own boundaries, not spilling out into the others. There is no common protagonist, no obvious connecting action or theme. If so, what unites them? It seems to me that the real protagonist of these stories is its setting, Benares.

This ancient, timeless city emerges as the true hero of the narrative. But what does Benares stand for? Why is Rao obsessed with it, both as a real location and as a symbol? It figures, in one way or another, in nearly every novel of his. Benares, it seems to me, stands for non-duality, for that principle which overcomes death. Death, of course, is a constant presence in this holiest of holy cities. But unlike elsewhere, death here is not just welcome but auspicious—a release, a liberation, moksha. In fact, what dies in Benares is death itself. That is why it is so important in Rao's scheme of things. It is Benares, which as a sort of miniaturized India, stands for the Truth of this world. It can unveil the mystery of human life and misery, by showing the way to transcendence through the dissolution of the ego.

Each of the stories in this delightful book touches upon this theme. Together, they portray an entire society, with all its strata and jatis and how each of these, in its own unique way, seeks the same thing—liberation, salvation, transcendence. In fact, what we see is not only a rich and diverse picture of society, but, in a sense, of the cosmos itself, both human and animal, and extending further, the animate and the inanimate—everything seeks the same Truth or emancipation.

5

At the end of such a detailed overview, one might as well ask, 'What is Raja Rao trying to tell us in this modern purana on Gandhi?' The clue is afforded in a lecture called 'Wisdom and Power: A Marriage of Necessity' he delivered on 24 May 1972, at the Woodrow Wilson Center, Washington, D.C., where he was a Fellow. I found it in his unpublished papers at the Harry Ransom Humanities Research Center. Rao's fundamental premise is that 'Every government promises its subjects happiness of one style or the other. Whether it be the holy Roman Empire or the American revolution or the Hindu state, they would create a condition or conditions for the total fulfilment of man, this fulfilment being that realisation of God, of Truth or Peace.'

But how is this to be achieved? According to Rao, it is by a combination of wisdom and power: 'Wisdom then would be the knowledge of Truth or God or Peace, and power will then be the means or techniques by which the ultimate (whatever name you give it) could be reached.' This goal can only be reached through sacrifice, that is making sacred, something that only 'the sage of sages: the Guru, the Raja Guru, the wise being behind the King' could do in the Hindu idea of polity. It was only Gandhi, according to Rao, who understood that politics was sacred, making holy the public life and organization of a nation. That was the true meaning of swaraj. It is this story of sacralization that Rao tried to tell in *The Great Indian Way.* This is how independent India should have turned into the ideal state: 'Gandhi who makes Nehru his heir, and gives him his blessing to rule in the name of India.'

This lecture, however, was delivered twenty-four years after Gandhi was assassinated and eight years after Nehru's death. The story of India had turned out somewhat differently, not working itself out as the collaboration of ideal archetypes that Rao had envisaged, like the combination of Krishna and Arjuna. Or, to change the terms of reference, the city of God ruled by the philosopher king. As Rao put it, 'Had Gandhi lived long enough, and had Gandhi attained the integrity of non-duality in himself, which he never claimed he did, Gandhi might have made Nehru, his Moghul Emperor, construct an India that might have resolved many of the intricate problems of internal and international politics in a truer perspective.'

Thus in 'Gandhi's Kingdom of Sri Rama, wisdom and power have to be divided only to be irrevocably married'. But, in retrospect, that was not to be: 'Gandhi failed himself, he never could be the Guru of Nehru, thus came the catastrophe of Pakistan, and the massacres and the failure of India as a moral force in the world.' That, to my mind, is why Rao's book more or less ends in South Africa, soon after the making of the mahatma. The rest of his life, as also his tragic death, are rapidly narrated in the epilogue.

Rao himself told me that on the eve of independence, he and a few close friends were desperately looking for a miracle that might avert the partition of India. They thought a true sage might, through an act of supreme sacrifice, avert it. Instead, Gandhi, the father of the nation, himself was assassinated. But wasn't that the sacrifice that Rao had been expecting? 'No,' he said sadly, 'it was too late. Gandhi died to save India from going up in flames. It was, at best, a desperate, last-ditch effort, after most of the damage had already been done.'[6]

To return to my inconclusive conversation with Rao mentioned at the beginning, it was Gandhi, more than anyone else, who represented the integrity of the non-dual ideal that India stands for. That is what he wanted to realize in his idea of Ramrajya and swaraj. But the oneness of Hindus and Muslims that he gave his life for could not be accomplished, nor the horrors of partition averted. India and Pakistan became two countries, soon at war. China also would attack India, occupying 38,000 sq km of Indian territory in Ladakh, along with another 5,180 sq km ceded to it by Pakistan. Later, Bangladesh would separate from Pakistan. Such events did not fit into the original neo-pauranic framework that Rao had devised to tell India's

---

[6]   I talk about this in my book, *The Death and Afterlife of Mahatma Gandhi* (New Delhi: Penguin Random House, 2015).

and Gandhi's story. Instead, the world's longing for non-duality needed an epic novel of the size and ambition of the Chessmaster trilogy.

Even so, I think it would only be appropriate to observe how we might tell the story of Raja Rao in the same pauranic manner that he himself narrated the *itihas* of the Mahatma. Rao, who was happily in our midst till 2006, has himself become a legend. It is meet that he gets his own chroniclers, his own *kathakaras*, to celebrate his deeds of grace and glory. It is this function that some of those who had the privilege of knowing him, as well as studying his works, must perform today. As Raja Rao celebrated Gandhi, so should we too sing of his magnificence, in a tongue and manner we have learnt from him. In my own way, I have tried to acknowledge and appreciate what he has done for us, to announce and celebrate what he means to us.

6

For we have learned from Raja Rao that the word is no less than a mantra. In its ultimate etymological or hermeneutical significance it is the Veda, truth itself, incarnated in the body of sound, gnosis embodied as sense. The word, in its pristine sense, is nothing short of *sruti* or revelation. It is *apaurishiya* or impersonal because it is not the invention of any human mind, but pure illumination, which negates and transcends the very medium through which it is revealed. The mantra contains the seed of light or the latent vibration which, when struck, unlocks the highest realms of consciousness. The gods descend into our world using the word as their chariot; we ascend to the world of the gods, reusing their very vehicle to take us back. Such is the symmetry and mutuality of heaven and earth.

In all religious traditions, the word has been sacred, but the modern artist alone sets himself up as a demiurge, an impostor, who would create an alternative universe according to his own whims and fancies. Pretending to democratize the word, he actually profanes it according to the demands of the market, thereby betraying his own gift and those so-called masses he feigns to please. Like the holy Ganga, which is polluted with industrial effluents and the untreated sewerage of modern cities, the perennial stream of language, which is the gift of the gods, is defiled by the greed and falsehood of its practitioners.

In this whole wide world, how many writers consider the word sacred and treat it as such? A handful, a dozen, or even fewer? Of these how many write in the English language? Of course, in the ultimate analysis, the word is divine and can never be defiled no matter how badly we may misuse it. Yes, we shall certainly violate ourselves in the process, but never diminish the grandeur of its transcendental sense.

When it comes to contemporary writers who actually recognize the potential of the word and strive to realize it, I can't think of anyone as readily as Rao. I know of no other Indian English writer to whom writing is a sadhana and nothing but a sadhana, the means of spiritual ascension. In recent times, the only other writer who treated language as such was Sri Aurobindo and that is why, despite whatever the critics may say, his epic, *Savitri*, is read by thousands every day as a sacred text.

We owe our respect to Rao because he has taught us how to revere the word. He has taught us how to preserve its sanctity. He has taught us how the life of a writer is to be lived. He has taught us what the Dharma of the writer is. And he has taught us all this not merely by his words, by his statements, or even by his novels, but by his deeds and lifestyle. I don't believe that he ever professed any other vocation, nor tried to earn a living by any other means. Throwing himself entirely upon the guru's grace, he lived by and for the highest standards that a writer can set for himself. In that sense, he has ever been Saraswati's priest, not a modern novelist. He has never cared for fads and fashions, for rewards and honours, for hype or publicity; in fact, he has not even bothered to write for an audience, let alone for a specific one. That explains why, even today, fourteen years after his death, he still has more unpublished than published works. No doubt, these works will one day be published and it will be proved beyond doubt that Rao is among the great writers of the last century.

But Rao himself sought only the Absolute, the pure and undivided consciousness of advaita, that which is truth and happiness beyond all doubt and duality. This Absolute, he tells us, can never be attained through accumulation or addition, but by dissolution and sacrifice. One may sacrifice the object, if one so chooses, or the subject. Either way, the primordial dukkha or duality, two-ness, separation from the source, the alienation which is the mother of all alienations, is undone. Rao says, 'In the dissolution of the object then is happiness' (*Meaning of India*, 80). In this sense, sacrifice is not just the outward act of consigning some offerings or oblations to the fire. Rather, 'Agni himself becomes a way of knowledge that would burn away every trace of ignorance' (*Meaning of India*, 6). As Ananda Coomaraswamy puts it, 'Sacrifice thus understood is no longer a matter of doing specifically sacred things only on particular occasions but of sacrificing (making sacred) all we do and all we are; a matter of sanctification of whatever is done naturally, by a reduction of all activities to their principles' (quoted, *Meaning of India*, 6-7).

Ultimately, however, Rao is an artist, not a philosopher. It is as an artist that he has to be appreciated and understood. As such, he has been true to his calling. In terms of language, style and theme, he has been perfectly consistent, fulfilling the promise he made in his foreword to *Kanthapura*. It is this consistency, this integrity of purpose, this concern with the ultimate reality, coupled with stylistic innovation and an inspired use of language, that makes him one of the most significant and interesting writers of the world.

Rao considered his writing a sadhana, a spiritual discipline. Reading him is also a sadhana. Like the great Russian writers Tolstoy and Dostoyevsky, his fiction pushes us deeper and higher into ourselves. 'I am a man of silence,' he said. 'The word seems to come first as an impulsion from the nowhere, and then as prehension, and it becomes less and less esoteric—till it begins to be concrete. And the concrete becoming ever more earthy, and the earthy communicated, as the common word, alas seems to possess least of that original light' (Makarand Paranjape, *The Best of Raja Rao*, 188). Raja Rao has returned to the silence from whence he came, merging into that light, that sacred luminosity that he managed to capture into words. I am convinced that the time is ripe to offer this and other Raja Rao works to a discerning reading public, not the least because India has changed so much. It is at last ready to receive his myriad gifts of heart, mind and spirit.

Makarand R. Paranjape
Professor of English, Jawaharlal Nehru University, New Delhi
Director, Indian Institute of Advanced Study, Shimla

Select Further Reading on Raja Rao

Dey, Esha. *The Novels of Raja Rao: The Theme of Quest*. New Delhi: Prestige Books, in association with the Indian Society for Commonwealth Studies, 1992.

Hardgrave, Robert L (ed.). *Word as Mantra: The Art of Raja Rao*. New Delhi: Katha Publications in association with University of Texas, Austin, 1998.

Mittapalli, Rajeshwar, and Pier Paolo Piciucco (eds). *The Fiction of Raja Rao: Critical Studies*. New Delhi: Atlantic Books, 2001.

Naik, M.K. *Raja Rao*. New York: Twayne Publishers Inc., 1972.

Narasimhaiah, C.D. *Raja Rao*. Indian Writer's Series. New Delhi: Arnold-Heinemann, 1973.

Narayan Shyamala, A. *Raja Rao: Man and His Works*. New Delhi: Sterling, 1988.

Niven, Alastair. *Truth Within Fiction: A Study of Raja Rao's The Serpent and the Rope*. Calcutta: Writers Workshop, 1987.

Paranjape, Makarand (ed.) *The Best of Raja Rao*. New Delhi: Katha, 1998.

Raja Rao: 1988 Neustadt Laureate. Special Issue of *World Literature Today* 62.4 (Autumn, 1988).

Sethi, Rumina. *Myths of the Nation: National Identity and Literary Representation*. Oxford: Clarendon Press, 1999.

Sharrad, Paul. *Raja Rao and Cultural Tradition*. New Delhi: Sterling, 1987.

Preface

The writing of this book has been an experiment in honesty. Facts of course are there, but facts are shrill. They have a way of saying more than they mean, and disbelievingly so. The silences and the symbols are omitted, and meaning taken out of breath and performance. Facts have to flow into event—there has to be *rasa,* flavour, to make facts melt into life. And the Indian experience is such a palimpsest, layer behind layer of tradition and myth and custom go to make such an existence: gesture is ritual, and each act a statement in terms of philosophy, superstition, historical or linguistic provincialism, caste originality, or merely a personal one, and yet it's all a whole, it's India. Thus to face honesty against an Indian event, an Indian life, one's expression has to be epic in style or to lie.

The Pauranic[1] style, therefore, is the only style an Indian can use—fact against custom, history against time (and I was going to say) geography against space, and it is these coordinates that have to change and make the life larger than it seems, and

---

[1] From Purana, legendary history, Rama and Krishna are parts of this legendary history, their stories being told in the *Ramayana* and the *Mahabharata.* See Glossary.

its small impurities and accidents and parts, must perforce be transmuted into equations where the mighty becomes normal, and the normal in its turn becoming myth. Prose and poetry thus flow into one another, the personal and the impersonal, making the drama altogether noble and simple. Hence the variegation of styles, Rama and Krishna run so naturally into the tale, the newspaper article (say of the *Times of Natal* or of the *Times,* London) treated first as reporting, then as history, so that, finally, when the whole as chronicle takes on a movement and rushes into the Gangetic flood, down the hill and wide as the plains, you speak in terms of song and anonymity, the crowd-singing story.

The Purana is never true except against the background of Truth—that is where the essence of fact shines.

If I have written thus another life of Gandhi, it's because most of the biographies (whether American or French, Greek or English) are true generally to facts but not so to meaning. There are, however, biographies by Indians—the official and monumental one is an extravagant dictionary of dates and facts, and the more able and personal ones exhausting demonstrations of the amalgam of human existence. A biography of Gandhi it seemed to me had to be written as it were from the inside, desperately, faithfully. It's an ambitious task. Should one dare it—I have.

Raja Rao

Part One

1

Fabled India

Every man's life is a fable. The not-two becomes two, and so the story. The great man is one whose life is a legend. A legend is just an epic fable, an hierophanous tale. The person becomes more and more one with the not-two, the principle. He who achieves the impersonal, the principle, he the great being, the Mahatma. He it is that's become the Law, from the laws that hold (*dhru*) the sun and the moon, the negative and positive in electricity, man and woman, the good and bad, and the law that makes the waters go down to the sea. When the sea and the waves are seen as water you see greatness. Greatness is not great. It is.

Once upon a time (that is now and always) there was a people tall and firm and fair, players of dice and betters on horses, who intrigued with godlings but supplicated the gods, especially Mitra the God of light, the sun, and Varuna the Lord of the water.

To gain thy mercy, Varuna, with hymns we bind thy heart, as binds the charioteer his tethered horse.

Since somehow the sun and the water were married, the world came to be and so this and that, you and me. They were an intellectual people, the Aryans were, and they speculated and wandered from some far icelands until they came towards the

3

land of the sun and of the seven rivers. That the sun was more
regulated here than in the cold north, in that the day followed
the night more quickly and the night the day, seemed to them
a continuous delight. So they sang praises to the sun. Also that
the rivers were warm and fordable showed that men could cross
over the water and conquer the sunlands.

The more south they penetrated, the shorter became the
day and the longer the night, and again the night was not so
long nor the sun so long gone, a temperate land it was with
mountains and innumerable rich valleys. Now they sang of the
valley and ripe corn, the colour of their skin. Man had only to
scratch and sow and everything grew as high as himself.

But further down there lived an astute and rich people, a
slightly darker men perhaps, but highly efficient with the bull and
the mortar, for they had built themselves great agglomerations
of permanent stone structures and lustral bathing places,
worshipping The Lord of All Creatures, the God of the Phallus.
They seemed contented and happy, with woman, jewel and the
pub. Today historians call them the people of Mohenjodaro. The
man of the swift horse defeated the man of the meaner bulls,
and the whole valley now lay for the northern nomad (far-seeing
and courageous) to conquer and subdue. The Aryan built himself
towers and fortresses and settled down to a more reasoned
existence. He now clothed himself in elegant bark of trees,
cultivated the cow, mother of milk and of gentility, changed
his gods as it suited his adventures (Mitra or Varuna, Indra
or Prajapati, they are all the same forces) and established little
republics or kingdoms, and around fire sanctuaries they loved to
debate. What is the nature of sleep or of death, of wifehood or
of wealth? Who hears? What knows? They split the word to its
background and thus found the principle of object behind sound,

and the coordinate system of consonants and vowels that makes for perfect speech. And the sound of all sounds that contains vowel and consonant and thus arising to its root showed the primary sound, the one which first moved from the unmovable Shiva, and so came all the world to be. The word is the world and the seat of breath, the hearth of wisdom. The learned went to kings for debate and the kings gave cows to the worthy, and so philosophy flowered all over the land of the Aryas, the Aryavarta.

* * *

Janaka, Emperor of Videha, was seated (to give audience) when Yajnavalkya arrived. The Emperor said to him: 'Yajnavalkya, for what purpose have you come here? With a desire for cattle, or to hear some subtle questions asked?'

Yajnavalkya said: 'Let me hear what anyone among your teachers may have told you.'

'Jitvan, the son of Silina, told me that the organ of speech (deity of fire) is Brahman.'

'As anyone who had (the benefit of being taught by a good) mother, father, and teacher should say, so did the son of Silina say that the organ of speech is Brahman; for what can be attained by a person who cannot speak? But did he tell you about its abode (body) and support?'

'No, he did not.'

'This Brahman is only one-footed, Your Majesty.'

'Then you tell us, O Yajnavalkya?'

'The (physical) organ of speech is its abode and akasha[1] is its support. It should be meditated upon as intelligence.'

---

[1] In the Upanishads, akasha is ether.

'What is intelligence, O Yajnavalkya?'

'It is the organ of speech, Your Majesty,' said Yajnavalkya. 'Through the organ of speech alone, O Emperor, are known the *Rig Veda,* the *Yajur Veda,* the *Sama Veda,* the *Atharvangirasa,* history, ancient lore, the arts, the Upanishads, verses, aphorisms, explanations, commentaries, (the results of) sacrifices, (the result of) offering oblations in the fire, (the result of) giving food and drink, this world, the next world, and all beings.'

'The organ of speech, Your Majesty, is the Supreme Brahman. The organ of speech never deserts him who, knowing this, meditates upon it; all beings eagerly approach him; and being a god, he attains the gods.'

'I give you a thousand cows with a bull as large as an elephant,' said Emperor Janaka.

Yajnavalkya replied: 'My father was of the opinion that one should not accept gifts from a disciple without fully instructing him.'

And the debate continued.

* * *

Meanwhile kings fought against kings, republics fought against republics and all the land was one large battleground, and since there was gold and spices, sugar cane and rice, and the white cotton pod for making garments with, a civilised life soon arose, that is to say, cities arose of carved wood or delicate stone, and great kings were born who sacrificed their kingdom for the Truth or mean ones who sacrificed the Truth for personal glory. But this glory does not last long, does it? Hence Truth-loving kings like Sri Rama destroyed monsters of egotism like Ravana who had abducted the great Queen Sita, herself holy wife unto

Sri Rama, and so with the populace, the monkeys, the bear and the very squirrel behind him, the king Ravana was conquered and his head fell at the feet of Sri Rama, incarnation of Truth. For what is evil but a shadow of Truth, as the world a reflection of the Self?

Then, perhaps thousands of years later, came Sri Krishna of the Yadavas, a Prince of Dwaraka, and when the two armies of the very evil Kauravas and the upright Pandavas faced one another (for there was base egoism and deceit behind the Kauravas, and Truth and love of dice play with the Pandavas) and so Krishna came to defend those who had Truth behind them. And he said:

'But know that That which pervades this universe is imperishable; there is none can make to perish that changeless being.

'It is these bodies of the everlasting, unperishing, incomprehensible body-dweller that have an end, as it is said. Therefore fight, O thou of Bharata's race.

'He who deems this to be a slayer, and he who thinks this to be slain, are alike without discernment; This slays not, neither is it slain.

'This never is born, and never dies, nor may it after being come again to be not; this unborn, everlasting, abiding ancient is not slain when the body is slain.

'Knowing this to be imperishable, everlasting, unborn, changeless, O son of Pritha, how and whom can a man make to be slain, or slay?'[2]

And so the *vira* then, the hero, he that leaps inwards before rushing outward. Mahavira, the great hero, was one such being

---

[2]   The *Bhagavad Gita*.

of aristocratic parents, of exquisite beauty, but he succumbed to the entanglements of the flesh only to arise, the hero, the monk, that wandering from far to further far inwardly, he discovered himself a combination of aptitudes, a bundle of fluxating memories, hanging on to a pure flowing stream of consciousness, and therewith discarding the accessories of being—for he was born again and again only for this end, as all men are—and he walked out now a free man and a friend of all living things. Achieving the one pure identity of his own being, he remained as it were, a star in some spaceless heaven, but brother to gnat and tiger, to tree and stone. His followers, the Jainas—from Jinna, the conqueror—contracted to severe moralities will not tread at night lest they should step on an insect, or drink uncovered water lest they should swallow innocent fleas, and they feed the wandering row of ants, or the lost bird for whom they build rest houses to this day. And of course they build hospices for old cows. They would worship monks too, the sky-clad (naked) and the white-covered (cloth-clad) ones.

Then came the Buddha, young and indomitable, a prince of the Sakyas, he fled from his kingdom and wife (and new-born heir and son lying under the Himalayan moon and snowshining silences)—he fled into the forest world of ascetics who asked serious questions and sat satisfied with half-answered answers. 'If you breathed this way you will reach that from which there is no returning', 'If you eat nothing and let the spine touch the stomach, and the stomach, the navel and the skin fall as powdered husk, and you've the perfume of celestial breath— then you reach that from which there's no returning' . . . etc. He did this and that as indicated, but did return to what he came from, and so he left the ascetics and their austerities, and reaching a solitary spot, tongue tucked to the roof of palate, he vowed he would not rise till the Truth was found. And Truth he found—the Aryan eight-fold path—suffering arises from desire, desire from the senses, and so on till the ego became a chemico-physical complex from which you escaped as you came, with discrimination (*buddhi*), with the clear understanding of the process. The process is life, is living, every second (wink of eye) an explosion of aggregates that illuminate and die forthwith—all is flux. The undoing of the process is *nirvana,* beatitude. And thus, therefore, freedom.

Buddhism's most historical hero was Ashoka, the Emperor. Having built the greatest empire India had ever known from the north of Afghanistan to the confines of Burma, and South as far as Mysore, Ashoka finally and stupidly went to war against a princeling, the king of Kalinga. And thousands on thousands of people were slaughtered on the battlefield. Dismayed with the sight of so much blood and sorrow, Ashoka then and there took a vow to turn his soldiers into messengers of peace and declared on stone edicts that stand to this day:

'When he had been consecrated eight years the Beloved of the Gods, the kind Piyadassi, conquered Kalinga. A hundred and fifty thousand people were deported, a hundred thousand were killed and many times that number perished. Afterwards, now that Kalinga was annexed, the Beloved of the Gods very earnestly practised Dhamma, desired Dhamma, and taught Dhamma. On conquering Kalinga the Beloved of the Gods felt remorse, for when an independent country is conquered the slaughter, death, and deportation of the people is extremely grievous to the Beloved of the Gods, and weighs heavily on his mind. What is even more deplorable to the Beloved of the Gods is that those who dwell there, whether

Brahmins, Sramanas, or those of other sects, or householders who show obedience to their superiors, obedience to mother and father, obedience to their teachers and behave well and devotedly towards their friends, acquaintances, colleagues, relatives, slaves, and servants—all suffer violence, murder, and separation from their loved ones. Even those who are fortunate to have escaped, and whose love is undiminished (by the brutalising effect of war), suffer from the misfortunes of their friends, acquaintances, colleagues, and relatives. This participation of all men in suffering, weighs heavily on the mind of the Beloved of the Gods . . .'[3]

Ashoka's Buddhism melted into different schools and churches and finally two groups gathered strength—the Hinayana and the Mahayana, the one flowing south into Ceylon and further still to the Malayan Archipelago, and the other, the Mahayana, going into China and Japan—and thus Zen.

Mahayana in its turn turned to the worship of the Buddha as god, and he in his final incarnation became Vishnu—many Buddhist sanctuaries became Vaishnavite temples, and with the Bhakti cult India was filled with the song of God.

Islam had by now entered into this holy land, and the challenge and defeat and victory and defeat again made the living god a need. And God walked India for seven centuries (some admitting that he could be approached but not touched, and others that he could be touched but not identified with, and yet others, the metaphysicians, the greatest, who continued to declare 'God am I. *Shivoham Shivoham*' but these were of

---

[3]   Romila Thapar, *Ashoka and the Decline of the Mauryas,* pp. 255-6.

necessity few and secluded away in the South and in the forests or on mountain tops). Finally the British came with ships, guns, Christianity and organisational ability, conquered India, or rather the India that was unheroic and ungodly, and out of this froth, as at the Churning of the Ocean, arose the glory of Vedanta with Ram Mohun Roy, Ramakrishna, Vivekananda, Dayananda Saraswati, the Theosophical Society—and Gandhi.

* * *

In the dim recesses of the fold that India takes above the belt of Bombay as she turns on herself tonguing away from the west, there arise a series of white cliffs and dun hills above the Bay of Cambay, called the Province of Saurashtra, or Kathiawar. Ancient and heroic, she has always been a battleground of kings and of philosophical ideas. Sri Krishna was prince of Dwaraka, after all. Vaishnavism and Jainism lived side by side in continuous dialogue and in healthy accommodation. Kathiawar and Rajasthan are the home of heraldic bards who sing of their heroes to this day.

> Once there was a Prince, Prithvi was his name
> And his glory I sing, I sing, I, Chand, the bard.

Each prince was of some ancient lineage going back through kings, emperors, sages to the very moon or sun, and each prince or princeling has done some heroic deed—or at least his ancestors had performed some historic or mystic act of courage or loyalty or of devotion, so that again and again it has been a land of fearless chivalry. Even the Mughals who had conquered the country so quickly could not so easily conquer

Rajasthan and so they often did the second best—they married the princess of the kingdom and thus the Mongols and the Rajputs created the magnificent civilisation of Mughal India. Shah Jahan, who built the Taj Mahal, had a Rajput mother and so did his father, Jehangir. And yet some Rajputs would rather fight in the hills than succumb to the formidable strength of the Mughal war machine. Even to this day, you remember, in every family history, which Raja or Maharaja's ancestors succumbed to the Mughal by the marrying of his daughter (for example, the Gohels of Jaipur) and some like the family of Udaipur did not and thus while they rushed to the hill or forest to protect their honour, the women jumped into the pyre that their wifely or virgin holiness remain intangible. I tell you Lord . . .

The princes of Kathiawar, like the Rajputs everywhere, claimed their descent from the sun and the moon, and belonged to the clan of Sri Rama (the Ikshavakus) or of Sri Krishna (the Yadavas). For, after all, Dwaraka was just round the corner of the peninsula, and that was where Sri Krishna ruled, so that most of the princes of course belonged to the Yadavas, or so they believed. Remember, Sri Krishna married his wife Rukmini at Madhavpur, and that is just down the curve of the bay, and the Yadavas once (and remember too) on that fateful day when they went gambolling to the sacred city of Prabhas Patan and got into a fist-fight, and then to a brawl and then to a real battle, they sent for Sri Krishna.

But he was not to be found—he'd so planned as to go and lie under a tree (and had not Gandhari cursed that the race of Sri Krishna come to an end)—and a hunter took Sri Krishna's heel for the head of a deer, and the greatest of Indians thus played the game even of death. He had planned it all, so everything happened according to his intent—for, for him intent and action were just experience, there was none to act, as it were for he was in action as inaction and in inaction as action.

And so too was that other game of Sri Krishna. He had, while at school, a poor Brahmin companion, Sudhama was his name and he was raggedly miserable. Life had been most ungenerous to him (again it was Sri Krishna's game)—Sudhama had a wife with a tongue of charcoal cinders and hair made as of rough-hewn hemp. When she called, even the street dogs would think it was one of their kind talking, and they started answering back. But Sudhama was so patient; he would always speak, when humiliated by his wife, of his friend Sri Krishna who ruled in Dwaraka. 'Fine thing to have such a friend. But what does he do for you, you son of tamarind tree hag.'

Hearing this morning after morning, Sudhama said one day to his wife: 'I go to see Sri Krishna today, this very day.'

'Oh yes you will go, you and your coconut-head and bursted-bleak belly, and seeing your tousled hair and bent back and bamboo limbs, even the guards will laugh at you.'

'Perhaps you're right,' said Sudhama, 'but give me please a handful of puffed rice and a piece of molass.'

'What for?' she asked.

'Well, when one goes to see someone, you don't ever go empty-handed, do you?'

'A beggar,' declared Sudhama's wife, 'has no manners, as the buffalo has no courtesies.'

'Well, so be it. Give what puffed rice and molass you have to me.'

Cursing her stars for such a rice-miserable destiny—that even the little puffed rice she had, she had perforce to give part of it away—she threw a handful of it to Sudhama's dhoti-edge, broke a piece of molass from the pot, and said with wide-fingered threatening hands: 'And don't you come back plain-handed, you coconut-head, after all this. I'll howl till the very spirits in the crematoriums will be frightened. Let's see what your great friend Sri Krishna is going to proclaim and perform for you. I take the name of God and tell you he will have you chased out of the city.'

Sudhama was so accustomed to his wife's tongue and breath, it was as if he heard sound but not meaningful speech. He picked his stick from the corner, and taking the thought of Sri Krishna, he started towards holy Dwaraka. Long was the road to Dwaraka, but such the sweetness of love, the trees seemed to open up and spread wide-limbed shade, and cool breezes blew from the northern mountains, and the sea seemed to churn in fevered joy. For when you take the thought of the Lord true, all things that seek him rejoice in your rejoicement—they also wave up and swell with your joy. Sudhama arrived at the city gates and these opened themselves as if by the vestal deities, and even the palace guards did not seem to mind his looks.

'Could you tell His Highness,' he begged, 'the Lord of Lords, his poor school-fellow, the Brahmin Sudhama is at the door?'

'Be so kind as to wait here, Pundit Sir,' said the guard politely, 'and I'll go and tell the Chamberlain.'

It was all as if the gods were playing a trick, the Chamberlain seemed just waiting for this event at the door, and Sri Krishna himself, when he heard the news, he had such joy, people could see tears run down his lotus eyes. 'Prepare,' he commanded, 'water to wash my guest's feet.' And as Sri Krishna clad in silken blue, his eyes clear as sleep, his gait as if made by the curvature of form when he stood, the washing-stool before him, there he appeared across the courtyard, Sudhama, his boyhood friend. In their high niches the pigeons and the parrots began to coo, and the ladies peered from the top apartments at this wondrous happening.[4] Krishna bade Sudhama stand on the ivory stool, and rich with jugs of silver swan-shapen and filled with water, first warm and then cold, and when these were thrown on the Brahmin's withered and dusty feet—then did Krishna taking the silken hand-cloth from his Chamberlain's arm, wipe his friends feet himself. Now Sri Krishna took his friend to the marbled court and before all his noblemen, he said, 'Friend, be seated,' and showed Sudhama the throne. Could a poor Brahmin occupy such an august seat? No. He would not. Krishna himself sat on a couch beside his friend. They now spoke to each other of all that had happened and passed by since their boyhood. They wept and laughed but all around there was as if a wall of luminescent silence. Everything moved in the palace as usual, the noblemen retired to the afternoon couch for their siesta, the servants moved with agility and calm, from corner to corner of the palace, the nine diurnal musics sounded, the elephants trumpeted after a good feed, the cows lowed for their returning calves, and when evening fell a great banquet was laid for the poor Brahmin, Sudhama, and he ate as if he was eating his own food, at his own home. For, for the first time he was at home with himself. Krishna enjoyed munching the puffed rice his friend had brought, and some of it was sent upstairs to Rukmini, and all the palace was given bits of it. It tasted, did this puffed rice, as nothing one has tasted before. It had the delicate saffron smell of Sri Krishna himself. And when the night drums sounded and the meal was over, the hands were washed, the betel leaves served, a carriage was made ready, and

---

[4] You can see this in many a Rajput miniature today.

beneath the high chandeliers, flower and fruit hangings, as Sri Krishna said farewell to his friend, he embraced him again and again, and they wept. Yes, Sudhama had to go. He had now to go back home. But he'd forgotten his promise to his wife. He had asked nothing of Sri Krishna. Pray what can you ask of a friend who is King?

Yet Sudhama was so happy the very mind-picture of Sri Krishna brought him tears. And when he came nearer and nearer his home, he began however to have fits of fearfulness. What would it be like coming back so plain handed? But when the town came it was all a different town—the very walls were shining as if white-washed and much repaired, and when his carriage stopped, his wife stood, a gold plate in her hands, flowers and *kumkum* water floating in it, and lighting the lamp of auspiciousness, she welcomed her lord befittingly, and fell at his withered feet. And from that day onwards the city came to be called Sudhamapuri, or the city of Sudhama, but due to the crookedness of people's speech, it became Puri, and later someone added *bunder*[5] to it so that today it's called Porbandar, Haven-city.

* * *

The Ranas of Porbandar, though they are Rajputs, do not come from the family of Sri Rama or of Sri Krishna, but from that of Hanuman. For this is how it happened: at the time when Sri Rama was preparing to fight against Ravana, Hanuman, the Monkey-God was secretly going to Ceylon to see where Lady Sita sat in imprisonment. Flying across the ocean, a drop of his thick sweat fell, and a crocodile drinking it brought forth a

---

[5]   *Bunder* means harbour, haven.

young human but with a monkey spine, and so to this day the Princes of Porbandar are called Puncharia. And the birth of the family happened so long and long ago that the bards say that till the beginning of the British conquest in the eighteenth century, at least 1098 of the Puncharias have been born and have died, and have ruled from Ghumli or Chayya, their ancient capitals, all of Kathiawar, sometimes all of North India, and sometimes, so the sagas say, they ruled till the frontiers of Samarkhand. For they were a maritime people, the Alexandrians and the Romans traded with them, and have left records of Baradaxima (Porbandar) in their geography books.

This was about the time of the good emperor Ashoka, whose exhortations and edicts stand cut on rock columns, in Kathiawar, to this day. 'King Priyadarshin, beloved of the gods, desires,' so runs the seventh edict, 'that everywhere ascetics of all persuasions should dwell in peace. He desires in all of them self-control and purity of soul. But people have different opinions and different likings. They may do all or a part of what they have to do. Nevertheless, for one who is not able to make large religious gifts, self-control, purity of mind, gratitude and firm devotion which last forever, are good.'

Meanwhile the Jainas begged for the protection of creatures big and small. They went to the princes, then to the kings, and later, much later, to the Emperor himself, that little creatures, helpless in their smallness or forlorn in their temperate natures, be saved from destruction. 'In the town of Rasmi,' so runs an edict on stone of Maharaja Chattar Singh, 'whosoever slay sheep, buffaloes, goats or other living thing is a criminal to the State: his house, cattle and effects shall be forfeited, and himself expelled from the village.' And again Maharana Jai Singh commanded the inhabitants of Bakrol, printers, oil-millers, and potters—that from the eleventh of Asadh (June) to the full moon of Asoj (September) when Jaina monks be in retreat 'and insects abound,' that they not be killed by the potter's-wheel or the oil-mill or the fishing net; hence 'none shall drain the waters of the lake; no oil-mill shall work or earthen vessel be made during these four rainy months'.

With the incursion of Islam into India the Ranas of Porbandar fled from one territory to the other till all they possessed in the sixteenth century was the small but ancient town of Chayya, and a few villages surrounding it. From there they looked about and while the Mughal conquerors were busy consolidating their vast and troubled empire, the Ranas carved out their own little kingdom, and unperceived, slipped to Porbandar, and established themselves there until the British came. 'While Colonel Walker was still in Kathiawar,' wrote Capt. Wilberforce Bell, 'disturbances broke out in Porbandar where Prathiraj, son of Rana Haloji rebelled against his father and seized the fort at Chayya. All the efforts to dislodge him failed and finally the Rana asked aid from the British. A force was sent to co-operate with him and after a siege lasting for two hours the fort of Chayya fell and Prathiraj surrendered . . . Porbandar was now placed under British protection and a detachment of one hundred men was stationed in the fort, for the protection of the Rana.' Later the Ranas were recognised as major princes of Kathiawar, and the Rana was now called His Highness, the Rana of Porbandar, and the right of a salute of eleven guns conferred on him. And quickly the city became once again an important trading centre sending out merchants and merchandise to the Persian Gulf, Arabia, the Red Sea, and to the ports of far Africa.

* * *

The Gandhis of Porbandar were a stout and subtle race. Like the marble house they lived in, where, stone after stone when cut from the quarry and laid one after the other, big, tenuous, nervous, the rains came and plastered it all to one constituent whole so that when you had to cut through for a door or stair you'd have to quarry like on the flank of the mountain whence they came—and once quarried and cut, you enter through the main door and you see to the left and to the right, rooms, apartments, corridors that connect one household with the other, and where birth, festivities, and kitchenings took place, and so floor after floor to the rooms of the elders, and further still to the rooms of worship, of Krishna, the Lord, and of Devi, the Benign Goddess, and since stone could no more bear on stone, the last floor was made of delicate, fine, chiselled woodwork, from under which one could survey the other tall and beflagged houses to the city walls, massive and in ruins, to the palace itself, mighty, mysterious, self-consistent, and now, farther still to the city walls again—and then the sea. The sea opened on Arabia and Africa, and down and around to the archipelagos of Malaysia, and the merchants and saints of Porbandar, had commerced with the west and the east, and had carried thither gold, diamonds and pearls, the religion of the Buddha, and of Shiva, the triple-faced.

The Arabs, able seamen that they were (they, the discoverers of the monsoon winds) dominated the Indian Ocean and founded entrepots on the West Coast of India and the East Coast of Africa as far as Zanzibar—selling incense and coffee against gold, ivory, spice or precious stone. Some of them too brought the strength of their faith, the loyalty of the race, to serve Indian princes, noblemen, patricians, as guards of palaces, courts and treasuries, protecting their masters from marauders of feudal wars or of palace revolutions. Here also in India they took wives, traded and prospered.

Therefore, to Africa, the Muslims of Porbandar went to trade, and finally to settle, so that this white city, despite its small population, came to be no mean port but an important emporium. The eldest among its citizenry were without doubt, the Gandhis of Kutiyala.

For indeed the Gandhis belonged long ago to Kutiyala, in the state of Junagadh, and Lalji Gandhi, somewhere in the eighteenth century, moved on to Porbandar, having served well his masters there in Junagadh as chamberlain at a minor nobleman's court, and now here in Porbandar he became daftari[6] or minister of state to the Ranas of Porbandar. And thus the Gandhi home (bought about 1777) in Porbandar, white, important and efficient. The rooms were small and dark, and sometimes smoke could smother you, but you arose out of it all a sturdy, serious, faith-held person, the doors indomitably opening on to the sea.

The house was the family, rooms connected with corridors, stairs linking veranda to courtyard, inner, outer, communicant, and thus brothers, cousins, friends, children, orphans, women, and servants all lived in active and inactive harmony. When so many live together the eldest lays the law by his presence, his brothers obey him with respect and devotion—often the elder brother would be at worship at the chapel upstairs, and the younger ones would have to consult him about matters of family or of the state, and before God and his flowers of worship, before incense and fruit offerings, he the eldest gives his opinion—and so the order goes out. Whether it be about some quarrel between servants, orderlies, coachmen, or they be relating to the Rana

---

6   Keeper of records.

himself, every gesture was a gesture made before God. You never go back on it. You stay and let the rains fall on the terrace. Little streams form and go down the drains back to the ocean. The marble is whiter, the cementing firmer, and high up in his sanctuary, the God himself seems to breathe and shine and to protect. Life is too serious to be lived any other way.

Lalji Gandhi had a son called Kishendas, who succeeded his father as daftari to the court of Porbandar, and he himself had two sons, Haridas and Govindadas, and they in turn became daftaris, so that by the time Ottum Chand Gandhi, the greatest of them all entered history, the daftari Gandhis held always a hereditary post, as it were. Ota (Ottum Chand) Gandhi himself was a man of firm fibre, of fierce loyalties, and of religious courage. He and his God mattered in all affairs of man and of the state. He was a person of few words, and when he said them they were to be like the stones of the hills that lain one over the other, silence and prayer would cement. But the Ranas of Porbandar were no easy masters to serve, and like when the monsoon rains came, they thundered and flashed and much damage could be done to the Gandhi household. But who can destroy what God has built and established? He who holds to God builds his home in another and superior dimension. Come summer heat or monsoon rain, the worship will go on.

One day when Ota Gandhi was still young and his uncle was daftari, the Rana sent for the daftari. The uncle was not there so Ota Gandhi went in his place.

'Well, there's a job to be done,' said the Rana.

'Why may I not do it, sire?' he asked.

'A troublesome job,' said the Rana.

'With faith in his sovereign and with devotion to the greater sovereign who rules over all, what cannot be achieved, sire?'

'Great words, son, but the deed is difficult.'

'Pray, may I try?'

'Yes, if you will,' said the Rana gravely impressed with such self-assurance in so young a man.

'Well, the matter is just this, Ota. My neighbour, the big fish of Junagadh, as you know, has his own tricks behind his beads. You know the Master of Customs, between his state and ours, pays me no revenue any more. And we are poor as you realise. Things are difficult.'

'May I, sire, look after the matter—have I a free hand?'

'As long as the evil does not spread, what greater good can I ask? Go, and you have my blessings.'

Then young Ota jumped on his Kathiawari mare and rode to his destiny. The villages of Junagadh and Porbandar were lying in each other's territory. To go from one to the other meant so much organisational structure, for customs, for collecting revenue, and for free movement for marriages, court cases or funerals. Ota Gandhi had a bright idea. Why not have the whole land surveyed, and barter that land against the narrow sea coast where nothing grew. Thus there would be a contiguous territory, and there would be no place for external intrigues? If you sent the silk shawl and betel nut to me, and I send back betel nut and silk shawl to you, he who wins wins. That settles the matter. However, there was another idea behind that idea. But this was never to be said before the right time came.

The Nawab Sahib of Junagadh was of course mightily pleased that one of his own subjects had made so fortunate a proposal— you got growing land against sandy shores. And you had them all together against these snaps and snatches of village lands. Once the treaty was negotiated and signed, and Porbandar now had one long tongue of territory by the sea coast, Ota Gandhi

built a dam over the river Sabra, and all the sea coast became
one vast garden. Thus the revenues of Porbandar increased and
it was then the British, impressed with the administration and
growth of the state, made the Rana a First Class Prince, with the
right to an eleven gun salute.

And then Ota Gandhi became the Prime Minister of the
State.

Fiercely honest, silent and religious, Ota Gandhi was not
an easy Prime Minister for the Rana to handle. Every event of
the state was for Ota a problem of princely pride and of divine
devotion. And what God wished to give He would give, for
Ota wanted nothing but service, service to his God and to his
sovereign. Palace intrigues and princely extravagances did not
worry him; he would slip through them with determination
and diplomacy. The people trusted him and he trusted his
sovereign and the sovereign trusted the people. In such a close-
knit hierarchy anything might happen, thus every gesture had
to be precise and prayerful. One false step before God and
all may be in shambles and ruins. For example, there were
betrothals, initiation ceremonies, ceremonies of marriage and of
pregnancy. The Prime Minister is all-powerful and merchants
and landowners would send in rice, pulses, cows-butter and
spices for the wedding of the Prime Minister's son. People did
not remember, the Prime Minister was the head of state, owing
fealty only to his lord. He loved his fellow subjects all. So the
whole town had to be invited for these festivities with priest and
music with 'swastika-mark on the city gate'.

The wedding was spread over a week. The Rana himself
was a constant visitor to the ceremonies. Therefore when Ota
Gandhi's son, Karamchand (father of the Mahatma), was
married off in ceremonies befitting a Prime Minister's son, Ota

paid back to every grain shop the price of the grain sent and to the treasury he sent all the jewellery received: 'It belongs to His Highness, the Rana.' The Rana would not hear of it. 'You belong to the state,' he said 'and the marriage of your children is a state function. Your sons are my sons.'

Thus did Ota Gandhi serve his master, Rana Khimoji, but when the Rana died he left only a boy of eight, Vikmatji, as heir to the throne. Therefore a regency was established, and the regent was none other than the Queen herself, Rupali Ba, efficient, intriguing and ambitious. Why should the Prime Minister be so powerful? True her husband had trusted him, but was everything people said true? Were there not flaws in the structure somewhere? Were not what the women in the palace said also true? How can a woman alone, and a regent, trust so powerful a Prime Minister? He has been too long on his couch of authority; he behaves as if he himself were the sovereign. After all, this cannot go on forever.

One day a man, the treasury officer, suddenly appeared at the home of the Prime Minister. The master of the household was not at home; he was at his office. The lady of the house, Lakshmi Ma, was there.

'Mother, my life is in danger,' he said, 'protect me.'

'You have my promise, Kothari Saheb. I will see that no harm is done. But what is the matter?' she added after a moment of silence.

'Mother,' said the Kothari, 'the Prime Minister knows that day in and day out people come from the palace asking for money. I am no gift-giving cow. I am sick of it all. I refuse unless I have written word from the Queen herself.'

'That is but right,' said Lakshmi Ma.

'But the Queen thinks somehow that I'm power-mad. She's a woman, Mother, and she's been poisoned by other women.'

'Come in, and be welcome and safe.'

And she hid him in the house.

'I've something to ask,' said Lakshmi Ma when Ota Gandhi returned from his office.

'Well, is anything the matter? Is anything serious the matter?'

'Yes, but the Master of the House must uphold my promise.'

'How can the Master of the House not uphold what his dharmic partner has promised? To whom is the promise made and for what? Have I refused you anything so far anyway?' were Ota's words.

'The treasurer Khimoji is in hiding with us. The Queen has decided on her vengeance.'

'But I am only her Prime Minister.'

'Justice must be upheld. I have given my promise,' said Lakshmi Ma.

'The promise will be kept,' said Ota.

He gave orders to his Arab guards to be ready for any consequence. Mohammed Makram, the chief, had pledged his sword to his master. It was there for every deed of duty.

The Queen wanted her treasurer back. Ota Gandhi now returned to the palace.

'Your Highness, this Khimoji is an honest and loyal man. If you can prove one dishonest act of his I will gladly hand him over to you. I know him. I pledge my word to you.'

'He's my treasurer and I, as Queen and Regent, want him delivered to me.'

'My job is to perform my dharma, Your Highness. The Kothari I know is an innocent man, and I cannot give him up to you.'

'Then you'll have to bear the consequences,' she shouted and dismissed her Prime Minister.

In the middle of the night the Kothari was given a duplicate key of the city gates and he escaped with his life. In a short while shells came hurtling on the Prime Minister's house. Either the fugitive is surrendered or the whole Gandhi house would be razed to the ground. Inside the house women and children lay in their rooms in prayer and fear while Ota went from door to door barricading them from within. The Arab guards fought with the Queen's regulars. Ghulam Mohammed died fighting. But such is the play of God—just when all hope was lost, the British who heard of these operatic events sent orders to the Queen to stop every move against her Prime Minister. Ota Gandhi had won but what victory could that be when it was against his own sovereign? God's ways are strange. Let us play the game knowing not where we go. The end is not here nor now. The end is where one is beyond the here and now. 'The strength of the weak is Sri Rama.'

After this drama Ota Gandhi retired to his ancestral home at Kutiyala, in the state of Junagadh. There he would cultivate his estate and perform his worships, and read the *Ramayana.*

But Ota Gandhi was too endowed a man to be left on his country estates. Whether the Persian wheels are greased or not, or whether this time cotton has to be sown instead of *jowar,* any agent could decide. Or frame petitions to His Highness the Nawab of Junagadh about this land dispute between neighbours or that money dispute between merchants, such functions any minor *vakil* could perform. The Nawab was not going to leave this important man in remote Kutiyala. 'Come to me,' he commanded. Ota Gandhi, always deferential to the rulers, jumped on his mare, and in obedience to the command soon found himself in the palace. When the Nawab saw Ota coming, the ruler came towards him with warmth and exquisite courtesy. Ota Gandhi, however, true to his race, offered his left hand in greeting.

'What, Ota Bhai, what's the matter?'

'Your Highness, the other hand is pledged to Porbandar,' he replied with deference and in sorrow.

'Anyway, would you be Prime Minister? I would give half my kingdom to have a minister like you.'

'How can I, Your Highness, my heart and care are all elsewhere.'

'Some of your heart must also be here. After all, you belong here. Give the bit of your heart that still is with Junagadh. However, I appoint you Karabari[7] of Kutiyala. And you and your descendants need never pay custom duties. Such is our love for you.'

'So be it, Your Highness,' he answered, and thanking the prince deeply for his generosity Ota Gandhi went back to Kutiyala, obedient and grateful, and jumped straight into his work, as if all work was own work and that work was God's.

For it was to God that he was truly dedicated. He believed in the richness of the Lord, in Sri Rama who could fill your heart with heavenly joy, and see you through the trials of existence as if they were nothing but minor irritations as long as you knew it was the hand of God that guided you. What was there in the world but Sri Rama? Rama, Sri Rama, he of the Raghu race, he would repeat and work himself up into an ecstasy. Life was a gift that one could love Sri Rama.

'Lord, may you help me perform my dharma, and be your devoted servant, forever.'

---

[7] Commissioner

But now Rupali Ba of Porbandar, she was dead, and her son, Vikmatji, became the ruler. The Nawab of Junagadh, on his own initiative, negotiated the return of the Gandhis to Porbandar.

'Would you be our Prime Minister again?'

'Sire,' replied Ota Gandhi, 'I'm now the servant of the Lord. Leave me to my Lord. But if you insist, may I say: There is my son Karamchand. He's already in your service, your personal secretary. Is that not like me being there?'

'Yes,' said Rana Vikmatji but remembering the devotion Ota Gandhi had poured into the service of the state, 'Karamchand Gandhi will be my Karabari,' he added smiling, 'and later my Prime Minister.'

Karamchand Gandhi was twenty-five when he accepted the silver inkstand and perforated sand pot—the traditional insignia of Prime Ministership.

This was probably somewhere around the year 1847.[8] And for twenty-eight years Karamchand Gandhi, also called Kaba Gandhi, consolidated the work of his father. Silent and steady, he did not seem to have the genius of his father. But he had the same devotion to his prince. Rana Vikmatji was no great ruler, but he was pious and devoted. Between them they built a state which became the jewel of Kathiawar. The British agent at Rajkot was so pleased with Karamchand that when the Supreme Political Court was established, Karamchand was automatically named one of its members. But, in fact, Karamchand thought, was it not an insult to the state? The Rana was King and Supreme Power in his state, and the highest justice should ever be his making. But the British, knowing the vagaries and malpractices

---

8   E.P., p. 179.

of the Indian princes, wanted the poor man to have some higher and more independent power to look to for protection. And thus they set up a sort of Supreme Court for all the Princely States of Kathiawar. The Rana of Porbandar, however, excused his Prime Minister's absence (at the first meeting of the court) on considerations of bad health, and suggested someone else should take his place.

'You have not considered,' wrote the Political Agent, 'as you ought to have, with whom the authority . . . rests, nor have you stopped to ask yourself how a thing once settled can be unsettled at the last moment. You are therefore informed that a penalty of five rupees a day will be exacted till Kaba Gandhi attends, and if he does not attend within ten days the amount may have to be enhanced.'[9] And this communication brought Kaba Gandhi straight to the new court. Later he was even appointed a member of the Rajasthanic Court, a court for the settlement of disputes between the Princes and their feudal chiefs.

Meanwhile the Rana got into further trouble. His son Madhavsinh, under the influence of his companion, Khavas, became a drunkard. And when he, the heir apparent, finally died of drink, the father was so angered that Raja Vikmatji had Khavas' ears and nose cut off. Thereupon young Khavas jumped down his balcony and killed himself. The British heard of it, and dealt a devastating blow to the Rana; he was degraded into a third class prince. This brought the Rana closer and closer to his God. But Karamchand Gandhi was unhappy with it all. What his father had built with such devotion, he wanted it to flourish in even greater splendour. However, when this could not be, and the state of Rajkot needed a Prime Minister, he left

_____
9 1 October 1867.

his brother Tulsidas at Porbandar, and went to Rajkot to put the affairs there in order. You know it is not always easy to be loyal and strong before your sovereign. But the Thakore Sahib of Rajkot admired the independence and sense of justice of the new Prime Minister, and never interfered with the workings of the state. People who went to appeal to the Prince against his Prime Minister were sent back to Kaba Gandhi. 'Tell him the truth and he will deal justice to the just and the unjust equally.'

Such was Karamchand Gandhi's reputation that the Thakore of Vankaner now wanted him as Prime Minister. But Kaba Gandhi would not go. Having left one Prince, the Rana of Porbandar, he'd become the Prime Minister of Rajkot. What more could one want? And the British had shown real respect for his administration.

'No, sire, I would rather stay with Rajkot.' But the pressures of other statesmen, cousins and friends were there: 'You can stay as long as you wish. After all, you can always go back to Rajkot.'

'But,' protested Karamchand Gandhi, 'once I take charge of a state and I do so in the name of God and of my elders, how could I ever leave it? Well, if you insist I'll take up the Prime Ministership, and only for five years. If the Rana allows me every freedom and I stay for five years, proper and good. But if he interferes with my administration, then I leave bundle and bullock-cart to where I came from.'

'Yes, you could, and that's a royal promise,' said the Thakore of Vankaner. And so Karamchand and his family now moved to Vankaner.

But if it's easy for a Rana to make a promise, it was easier still for him to break his promise. He started interfering with the administration but Karamchand held out with courage, disinterestedness and simplicity. For the Gandhis were a simple people. And once when the Rana intervened in an affair of state about some sale, and settled it against the best interests of Vankaner, the Prime Minister went on a fast. He would now go back to Rajkot from where he came. He was finally allowed to leave but then the Chief, after due apologies, begged him to come back. Kaba Gandhi went back to work with humility and devotion, on the promise that no interference would ever come from the Thakore Saheb again.

'You will have your way. I promise you that.' However, very soon the promise was broken, and Karamchand asked to be relieved of his responsibility.

'What matters are the people and the Truth. So I go back where best I can serve the people and the Truth. The contract, sire, was for five years. A word is a word given before God. And, remember, it's a King's word.'

'You know, Karamchand, there's no king who'd be as generous as I am. For just a few months of service, here you are, and I am giving you ten thousand pieces of silver.'

'Sire, I would want only the word honoured.'

And the carriage was ready. He went home to see if all his belongings had left. They had. When he came back to his carriage he felt the seat underneath him uncomfortable. He jumped down from his seat and lifted the seat cover. The Chief's silver was hidden under it.

'Take it down!' shouted Karamchand, for he was also a man of fierce temper. 'Take it down, Puniya!' he shouted to his favourite servant. 'And this as well,' he added, when he found more money elsewhere in the carriage. The two sacks of silver were left on the doorsteps. And the carriage moved on.

The Gandhis were difficult people. Always scrupulous with others' money, they themselves never cared for money. When later Karamchand became Prime Minister of Rajkot again, and the Rana offered him any land he wanted to construct a house on, Karamchand chose just four hundred square yards. 'Take more, Karamchand. Remember you are an important man, and you have a large family.'

'For me and for my family, sire,' replied Karamchand, 'this length and width of land is sufficient. What shall I do with more?'

Such austerity frightened and humbled the Rana. A drunkard, he would be afraid to show his weaknesses before his Prime Minister; fond of women, he was terrified of what the Prime Minister would do to balk his adventures. Once a Brahmin woman, the young bride of one of his subjects, was seen by the River Aji. The Rana found her beautiful. Word went out that night that with ladder and police the woman would be seduced by him. When the servants of the Rana arrived with the necessary ladder, they were arrested and locked up. The Thakore Saheb's tricks were undone.

Yet Kaba Gandhi would not let the British agent show the least disrespect to his ruler. Once when the British agent lacked courtesy even to Karamchand himself, the Prime Minister just went back home. 'Tell the political agent of Her Majesty that the Dewan of Rajkot came on appointment. Since the Saheb is not free, he has gone back. If the Saheb wants to discuss anything with me, let him write to me.' The British agent had to apologise for such misdemeanour on his part. A word given is a truth stated.

And it was the same in his private life.

Karamchand Gandhi was married when he was fourteen years of age. He had a daughter by this union. He married again on the death of his first wife. He was twenty-five years of age then and this wife again died leaving another girl behind. He married for a third time, but this new wife, being ill, never bore him a child. As you know, without a son no manes are ever satisfied. And in case your wife gives you no son, ask her permission and marry again for the birth of an heir, so goes the tradition.

'May I marry again?' he asked his wife.

'Yes, you may,' said she. It was good for her that there should be an heir for the unearthly satisfactions even of her own soul.

'Yes, find a good wife and for your sake and mine, marry her.'

But, who would give his young daughter to the Prime Minister of Rajkot in marriage? He was already over forty years of age, and this would be his fourth marriage. No upper class family would, and no one in one's own community will.

But a bride was at last found—Putli Ba (or the Toy Lady) was her lovely name, and she came into the house not just as bearer of an heir, but as a noble wife to a truth-dedicated and powerful man, and finally as mother to the Mahatma.

Putli Ba's humbler ancestry was made up by her benignity. Young and devout, her song and silence, and brief words, equated the house into discreet little patterns; apartments were linked with apartments (for it was a wealthy and large family) where after all five generations had grown and prospered in tolerance and in piety. Putli Ba's own worships sounded from floor to floor of the house, and who would not have loved her chants and her *tulasi* adorations? Krishna, the Lord, was born in Brindavan, on the banks of the Jumna, and was smuggled away to Dwaraka on the Cambay sea. And Devaki the mother had to slip through the night lest the Uncle's minions discover him, such one's grave anxieties. And Devaki with the blue-bodied baby, little Krishna, came to Dwaraka. And he the Lord later killed Kaliya, the serpent, riding over him, stole butter from his foster-mother's kitchen and hid himself in the *tulasi* groves.

'Oh Lord of Dwaraka; would I not have a son too,' so ran Putli Ba's desperate prayers.

The kitchen smoke burnt her eyes, yet the womb-longings, who would answer but the Lord?

* * *

'Kaba Gandhi's was a large household,' writes the biographer. 'The number of guests who sat to eat with him was seldom less than twenty. They included not only members of the family but also guests, secretaries, officials, who together with the members of the family constituted the wider family.

'The keystone of this domestic edifice was Putli Ba. An ideal housewife, she was the first to rise and the last to go to bed . . . In spite of all this she was always cheerful and smiling. No one had ever heard her raise her voice. She never made any distinction between her own children and other children in the family . . .

'Kaba Gandhi as the head of the family looked after the well-being of every member of his clan—getting them married, settling them in life, securing them jobs, etc., besides helping Putli Ba in her household work. It was a familiar sight which people in Porbandar still remember, of him sitting in Shrinathji's temple day after day, peeling and paring vegetables for his wife's kitchen while he discussed with his visitors and officials affairs of the state.'[10]

Putli Ba herself, whether peeling vegetables or making her worship, would be sent for by the Palace. She would neither put

---

[10] E.P., p. 192.

on especial jewellery or wear the silks or velveteens; she would go to the Queen Mother with her usual 'Kathiawari sari and kamkho—a narrow vest open at the back that came only half way down the stomach'. Her Highness would seek Putli Ba's advice, for though the Prime Minister's young wife had no formal education, she was not only a deeply discerning person but kindly disposed to one and all. Her simple, unadorned presence, except for the sacred *tulasi*-beads at her neck, seemed to carry a sainted, an auspicious wisdom.

The city was always full of movement. Elephants and camels passed by the streets, horses with Kathiawari caparisonings, and the continuous sight of palace activities reminded one of Ayodhya. Sri Rama—is he not the Prince, and Dasaratha the King? There's always a Kaikeyi somewhere. But God hides behind every tapestry to absolve and to abide. Palace intrigues are like so many secret streamlets that run to the watertank below—once the water settles into time, the red earth sinks and the water is clear. Prayer is the making of silence. And silence is of love and wisdom. To survive a kingdom's politic one has to stand by noble truth.

> Disregarding the fault of others
> Those who accept the good in them
> Who are willing to undergo hardships
> For the sake of Brahmins and cows
> Whose good conduct serves as an example
> To others in the world
> Their good minds are their home
> In him who knows thy goodness
> And is aware of his own shortcomings
> Who depends on Thee in every way

Who loves the devotees of God,
Live in the hearts of he, O Rama with Sita.[11]

And God gives one children, one, two, three and four.

In a little apartment of the Gandhi household, on the ground floor, Putli Ba was to bear and bring out her offspring. It was a room nineteen-and-a-half feet long and thirteen feet wide and eleven feet high. In its original condition it used to be so dark that 'even at midday one could not see without artificial light'. The mother-in-law lived across the door with Tulsidas, her last son, her daughter-in-law, and grandchildren. Thus with the many many children and the women of the larger household, the slippery hushed voices of the servants, the lowing of the cattle, the beating of the drums (on the palace gateway) and the naming of the Name by some parrot from a neighbourly window, was child after child brought into this our world. The first was a boy, and then a girl, and then a boy again, and finally a boy too, and he the last, Mohan, came into the world on 2 October 1869. 'Devotee of the beautiful,' they called him, thinking of Dwaraka, Sri Krishna. The bells must have rung to announce the birth but there's always an edge of sorrow at every incarnation—what joy can birth bring to man except the sorrow that birth also has death at the other end? Where birth is, death also is. And thus the cycle.

'Lord, my Lord, release my child from this cycle of existence. Lord, Lord of Dwaraka.' Yet the Mother's joy must have shone on her forehead, and through the smoke of incense, and of garlic, the child lay on the lap in depth and terror.

The women must also have burnt broom grass and sea salt to ward away the evil eye. And the eunuchs must have drawn birth

---

[11] Tulsidas, *Ramcharitmanas*.

marks on the wall to announce to the world: A son, yes, a son has been born to Kaba Gandhi, our Prime Minister. The palace must have sent sweets and jewels, the palace servants bringing it all in gilded uniforms, proud of the Prime Minister's progeny. Wherever there is birth there's a feeling something grows. And growth is auspicious. Give sweets to the visitors, beat drums in the temple. The birth of a son is like a rebirth for oneself—it's a secret announcement somewhere of one's endlessness.

> Like Devaki's son, the Lord,
> Who was born on that night,
> Lest the populace know the secret,
> The father left in the thick of night, the city,
> For Kans the monster, was there,
> The monster, the monster,
> And Devaki brought forth the baby God, he the Cloud-blue Lord.
> And now the Prime Minister could go back to his work.

* * *

But work is not so easy, is it? The palace intrigues made for such contrasts of humour and of achievements. The simple is never so simple with a prince about one, nor the true ever so easy. Intrigues in Kathiawar, so people say, are like the twists and folds of their turban—even Krishna could not resolve them. His clan, the Yadavas, destroyed themselves and that is why even today the word Yadavis, means the complexities of a Kathiawari existence. Two hundred and twenty dynasties, with little principalities, sometimes not larger than a village, rule the peninsula, and yet going back through history and tradition—each one entitled Lord of the Universe, *Mahabhupala,* one and one-fourth Raja (*Sevai Raja*), the Shine of Empire, the Jewel of the Continent, etc., etc., and with the British came other titles, Knight Commander of the Indian Empire (K.C.I.E.), Grand Companion of the Indian Empire (G.C.I.E.), etc., and with appropriate retinues and concubines, and the intricacies of court jealousies—nothing could ever be straight. And a straight man like Kaba Gandhi was a gift of the gods, and a painful luxury. He never saw anything but straight, yet even the Kathiawari shoreline is more crooked than any in India. How will one survive it all?

'Kaba Gandhi,' says his biographer, 'was deeply attached to his children. Manu (Mohan) was his favourite. He had a cheerful sweet face, slightly curly hair, a broad, radiant forehead, finely chiselled features, and lovely eyes. Unlike other children he was not given to crying. He had a hearty ringing laughter and everybody liked to fondle him.'[12] And as it often happens in our Indian households, the first person to look after him was a sister, Gokibhen. 'Moniya' she said to the biographer, 'could be said to have grown on my lap . . . Mother was worried lest I should drop him or lose sight of him. Moniya was restless as mercury and could not sit still even for a little while. He must be playing or roaming about. I used to take him out with me to show him the familiar sights in the street—cows, buffaloes and horses, cats and dogs. He was full of curiosity. At the first opportunity he would go up to the animals and try to make friends with them.'

Once there was a festival—the Molakat—and he was lost among the gaysome crowd. Nobody could find him. And at long last, late towards the evening, he was brought home by some girls, but he did not feel too well. He had eaten something that

---

[12] E.P., p. 193-194.

burnt his tongue. He had swallowed some strange poisonous flowers. The doctor finally set him right. But the boy was never to be left alone again. It was then that Rambha was engaged as a nursemaid. Rambha who was to leave such a deep impression on Mohan's life.

His first schooling was at Porbandar. It was at the Sand-House where pupils sat on the floor and learnt their alphabet—A AA, EE EEE, UU UUU, etc., drawing them carefully over the stretched sand with their bent little fingers.

However, before that he must have been initiated, by Joshiji perhaps, to the sacred syllable itself. Bathed and new-clad on an auspicious day he must have worn the *tilak* on the brow, and at the appointed conjunction of the stars, his teacher, his Guru (or the Guru of the household) must have made him write the syllable, the syllable among syllables, the most potent, the most sacred; the triple lettered AUM which contains in its symbolism all that heaven and earth could compute, of the waking state, the dream state, and the deep sleep state, and the average of sound that remains over, the most subtle, that which leads back sound to the silence from which it arose. And the child be told of it all in the ear: Did Mohan understand it? Who knows? Knowledge is pre-nescient. It is there before you know you are, or rather, as the sacred syllable says it, you know you are itself it, you are all knowledge. There is none beyond, Pray what is there beyond the 'I'.

* * *

School however did not stop Mohan from his mischief. He loved to play pranks with his family; he would rush to the sanctuary, he would look at all the gods, and once, it's said, he even took one of the idols from their sacred seats, and placed himself in the god's place. Why not, I ask of you? Is not oneself somewhat of a god! Are you sure the gods don't like this play? Look at the play of Lord Krishna. He once, you know, stole away the clothes of the bathing village-maidens—they had all gone into the river and were enjoying themselves in the cool waters of the Jumna. Krishna, the mischievous god, came on to the shore of the river and said to himself. Well, mothers, I will play a trick on you. And he took the bundle of saris and rushed up the tree. And did he not laugh and laugh. For when the ladies, once the bath was over, slipped up to the shore: Lo and espy there were no saris left. They looked here, they looked there, trying to hide their big bosomed nakedness, and their central feminine secrets, their hands now here, now there, and yet where were the clothes? The Lord had stolen them all.

Finally he laughed, and they looked up and saw the baby boy, there he was on the high pipal tree and his bundle in such disarray. Lord, give us back our clothing! What will the men think? 'Throw it, oh divine child,' they begged. And mischievously he spoke, and said, for he was so tender, young: Come up, come up and take them yourselves. 'No,' said they, 'for our marriage necklace's sake, drop them, drop our saris, Lord.' And he asked: 'And what will you give me, O ye mothers?'

'Well,' said they in their abashedness, 'we will give you milk,' said one. 'Butter,' said another. 'Hold you to our breasts,' said a third, and so on. And in his mischief, he said, 'Close your eyes.' And they closed their beautiful bee-black eyes. And he slipped down the tree and gave each one her sari, for he *knew* them all. The Lord knows, if anyone knows, the clothes you wear is the ego. For before him how could you be clothed? But even the clothes are what he gives, says Mother. And that's the truth of it, Mohania. Who knows us, women, if Krishna, the Lord did not know us! And will you, Mohania, when you grow up also understand us? All the rivers of the world, my child, are made of our tears. We suffer silently we give, but man is too much in a hurry. He has no time to take; there's the palace, the horse at the door, the sword in the scabbard, the Turks at the frontiers. Once upon a time, you know, in Kathiawar they even killed their daughters that they may not suffer. Will you always be by me, my son?

* * *

But Mohania had other tricks to play. When nobody was about he would take a piece of coal and do his 'writing'. He would scatter imaginary letters and words on pillars, walls, doors. If Father sat and wrote in his office, why should not Mohania write where he wished. Rambha had always to be just behind him. He did not like his nurse to be everywhere about. He would push her away and ask her to get out of sight. But she would watch him from behind the door. And now what trick was he thinking about? He would rush to the garden (when Rambha was looking at something else), rush up the guava tree and slither down in glee. Sometimes his brother would discover him and pull Mohan down the tree. Oh how it hurts. 'Mother, Mother, look at what Elder Brother is doing! Mother scold him.'

'You are a big boy now. You must square up the quarrel yourself. If he hits you, you should hit him back. That will teach him a lesson.'

'Mother, is that all you can tell me? No, I will not hit him back. How can I?'

'Oh Mohania!' she would cry in pride and shame. 'Where have you come from? And who has taught you all this? What were you before you came to me, Son?'[13]

What does Mohania know? He is now busy with some other thought. Rambha of course is behind him. 'And now to the studies,' she says. And like all those tall, big people, he will place his book before him, and try to learn his lesson. One day he will grow big and be a very learned man—like Joshiji. Why not? Joshiji not only knows all the sacred books. He also looks into his oily book and tells Mother, what festival is on which of the fortnights and what worships should be done on that sacred day. In fact, what would life be without festivals? For men and women dress gaily—sometimes one fasts, sometimes, and most often, one feasts, and there are always lamps to light, incense to burn, and the men sit and throw flowers at the gods whilst women sing. What should one do without chants and *aratis?* It will ever be such fun for Mohania. And especially the festivities in which the palace has its elephants and its horses out. You never see anything as beautiful. It's like the *Ramayana.* Jewels on the elephant's head, and the horses all adorned with colour and ornament. Sometimes the Royal Steed has a deep yellow tail, and his caparisonings are in gold. They offer the horse and elephant worship, and when the offerings are taken to His Highness, His Highness touches them and offers silver rupees to the Brahmins. After that in gay and muslin clothes everyone goes to the Maharaja, and offers him gold coins on a silken handkerchief: The king touches it and gives it back to you. But, oh, the throne, the crown! They are so grand. The king is indeed a noble being.

---

[13] E.P., p. 195.

Music plays outside, and with perfume, betel leaves, and sweets you are sent home. Father stays back. He has a lot to talk to the Maharaja. For Father is an important man. He is the Prime Minister.

But when morning comes you go to school as usual. Mohan never likes to go late. Whether his meal is ready or it is not, he must be at school exactly on time. If the food is not ready—the vegetables or pulses late in cooking—he would just take curd and *khakras,* and run to the school. Father says, however: 'Son, take your meal. And you will go in our horse-carriage.'

'No, father, I prefer to walk.' Why not? And as he walked to school, one could see how spotless were his clothes. He had washed them himself and dried them and had pressed them.

At school, however, he does not shine. He was not really a bad pupil. But he was not bright either. He did his best. But he never could do very well. One has to accept this fact, as many other facts. There are widows in the world or monks or servants. That one is not clever is a fact similar to that.

But, what is an untouchable? This he could never understand. His mother and nurse Rambha, they explained again and again what an untouchable was. An untouchable is one who is dirty. An untouchable eats carcasses of dead animals. Besides, he cleans our latrines. So he is not clean. And that is why he has to stand so far away from us. 'Mother, what's an untouchable?' he asks again.

'Son, an untouchable is an untouchable!' Be that an answer? No. He would investigate it all for himself. So he went to the untouchable, touched him ever so quickly, and ran away into the house. What does one do about it now?

You just have to go and tell Mother. And that does the trick! 'Mother, I touched the untouchable. What do you say to that!'

'Oh, you joker,' she laughs. Her Mohania would never do any such thing. No, he will not.

But he would never stop mischief. All the boys gathered together and decided they would perform a grand swinging-the-swing game. The gods are put on swings and with songs and camphor you give them a grand push. Now, when children played the game they had to make clay images. And then after the swinging-the-swing ceremony throw them away into some water—the well, the river, or the sea. The boys this time decided they would have the real ones—gods in metal and from the temple. Some young boy had heard there were idols in a side room. Of course, one could not steal the idol from the sanctuary—one would never do such sacrilege. However, why not the other gods who never had much worship given to them anyway? We will offer them worship and give them a good push on the swing. The plan was discussed and decided on; who would steal the images, and from what room of the temple, and when. 'The priest awoke. The band of robbers took to their heels. The priest gave chase but was outpaced. The leader of the expedition threw the stolen images into the compound of another temple to get rid of the incriminating evidence, and with the rest of the boys ran into Ota Bapa's house for shelter. Most of the boys belonged to the Gandhi family.' When asked, they all denied having done it. 'When Mohania's turn came he told the whole truth and named the cousin who had removed the images and he alone could tell where he had thrown them, when he, along with the rest, was pursued by the priest. The boys realised that Mohania was differently made, and thereafter never invited him to join in their pranks.'

Yet they always wanted his presence, his company. He did not like 'boisterous games' but he would be the umpire. Hindus or Muslims, Jainas or Parsis, he seemed never to have worried about their religion, their family; he would be just, and that was all which mattered. 'He had a reputation for strict impartiality and everybody respected his award. When disputes arose among the players he invariably acted as the peacemaker . . . To compose differences among quarrelling parties had always been the passion of his life.'[14]

Yet school had to go on. He worked hard and ever the multiplication tables were so difficult.

'The fact that I recollect nothing more of those days than having learnt in company with other boys to call our teacher names would strongly suggest that my intellect must have been sluggish and my memory raw.'

* * *

Mohania was about seven years of age when Kaba Gandhi had moved from Porbandar to Rajkot. Once again the father had settled down to his ministerial functions, accommodating himself to the intricacies of Kathiawari political manoeuvring and the superior skills of British diplomacy. The British power was slowly settling down, adjusting itself to a new way of looking at human problems—the tricks and traffickings of the Indian mind were, to say the least, somewhat bewildering. The Indian mind never seems to go straight—it seems rather to go round and round itself, as if every event a superior joke—the consequences never seemed to matter whether you won or whether you lost. Look at the *Mahabharata*. Dharmaraja sold his kingdom and his wife for a throw of dice. It all seemed to make little difference; the

14 E.P., p. 197.

game was interesting in itself. The hide and seek, the kill-and-get-killed ventures and adventures of the Rajput chivalry face to face with the Mughals had further given the Indian ruler a feeling of transience and of recklessness. The King of Kings, Rajadhiraja, is coming, his army may be but three hundred and thirty strong, and yours thirty five thousand big, but he has grit in his pride and virility in his loins. To die a hero is what matters; we live heroes.

Our past is our future, and our now will be tomorrow. But when the action could no more be reckless in war or peace, the prince settled down to most complex intrigues—the human mind had to be busy with something, and why not eunuchy tricks be ours now? And since there were hundreds of princes in Kathiawar, the tricks became so intertwined the only way to play was the straight way—the Kaba Gandhi way. You never lose when you are truthful and disinterested. The worst that can happen is you go back home—that's where you came from—to Porbandar or Kutiyala and your Tulsidas *Ramayana*—or rather have it read—or again discuss the manyness of the one and the oneness of the many, with Jaina monks, thus the controversies of being and non-being—and Kaba Gandhi could always go back to it. He had suspicions his wife Putli Ba had some inklings of it all. But he had no time for such dialogues now. He was called by the Thakore Sahib of Rajkot to set the affairs of the state right. He had been entrusted with full responsibility, and he would answer to it. And the British also relied on him. He was now an important member of the Rajasthanic Court. God would help him to do his best. Everything was His Grace. Who would help if Sri Rama did not help?

For those in bitter need
No other solace is there, Lord, except thyself,

Thou art the end and the beginning.
Thine is the kingdom and the might . . .
Thou staunch Defender of the helpless and bereft.
Om Jaya Jagadisha Haré!

It was in the midst of these long silences, quiet sufferings and household sounds that Mohania grew up. He was energetic, unorthodox and forgiving, so that everything seemed miscalculated about him. He was never a quiet boy but he was very devout—especially in relation to his parents. He deeply respected his father and revered his mother. 'My mother was deeply religious,' he wrote later in his autobiography. 'Fasting and austerity were an integral part of her life. She recited only one mantra: *Sri Krishna sharanam mama;* Lord Krishna is my refuge. The *Gita,* etc. she could not read.'

Life, nevertheless, still seemed a play for Mohania. The school was play too, but it was a serious play. The fact of the matter is, when you look at it truly, all play is serious. And so you go to school as if it were a play. And yet school is not so enriching. One had to learn things by heart and there isn't much joy in that, is there? And when study is thus it becomes painful. Especially after a while when English became the language of instruction. Oh, how difficult it all was. 'I read nothing outside my school books,' he wrote. 'Even story books had no attraction for me.'

When the English language was still young in India, the spelling of the word 'kettle' once enunciated a moral problem. Our teachers of English were in awe before the majesty of this language, their awe often in equivalence to their ignorance. And especially when a white man, a real Englishman, was going to visit the Alfred High School there was terror in the air. The gods themselves seemed to come down the Himalayas, to test you as it were, so that the teachers went to their classes in terms of their own awkwardness, sneezing and snuffing, and wondering how it would all turn out. The Englishman, Mr. Giles, came to find out how English education was faring in Kathiawar. He would visit this school, as he would any other school, write a report and forget about it, one supposes. The British Raj was consolidating itself, and it was only a question of time as to how long it would take to make the language of the rulers the medium of instruction, and of administration. Someday India would have to come out of this medieval darkness and mess. Macaulay and the Indian leaders had decided it thus, and thus it was going to be.

The class was all a tremor at the prospect of the Sahib's coming; the school teachers more so than anyone else. And when the time for the test came, Mohan could not spell the word 'kettle' correctly. The master saw the mistake and was overcome by the image of the consequences. He would help Mohania (after all, the son of the Prime Minister) but the pupil would not listen to the teacher. Mohania would not copy from his neighbour or teacher were the British Empire to fall. Truth is more important than any earthly power. After all, Harishchandra did it. Why not Mohandas Gandhi?

The ire of the teacher was on Mohandas Gandhi. The teacher would take his revenge one day.

* * *

If English was difficult, Sanskrit, with its complicated grammar, was ever more trying. And the most difficult of all subjects was Euclid. One could never grasp in full the reasoning of Euclid. Is one so dense, then, he began to ask himself? But in the middle of this struggle, it was about the thirteenth proposition of Euclid, there's a flash and a sudden apperception of an evident law.

Forthwith everything became lucid and exalting. In fact, reasoning is such an exciting experience. It makes the unclear organic with itself, and so explains the inner movement of the whole. Even with Sanskrit grammar this is so when the pandit knows how to explain it. A fact may be confusing, never a principle. A principle is only the law behind events—it makes the concrete abstract, and thus intelligible. And from law to law is a leap that takes us straight to the truth.

But there are other and more mysterious ways by which the truth functions. For example, Rambha was an 'unlettered' nursemaid but there was much she understood that others did not seem to. Now, when one is afraid of ghosts what does one do? One can say they exist, or do not exist, and yet again you may say there's fear. To say the ghost is a ghost does not take away your fear. To say there is no ghost does not prevent you from looking for those forms behind doors or out there when the eye peers across the room behind the blanket and sees movement. Rambha of course believed in ghosts. They sometimes hang from trees, or tear their hair, and sometimes they cry out in strange voices. Mohania would hide himself under the blanket and would not want to see them. But Rambha had the remedy— the remedy of remedies. She gave him a mantra. 'Rama, Rama' you say, and what ghost will ever face you after that? Think?

And indeed whensoever a ghost seems about, just the name of Sri Rama seemed to drive it away. In fact, not only ghosts but all fears seem to go away, just with the name of Rama. No ghost or fear could trouble you for you have now the name of the Helper of the Helpless, Sri Rama. And He would protect us all.

And the school—the Alfred High School had all sorts of boys and all sorts of teachers as well. But when one is so serious, friendships are difficult. You admire most those who are most unlike yourself; his friend, Mehtab, for example, from the opposite house. Son of well-to-do parents (Somali Negroes settled in India for generations), he could fight with his fists, laugh loudly and perform such things of town or country one does not talk about before parents. 'Why do you think, you fellows, you all look like bamboos and widows? You don't eat meat. Look at me how strong I am! I can fight the very devil of the tamarind tree. And as for women . . .'

And cigarettes too. To be a man you must smoke like an elder, like the Englishman. You must take stumps from your uncle's leavings or buy them with hard pice, when one has the pice to pay. Pray how? Steal them from the servant's pockets. If not, you can always make cigarettes from herbs. They smell bad. But they would do.

However the meat and cigarettes could wait. One has so much to do at school.

'Sir, I am sorry to be late. My father is ill.'

'Yes, of course, everybody's father is ill when they are late.'

'Sir, I beg of you to believe me. I did not tell a lie.'

'Of course you never spoke a lie in your life, did you Mohandas Gandhi?'

'Never, sir.'

And what sorrow one has when the elders do not understand what the young heart knows. But the father is a truthful, an understanding man. He will vouchsafe the truth to the schoolmaster. 'Yes, my son Mohandas was looking after me. I have been very ill, it is only because of this he did not come to school. In fact, I want him excused from school gymnastics for I need him.' Thus wrote Kaba Gandhi.

Mohandas came back, therefore, and continued nursing his father. And what interesting people came to see him. The Parsis with their funny flat and hollowed-in caps, the Muslims with their fingers on the beads, the Jaina monks, the Brahmin readers of the *Ramayana*. It is always so impressive to see the Parsis, white-clothed, deferential and so honest. A Parsi never told a lie and never cheated you in business. You do not come thousands of miles away from your own country so as to protect your religion, your sacred fire, and sell yourself for a silly lie. No, never will a Parsi do this. One must fight for one's god. And the Muslim too who drove the Parsi out of Persia; what fervour he has for his god, and what feelings of fraternity for his mankind. He it is that loves all his fellow-men. For him there was no untouchable. The Christian missionaries who stood on street corners and spoke abusively of Krishna (the lover of many maids and dishonest man in war and in peace, and of Shiva who had such a shameful symbol, as everybody knows! etc. etc.), these missionaries were all wrong even about brotherhood. Look at the British. But as for the Jaina monks, what creation they carried with them, what purity, what beauty. Why not become a monk and be devoted forever to God? But Sri Rama too was devoted to God, was God himself. Listen now to Tulsidas:

Homage to the Lord Hari, whose name is Rama, to whose illusive power is subject the whole Universe with Brahma and all the gods and demons; because of whose true being all this unreal world seems true as when a rope is thought to be a snake; whose feet are the only boat for those who would cross the sea of birth and death: first cause beyond all causes! . . . I

do homage to the lotus feet of my guru, ocean of grace, Hari
in human form.

The school may be an excellent place, but the best school
was home: Mother with her prayers and fasts. Mother fasted as
you know on every *ekadashi* day. But when the *Chaturamasa*[15]
came she fasted every other day. And when the day of fasting
was over, and she had to break the fast, the sun had to be seen
before she would put food into her mouth. Oh, it was so grand
standing on the veranda and waiting for the sun to appear. But
the sun would not appear. Then suddenly the winds would rise
and the clouds pushed away.

'Mother, Mother! The sun, there,' and he and his brothers
would rush to the kitchen. Putli Ba would come to the veranda.
The sun had by now been swallowed up by the clouds. 'Oh,
Mother, we saw it! I assure you we saw it.'

'But I did not see it.'

'Why must you see the sun? Is it not enough we have seen
him?'

'No, son, such are God's ways.'

And she would not eat that day. Yet mother was so gentle,
so devoted. She went about her job, serving the elders and the
young the whole day. When one has God's name on one's lips
what need have you of other energies?

For there's mystery in the fast. It seems to give clarity and
power, power of devotion, power of self-forgetfulness. Fasting
draws power from the very heavens. And there's God's breath
in worship. When the camphor burns (after the fast) before the

---

[15] A sort of Lent lasting four months when people fast regularly, sometimes
for several days at a time.

divinity, so rich the world seems, and so true. Why do people tell lies? Why does not everyone worship father and mother, the elders, and the gods, and live a measured and mystery-rich existence? There is no truth without mystery and no mystery without truth. Look at what happened to Sravana. Look at Harishchandra. How moving it is to go to the *Kathas*[16] and hear those stories again and again. You never return home without wetting your clothing, or your sari, with tears.

* * *

For once upon a time (he, the *Kathakar*,[17] would start, with offerings of incense and camphor—worship to the divinity, whether at home or in the temple), for once upon a time there was a king and his name was Harishchandra, the Moon of Hari, the Lord, the moon being the symbol of the mind, and Hari being pure, it meant the mind of Hari, or He of Pure Mind. And the pure mind, what does it say? It speaketh nothing but the truth. How could the pure mind make the tongue say an untruth? It certainly would not. Harishchandra was known over nations and continents as he that spoke the truth. Truth alone was the ingredient of his words. He also had a wife, fair and true, Saibya was her name, and a son by the name of Rohitaswa, four years of age, tender, intelligent and devout. And the king ruled his country with justice, compassion, and fearlessness. What he said was so true, the rabbit held itself on the fence-grass, never stole a blade from field or garden and the elephant shuddered and stopped straight before the king's sudden presence, trumpet

---

[16] A divine story.
[17] One who tells a divine story in verse and prose in accompaniment to music.

and bow down—such the power of truth. Every evil is conquered by the truth. So even the wild tiger will stop and let you pass by. And the whole state was in a continuous festival of marriages, child births, harvests and sowings, initiation ceremonies, the fire of sacrifice ever sending curling smoke into the air while ascetics meditated safe in the wilds, and women's virtue was never in question. Such the kingdom of Harishchandra.

One day, however, Vishwamitra, the great sage, wanted to test the mighty monarch. Be it true that truth alone is what he speaks, breathes and lives? 'Let us try,' said Vishwamitra to himself. And the gods rejoiced at this for their own power would diminish with such unique austerity on earth. And Vishwamitra now sailed down to the court of Harishchandra. The king rose from his throne.

'O great sage, what may have brought you to our humble abode?'

'Nothing other, sire, than just a friendly visit to a great king.'

'Is there anything I can offer to the great sage?' he begged and once he had wiped the sage's feet with silken towels he fell, did Harishchandra, before the sage in reverence and in total adoration and said.

'All of me, gold, my son, wife, body, kingdom, good fortune—everything of mine is yours, O sage, O sage of sages. Deign bless me that I live according to my dharma to the end of time . . .'

'You have my blessings, son. And since you kindly said all of yours is mine, may I, it just came to me, ask of you your kingdom?'

'You have it, O great sage.'

And the *dakshina*,[18] the gold-of-gift, where is it, O king?'

---

[18] Dakshina, a piece of silver or gold that should accompany every gift to an elder, a saint, or sage.

And the king at once realised he had no *dakshina* to add
to the kingdom he had just given away—all the kingdom,
including palaces, treasury, elephants, horses, houses, trees,
rivers belonged now to the sage Vishwamitra.

'King, take a fortnight, and you could give to me, the
auspicious piece of gold—and in good time.'

'So be it, O sage.'

'And you have my blessings . . .'

And Harishchandra going into the inner apartment
called Queen Saibya and told her of the happenings, and with
Rohitaswa between them, they walked down into the forest. It
took them three days and three nights to leave the kingdom,
and everywhere where people heard the news, they gathered and
bowed low before the king, for the king was leaving the kingdom
(with his delicate wife and young child) in answer to a given
word. For the word is truth, and a king rules because Truth
rules. Truth burns on. Victory is ever to the Truth. 'Victory to
Truth!' they cried: *Satyamaeva Jayate.*

Harishchandra, his wife, and child now came to Benares,
city of splendour and of the gods, city of sandalwood pyres, of
delicate gold brocades, of horse-marts and bird-marts, and of
subtle musicians, emporia of silk and of pearl; where else could
one go for god or gold but to holy Benares? And day after day
the royal couple wandered through the streets in search of work.
And fifteen days do not last so long, you know! How to make
money? Oh what could one make money with? Nobody would
buy or sell for nothing. Thus bereft of hopes, and all sorrowful
they finally went to the slave market.

'Here is a goodly woman for a housewife,' said a round, big
merchant looking at Saibya.

'Yes, so she is, sir.'

'And how much will you sell her for?'

'She and the son as well, merchant sir.'

'Well that makes a difference, does it not? When she chores the son will come in the way.'

'I promise you I will work well,' assured Saibya. Her voice was so sweet and clear the merchant knew he could trust her. And for two gold pieces she was forthwith sold. Such, Lord, the game of fate.

And Harishchandra sold himself to a *dom*[19]—after all somebody must own and keep clearing the ground, and get payment for the right to burn a body there. And so he became, did Harishchandra, a guard of the crematorium grounds. Day and night he had to ask a small fee for the right of entry, and then only could the dead body be laid on its pyre. Thirteen days were over yet no money came to make the four pieces of gold for Sage Vishwamitra's gift offerings.

One night, and it was the new moon night, dark as a crow's flat wing, and as inauspicious. It rained heavily, jackals cried. A woman came with a child in her arms. She laid him on the heaped-up wood.

'Lady, where's the fee?'

'I am poor, sir guard, and I cannot pay. I am piceless. I am a poor working woman in a rich man's home.'

'You cannot burn your child till the fee is paid.'

'I have nothing. I beg of you, I have nothing, nothing, sir guard.'

'Go and ask your relations.'

'I have no relations. None. I am an outsider, sir.'

'Then you must take away the corpse.'

---

[19] The owner of a crematorium.

'How can I, sir guard?'

'Then what can I do?'

'Help me, sir. This my only child. And he bitten by a snake. My only child.'

'Only child or not, I see a glittering piece of gold at your neck. Why not give that to me?'

'My husband, sir guard, is still alive. How can I break my holy marriage necklace?'

'The merchant does not care. The boss does not. He wants his fee.'

And as, praying to her husband, and thinking on the Lord of Lords, Shiva Himself, He full of compassion, she put her hand on the marriage necklace, the very heavens opened wide, and music and trumpets sounded in the upper worlds. 'The vow of Pure-Wife is stronger than any law of man. It's like the law of the sun and the moon, the law that makes the fast pure, the monk celibate, the king powerful.' And the golden chariot of Indra descending took Saibya and Harishchandra to Satyapuri, the City of Truth.

Vishwamitra was waiting for them at the palace door.

'Great are you, Harishchandra. Truth is greater than man. Truth is God Himself. May you live a thousand years,' he blessed and with the clapdash sound of the moving sandals of his feet, he left, did Vishwamitra, the capital under a shower of flowers.

And Harishchandra and Saibya and Rohitaswa lived happily on, and the kingdom flourished as never before. 'Hence,' said the *Kathakar,* 'the Harishchandra Ghat in Benares to this day, and the *dom* chief, you remember, who has a palace on the banks of the Ganga—descendants of the cremation-ground *dom* who had hired Harishchandra, guardian of the crematorium. And the River of Truth flows.'

'And why not?' Mohandas asked himself that night, 'why not everyone be like Harishchandra?' Why not, I ask of you?

* * *

When Mohan was thirteen he was married off. Round and thirteen, wilful and innocent, Kasturba was a match to her future lord and guide. A rich neighbour's daughter from Porbandar, they had played together, and it would seem as if life had managed them to play games all their life for each one went his and her way, and each one did what she and he had to do, and if the moments were difficult, so was the whole mechanics of existence. In fact, Mohan was engaged when he was only seven years of age. The two other previous engagements had ended with the death of his prospective brides—and neither Mohan nor Kasturba knew what was which anyway. How could they? The elders had so decided on it and who, after all, understands the acts and intentions of the elders except the great god himself? And so the marriage had to be. And it had to be at Porbandar, the family home of the Gandhis and of Kasturba. It was also going to be the marriage of Mohan's elder brother and a cousin of his so that all in all the pomp will cost less and the elders would be more satisfied. For the more the marriages, the more the satisfaction of the living and of the dead. The living because they will die and so would rather see the children settled, and maybe see the birth of grandchildren, and the dead because their manes would thus be satisfied. What is the future of a house with unsatisfied manes? The hanging shadows of the dead that swirl about the earth need to be pacified, need to be fed and exorcised so that they too will dissolve and their psychic forms vanish forever from every trace of existence. The forms of the mind, whether of hatred, affection or desire, remain shadows and the dissolution of psychic entities bring peace to mankind. Thus marriage and son-birth, and the annual offerings to the manes.

For Kaba Gandhi was growing old. He never recovered from his illnesses in Rajkot, and may be he felt the end was nearer than anybody knew. In fact, if you lead a serious life death gives you intimations of its visit, august and inevitable. Since man has this desperate edge of sorrow, the deepest and yet not the most lasting—the dying body dies but the undying is already reborn while this body is being prepared even for the crematorium—like the caterpillar that does not leave one blade of grass till it has found another, such your being that you will not leave from one body till you've chosen a proper womb for your soul's receptacle at the other end—hence these psychic intimations. He knew, did Kaba Gandhi, somewhere secretly inside himself, the end was coming, and so beat the drum from gate-tops and proclaimed to the world, my son Mohania will be married to Kasturba and it will be the most resplendent marriage I have performed. Let the courts of Rajkot and Porbandar know that Ota Gandhi's last grandson was getting married to Makanji's daughter, Kasturba, and so distribute flowers and sacred-rice invitations to the whole city, make marks of swastika on the houses of all the invitees, and let there be music and elephants and all the best cooks Porbandar and Rajkot can find, be demanded and paid for. Let milk flow into the cauldrons, and rice and lentils and vegetables into the granary and stores, smell the spices curried into powder, examine the *puri* flour being weighed, hear the sweets being discussed. Marriage to be grand must have horses, noise, and strong smells.

Kaba Gandhi, however, could not be present immediately. From Rajkot to Porbandar (one hundred and twenty miles) it took five days by bullock-cart in those days. He had urgent official duties to perform at Rajkot—the women and the party could go first, he would join them soon. And so the marriage party left with auspicious *kumkum*—adorations to the women, with bags, new clothes and perfumes, and after five days the marriage party did arrive at Porbandar. And the door decorations had to be hung, the poles to be fixed for the reception halls, and tents and drum-stands, and carriages arranged for people to go from house to house. There would be palace elephants, too, trumpeting somewhere as if to make the confusions of the wedding house more exalted while the flower-sellers came to offer jasmines and roses and marigolds, for worship and for garlands. To Mohan all this was fun. Does marriage always mean big noise and movement? Then marriages are indeed splendid. 'And I will be married, too.'

Women, of course, cast shy glances at Mohan and whispered things to each other. And sometimes men pinched his arms or cheeks and laughed. He would see what he would see. He did not like it all, but there were intimations of feelings that arose in him, and yet they had no name; what they seemed to hint at he just did not know. One day his sister-in-law took him aside and told him all about it. On the first night this happens this way, and this other has to be done for it to be this, and not that. And with flowers, perfumes and sweets, it will, you will see, be beautiful.

Of course one never saw Kasturba. She was hidden away in her house. And she was being smeared with turmeric and the oils and being given little hints of the ups and downs of events so that when the time came for the ultimate discovery, it would be something so tender and total—the like of it a woman will never know again. The womb of woman is the fount of holiness.

That is why every man, every father, that 'gives away the womb', is giver of prosperity.

Tell them on the veranda to start the music. And the women start their songs.

> When Yasodha's son was going in procession
>   was going in horse procession,
> Did not the stars weep, did not even the stars weep,
>   for such the joy of Rukmini
> 'Look, the horse-rider will come, and he will come,
>   and elope you away, O Rukmini.'

Meanwhile, the streets were being swept and the carriages stood with horses and bullocks, and the very palace shone and looked as if it also took pride in this performance—every breath of happiness that shines, shines on the walls of he that rules—and so many chants would go up into the heaven, and the heavens will be bright. But Kaba Gandhi had not yet arrived. The Master of the House had not yet come. When would he come?

The Thakur Saheb of Rajkot had sent relays of bullocks so that what could be done in five days be done in three. Of course it can be done, despite boulder and dust and hollow stream and the vast desert spaces and then the hills, and, finally, the fitful descent to the shores of the sea. But somewhere in the middle, the bulls slipped, and the cart fell, and the Prime Minister had toppled on his belly. The servants lifted him and bandaged him, and with blood on his face and arm, he went back to his bullock cart—he would not be defeated. The pipes were already playing when he arrived—stern and sure, he the father of the bridegroom and ready for all the ceremonies. Putli Ba was in misery—was not all this inauspicious? The gods know better.

Make a vow, woman, and hang a magic-knot at the temple. The gods will ever listen to sincere prayer.

And was not Mohan splendid on his horse! So were his brother and his cousin. But there was always something a little special about our Mohan. He did what others did not do, and what he did seemed right. For example, he would consent to ride the bridal horse but he would not touch the gold necklace. Why all this fussation when life is so unpredictable, anything may happen to anyone, and any day, like Harishchandra, one may have to leave the kingdom and wander away for a given word. Life has meaning only when truth has meaning. And truth has meaning only when you possess nothing.

And Mohan sat through the chants and the implicate sophistications of marriage liturgies with the seriousness of one to whom this would all be a blessing and a beginning. It would mean for him the beginning of his manhood—he is going to have a wife. He would have to be a husband. Remember Tulsidas. When Rama was married to Sita.

The bride and the bridegroom gracefully circled the fire, and all with reverence feasted their eyes upon them. No tongue can describe the enchanting pair, no simile suffice. The lovely reflections of Rama and Sita glittered in the jewelled columns, as though Kama and Rati, taking many forms, were watching Rama's peerless marriage; again and again revealing themselves, curious to see the sight, and then, overcome by modesty, vanishing from view.

All who looked on were enraptured and, like Janaka, lost consciousness of self. Joyfully the sages bade them circle the fire; they distributed gifts and performed every rite. Rama applied vermilion to Sita's head, a scene of unutterable charm. As red powder fills a lotus full, so the vermilion filled Rama's hand;

desiring her beauty, his outstretched arm adorned her face, as a serpent reaches out to the moon when greedy for ambrosia. Then at Vasistha's bidding the bride and the bridegroom sat together on one seat.[20]

Yes, all weddings on earth must happen at Janaka's capital. If every wife has to be a Sita, every man has to be a Rama. Lord help me that I do not fail—fail neither my Father nor my Mother, and fail not especially my wife. 'Make me a devotee-husband, Sri Rama.'

Kaba Gandhi, his face and arms in bandages, seemed so intent and fatherly as Dasaratha himself. The laughters and the noises seemed so crude before this august occasion, when man took woman to wife, and the father and mother stood by and said: Go children and fulfil your tasks in the world. The chatter of women seemed so improper, and the mechanical chants and movements of the Brahmins so little elevated. Yet the splendour of the Sanskrit language seemed to make marriage sacred. Amidst Sanskrit chants and the rising of the music, auspicious flowers fell on the cloth-linked couple. They held each other's hands before the Witnesshood of the Fire and of the Elders of the city and the very gods now proclaimed Mohandas Gandhi had married Kasturba in proper Vedic wedding. May they prosper and have a hundred children, blessed the crowd as flowers fell on the holy couple. And the women and the servants wept.

Everything after the tying of the marriage-thread seemed so different. Suddenly manhood seemed to have surged up as if released from another existence. Is it because we remember from a past life that a boy of thirteen can feel passions rise in him and his limbs and arms search for appropriate gestures? The fun-

20 Tulsidas, *Ramcharitmanas*.

making at the feast seemed so incongruous, the laughter of the ladies profane. Would they have to be so irritatingly salacious in their looks? Was not the discovery of woman by man something so secretive, no eye should peer into its anguish, its mystery? It was as if one woman became all women, and her touch the cosmic knowledge of a law. But all eyes seemed only open for that pure moment, and some men even sang ribald songs, and the women remembered Kasturba with envy and wonder. Yes, you will see it will be true, wondrous, beautiful.

The world was all awake when the moment came. The whole town knew, including princes and princesses, daughters and concubines, tonight Kasturba would discover Mohan, and the women's songs could be heard from the tops of the houses and from all around. The men were seated under the *shamiana* eating pan or smoking or gossiping. What was happening at Rajkot? And Kaba Gandhi, how long was he going to stay here? What was the new British Agent like? And how did it feel to sit at the Rajasthanic Court? Would he not be coming back home soon? There is nothing like Porbandar in the vast and wide world. Ota Gandhi's prayer room is at the top and one remembers where one's gods are. Putli Ba was in agonies. Her tender son was going to discover life. And life is not easy to live, Mohania.

In the nuptial room, however, with the scented oil-lamps and the flowers around, and the shine of the carpets and the silk of the pillows, there was a tender demand as of two children playing a serious game. When the play started it took Man and Woman to such depths the World was forgot. The noises outside seemed irrelevant. Discovery had its own strength and one went back to it again and again, a new play of children and so very luminous. It is good to be a man. And holy to be woman,

and worship her man. There's no end to Radha's love for Sri
Krishna.

Krishna Haré, Krishna Haré
Radha Krishna, Krishna Haré.

* * *

Marriage and husbandhood go ill together. The luxury of
the young body felt layer after layer in shyness, wonder, and
accomplishment, seems, when one is but thirteen, like a precious
possession to be feared but tasted, and indeed as if the other
were not a wife, but someone one has known always, so close, so
familiar, so opportune, in fact she seemed a cousin, one's own
mate and self, a sister. There's nothing in the other except that
it be the proportions and privacy of the woman's body, which
seems more vocal, more sumptuous, and more vulnerable.
Beside the woman's body, the male's looks austere, lonesome
and so abstract; it has vitality and no depth, the woman's has
depth and mystery, and a sense of the deathless. Woman's body
seems assumptious and the man's presumptive. And when, after
betel-nuts and perfumes, and the wonder of wise shyness, the
male redeems himself in the purity of his mate's upsurgence,
he's lost to himself forever. There is no depth where you find
yourself—but the woman, the girl has found herself. Not only
has she found herself, she smiles in the innocence of her gift, in
the beauty of her brother's face. All the folkloric meanings come
up to your images; the brother, the hero, the protector, the
bridegroom. O brother, I love you. O husband, I am yours—a
dasi, an adorer, a slave. A slave to wash your feet, to feed you on
almond and saffron, and give to you night after night the true

honey of being, like Radha must have given to Krishna. Brother take me, and take me far and away. Let us elope on the awaiting white steed.

Yet the school in the morning remains. And the multiple functions of a new-come bride brought into the household. The cattle, my daughter, have to be fed at this mid-hour of noon, and the clothes have to be given for washing before the cattle return. When the palace servants bring something from Her Highness, the *Ranisaheba,* you must make them stay in the courtyard, and give to them according to their status, either *kumkum* and flowers or a small coin or just send them away. And when the Brahmin astrologer comes you must give him a wooden-seat to sit on, and puffed rice and molasses and even a few dry figs if you can find some. And may be he would tell you what pujas to perform that you have an heir and a son. 'What's the use of a woman's womb that bears not even a granary rat?' You might, now that the sun is getting hotter, cut vegetables for the kitchen. You know, your father-in-law is such a humble man he has often sat in the temple cutting vegetables with your mother-in-law. Even the king's men would come and ask for advice, and he would give it to them cutting his cucumber or snake gourd. And you can have such a grand look at the divinity in between whiles. 'Only He gives and He takes. Lord Krishna, he the Bearer of the Mandhara Mountain. He protects us always.'

Meanwhile, Mohania is busy at his school. His English is still poor and his Sanskrit continues to be indifferent. Sanskrit grammar seems such a complicated construct—you may only learn it by heart. And one always has a feeling one is wrong somewhere when one is at school. The big boys dominate the establishment with their physical prowess, and you look up to boys like Mehtab with admiration. Look at his muscles, his courage. He is even unafraid of ghosts. It all comes of eating meat. Then why not eat meat?

> Behold the mighty Englishman,
> He rules the Indian small.
> Because being a meat eater,
> He is five cubits tall.

If it's true then meat may be the answer.

And when you go on eating meat again and again it becomes interesting. It becomes even delicious. One will become strong one day like Mehtab, like any Englishman, and thus the world could be changed. Somehow the eating of meat seems to make you more of a man.

'How was it last night, young man?' asks Mehtab of Mohan.

'It was good, thank you.'

'Not just good, my dear boy, don't you feel when you're at it you're more of a man?'

'Perhaps, yes, I do not know.'

'Go on persisting, Mohania, and you'll find meat and woman go together. What goes in goes out, and what goes out comes back, and goes out again. What a wonder god's creation is.'

'Yes it is, I think,' says Mohan shyly.

'And your young wife,' says Mehtab all knowing and protective, 'when you're away at school you're sure there are no men around?'

'Men around?' says Mohania. 'There are always men around in Hindu houses—uncles, cousins, and servants, and other boys brought up in the household that go to work or come searching for jobs. Our house is no home, you know, friend, it's like a *dharmasala*.[21]

'You realise what *dharmasalas* are like?' remarked Mehtab with an all-knowing air and winking his bright eyes. Of course, Mehtab was a strong fellow and he knew the world better. Who would know if he did not know?

That day the school was long and difficult. The imagination took hold of shapes and acts and brought them before you; such and such a man is there at home, what may he be doing? Where is she? And the longer the delay the fiercer the pictures. But when Mohania came home, there was great sweetness in the household, the corn was being ground, perhaps the cattle were being given grass, the horses were being groomed, and maybe Kasturba was in the backyard placing the clothes on the washing line, or helping the mother-in-law with the pickles. And the servants were drawing water from the deep splashes of the well. The right eye has been winking the whole day—the left arm shakes. What may it all mean? Lord, what? Seeing her husband, Kasturba comes in like a wife to her husband. Outside her room she's no sister and bride but a devout wife. The mother-in-law made her into a wife. Mohania is like this. Mohania likes sweets and not so much salties. Mohania is so precise, he does not like a scratch or a thread on his clothes. The wife has to learn about her lord from her mother-in-law. If not, who is there to teach you? And now for some afternoon tiffin.

But when the night comes there's a premonition of the disaster to be. Mohan does not speak to his wife.

'Why, what has happened today?' No answer.

---

[21] Hospice for travellers, pilgrims.

'Was the teacher difficult? That matters little. When one goes to school, I am told, the masters can be very unreasonable.'

'How do you know? You have never been to school!'

'Then why not teach me? I will also learn.'

'Why don't you ask someone else in the house to teach you?'

'As one knows, there is no one. The women know no alphabet and no man should teach me. So, what?'

'There are so many elders in the house.'

'But I cannot talk to the men. And the women of course do not know how to read or to write.'

'You mean you talk to no one when I am at school?'

'To whom shall I talk except to mother-in-law, and sometimes to her mother-in-law?'

'That's too simple. You mean you never see any man while I am away?'

'What an idea!' remarked Kasturba in fury. 'What does one think I am? Born in a cowherd's home or amongst the untouchables?'

'Oh don't be so angry,' says Mohania trying to be a little more friendly. 'I was just wondering.'

'If this is what the school teaches one, send me home. I would rather be a slave at my parents' home than a daughter-in-law here.'

'There's nothing to be angry about. It's man's privilege to be jealous.'

'And the woman's to go back home,' said Kasturba. 'I'll pack my trunk tomorrow and be back home. Send me back home; I beg of you.'

'Anyway you are going back home in a few weeks. Your family is coming to fetch you.' Kasturba did not answer. She laid herself on the bed and tried to sleep. Tears trickled down her eyes. What was all this and why did I come here? But Mohania came to her and knew he was very unreasonable. He knew her somewhat as he knew himself. And now that their irritations had subsided they felt once again brother and sister-spouse, and enjoyed the never ending game of love.

Beautiful though the game be, how sad one feels after it all. You go back to it to right it, and the more you want to be right, the more miserable you become. May this be true? Is this how a man feels? Dejection follows wonderment? Heaviness follows innocence? If God were true could there be sorrow? May be this is not God's will. God could not make a wrong world and give us pain. And this mess—could God make a mess? Lord, protect me and give me understanding.

Exercises and examinations of course are important. But it is truth that matters most. How hide it, slip between the elders and rush through the studies and wander through the house aimlessly as if everyone knew what was what, and yet nobody really saw under your mind. How hide a thing that seems like a bubo under your thought or heart, or visible like a pimple on your nose to everyone, and yet nobody understands. Truth alone should shine. Truth alone shines. Should not one rather be like Harishchandra? Is that not the only path of normal human existence?

But now to the studies.

Mohania had important problems. He did not think he was very bright. And yet the whole family seemed to have great expectations of him—he will succeed his father as Prime Minister. A Gandhi has always been a prime minister of Porbandar for at least two generations, and home ministers for six. As if all the ancestors were awaiting this fulfilment, such the gentle pressures around him. But how could this ever be, and these constant thoughts of Kasturba at school, or in between books, in the evening. Night seemed exhaustedly delicious with the pungent odours of fulfilled bodies and that long rest of prurient limbs. Life's measures seem improper when you looked at textbooks on the table. So, exasperated, Mohandas would take an elementary book in Gujarati and teach his wife the alphabet. At least if he would not study, let her learn how to read and to write. And then one could always go back to the sweetness of the anticipations, and the slipperiness of man's urge and of the woman's shy self-revelations. How could this be wrong? From the woman's face shone a splendour that seemed to annihilate any questions. Indeed, the woman's eyes were demanding. Do you . . .? Of course, how foolish of me to ask. And the gentle play begins again. The whole house is awake to its own activities. Is this how mother and father have been? Is it how it always is? And there is no one to ask. Even when father is ill and he needs a massage or a hand to help him go to the latrine, how luxurious it is to lie on the awake woman's body. Mother or brother would look after father. Come wife, let us play the game of husband and wife.

It was so like a doll's play. But at sixteen one is no more a doll. A baby was shaping itself in the bride's belly. Would he be a boy?

Sheik Mehtab was not only friend and chum, but ever the hero of the school. Mohania's own beginnings of adolescent distress and faint rumours of revolt, combined to draw sustenance from him. Mehtab's courage and knowledge made him the object of deep respect, of gratitude. If he did not know 'Life' who would? Meanwhile, Mehtab had other and more elaborate plans to educate his friend to sturdy manhood.

One day Mehtab said to Mohania, winking his eyes, 'Be ready for an adventure!' It was spoken in such a manner that if you said 'no' not only would you be coward in his eyes, but in your own. What in the world could you be afraid of with Mehtab beside you?

'Yes, brother, and so I will.'

And when the appointed time came Mehtab was all dressed in gay muslins and smelt of excellent perfume. One would think one was going to a marriage party.

'Whose marriage are you taking me to?'

'You'll see when you come there. And for the moment just follow me, you understand?'

Mohania, silent and wide-eyed, followed his leader. And they came after twisting through many lanes and slipping in between houses to a strange looking dwelling. It seemed a little less clean from outside, besides the doors were closed.

'Where are you taking me to, brother?'

'I told you to your marriage, Mohania. Where else!' and the boss seemed almost angry.

The door was opened by an older woman, dirty in her clothes, but bejewelled and magnificent in her beaming look, who welcomed them in. There was something well-bred about her whole appearance except when she talked, and she talked like a servant. Suddenly Mohania understood. They were visiting a house of concubines. You are not a man if you do not know concubines. Why they have more knowledge and riches in their heart and body than all the wives put together. Suddenly, as if by instinct, Mohania began to take the name of Rama. Whether you fear ghosts or the concubine, the same mantra would work: *Ramanama* is the most potent force against evil. 'Lord Rama, He of the Raghu race, protect me!'

Soon the older woman disappeared with Mehtab to a room, and came back and slipped Mohandas to another room. There was a lovely young woman lying on a bed, and her limbs were shapely and full of desire. Mohania had such virility, his body tingled and his hairs stood on end. Frightened and fascinated, he sat on her bed contemplating her bosom, her lips, her thighs, and drawn in by the net of his own desires. What fulfilment there could be if only this body could fit into the woman's and holding it in its total tightness suck the very juice out of existence. How could this be bad? Why should, if one ate meat and smoked cigarettes, why should not one also slip into the vulnerability of woman, and bite her out into waving upsurges and still her down into fluid satiations? Yet, behind this woman he saw the face of Kasturba, tender, innocent, firm and devoted. How could one ever betray such a wife? Of course, never. And the face of Putli Ba rose behind his eyes—not in admonition but in prayer. 'Mohania, are you not my son?' And this made the trick. Strength flowed from everywhere. The gods seemed, suddenly aware, to have come out of the heavens. They were there to help and to protect. The woman seeing such cowardly ambiguity on the man's face, started to abuse, 'You son of a donkey, what do you think you are? Be a man and if you cannot be, get out. Because you have paid me money, you think you can just sit there and watch me! Besides, I have other clients. I can tell you if you do not like my body, there are others better than you, richer than you, who want me. Get out.'

Mohania, perplexed and frightened, stood up and walked out. 'God in His infinite mercy protected me,' wrote Gandhiji later, 'against myself. I was almost struck blind and dumb in this den of vice. I sat near the woman on her bed, but I was tongue-tied . . . I felt as though my manhood had been injured and wished to sink into the ground for shame.' Next day he could never face Mehtab. Was Mohania a coward?

'Idiot,' shouted Mehtab, 'it's not my money that matters. But the shame on your manhood!'

'I am sorry to have humiliated you,' sputtered Mohan. He was so shy. After all, Mehtab was a very good fellow. Only he does not understand a married man's scruples. Otherwise who knows what might not have happened? Who can foresee the acts of a man of passion? When his own father was ill and needed massage, did not Mohan quickly finish his task and rush to his wife to have coitus. The male organ is such an unruly thing. What is one to do? Lord, who can help us? Lord, who will help?

* * *

Yet what expectations can one have for this country—look at the pomp and vulgarity of the priests, the gold dome, the spire, the silver vessels clinking in the sanctum, the head-dresses, the limb-brocades, the very hair of the goddess gold-covered to shine and to bewilder, the rituals, one more elaborate than the other—it always costs more to have a 'thousand-names' said than a 'hundred-names'—and the camphor and the bell, the sloth, and the slumber in which the priests lived, and look at the rings on their fingers, filigree on their bodies, and their eyes so full of mist and lust—concubines, people said, are who the priests spend their nights with. The priests did of course, but not with the street-corner concubines, but those devoted to Krishna, the Lord. And since Sri Krishna, He the Splendour of the Universe, He the joy in enjoyment, had so many, many *gopis,* and to each one he was the male, and the fulfilment, then why not each priest be a Krishna, and each concubine a *gopi? Bolo Sri Krishna*

Maharaj ki jai—Shout the Glory of Sri Krishna, the Lord. He the Sun of the *Gopis*.

Such the sumptuousness of the apparels and jewellery on the women-of-Sri-Krishna, eyes would stare at them rather than on the god, their half-veiled, nose-ringed faces, a more intriguing presence.

How then take the sacraments offered by the priests against tinkling silver and the high and low of chants that they murmured with such graceless garrulity? Was this worship?

Look at the Jainas. Look at the Muslims. And yet we talk of the greatness of Hinduism. Look at our Untouchables. In Rama's kingdom there were no Untouchables. Yes, there were none.

Even beast to beast act not in superiority. Do beasts ever harm one another in amusement or for a meaningless act? Look at that boy who struck me the other day. And I complain to Father about him. (How can I bear him a grudge?) What made him strike? Do I know? (Does anyone know anything at all?) Do not the Jainas say you can prove nothing? You cannot say even what a jug is. So, how judge a man, any man? Therefore do no harm to anyone. Purify yourself. Thus it was Mohan would bathe early, wash his clothes (whiter than anyone else's) and go to his room, serious and meditative, and after that to school. Every footstep should be a ritual, every word a mantra. One says one's beads as it were, as one walks or talks or works. All the world is a temple, the Kingdom of Sri Rama. In the Kingdom of Rama nobody hurts another, nobody complains against another. The right rights all and goes forward to the truth from which it arose.

When Rama sat upon his sovereign throne, the three spheres rejoiced and there was no more sorrow. No man was any other's enemy, and under Rama's royal influence all ill-feeling was laid aside. Everyone devoted himself to his duty in accordance with his caste and stage of life, and ever found happiness in treading the Vedic path. Fear and sorrow and sickness were no more. In Rama's realm no one was troubled by bodily pain, ill fortune or evil circumstance. Every man loved his neighbour, walked in the path of his own duty and obeyed the injunctions of scripture. Piety with its four observances prevailed throughout the world and no one ever dreamed of doing wrong. Men and women were Rama's earnest votaries, all heirs of final release.[22]

Life is such an agglomeration of incidents. The pure act the path. It cuts through unnecessary involvements in time and location, it creates its own universe. After all, like Prahlada, you take the name of God, and you are never abandoned. The poison becomes sweet, the wild elephant mild, and God breaks out from the very pillar to protect you. Such the Vaishnava. Did Mira Bai have to say to herself, she a princess of Marwar, whether the Rana, her husband, would understand her devotion to Sri Krishna? No. Sri Krishna once loved would truly make the Rana understand. Who cares if the family or friends forsake you? You sing the name of the Lord at the temple, and the Lord knows what he does with you. So let us sing the name of the Lord. Lord, what a sight when man sells himself for a commodity. Hunger is bad, is evil, but to hunger for God is good. Mother, let us go to the *katha* again.

And this time it would be about Sravana.

Sravana, the young Brahmin, who carried his blind father on his shoulders and who, whilst on a journey, being thirsty both, left

---

[22] Tulsidas, *Ramcharitmanas*.

his father on a roadside, and while drinking water—lapping it up in his great need, by a river—the sound was so animal, Dasaratha, father of Rama, shot an arrow, thinking the noise came from a deer. Sravana had but strength to hand the water-pot to his father, and seeing Dasaratha cursed him and said, because of the act he be separated from his son, like he himself would be from his father, by death—and he died on the spot. And thus the *Ramayana,* the exile of Rama and Sita, and the sorrowful death of Dasaratha.

Now, the world around one, moved its usual many-mansioned, measured course. The mind and the body, the high and the humble, they all live as in a city, a city of the palace and of the beggars' huts. Demands are made by the world, by the mind, by the body, and do what you will they will go their own way. Like the wandering washerman's donkey goes along its path, its own straight course. Life is never so simple, not like a simple stream that flows; it's like a high river that throws itself into the ocean. The universe within us is so multiple in shape and colour. Lord, who will help us if not you, the helper of the helpless?

* * *

The secret adventures with meat-eating went on. (How could they not?) It lent mystery to common living, made secrecy an enchantment in courage, and the very hide and seek of it was exciting. Besides as Mehtab said, it made you strong. There was no doubt about it whatsoever. But where find the money for it all? For meat is expensive. Brother had a nice idea however. He had an amulet in gold. A piece of it—the crown—once removed would perform the trick. For you had only to cut it off, and sell it, and you pay off all the debts, and maybe even have a little left over for other adventures. And why not! But when after the selling and paying they came back home, Father and Mother of course noticed something was amiss. The crown of the amulet indeed was no more there. Who knows where it fell off? Of course nobody. And the parents accepted the explanation. Why would the boys lie? Yet Mohan was not happy. He went to his room, he had much school work to do. But he could not work. He went to his mother and told the whole story to her.

'Go and say it to your father,' she pleaded.

But Father would probably thrash him. 'No, I will go myself and tell him,' she added. 'If I tell him he will not hurt you. I know that.'

'No, Mother,' said Mohania, 'I will do it myself.' And so he sat himself down and wrote his confession and gave it to his father.

'Father, give me the maximum punishment. Do not be lenient. And above all do not hurt yourself, in not wanting to hurt me, things like, fasting, speechlessness, silence, etc. So, Father, your son in your eyes is nothing better than a thief.'

The father read the confession. And he was absolutely quiet.

'Pearl drops trickled down his cheeks wetting the paper. For a moment he closed his eyes in thought, and then tore up the note. He had sat up to read it. He again laid down. I also cried. I could see my father's agony . . . Those pearl drops of love cleansed my heart and washed my sin away.

'This sort of forgiveness was not natural to my father. I had thought he would be angry, say hard things and strike his forehead. But he was so wonderfully peaceful, and I believe this was due to my clean confession . . .

'From that day truth-telling became a passion for me.'

* * *

One day, and it was to be an unforgettable day, father seemed in normal discomfort, but there was a great sense of anxiety all about the house. People of course went around as if nothing strange was the matter; children went to school and came back, the *tulasi* platform was adorned and lit, and the evening chants from the temple came in harmonious intervals. The breath of life seemed the norm of existence. Bells rang to announce the time of evening worship, and the women went to the temple next door and came back with flowers in their hair and *prasadam* in their hands. The *prasadam* was also brought to the master of the house. Though ill, the master of the household looked bright with *kumkum* on his forehead and flowers behind his ears. The dinner was served as usual, the men and boys first, and after that each one went to his own room or job, and soon the night would settle unto itself. The women would now eat and wash up the vessels, the floors, and then each one would go to her own room. Meanwhile, Mohania would sit by his father and massage him. How moving it is, this wrinkled limb, this heavy bone, these nervous hands. This is the body which created this other body, mine, just as this my body has created that further one, still in the womb and to come out in a few months. Thus the rhythm of life from father to son and from Gandhi to Gandhi, and for all time to come.

'Father, are you well?'

'Not worse than before. Perhaps just a little.'

'Are you sure, Father?'

'Yes, of course I am. When Uncle comes you could go.'

'No Father, I was rather thinking you do seem a little bit more uncomfortable than usual.'

'Well, it is natural. Is that not so? When disease has its way the body does not have its own way. The two quarrel.'

'Is there anything I could do, to soothe you, Father?'

'No, son, your massage is doing me a great deal of good. Your wife must have gone back to sleep. Is it not time you went to her?'

'No, Father, let me (go on serving you) as long as you need the massage.'

'I may need it the whole night. And you should not be spending your time looking after me. You are so young. There are so many others in the household; they will come.'

The father knew his son. The son was often like his own image. The uncle soon came. Somehow there was joy in Mohan's heart at the sight of his uncle. Suddenly he understood. Behind every gesture and thought was Kasturba. Her limbs, her chest, and her rounded belly. Night after night despite every book he had read—during pregnancy the male should keep away from the female—the demand became so overpowering, every resolution was broken. Yes, it would be sweet to go back to Kasturba. What if it's too late and she be asleep? After all you could wake her up and take what you want. The woman's surrender is man's privilege.

'Go, son, I'll look after your father. It is so late already. And you must have your school to think of.' This was the uncle speaking.

Mohania rose up to go. He was not thinking of his books. He was thinking of Kasturba. It felt so crude before the nobility of his father's body, to live the lie of studies, when the thoughts that came uppermost were those of passion, manly function, fulfilment. So Mohan left his father and went to find Kasturba. She was indeed asleep. He did wake her up. He caressed her to his passions and when he'd delved and risen, delved and risen, and delved in again amidst the juices and salivas of folly, he heard great big commotions in the house. A knock roused him out of exhaustions, smells, and awkwardness. Then with his re-found truth he heard his father's condition had suddenly become worse. And by the time he reached the apartment his father was dead. The heart had stopped. His father lay as if in deep sleep, but the whole family was in sobs. More and more people came from all over the house and the usual lamentations arose. Neighbours came, and then all the town quickly knew Diwan Karamchand Gandhi had just breathed his last. What a loss. And yet, he was not so old. But death when it comes, does not ask your age, or does it?

Mohandas was just amazed. Is this what people call death? This living limb that he'd massaged but a moment ago is cold, will never move. Mohan's clothes were still crumpled and tainted with his body's passionate adventures. So this is how the virile body shivers out into a simpleton sleep—and then there's only the fire.

Of course, Brahmins will come and courtiers from the palace. The former Prime Minister will be given a befitting funeral. Shawls and flowers will cover him and when the washings and the chantings are over, the eldest son lights the pyre and the dawn reveals a happy leaping fire. The virtuous burn out soon and their heads split with such ease. The end of man is so simple. It's all beautiful ash.

And what a lot of noisy ceremonies to say what is ended is ended. Putli Ba's silence and simplicity seemed to make even the Brahmins' chants somewhat purer. The smell of money kills ceremony. The Brahmins will go back with shawls and cows, but the dead will never return. Yet, when the night comes back after the emptiness and inevitabilities of the day, man seeks his woman and so goes round the circle of existences. How vile seems the body then. You could spit on yourself. Only the innocence of the giving woman comforts the situation. There's no ugliness in her. It is only in the attacking man.

A few weeks later, Kasturba had vicious pains. While the women of household gathered around her, the washer woman coming in with her sure surgical knowledge, the ungrown child emerged (amidst so much blood and torn ligaments) and the midwife carried it all, and buried it under a tree. For, Mohandas's first child was never born. The foetus had a brief karma. It came for a short visit into this world. Some superior being he must have been which needed only a brief sojourn into human awareness. With the death of that child something in Mohandas was defeated.

* * *

Of the woes of woman, widowhood is the most final. Or so it seemed to Putli Ba, and to the India of her times. If only it had been a hundred years earlier, and like the sati-stone after sati-stone that stand by road and temple and sing the glory of the woman who, on the death of the Lord, having lost dignity and desire, followed the procession and in tender surrender walked up the pyre to be dissolved. What life for a woman without her man—an inauspicious, white-clad creature that had to slip between streets and sacred occasions, lest the good turn not away from one. A house without a man is a mournful establishment. The very cattle seem to look up—and ask: Mother, where's the Master of the Household? And the lizards too. The dog will bark all night, and the parrot of the house will not eat its grain; he will sit silent on his perch. Even the serpent that used to slip in and drink its milk in the backyard does not come. Life is a cosmic rhythm, there are connections between fact and fact and he who understands it—the wise man, the true hero, and the husband life after life.

To Putli Ba breaking the bangles or tearing away her marriage necklace seemed the least sorrowful. That the Master of the House did not walk up the steps of the home, coming back from the palace, with the dignity of appropriateness, as if foot after foot told a truth: this was the tragedy. Would Mohania grow up and become like his father? Such a thought never appeared clearly to the mind. But like a flash, and it seemed a prophesy, a reality, and disappeared among prayer. The gods know and only they know, what might appear and disappear in existence. And prayer is a way of knowing the saying of the gods. The temple bell or the shooting stars speak if only you can perceive. And Putli Ba was someone who heard and sometime understood what she heard: 'O Mother, may I be worthy of the children.'

Mohania's eagerness to study increased with the sense that father to son he had now his family responsibilities. When the household priest Joshiji came he would indicate by suggestion and doubt, how there's always been a Gandhi who was Prime Minister of Porbandar. It's like an astronomical law, like the sunrise or the eclipse. It cannot help happening unless we fail it. 'Who else could be,' Putli Ba would whisper between her sari-fold, 'but Mohania?' The other sons, though good and nimble, yet never seem to rise to the occasion.

'Yes, Mother, but he's to study better. Besides, these days with the British about us you do not become prime minister like it used to be in the olden times; educated or uneducated, you had your learning in your blood, and so you ruled. But today you need degrees. I think Mohania should have the highest degree of the land to be Prime Minister.'

'But,' Putli Ba would object, 'Mohania says he is poor in his studies. What would one do then, Joshiji?'

'I have his life as in a written book. I have told you he has such a strong Jupiter, and in the tenth house, he must be a prime minister.'

'But,' says Putli Ba, 'he says he would rather be a doctor.'

'Yes, that might be good. But a doctor will never become a Prime Minister of Porbandar. Have you ever heard of such a case, and especially under the very difficult British?'

'You are right, Panditji. What studies do you think he should undertake then?'

'I have heard it rumoured about if only one went to London and came back, all jobs are offered to you, as if on a silver plate of the sanctuary. A lawyer—Mohania would be the first one of the community to go across the seas, and to come back a barrister. Mother, what do you think of that! It would be grand, and he would be made prime minister immediately.'

On this they both became silent. Putli Ba gave Joshiji his betel leaves and nuts, and some fruits, and fell at his feet. 'May you live a hundred years, and may your children be happy and fulfilled,' he said in blessing.

Mavji Dave, or Joshiji as they used to call him, was a kind and highly esteemed man. And his son, Kevalram, had an important position at Rajkot as a lawyer. Pure as his forehead, Joshiji seemed to bring peace wheresoever he went, and he came to the Gandhi house often, exactly as his fathers and grandfathers have always done. Why are we born all together except that we help each other? Life after life as priests, neighbours, kings, and prime ministers, we have exchanged existences only because we have to bring to each other that by which we rise to final dissolution. After all, even Ravana has to be born again and again only for his ego to be dissolved, by Sri Rama. Joshiji knew more than he said. And others knew that he knew.

Mohandas would still be a doctor.

'No,' said the elders.

'Why not!' said he.

'Because, because,' said they, 'because you cannot cut a corpse and see what's in it.'

'Why not?'

'It is not done. We have already told you so.'

'The corpse is dead . . .'

'Who could argue with you!'

'Revered elders,' he persisted, 'after all, a dead body is a dead body. And it's only when you cut it open and see what there is in it that those who are alive may know the nature of the deceased. The dead cease to exist whereas the living will have to go on living and suffering.'

'You cannot do it. That is all. The caste rules are against such a profession. For generations, for hundreds of years no one in the Modhi-bania community has ever done such a thing. Nor amongst the Jainas or the Brahmins.'

'And so?'

'And so, you must do something else.' Mohania was conciliant but not defeated. 'Besides,' they added, in order to convince him, 'you know your father was against it.' This was the final argument. And that did the trick. How could it not?

'What next, then?'

'Go to London and be barrister.' To the Bar. That sounded good. And to London.

After that the conversation fell into a long, normal silence.

'Mother,' he said one day. 'Mother, suppose I go to England.'

'No, Mohania, you will not play such pranks with me. I know my son.'

'But your son knows you too,' he laughed. 'Your son says he goes to England. He will come back a big *Vakil,* a barrister, and bring great lustre to the family.'

'Your mother says the son's family for generations have been ministers and prime ministers, and never have drunk but the good Kathiawar rain-water.'

'But times have changed, Mother, even in Kathiawar.' The conversation stopped abruptly.

On another day he began again. 'Mother what if I went to England? Say yes, Mother.'

'I will say yes if the elders say yes. What's a woman's word? It's the elders that decide.'

'And so?'

'And so ask your uncle. He is the head of the family now.'

'Therefore, I will go to Porbandar. And if Uncle is convinced you're convinced. Now, say yes Mother.'

'Yes, Mohania, so it will be.'

What's in a woman's life but what comes to her? Birth and marriage, wealth and death, come to her just as the seasons come and go. She only a woman who accepts the law that what happens because it could not happen otherwise. Men do other things. That is their affair.

'Then a day was fixed for my going to Porbandar,' wrote Mohandas Gandhi later.

'Twice or thrice I prepared to go but some difficulty came in my way . . . Once I was to go with Zaverchand but an hour before the time for my departure, a serious accident took place. I was always quarrelling with my friend Sheik Mehtab. On the day of my departure, I was quite engrossed in thinking about the quarrel. We had a musical party at night. I did not enjoy it very well. At about 10.30 p.m. the party ended and we all went to see Meghjibhai and Rami. On our way I was buried in the madcap thoughts of London on one side and the thoughts of Sheik Mehtab on the other. Amidst thoughts I came unconsciously in contact with a carriage. I received some injury. Yet I did not take the help of anybody for walking. I think I was quite dizzy. Then we entered the house of Meghjibhai. There I again came in contact with a stone unknowingly and received injury. I was quite senseless. From that (time) I did not know what took place, and after that I am told by them I fell flat on the ground after some steps. I was not myself for five minutes. They considered I was dead. I came to my senses at last. The mother was sent for. She was very sorry for me.'

This was Gandhiji's first attempts at using the English language. His awkwardnesses are made up by his precision.

'She (the mother) was very sorry for me, and this caused my delay though I told them that I was quite well. But none would allow me to go though I afterwards came to know that my bold and dearest mother would have allowed me to go to London. But she feared the calumny of other people. At last with great difficulty I was allowed to leave Rajkot for Porbandar after some days.'

He was eager to settle the matter—and get to London quick. His cousin Madhavji had also promised financial help. Mohania must now get to Porbandar as early as possible. He jumped on a bullock cart though still weak from his fall, then on the back of a camel—he was in such a hurry. He came back to Porbandar, the family house, the old servants, the comings and goings of courtiers, the staircase, the brother, the cousins, the uncle. The uncle had a large heart for the nephew. The uncle was himself, however, preparing his pilgrimage to Benares.

'So Mohania what may it be?' he asked, did the uncle.

'Uncle, I have finished my matriculation, you know. I was not bright but I was all right. Then I went for a few months to the college at Bhavnagar. It was so dull—and my health poor. There was nothing to learn. Our teachers are still new to English education. I must go to England. I must return a barrister. Then I can do something worthy of the family.'

'Your father,' said the uncle gently, affectionately, 'your father had high hopes for you. We felt you would bring lustre to the family name.'

'I don't know whether this will ever be true. I am earnest, however, or rather I am trying very hard to be more and more earnest.'

'Of that, son, we have no doubt.'

'But I have,' insisted Mohania. 'There is no end to the discovery of what is true. I work so hard. And yet I fail, all the time. It's not so easy, Uncle, to love the truth, to attain the truth. Only Harishchandra could.'

'Why could you not be Harishchandra? Who knows!'

'Oh, Uncle, how could that ever be? I am such a simple, unendowed person. All I can do is to seek, seek hard, reach if possible the core of things.'

'We, the Gandhis, have always been somewhat difficult with the world. You will succeed, though, son. My thoughts are now bent on Benares. If you want to go to England, you can go. If your mother says yes, I say yes. And you have my blessings.'

The uncle was not only kind. He was diplomatic. He was not only humble and truthful, he was also ambitious and proud. Yes, Mohania will bring lustre to the family. Yet, would he help?

'When will you be going?'

'As soon as I can get the money. It will cost between five and ten thousand rupees. Madhavji has promised to lend me the necessary sum. I can return it when I make my own money.'

'If Madhavji says so he means it.'

'So you think, Uncle, I can go?'

'Yes, of course, you have my blessings.' Mohan was overjoyed. So now he could go, he will go.

With this consent extracted he went to his cousin, Paramanandji. To promise money is one thing, but to give it another. Especially a loan, and to such a stripling of a boy. And he going off to far Europe. The family will not permit it. The caste will not permit. It never will. Thus spoke the wise cousin. So what's to be done now? Perhaps the princes of Porbandar or of Rajkot might give him a scholarship. Would not Mr. Lely, the English administrator of Porbandar, do something to help him out?

'For the first time in my life,' wrote Mohandas Gandhi a few years later, 'I had an interview with an English gentleman. Formerly I never dared to confront them. But thoughts of London made me bold. I had small talk with him in Gujarati. He was quite in a hurry. He saw me when he was ascending the ladder of the upper storey of his bungalow. He said Porbandar was very poor and could not give me any pecuniary help.'[23] Our Mohania may ultimately have to depend on Paramanandbhai.

---

[23] Here again it is the first use of English for self-expression. These lines are taken from his *London Diary.* C.W., Vol. 1, p. 6.

Yes, the money would come. And with such an assurance he went back to Rajkot.

And then again there was Mr. Watson, the Political Agent to Kathiawar States, and he may, remembering the service of Kaba Gandhi to Kathiawar, render some help. Meanwhile, another cousin, Madhavji, who had promised help, withdrew his offer. He was frightened of caste-opinions. Not only did he not want to loan out any money (to this wiseacre kid of Kaba Gandhi's!) but he even spoke ill of Mohandas. This made his mother very unhappy. 'I could easily console her and I have the satisfaction to see that I have often consoled her with success and have made her laugh when she, my dear, dear mother, would be shedding tears on my account. At last Colonel Watson came. I saw him. He said, "I will think about it," but I never could get any help from him. Then they sought the Thakore Sahib of Rajkot. Nothing came of this either. Then for the last time I saw the Thakore Sahib and Colonel Watson, received a note of introduction from the latter, and an autographed photo from the former. Here I must write that the fulsome flattery which I had to practise about this time had made me quite angry. Had it not been for my credulous and dearest brother, I should have never resorted to such a piece of gross flattery.'[24]

But it was so willed by the gods, Mohan's eldest brother was with him in this great adventure. Yes, Mohan must go to England and come back a barrister.

And when he returns he would be prime minister anywhere in Kathiawar. The Gandhi name will continue to shine high on the brow of Porbandar.

---

[24] C.W., Vol. 1, p. 10.

But the community, roused from its inertia, woke up one day to find that a distinguished member of the Modhi-bania caste was going away to England. This shall not be done. The Gandhis of Porbandar will be excommunicated if they went against the consensus of the community. Yes, we will do it for all the manes in the heavens; the very gods will desert us, if we did not respect our tradition. No, Mohandas Gandhi, son of the revered Kaba Gandhi, will not leave the sacred shores of India.

'Son, you must not go,' said the mother.

'Why not, Mother? You had given me a promise . . .'

'Yes, that is so. But look at all the community. What will happen to us who remain behind?'

'Mother, after all, the world has always gone and will go on were the community to say no, and yet again no. The fact, Mother, is this. Do you really believe I will lose caste by going away to England? Do you?'

'Not really, Mohania. But they say women in England are easy of ways, and further that you will have to eat meat and drink wine.'

'Is that all that worries you, mother?'

'Yes, only these . . . and other things as well.'

'Will you not trust me? I shall not tell you a lie. I swear I will not touch any of those things. Would that do?'

'I can trust you,' said Putli Ba. 'But how can I trust you in a distant land? I am dazed and know not what to do.'

'God is everywhere, Mother. He is not present only in Gujarat. And He will help me if anyone will . . .'

'Yes, that is true.'

Who could argue with Mohania? He was so true, so very clever. Yes, he will do something worthy one day. She would ask Becharji Maharaj, the Jaina monk. He was once a Gandhi.

'Swamiji,' said the mother to Becharji Maharaj, when he came visiting them a few days later. 'My son Mohania insists on going to England. He says he will not touch meat or wine or women. Our Joshiji said: Let Mohania take a vow "I will not touch meat or wine or women" and then he could go. What does the Swamiji think of it?'

'If he would take a vow he would keep a vow,' assured the Swamiji knowing Mohania well. 'And I will administer it myself.'

Kasturba, however, was inconsolable. Not only the community was against her and him but he was going to a far-off country with easy women, meat and drinks. 'And now what will happen to me? Lord, why do you give me this, this, this?' Her parents too came round to her view. 'How could you do that to us?' And day after day he had to argue with them, console his wife. After all, it was going to be only for two years, the separation would be, and when he comes back he will be a barrister. That means money, position and great dignity. Yes, it is right he should go to England.

Of course, the body's fires who will quell? But life is sorrow, especially the life of woman. She bears pain while men go and fight in the world. Look at our ballads—the Jauhars. Men go to battle to slay the Turk or be slain by him. The women will sit around the fire, reading the sacred texts. If men come back the women will welcome them with *kumkum* water and flower garlands. If not, they adorn themselves with *kumkum* and garlands and jump into the blazing pyre. Such the tradition, such the women of Kathiawar. Yes, of course, the body cries. Its agony seems sometimes unbearable. Passion is not anybody's friend.

Who can bear the submarine fire? Yet must husband and wife know that man must do his duty—he must go to his wars, his conquests. The woman looks after the brood, the little ones. Now that they had a son, he will keep Kasturba busy. A son on the lap is part of his father at home. 'Harilal will look after you!' Thus the arguments and explanations, and reversals of arguments, to come to one decision: Yes, Mohandas will leave for England.

'Then a day was fixed for my departure. At first it was the fourth of August. The matter was brought to a crisis . . . My brother was asked by some persons about my going. Now was the time when he told me to leave off the intention of going but I would not do that. The tenth of August came and I started . . .'[25]

'Mother,' he said, 'Mother, I go and come.'

'Go and come, son,' she answered but before she could say her blessings, tears streamed up in her eyes, and she hiding her face behind her hands, spoke nothing. Would she see her son again? This was the only question that needed an answer, but who could tell her? Widowhood is sad, and death the holy termination of this existence. For how long could one carry one's inauspiciousness about? And Mohania not there.

'Son, go and come,' Putli Ba repeated while the whole house was already bustling with the confusions of departure. Kasturba was inconsolable. She sobbed and sobbed. But now she had a son too, to look after, the little Harilal. 'Can you not stay back, at least for your son's sake? Must you be so obstinate? There is still time . . .,' and she would break into big fits of sobbing.

'I kissed her,' says Gandhiji, 'and she said, 'Don't go!' What followed I need not describe.'

The carriage was ready. The servants were in tears. All the family came to the front door; uncles, cousins, aunts, retainers.

---

[25] C.W., Vol. l, p. 10.

The neighbours too opened their windows to see this great departure. Perhaps when one goes to London one never returns.

Karsandas, the elder brother, was accompanying Mohan to Bombay. The faithful, the irrepressible Sheik Mehtab too would travel as far as Bombay with his friend. After all, one does not go to England every day from Kathiawar. Mohandas Gandhi's journey abroad became such an event that even the *Kathiawar Times* spoke of it. 'I hope some of you will follow in my footsteps, and after your return will work wholeheartedly for the big reforms in India.'[26] These were his final words to friends and fellow young men.

* * *

At least it was good to be going to Bombay. From Bombay everything will look different, and London near.

The city of Bombay with its tall Victorian structures, its many fine and honoured statues, its parks, grounds, its harbour, seemed a real metropolis after Rajkot. And the number of Europeans who went about in carriages showed it was an important one too. The buggies were more splendid than anyone saw at Rajkot, with outriders, brilliant horses, and coachmen dressed in black and gold. Ships came and went (though not too frequently) and this in itself seemed to make the city larger than it was. More humanity came in, and some went out too. Goods came in, and raw materials went out. The Kathiawaris were excellent merchants, and they made money with this buying and selling, then selling and buying again. The Modhi-banias, to which sub-caste Mohandas belonged, were

---

[26] C.W., Vol. 2, p. 2.

a prosperous community in Bombay. You could make money from the foreigner; you could make much money, but you will not go to his land. It was evil to do so. How dare, said they, does Karamchand Gandhi's son go to London? The community became excited over it all. Elders went to elders and talked about it on verandas, and the women inside their courtyards could not think of such sinful things happening. And, too, with a wife and child. Was it plausible? This indeed was the iron-age, the *Kali-yuga*. One day some Modhi-banias seeing Mohandas on the street, surrounded him and booed him. 'Look at that fellow, and he be going to pariah London, so he says, for higher studies. Does not he know in England—and we in Bombay know it for we see it all the time—the Englishmen do not wash every day, they've no knowledge of the pure or the impure, the touchable or the untouchable, in fact meat and drink is all they know, and the easy way women yield to men. Just see it in Bombay any evening on Malabar Hill or in Colaba. And the way women and men hold each other tight and dance! You can see it all with your own eyes. Come!'

Mohandas was ever shy. Words did not come to him easily. Nor did hatred. He simply said, 'I go to study. I will become a barrister and return. I have taken my vows and to those vows am I wedded.'

'The better-than-you have succumbed, my dear fellow. You will not go.'

'I will go,' said Mohandas firmly, and walked out of the angry crowd.

Day by day events began to grow worse. The brother began to wonder if Mohandas was doing the proper thing. 'Brother,' he answered, 'You know I've promised Mother. And Mother for me is like the Goddess herself. I will not break my promise.

Anyway, the vows were administered by a Sadhu. How could I break these.'

'Yes, you must go,' remarked Karsandas. 'Father always imagined you holding big posts in government. How could you do that if you did not get a London degree? Go, brother, and you have my blessings.' One could not wait indefinitely in Bombay after all. So Karsandas left for Rajkot. However, monsoon weather was not appropriate for a novice's sea-voyage. Somewhere a ship had sunk. Thus one had to wait till the climate changed. But this made the waiting worse. The community was getting angrier. One day they called a big meeting. Anybody who did not turn up would have to pay a fine of five annas per person. Mohandas had to answer to the whole community, and be condemned by them if he foolishly persisted in his decision. He went to the assembly nervous but courageous, fearful not of what they would do to him but as to what he would say. And then again to address a whole assembly, the elders amongst them!

They said the same things (at the meeting) they had spoken before; the immorality of the British, the meat, the wine, the women. But he insisted his vows would see him through them all. Remember, there is such a thing as Truth. And Truth protects. Look at Harishchandra. This is not what he said, this is what he thought. And it gave him strength. 'Rama, Sri Rama,' he chanted to himself. That is the refuge of the meek and the true. He would go to London and come out a better man. Of this he was certain. He could not say it to the assembly but he knew he would see a new humanity, and he would return a wiser man. 'I am sorry,' he said, 'that I cannot alter my decision. What I have heard about England is quite different from what you say; one need not take meat and wine there. As for crossing the waters, if our brethren can go as far as Aden, why could I not go to England? I am deeply convinced that malice is at the root of all these objections.'

'You and your family will be excommunicated.'

'Who can, revered sirs, stop you from doing what you think just. And so I go.'

'The elders of your family too might be excommunicated.'

'Well, they will have to take their own decisions. I have taken mine. And it is immutable.'

So young, yet so strong, never had a Modhi-bania boy behaved with such lack-reverence to the community, as this Mohandas Gandhi, son of Karamchand Gandhi of Rajkot. And what do you think, the whole family would duly be excommunicated! One might neither eat with them nor drink with them. No one will ever cross a threshold where the Ota Gandhi family lives. And, of course, there would be no question of any of us giving our daughters in marriage to the Gandhis.

'This boy has lost his senses!' they cried. 'We command everyone not to have anything to do with him. He who will support him must be treated as an outcast, whoever helps him or goes to see him off at the dock shall be punishable with a fine of a rupee and annas four.'[27]

* * *

The *S.S. Clyde* was a ship that had sailed many seas. When it berthed in Bombay it seemed a wonder and a promise. Mazumdar, the well-known Junagadh lawyer, was going by that ship. If Mazumdar could risk his life going on September seas, why not Mohandas Gandhi? People thought it a wise

---

[27] C.W., Vol. 1, p. 2.

decision. But when he went to get his money—Karsandas had handed it over to Mohan's brother-in-law to keep—the brother-in-law would not give it back. Mohandas then went to Ranchoddas Patwari, a friend of the family; the good man, he willingly gave Mohandas the necessary money. The ticket was bought. And so too the clothes and accessories. 'Some of the clothes I liked, and some I did not like at all. The necktie which I delighted in wearing later, I then abhorred. The short jacket I looked upon as immodest.'[28] The boat was going to sail the next day. But who knows what can still happen, after all there's the excommunication? He would go anyway. There was no question whatsoever about it. He would go to England, 'the land of philosophers, poets, the very centre of civilisation'.

The *S.S. Clyde* left Bombay for England on 4 September 1888, sailing a quiet, monsoonless sea. He had left his mother.

---

[28] A., p. 41.

2

England of the Fabians

Sir, how be a gentleman? What marks and modes of thought and clothes, what inflections of sound and temperament, make a young man a gentleman? And if one is a vegetarian, a little too young and a little too awkward of word or gesture, what then? And what then, too, if one's English is imperfect (Indian schools, you know, have only just started the teaching of English and, sir, albeit a great language, it's still an alien tongue to us, and forgive us our abuse of it!). And the way you hold that needly fork and that ever slippery knife in your hands, and ask the waiter in whispered and almost inaudible tones, 'Be there any meat in it?' While the ship rolls over to its sides—it's sort of the monsoon months yet—what then do you do when the waiter does not understand? 'I do not eat meat,' you repeat, but the waiter still does not understand. How then, Lord, be a gentleman? You can eat bread and butter and say no word to anyone, eat jam or cheese and endure it all. This does not leave you alone. For a few friendly Englishmen are about and they will not let you in peace. 'Unless you eat meat, and smoke and drink you will never make a gentleman.' They more or less mean what they say, though it is not always easy to understand what they say. The best thing then is to go back to one's cabin and eat little tidbits brought from home, and be hungry. You can at least walk on the deck and show in your clothes that you're a gentleman. There are still decent people in the world, even among Englishmen, who think you are not a boor if you do not eat meat but who will try and persuade you to do so. Their arguments sound authentic, even true. But there's the vow. And so you go back to your tea and tidbits, and let God decide the rest.

Mohandas would not yield to the persuasions of others. Of course, what they say may be true, especially as everyone seems to be saying it. And he would suddenly think of the austere, the trustful, and the sacred face of his mother. Tears would come to his eyes. God will help him. He would keep to his resolve.

God does help. This is what Mohandas' experience tells him again and again. God's hand helps those who have trust in Him. For, finally, the ship's authorities gave Mohandas and his companion, another Indian and a vegetarian, a boy to cook vegetarian meals especially for them. And thus the very first test was won. You could still sit at table, tuck your napkins the right way, use the proper knives and forks, and withal become more knowledgeable in your ways. It's just a question of observation, of practice. And soon Mohandas was able to behave more and more like the others. He was however still shy and could not talk English to his satisfaction. He had to formulate every sentence first in his mind, duly translated from the Gujarati, and then only would he pronounce his words. It was a difficult task but not an impossible one. Others besides him do it and do it so well. It's all a question of time.

Meanwhile, the ship stops at Aden. You admire the Arab boys plunging into the water in the wake of your pennies, or later at Port Said be pestered by vendors: You want carpets, watches, walking sticks? You want carpets, watches, walking sticks? The first glimpse of Europe was at Brindisi, with its narrow streets, its cobbles, its dirt, and its high, aspiring houses, perched churches, and clothes hanging across the streets (so much like in India) and curs and dirt, and the ever present tricks of the procurer and pimp, 'Girls of fourteen for you, Indian gentleman, plump, white, and pretty?' The world is ever the same. But how beautiful the blue of the Mediterranean, the magnificence of the Santa Maggiore on the top of the Hill. Six hundred years old they say, that is about the time of the invasion of Mahmud of Ghazni to India. Old, yes, but not old enough. Yet how melodious the city was in the gentle Italian night.

The European was a kind man after all. He was neither so distant in his own country nor was he so immaculate. Therefore every European is not a 'gentleman'. There's something protective about such a realisation. One's awkwardness somehow seems less awkward and one's clothes (especially when one is hardly nineteen) shine the brighter. Thank the Italians for making us men again.

After Brindisi the weather became cooler, and the Mediterranean is enchanting. Malta, first, with the cathedral of St. Juan, the Armoury Hall, and the beautiful carriage of Napoleon Bonaparte. Then, Gibraltar. Gibraltar again is a sign of Britain's might and high power, and after tossing on the Bay of Biscay, you feel you cannot bear it any longer. There's such hunger in the stomach. Kind Englishmen—and they can be so kind—try to persuade you, once again, it is time you decided to eat meat. You might not smoke or take liquor but without meat you will starve to death, young man. Yet Mohandas would not be persuaded. Plymouth revealed the circular splendours of great England. There's something divine about these strange embattlemented isles. God would not have given them this strength had they not been so worthy. Look at the whiteness of those ships, and the measured and comfortable architecture of those houses. People seemed so quiet and going about their business with simplicity and pride. They puff at their pipes and go their way. The proud Englishman was a noble creature to watch. Would Mohan be ever like him?

From Southampton he and his companion (another Indian) travelled to London. The landscapes, the houses, and the people, seemed just as the pictures in textbooks. When you see what you've imagined and it's found true, you always have a secret sense of self-assurance. The world seems less uncertain, and a place of some hope.

The Victoria Hotel in London was a marvel.

'I was quite dazzled,' says Gandhiji, 'by the splendour of the hotel. I had never seen in my life such a pomp . . . There was all over electric light. Then we were to go to the second floor by a lift. I did not know what it was. The boy at once touched something which I thought was the lock of the door. But as I afterwards came to know it was the bell, and he rang in order to tell the waiter to bring the lift. The doors were opened and I thought that it was a room. But to my great surprise we were brought to the second floor.'[1]

October can be beautiful in England. The autumn light can be magnificent, with more gold in it than any you ever see in India, and the way it colours up the whole perspective on church, bank and bridge. There's a splendour about England that seems almost mythological. The barges, the Thames, the ships, the high buildings, the Palace of Westminster, the clean and quiet ways of a civilised land. Everything is so instructive

---

[1]   C.W., p. 21.

to behold; the gentle but steady tread of men, the elegant and furry clothing of women in high carriages. And one's own awkwardness seems the bigger in the midst of all this. Mohandas, thinking that white flannel was more becoming than serge or dark wool (he'd left these clothes behind to be shipped to his London address), found himself the only inelegant man about town. He was ashamed of himself for such ignorance. He could hardly walk about without realising his clothes attracted undue attention. And the Indians were not without telling him how very stupid it all looked.

There was, for example, the great Dr. Mehta who had become a gentleman. Many years in the British Isles had given him this rare privilege and accomplishment. Morning coat and top hat and an affected but impeccable way of English speech had given him (or he had given himself) elegance and authority. Mohandas had sent him a telegram from Southampton.

'My dear fellow, how nice to see you,' he said as he entered the Victoria Hotel where Mohan had taken a room. Mohandas was pleased to see a man so expert in dealing with this bewildering world and was willing to be his pupil, his protégé. Mohan, however, seeing the extreme softness of the top hat, took it in his hand and tried to feel its texture. The Indian gentleman was shocked.

'Mr. Gandhi,' he said in a high and imperious tone, 'do not touch other people's things.' Mohandas instead of being offended was ashamed and apologetic. 'Do not talk loudly.'

'I am so sorry I do not know English etiquette.'

'In this country etiquette is morality,' he pronounced. 'What you do does not matter. How you do it does matter.'

'I am deeply sorry for my inadvertence. I will never do it again.'

'My dear fellow,' continued Dr. Mehta, 'this is a prohibitively expensive hotel.'

'I did not know,' replied Mohandas. 'My companions from India came here. And I followed them.'

'I know a better place,' remarked Dr. Mehta with much assurance. 'I will fix you up at a cheaper place soon. Besides, you must learn the English language. And for that you must stay with an English family. In this country, language shows your class. In England,' he added, trying to educate his fellow-countryman, 'in this country there is no caste, but there is class, and class distinctions are worse than caste distinctions. And the class of a gentleman is known by his language. You must learn English well,' he admonished and took his friend on a stroll through London streets. It was an education in itself. The way you cross a street or hail a cab, all this is to be learnt. You never brush past a lady, and if you entered a restaurant and met a lady at the door, you always lift your hat in recognition of her gentility. And this is England.

And once in a restaurant you wait for the waiter to come. He gives you the menu card. Mohan examines it carefully. He sees nothing to indicate there what is vegetarian and what non-vegetarian. Besides, many of the dishes have French names. When the waiter comes to take an order, Mohan whispers, 'Have you anything vegetarian for me? I am a vegetarian.'

The waiter does not understand. The London Indian, angry and humiliated, explains to the waiter the needs of this young man from India. Of course, there are cabbages and potatoes, cheese and bread.

'What about that?'

'Thank you very much.' Yes, Mohan could eat. And when the waiter goes away with the orders, the London Indian's ire was all upon his young companion.

'My dear fellow, this is England and not Kathiawar. You should be ashamed of yourself. Why, you mean you have never eaten meat?'

'No, I have. Some years ago I and my brother wanted to experiment on eating meat. We did it. But I hated to tell a lie to my parents. So I gave it up. In fact,' confessed Mohan, 'I rather liked it.'

'If you ate it in India, what's wrong eating it here?' laughed the London Indian.

'Nothing wrong. Only I have taken a vow never, never, to touch meat. It was done to satisfy my mother.'

'Your mother, my dear young man, knows nothing of England. And a vow taken to please an illiterate woman is no promise at all. I tell you as a man with a wide experience. Life in England is impossible without the eating of meat.'

'Then I had better go back.'

'Have you ever read Bentham? If you have read his *Theory of Utility* you will never argue this way.'

'But, sir, a vow is a vow.'

What a dunce, the London Indian must have thought to himself. The young fellow has come here and to study. His family has spent so much money to send him here. When shall we ever get civilised?

'Well, please yourself,' said the London Indian and never tried to change his companion again.

But Dr. Mehta, true to his promise, fixed up a place for Mohandas to stay. It was with an English family in Richmond. Mohan spent a miserable month there. He had to eat only bread and cheese and porridge, and for the rest he slipped into English restaurants to feed himself. Winter was coming on, and the cold gave him greater hunger. Lord, help the hungry in cold climates.

Mohandas now moved to a private apartment. It cost less and one could cook one's breakfast and tea, and for dinner one went out. One could live on about ten shillings a week thus, and with room-rent, it was not ruinous. Yet how long would 666 English pounds last? Would they last three years? He paid a pound and joined the Inns of Court. The Inner Temple was the most distinguished one—or so they said—and he would get there the best education. His mother and family had sacrificed themselves greatly for his sake. He would be worthy of them.

Meanwhile, his vegetarian experiments continued. Once an Indian, Mr. Shukla, invited him to dinner. He wanted to trick him into a decent English meal. So they went to an expensive restaurant. After that they were going to the theatre. It was all a part of being a man about town. This is the way to live if you want to live a civilised life. They entered the Holborn Restaurant. It was grand and so very gay. They sat at a table and the menu was brought. Mohandas did not know what to choose, so he whispered to the waiter once again.

'I am a vegetarian. Can you tell me what I can eat here?'

Mr. Shukla got very angry. 'Mohandas Gandhi, if you cannot eat like a civilised man, get out, eat where you like, and we'll meet at the door of the theatre at the fixed hour.'

Mohandas was not hurt. He was sorry to have put his friend to so embarrassing a situation. Mohan now went out, but it was dark and cold. Friendly, and a gentleman, he waited at the door of the theatre, unable to have his meal. It had been too late. His friend never knew of it. The ways of God are strange. 'I could see and appreciate the love by which all my friend's efforts were actuated and my respect for him was all the greater on account of our differences of thought and action. I decided . . . I should assure him that I would be clumsy no more but try to become polished by cultivating other accomplishments which fitted one for polite society.'

But the process of becoming a gentleman was not so simple. You had to have the right clothes. So he chose for himself a nice suit on Bond Street. Nothing could be more elegant. And a bow tie—this was the appropriate thing. And someone said one must learn French to be a gentleman. So he paid some money and started learning French. And dancing, too. If, when you go to a party, and most parties have dancing in the evenings, and you say you cannot dance, it would be so awkward. Therefore he had to take dancing lessons. But the measures of the Indian musical scales were different from the English ones. Mohandas could never follow the steps—he just could not, and so gave up ballroom dancing. He would learn violin instead, to understand European music. Thus he bought himself a violin. Further, the wise among the Indians in England had told him he must speak English with the correct upper class accent. He must therefore learn elocution. Now he went to a teacher to learn elocution. *The Standard Elocutionist* was the book he had to follow. After some time he gave that up too. He also gave up the violin lessons: 'The violin was to cultivate the ear. It only cultivated disappointment.'

Meanwhile, a very significant event took place. Going along the road one day, suddenly he saw a vegetarian restaurant: the Central Restaurant, on Farrington Street. 'The sight of it filled me with the same joy that a child feels on getting a thing after its own heart.' For the first time since he arrived in England, he ate a real meal. He also bought for himself at the restaurant *A Plea for Vegetarianism* by Henry Salt. He now had arguments to prove his case. Vegetarianism was no more a barbaric practice. It was the most civilised way of eating, and also the most scientific one.

And he began to read newspapers. What was happening in the world around was fascinating. There was that big problem of Ireland. And the English seemed to be in such a confusion. And the Irish too. Look at Parnell and the scandal against him. It won't do to fight against an enemy if you're not morally his superior. The way of Harishchandra is the only way to live in a world filled with contradictions and corruptions. Somehow one knows truth always wins.

The readings of the English papers also taught him to understand the English language a little better. Could he not aim at a higher degree now that his English had improved? What degree? Oxford and Cambridge were too far away (in terms of the time needed)—and too expensive. Why not take the London Matriculation? Mohandas went therefore to a tutorial school and learned Latin to pass his exams. 'It was an almost impossible task for me. But the aspirant after being an English gentleman chose to convert himself into a serious student.'

London towards the end of the nineteenth century had become not only the financial metropolis of the world, but its political megalopolis as well. The Good Queen's rule had laid the foundation of an empire that stretched from end to end of the world, and as goods went and gold came, ideas came as well. The wisdom of China and of India mingled with the ideologies of the philosophers (the French Revolution was not so far away, it seemed, because of Carlyle) and prophetic concepts came to be born. Indeed, refugees from Germany and Russia, from Italy and even from far-off China, sought new and revolutionary solutions to world's problems. Meanwhile, the English themselves were not yet basking in the splendour of their own glory. The poets had stated their utopian ideals, Wordsworth, Shelley and Blake, and the philosophers followed them. Bentham and Mill had searched for universal values, and their discoveries had changed the whole perspective of English political life. Bentham had in fact sat at the table of some of the directors of the East India Company and had forced them to think of more humanitarian ways of dealing with their vast domains, while Mill's liberalism and the hope of human dignity seemed to go so well with economic prosperity. Further, Spencer's new sociology had aired the stuffy precincts of established English institutions, and thus change seemed inevitable. But the man who had started it all was Darwin. Darwin having removed the theological contexture of man's being, and man becoming duly freed, the politician abandoned his double standards—the one practical, the other religious— thus the practical became philosophical, and finally the philosophical practical. The mess the Continent was in— look at the France of 1848, and of Germany, of Prussian expansionism, and the revolts of the Russian subhumans and their turmoils, and of Italy's elegant protests—it all spelled of something grave. In England it will not be thus, for England, is, after all, England. The English can solve all problems with a shy smile and a puff of common sense. The British were a practical people (unlike the French who always quarrelled over ideas and left the reality to be looked after by dictators and emperors) and Britain was going to enter the modern industrial age, a nation that believed in and practised freedom both in trade and politics. When the whole world was British what restrictions could one have? A gunboat here, a few soldiers there—some diplomatic move, now here, now there—and the world not only went the English way but indeed was grateful to England. Britannia ruled the waves, and the Good Queen as head of the red, round world?

At the frontier of this great confidence lived the revolutionaries—the aliens. Marx had fled from a backward

Germany to seek political and intellectual refuge in England and he, his aristocratic wife and his friends and his friends' friends, evolved long continental philosophies that seemed to have little relation to facts. And these arguments came out in big tomes or in arrogant pamphlets. How could one have chains—leave alone break them—when boats ploughed through the Thames with such natural self-assurance and the ships that came and docked at the British harbours pouring out such variegated and hopeful humanity? What did they lack? Freedom? No, of course not. When Marx did not sound ridiculous he sounded Utopian. True, there is misery among the working classes but as everybody gets rich there will be no poor man left in the realm of England. The hard English pound with the heavy round Queen's effigy on it carried such absolute concreteness. One must be mad thinking on revolutions. To use Darwin—so English—to the un-English thinkings of the European revolutionary was to forget the real point; whatever you may say about the universe, there is an order, and that order is unearthly. We must bow to it as the primitive peoples (and their religions were being studied by the new scientists, the anthropologists) bow to the sun. However, Mazzini had other ideas. He accepted the Superior Power, God, but wondered why Austrian humans and others leagued with them, behave as they do towards Italy. The Italian working classes were as good as any—in fact, more humane and more cultured than any in Europe for they had Jesus Christ and Dante. It was Mazzini's ambition to unite the revolutionary fervour of Marx (without Marx's abusive language, his free morals, and his intellectual haughtiness) with some form of divine guidance. God (and so Christ) was to be made the revolutionary. It was, if you remember, an old dream of Savonarola. To be one with God was to be a revolutionary,

and to be a true revolutionary one had to be a good Christian—
not necessarily Papal (for the Vatican was corrupt as everybody
knew) but Catholic. Kropotkin, on the other hand, had come
a long way from backward Russia—he had paternalism in his
blood, and so he wanted all mankind to be free, like himself.
The abstract man was the Father, and all was noble when he was
in true authoritiless authority. Eat, mate, come and go, and do
what you like for the world was a happy place with everything
in plenty, and purity and nobility in the hearts of man—all was
well except a few tyrants and tyrants are easy to get rid of. You
can shoot a few of them dead, and when thrones fall, freedom
comes. Then there is peace and plenty for all mankind. Man will
thus reign supreme.

All this sounds pretty un-British, but what harm could come
if Prince Kropotkin aired his views? A little embarrassing for the
British but England being an isle, aliens are easy to control, and
so let these cranks go their ways. And it was also such a pleasure
to embarrass the Russian cousin.

However, the English also had their own cranks. These
cranks were reasonable people, but reasoned so well that for the
practical Englishman they looked eccentric. Some, for example,
were against vivisection. This absurd and cruel theory held that
diseases come from parasites, and so as to see that you do not
get those diseases, you have just to have those diseases grow
on an animal—a cow, a horse—and once they, the doctors,
inject a bit of this disease into you, you are freed from that
danger almost forever. Dreaded diseases like the plague and
the smallpox could thus be controlled, it was argued, and this
way we would wipe out epidemics over the face of the earth.
Effective as it all might be, how give so much pain to the poor
animal. The British, you know, love animals—especially dogs,

horses, birds, cats—and as such, they came to the rescue of the cow. There were others however who said not only must you not torture the cow, but you must never eat her. This was of course going too far. For if you argued the point correctly, how could you ever talk of saving cows from torture, but would not mind a chunk of one of them on your table? Thus the vegetarians came into the picture. Meanwhile, socialism— that vague humanitarian expression which came from the continent—brought in some new ideas. Not only were the working classes to have better pay, better houses, etc., but all men being equal, no man should exploit another man. Man is born with noble human impulses. He must love man, not in the Christian way alone—though this too was permitted—he must especially allow man to be free from all economic strain. There is enough in the world for everyone to be happy. So let us share the goods of the world. This philosophy—called the Fabian—emerged from among the intellectuals, men and women. For by now women too had joined the game. If all men are equal, by definition woman is equal to man. So one man, one vote should be really, one woman, or man, one vote. You could carry flags in procession announcing this, and sometimes if you were too noisy and obstreperous (and the English upper middle class flag-waving women had strong biceps and connections, anyway) you were thrown into prison perhaps for a day or two, perhaps even physically uncomfortable there, but nothing really ever happened to you. You were let out after some time (too many questions are asked in Parliament) and you became a heroine. And so on to the next march.

  Now if you are a woman and you are free (like a man), it seemed improper to have so many children imposed on you. Why should woman bear children merely because man imposes them on her? Since God was no more the problem, society could control human productivity in all womankind. Contraceptives were, after all, innocent little rubbery things that could stop you from having babies. If you believe that God does not give you babies but you do, then your woman could also decide not to have babies—now that man and woman are equal. This should be even more obvious to anyone who knows what Malthus had said: Population does not grow on principles of addition but in terms of multiplication. It is a question of simple common sense, and of arithmetic. Therefore, one day, the whole world would be peopled by mankind and there will not be enough food to eat. The British Empire may still be generous and stable and protective, but when there is no food there is no food. There is no solution to the problem except ration the birth of babies. This appealed to the vegetarians as well. Do not kill the cow (or ox or sheep) came to be sometimes united with: do not have more babies. Sometimes the two quarrelled, for the vegetarian was often a God believer, and the birth-control propagandist a more scientific person, and as the latter, he or she, described the human body in its procreative functions too openly, and were being prosecuted for obscenity (in literature), there were some acute difficulties in mutual understanding. However, with a little goodwill, and England at that time was flowing with goodwill, everybody became friends again with everybody else and the procession moved on.

And then there were the poets, the sociologists, the mighty atheists (Bradlaugh amongst them). Finally, the Theosophists. Sometimes the Theosophist was a contraceptionist, the Fabian a vegetarian, the socialist a free-love theoretician and a nudist, and all of them here and there (and through Theosophy and Max Mueller) somehow dipped into Eastern wisdom. Schopenhauer believed wisdom always comes from the East, thus free love and nirvana, and why not, I ask of you?

* * *

Such was the world Mohan entered. Naive and passionate, he was convinced of what was logical, and what was conviction immediately took effect in action. If he believed in a non-carbohydrate based diet, he not only understood the science of it but cut out all elements such as potato and rice from his menu. If he believed in fruit and salads, from then on no cooked food would ever tempt him. The mind makes the palate. And since money was so scarce one should live on £1 a week. Bradlaugh did it. Why not Mohandas Gandhi?

Good health was a basis of moral living. And thus dietetics went with truth. And now (after meeting Henry Salt and having read his books) vegetarianism was no more a question of keeping to his vows, it had become a creed. It was based on scientific thinking. If apes from whom came man were herbivorous, how could man go back to his carnivorous instincts? It was a retrogression, it was a going back to some form of cannibalism? For, if, after all, animals had souls then must the eating of flesh be a form of cannibalism. What higher state of civilisation than that man kill not a living soul?

The Christians, however, objected to this. Christianity, of course, had to be purified, its essence was missed by the church. Harm no other Jesus said, and so harm no man. But if you harmed an animal would it be Christian then? Gandhi believed it was not so. Others did not agree with him.

So Gandhi read the Bible. The Old Testament was, he felt, somewhat a little too bloody, but the New Testament was indeed a great book. Then pray why not become a Christian? Yes, why not? Only before you leave what is yours, may it not be better to know what you have inherited? Then alone could you compare and be totally convinced, only after that could conversion be proper. One vegetarian gave Mohandas a copy of *The Light of Asia* and *The Song Celestial*.[2] For though a Hindu and an orthodox one, Gandhi knew only the Tulsidas *Ramayana*, and a few sacred verses from the texts. But he knew not the great *Song Celestial*, the *Gita*. He concluded after reading it that there was more reasoning in the *Bhagavad Gita* than in the Bible. The *Gita* was more scientific, he concluded, and the Bible more religious. The Theosophists here intervened and showed the wonder of Hinduism. Though all the religions of the world are great and ultimately one, Hinduism was the eldest and the richest. There were, said the Theosophists, Masters in Tibet who guide humanity; Madame Blavatsky had seen them through her supernatural vision, had talked to them, had been guided by these great beings. The esoteric Christians, on the other hand, were trying to revive the more mystical aspects of Christianity, the Gnostic traditions, in particular. The vegetarians gathered them all into a humanitarian fold; thus the vegetarian restaurant became the debating centre for every radical thought. For there you met not only cranks but great men—sometimes, even members of parliament. The atheists too joined the game and their vehemence was no meaner than that of the theists. Bernard Shaw crushed the greatness of God with his carrot. The jump from pure atheism to theism was a magnificent jump—Madame Blavatsky had shown the trick.

---

[2] Both by Edwin Arnold. One tells the story of the Buddha. The other is a poetical translation of the *Bhagavad Gita*.

And Shaw's former companion, Annie Besant, now able to see Brahmanic auras, sailed away pilgrimaging to India, India the home of true God.

Vegetarianism thus became the unique creed in revolutionary thinking. And even if you were not a vegetarian you could go to the Central Restaurant on Farrington Street and meet a curious spectrum of interesting people. During those days one often saw a young Indian in black frock coat and with passion-filled eyes, listening to others dialoguing but barely saying anything himself. When he did say something it sounded more passionate than true. Yet he seemed so gentle. His fervour was inspiring, and Henry Salt therefore had him elected to the executive committee of the Vegetarian Society. When people disagreed, as for example, Mr. Hills the capitalist financing the propagation of vegetarianism, and Dr. Alcott the propagandist of birth-control (he even wrote an 'obscene' book on it), Gandhi tried to see reason on both sides. He even made a short speech— rather he tried to make one, for he wrote down what he wanted to say but could not say it. He was too shy, and tongue-tied. His silence however was rich. It made him think before he spoke. He realised in the midst of all these confusing debates that every thought was valid in terms of itself, but that creative thought was only the gift of 'the inner voice'. No arguments could frame the conclusions the inner voice gave. Reason was only a step-stone to the inner being. Listen then to the inner being—it is God speaking. For God always speaks. Only we do not listen. God not only speaks, he acts for us, if only we allowed him to act. And here is a good example of his 'miracles'.

Sensuous, subtle and austere, every Indian is somewhat of a Karamazov. Look at India's temple sculpture and palace paintings—full-bosoms and thick-buttocks go with bearded ascetics sitting on top of mountains, or under ancient banyan trees merged in hot meditation, but when the gods, worried that their kingdom might be upset with so much yogic power, suddenly decide to send a Rambha or a Menaka (with full-bosoms and thick-buttocks again), there you are, the austerity melts into active semen, and this semen when drunk (because of the water in which the ascetic bathes or washes his under cloth) by deer or fish produces heroes. Thus India's epics, her Puranas, her traditions. On the other hand, even in historical times, for millennia, since Megasthenes at least, India has been famed for her truthful, her measured people (who can believe it today?)—and just people at that. May it not be that truth was so necessary because Indian passions rise so pointed high; is it not because Indians wrote long-winded sentences that *sutras,* aphorisms, became necessary? The Himalaya and Cape Comorin both are integers of the Indian scene, as are the Dharma Shastras and the *Kama Sutra,* both written by sages. And when an Indian slips into a puritan, an Anglo-Saxon world, many comic things can happen—the loser always is the Indian—sometimes edging on the bizarre. The myth is more real than reality.

For Mohandas was not naturally moral. Who is? His vows had tied him into noble austerity, as his meagre finances had made him economical. Passion in him was uppermost, and passion applied to truth became satyagraha, later. Kasturba was a lovely woman by now, and certainly the play of love must have been sumptuous, inexhaustible. And when you live among families where women rarely talk to men, or when they do so, it's in the courtyard, on the veranda, in between rooms, the servants going about and the old women grinding corn, or sieving stones out of granary rice, there's usually no place for subtle fascinations of man and woman to play on each other.

And even if it ever does happen, you slip out of it into larger family confusions. Virtue is not merely moral, it's practical. And thus the strength and continuity of the joint family. But here in England where men and women talk together as if there were no differences between one and the other, and they play cards together, go to the theatre together, and are, sometimes, even left in the same room by elders for obvious possibilities, the Indian unaccustomed to these restrained subtleties, jumps on his female companion, or runs away from her—there are no intermediary stages. The puritanical disciplines that permit men and women's bodies to touch (as in ballroom dancing) and have no serious moral or physical consequence is an experience the Indian just does not comprehend.

Mohandas Gandhi was an honest man. He knew what was what, and hence the drama.

One day in Portsmouth—for it must begin in Portsmouth, after all—where he'd gone for a vegetarian conference, he was staying in a lodging house. Lodging houses at seaports are often run by knowledgeable round women who know men as their men know the sea. Returning after some strenuous discussion on dietetics, Mohandas came home, and was requested to play cards with others. He needed to relax after his exams and the strains of the conference afterwards. He was as good or bad at bridge as anyone else. The atmosphere was fall of gaiety, indeed it was all such fun! But suddenly something was happening. The landlady's gestures, her smiles, her words, became so beguiling. The Indian companion who knew more about such things than Mohandas, warned his friend, 'What's happening to you?' Indeed, what was happening to Mohan?

And the vow to his mother, and her austere tear-filled face. He ran for his virtue. 'To my room I went,' he wrote later,

'quaking, trembling and with beating heart, like a quarry escaped
from its pursuer.' This was the first time passion for another
woman had ever taken hold of him. He would now flee from
Portsmouth but he had a paper to read: 'The Foods of India'.
After Salt's apotheosis on the exaltations of 'Return to Nature',
and Mrs. Harrison's 'Hints to Housewives and Caterers',
Mohandas read his paper which led the assembly to laborious
discussions on the uses of oil for cooking, and sesame oil was
proved to be the most eminently suitable for all culinary needs.
And after this important debate, and feeling satisfied that he
had done something good and fresh for English vegetarianism,
he fled to Ventnor and to the Shelton's Vegetarian Hotel. The
Portsmouth experience had led him to the door of God.

'I did not know then the essence of religion or of God, and
how He works in us. Only vaguely I understood that God
had saved me on that occasion. On all occasions of trial he
has saved me. I know that the phrase 'God saved me' has a
deeper meaning for me today, and still I feel that I have not
grasped its entire meaning . . . but in all my trials . . . I can say
God has saved me. I have not the slightest doubt that prayer
is an unfailing means of cleansing the heart of passions. But
it must be combined with the utmost humility.'

Nirbala ke bala Rama: The strength of the strengthless is
He, Rama.

However, the end of his stay in England was approaching.
He had to bid goodbye to friends and fellow members of
vegetarian societies. For someone as sensitive and warm-hearted
as Mohan, this was a painful period. But he had to go back,
he would, to his mother, and to his wife, 'my sister, my bride'.

They were awaiting him with anxiety and hope. He had to go back, the light of the household.

Mohandas gave a well-planned vegetarian party to his friends before he left. It was at the Holborn, a very fashionable restaurant at that time. There was even some music. And, of course, there had to be speeches. Mohandas had prepared his speech but he was nervous.

When he rose up to deliver it, he stood in bent solemnity. But forgot all things. 'I thank you, gentlemen, for having responded to my invitation,' he said abruptly and sat himself down.

He had by now finished his terms and was called to the Bar. Two days later (12 June 1891), and more than two years after his arrival there, he left England for home. Many things he did which he had not liked, and some things he had done which were useful and good. But above all he was on the edge of finding God. This trip to London had become a pilgrimage.

3

South African Genesis

Of sorrow is the edge of life—whether in departure or in arrival. Or in birth or death. The cycle of existence goes on from life to life, from epoch to epoch, and every departure is premonition of an awkward arrival—the image never fits the reality. Besides, there's fear not only in every departure but in every arrival. What might happen when the now has become the gone past? The ingredients of the past—your karma—make you face a new world of other, and more concrete, images. Husband and wife, or mother and son, or the cab driver's insistence on better payment, or the servants' hurried help to bring down your luggage—or the midwife's announcement it's a boy, but what a boy, yet it's not what you imagined him to be—and thus the circle of awkwardness and sorrow. The brother himself might come to welcome you—the ship is so full and involved in loud metallic activities of the arrivals, goods and men, and the gangway the logic of inward coming event. People suddenly come up now, and garlands smother new arrivals, people embrace each other, cry over each other, mother and son, wife and husband—yet it is all so different. Time deceives. And the face as well.

'Well, how is Mother?'

'Well, so to say, she's all right.'

It's an awkward statement. Karsandas, Mohan's brother, was not given to much ambiguity. They walk down and out and drive along again through Bombay.

'And how's everybody?'

'Everybody is as well as they could be.' And after a moment he said, 'And the baby and the wife are well, too. You will find them much changed.'

After London Bombay looks so provincial, so parasitical. The Indian too seems so thin, so drab. The British look the master race that can rule a country with high elegance, with shrewd competence. Their offices even here look shining, and clean, the peons in splendid uniform, and the British flag flies on the masts with delectable self-assurance. The Britisher is so certain of himself—he's at home everywhere. But the Indian, he seems so lost, even in his own land, among his own people.

'So all is well at home.'

'No, Mohania, not quite.'

'What may you mean by that?'

'Well, mother has passed away. She has passed away.'

Somehow one knew about it all the time. The tragedy of an event is not in cognition but in recognition. You know a thing is true, but you also feel it's not quite so true. So when it's true the real faces the real, and there are not even tears in your eyes. You had wept before on some unknown night, and of other and more cognate things. But this was it. You had lost your mother.

'We did not want to disturb your studies. What was ours was gone. That is all.'

'And I was not there.' But he'd kept his vows. It's as if his mother was present in every deed and so had protected him in Portsmouth, in London.

For mother's love is infinite. Because mother is, man can live the world.

'Rama, Rama,' said Mohan and took his funerary bath.

* * *

England had not made him forget his Hindu instincts. One is born where he is born, for that's the pathway to his God. One's actions should be his dharma. Thus the world is redeemed. Sorrow then merging into the Law becomes peace itself. And peace centred is nirvana.

For, truth, that's the problem. Whether to accept the ego as entity and accept the manyness (*anekatwa*) of the one or the manyness of the many, whether there's a Principle that looks after us—and so of life and death—or be there nothing but the One, or rather the Not-Two, wherein once established, one has no equals (for to say equal is to state another), so, when there are no two entities how refer to another when there is no other—such the intricacy of human existence, and he who's answered it truly and surely, he the human that knows there's no problem. And if there be no problem, then you're free. If freedom is all that I desire, why feeling free—for example as Mohandas Karamchand Gandhi—am I not free? Yet there's the cycle of life and death, and Lord how shall one accept that! The death of the mother is not merely the death of mother—it's the assurance that nothing remains, that death is, and if death is death, if nothing remains, why live at all? Why suffer? What's vegetarianism or esoteric Christianity, or, for that matter, what has Hinduism to do with it? Lord, be there no way out? Once again, when I say Lord, what do I mean by it? A man? No. A superman, perhaps. But since superman is not all men, there's an illogic about the statement. If God exists, and he does exist, then the oneness and the manyness must be dissolved in him. If so, who is there to know it? If one does not know this dissolution there is only the moral world: I am, so the world is. I am but I see the many; am I the many? Since the world is, then I must be honest, good, faithful to my wife, clean in my business, etc., etc. But, again, since the many are so many manies, seen by so many manies as many, and so on. Thus no one of the 'manies' is one, and everyone is a many seen by other 'manies'. So what? What then the answer? From wherever you start there's no solution. Logic stops returning to its own beginning. I stop where I am. And yet I know there's a way out. How to find it? This wheel of fire, where's the chink in it that I, like a flea or an atom, can escape around and out?

The Guru, he who stands outside the fire, and since outside the fire all is It, the nameless pure Principle, that in and by its reality makes even the fire whirl, for the fire is the whirl, and the whirl the fire, and the fire and the whirl but it—the Guru then is It, the Truth, he, neither man nor superman. What is in and through every thing is the Truth affirming there is no other Thing, hence just Isness Is, and so no thing. And as I see Isness and know Isness, I am none other than the Isness. So I am It. The boat awaits you then to take you to the other shore, the 'I'. The Guru in his infinite love—the 'I' that knows none other, awaits you. Will you jump to it, that's the real problem. Do you see it? Jump, and . . . Truth will take you where it will.

* * *

Kevalram Jugjivanram Jhaveri were a firm of Bombay jewellers. A partner of this firm was an elder brother of Dr. Mehta with whom

Mohandas and his brother were now staying. And Rajachandra (a brother-in-law of Dr. Mehta's brother) worked in the firm, a specialist in precious stones, he was also a poet, hence called Kavi by everyone around him. A man of high, very high spiritual attainments, Rajachandra was famous for his hearing-a-hundred-things-at-the-same-time, the power of the *shatadhvani*, someone could talk to him in German, Latin or French, and another make a statement of geometry, a third one speak of politics in English, and a fourth one recite poetry, say in Hindi, and each of these would be repeated by the *shatadhvani* whensoever you asked him. This is a part of Indian tradition, as you know, and though it implies no great spiritual worth, it does signify an unusual power of concentration, which is, in some ways, a beginning of spiritual power. For the spirit be power and understanding, which leads one beyond the opposites to the shore from which one never returns. Rajachandra was austere, humble and efficient. He ate sparsely. He slept little. He was shrewd in his business yet so honest that a lie in another would be an excruciating hurt to his very self. He found no reason why business and the life of the spirit would not go together; while evaluating a precious stone or discussing the price of gold with another—he would note down a few statements of philosophical or of spiritual significance. Or he would write a poem. Then he would go back to his business. Indeed, so scrupulous was his word, and so weighed his speech he is supposed never to have said one word more than was imperative. Such was the man who came nearest to being a Guru to Mohandas Gandhi, and certainly the most potent factor in young Mohandas's development. For by now Gandhi knew what he did not want. His London life had taught him that. He could not yet know what he wanted. And since what he did not want were so many, Rajachandra's moral help became a deep necessity.

Mohandas met Rajachandra dramatically on the night he heard of his mother's death. This saintly man's philosophical and healing presence gave to the young man the tender care an orphan needs. The sudden discovery of spiritual direction thus seemed the pathway to the discovery of his mother. For it's Mother who really helps in the discovery of Truth: *Mata mé Parvati Devi.*

Rajachandra was a Jaina by birth and a consummate yogi. He felt that one could pluck out evil from oneself as one could, if one wishes, hairs from one's body—hair by hair. The body thus becomes pure and straight in the face of space, of time, of truth, will attain altitudes of shining immortality. Mohandas had just discovered truth. To him nothing mattered except what was experimented on—after all, he'd emerged from a Fabian world (vegetarianism was a form of Fabianism too) and only the proven was the true. Rajachandra had one defect that went against Mohandas's metaphysics. If Rajachandra were right he could never be ill. For illness came of bad diet, it's a sort of bad manners, and bad manners had no place in an ethic of perfection. How then could you be a sage? A wise man, yes, a sage no. Hence an elder Rajachandra would be to Mohandas but not a Guru. Rajachandra believed in caste-rules, and all such orthodoxies. It was a tragedy not only for Mohandas, it was to be for India. In the modern times not to eat with another because he's not of your caste, is, so to speak, a sort of sin. And, again, Rajachandra was not a monk, he was a jeweller. If you seek the truth (or God, if you will), you must pour your every fervour towards it. If you had two masters, your God and your shop (or gold or pearl), something was wrong with the system. Yet one could see Rajachandra was a great man. He spoke the truth with such conviction there was no doubt he could help

Mohandas. And whenever Mohandas was in need, he could always write and get an answer. The answer did not always satisfy but it was ever strong and earnest. And this made you think better, and finally act with greater wisdom. Mohandas ultimately had to find his own solution to his own problems— therefore the dilemma and the tragedy. For to feel many and to think one is whole is to live in contradictions. The pursuit is all that matters—the means more important than the end—this is the first axiom of all freedom.

It's with such thoughts he went back to Rajkot. Meanwhile because of his mother's express wishes, he had been to Nasik on pilgrimage and on the banks of the Godavari, the proper Brahmins purified him from his impurities of having gone beyond the seas and thus having satisfied the wishes of the elders he returned to Rajkot, to enrol himself as barrister. In fact, so great were the hopes of Karsandas, the elder brother, that the family house was whitewashed and refurnished, chairs and tables were added on for the London-returned man to enjoy himself in a 'civilised' way, and indeed Mohandas himself was convinced his newly acquired habits were the basis of civilised existence. Not only forks and spoons were essential ingredients of gentlemanly living, but so were oatmeal and cocoa—a late London discovery. Further, to be the proper wife for a barrister, Kasturba was to study Gujarati and English, sit at table and behave like a lady. Mohandas was happy to rediscover his son, Harilal, now four years old, and if he could not turn everybody into a gentleman, he would at least make his son into one. The English way of life was, after all, the only true way of living; London, a new Ujjain.

The confusions of the day—the servant's salaams, the elders' blessings and silences, the women's whispers (behind semi-closed doors, sari-edges drawn over half-covered faces), the cows' lowings, the horses' neighs (for horses do recognise their masters are back)—the palace chamberlain's son's visit, the young uncles, the cousins, the neighbours' enquiries, laughters, admonitions (Oh, be you careful, the evenings, for witch-eyes cast spells at dusk, and jealousy and passion roam the streets—beware!) and the look of the young (Oh, one day I, also, will go to England and return and be barrister and be received with Brahmins at Nasik and pipe-music at home, coconuts breaking at my feet) all this is exciting, confusing, but, finally, when the day is exhausted and night comes there's the secrecy of one's room, and Kasturba, so rich, so natural, so whole. And just a look, and one knew forthwith the surging passions had not waned. If anything, the house had no mother-in-law and the love-play would be more free in accomplishment. The other women may go about their business, washing the kitchen or drawing well-water for early morning baths—but here was a new type of husband come, the London-returned barrister equal to any prince or prime minister, and so well dressed. He looks true and beautiful. Seek him and worship him and be taken and discovered. The barrister being London-returned is above all rules, and so night or day will make no difference, if you understand. The fact was, as anybody could see, the husband had come back to his wife, whole and holy. Let the world stand on their terraces and see it, see it firm and clear as a pillar. And Kasturba's chastity having matured her needs, she the willing rediscoverer of this more manly world. For Mohan's manliness was his fortune, his pride.

* * *

Whatever your academic acquirements, to be a lawyer in a small town however brought you no great success. True, Kewalram (son of Joshi, the same who had persuaded the family to send Mohan to England) was a lawyer himself at Rajkot but when you have a London degree you need a superior clientele. Everybody was in debt, including the Maharaja himself, and so not much money was forthcoming to pay for the services of a barrister-at-law. One could, of course, write petitions to the benign government for better emoluments or for the return of lands confiscated by an adventurous nobleman—or for stolen jewels or for more money to be given to some young prince whose property was being looked after by the court-of-wards, but an important legal consultation was out of the question in Rajkot. There was only one escape and the elders all agreed to this. Go to Bombay, for who had not heard of the legal exploits of Sir Phirozeshah Mehta and of Badruddin Tyabji? And in the emergent Indian world they were already important names and prosperous barristers. Phirozeshah Mehta was called the Lion of Bombay. So Mohandas now went to Bombay. He took an apartment, engaged a brahmin cook, and he seemed to have spent more time on teaching the brahmin to prepare European style vegetarian dishes than in the practice of Indian law. Mohandas Gandhi's natural honesty forbade the use of touts. So day after day he would go to the High Court, listen to the intricate Indian cases in law (his knowledge of Indian Law was, in any case, sparse), and yawn and go to sleep. He tells us after some time he realised going to sleep at the Bombay High Court was a sign of distinction. All the better lawyers had this habit. It gave you rest before your case was heard; it also indicated your superior confidence in yourself.

One day, however, a client sought his services. It was in connection with a minor case before the Small Causes Court. Mohandas appeared before the magistrate and he could never bring himself to utter a word. His shyness took the best of him. He apologised to the court, then to his client, and now decided he would never never make a barrister. So he applied for a post of high-school teacher. He was discarded for not having a degree. 'I have taken Latin for my Matriculation in London,' he protested. But the school wanted a graduate. The laws said so. Thus he could not, having spent so much money in London, even be a school-teacher. After six months of an existence unrewarding and hopeless, he decided (on the advice of his elders once again) to go back to Rajkot. After all, his brother might find something for him to do. His brother and another friend were partners in a legal firm. He might still draw up petitions for important clients. This time however he had greater success. He was able to earn more money and was not altogether unhappy. Yet, was this all?

The British at that time had already consolidated their power. Someone with a degree from England must surely get a ministership. But who would give it? The Gandhis had by now lost their influence. The Princes, whether of Porbandar or of Rajkot had become weak, and the British had their own administrators. Mohandas was too highly qualified to be a semi-important administrator—remember his father was once a Prime Minister—but not being an Englishman, he could never be a high official. Further, a small but very significant experience confirmed that he could never, would never, collaborate with the British.

A Mr. E.C.K. Ollivant (later Sir Charles) was then Agent to the Kathiawar States. Mohandas's eldest brother, Lakshmidas, was an advisor to the Rana of Porbandar. The Rana, like innumerable other princes, was involved in some hide and seek game with the British. The state jewels, he claimed, were his personal property. He illegally removed these from the treasury to the palace. Lakshmidas was supposed to be in league with the Prince in this adventure. Mr. Ollivant was enraged by such dishonesty and was determined to impose good behaviour on this unprincipled ruler.

Mohandas had met this British administrator in England briefly. Mr. Ollivant was, in his own home country, indeed very friendly to the young Indian. But that was just the tragedy of the British administrator—a gentleman in England, he would be a Sahib in India. A Sahib too is a gentleman, of course, but he's the Indian version of an Englishman. Superior as a race, courageous, skilful and educated (often at Oxford or Cambridge), the British civil servant believed he was a class by himself—a gentlemen's gentleman, as it were, and as such superior to all, Englishmen and Indians. Convinced the Indian was often a liar, and usually a complicated fellow (especially in Kathiawar), the Englishman had to make quick and irrevocable decisions. Generally he did this for the good of the administration, and often it was for the good of the country. It had also, by deeper implication, to be good for Great Britain. What is good for the I.C.S.[1], the unformulated argument would run, is good for India and England at the same time. Thus an Indian liar (or dishonest man and 'getting away' with his lies) was a blot against the British Empire. The Princes of India on the whole were a set of unscrupulous adventurers (the civil servant believed), who had no interest either in their subjects or in the British Empire, but being useful to the British Empire (by paying tributes or by supplying armed forces in times of Britain's needs) they were, so to say, useful to India, and finally not so bad to their subjects, etc. But when one steals a crown jewel and wants to dispose it

---

[1]   The Indian Civil Service—the famous 'Guardians'.

off (perhaps to pay a debt or reward a concubine), it smells bad.
And Lakshmidas Gandhi, who's supposed to be involved in all
this, was a rascal. In fact, the whole lot are bad fellows. To hell
with the yahoos!

But the Indians argued it another way. What is good for the
British is good for India, for the Britisher is honest and able, and
so he loves our country! He builds bridges and roads, he brings
in the railway to unheard-of places (like Rajkot, for example),
imposes a just tax on the cultivator, and, if unjust, would
sometimes repeal it. Which Maharaja today would ever dream
of being so honest? The Englishman too believes he comes of a
superior race. Perhaps he is of a superior race. If they be of such
moral superiority, why then do they sometimes miscarry justice,
believe in what no Indian would believe, and generally act as
if they had no human understanding? If superior, they should
understand the Indians. Superiority comes from wisdom. If they
do not understand the Indian, they would not possibly be so
able, or so superior. Such the basis of tragedy.

Let Mohandas himself tell the story.

I could not refuse him (my brother) so I went to the officer
much against my wish . . . I opened my case. The Sahib was
impatient.

Your brother is an intriguer. I want to hear nothing
from you . . .

But selfishness is blind. The Sahib got up and said, You
must go now!

But please hear me out, said I. That made him more
angry. He called his peon and ordered him to show me the
door. I was still hesitating when the peon came in, placed his
hands on my shoulders and put me out of the room.

The Sahib went away as also the peon, and I departed fretting and fuming.[2]

Sir Phirozeshah Mehta happened then to be in Rajkot for a case. A friend of Mohandas Gandhi told him the story and asked advice.

'Tell Gandhi,' he said, did Sir Phiroze, 'such things are the common experiences of many barristers. He is still fresh from England and hot-blooded. He does not know British officers . . . He will gain nothing by proceeding against the Sahib, and on the contrary he will very likely ruin himself.'

'This shock changed the course of my life.'[3]

Just at this moment of deepest despair, the hand of God showed itself. There was a firm at Porbandar which had important connections with South Africa (Porbandar had ancient contacts with Arabia, and for over a hundred years or so, with Africa). Dada Abdulla and Co. was a rich firm in Durban in litigation with another rich Indian firm in the Transvaal. They wanted legal help, especially from an Indian. Would the son of Karamchand Gandhi, just returned from London, go to Durban and help in the progress of the case? In fact, Mohandas Gandhi would not have to plead before the courts—he had just to give legal help with the documents, translate the letters from the Indian languages, etc. It was really a clerical job. It was not even well paid—a return boat-fare, and a fee of £105 was all that was promised.

'This was hardly going there as a barrister,' wrote Gandhiji. 'But I wanted somehow to leave India. There was also the

---

[2] A.
[3] A., p. 124–126.

tempting opportunity of seeing a new country, and of having a new experience. Also I could send £105 to my brother and help in the expenses of the household. I closed with the offer without any haggling and got ready to go to South Africa.'[4]

* * *

The Republic of South Africa is, among the territories of the world, both geologically and racially, one of the most extravagantly endowed. The Zulus and the Boers, the Hottentots, the British and the Malays, the Coloured, the Indians, each a nation by themselves, with their customs, prejudices, and gods, had time and space to cut out their own bit of land, and if threatened in their liberties or customs, took to the trails like the Zulus did or the Boers, and night after night of going up the steep pathways and coming down mountainlands to the rich valleys, they started other nations, other empires, and thus each part of South Africa has a cragged and noble story to tell.

The hasty judgement of politicians often goes against history. To the Aryan invaders, the dasyus of India, dark and flat-nosed, were not a civilised people. The conqueror conquering, he automatically became superior—or so he thought. So, too, with the Dutch, the British. And just as today historians are beginning to uncover (another and more important fact) that it's perhaps the Dravidian that's the most civilised man of the Indian continent, maybe, history which has proved the first man among men to be an African, may yet prove through archaeology that other and more splendid civilisations have arisen in this vast and rich continent, with cities, temples, laws and noble,

---

[4]   A., p. 129.

indecipherable texts; that the Zulu, the Bantu, and the Amharic peoples have perhaps said and done impressive things that historians have to catch up with, but not so history. Again there is in the geographical parallelism between the peninsula of Asia, which is India, and that peninsula of Africa, which is South Africa, something perhaps historically akin. Indeed, India's Puranas—of unknown dates—seem to have known of this extraordinarily rich continent, high with the Moon Mountains, and the blue Nile—and maybe they even knew of the mysterious Mlanje heights and of the golden Nyasa. Indian divinities, too, from the Deccan and the Chera lands, did they not know of the great Unkulkulu and the Zimbabwe, of their hero gods and the lion-incarnates? Again the riches of India (which remember made for the very discovery of the Cape of Good Hope, and of the continent that Columbus landed on)—the same mineral wealth, gold and diamond (one should not forget, diamond was first mentioned, used, and sold by the Indians)—these are to be found in South Africa, have made South Africa. Then too are common the variety of birds, beasts and shrubbery. The descriptions that the Roman historians have left of India (and the Greeks as well) seem so much akin to the splendours of the elephant, the zebra and the giraffe, the orangutan and the hippopotamus, the lion, the great size of birds—one should think one was talking of Africa, for all wonder was 'Ethiopic'.

Into this splendrous land came Mohandas Gandhi (leaving his wife and son behind), then just twenty-four years of age, carrying with him the multiple riches of India, recognised and unrecognised, with a thousand little understandings from the British—not just the long, dark frock-coat, his impeccable shoes and tie, yet also his British way of courtesy and independence. No sooner Mohandas Gandhi landed in South Africa than he discovered himself not only an Indian, but a subject of the British Empire. This was at once his pride and his tragedy. For South Africa was not British. It was British and Boerland and Zululand. Yet, looking back, one realised India was magnificently British. A British administrator may misbehave, and the might and complexity of the young British Raj could still drive Mohandas Gandhi out of India to seek employment elsewhere. Yet, Mohandas knew the British were otherwise. They had sound laws, a shy relationship with one another, dependable yet distant; on the whole they tried to be gentlemen. And Gandhi would be a gentleman in South Africa, and thus be true to what was noble and contemporary. Wherever anybody behaves a gentleman, automatically that becomes a civilised land—the land of the Aryas, the *Aryavarta*.[5] For an Indian all the world is *Aryavarta* and so the Englishman some sort of an Indian. Thus an Indian out of India becomes, as it were, an Englishman, the universal man.

When Dada Abdulla Seth, the great merchant from Durban welcomed Mohandas Gandhi at the docks, little did he realise the great event of history this meeting would unfold—not only to Africa and to India, but to the whole political structure of the world. For to behave like a gentleman in a British land but with fierce Boer traditions was to make one a slave or a gentleman. And with Krishna (of the *Gita*) behind one, one becomes not merely a gentleman but a gentleman of God, a templar, a holy warrior, an *Aryaputra*. The Dharma-performer of the *Gita* then is just one step removed from the office of being a gentleman—hence satyagraha, Smuts and the freedom of India, the decolonisation of the whole world. Thus the drama of the

---

[5]   The name of India, meaning Land of the Noble.

world was being enacted in the territories of South Africa, just as the colonies were at last getting more or less settled into their own. The moment of their fulfilment started the beginnings of their disintegration as well. The world will be free because India is going to be free. A new Zionism was in the air—all people will have their own Jerusalem.

Dada Abdulla Seth was a man of great wealth, courtesy, and humility. Like many Indian merchants of his time, especially Muslim, he had little learning but a great heart. He had large houses, many servants and clerks, and was lavish with his hospitality. In fact, Barrister Gandhi was not really necessary in the case he had filed in Pretoria against Mohammed Seth (another Indian merchant) for the recovery of a sum of forty thousand pounds. There were good white lawyers looking after the whole matter, and the idea of having an Indian helper was purely in the heads of his colleagues of Porbandar. But since Barrister Gandhi is come, he be thrice welcome! Yet this new arrival was a different type of Indian to any that Dada Seth had ever encountered. Mohandas Gandhi spoke faultless Gujarati (after all, a son of a former Prime Minister of Porbandar, the grandson of the famous Ota Gandhi himself)—even so the young Gandhi was also very much a sahib. He not only dressed in impeccable British manner, he also ate with fork and spoon. The only difference, however, was that Barrister Gandhi never touched meat or fish. Nor for that matter did he touch spices. He ate plain, boiled vegetables and English porridge, sometimes even fruit and raw vegetables, but never anything very complicated. The only Indian thing about him was his turban. It made him look what he truly was, that is, a coolie Barrister. Now the word coolie, Dada Seth enunciated and explained, had a particular meaning in South Africa. A coolie was not an Arab or a Persian or a Chinaman, a coolie was always a Hindu. For the Indian merchant here, being rich and being Muslim, could claim Arabic descent. The Parsi, though having settled in India, could claim Persian descent. Yet the poor peasant from some obscure South Indian village, he with his deep Dravidic traditions and layer after layer of religious sensibilities—his people having died of famine or of poverty, had hired himself as a legal slave for five or ten years to his Boer or British masters—he could not be anything recognisable. He could not be called a slave (the British Empire would tolerate no slaves on their territories)—so he became a coolie. A coolie is one who is bound to a master for a fixed period within which period if he escapes he is brought back under police escort for work or prison, but once he'd finished his contract, he could, if he cared, reengage himself in plantation work, or go out into the world a free man, but ever a coolie; that is one who would do menial or small jobs. It sometimes saved you from humiliations if you changed your religion and became a Christian and sported an European hat. In the eyes of everybody that was higher than the lowest but you could never reach the highest. So why not remain a coolie? And the coolies produced other coolies who went to school, read books, and became clerks in offices, shops, or later in the railways—minor jobs that needed a little education and much adaptability—and so you never had a large coolie colony. They, the coolies, had their own shops and temples, their own 'locations', they were befriended by the so-called Arabs and the Persians, but never equal to them—yet you know it was not so terribly bad. Suffering, after all, is man's inheritance. What karma was it that made us come to this distant, forest-ridden Africa? We can still observe our festivals, marry our children according to Hindu rights, and when we go they will still give us a good funeral-fire, and feast.

Mohandas Gandhi was the first Hindu who came to Africa that was not a coolie. He was a British Indian gentleman. And this set more problems than politics or goodwill could resolve.

The first experience of such a problems was when Mohandas went as a visitor to the court at Durban. The magistrate had never seen such an educated Indian. For him, as to most Boers, the Indians were a semi-barbaric race. Gandhi was a barrister but an Indian barrister. He came with a frock-coat and tie to the court at Durban, but had a neat turban on his head. The magistrate said he, Mohandas Gandhi, could not be seated in the court of Durban with a turban on his head. Now, this could never happen in Great Britain. It cannot happen in India. It should never happen in the British Empire. Gandhi refused to remove his turban. So he walked out of the court. But the problem remained. He was a coolie barrister. What was he going to do in this God-forgotten country? Would he find God? Or rather would God find him?

The fact is we serve many gods. The gods of the Boer are different from the gods of the Bantu, as the British god is different from Sri Krishna or Sri Rama. The Boers were Dutch by extraction. They had once worshipped Odin, and the dark gods of Germanic forests. Civilisation and Christianity came late to them. Tacitus had said of them:

The Germans have no taste for peace; renown is easier won among perils, and you cannot maintain a large body of companions except by violence and war . . . It is always 'give me the war-horse' or 'give me that bloody and victorious spear'. As for meals with their plentiful, if homely, fare, they count simply as pay. Such open-handedness must have war and plunder to feed it. You will find it harder to persuade a

German to plough the land and to await its annual produce with patience than to challenge a foe and earn the prize of wounds. He thinks it spiritless and slack to gain by sweat what he can buy with blood.

But again the Zulu Cheka was a magnificent Tamberlane who destroyed townships, killed nations, and did not mind drinking man's blood. The Hindu with his several thousand years of civilisation (and what do, after all, several thousand years mean in biological history?), when he went to his first forests, his gods too, Mariamma and Badakamma, came into existence. They asked too for blood sacrifices. The Calvinistic edge of severity among the Boers was only the Odinic demand for blood-rights. It was still the mood of the Valkyries. The supplications of the coolie were no different from what his demonology demanded. The Englishman was arrogant and uninvolved, he already belonged to the nineteenth century, or so he thought. He did not face his back to the forest, he could always step into a British gun-boat, his god was his flag. The Zulu and the Boer fled to the forest and would create other empires. The Hindu was totally lost in their midst. And there were mountain tops on which, as ever, the gods fought. One such drama took place on the heights of Pietermaritzburg. All the gods howled at each other, it would seem, in a unique drama of mankind.

For Barrister Gandhi, an Indian gentleman, left Durban on a nice bright day, with respectful adieus from Dada Seth and many of his countrymen, for Pretoria. Now Pretoria in those days could only be reached from Durban first by a stretch of railway—some seventy-five miles—to the frontier town of Charlestown. From there you took a stage coach, crossed over to the Boer Republic of Transvaal and thus on, shifting and shuffling, to Johannesburg. And once in Johannesburg, you take a train again, and reach the Boer capital of Pretoria. A magnificent journey by itself, full of high grasses, steep and treacherous mountains and finally the wide rolling veld—with quiet, sparse, new agglomerations, in which citizens solved one another's problems with morality, probity and finality. The Boer Republic was courageous and clean, cruel and God-demanding. Kruger was the President of Transvaal, a rough and honest man who wanted to abide by his God, and be interfered with by no Englishman. The English never understood the Dutch God. Anyway, look at William of Orange! A new kingdom by the grace of God would now be established, and Kruger would be its hardy architect, its messiah and chief burgher. And, God willing, they would succeed.

High on the veld and surrounded by many green and rugged hills through which a cold wind blows, Pietermaritzburg, capital of Natal was founded long ago by the two Boers, Pieter and Maritz, who were fleeing from the persecution of the British. And once established, in its turn it became a British city like Cape Town, and capital of the crown colony. The Boers fled once again and across the Vaal to found with flag and Bible, their own republic, the Transvaal. They always revered their ancestors, the Voortrekkers.

The Boers brought out, as their fathers had done, their whitetilted wagons that could hold a family; they assembled their kine and their kindred; once more an exodus began, but an exodus now in thousands. Between 1836 and 1840, six thousand trekkers left the Cape for the unknown east and north. The very Trek of Treks was on—the Great Trek.

Perhaps the Boers were not less free under English rule than under the rule of the Dutch East India Company;

perhaps they had, but for the slave business, prospered. They had trekked, however, in the old days, before even the English came to the Cape, because each man wanted to do as he chose and not as others chose for him; because, in fact, those early Dutchmen had so learnt to hate any kind of government that, even on the Trek of Trek, they trekked away from one another.

They must have been a difficult people indeed to manage. Yet their pride in their achievements—the increasing pride of their descendants—is not unjustified.

They had prepared to face dangers, known and unknown, in the cause of independence, and they had greatly met them. They called themselves, they are called today, the Voortrekkers: those who went before.[6]

The difference between the Britisher and the Boer by now was just this, the Englishman, since all was England, he was unafraid and could afford to be courteous, if not always gentlemanly. For the Boer who was neither Dutch nor Huguenot but a mixture of all including the Hottentot, this was their home, their own land, where they could practise their own dogmas. The English would always go back to England. But where was the Boer to go? He would, like the Zulu or the Hottentot, go elsewhere in Africa—and this continent is so large—and build other kingdoms or republics and lead his own ordained way of life. Further, his own religion told him there were some whom God has chosen—and you would not bear all this suffering and not be chosen by God, for look at the ways God showed his Grace, now by appearing through a voice in the mountains, now

---

6   Sarah Gertrude Millin, *The People of South Africa*, p. 25.

through a healing presence, and now through a pure Burgher authority. God was on their side. So God was not on the other, on the black side. Hence the Zulu and the Hottentot were going to be the Boer's hewers of wood and bearers of water, to whom the Boer would be as father to the slave. There was nothing wrong in this scheme, for that is how God had ordained. The black man was somehow black, the white man was white, and between them there would be no other relationship than as between a man and his ox.

Now, if the fight was between the black and the white, between the Britisher and the Boer, the problem would be easily settled. Everyone knew the other's propositions and positions, and thus arrangements could perhaps be made by which each one would mind his own business, as it were, the Boer the overlord of them all. But the Indian created a new problem. He was neither black nor white, civilised to the barbarian, and barbarian to the Boer, and withal British, being a subject of the beloved Queen Victoria, and Victoria herself not so far, so to say, for she too was a German by birth (was not her mother German?), and Dutch and German were brothers after all. The very word Dutch was very revealing. Then how solve this complex problem?

Though the Boers, driven by the British, had gone to settle in Transvaal so as to have their own republic, they also had another republic, the one of the Orange Free State, on the other side of the Vaal. Even so, the Boers had much to say in the Crown Colony of Natal. Of course, the British ruled here but the Boer could still have his way. Also, the Boer having preceded the British had left behind him an inheritance of actions and reflexes that had stayed. The Englishman might be courteous, but he demanded the same pound of flesh. If found wrong, however, he would apologise—but not so the burgher. The burghers could never be wrong, for, after all, by now history had proved them a people of God, the chosen tribe. The republics therefore prospered.

* * *

On this cold winter evening—it was in the month of June (1893) and in the Southern hemisphere it can be as cold then as December in the North—the train drew up at Pietermaritzburg. Mohandas Gandhi was travelling in his frock coat and striped trousers, and Bengali turban—every inch as distinguished as any first class passenger should be. He also seemed kind and deferential and polite. Pietermaritzburg being the capital of the State, many people got out, and others got into the train. But from Pietermaritzburg the train was going towards Transvaal and thus it was already, as it were, a Boer train. Do you think material things, trains, coaches, or cars do not change with circumstances, just as men do? Yes, they do. And you have just to look at the very way the railway line that goes hurry scurry through bramble and high brush, and down and breathless through the sonorous valleys, by solemn lone waterfalls, and now along vast and round sizzling terrified spaces, the way the engine exhausts its smoke in wild curls or short sweeps or the wagons hold one another with fearful tightness—or so it would seem—and, of course, the guard too behaves differently. The guard was taking the train to the Boer country. He was the guardian of all laws, the railways' breath and speed, and magician of its destiny. So the guard too had to take his responsibilities. One was indeed entering totally different region of the human universe.

A white man—one never knew whether he was a Boer or an Englishman—entered the compartment where Mohandas was seated comfortably feeling the exquisite freshness of the mountain air, and noting the ways, the voices, of these westerners settled in the heart of the African wilds. They were different from the Europeans he had known, but yet not really so. One might as well be on any wide Scottish countryside. They seemed sturdy and somewhat fierce but they were civilised after all. The white passenger having looked at Mohandas Gandhi jumped out of the wagon in a hurry, and returned with the guard.

'You will have to go and sit in the van.'

'Why?' said Mohandas, with as much fear as sweetness in his voice. 'Why, I hold a first-class ticket.'

'For ought I care you might hold a ticket to heaven, but you must get out. This man wants to travel in the compartment.'

'I don't object to his travelling. There is room for him here, and for many others as well.'

'I have no time to waste.'

'I will not leave.'

Here the guard called a constable who, in turn, threw the luggage down and pushed Mohandas out of the compartment. The white man got in. All was right now. The laws were upheld. But who made the laws? And did such laws truly exist?

And in the whole jostling humanity that evening there was not one man or woman who could feel the agony of an anguished young Indian, son of a former Prime Minister of Porbandar, a barrister-at-law at the Grays Inn, London, the beloved child of his mother, who had come as legal adviser in this far off land—legal adviser to a merchant prince like Dada Abdulla—there was no one to listen to his cry. Would the gods hear? Would God hear?

Mohandas went into the waiting room hoping to find some solace in rest and sleep. But no sleep would come, and it was bitterly cold. He could, of course, go and fetch his luggage. It was left behind on the platform where it was thrown. There was an overcoat in the trunk. But fear and pride forced Mohandas not to venture out. Anyway, what could happen to him? Pneumonia? Was there a God? If so, why this world of humiliation, of injustice? Was not Mohandas at least as well educated as any of those white men, and certainly more than most? Was he not ever courteous to the Zulu or the Boer? Why then this plight of man—not only the young Indian barrister's plight but the suffering of all men, of man as such. There's a brotherhood of the sorrowful as there's a brotherhood of the joyous. For in the intensity of suffering as in the intensity of joy, we slip beyond ourselves somewhere, and feel the feel of every other. Or so it seems. The edge of sorrow and the beginnings of joy are one and opposite. The ambivalence of man is at the circumference. There is none at the centre. It is. Is is. Is.

The look of 'things' changes with subterranean changes in you. So the world is illusory. Where are you, then? What is you, I? And the 'I', is this what one calls God? Then what is an Indian? A Boer? The Zulu, the Englishman? What?

This was the most creative experience of his life, Gandhiji said almost half-a-century later. And he went out of it a new man.

After all, Harishchandra walked this truth wherever he wanted, in his palace or to his crematorium. And so did Dharmaraja. And Bhishma. There is no problem, then, except that there is no problem. This reconversion (or rebirth) indicated the wherewithal of the free. Not that man will be free. Man is free.

For in the history of civilisation each God or hero wanted his cauldron of blood. Each Odin or Chengiz needed his millions of dead. Unless man goes beyond God, he will never go beyond history. God—the European or the Asiatic—we make him as we grow.

So on that night at Pietermaritzburg at the train station—something important happened to history. There was a man—neither black nor white, yellow nor brown—there was a man who was just suffering under the aegis of no God he could name or even know. One has to be alone to find one's God. The British Empire was ending here at Pietermartizburg (for Natal was still mostly British) and the Boer Republic started on the other side of the frontier. You changed gods as you changed trains—and in between was the engine—changing station, you shivered in your fright and mountain cold. The day Lenin knew his beloved brother was hanged changed the face of history. On that June night at Pietermartizburg was Gandhism born, and the two face each other before civilisation. For one to whom History (or Marx) is God. For the other to whom Truth is God. They are not irrevocable positions, they only function at different levels. The historical man would create his paradise on earth. The truth-seeker will go beyond man and be sacrificed.

Mohandas now walked out to send telegrams to the wide awake world. The world indeed was so differently aspected now. Objects seemed to escape their dimensions and affirm a newer reality. Even the colour of earth and sun seemed different. One had changed perspectives, as if one were fresh and young and in a subtler universe. For the universe grows with one's growth and dissolves with the ego's dissolution. The inner and the outer pilgrimages thus are one.

Of the telegrams sent, one went to Dada Abdulla and the other to the Manager, Natal Government Railway. And

Mohandas went back to the waiting room and sat for an appropriate answer. It would come.

Indian merchants, as soon as they had heard from Dada Abdulla of the anguished traveller, went to his immediate rescue. But the tragedy was now no more a personal tragedy. It was as if the tragedy was a part of a law, a cosmic principle that had to be reckoned with. It was not that Sita, the wife of Sri Rama was prisoner of the ten-headed Ravana, the King of Lanka. It was the sheer incomprehensibility of this event. That Ravana, the great monster, once the worshipper of Shiva, who had shaken with his austerities the very trident-bearer, Lord of the Himalayas, Shiva Himself, such Ravana's fervour—that Ravana had to have ten heads and be the Sita-enticing demon, this was the tragedy. But when the understanding came, that Ravana's fervour translated into a quick demand for liberation, and meant he had to be born a monster and die at the hands of Sri Rama himself— then one wholly understood. This is the nexus of tragedy. Not that Sita is prisoner of Ravana—yes, of course, she is, but that Ravana's liberation came from Sita's imprisonment. If not what would Hanuman have been—he the monkey-messenger and fighter who saw Sita under the Ashoka tree and finally set fire to Ravana's capital. Everybody is a Hanuman—the monkey and will build the bridge to the island of Lanka, destroy the devout 'enemy,' and, freeing Sita, bring her back in an aerial chariot of flowers. Thus the law. (Evil is only a roundabout way of affirming good.) For the affirmation of evil as an indicator of good leads one beyond the good and the evil—and thus liberation. There is, in fact, no personal tragedy, as such, for any man. All sorrow is the ignorance of its implication of joy. The suffering of Pietermaritzburg was an indicator that man will be free. So that when the Indian merchants of Pietermaritzburg beheld

Mohandas Gandhi, it was to discover a young man sorrowful but with an inward radiance. Something had happened to the young man that nobody could name.

Once Mohandas went into the city of Pietermaritzburg all the well-to-do Indians gathered around him. What happened to you, brother? Oh? Only this—well, that happens to us every day. What else can one do? We are ignorant people. We come here to make money. We make money, and gobble down the insults. After some time it seems as simple as a boil on the face. It comes and goes. Allah is great.

This was too simple an argument. Something must be done about it all. It must change. It will change. Let us change it, shall we?

The Manager of the Natal Government Railways, Durban, had wired back; a berth was reserved for Mohandas Gandhi up to Charlestown for that very evening. With trepidation but with a new burning faith in himself, Mohandas boarded the train and reached Charlestown the next morning without drama. At Charlestown, however, they had to take a coach. The coach could seat only five at a time. What will one do then with this coolie, however well he might be dressed, and though he may bear a first-class ticket?

'You missed your reservation yesterday. There is no seat,' so spoke the agent.

'But I have a seat. Look at this ticket.'

'Yes, you have a ticket, I see. But you cannot take this coach.'

'I have this ticket. I have a right to the seat.' Mohandas was affirmative but not vehement.

'Well, we'll see. You can sit on the box next to the Hottentot servant.'

'Give me a seat is all I ask.'

Mohandas was now accommodated on the box seat next to the coachman. The 'leader' of the coach, a big and grumbly man sat inside, where Mohandas should have. Fear possessed Mohandas Gandhi—to be in this far-off countryside amidst strange and rather cruel looking people, and to have no one to come to his rescue. Such are the ways of God. Let us pray and hope. Hé Ram, Hé Ram, he started saying to himself.

In the afternoon, however, a crucial situation arose. The burly Boer leader needed to have a few puffs—he wanted to smoke. It could not be done inside the coach. Therefore he had to go up to his own official seat. What will one do with this coolie barrister then?

The 'leader' laid a cloth at his own feet.

'Sit here. Now we can go.'

'No, I will not sit there. I have a right to a seat inside.' But he did not want to fight.

'Here is one for you,' shouted the 'leader' and boxed Mohandas so fiercely Mohandas almost fell on the ground. He held on however to a railing of the carriage, while the Boer went on hitting and kicking him.

'I clung to the brass rails,' 'Gandhiji wrote later, 'of the coachbox . . . determined to keep my hold even at the risk of breaking my wrist bones.' The white passengers, at first indifferent, now separated them, and finally with Gandhi in his legitimate seat and the Boer next to the Hottentot, the coach finally reached Standerton. The Boer leader never seemed to stop swearing and threatening what he would do at the end of the journey. 'My heart was beating fast within my breast, and I was wondering whether I would ever reach my destination alive.' Nothing happened, however. Other Indians met Mohandas at the end of this journey, and he was taken away to their homes, and once again Mohandas heard all the woes of the community. 'Oh, only this! Of course we are not educated. But this happens to us every day.'

From Standerton he reached the Vaal River, the boundary between Natal and the Transvaal, without any further incident. That night he reached Johannesburg by another coach. He spent the night with some friendly Indians. Mohandas Gandhi read through the railway regulations. There was no mention anywhere that a coolie could not travel first class.

From Johannesburg to Pretoria is only thirty-seven miles. The railway journey was a quick one. How about getting the proper ticket? 'I am an Indian Barrister,' wrote Mohandas to the station master. 'I always travel First Class. I hope you have a ticket for me. Since there is no time for reply, I shall present myself to you before the train starts. Yours truly, etc.' So his host and a few others went to the station. The impeccably dressed Indian barrister asked for a first-class ticket. The station master, a Dutchman, and not a Boer, gave it to him, and said, 'Good luck to you', and winked and gave a friendly smile. Now Mohandas entered the carriage and sat himself down. There was only one other passenger—a white one—but there was no drama. The drama seemed over.

In the middle of the journey, however, the guard came to examine the tickets. Seeing a coolie in the first class compartment, he became red with anger. 'Get out and sit in the van!'

'No I will not. I have a first class ticket.'

'You might have any ticket you like, but a coolie must travel in the van!'

'I have studied all the rules of the railways. Nowhere do they mention it.'

'I won't argue with you. If you won't listen I will have you pushed out!'

'No,' protested the white passenger. 'He is quite harmless. Why do you want to do that to him? He has a first class ticket. He will do no harm to me.' The passenger was an Englishman.

'In that case, please yourself!' shouted the guard, banging the door behind him. What can one do with such behaviour, and he a white man? Strange indeed are the ways of us humans! But it was now a peaceful journey through the flat veld, quiet, open and ingrown—the railway running through it all with civilised reliability, then suddenly it turned down a bend and rushed whistling down to Pretoria, the proud new capital of the Boers.

* * *

Pretoria in the nineties of the nineteenth century was just a sprawling little town, a frontiersmen's capital with low wooden houses, wide streets spreading between them, and with sidewalks and long avenues. A broad, squat house with a round roof on it, and being nothing different from any other except two artificial lions at the veranda steps, and the sentry at the door, was the home of President Paul Kruger. Affable, large and bearded, he was a kind father, Oom Paul, to all—a pioneer who had faced the wilds and the Hottentots and the vile trickery of the Englishman to establish here a government worthy of his Christian forebears. A new Jerusalem this would be after all these treks—the Englishman put in his place, the Hottentot and the Zulu in theirs, and the Coloureds after all were never a people, being neither black nor white they belonged to none. The Indian merchant was a busy nobody who made his pile and slept on it. Who could or should worry about them? Among God's ordinances, the Hindu had no place. He existed just enough to show he does not exist.

Into this isolated universe arrived Mohandas Gandhi, the coolie barrister—he arrived to give legal help in a small court case between two Indians. Among two non-legal entities a fight is no matter. The coolie barrister would settle into his dirt and his murky ways, and persuade himself into the rightness, nay, the righteousness of whatever the white man's law would impose. There was already, as we have seen, a white man's lawyer engaged for the case by Dada Abdulla. Mohandas Gandhi was just to look into the accounts, read the correspondence in the devil's own tongue, Gujarati, and advise the lawyer accordingly.

A.W. Baker, the attorney, was an excellent man. Belonging to the African General Mission, he was as intent on conversions as on moneymaking. Having no colour prejudice whatsoever he welcomed Mohandas Gandhi with warmth and hope—hope that a new convert, and a high-class Hindu at that, may be in the making. Baker found a room for the Indian barrister in a white woman's house—Gandhi was to pay thirty-five shillings a week. And between his ventures into accounts and the Gujarati correspondence, Mohandas had plenty of time to examine the new land, and its religion, Christianity.

'Why don't you become a Christian, Mr. Gandhi? There's salvation only through Jesus Christ.'

'So it might be,' answered back Mohandas Gandhi. 'After all, God has guided me here. I should not however think of embracing another religion before I fully understand my own.'

But he went to Baker's church. There everybody prayed that 'the new brother who has come amongst us . . . may the Lord Jesus who has saved us save him too.'

There were a few Quakers too among the assembly. They invited him to tea. Mr. Coates, a Quaker, and he became warm friends. They met often and discussed the religion of Jesus Christ passionately. Books were given for Mohandas to study incontrovertible documents to prove that Jesus was the only saviour. But the arguments were not really convincing. If compassion was Jesus' greatest gift, the Buddha with his love for all creation—and not only for mankind but for trees and animals— seemed to be a great prophet. If sacrifice was the greatest proof of Christian greatness, the sacrifices of the Hindus seemed so much more lofty. Until the other day the Hindu woman burnt herself on her husband's pyre. Yet Christianity, especially the Sermon on the Mount, had a very special fragrance of its own. It brought Mohandas Gandhi again and again to the church. And one day Mr. Coates, the Quaker, went straight into the problem.

'Those beads you have at your neck, Mr. Gandhi, do you believe in them?'

'Believe in them? As a matter of fact I have never thought of it to this day. My mother gave them to me with love and I wear them. That is all. The necklace has nothing to do with my religion.'

'If so it's only a superstition.'

'May be it's so, who knows?'

'How can you live with such a superstition? Come, let me break it for you.'

'No, thank you, Mr. Coates. As I told you, my mother gave it to me with love. Unless it breaks of its own accord, I will not throw it away. Thank you all the same for your deep concern for me. I appreciate your sincere feelings for me.'

Meanwhile, one day while Mohandas was passing by the President's House something unexpected happened to him. The sentry at the President's gate, seeing a dark man on the pavement, gave him a rollicking kick. The coolie barrister fell yards away— so unexpected was this act, and so frail the offender. Mr. Coates was passing by on his horse. In good Dutch he reprimanded the sentry and told him who the victim was. The sentry seemed surprised and shamefacedly apologised.

'Gandhi, if you will go to court, I shall be your witness.'

'Oh, why should I go to court? Poor man, he did not know anything better. I have already forgiven him. Besides, I have decided: for no personal reason shall I ever take any man to court.'

'A brave statement.'

'But a true one,' said Gandhiji and smiled.

Not only Mr. Baker and Mr. Coates but there were others very kind too to Mohandas. For example, F.E.T. Krause, a young lawyer that took Mohandas to his brother, A.E.J. Krause, who was the Attorney General of the Republic. With Coates and the Krauses about what ugly event could ever happen again? Even so it was in the very Krause household that the coolie barrister could not be served at the table. The coloured servants refused to serve a coolie. However, when Gandhi was explained to be a Native Chief all went well and the problem was solved once and for all.

Such the problems of a pioneer civilisation. The elder Krause gave Mohandas Gandhi a pass so that the coolie barrister could walk the sidewalks without being stopped or kicked by the police, ever again.

Meanwhile, however, the light of Christianity pursued Mohandas too. He read book after book of the Christian doctrine presenting different aspects of this great tradition. Much as he admired Jesus Christ, when it came to His being the

only incarnation of God, the logic in Gandhiji asserted itself:
How could God have only one son, one incarnation? Why this
partiality of history? Did not each epoch present a different
aspect of mankind, and just as the *Gita* said, did not God present
himself to mankind at each epoch in terms of itself? How could
a God, as seen by a certain people, at a certain time, be thus the
only God? Yet there was something so utterly beautiful about
Jesus, he, Gandhi, would not give it all up so easily. So he went
to study circles, to church, and to conventions. In the case of
one convention he had to travel with a special permit for he and
his companion to travel together, and again for he and his white
companion to stay in the same room in a special home. But once
in the convention everybody he found was praying for his soul:
May the young Hindu amidst us be saved. May Jesus show him
the Way.

What was indeed so unique about Christianity that other
religions did not possess and, sometimes, even in a more exalted
form? And, again, why are we here and what are we about, and
in the words of Sankara: *Koham Kutham?* Young Gandhi did
not know these words, but it was the same question, it came
from the same background. If there is a world, who made it?
And why am I here?

And what then of Islam? Here was perhaps the most
monotheistic of all religions, he felt, which not only preached
brotherhood but practised it—Arab or non-Arab, white or
black, it never thought in terms of a race, of a community.
There was but only one God of Gods, and Mohammed the
Prophet, the Elder as it were of humanity. If Christianity
preached love did not Islam also preach the same love? Did not
Dada Abdulla and his community show more warmth than any
Christian community towards its fellow-man—in fact, did not

the Muslim show more love than the Hindu? The Hindu, sunk
in his philosophical pride, seemed as narrow as any, and yet with
less love. Where was he to turn now?

* * *

By this time he had met every Indian in Pretoria. He had gone
personally to see them, one by one, and he often called meetings
to discuss social and political matters. Sometimes they met once
a week, and they all spoke of their woes.

'Do you think this will continue?'

'It only continues because we are indifferent to it.'

'We do not know how to read and write, Mohan Brother. If
you will help us we will follow you.'

It was a big responsibility. But he was not unwilling to bear it.

God, or whatever that force was which guided man, would
show him the path. First, every Indian has to live hygienically—
that is, his house and the surroundings must be kept clean. Look
at the way the Boer and the Englishman live. Do you suppose
any Boer or Englishman—however low he might be—will
tolerate the muck that we amass at our doors? And the careless
way we dress? To be clean is to respect oneself. Yes, I know the
story of how the Hindu, the Indian, bathes every day, etc., etc.
Then why not also wear clean clothes? Besides, clean garments
help you to think cleanly.

Secondly, all of you must learn the language of the rulers;
the English language. To speak Tamil or Gujarati is of no use in
a land where the English language prevails. How many among
you would like to learn it? he asked. Three offered to learn the
English language. Two Muslims and a Hindu. One, a barber,
another, a merchant, a third, a freed coolie. Gandhiji went day

after day to their houses to teach them English. Sometimes his pupils were busy with their trade. He would wait for them to finish their jobs. Why not, I ask you? Everybody at his job must be respected. If one man changed for the better in this universe, all men are participants in this hypostatis. No man is alone but is brother to another, in job and in worship.

Finally, and this is the most important factor, one must ever be truthful—truthful in business, truthful in human relationships, truthful to your God. For where truth is, there's neither colour nor religious difference. All men are equal before truth. And every Indian that does not live by truth is thereby betraying his religion (be he a Muslim, Hindu or Parsi or Christian) and his country. For every Indian in Africa represents the whole of India . . . represents our beloved country. Let us know our responsibilities. Let us beware of what we say, what we do.

Sobering words, but so simple, they went into the heart of his audiences. Nobody had so far spoken to them in this manner. In fact, he had never himself spoken so clearly nor understood his own responsibility. He spoke to them as he would speak to himself. There was no pride in his education, in his being the son of a prime minister, nor in his already acquired position among the whites. He spoke naturally as one of the Indians here for he could easily be one of them. There was something happening to the Indian community.

The ideas caught fire. The first issue taken up was the question of railway travel—could the Indian travel in all the classes or could he not? Mohandas Gandhi studied all the regulations. Nowhere was it specifically stated the first class was reserved for the whiteman. He therefore wrote to the directors of the railways. An assurance came that indeed as there was no such law regarding first and second class travel by Indians, any Indian who was 'properly dressed' could travel any class he liked. It was a first but a symptomatic victory. It gave zest and purpose to the Indian community. They were not going to be there just to fight for money—they were going to fight for their rights as well. From Pretoria the news travelled to Durban. There was strength and victory in the air. An Indian merchant, Tyeb Mohammed, was ejected from a second class compartment between Durban and Pietermaritzburg. He appealed to the courts for redress. The white man had threatened the Indian, he wrote, to 'knock the hell out' of 'the stinking coolie'. The witness, a railway official, denied having heard any such thing. But the magistrate differed. He condemned the Natal Government Railway authorities for such bad behaviour of one of their own officials. It was a decisive event. It broke the white magic circle. Indians could still be free.

'The verdict,' wrote the *Natal Mercury,* a white paper, 'may not be a popular one—but we cannot but admit that it is a fair verdict. Our merchants do business with the Arabs and mingle with them at public sales and there ought not to be any reasonable objection to travel with them provided they conform to the regulations. Very many of the lower classes who travel on the Home Railways are infinitely more objectionable from the mere point of cleanliness to the better class Indian merchants of Natal.' There was a touch of truth in this. Facts rubbed against facts, and the community was suddenly on the verge of discovery. The world could and would still be different.

* * *

Food is Brahman, food is the Absolute, our ancestors have declared. The essence of food is vitality, the essence of vitality life, and the essence of life is Consciousness—so indeed essence flows back into essence, through essence—and therefore is Brahman itself. Thus he who knows food knows Brahman. So said the commentators. Let us then cultivate the right foods. For from right foods you get right thoughts, and also from no food you get into the state of naught-thought where the Absolute shines in its own splendour, for the self-mirroring mind is it. Hence fast, hence be perceptive in foods. The onion or the cucumber may give you passion or flatulence according to your temperament, so be of care. The essential foods, the foods of the wise, are fruits and light vegetables, fine cooked rice or wheat, and sometimes milk. A wise man can live on these for a hundred years.

Gandhiji knew all this from his mother. But he came to it from another end. He came to it through the London Vegetarian Society. Mr. Hills of the London Vegetarian Society had worked out a perfect system of dietetics—he called it the vital foods. It was to consist of wheat (or grains) and pulses uncooked because it kept the sun's rays intact. And also nuts and fruits and sultanas. Gandhiji was charmed by the idea—for it meant neither cooking nor washing dishes nor being unsure whether the landlady's kitchen be clean or somebody might have, by mistake, put some meat sauce into your soup. This does happen, you know, and not always pleasant for the vegetarian when he discovers it. Whereas with the vital foods no such problem arises—and also you can dispense with your servant. Besides, these foods are so refreshing. Hence let me try vital foods. Gandhiji had decided on this already in Bombay and had tried hard to teach his servant this new science of pure foods— but that brahmin servant was a dunce and was, moreover, very unclean. He understood nothing of the pure foods or of a clean kitchen, and so Gandhiji had given up his scheme of dietetic regeneration.

But now here in South Africa there was plenty of everything—of time, of pure vegetables, and a new and maturer temper for experiments.

'August 23rd: Feeling hungry, had some peas last evening,' so he wrote in his diary. 'Owing to that I did not sleep well, and woke up with a bad taste in the mouth in the morning. Had the same breakfast and dinner as yesterday. Though the day was very dull and it rained a little, I had no headache or cold. Had tea with Baker. This did not agree at all. Felt pains in the stomach.

'August 24th: In the morning woke up uneasy with a heavy stomach. Had the same breakfast except that one spoonful of peas was reduced to half. The usual dinner. Did not feel well. Had feeling of indigestion the whole day.

'August 25th: Had no appetite for dinner . . . There were undercooked peas for dinner yesterday . . . Got headache in the latter part of the day. Took some quinine after dinner.

'August 26th: The mouth did not taste well throughout the day . . . Had the usual dinner. At 7 p.m. had a cup of cocoa. I feel hungry (8 a.m.) and yet no desire to eat. The vital food does not seem to agree well.

'August 29th: Woke up well in the morning. For breakfast had one and half teaspoonfuls of wheat, two of *sultanas,* one orange, and twenty nuts. For dinner had three tablespoons of wheat, two of currants, and twenty nuts and two oranges. In the evening had rice, vermicelli and potatoes at Tyeb's. Felt weak towards evening.

'August 31st: Felt extremely weak throughout the day. I can take the walks with much difficulty. The teeth, too, are getting weaker, the mouth too sweet.

'September 1st: Feel very weak. Teeth are aching. The experiment must be left off. Had tea with Baker as it was his birthday. Felt better after tea.

'September 2nd: Woke up fresh in the morning (the effect of last evening's tea). Had the old food (porridge, bread, butter, jam and cocoa). Felt ever so much better.'

Then he came to the conclusion. 'Vital food may have its great possibilities in store, but it will surely not make our perishable bodies immortal . . . the vital food will not, cannot, as such minister to the wants of the soul. And if the highest aim, indeed the only aim, of this life be to know the soul, then, it is humbly submitted, anything that takes away from our opportunities of knowing the soul, and therefore also playing with vital food and other such experiments, is playing away to that extent, the only desirable aim in life . . . What a sacrifice of time and trouble . . . which falls short of the highest. Life seems too short for these things.'

His spiritual dilemma was exhausting. Christianity was of course beautiful, touching, and all-embracing, but it could not be his. Hinduism with all its extravagances, corruptions, and intellectualisations, had in it a kernel of something shining, something so exalting, and yet it could not be for all. And there was Islam too—and most of the Indian merchants in South Africa were Muslims—which with its creed of universal brotherhood, charity, and frugality, was an upright and a clear statement of God. What then was the solution? How could he, a Hindu by instinct, join with all in the worship of the One? Here a book came to him which was to have perhaps a permanent effect on his passion for religious syncretism. The book was called *The Perfect Way*, written in an impassioned and dramatic style by a 'mystic' who'd had the revelation of the unity of all religions, especially of the Indian and Christian, the Islamic thrown in

with imaginative precision. For, said the author, Mrs. Anna
Kingsford, there's no doubt Truth or Knowledge was given as
a 'revelation' once and once for all. In the West it was called
Gnosis, which for reasons of politics the Church had put aside
and had forgotten. All religions contained the Truth and in
differing degrees, but Buddhism and Christianity were, so to say,
supreme in the divine scheme of things. The Buddha, and with
him goes Pythagoras (the two were, remember, contemporaries),
were none else than what the Bible calls Abraham and Elias. The
Buddha was the forerunner of the Christ, he the true John, the
Baptist. Buddhism and Christianity are so interrelated that one
could boldly say where one is philosophy and the other is religion,
where one is circumference the other is within, and where one
represents man, the other woman. 'But for Buddha,' declared
Anna Kingsford, 'Jesus would not have been . . . wherefore
no man can be properly a Christian who is not also and first
a Buddhist.' Hence the future of the world and its redemption
depends on 'the relation between the two peoples through whom
on the physical plane this union must be effected. Viewed from
this aspect, the connection subsisting between England and India
rises from the political to the spiritual. And thus the marriage of
dark and fair, Man and Woman, of Humanity' which in due
time will constitute one Man made in the image of God . . . And
so shall the 'lightning from the East' after 'illuminating the West'
be reflected back purified and enhanced 'a light to lighten all
nations and to be the glory of spiritual Israel'.[7]

Therefore if you said Brahma instead of Abraham ('for
they are one and the same word, and denote one and the same
doctrine'), the prophesy of Genesis XV.16 will be fulfilled.

---

[7] C.W., p. 250.

'Many shall come from the East and the West and shall sit down with Abraham and Isaac and Jacob in the kingdom of heaven.'

Anna Kingford was not only mystical, she believed herself scientific. She had studied medicine in Paris and she did not want to listen to outworn and superstitious concepts. She wanted the mighty aid of reason and of science to fulfil her mission. And so she used not only mystical and philosophical language but also the scientific. The soul, for example, 'may be likened to the nucleus of a cell. The protoplasmic medium which is found within the capsular envelope and in which the nucleus floats may be likened to the astral fluid, whether interplanetary or intercellular . . . All the elements of the cell, however—the nucleus included—are material, whereas Matter itself is a mode of Substance of which the nature is spiritual.'

And Substance is God.

But for those who'd proclaim the difference between the Hindu and the Christian traditions, she would give every satisfaction by quoting from the scriptures and from the tradition itself. Take the example of the transmigration of souls. This is supposed to divide the Hindu and the Christian religions. Actually it should not, for both thought alike—metapsychosis was also believed true by the early Christians. The early Christians also spoke of the evolution of man from tree to animal and from animal to man. The plan of God could be viewed as a triangle. God came down to earth to manifest Himself (one side of the triangle) and became Matter (the base of the triangle). And now Matter is going upwards to be united in God (the third side of the triangle). This is the pure Hermetic tradition, and known through the Mysteries of Egypt and of Greece. Thus also the feminine and the masculine aspect of the divine. 'As living Substance God is one. As Life and Substance God is Twain. He is the Life and She is the Substance.' She appears as daughter, Mother or Spouse. And she will make him, in the highest sense, Man. Thus the Immaculate Conception is the 'foundation of all Mysteries, so the Assumption is the crown'. This explains the statement of Jesus to Nicodemus that he, Jesus, was the Son of Man. The Buddha completed the regeneration of the Mind and prepared 'for the grace which comes by Jesus'. And therefore the hope of humanity is the spiritual union between the two.

And it must have gladdened Gandhi's heart that Islam too was a part of this dream, according to Anna Kingsford. 'Between the two hemispheres stand the domain and faith of Islam, not to divide but as umbilical card to unite them.'

Anna Kingsford died in the year 1888.

Dr. Maitland continued the work of Anna Kingsford— he now made magnanimous marriage between vital foods, Christianity, and eternity. After all, God was like the Sun, he argued—the Sun radiated his heat and warmth through air and mist to the awaiting earth, giving pulses and fruits and nuts and sugar cane the vitality that's his own. The sun that wheels round the earth—or rather the earth that circles around the sun—is God's work and we must eat the sun's food, solarised food; the meat of God for our soul. Spirit and matter have not to be separated. Transcended the spirit must rise to the eternal. Therefore the Christians who declare Christianity is the only way know neither the history of the great religion nor its mystery. For Christ is the Truth. Every religion has the Truth in it. Maybe, and who could gainsay it, Christianity might possibly be the most recent and the most pure manifestation of the Divine Principle. But the pagans and the Orientals too had their great religions. We have no quarrel with them—after all, we cannot quarrel with God and his manifestations. There's a mystical marriage that takes place in the soul, it's that the centre and the end of spiritual life. The eternal man and woman are united in oneself.

In Alexandria this drama of spirit and matter was understood long ago. The mystical Christian was born heir to all that was great in Egypt and the Orient, heir to the mystery of Osiris, Mithra and the Buddha. Christianity, of course, did not invent anything new. It only expressed the mystery in new symbols. In fact, the whole of the Gospel is nothing but a poem in mystical symbolism. He who reads these scriptures literally does not understand its essence no more than he who sees the body as the man know the soul. To prepare the body for the discovery of the soul is true religion, the true mystical life. This is Hermetic Christianity, the Esoteric one. Let us therefore get to the source—the vital foods helping us to be right and pure—and we'll all find God our own way.

To go inward is to discover the true Christian way. 'One purified oneself through Abstinence, Prayer, Meditation, Self-restraint, Fearlessness and Voluntary Poverty.' One must completely conquer the body. This was the Perfect Way, the way one enters little by little the realm of the spirit—to union with God. For 'God is nothing that man is not.' Thus with spiritual discipline one abandons one's will to God's will. 'This unification of the human will with the divine will mystically termed the At-one-ment or the reconciliation between man and God.' And this way one attains Christhood.

'And he is a Christ who in virtue of his observance of this process to its utmost extent while yet in the body, constitutes the full manifestation of the qualities of Spirit.'[8]

---

[8]   Hence the London Esoteric Christian Union of which the leading figures were Anna Kingsford and Dr. Maitland, both also fervent devotees of vegetarianism.

Mohandas Gandhi was convinced this was indeed in the direction of Truth. Why should he not in some way participate in this unique, this transcendental movement for the spiritual unification of mankind? He would therefore be the representative of the Esoteric Christian Union (London) in Johannesburg.

He would sell their books and write about them. 'I promise that after a perusal, he (the reader) will become a better man.' For the 'Union establishes the unity and common source of all the great religions of the world', and shows 'inadequacy of materialism which boasts of having given the world a civilisation which was never witnessed before . . . forgetting that its greatest achievements are the invention of the most terrible inventions of destructions, the awful growth of anarchism, the frightful disputes between capital and labour, the wanton and diabolical cruelty inflicted on innocent dumb animals in the name of science "falsely so called".'[9]

This new version of religion appealed deeply to Mohandas Gandhi. Here were people, he felt, who had understood something that he had been discursively feeling but never formulated. So Christianity might not be the final answer. Besides transmigration and such other Hindu concepts—and Dr. Maitland seemed to find them quite rational, and rational a man must be—so these Hindu ideas were perhaps not so absurd. But where to seek the right answers? He should ask Srimad Rajachandra. And so he wrote the famous letter of the twenty-eight questions which asked about every religious problem a young man might ask of an important spiritual figure. To put God in the heavens and not worry about what one does here had no meaning for Gandhi. Everything had to be God's way—that is if God existed—and

---

[9]   Letter to the *Natal Mercury,* 3 December 1894.

the ultimate answer had to be to see 'God face to face'—the true aim of every man in search of Truth.

'What is the soul?' Gandhi asked of Rajachandra. 'Does it perform actions? Do past actions impede its progress or not?'

And again: What is God? And if God exists, did he create the universe?

If past actions bind one, and if God exists, then what is the relation between the two—how does one attain *moksha* or liberation? And if indeed *moksha* or liberation could be attained, could it be so while one is still alive?

How could one be alive and be perfect and free? How is this at all possible? Besides, be it true that when a man dies he could be reborn 'an animal, a tree, or even a stone?' What do you have to say to that, Rajachandraji?

What then also is Hinduism that people call the Arya Dharma or the religion of the Aryans? Did every Indian religion originate from the Vedas? Are the Vedas eternal? Anyway, who composed them?

And again, sir, who is the author of the *Gita?* If God is author of the *Gita,* as many Indians believe, where is the proof?

And also, how does one know his religion is the best? Do you, sir, know anything about Christianity? Was Christ the Incarnation of God?

It is said some great souls have attained liberation or *moksha.* How does one know about it? How do you know?

Can an illiterate person attain liberation by the pure love of God?

'Rama and Krishna are described as incarnations of God. What does that mean? Were they God or only part of Him? Can we attain salvation through faith in them?'

'Who were Brahma, Vishnu and Shiva?'

'If the snake is about to bite me should I allow myself to be bitten or should I kill it, supposing it is the only way I can save myself.'[10]

Rajachandra, seated on his white, immaculate *gaddi* in his shop, reading the letter, and pondering over it between selling his diamond or ruby sapphire or gold to the marriage-making elder, the concubine, the Maharaja, must have written down his answers in the little notebook he always kept at his side. Thin, tall, and fiery-eyed Rajachandra was only a few years older than Mohandas Gandhi. But he had received his answers from his own Guru. And he knew. Every path leads one There. Religions are little pens in which men, like cattle, are huddled. One must get out of them and be free to know the truth. There is nothing wrong with religion as long as you know it's a pen. And one's own pen always seems the best to you because you know it best. Therefore, why not see every stone and nook of it so that you know what it is before you are free.

> O for that hour of unique bliss,
> When all the knots untied within without,
> And all the subtlest bonds removed, I shall
> Walk on the blessed path that sages tread of yore.
> Transcending mind and all its fleeting moods
> And fixed in deep detachment evermore,
> Regarding body only as the means
> For self-discipline,
> And nothing else for any cause whatever,
> No more deluded I shall be,
> By this sense-magic or this earthly frame of mine.[11]

---

[10] C.W., p. 90-91.
[11] E.P., p. 274.

And Sri Rajachandra wrote back: God is Atman freed from all bonds of karma. Atman in its pristine state is pure consciousness, total intelligence, all strength, all knowledge. There is no first cause mightier than or exterior to the Atman in its pure pristine state.

Both the Atman and the Universe are eternal—without being and without end . . . Both Cosmos and the Atman are in a perpetual state of flux and will endure for all time.

Passions like hatred and attachment, greed and lust, etc. bind the soul to matter and are the cause of its bondage. Liberation, or *moksha* is complete freedom from these.

Good and evil are like any other category of thought . . . Every individual is free to choose between good and evil, and it is the moral duty to embrace the one and eschew the other.

The antiquity of the Vedas cannot be denied. Before the Buddha and Mahavira were the Vedas . . . Both the Vedic and the Jaina ways of life may be said to have existed from the beginning; the question to be answered is, which one of these answers meets the needs of the soul best?

All the miracles of Christ pale into insignificance before the omnipotence of the perfected Atman.

Moksha or liberation can be attained only by the complete deliverance from the passions of hatred and attachment and the resulting ignorance . . .

And so now to the question, 'Shall I kill the attacking snake or shall I not?'

'If you have realised the transitory nature of the perishable body and the eternal glory of the immortal soul and its boundless potentialities, you will not wish to barter the latter for prolonging the momentary existence of the former.

'The question therefore is not what I would wish you to do but what you would wish your choice to be. The choice will depend upon the degree of your illumination or enlightenment.'[12]

Hence be a better Hindu is more or less what Rajachandra said to Gandhiji, and sent him a number of important philosophical books: *Panchikarana, Maniratna Mala, Mumukshu Prakarana* (of *Yoga Vasistha*), and the famous Jaina text, *Shaddarshana Samuchaya*.

Thus you get out of your pen your own way. There is no other way. Your way is the all—for you. Gandhiji now returned to his study of Hindu philosophy. If one does not find in it what one wants, one can always find it elsewhere. Start then from where you are.

* * *

Facts are three-fourths law, an Englishman had told Mohandas Gandhi. And so having studied accountancy he plunged into the accounts. And having plunged into the accounts he studied the letters and the documents. Law was not merely a series of ethical edicts, it was something more final. The fire of truth lay behind it, something very living, impersonal, and that took you from depth to depth of perception. It seemed to take you from frontiers of facts to the discovery of some central power, vision, presence, in which all dissolved, and you enjoyed yourself. Such an enjoyment brought not only deep fulfilment but light.

By now Tyebji Seth, the merchant, and Gandhiji had become true friends. Indians met at least once a week and they met at Tyeb's house. After all, he was a merchant-prince

[12] E.P., p. 328-29.

like Abdulla Seth, and he could be so generous and brotherly. Further, Gandhiji had finished the full study of the litigation case—the accounts had been minutely examined, and so was the correspondence. There was no question, any court of law would have given cause to Abdulla Seth. And the proceedings would take up so much time and would cost so much money, both the parties would be ruined here, and forever. This was no way to behave between man and man, between Indian and Indian. What would Dada Abdulla Seth say to arbitration? Dada Abdulla Seth accepted it but with reluctance. He knew he was going to win, and the costs would be paid by the defendant. There was no question this would be the ruin of Seth Tyeb. Is this what Dada Abdulla would wish for a fellow countryman, besides a relation of his own? Of course not, said Dada Abdulla. Then what about an arbitration out of court? If Tyeb accepts, why not? Gandhi was deeply moved by this experiment in human understanding. People given the right opportunity could behave decently. The problem therefore is only one of patience and understanding. Nobody was fully wrong and no man fully right. It all depends upon how you look at any situation. This is what Jainism had declared: You can look at an object in six different ways, and yet not be able to prove its reality. If so, is it not more difficult to find a man wrong? The crux of existence absorbs and absolves.

The arbitrator of course gave cause to Seth Abdulla. Not only Seth Abdulla won his case, but with so little cost. Now came the question of payment. Pound 37,000 is a big sum of money. If Tyeb Seth paid it all at once, he would go bankrupt. And that would be suicide. Would not Seth Abdulla, as a magnanimous gesture, suggested Gandhi, accept regular payments at fixed intervals? This would be human and brotherly and true. Dada Abdulla accepted the terms. The

agreement was duly drawn up. Gandhiji had tried his hand—
so young yet, he was hardly twenty-five years of age then—at
disentangling the strands of complicated human relationships.
By applying the twin arguments of understanding and truth
he had won this, his first experiment. Naturally, this could
be applied to every human predicament. Why not? For all
problems are no different than the case between Dada Abdulla
Seth and Seth Tyeb. Two men went to fight. Over what?
Over a mere misunderstanding about accounts. Passions rise.
Insults are hurled at one another. The rupture takes place. For
complete satisfaction, one party or the other would have to be
ruined. In every fight there is a loser. And the loser wants to
rise again, fight and win. If this is human law then humanity
is doomed. Are we still at the state of beasts? Yet, to say beasts
is improper. For even beasts behave better. After their physical
satisfactions are over, they leave one another at peace. If so,
why not the higher being called Man?

Seth Tyeb rejoiced at the way the case was settled. Gandhi
had been like a brother. Not only to Seth Tyeb but to everyone
around him, to the barber, the cook, the tailor, the mechanic,
the coolie. But now there was no more reason for Gandhi to stay
in Pretoria. He had spent eight useful months here. Now it was
time to go back.

It was sad to leave all his friends. But this had to be.
Kasturba was at home waiting with her two children. Kasturba
with her full square face, her luxuriant body, and her many
tricks, tempers and withdrawn silences. She was a clever girl, was
Kasturba. What a long separation it has been. Yet, somehow,
the passion for work took away the passion from the loins.
What next, however? And then again there was the brothers,
Lakshmidas, Karsandas, their children, and others.

Gandhiji now left Pretoria with pain and gratitude. Of course, he would come back to meet his old friends. They, his friends, would never forget him.

Durban was a bigger image of Pretoria in every way and Dada Abdulla Seth had been closer to him than had Tyeb Seth. Of course, Gandhi Bhai[13] had now to go. There was no question. It was such a pity, however. But one has to go back to one's home— to India, to Porbandar. The Indian community in Durban had to arrange a fitting adieu to this young and spirited barrister. Somehow he had, within these few months, changed the face of things for the Indians. Who would look after them now?

Sydenham is a seaside resort (full of parks and pleasant avenues) by Durban, and here people came for their holidays. It was such a lovely place where the whites enjoy themselves, why not the Indians enjoy themselves too there? Dada Abdulla Seth was after all a rich man. And he should do something befitting this important occasion. For when Gandhi Bhai goes from here who knows when he will ever return? Every departure is a movement in the great, and eternal, pilgrimage.

As the Indian holidaymakers were enjoying themselves, Gandhiji's eyes caught a short note in the *Natal Mercury*. It was significantly called, 'Indian Franchise'.

'The Asiatic comes of a race impregnated with an effete civilisation,' it began. Of course, he, the Indian, has no knowledge whatsoever of representative government. He is truly a political infant. And it would be unjust to ask him to have sympathy for our political aspirations. Besides they hardly know how to read a newspaper. So few of them know the English language. 'He thinks differently and reasons in a plane unknown to European

---

[13] Gandhi Bhai—brother Gandhi.

logic.' Our political systems are as mystical to him as his Vedas be to us. Besides, they are a parasitical race. God knows why we ever gave them franchise. They would perhaps be so happy to have this responsibility removed. 'If the Colonists arrogated to themselves the sole duties of government, they took upon their shoulders responsibility that the government should be fair and just, and by claiming to be the dominant race they understood that their rule should be one of generosity and justice to the unenfranchised.'[14]

Therefore it behoves the whites to disenfranchise the Indians. That sounds logical. Does it not? And a bill was accordingly brought before the Natal legislature. 'Do you know anything about it, brothers?' asked Gandhi.

'What can we understand of these matters?' answered Dada Abdulla. 'We can understand only things that affect our trade.'[15] Besides, similar things had already taken place in the Orange Free State, continued Dada Abdulla. 'Indians were driven out by the colonists. No Indian could own property there or settle in trade.' And listen, brother, here in Natal it all started in this manner. 'A European attorney got a few of us to vote, and we voted for him. That is all. We know nothing.'

'Something must be done,' said Gandhiji gravely pondering over the situation. 'Yes, something must be done about the franchise question, and forthwith. There is no time to lose.'

'What shall we do, brother?' they all said. 'You say, and we do what you say.'

'But I am going away.' He had been almost a year in South Africa.

---

[14] 25 June 1894.
[15] A., p. 173.

'No, you must not go,' they insisted. 'Abdulla Seth, you must detain brother Gandhi.'

'Of course, and how wonderful that would be,' answered Dada Abdulla, adding diplomatically, 'but you too have the same right to detain him. Let us all persuade him to stay.'

'Of course.'

'But you must not forget he is a barrister. What about his fees?'

'Abdulla Seth,' said Gandhi, 'I need no fees for this work. There can be no fees for public work.' But naturally there would be other expenses—postage, stationery and fees for the attorneys. 'Everybody will have to cooperate with me. We will have to fight the Bill[16] with courage and sacrifice. It cannot be a one-man show. I will postpone my departure by a month provided you all promise me your full cooperation.'

'Allah is great!' they all shouted. 'And of course money will come. And you can have as many of us at your service as you like. Stay with us then, Gandhi Bhai, stay with us.'

'Yes, I stay,' said Gandhiji and thereby his political vocation started.

* * *

Geologically speaking, the Deccan[17] is one of the oldest chunks of this rotating planet. Sturdy with laterite and gneissite, it once formed the cretaceous part of a continent, the famous Gondwanaland, of which Africa and India and South America

---

[16] Called the Franchise Amendment Bill, 1894, which specifically stated: '. . . Persons of Asiatic extraction shall not be qualified . . . to vote as electors or of any law relating to the election of members to the Legislative Assembly.'

[17] South India.

are each a third of the whole landmass. But at some unknown time a mighty geological movement shook the earth—and this split it into many different parts, each with its own peculiar mutation of fauna and flora, in mountain, river and plain. For example, in that bright young past there were no Himalayas— they came much later—and they began to grow little by little and from their slowly emergent uplifts, little streams began to flow, which gurgled and watered and fed the oceans till the silt formations built up in millions of years the large spacious and auspicious Indo-Gangetic plain, the home of the Indo-Aryans, the *Aryavarta*. And the Aryans coming from the cold North when they met a dark-skinned, flat-nosed race, but mighty and highly civilised so historians conjecture, they fought these darker folk and defeated them and called them the slaves, the *Dasyus*. But as it often happens in history, they, the Aryans, probably took most of their civilisation from the *Dasyus,* and ruled happily their own republics and kingdoms according to *Dasyu* concepts—each village a little republic, with canals and aqueducts and collective grazing grounds. Five persons ruled each village by election, and thus from age to age, the *Dasyus,* now called Dravidians, ruled their own new territory, the Deccan. The rich thick velds, the Dandaka Forest, divided the Aryan and the Dravidian, so each one lived his own life. Again and again the white Aryan tried to conquer the South and again and again he was defeated for the thin and blue-coloured Dravidian is rich in intelligence and a mighty brave man. He has a speech of his own—among the most ancient of the earth—called the Dravida, from which rose Tamil and Telugu, Kannada and Malayalam, among the great languages of India, and with at least about one thousand years of literature each. Cultivating his great belt of rice fields, green and gold against the monsoon-blue sky, blue of skin, and singing his rich realistic songs, he made South India among the most civilised parts of the earth. Cities and emporia arose one after another, and from the ancient Egyptians, the Hebrews and the Chinese, the Greeks and the Romans—they all traded with the Dravidian and in fact Queen Sheba even received an Embassy from the Kings of Dravida, with gifts of ivory and the peacock. And the Roman emperors got the elephant instead. Thus the fame of the Dravida land wherever trade and learning flourished.

Meanwhile, however, long before man was imagined anywhere Africa had been, because of some biological mystery, shaping a new, erect-standing and babbling baboon so that whether we like it or we like it not, we are all of African origins. That is what archaeologists and biologists are beginning to tell us. The African North, of course, is cool and lush with the Mediterranean sun and the splendours of the cypress and the olive, but where the deserts begin is a vast human silence which is cut through only by the narrow habitations of the Nile. Man who had gone from the African South to the cold polar North, and thus become pale and finally white, he, tired of the sudden changes in temperature—it was getting colder and colder on the North and brighter and brighter in the South—he returned slowly South and being of a sturdier build—cold and snow had made him struggle hard to live—he defeated easily the Mediterranean dwellers and established himself in their place. One branch however, and an earlier one, had already gone towards the East and so they had discovered India. The others, late-comers, went West and having conquered the darker and more civilised peoples there pushed them further and further down till, frightened by the deserts, the Northerner remained behind while the ancient Mediterranean man went downwards and was lost somewhere in the African oasis and wilds. And he too must have met other, earlier inhabitants of the land: the Bushmen. Short and yellow-faced, they looked much closer to the animal than to civilised men. But they were skilful both in archery and in art, and for language they had but 'clicks and croaks'.

Between the Mediterranean man, the Zulu, and the Bushman, wars went on and nobody could truly win for the Bushman would always run away from wilderness to a further wilderness. The civilised and browner man could not run so fast—he loved dwellings and wished to stay on the same spot more effortlessly. Thus between the two heroic wars went on till the Bushman came to the southern-most tip and stayed there on the table land of the South, a high and temperate territory with much wild game to hunt and simple, rich vegetation to help him feed himself and his cattle on. Sometimes, however, the two races met and mated and produced the Hottentot. The Hottentot too had now become a tribe of his own, and the Zulus therefore fought with the one and then with the other, but Africa was large and you could have wars for a million years, and yet more land could be conquered and more men born to fight and to kill and to die again.

At this moment—at some particular and recent period of history—the Mediterranean man having heard of the riches of the country called India by the Greeks, and which once Alexander had tried to conquer, and a great merchant, Marco Polo, had described as having so much riches (the Greek historians too had extolled her wealth and her civilisation)—these European merchants wanting to go to the rich Indies, had big ships built for long voyages and had, under the order of kings, made maps based on the tales of the travellers and so a flat picture of the earth produced a long-nosed Africa around which, on one side, was a small island forever called India and sometimes mistakenly called Ethiopia as well. To reach India and get its pearls, diamonds and precious stones, its spices, and see its famed women became the dream of merchants and adventurers. Charted first by King Henry the Navigator, great expeditions set out and finally discovered the Cape of Good Hope, and later Vasco da Gama reached India itself. The Portuguese had, of course, discovered the routes to India but the Arabs had been masters of the Indian Ocean for more centuries than anyone could remember. The Portuguese, therefore, the Indians, and the Arabs made naval-war with each other, and finally endowed with more military skill than the Arabs, the Portuguese won, and all the Indian Ocean came officially under the Portuguese flag.

And now to go around to India, the Cape of Good Hope became the little halting station. In fact, there was not much to grow there and the land did not, to speak the truth, seem inviting. At first it was just a small settlement, to water and victualise, on a great expedition. Little by little the whitemen began to fight with each other. The Dutch defeated the Portuguese and established a small encampment there. And there for the first time they met the Bushman fleeing from the Zulu. The Bushman seemed harmless and willing to live and let live with the newcomers. Finally, finding ivory, the whiteman could not resist fighting, and almost exterminating, the Bushman. But the Hottentot and the Zulus were more difficult to conquer. Thus the whiteman slowly pushed the Zulus northward, that mighty and hard race of beautiful men and reckless fighters. The whiteman had to come floating down in ships from some godforsaken country, and he could therefore only be a handful against a whole tribe, against a whole race. But tribe fought against tribe too for dominion, and sometimes wiped out a whole entity of opponents. The still-remaining Bushmen skirted the fights, and chuckled and clicked at their own happy destiny. While the others fought, Bushmen could at least propagate their tribe and lead their own hunting lives. Nobody was alarmed or worried—for the world (of Africa) was very large, and killing and dying after all was a natural affair. When the great Zulu chief Cheka heard his mother was deadly ill, he, a mighty warrior, rushed through the harsh African forests to her side. And when she died and had to be buried it was going to be a whole tribe in lamentation—indeed, not only a tribe but the whole of creation in mourning. He had one thousand men beheaded at the same time so that the husbands and mothers could cry for their dear ones, and thus add to the agony of the world—and a ten thousand cattle butchered so that their cries too would fill the heavens in sorrow. In the middle of this great sorrow the hero stood by the grave, lifting his own mother into the earth. And corn-bugles blew.

* * *

The whiteman had not only settled in South Africa, he had conquered India as well. One king of India was warring against the other, the northern one against the southern ones, and southern Muslim king against a Hindu Maharaja, the Hindu Maharaja against his brother, his cousin, his prime minister, and finally when a Mughal emperor died, his sons started a whole series of dynastic wars. Brother ran against brother, and sometimes killed all of them to win the throne. And since the emperor could have many wives, there were also many brothers to kill. The emperor had to have again one eye on his brothers' children or royal bastards, and the other eye against the Hindu kings, the Rajputs—and finally here comes the whiteman. The whiteman had one superiority over them all. Having discovered gunpowder from the Chinese, and the compass, and having developed remarkable military and navigational skills, he could go round the seas as he liked and blow up fortresses with an ease that astonished the bravest among the brave. The Maharajas, the Nawabs, the princelings and the claimants (to various thrones) having discovered how eager the whiteman was not only to trade with them but to fight for them, employed Frenchmen, Englishmen, even Italians, as trainers to the local armies, and later had many mercenaries fighting for them. The mercenary is always more reliable than the native soldier. You pay the European and he obeys. The mercenary and the merchant, however, to make things work, had to have more and more organised authority with the result that all India, little by little, came under British rule. If a prince (like the Rana of Porbandar or the Thakore Sahib of Rajkot) obeyed the British they would be protected and allowed to live more or less as they liked. If they did not, like the Nawabs of Carnatic (in the far South, the land of the Dravidians), the British took over the territory, organised it in districts and commissionerates and provinces, and ruled the land with a fair quantum of justice and some humanity. The great God in his compassion has sent the whiteman to protect the feeble from the tyrant, the Hindu from the Mohammedan, so some thought. Indeed, in good time, after the mistakes made by the over-hasty acts of the whiteman—for he went on annexing territories too quickly, too irresponsibly, and never seemed to understand the ways and thoughts of the 'natives'—the white Englishman was almost defeated in 1857 in a historic revolt, called the Mutiny by the British, and the First War of Indian Independence, 1857, by the Indians. When the Parliament of England rose in rebellion against this inhumanity going on in their name, the Queen herself, magnanimous, brave, and understanding—and loving—took the whole Empire under her own authority. She became the Empress of India and declared in her famous proclamation:

> 'We hold ourselves bound to the natives of our Indian
> territories by the same obligations of duty which bind us to
> all our other subjects, and these obligations, by the blessings
> of Almighty God, we shall faithfully and conscientiously
> fulfil. It is our further will that, so far as may be, our subjects
> of whatever race or creed, by freely and impartially admitted
> to offices in our service, the duties of which they may be
> qualified by their education, ability and integrity . . . duly to
> discharge.'

So all Indians became automatically British subjects, and true justice and humanity would now rule the whole land.

Meanwhile, however, goods and administrators flowed into India from Great Britain, and more and more gold went out and produced such prosperity in the Home Country that some early industries paid as much as three hundred per cent profit. Long live free trade and the Empire! Jeremy Bentham rejoiced his principles had proven right and he became a friend of India.

The same historical process would have taken place, might have taken place, in South Africa as well had the Zulu and the Bantu a more stable civilisation. Besides, there was so much empty land in Africa—the more you pushed the native the larger and the vaster became the empty space—fold behind the fold behind the horizon seemed to be such magnificent territory. You just erected a log-cabin, settled with a few oxen, cut yourself a plough or wagon and there you were. And the

Hottentot women were so greatly happy to have round, white children—indeed the first Boer was born, so says the gossip of history, round the corner of the nine months after Jan Van Riebeeck landed at the Cape in 1652. To the Hottentot added the Huguenot (the edict of Nantes had done this) and thus the Dutch, the Hottentot and the Huguenot, created a new type of man—the Boer. Devoted to his Christ and to his Calvinistic creed, fearless (Kruger, their chief, killed a lion when he was just eleven years of age) and paternal, he looked after his family, his cattle, and the natives, a zealous devotee of God. God had sent him to this rich and vast land and he would be a master here. Both science (the new theories of Darwin) and the Bible had said the black man (son of Ham)[18] was an inferior being. So he would be the slave. Thus with cattle, children and slave—and a devoted, hard-working wife—the Boer could live happily here as never in his own ancestral lands. Here was the new Holland, the new France, the new land of Almighty God.

In India, however, the civilisation being more ancient, the people were more easy to govern. Formerly, as king after king had fought, conquered and gone, each village had become a republic—who ruled mattered so little—a state by itself, paying dues to its masters whoever they might be—the Hindu, the Muslim, or the white king. As long as the Hindu was left with his gods and his festivals, his particular foods, and his marital and inheritance laws anybody could do anything in the upper reaches of the state. Who cared? But the villages became bigger and bigger—population increased. The whiteman had built cities and roads and even brought the long chugging trains and the mysterious humming telegraph wires. A magic surrounded

---

[18] Genesis 9: 18-27; Joshua 9: 21-27 (Quoted by John Gunther, *Inside Africa*)

the whiteman's empire. But even when he built roads and dams there was, however, not always enough to eat. More mouths arose every year, and less food grew. And the few kings that remained, these again seemed more interested in worshipping the whiteman and playing with the concubine. For wherever the Rajas were good, there was some prosperity even after the British came. There might have been less English education but more food. And more culture, that is more music, more Sanskrit-learning. And you could deal with the Maharaja's government as if they were your own kings, your own chiefs, your own god's men. It was different with the British. They were more reliable—if you were just, they were usually just. But they sat so far away and, somehow, one never got enough to eat. Thus the gold, the jewellery, the rice and the wheat were drained out of the country unperceived, and the once fabled country sank from poverty to greater poverty. In fact, such poverty was never known in all of Indian tradition and history. Famine one has known; but rarely it came, it went. Famine too came now and with it came disease. The bubonic plague, the syphilis, and the gonorrhea, and so many new illnesses came to the land. The goddess of the land seemed to have grown angry. So you sacrifice your goat or hen to the goddess and she forgives you and sometimes gives you rain and health and many children. Year after year goes and marriages and nuptials and childbirth, adolescence and marriage again take place; the rich and the poor both became poorer every year.

In England, however, the mighty factories were working, urging man forward to the new civilisation. Cotton went from India and became fine cloth in Manchester and returned to India as *dhoti* and towels, frocks and *choli*-cloth for men and women to wear. Trains took cotton forward to the ports, and ships brought cloth and little machines in. The villager could see the flying trains and wonder where men went and why. He stayed with his cattle and his bullock-cart, went to the fair every week to buy or to sell, and returning home would procreate, go to sleep and go back to his fields the next morning. 'The wretch, the rain, she seems not to come this way.' And thus year went by year and nothing whatever happened.

One day, however (in the early 1860s), among the pigs at the gutter, or the cattle on the commons, drums began to beat. The whiteman needed men far away to work—to work on large gardens where coffee and sugar cane grew. They would have a pay of seven rupees eight annas per month[19] for each able man, and if women wanted to go they too could go. It's a land far across the seas. If you did not like it, brother, you could always come back.

Five years you must promise to stay. You cannot leave the plantation before that. But after that you can jump on a ship and come back, if you will, and so to your village, and to your family. And to your temple.

'But can we not take our gods too?'

'Fool, who could be against your gods and goddesses? You can take them if you will. But there are no temples there.'

'So what shall we do?'

'You can build some if you like.'

'Thus,' concluded the wise visitors, 'seven rupees eight annas a coolie, and five years of work there. And if you do not want to return because you find that land kind and good, you can settle there. The government will give you land. And for that country is so vast, you can never imagine how vast it is. Now you grow your own rice and vegetables and live happily ever after.'

---

[19]   10 to 12 shillings.

The elders and the men thought it all over in silence. They met again at the panchayat house. It sounded nice, so nice to go and earn seven rupees eight annas a month, and later have a large stretch of land and call it your own. 'What do you say to that, wife?' they asked on returning home.

The wives said: 'And after all I am a woman. What do I know? Whatever they[20] decide will be my decision as well.'

Most men decided they would not go. Some however agreed to go. And eventually there were many, many who would go.

And the first ships left the shores of Madras (1860) taking the coolie across the seas to the new land. Great and big was that land they were told again and again even in the boat, and the whiteman ever so kind. Even in India you know the whiteman is not so bad. He gives you medicine when you are ill, and builds schools for your children. And there would be bigger schools and more medicine in that new land. The God you know, who brought us to this earth, would not want us to eat grass. Would he?

And clipper after clipper crossed the evil seas to Africa.

The Boer had one problem: God did not want slaves. This the Bible had explicitly stated. Man being made in the image of God, no man was to be a slave. But the blackman, did he have a soul? It was a devilish question. If he had a soul he could not be black. He will be a slave. But what about the Englishman, who would slave for him? A solution was found. Get Indians from India. It's said they are poor, dying of famines and of hunger. The British rule them, and they could therefore deliver to us Indians to labour on our sugar cane fields. Since the Kaffir will not work the brownman will. He will come here and work, but he will not compete with us because he is barbaric and brown.

---

[20] Meaning the husband. The woman uses the plural as a sign of respect.

So there could be no problem. God's plans are mysterious, so magnificently rich, so loving . . . And ship-loads of coolies came.

As the ocean rolled and the winds howled outside, 'Hé Ayyapan', 'Hé Murugan', they cried, the coolies did, rolling in their blankets.

Down it went, the ship,[21] struggling to know where she was, she suddenly jumped up and lurched again, and when sometimes mists and monsoons covered her up, the ship hooted and cried, bringing desperation to their hearts. It's then that Velayudhan or Ponnan thought of pilgrimages to Shabarimalai or to Palani through mountain paths, strewn with the bones of animals dead that the tiger or panther had killed, or the tree that the elephant had felled and broken, eating away most of the leaves—their turds still fresh on the shining dew-wetted grass—while with children on their back, and beards on their faces (the women carrying the bundles), the men in front walked, bells tied to flag poles, chanting 'Ayyappa Sami, Ayyappa Sami', till on that cold and crowded morning, shivering in their wetted clothes, their jawbones clutched in dew-cold, the temple door opened, and the whole assemblage had suddenly seen God face to face—yes, that was so good, and had brought deep spaciousness to their hearts. The Ayyappan that called them, and saved them from tiger and elephant, would save them also from the rugged seas— and the whiteman for whom were going to work. For, people on the deck were full of such tales, the whitey ate meat so big no panther could swallow, the whitey used powder to hide the bad smells, their women were not like our women—their women were fat and showed their bosoms. Our women too showed

---

21   In those days the ships were small. See G.W. White, *Ships, Coolies and Rice*, London 1937.

their bosoms but not in the same way. And they drink, their women do. And how does that proverb go: A drinking woman is like a tail-less dog; it does not bark. And they, the whities, drank not from pots but from bottles. That must be more strong. That is why they drank so little. Look at the whites on the upper deck. Look at their red eyes. Were the sugar cane planters the same?

'No,' says the Ramsay who'd been to Africa before and was bringing back his new fold. 'Oh no, the whities on the plantations are more fierce—but when they are kind they are kinder than the whites of the city. . . .'

'Well the great Ayyappan alone knows. What do we know!'

As if to ease the minds and hearts of every man and woman—and that nothing should go wrong till you get to the plantation—the Ramsay or the Wells says, 'Wait and see. It will be grand there. You will have beds, solid houses to sleep in, and a lot of land to grow vegetables on. Nothing like that have you ever seen, my son.' This go-between had never seen anything better—he was a Christian. He had changed his religion in Africa, understood the whiteman better. And, of course, he understood the Dravidian so well, for once he was one of them. And he spoke for both.

'Well, everything will be good when we get there,' they, the Dravidians, decided, spat over their shoulders, and went to a soothed sleep. 'Hé Ayyapan, Thy Feet are our only Protection. Protect us. . . .'

'If life is, it is this, it is this,' cried the young among them, and dreamt of great adventures.

As the ship berthed and the Ramasamy and the Virasamy,[22] the Velayandhan and the Govindan fearfully came down the

---

[22] The termination of South Indian names with 'sami' (a corruption of the Sanskrit word swami or a divine being) became one of the generic names for the Indian. Finally, the word Sami had the same connotation as the coolie.

gangway, they were impressed by the simplicity of everything. The whiteman was not so angry nor the blackman so terrifying—the world seemed less distressing than they had imagined from afar. And when they passed through Durban and on to the waiting road or train, they felt more reassured. It was not going to be so terrifying, after all. Look at those broad, mirroring streets, those neatly dressed whites going in buggies. Bigger than anything they'd seen ever was Durban—she seemed a capital of many propositions. And when the train chugged and eked for breath and pulled into the countryside, how wide the world seemed. There was a breath of God upon this African earth. Twist after twist brought them to higher and yet higher hills, and once the train had jerked and stopped, jerked and stopped again, they were descending towards large, garden-like territories—round and gentle flowing, and unending, the plantation land seemed friendly, almost familiar. The gods had not sent them to the heathen for death. This was a sweet land, and they would live here, work, grow, make money, bring the family from Puttur or Arcot, and thus end their days in peace amidst waving harvest fields. Such a land it was—and so like Karnatak or Malabar.

And the whiteman, too, once you went up the plantation, with his strange, short-haired head and pipe, and speaking a harsh ununderstandable language, seemed, nevertheless, benevolent. He spoke and did not spit. Here they could not be beaten (thus the go-between had declared) for Christianity was a kindly religion. Their god had sacrificed himself for love, so someone had said.

Thus with tender and hopeful dreams they looked here and there, on the splendours of the latrines, the comforts of the cots—and Ramasamy and Virasamy went to an unaccustomed sleep. It was cold but there were blankets. The sugar cane stalks rubbed against one another and made strange noises, like the noises of gently hissing snakes. Row after row of sugar cane lines could be seen, tall and severe, and in between one could see the running land—the lane of fire-protection, endless and mighty, lifted against the sky. Somewhere lions and lionesses and lion-cubs must be roaming, or wild elephants, but as the go-between had assured everyone, the sahib had guns to shoot them down. Thus one could sleep in peace and wake up on a morning to the glory of work. God is compassionate. Of this there was no doubt. Otherwise would he have made this land, and its line after line of sugar cane, as if planted straight from Indra's heaven. And a Velayudhan or a Govindan from far Madurai, sitting on his bed after work, would go on dreaming of his own garden. He also would plant sugar cane one day. And his wife will by then have come. Were they only dreams? No, look at the Coloureds here, the half-white, the half-black and the half-anything else. They seemed so happy.

After all, the worst that can happen to you is death. The best would be a house and a garden. God would give it. For, look, the land is so vast!

'I will remember,' wrote Sir John Robinson, who became the Prime Minister of Natal later, 'one evening . . . watching from a height overlooking the sea, the ship *Truro* sail up the anchorage. Her white canvas towered over the blue line, and we all regarded her as the harbinger of a new dispensation.' And such the prosperity the coolie brought that the revenue increased fourfold within a few years. And after five years of work on the plantation, or ten years, the coolie won his freedom and set up his modest shop anywhere in town, or hawked his vegetables—carrots, turnips, cabbages—for no whiteman would grow them in Natal. 'The Asiatic has come to stay in South-east Africa'. Sir

John concluded, 'At any rate under such conditions as restrictive legislation may impose.'[23]

Thus Indian communities rose in Durban and Pretoria, and in the Cape Province. They knew nothing of what was happening anywhere in India or in Africa. They made money, built better and better shanties, obeyed the laws of the land, were peaceful, and wonderfully happy.

Meanwhile, beat the drum and sing:

There's no lie with us,
Lie is our god.
The ant builds a wall, I saw it.
The cat baked the bread, I saw it.
I saw the pimento, Mother—big, big as a man.
I saw the cock conquer a fortress,
And the bird weave a blanket.
I saw, Sister, a bean-pod big as an elephant.
There is no lie with us,
I tell you,
Lie is our god.

And happy, too, were the scattered 'Arab' merchants. These also came from India, from North India, spoke a different language, built mosques and mansions, and lived very much like the whiteman. One only went to see them on occasions to ask for help, or for understanding the laws of the land, and though they were Muslims they were full of love and kindliness. They gave excellent advice and sometimes even money. They grew rich, too. All the rich people grew richer. Diamond and gold had

---

[23] Sir John Robinson, *A Lifetime in South Africa*, p. 75-76, London, 1900.

now been discovered and made South Africa the boom country. The English too now arrived on crowded ships, and they also went over hills and through long and lion-haunted valleys to the great land where you could scratch and find a diamond or, better still, dig a little and find endless corridors of gold.

The blackman however seemed to go nowhere, to do nothing. What was he going to do? Would the blackman always remain black?

To President Kruger of Transvaal, everything was clear. He read the Bible and everything was written there in it. He always believed the earth was flat, and not round, for the Bible said so— and became wrathsome if anyone contradicted this statement. Like Moses he had led the Boers into the promised land. The Boer was the eldest of God, austere, clean, and homely, they had no problems of their own. The real problem was the English, these Uitlanders, the outsiders—they sat outside the door, as it were, and wanted all the rights of the Boers. This was un-Godly. Either become a Burgher of the Republic or go back to your own country. The English backed by London neither went back nor did they become citizens. Nor would they fight with the commandos whenever a rebellion had to be suppressed. And the English had, further, brought these Indians, these god-forsaken peoples, neither totally black, nor in any way white. Alien to God and to this country, they were too clever to be left alone. And the British seemed to protect them. What is there to protect when the good Boer was there?

And he was making this wild, savage land into a paradise. And God in greatness and compassion had brought not only milk and honey to this land but revealed those wondrous mineral treasures as well.

Such his bounty. Africa, South Africa, will belong to the Boers. The English must go back home, these Johannesburg moneypots. And somehow or the other the wretched Indians have to be pushed out too. After all, one had almost done it in the sister Republic of the Orange Free State. What could happen there could happen here. So an Indian delegation went to see President Kruger. His contemporary, Calgnhoun, has described the scene of how he received his people, 'seated on a leather-covered arm-chair, in dirty-looking clothes, his hair and beard long, a big Dutch pipe in his mouth, and a huge red bandana handkerchief hanging out of the side pocket of his loose jacket.'[24] The Bible always lay before him, his cup of coffee beside it. He offered his friends a seat without even rising to receive them, and a hot cup of thick Dutch coffee. But the Indians were left standing. President Kruger, after listening paternally to the woes and fears of the Indians, after a few grumbles and silences, lifted his Bible, and spoke as follows:

> 'You are descendants of Ishmael and therefore from your very birth bound to slave for the descendants of Essau. As descendants of Essau, we cannot admit you to rights placing you on an equality with ourselves. You must be content with what rights we grant to you.'

And he added: 'You must see that the Volkraad (Parliament) has placed me in the position of Abraham, and you will have to obey the law, and live outside as Ishmael did.'

---

[24] Cecil Rhodes, p. 288.

4

The Triangle of Facts

Briton, Boer and the Indian

Elections would soon be held all over Natal—Natal would become a self-governing colony on 4 July 1893. A certain Harry Escombe, attorney to Dada Abdulla, had in the 1882 elections, when Natal was still a Crown Colony, a powerful rival in a wharf engineer of Durban and everybody knew the contest would be hot. Mr. Escombe had then told the Indians that according to law, 'every adult male not being a 'native' or alien who had been naturalised, above the age of twenty years and who possessed an immovable property worth fifty pounds or a rented property of ten pounds was entitled to vote provided he had not been convicted of any infamous crime or offence without having received a full pardon.'[1] Thus many Indians had registered themselves to vote—and some had started to vote. And, of course, they would vote again in the elections of September 1893. And since each candidate was trying to outdo the other, he found every plausible reason he could to fight his opponent. And one of the easiest propositions for any white

---

[1] E.P., p. 395.

settler was the position of the Indians in Africa. For, he said, if you gave them rights they will swamp us and they will drive us out. But, objected the opponent, they are British subjects. And what is more, when contests were taken to the Supreme Court again and again, the justice was on their side. If the Briton voted and the Indian does not vote, the Briton could not vote either. What can you do with such a situation? 'One way or the other,' the *Natal Advertiser* wrote, 'all Asiatics must be prevented from exercising the franchise in this colony. If this is not done then our children will have cause to curse us for our folly.'

But the problem was not so simple. If you threw the trader and the free Indian out, then you must also stop all Indian immigration. There would be no shiploads of coolies coming anymore—into this green and sugar cane-waving lands—and thus our land will lose value. Hence the coolie must come. But the trader must go. 'Without doubt the Asiatic is the most undesirable addition to the population.' And then again:

'If instead of thus hauling them into the same sack and consigning them *en masse* to perdition, a little discrimination is exercised it will be seen . . . that the coolie as labourer, hawker and servant is the least objectionable, and the Indian trader the most dangerous and harmful of all.'[2]

And Natal only followed what others did. The Orange Free State was an independent territory. The British had little influence in that state. The first Indian merchant, Abubaker, settled there and quickly, much too quickly, made so much money other Indians joined him. And not only did they prosper, but Abubaker went over to Pretoria and bought himself more shops and lands so that the white traders said to themselves: And

---

[2]   *Natal Advertiser*, 15 September 1893.

now what shall become of us? And soon, very soon, the Indian merchants were asked to leave the Orange Free State—anyway they were so few—but in Transvaal it was another matter. The Indians there had invested more money and had amongst them petty shopkeepers, barbers, bakers, hawkers, vegetable sellers and others, and these were more difficult to be rid of—every British subject had the same rights, whether in England or anywhere else in the far-extending Empire. Hence the British Agent in Pretoria was also the protector of the Indians. However, the Uitlander—the Englishman—himself was seemingly being threatened (but everybody knew the intrigues going on behind the back of the Boers by the English, what with Cecil Rhodes and his Kimberley territory, nobody, not even the Boer was going to stop them), therefore what could a poor Indian do in this very complicated world? Children of Ishmael or not, they were doomed. They were too clever in business, and often the whiteman had to close his shop and find something else to do. If this continued Transvaal and Natal would finally become all brown—the semi-barbaric Indian would drive the white out, and rule. Already there were as many browns as whites in Natal alone. What was one going to do about it?

And here opened a decisive drama of the Empire. The great Empire builders were men of adventure, as much drawn by money as by the lure of impossible tasks. Clive was not only in love with gold but so was he with his sword. Thus the Empire was built without anybody knowing how. But the English gentleman, be he a Burke, a Bentham, or a Mill, wanted gentlemen to rule. Hence the fight between the adventurer and the gentleman all over the world wheresoever the British influence was felt. The gentleman would, like Burke, uphold the British sense of justice and freedom everywhere, even there where they were not concerned. An adventurer like Rhodes dreamt of Empire and diamonds at the same time; though Oxford and adventure did not always go together, but Marcus Aurelius and Gibbon did. The Boer, however, was just as stubborn a man of God,—both the Englishman and the Indians were to him intruders. Both had to go—the Indian first because he was brown and the easier to get rid of, and the British because they were so shrewd, the Boer would be finally fooled. So, beware of the British!

And among the British representatives, either settled in Africa or as representatives of Whitehall, there were once again gentlemen and adventurers. Some would uphold the laws of the Queen to the letter and see that justice be done, and others, and amongst them some of the ablest men who established the Empire, would combine the most astute diplomacy and sharp methods with the highest ability in the service of the Empire, like Sir Alfred Milner. And the Kipling figure was the one that tried to combine the two, and failed only to be forgotten.

The Indians, therefore, when they approached the British representatives in Pretoria or Pietermaritzburg received very confused advice—of course, they, the Indians, were British subjects and naturally the Queen's great proclamation was true and for all places and at all times. But the Boer was being difficult. Let us be patient, said they. Leave the British authorities to look after the matter. There is nothing to worry. Go home and sleep on your treasures. Nothing will happen to you.

And this state might have gone on forever, the Indian being well-protected or ill-protected according as the British Agent in power, a gentleman or an adventurer—but the politician now came on to the scene. Under the new Constitution the Boer and the Britisher would both have power and perform whatever they conjointly wanted! The Boer in the name of God, and the

Britisher in the name of Queen Victoria, they could, if united, build a prosperous and a bright Natal, rich in wealth and dignified in its citizenry.

Caught here between the Boer and the Briton, the Hindu became the cause of all evil. 'The dirt of Asia,' 'the real canker that was eating the vitals of the community'. They swarmed like locusts, 'squalid coolies with truthless tongues and artful ways.' Further they were 'pigs' or 'swine' or 'vermin'.

A thing black and lean (ran a doggerel)
and a long way from clean,
which they called the accursed Hindoo.

And again:

He is chock-full of vice
And lives upon rice.
I heartily cuss the Hindoo.

Finally, the *Natal Advertiser* openly declared:[3]

'These wily Asiatics . . . taking advantage of the wholesale (white) dealers . . . have also driven out the small European trader. The place he once occupied is now taken by these wretched Asiatics who live a semi-barbaric life, spend nothing, send all their savings to Calcutta and go insolvent when they please . . . With respect to these 'Indian traders' there should be no hesitancy shown and no quarter given. They must be expelled if possible, and if that cannot be effected forthwith,

---

[3] 15 September 1893.

at least they can be taxed as not to make it worth their while
to remain longer in the colony.'

* * *

It is here Mohandas Karamchand Gandhi enters history. He
touched the nerve centre of empire building with a gentlemanly
geste and an elegant argument—meek in voice but firm in
statement which eventually broke, in fifty years, the most firm
foundations of the Empire. He himself did not know what was
happening. But this is how it happened.

The Natal Legislative Assembly was duly elected, the first
free one of the colony, in September 1893. Already a new
governor had arrived to face a new situation, an African self-
governing colony. He had to face, as we have seen before, the
triple factor of the British, the Boer, and the meek Indian, living
side by side. The native, however, the most populous of the
land and who ought have most to say had, of course, no voice
whatsoever. An Indian delegation met the new governor, as the
high representative of Her Majesty the Queen Empress.[4] He had
perforce to speak with two voices: of course, said he, the Indian,
as a loyal subject of the Queen would have all the freedom and
the rights he ever had in the vast Empire that Her Majesty ruled.
But when the governor opened the legislature—all-white—he
had to say his sympathy lay with the whites; the Asiatics had to
go. And no sooner had the new government come to power than
a delegation was forthwith sent to India. If the Government of

---

[4] His Excellency the Hon. Sir Walter Francis Hely-Hutchinson, K.C.M.G.,
    Governor and Commander-in-Chief in and over the Colony of Natal,
    Vice-Admiral of the same and Supreme Chief over the Native Population.

India does not understand the game so much the worse for it. If it insisted that every Indian was a British subject, and as such welcome all over the Empire, then one could say this might be true and right elsewhere but not so in Natal. The Indian coolie must come and work on the plantations and after his five-year contract is over—or if he preferred to stay longer he could for another five years—he must get out. And if he insists on staying back in Natal, he must pay an annual poll tax of £25. If this is not understood by the Viceroy and the Government of India, then no Indian would ever be allowed to enter Natal and thus the problem would forever be resolved. But the Indian Government knew the exact situation. If Indian labour did not go to Natal, the prosperity of Natal would soon come to an end. Yet what no other colony—the Mauritius or the West Indies—had asked for, the governor of Natal would ask. What then was the proper way out? The British are great masters of compromise. They are pragmatic, human, and generally decent.

They agreed to a sort of residence-tax which each Indian would have to pay to remain in the colony. This would make him equal with the British all over the Empire but specifically differentiated only in Natal. Everybody was satisfied.

But now what about the franchise? Among the first bills to be introduced in the new legislature was one which said, 'no person who is of Indian, Asiatic or Polynesian descent or origin shall be entitled to be placed on a voters list or to vote at the election'. In the next session the government itself introduced the Franchise Amendment Bill. Sir John Robinson, the Prime Minister, was explicit on the nature of the Bill.

'He thought he might lay it down as an axiom that the franchise right was a race privilege . . . It was the most

precious inheritance of an emancipated race and the product
of civilisation among the Caucasian races, and especially the
Anglo-Saxon . . . The Asiatic . . . could not be considered
as an offshoot of the soil or an offspring of the races that
had undertaken the duty of colonising South Africa. The
men who had occupied and colonised South Africa were
determined to affix and impress upon South Africa in the
future the character and institutions of a Christian and
European civilisation. And if this continent were to be
properly reclaimed from barbarism . . . it would only be
through the recognition of these principles.'[5]

Actually, he went on to remark, discrimination and
Empire could go together and, in fact, went very well together.
Otherwise, imagine what might happen if having learnt the
powers of franchise here the Indians 'became propagandists of
agitation and instruments of sedition in that great country from
which they came.' After all—and rightly—the colonists argued,
if the Indian did not vote in his own country, why and how could
he vote in Natal? What an absurd argument, the opponents
remarked. For if this proposition held what would happen to
the Queen's proclamation, and the logic of the Empire?

Nobody had an answer. It was a historical situation which
only one step at a time could slowly clarify. For the moment the
whiteman was powerful, and he would rule. Let the Queen look
after the rest.

The most perplexing aspect of it all was no Indian seemed
to worry about the problem. There were however some white
people and some white newspapers in the colony of the Cape

---

[5]   *Natal Mercury*, 22 June 1894.

that seemed agitated about it. The whites, mostly British, in the Cape spoke against disenfranchisement. 'He (the Indian) may be objectionable in many ways,' wrote the *Herald*, 'so are many Europeans . . . but he is a British subject.'[6] However, with the Transvaal and the Orange Free State on their borders, and the Boers building a solid civilisation of their own, the British in Natal could not very well go native. The first reading of the Franchise Bill was passed quickly. The second reading was also hurried through. It was a pity, however, some felt that the Bill only talked of franchise for the legislature—it did not talk of municipal elections as well. 'A Ramasamy in or near town is all very well as a grower or purveyor of vegetables, . . . but he is an insanitary nuisance,' wrote the *Natal Witness*. 'We don't want him to make Town Councillors or be himself made such by the votes of his fellows.' And if he still wanted to stay on, we could build him his shanty areas where he could practise as he liked his own filthy habits. He is meek, it is true. He is law-abiding, it is true. An Indian had never been condemned by any court of law in all South Africa for any crime, or even of theft. This also is true. But he must stay out of the City of God the whiteman was building for himself. We will not meddle with his ways. Let him not interfere with our noble civilisation.

The third reading of the Franchise Amendment Bill was to be brought before the Natal Legislature on 27 June 1894 and, then, with the Royal Assent it would soon become law. Thus one of the thorniest problems of the Empire would once and forever be resolved. Long live the Queen!

And so an Indian agitation had to be launched. All the Indians in Durban had gathered that evening at the splendid

---

[6] Quoted by E.P., p. 409.

house of Dada Abdulla—the rich, the poor, the learned, and the ex-indentured coolie, the Hindu, the Muslim, the Parsi, the Christian, and it was august and happy as a marriage party—for the first time they had all met, and felt as one family. The poor clerk had never seen a boss's house and be received there as a guest. The Christian, the Muslim, and the Hindu were like one, and there was about it all a festive, active air. And just as at a wedding, everyone says, 'And, Elder Brother, what shall I do now?', and, 'Mother, what next for me to perform?', the whole community was asking what it could do for the occasion. One thing was certain. That very evening a telegram had to be sent to the Speaker of the Assembly, the Prime Minister, and the Governor: a petition is being presented to the House, therefore please stop the Third Reading of the Bill.[7] So it must all be done at once. Mohandas Gandhi started preparing the petition. It was one of the first important documents of Indian Independence. It did what every other Gandhian document tried to do later— it never accused the adversary of bad faith. Human differences are always a question of misunderstanding. If your adversary behaves as he behaves there must be reason for it, just as valid as the reason that makes you do what you do. Nobody is evil unless you can prove him so. And nobody, in fact, can be proven evil in terms of our limited understanding. So pray give him, always, the benefit of doubt. But state your case clearly and firmly. State your adversary's case also with understanding and goodwill, and you might see wonders happening. Who can know the will of God?

The petition that Gandhiji drew up first spoke about the accusation that Indians are semi-barbaric and uncivilised

---

[7]   The Royal Assent was only a matter of form.

hoarders. This, certainly, he argued, comes from ignorance. For any book of history, and there is no reason for the Boer or the Britisher in Africa to know it—any historical survey of India would tell you the great antiquity and richness of Indian civilisation.

You say having never exercised franchise Indians are not fit for the exercise of franchise here, in Natal. However, facts and history speak differently. 'The Indian nation has known,' writes Gandhiji, 'and has exercised the power of election from times prior to the time when the Anglo-Saxon races first became acquainted with the principles of representation.' If you so wish you have just to consult Sir Henry Maines's *Village Communities* which speaks of how India was 'familiar with representative institutions from times immemorial'. That learned writer has also shown 'that the Teutonic Mark was hardly so well organised or so essentially representative as an Indian village community until the precise technical Roman form was engrafted upon it.' Further, the petition went on to say, 'the word Panchayat is a household word in India, and it means, as the Hon'ble Members are well aware, a council of five elected by the class of people to whom the five belong for the purpose of managing and controlling the social affairs of the particular caste.' Further 'even today in the State of Mysore, in India, there is a representative parliament called the Mysore Assembly on the exact model of the British Parliament.' Even in British India there were (in 1891), Gandhi goes on to state, 755 Municipalities, 892 Local Boards with some 20,000 Indian members, etc., etc. And as to our moral integrity, Sir George Birdwood has said: 'The people of India are in no sense our inferiors, while in things measured by some of the false standards, false to ourselves, we pretend to believe in, they are our superiors.' But, above all, listen to what

Professor Max Mueller of Oxford has to say about the 'much abused and misunderstood Indian'.

'If I were asked under what sky the human mind has most fully developed some of its choicest gifts, has most deeply pondered on the greatest problems of life, and has found solution of some of them which well deserve the attention of even those who have studied Plato and Kant—I should point to India.'

Finally:

'Your Petitioners have purposely let the English authorities speak on their behalf without any comments to amplify the above extracts. It is yet possible to multiply such extracts, but your Petitioners confidently trust that the above will prove sufficient to convince your Honourable Assembly to reconsider your decision; or to appoint a Commission to inquire into the question whether the Indian residents in the colony are fit to exercise the privilege of franchise before proceeding further with the Bill.

'And for this act of justice and mercy, your Petitioners, as in duty bound shall for ever pray, etc. etc.'[8]

The text was copied out by a court copyist, in bold, clear characters, and four copies made of it, one of which was to go to the press. The rich and the poor then separated, and each went his way on foot or in their own carriage, and when necessary fares were paid for those who had to go far, and the petition carried overnight five hundred signatures. The Bill having been

---

[8]   C.W., Vol. I, p. 92-96.

delayed by the Speaker by one day, when the petition was going to be presented to the House, the visitors' gallery was 'for the first time in the memory of man . . . invaded by Arab and Hindu clothed head and foot'. So much so indeed when daintily dressed European ladies came to occupy their seats, all the front seats being taken up by the Indians, they had to retire humiliated. It was now a question of pure sedition as everyone could see. The Bill, however, was briefly debated and passed by the Assembly. And now it went up to the Legislative Council.

But by now the ideas had caught fire. Yes, indubitably Indians are British subjects, and they would get the best and most civilised treatment from the people and the Government of Natal. Yet to imagine they could share power with the whites, that is altogether a different matter. In fact, it was absurd. Of course if all Indians were as educated as Mr. Gandhi the problem would be quite another, but they are not. And that definitely settles the issue.

Gandhiji was not to be dismayed with such finalities. He was ever ready to appeal to the higher traits of human reason. It was easier, he wrote to the *Natal Mercury*, to create dissension and show how different we are. May it not be a nobler thing to show how as subjects of Her Britannic Majesty we should bring all the people of the Queen closer together.

Meanwhile, the Indian papers that had received copies of the petition started commenting. The *Times of Natal* got angry with the *Times of India*. It was 'mendacious rubbish', to say Indians are ill-treated in Natal, it wrote in an article called 'Ramasamy'. 'Every black man in the colony,' it declared, 'receives the justice and protection extended to the white man, and we see nothing more the black man can expect.'[9]

---

[9] E.P., p. 424.

Gandhi here intervened and said both the African and the Indian should have the same rights. 'Indians would regret it if it were otherwise.' Anyway, what had dark skin to do with the franchise?

'You would look to the exterior only . . . So long as the skin is white, it would not matter to you whether it conceals beneath it poison or nectar. To you the lip prayer of the Pharisee is more acceptable than the sincere repentance of the publican. And this I presume you call Christianity. You may, it is not Christ's.

If He came among us will He not say to many of us I know you not? . . . Will you ponder over your attitude towards the coloured population of the Colony? Will you then say you can reconcile it with the Bible teaching or the best British traditions? I can have nothing to say . . . Only it will be a bad day for Britain and for India if you have many followers.'[10]

The *Times of Natal* would not permit Christianity to be quoted back to the Christians. The correspondence was therefore closed.

Now he would move British public opinion. It was, in its time, not only the best informed but the most vigilant in all the world. There was always an eccentric Englishman, a Burke for America, a Burke for Greece, a Bradlaugh for India, who would fight for a cause and be heard. And hearing it again and again it would become a great cause not only to fight for but to die for. One such Englishman was Allan Octavio Hume. A former servant of the Crown in India, he knew India well and loved it much.

---

[10] The *Times of Natal,* 26 October 1894.

He knew British rule in that great land—he knew and many others like him, William Digby and Sir William Wedderburn, all civil servants, knew—was often un-English. And at that time there was also an enlightened English Viceroy, Lord Dufferin, who decided that Indian opinion had to be heard first because it was right that it should be known, and further, if unknown, it might ultimately create an overpowering situation—hence Indian opinion had to be organised and allowed to express itself. Who but the British could foster such public spirit? Since the Mutiny (1857), however, there were voices—Indian voices—that were learned and angry. Someday it would explode. Actually, unimpeachable evidence had proved a revolutionary situation developing to which, in answer, 'Russian methods of police repression arising.' The countryside impoverished by famine and over-taxation was stirred by 'vague dreams of violence, even revolutionary change'. Thus something had to be done, and forthwith. And it was under these circumstances that the Indian National Congress was founded—it was founded by A. O. Hume with the tacit approval of the Viceroy. It first met at Bombay (28 December 1885) with W. C. Bannerjee[11] in the chair. Elegant and most noble speeches were made by the Indians and the British and after expressing their deep loyalty to the Queen they mentioned their grievances in their petitions; may it please Her Majesty's Government, etc. The Congress was held again the next year in Calcutta under Dadabhai Naoroji and the year after in Madras under Badruddin Tyabji, and each year it carried its own momentum. By 1888 it had not only become an impressive organisation heard with respect by the British (and with dismay by the more die-hard elements of

---

[11] Eminent Indian (Christian) lawyer from Bengal.

the Empire, and hence of Kipling and all that)—but a sister organisation was soon set up in London and its members were Sir William Wedderburn (Chairman), Dadabhai Naoroji, W. S. Caine, M.P., W.S. Bright, McLean, M.P., W. Digby (Secretary).

Dadabhai Naoroji,[12] called the Grand Old Man of India, was perhaps the most eminent Indian politician of his time. A businessman in private, he represented Central Finsbury, a district of London, in the British House of Commons. It is said that when Disraeli remarked he was surprised to see this black man in the great Mother of Parliaments, Dadabhai Naoroji answered back: 'If the Honourable Minister could look at his own face in the mirror and then look back at mine.' For, it so happened, that being a Parsi, Dadabhai was fairer than the English Jew.

A man of great learning and of immaculate, almost religious, integrity, Dadabhai roused public opinion for India in Great Britain, and later all over Europe. He also brought the Indian issue from the political to the cultural fold, for to talk sense of India one has perforce to talk of culture. He spoke of the great past of India and begged the English people who were ultimately responsible for the welfare of India not to be misled by the newspapers which represented only vested interests. Spirited but humble, he never said an unkind word to anybody. He revealed his truth by his own life. When Mohandas Gandhi was a student in London he was so awed (at Indian public meetings) by the presence of the great man, he sat and listened to Dadabhai overwhelmed with emotion but never said a word to the eminent Indian leader, though he had carried a letter of introduction to Dadabhai from India. What a man, and how

---

[12] 1825-1917.

proud that he belongs to India. He would, would Dadabhai, fight with us when the fight came.[13]

So now that the fight had come, Gandhiji wrote to him from Durban, 5 July 1894.

'I am yet inexperienced and young, and therefore quite liable to make mistakes. The responsibility undertaken is quite beyond my ability. I may mention that I am doing this without any remuneration. So you will see that I have not taken the matter up, which is beyond my ability, in order to enrich myself at the expense of the Indians. I am the only available person who can handle the question. You will therefore oblige me very greatly if you will kindly direct and guide me and make necessary suggestions which shall be received as from a father to his child.'[14]

And now that the Third Reading of the Bill was passed by the Natal Legislative Assembly, Gandhiji again wrote to Dadabhai Naoroji (14 July 1894). Only the British Government could now stop it from becoming law. To this end a petition had to be sent to the Home Government. Ten thousand signatures of Indians were being gathered—Indians went from house to house, from village to village, travelled by cart or train or on foot. Thus almost every Indian was met personally, the implications of the petition fully explained to him and only then was the signature asked for. No one would accept or should accept a hastily given approval. This would be untruthful.

---

[13] Compare Lenin's admiration for Plekhanov which was 'respect, reverence, infatuation'.
[14] C.W., Vol. l, p. 106.

The petition said those Indians who were already on the voter's list were about one Indian to every thirty-eight Europeans—the Indian could therefore hardly threaten the white supremacy in the colony. Besides, the property requisites were beyond the competence of most Indians at that time, and would thus be so for a long time to come.

Further, you will not do this to the Indians who had by their labour brought prosperity to the colony. How could one be so ungrateful?

The petition was submitted to the Governor, and through him to the Colonial Secretary in London. The petition was now also printed (a thousand copies) and sent all over the world. Let everyone see what was happening in Africa. Both the *Times* of London and the *Times of India* (Bombay) agreed with the cause. 'They want to put Indians,' wrote Gandhiji to Dadabhai, 'under such disabilities and subject them to such insults it may not be worth their while to step in the colony. Yet they would not want to dispense with Indians altogether . . . they want indentured Indians very badly; but they would require, if they could, the indentured Indian to return to India after his term of indenture. A perfectly leonine partnership!'[15]

A memorandum was also sent to Lord Ripon, Her Majesty's Secretary of State for the colonies. So now that things had begun moving appropriately, Gandhi felt he could start thinking of going home. He must now go back to Kasturba. After all, he had promised to stay about a year. And that period was almost over now. But the Indians feeling 'a taste of combat, would not hear of it'.

'You yourself told us,' they argued, 'that the Franchise Amendment Bill was only the first step towards our ultimate

---

[15] Letter of 27 July 1894.

extinction. Who knows whether the Colonial Secretary will return a favourable reply to our Memorial? You have witnessed our enthusiasm. We are willing and ready to work. We have funds too. But for want of a guide, what little that has been done will go for nothing. We think it is your duty to stay on.'[16]

Yes, he would, if needed. But how to stay on? On what was he going to live? 'My work would be mainly to make you all work. And could I charge you for that?' Further, if they paid for his stay and he would have to, sometimes, tell them unpleasant things—and truth as you know, can be unpleasant—what becomes of him then? No, if he stayed it would have to be as a professional man. If they could offer him legal work and give him retainers—and he would, according to his estimates, need 300 pounds a year—he would stay. Twenty Indian merchants gladly and forthwith accepted him as their legal adviser, and Dada Abdulla, the eldest among them having discovered a house, had it decently furnished.[17] 'Thus I settled in Natal.'

* * *

But what is Gandhism? It is not a creed; it is a perspective on life (*darshana*). Its first attribute is a love for facts, a search for the precise. In human actions every gesture is an attempt to go towards reality, reality in facts, to the reality beyond facts. Through the manifested to the non-manifested, that's the great path of man. Then, again, if this be so, there are as many paths as there are men—that is to say each man looks at his problem

---

[16] S.S.A., p. 44.
[17] From the money he was going to give Gandhi as 'purse' at the moment of departure.

from his own station, his facts. Hence one must always be ready, at all moments, to try and understand the facts, and, therefore, the perspectives of others. These are as important as your own. And sometimes you may think your fellowman does not face facts—but there's always a chink by which the truth speaks. Seek out that little emergence of truth and seek it back to its source. Thus you can always try and convince him of his own truth. For example, when the Third Reading of the Bill was taking place, the Premier, Sir John Robinson, said all Indians are not illiterate, dirty, and irresponsible—there are some who are eminently educated, men of integrity and highly civilised. Gandhiji immediately took up this thread and said how the statement 'breathed honest sentiments of justice, morality, and what is more, Christianity'. And, he went on, 'if only we could settle all matters in this manner we would never despair of right being done in every case.' Later he remarked, as if it were an aside, 'However, we beg to point out that both the Anglo-Saxon and the Indian races belong to the same stock.' Then he added, lest it should sound just a boast, that scholars like Max Mueller, Morris, Greene, 'and a host of other writers with one voice seem to show very clearly that both the races have sprung from the same Aryan stock, or rather the Indo-European as many call it. We have no wish whatsoever to thrust ourselves as a brother nation on a nation that would be unwilling to receive us as such, but we may be pardoned if we state real facts.'

And again, since in human affairs there are bound to be so many points of view, be ever ready to compromise not on a principle, but on details. For example, later when he was to join the Bar at Durban (which he did), the Judge of the Supreme Court asked him to remove the turban on his head. It was contrary to the rules of the Natal Bar. Once before, in Durban itself, he had refused to do so on principle. He did not belong then to the Natal Bar, he was only a visitor. But a year later things were different. One must respect, when one is going to live in a country, its ways, its laws, and now as he was going to live in Natal, at least for some time, he must respect the laws and customs of the country. 'In Rome do as Romans do,' he quoted to himself. His friends including Dada Abdulla were not very pleased with this concession made. But Gandhiji was convinced he was right. And so here again another point of Gandhism was made clear. 'I pacified the friends somewhat,' he wrote in his autobiography, 'with these and similar arguments but I do not think I convinced them completely, in this instance, of the applicability of the principle of looking at a thing from a different stand-point in different circumstances. But all my life through the very insistence on truth has taught me the beauty of compromise . . . It has often meant endangering my life and incurring the displeasure of friends. But truth is hard as adamant and tender as a blossom.'[18]

* * *

And now to work. And Kasturba and the fierce longings for her, those would have to withdraw and wait.

A few days after he decided to stay back in Natal, a meeting was called of the Indian community. If you want to do anything in politics you must have an organisation, 'a public organisation of a permanent character'.

Dada Abdulla's immense room was 'packed to the full on that day'. What was the organisation going to be called? Of

[18]   A., p. 184.

course, it must have the word Congress as part of its name. The Congress had already become a symbol of freedom in India: 'I was a Congress devotee.' The conservatives in England and elsewhere may think it smelt bad.

> 'It savoured of cowardice to hesitate to adopt that name. Therefore with full explanation of my reasons I recommended the organisation should be called the Natal Indian Congress and on the 22nd of August 1894, the Natal Indian Congress came into being.'

It had to be able to work well and be effective, have highly demanding conditions for membership. Five shillings a month was to be paid by every one, and those who could pay more should give more. Gandhiji subscribed himself for one pound a month. 'This was for me no small amount.' A large number of others subscribed according to their capacity and became members. And next, what were the aims of the Congress?

1. To bring about a better understanding and to promote friendliness between Europeans and Indians residing in the Colony.
2. To spread information about India and the Indians by writing to newspapers, publishing pamphlets, lecturing, etc.
3. To educate Indians, especially the colonial-born Indians, about Indian history and induce them to study Indian subjects.
4. To ascertain the various grievances the Indians were labouring under and to agitate by resorting to all constitutional methods for removing them.
5. To enquire into the conditions of the indentured Indians and to help them out of special hardships.

6. To help the poor and needy in all reasonable ways, and
7. Generally to do everything that would tend to put Indians on better footing morally, socially, intellectually, and politically.

The Congress was not only born. It was going to work. It already had three hundred members, Muslims, Hindus, Parsis, and Natal-born Christians. And from its very foundation it was run on very severe discipline. If you did not attend six meetings consecutively, you were not a member any more. You could not come late either. 'Late comers had to pay a fine of five shillings for each offence.'[19] And nobody was allowed to smoke at the committee meetings. Further, 'every member shall use Mr. in addressing one another at a committee meeting'. Questions were asked freely at these gatherings and anybody could rise and say anything he wanted. People who had never learnt to speak in public became accustomed to share their experiences with others. Non-Indians also could become members. 'The Hon. Secretary,' so ran one of the rules of the Congress 'shall if he chooses invite a European who takes interest in the welfare of the Congress to be a Vice-President.'

And to make the Congress known all over Natal and for gathering membership, volunteers were asked to go from door to door, explain the nature of the new organisation, and to collect the subscription. Even the rich merchants started canvassing for membership. Gandhi himself thus came into contact with Indians all over the colony. There's a beautiful story told how

---

[19] The same severe fines were imposed by Trotsky in the early days of the Russian Revolution on chronic late-comers, and the Russians seemed not a whit inferior to the Indians in this respect.

one Indian who was to have paid £6 refused to give it when Gandhi and some others came to see him. The day became night, and yet the man would not pay. He would only give £3. So there was only one solution to the problem. Be patient and try to convince him of the wrong he was doing. 'If we had accepted that amount from him, others would have followed suit, and our collections would have been spoiled.' Gandhiji and his companions were hungry. But they would not leave. Other Indian merchants came to persuade the wrong-doing merchant. But he would hear no one. They spent all of the night hungry and patient. 'Most of my co-workers were burning with rage,' continued Gandhiji, 'but they contained themselves. At last when the day was already breaking the host yielded, paid down 6 pounds and feasted us. This happened at Tongaat but the repercussion of the incident was felt as afar as Stanger on the North Coast and Charlestown in the interior. It also hastened our work of collection.'

'But collecting funds was not the only thing to do. In fact I had long learnt the principle of never having more money at one's disposal than necessary.'

And every penny was to be accounted for. In fact, there is a famous anecdote of a six pence that was missing in the annual budgeting. How did these extra six pence come into our coffers? Gandhi had no sleep the whole night through. Finally the cause was discovered. The discrepancy came because 'one member had paid two-and-six once and three at another time. The 3/- could not well be represented on the list . . . Without properly kept accounts it is impossible to maintain Truth in its pristine purity.'

The most important object of the Congress was not merely to educate the Indians with regard to outward activities but to

make them think, to make them understand each other and all.
And you can only understand others if you understand yourself
first. Hence, 'attempts were always made to draw attention
to their own shortcomings. Whatever force there was in the
arguments of the Europeans was duly acknowledged. Every
occasion, when it was possible to cooperate with the Europeans
on terms of equality and consistent with self-respect, was heartily
availed of.'[20]

Thus win the hearts of the adversary—one of the principal
propositions of the Gandhian law.

Meanwhile, Gandhiji having enrolled himself as a barrister,
not only did he fight for the merchants but even more so for
the common Indian who had everything to lose. Of course in
such cases he would accept no payment for his legal services. For
the laws of Natal were strange; no coolie should ever be found
on any public highway without a proper pass. This pass should
be given to him by his employer otherwise the coolie would
go straight to jail. And some coolies spent years in jail because
they did not want to go back to their harsh masters. Some even
hanged themselves while in prison. Even were you not a 'coolie'
but a 'free' Indian, you should have a pass, especially after nine
o'clock at night. These passes had to be issued by the proper
government authority. And little by little funny little incidents
came into one's knowledge, which either the press reported or
the Indians themselves came to complain of, and each case was
a story all by itself. For example, two Indians excellently dressed
and speaking 'faultless English'—and so of no suspicion ever
to be taken for a coolie—were one night coming home slightly
after nine from a party. They were immediately molested and

---

[20] S.S.A., p. 48.

arrested by a policeman under the Vagrant Law and thrown into custody. They had no passes. One was a school master and the other a civil servant. One of them was called Samuel Richards and the other John Lutchman Roberts, both of them sons of Indian indentured labourers and both lately converted to Christianity. Hence their names.

Superintendent of Police: How long have you had that name?

Defendant: Eighteen months. Since I was converted.

Superintendent of Police: What were your parents?

Defendant: Indentured Indians; father's a dhobi.

Superintendent: Since your family name was not good enough for you, did you inform the police that you had taken an English name that would excuse you from Indian laws?

Defendant: No.

Superintendent (to the other man, Roberts): Who were your parents?

Defendant: Indentured Indians.

Superintendent: Why should a constable pass you anymore than your parents?

Defendant: My face is sufficient.[21]

The Magistrate dismissed the case. And this made a great impression on local public opinion. The *Natal Advertiser* said it was 'a departure in the administration of law as applied to Indians'. It was a 'test case' said the *Natal Mercury* a government organ. 'Everyone will admit this law presses harshly on many people.'

Gandhi defended the two young men before the courts (of course he would never charge a fee) and also wrote a letter to the *Natal Mercury* explaining the case and its implications.

---

[21] *Natal Mercury*, 29 January 1896.

'I humbly think theirs was a very hard case and the police erred in arresting them and afterwards in harassing them. I said in the court, and I repeat, that the Vagrant Law would cease to be oppressive if the police showed some consideration for the Indians and used discretion in arresting them. The fact that both are sons of indentured Indians should not go against them, especially in an English community, where a man's worth, not birth, is taken into account in judging him. If that were not so a butcher's son should not have been honoured as the greatest poet . . .

'The Magistrate (in regard to the first defendant) made no order, but he, in his fatherly and kind manner, suggested that I should advise him to get the Mayor's pass. I submitted that such was not necessary but said in deference to his suggestion I would do so.'[22]

The Superintendent naturally came to the rescue of his constables. He wrote to the same paper and showed how difficult was the task. Gandhi admitted anybody could make a mistake: 'Whether a man is an honest Christian or a Satan . . . in Christian garb.' And he went on. 'I appeal to him and entreat him to consider well whether he himself would have arrested these two boys. I say in his own words: 'If his whole force were as considerate and amiable as himself there would be no difficulty'.'

Superintendent Alexander, for that was his name, and Gandhi ultimately became very good friends. And also Superintendent Alexander became his staunch supporter 'and one of the best friends of the Indian community'.[23]

---

[22] C.W., Vol. I, p. 295.
[23] E.P., p. 455.

For example there's another story, the story of Mrs. Vinden—an Indian school mistress in Ladysmith (wife to Mr. David Vinden, a clerk at the court) who, when she was returning home one night, was mishandled and beaten by a Kaffir policeman. Her only offence was she had, as a coloured person, no pass on her. And when she arrived at the police station a policeman threw her with such violence into the prison that she lost consciousness. When discovered by the white officer on duty and taken home still in an unconscious state, much was the ire of the community—an innocent and educated woman, going her way—was this human, civilised? But what could one do. Of course, the case was brought up before the courts.

Q. (addressed to William Macdonald, Chief Constable): Did you take any steps to ascertain whether these policemen who made arrests had behaved in a proper manner?

A.: Nothing beyond asking them if they had done so.

Q.: Did you report Vinden to the Government as you threatened?

A.: No, not yet.

Q.: I suppose if he loses this case there will be no need to do so.

A.: I don't know so much about that.

Sir Walter Wragg: Did you tell your constable the arrest was a mistake?

A.: I did not tell them then but I have told them since.

Sir Walter Wragg: We have been in the habit of arresting Indians and natives for being out after hours.

Q.: Do you arrest Arabs?

A.: No.

Q.: Why?

A.: There seems to be an understanding in the Colony not to arrest them.

Q.: An Arab is a person of colour—why do you not arrest him?

A.: For the same reason that we do not arrest Vinden.

Q.: Why?

A.: I do not consider he is a coolie.

Sir Walter: Coolie has nothing to do with colour. Why is not an Arab arrested?

Witness: Because I don't think he comes within that meaning of the law.

Q.: Why?

A.: I will leave that to your Lordship to decide . . . (Laughter).

Mr. Justice Mason: I suppose you don't deal with people of recognised positions, and whom you know, even although they are of colour?

Witness: No.

Sir Walter Wragg: Then it is the position and not the colour?

The Chief Justice was severe in his strictures against the authorities. An innocent person of 'superior status and blameless character whose identity was not in doubt' to be treated thus was a behaviour 'unjust, harsh, and tyrannical'. And he went on to add: 'She suffered indignity, she suffered pain, and she suffered agony.' That Mrs. Vinden should be called a 'coolie' was 'as monstrous a misuse of the word as to call an Englishman a Frenchman'. And since a European in Maritzburg for the same sort of offence was awarded twenty pounds by the court, the judge thought Mrs. Vinden 'could not complain if she was put on the same footing as white person'.

Thus 'colour' began to take on a new legal definition, which as the *Natal Witness* added, 'will not pass unnoticed by Mr. Gandhi'.

The Africans now felt they too could challenge the authorities. 'Superintendent Alexander,' wrote Mr. Nyovgwanna in the *Natal Witness*, 'and others will in the future learn that the fact of being a coloured person is not in itself sufficient cause for punishing a person. Justice Wragg in a previous case against a native had said, 'a tiger cannot change his spots'. And now it looks as if His Lordship has changed his mind. If one could change Mrs. Vinden's colour then surely he will admit there can be a law to change Mr. Lutuli's colour?'[24]

Again, Gandhi loved the law. If he were faithful to the facts, the facts would be faithful to the law. The law never went wrong—if one judge misinterpreted the law another would correct the mistake, and if he in return misinterpreted his texts then there would always be someone, be it the public, that will set matters right. We should do our duty anyway, and the rest is not in our hands. In his public career, as in his professional activity, he took great pains to study the case, understand the legal points with honesty and precision and only then would he present his arguments. For example, there was, sometime earlier, that case before the Durban court about an intestate inheritance. The Chief Justice had asked Gandhiji to 'frame a plea of distribution according to Mohammedan Laws'. Mohammedan Law differed in this matter, both from the common law and the Hindu Law. The point was, in Islam the gift to the poor had always had a very special legal status. Once this is misunderstood all division of property became difficult, if not impossible—the gift being a religious part of the whole, therefore the most important part. But it never is entitled 'to any part of an intestate estate'.[25] This

[24] E.P., p. 456-458.
[25] C.W., Vol. I, p. 171.

point did not come easily into the comprehension of the British judges; truly to say they often misunderstood it. But Gandhiji had not only thoroughly studied the Mohammedan Law—he had read the *Koran* as well to be sure of his position. And he also spoke to Muslim divines about certain interpretations of the doctrine and the law. The judge—and after all it is human to make a mistake—thought Gandhi's point of view was erroneous; being a Hindu he could not know Muslim Law. 'He is,' said the judge, 'as great a stranger to the Mohammedan Law as a Frenchman. For what he has stated he would have to go to a book as you would; of his own knowledge he knows nothing.'

Mr. Tatham pleaded for the successors.

Mr. Tatham: The question is whether we shall take Mr. Gandhi's view or the priests'.

Sir Walter Wragg: The priests'.

It was according to Gandhi not merely a point of law but something that was to affect the whole of the Muslim population in terms of inheritance. Quoting the *Koran*, Gandhiji showed how inaccurate the judgement had been.

'But the report says', he wrote later to the *Natal Witness*, 'that the priest and I differ. If you eliminate the 'I' and put 'the law' instead (for I simply said what the law was) I would venture to say the priest and the law should never differ, and if they do so it is the priest and not the law that goes to the wall.'

Gandhiji thus did not argue for himself. He argued for the law. Who was ever going to go wrong then?

'It seems to be a fashion . . .' wrote a commentator in the *Natal Mercury*, 'to sit on Mr. Gandhi himself. I should like even at this late hour to raise my feeble protest against the rather 'hoity-toity' remarks indulged in by the judge in a recent case to the effect that Mr. Gandhi knew nothing of Mohammedan

Law, that whatever knowledge he might have of it he would have obtained from books, and that of his own knowledge he knew nothing . . . I fancy if the learned judge were stripped of all knowledge, he had got from books he would appear legally and intellectually rather naked. Then why should not a Frenchman know Mohammedan Law, and why should not Mr. Gandhi and why should the learned Judge? Whence does he himself derive his knowledge of the law which is sufficient to enable him to deliver his *ipse dixit* upon a matter whereon he seems to think nobody but a Mohammedan can give an opinion. Is it from the derived source or does it spring from his 'own knowledge'?'

Thus was Gandhiji defended by the press again and again. In due course the press got involved each time there was a conflict between the Indian community and the whites. A few shops would suddenly be burned down by an angry white mob or some angry European would take a shot at an unknown Indian, and Gandhiji was always there in defence of the victim. Scrupulous with his facts, and always erring on the side of kindness rather than of accusation, he received the sympathy of both the press and the public. For example, in a legal matter—a matter involving insolvency—Mr. Tatham was the adversary. Mr. Tatham lost the case and he laughed and made all the court laugh with the remark: 'Gandhi is supreme . . . The triumph of black over white again!'

* * *

Now it was time to address the whole white community. He sat and wrote his famous 'Open Letter'. It was addressed to the members of both the Legislative Council and the Legislative Assembly of Natal. The 'Open Letter' became perhaps the first

manifesto of nationalist India. Indians were going to repeat it
again and again for the next fifty years or more so that every
school boy would know to say—of course we're poor but
we're ancient, of course you may, you white people, rule us
today but remember what you owe to us—in fact who we are.
From Megasthenes and Strabo among the ancients to Goethe
to Schopenhauer and Victor Hugo, we put our quotations on
placards and we would walk through contemporary history
shouting: *Vande Mataram*, Victory to the Mother. Don't you
please judge us by the coolie, Indians went on saying—of course
he's illiterate, of course he may not know how to read and write,
but don't you lift your finger at us, and pray, remember what
were you yourself five-hundred years ago, a thousand years ago?
But let us see what's writ on our placard. The great (English)
historian, Sir William Hunter hath said:

'This nobler race (meaning the early Aryans) belonged to the
Aryan or Indo-Germanic stock from which the Brahman,
the Rajput, and the Englishman alike descended. Its earliest
home visible to history was in Central Asia. From that
camping ground certain branches of the race started to the
East, others for the West. One of the Western offshoots
founded the Persian Kingdom; and another built Athens and
Lacedaemon, and became the Hellenic nation; a third went
to Italy and reared the city on the seven hills which grew into
Imperial Rome . . . And when we first catch a sight of ancient
England we see an Aryan settlement, fishing in wattle canoes
and working the tin mines of Cornwall.

'The forefathers of the Greek and the Roman, of the
Englishman and the Hindoo, dwelt together in Asia, spoke
the same tongue, and worshipped the same gods.

'The ancient religions of Europe and India had a similar origin.'

And Gandhi added to this the following remark:

'If I then err, I err in good company. And the belief, whether mistaken or well-founded, serves as a basis of operation of those who are trying to unify the hearts of the two races which are legally and outwardly bound together under a common flag.'[26]

And Gandhiji goes on:

'As to the Indian philosophy and religion, the learned author of the *Indian Empire* thus sums up: The Brahman solutions to the problems of practical religion were self-discipline, alms, sacrifice to and contemplation of the Deity. But, besides the practical questions of spiritual life, religion also has intellectual problems, such as the compatibility of evil with the goodness of God, and the unequal distribution of happiness and misery in this life. Brahman philosophy has exhausted the possible solutions of these difficulties, and most of the other great problems which have perplexed the Greek and Roman sage, medieval, and *modern man of science* (the italics are the author's). The various hypothesis of creation, arrangement and development were each elaborated, and the *views of physiologists at the present day are a return with new lights to the evolution theory of Kapila* (the italics are again the author's). The works on religion published in the native languages in India in 1877 numbered 1,192, besides 56

---

[26] C.W., Vol. I, p. 149-150.

on mental and moral philosophy. In 1882 the totals had risen to 1,545 on religion and 153 on mental and moral philosophy.'[27]

And now, of course, Max Mueller's famous statement has to be repeated:[28]

'If I were asked under what sky the human mind has most fully developed some of its choicest gifts, has deeply pondered on the greatest problems of life, and has found solutions for some of them which well deserve the attention even of those who have studied Plato and Kant—I should point to India; and if I were to ask myself from what literature we here in Europe, we who have been nurtured exclusively on the thoughts of Greek and Romans, and of one Semitic race, the Jewish, may draw that corrective which is most wanted in order to make our life more perfect, more comprehensive, more universal, in fact more truly human—a life not for this life only, but a transfigured and eternal life—again I should point to India!'

Now look again at what the great German philosopher, Schopenhauer has to say about the grandeur of our philosophy, especially of the Upanishads:

'From every sentence deep, original and sublime thoughts arise, and the whole is pervaded by a high and holy and earnest spirit. Indian air surrounds us . . . and original thoughts of kindred spirits. In the whole world there is no study, except that of the originals, so beneficial and so elevating as that of

---

[27] William Hunter, *Indian Empire*.
[28] Max Mueller happened to be not only the greatest Orientalist of his age, but was also a trusted friend of the Queen and of the Prince Consort.

the Oupnekaat.[29] It has been the solace of my life; it will be
the solace of my death.'

But let us go back to Sir William Hunter for a moment:

'The science of language indeed had been reduced in India
to fundamental principles at a time when the grammarians
of the West still treated it on the basis of accidental
resemblances, and modern philology dates from the study of
Sanskrit by European scholars . . . The grammar of Panini
stands supreme among the grammars of the world . . . It . . .
stands forth as one of the most splendid achievements of
human invention and industry.'

Besides Sir H.S. Maine, in his Rede Lectures, has lately declared:

'India has given to the world Comparative Philology and
Comparative Mythology . . . For India . . . includes a whole
world of Aryan institutions, Aryan customs, Aryan laws,
Aryan ideas, Aryan beliefs, in a far earlier stage and growth
than any that survive beyond its borders.'

Says Sir William Hunter:

'In certain points (of astronomy) the Brahmans advanced
beyond Greek astronomy . . . Their fame spread throughout
the West and found entrance into the *Chronicon Paschale*.
In the eighth and ninth centuries the Arabs became their
disciples . . .'

---

[29] The Upanishads.

Further, Sir William Hunter goes on to speak of the way
Indian medicine 'had made progress' before 350 BC:

'Arabic medicine was founded on the translations from
the Sanskrit treatises . . . European medicine down to the
seventeenth century was based upon the Arabic . . . The
Brahmans regarded not only medicine but also the arts of
war, music and architecture as supplementary parts of their
divinely inspired knowledge . . . The Sanskrit epics prove that
strategy had attained to the position of a recognised science
before the birth of Christ . . . The Indian art of music was
destined to a wider influence . . . This notation passed from
the Brahmans through the Persians to Arabia and thence
introduced into European music by Guido d'Arezzo at the
beginning of the eleventh century.'

And what about architecture and arts?

'It seems not improbable that the churches of Europe owe
their steeples to the Buddhist topes . . . Hindu art has left
memorials which exhort admiration and astonishment of our
age . . . English decorative art in our day has borrowed largely
from Indian forms and patterns . . . Indian art works, when
faithful to native designs, still obtain the highest honours at
the international exhibitions of Europe.'

Coming to architecture, even Andrew Carnegie was dragged
in to prove the greatness of India's achievements.

'There are some subjects too sacred for analysis, or even
for words. And I now know there is a human structure

so exquisitely fine or unearthly as to lift it into this holy domain . . . Till the day I die, amid mountain streams or moonlit strolls in the forest, wherever and whenever the mood comes when all that is most sacred and most elevated and most pure recur to shed their radiance upon the tranquil mind, there will be found among my treasures the memory of that lovely charm—the Taj.'

What about our literature, our drama? Who else but Goethe could have said of *Shakuntala*, our most famous play:

'Wouldst thou the young year's blossoms
and the fruits of its decline.
    'And all by which the soul is charmed, enraptured, feasted, fed, Wouldst thou the earth the heaven itself in one sole name combine.
    I name thee, O Shakuntala! and all at once is said.'

But let us go back for a brief moment to Megasthenes and what he had to say about the Indian in terms of character and social life. (Once again from Sir William Hunter, and his *Indian Empire.*)

'The Greek Ambassador (Megasthenes) observed with admiration the absence of slavery in India and the chastity of the women and the courage of the men. In valour they excelled all other Asiatics; they required no locks on their doors; above all, no Indian was ever known to tell a lie.'

But why talk only of the past. Sir George Birdwood says of contemporary India:

'They are long-suffering and patient, hardy and enduring, frugal and industrious, law-abiding and peace-seeking . . . The educated and higher mercantile classes are honest and truthful and loyal and trustful toward the British Government, in the most absolute sense that I can use, and you understand the words. Moral truthfulness is as marked a characteristic of the Settia (upper) class of Bombay as of the Teutonic race itself. The people of India, in short, are in no intrinsic sense our inferiors, while in things measured by some of the false standards—false to ourselves—we pretend to believe in, they are our superiors.'

And let us not forget Bishop Heber either. Speaking of the people of India he says:

'They are men of high and gallant courage, courteous, intelligent, and most eager after knowledge and improvement . . . They are sober, industrious, dutiful to their parents, and affectionate to their children; of tempers almost uniformly gentle and patient, and more easily affected by kindness and attention to their wants and feelings than any man whom I have met with.'

There's always a Frenchman who'll go ecstatic over some culture. Here's certain Louis Jacolliot and his paean:

'Soil of ancient India, cradle of humanity! Hail! Hail! venerable and efficient nurse, whom centuries of brutal invasions have not yet buried under the dust of oblivion. Hail, fatherland of faith, of love, of poetry, and of science. May we hail a revival of thy past in our Western future.'

Thus Gandhiji showed through documents to the Boer and the Briton India's certificates of the past and the present. But one could rightly object, what about the Indians one sees in Natal, in South Africa, the coolie, the merchant? 'If what you say is true, then the people whom you call Indians in the colony are not Indians. See how grossly untruthful they are!' And here we reach what came to be one of the infallible tenets of Gandhism: To admit a fact when true. Never base success on a lie. For truth always wins—in its own good time.

'To a limited extent,' said Gandhiji, 'I admit the charge . . . Much as I would wish them to be otherwise, I confess my utter inability to prove that they are more than human. They come to Natal on starvation wages (I mean here the indentured Indians). They find themselves placed in a strange position and amid uncongenial surroundings. The moment they leave India they remain throughout life, if they settle in the colony, without any moral education. Whether they are Hindus or Mohammedans, they are absolutely without any moral or religious instruction worthy of the name. They have not learnt enough to educate themselves. Placed thus they are apt to yield to the slightest temptation to lie. After some time lying becomes a habit and a disease. They would lie without any reason, without knowing what they are doing. They reach a stage in life when their moral faculties have completely collapsed owing to neglect . . . They cannot dare tell the truth, even for their wantonly ill-treated brother, for fear of receiving ill-treatment from their master. They are not philosophic enough to look with equanimity on the threatened reduction in their miserable rations and severe corporal punishment, did they dare to give evidence before their master. Are these men then more to be despised than pitied? Is there any class who would not do what they are doing under similar circumstances?[30]

'But,' he continued:

'I will be asked what can I have to say in defence of the traders who too are equally good liars. As to this I beg to submit that the charge against them is without foundation, and that they do not lie more than the other classes do for the purposes of trade or law. In fact the reason for such a conclusion is that very few Indian traders speak English, and thus the great causes of misunderstanding—adding colour to other differences and misunderstandings.'

And he asks:

'Is their present treatment of the Indian in accordance with the best British traditions, or with the principles of justice and morality, or with the principles of Christianity?'

No. The Indian, one must admit, is hated. He is whenever possible spat upon. The press find not sufficient words to damn him.

What then should one do in the best Western tradition? 'We are free,' wrote Macaulay, 'to little purpose if we grudge to any portion of the human race an equal measure of freedom and civilisation.' Just remember your Mill, Burke, Bright, and Fawcette.

---

[30] Open Letter, C.W., Vol. I., p. 158.

'To bring a man here on starvation wages, to hold him under bondage, and when he shows the least sign of liberty, or in a position to live less miserably, to wish to send him back home where he would become comparatively a stranger and perhaps unable to earn a living is hardly a mark of fair play or justice characteristic of the British nation.[31]

'It now remains for me only to implore you to give this matter your earnest consideration, and to remind you (here I mean the English) that Providence has put the English and the Indians together and has placed in the hands of the former destinies of the latter . . . In conclusion I beg of you to receive the above in the same spirit in which it has been written. I have the honour to remain, your obedient servant, M.K. Gandhi.'[32]

* * *

It is so simple to say—and so complex to know—anything. For example, one could talk so much and so movingly of indentured labour but till one meets Balasundaram, how abstract, how almost irrelevant it all looked. To see suffering face to face is to know something more than suffering—that man has no right to suffer, and not that suffering is evil, but the suffering of suffering is irreverent to human existence. Why should one suffer? And who was Balasundaram?

Gandhiji sat in his law office, occupied as usual with the business files on the one side and the problems of the Indian community on the other. In fact, the former was only a

---

[31] Open Letter, C.W., Vol. I, p. 161.
[32] Open Letter, C.W., Vol. I, p. 163.

justification for the latter. 'Service of the poor,' he said, 'has been my heart's desire' and if one loves anything with all one's heart, there it comes, the thing asked for. And so Balasundaram, the child-beautiful, appeared.

With broken teeth, blood flowing from his lips and face, on to his low-held turban, he stood, did Balasundaram, with torn clothes, in front of the barrister. He was speechless with fear. He had heard of this great man—somebody had told him of this young Indian lawyer, equal every whit to the whiteman, and whom anyone could go to, and he would defend you against the whites or the government. It was like a fable, like something from a Purana. But perhaps it was true. God does send such men on earth. But when the coolie Balasundaram stood before the great man he felt tongueless. He needed some comfort, but what he could not say. How would he know? He had a broken body and broken teeth, and an intense fear that anything might happen to him, at any moment, in this strange and fierce land, a land where the coolie is caught between the Kaffir and the white man—and the rest is a no-man's land. Where was one to go? One's land was far away across the seas. And in any case what was there to go to?

But, here in Africa, the Sahib and his wife were fierce people. When they got angry they really could tear anything, break anything to pieces. Balasundaram learnt, of course, to tell lies. How could one be straight with this Sahib or his great big lady? So one told lies. It made life simple. But the more the lies the more the anger of the Sahib. Now what was one to do? One told ever more lies. The Sahib today had got so furious, he'd slapped Balasundaram, had kicked him, beaten him. Balasundaram well deserved it. In fact, that's what he thought. But what was he to do? He was just frightened. So he ran away. Where was he to go now? He first went to the Protector of Immigrants, a white man, and in charge of all the coolies. 'Come tomorrow,' said the officer. What did that mean? Would the Sahib have him back? No, he would never again serve the Sahib. What then to do?

So he ran to that new Indian, the great man, the coolie lawyer.

Gandhiji immediately stood up and asked Balasundaram to put back the turban on his head. Gandhiji was not a white man, he was not a boss. There was no need for abject respect to be shown to a fellow human being. And now go to the doctor. And here is a letter to the doctor.

The doctor was a white man. He was shocked with what he saw. He not only poured medicine on the wound and bandaged the poor coolie, he also gave him a certificate of Balasundaram being of a victim of clear brutality. And now with certificate and bandage, Gandhiji and Balasundaram went to the magistrate—the same type of court as the ones in India, the same Queen on the wall, and the same shape of table and magnificent servants about. The magistrate was angry, very angry, when he heard the story. He would prosecute the culprit immediately. Gandhiji averred: 'It was far from my desire to get the employer punished. I simply wanted Balasundaram to be released from him.' The magistrate kept the 'turban as an exhibit' and sent the wounded coolie to the hospital. Here he was well-bandaged and cared for, and once discharged he went straight to Gandhiji. 'Revered sir, I never want to go to the old Sahib again.' He could not articulate his words well. His gash was still unhealed. 'I would like to be free.' Gandhiji immediately went in search of the employer. 'I do not want to proceed against you,' said Gandhiji to him, 'and get you punished. I think you realise you have severely beaten the man.

I will be satisfied if you will transfer the indenture to someone else.' The master agreed. So now Gandhiji went in search of a new white employer—for according to law, he had to be white, or Balasundaram would have to be escorted back by the police to the old master. A European agreed to take Balasundaram in his service. During this time however the old employer had changed his mind. He and his wife liked Balasundaram, and very much so. He's such a good servant. Where will one find someone like him? After all, one has paid for and signed documents to have him. Yes, Balasundaram must come back to him. So the white master went to the Protector again.[33] The Protector was out. The coolie, meanwhile, had come back to the Protector. Gandhiji had sent him alone. Everything would now work out well—it was only a question of formality. After all, a white master had been found.

Meanwhile the Protector, on his side, had an excellent idea. The coolie had failed in his duty. The Sahib was right. Balasundaram had done something very wrong. In fact, he could be arrested and sent back for desertion. But he would let the coolie go with just a simple signature to a document, a thumb impression. It would cost nothing to the coolie. And after that signature, of course, he would go back to his master. Why not? The law said it. And being beaten by his master is after all not such a big offence. It happens everywhere, and all over the world.

Balasundaram returned to Gandhiji. Now there seemed no way out. Balasundaram would not go back to his old master. Yet he had signed a document and said he was wrong. And the

---

[33] Protector of Immigrants who looked after coolies—indentured Indian labourers.

white master wanted him back. Sick at heart, Gandhiji returned home and wrote a letter imploring the master to consent to the transfer. He refused. So now they went back to the magistrate. The magistrate was very angry. The employer had taken the law into his own hands. He had beaten the poor coolie 'as if he were a beast'. Balasundaram must be freed from the contract at once. If not, the law would take its own course.

With that he adjourned the court, giving the employer one day to make up his mind. On sober reflection the latter climbed down.[34]

The white master now agreed to Gandhiji's offer. If Balasundaram could find a new master he would let him go, though with deep regrets.

One now went to the new white employer. It was Mr. Askew, the sole European who attended the meetings of the Natal Indian Congress. He would employ Balasundaram, and sign the papers accordingly. The white master of Balasundaram finally gave Balasundaram his freedom. He now went to settle down to work with Mr. Askew.

The news of Balasundaram's case spread from town to plantation and by mouth and letter all over Natal and Orange Free State, and the Colony of South Africa. The news crossed the seas and was heard of in faraway Madras in India from where Balasundaram had sailed. Somewhere the whiteman was not all in all. And this frail, tall, austere lawyer from India was winning. If things went this way, what would happen to indentured labour, the sugar cane and the new gardens of coffee and of tea? And if the Balasundarams once free, set up their shops, and sat underselling the white man—besides

---

[34] E.P., p. 495.

they had so many children they would soon outnumber the whites—what was to become of Natal, and the dream of the Cape Cairo Railway, and the Queen's red map of earth? The mystique of the Empire in its own way was based on God. There was a secret between heaven and earth, Cecil Rhodes thought, that made for the glory of the British Empire and, ultimately, of the human race. And somewhere deep down Gandhiji and Balasundaram also agreed with this truth. Who can know God's ways?

Others and yet other Balasundarams followed. And each one ever more courageous. A certain Thangavellu ran away from his master, a baker, one day. He went straight to the Protector and the Protector gave him a three-day pass. Meanwhile, he had to appear before the Clerk of the Peace for an appropriate settlement. Thangavellu was ill-treated by his white master. And he will not return to the same master. But the police meanwhile arrested him.

'Ho, ho, what! How dare you go about so free?'

'Why, I have a pass.'

'Is it your master's?'

'No, it's the Protector's.'

'No good for us. Come then to the police station.'

And, of course, according to the police he had no business, without his master's permission, to be out on the streets. He was officially loitering. Taken before the Magistrate, Thangavellu said he would rather be in prison than go back to the master. Anyway, for all positions and practices the little pass of the Protector had no value whatsoever. Therefore the Magistrate found the Protector had gone too far. But by Natal-British arrangement, the Protector had the right. By Natal laws, however, he had none. Now, who was right? Thus the coolie had to go back to his master. The Protector, with now the Governor's consent, cancelled the contract. Finally, the Indian found another job.

But one could not go to the Governor for every case of desertion of a coolie. Everything was in confusion. What then was the law?

A little later a certain Guppi Gownden, Naransamy and a great many others (working on the Beneva Estate) were brought before the Umzinto Magistrate for having left their homes without permission, and having gone out in a body to the city. They pleaded (but how true was it?) that they had gone to perform memorial rights for a fellow Indian. But the Magistrate contended that they had gone to Umzinto to see him so as to be able to protest against their employer. The first two were condemned to two months imprisonment and the rest each to a fine of ten shillings. They had all pleaded guilty. The Supreme Court, where the case was now taken, ridiculed the Magistrate for such a decision. The day the Indians had gone to the city was a Sunday. Thus they were not on duty. But the grossest error was that the Magistrate had condemned them under Section 101 whereas it should have been under Section 31.

Sir Walter Wragg: It is no offence to leave the Estate in a body. You might just as well charge them with going up in a balloon.

The Chief Justice: The most extraordinary thing is so many Indians should plead guilty.

Sir Walter Wragg: The Magistrate has not only taken the wrong section but has quoted the section wrongly and created the offence . . . It is a terrible thing that these men should have been imprisoned for a fortnight. The fault of the Magistrates was that in dealing with cases they would not look at their law books.[35]

And now more and more white people were shocked and amazed with what was happening about them, and in their name. Was this the way to behave in civilised society? And with the support of enlightened white opinion on one side and under dedicated leadership of Gandhiji, the movement carried a secret and astonishing momentum of its own. For example, in the sugar estate of Reynolds & Co. at Umzinto, the Indian labourers were so miserable they went to the Protector at Durban for relief. The Protector sent their complaints to the Crown Prosecutor, back to Umzinto. The summons were issued. But the coolies refused to return to Umzinto. The police then came to arrest them in Durban, on the spot. They were all taken to the compound of the Protector's office. From there they would be marched down to Umzinto. Meanwhile, 'eight men of the party snatched their loin clothes, which they managed to fasten round their necks and attach to the branch of a tree in the compound before the police could stop them. The branch of the tree was too low to suspend the coolies but as they strained and tried to strangle themselves, they presented a horrible spectacle with their eyes starting from their sockets and their tongues lolling out of their mouths. The women belonging to the party gathered round howling and weeping.'[2]

The Protector's chief clerk however came to rescue them and cut the noose. But the police would have their way. The Indians were now handcuffed. People gathered round to see what was happening, 'some cursing and some commiserating the Indians'. This frightened and pushed the police to more

---

[35] *Natal Mercury*, 12 November 1896.

brutal action. 'The Indians continued to struggle after they were carried out of the compound, and the constable finding them too heavy to carry dropped them on the road which made them howl louder than ever, as their backs which were bare came in contact with sharp stones on the road.'[36]

The Police Superintendent Alexander noticing this immediately asked the police to stop such 'brutal treatment' and they were taken to the station in rickshaws to board the train, and finally be placed before the Magistrate at Umzinto.

And thus from tragedy to tragedy, and often from victory to victory.

* * *

Meanwhile, the Indian traders were not to be forgotten. In the Boer Republic of Transvaal they were to be herded ('for sanitary reasons') into little community settlements called locations, where alone they could buy their lands, build their houses, and often ply their trade. Things were slightly different but generally difficult even in the Cape Colony. However, the British Government was now in a dilemma. It has to side with the Indians, on principle, because of the Empire, for without India there would be no Empire. And with Indians creating trouble elsewhere, in other African colonies, each with its own peculiar problems, what was to be the position of the home government? Some who had the mystique of the Empire sided with the Indians. For them the Empire was beyond a question of colour. It was somehow holy, divine. For others—and these were the white settlers in the colonies mainly, and the conservatives at

---

[36] *Natal Advertiser,* 7 October 1896.

home in England, the Empire was—if ever it was going to be what it was destined to be—white. Thus the agitation began not only in Africa but in England as well. Indian delegations, helped with every detail by Mohandas Gandhi, waited on the Secretary of State for colonies, often led by the venerable Dadabhai Naoroji himself. The Secretary of State's decisions depended on his party's policy.

At one moment Mr. Chamberlain came to be in charge of the colonies. He was a man of great ambition, precision and courage but he had to deal with a growing Empire. Of course, he understood the Indian case. But then the truth was not just a question of the white or the brown—there was also a deeper fight between the white and the white, between the Boer and the British. In Transvaal, for example, and in other Boer republics there was always the problem of the Uitlanders. For there were more Englishmen in Transvaal than the Boer. And the English had all the money.

Rhodes had called Kruger 'a dirty, uneducated Dutchman, backward, primitive and impossible, an anachronism, a throw back to the time of Moses who ought to be cleared away'. Kruger had, so the legend went, killed over two hundred lions with his own hands, so hardy, resolute, indomitable was this man. He could look after his Boers, with their farms and their babies, their bellowing cattle, their Bible-readings. The Boers will never be British, will never belong to the modern world. And Kruger on his side did not sit mute. He called the Uitlanders, these new-comers, 'dirty vultures' and the gold they had discovered, the very source of corruption. 'Every ounce of gold,' he declared, 'taken from the bowels of our soil will have to be weighed up with a river of tears, with the life-blood of thousands of our people in the defence of that same soil, from the lust of other's yearnings for it, solely because it has the yellow metal in abundance.' He hated Johannesburg, therefore, and all its corruptions of Sodom. The English dominated it all. He hated to even go there. And asked once to open a public hall in the city, he grudgingly accepted the invitation, went, and spoke thus from his mountain top. 'You foreigners, you new-comers, yes, even you liars, thieves and murderers.' And he returned to his Boer capital of Pretoria, satisfied he had his say. Then he sat with his pipe and coffee pot, till the next Burgher came.

Beware of the British. And now they bring in the Indians. Of course the British need them on their plantations in Natal. And so we have to suffer. Strange.

The Orange Free State, when it discovered the seriousness of the problem, had already made it impossible for Indians to stay on its territory. Transvaal was making it more and more humiliating for them every day. Between the Britisher and the Indian, London would choose the Britisher, of course. But what if it came to a choice between the Boer and the Indian? The Empire came first. And, yet, how could one go against a white man and for a brown man?

'It sometimes happens in life,' wrote St. Leger, a famous journalist, in the *Cape Times*, 'that men are called upon to decide decisively between the claims of justice and claims of self. With men of honourable inclinations the task is . . . a far heavier one than with men whose natures have long ago cast overboard any conscientious scruples with which they may have been endowed at the outset of their unlovely existence.

'When one reflects that the conception of Brahmanism, with its poetic and mysterious mythology, took its rise in the land of the 'coolie trader', that in that land twenty-four centuries ago, the almost divine Buddha taught and practised the glorious doctrine of self-sacrifice, and that it was from the plains and mountains of that weird old country that one derived the fundamental truths of the very language we speak, one cannot help regretting that the children of such a race should be treated as the equals of the children of black heathendom and outer darkness. Those who, for a few moments, have stayed to converse with the Indian trader have been, perhaps, surprised to find they are speaking to a scholar and a gentleman.'[37]

Africa could not do without the Indians. It could not do with them. The British could well do without the Boers. But where were the Boers to go? They were no more Dutch. They were Afrikaners. 'Africa is my mother's country. I do not know exactly how long my mother's family has lived in Africa, but I do know that Africa was about and within her from the beginning.'[38]

The Indians however could always go back to India. A few thousand more or less (there were about 50,000 Indians in Natal at that time) would make no difference—they may, when back in their own country, even bring some spirit of reform, of adventure. Then why not go back? Now, if this is the argument, why don't the British go back? They did not build South Africa. In fact, the Indian in the earlier days had done more for South Africa than had the Britisher. And in all this wrangle nobody thought of the Kaffirs. They were beneath any consideration; they belonged, like the forest and the rivers, to the country of Africa. Savage and sometimes even cannibals, just a little superior to the cattle, they would be looked after in their own territories with their own chiefs whom you could buy or sell or kill.

---

[37] E., p. 535.
[38] Laurens Van der Post, *Venture to the Interior*, p. 17.

Thus between the Boer and the British there was no love lost. Between the Boer and the Indian there was no problem either—the Indian was inferior. So where was the problem? He, the Indian, will stay where he has to stay. We will see to that. Between the British and the Indian there was sympathy because of the Empire. Between the Dutch and the Boer too because they once were of the same stock. Between the Boers and Kaiser Wilhelm II because he did not have any share in the wrangle. The Germans also needed a place under the sun. So they became the unofficial protectors of the Boer.

Hence the British sometimes sided with the one sometimes with the other, according to circumstance or whims of the parties in power in London, Pretoria, Durban or Berlin. But somewhere deep down where the biggest fears were dormant, the Kaffir was the problem. When the giant would wake, what shall we do with him? Would he waken? And if the Indian did not go back, the Indian and the Kaffir will join together, the brown and the black, and throw the white into the sea. What then?

Gandhiji, still young and his ideas not distinctly formulated, did not think so. The Indian came from an ancient race—in fact, the same race as the Britisher. The Queen was our Queen Empress too. Proud of the Empire we will fight indeed in the name of the very principles of British justice, of British civilisation. We will not go back to India. And if we do, no Indian will ever step here again. So, choose!

* * *

The art of compromise is a legitimate, a noble species of human activity. Facts are never too noble—all situations a South Africa.

The edge of fact is poetry, and the gentleman, the poet in action. Every Englishman is somewhere a poet, hence his willingness to compromise—the misunderstanding call it hypocrisy. However in the end the compromise ever seems to serve the British. That's the paradox, the extraordinary aspect of the international drama. Is God, then, on the side of the English?

Lord Elgin, the Viceroy of India, was a noble person, a gentleman. He would feel it beneath his dignity, beneath his Englishness to be unfair to the Indians. He could not either be unfair to his countrymen in England. Nor for that matter to the English in South Africa. The situation in South Africa was quite serious. The English were on the edge of being thrown out. So were the Indians. He, the Viceroy, therefore agreed to a poll-tax. The Boers wanted to make every Indian pay twenty-five pounds for the right to stay in Natal. That would be too much. It was unkind, ungentlemanly towards a people who had brought so much prosperity to the whole of South Africa. Hence three pounds would do. (Three pounds were about four to six months wages of an Indian.) And if each Indian had a family of seven or eight adults—and which Indian did not have a large family?—you make it up in numbers. Thus facts remain the same, the perspective is different, and the whole solution honourable. What do the governments of Natal, of Transvaal, think? This way the Indian is at once free—and as British subject has all the rights, more or less—but he will thus be forced to go back to India as being the only economic solution. And each year the indentured labourer can always come into the African territories. Nothing changes except the way of looking at it all.

The Boer was a fiery, proud, puritanical creature. All these 'arrangements' seemed to him so much moral confusion. The Britisher always lives in a mess, the Boers had long ago decided.

But facts are facts. The white man will rule South Africa. The brown man might serve him on the plantations. It's such a pity the Kaffir will not work. Thus the only way now left for the white man is to get the coolies from India, and send them back to their God-forsaken country after the contract is finished or over. What is wrong with that anyway? Gandhi had become the obstacle. And not only Gandhi, but look at the British press. The *Times* in London sat on its imperial perch and seemed to dictate to the whole world how to behave. 'It is to be feared,' wrote the *Times*, 'that the ordinary colonist, wherever settled, thinks much more of his immediate interests than those of the great Empire which protects him, and he has some difficulty in recognising a fellow subject in the Hindoo and the Parsee. The duty of the Colonial office is to enlighten him and to see that fair treatment is extended to British subjects of whatever colour.'[39]

This advice pinched the South African press on its most sensitive side, and quickly came the reply.

'Frankly, whites do not recognise Hindoos as fellow subjects in the sense in which the *Times* uses that expression . . . Rather than see him swamping the white voter at the polling booth or sitting in the legislature, there are thousands of whites who would fight tomorrow, and the sooner Mr. Chamberlain thoroughly assimilates that unquestionable fact, the more successful is he likely to be in his dealings with South Africa.'[40]

Could not the Right Honourable gentleman, the *Star* went on to ask, find some other way of achieving 'the same end by other means' than by forbidding the disenfranchising of the Asiatic? One day the British will understand the truth about it all.

---

[39] E., pp. 555-56.
[40] *The Star*, 31 August 1895.

'Perhaps in the presence of some common danger from outside something will come of the ideal which most of us cherish, of South African Union, and it is not too much to say that there will be considerable hesitation in admitting to the South African family any state which is cursed with a coolie vote.'

For, the press in South Africa argued, if the coolie were given the vote, 'a Parnell or even a Tim Healy and the coolie will govern the country'. And you say they are British subjects. 'They are in every respect as completely aliens in this country as Polish or Russian Jews are in England . . . The colonies have no interest in India, and except as a mere matter of sentiment, would care very little if it ceased to be an appendage of England.'[41] Actually if you went on in this manner, the *Natal Advertiser* said, there will be a tragic-comic side to the story. Imagine, for example, by 1900 you will have a government composed somewhat in this wise:

Prime Minister:	Ali Bangharee
Colonial Secretary:	Dost Mahomed
Attorney-General: Treasurer:	Said Mohomed Ramasamy
Secretary for Native Affairs:	Dhurra Walla

What would the sacrosanct *Times* think of such a predicament?

By now Gandhiji's presence was felt everywhere, not only in South Africa but in England and in India as well. He wrote letters to the Natal and the South African papers in general—always courteous, ever ready to accept a fact when true, and asking only for fair play, both from the Boers and the British. Nobody could find fault with his arguments—so disengagingly honest were they.

---

[41] *Natal Witness*, 13 August 1895.

His reputation had by now grown so vertically that nobody spoke of him but with respect—even the South African press.

'There are Indians here like Mr. Gandhi, for instance,' wrote the *Natal Mercury*, 'who have come into the Colony to stay and who are more capable than many Englishmen of exercising their vote in an intelligent and patriotic manner. They are practically naturalised Natal colonists and there can be no more reason against their possessing franchise than there would be against the Frenchman and the Germans who form a portion of this community.'

What the South African press did not tell its readers was that the business community wanted the Indian trader out. But not the coolies. Thus one came back to the same dilemma. Chamberlain would not agree to the opinions of the Natal Government with regard to the disenfranchising of the Indians.

'Your Ministers,' he wrote, 'will not be unprepared to learn that a measure of this sweeping nature is regarded as open to the very gravest objection. It draws no distinction between aliens and subjects of Her Majesty, or between the most ignorant and the most enlightened of the natives of India. Among the latter class there are to be found gentlemen whose position and attainments fully qualify them for all the duties and privileges of citizenship and within the last few years the electors of important constitutes in this country have considered Indian gentlemen worthy not merely to exercise the franchise but to represent them in the House of Commons . . .'[42]

The Franchise Bill, in its original form, had better be given up then. Her Majesty would never give her assent to such an iniquitous legislation. The Natal Indian Congress was going to

---

[42] E., p. 378.

win its first victory. But the young self-governing colony will suffer a historic defeat. It would, however, go on fighting for its rights, its own way.

The time had come, Gandhiji decided, to appeal to the whole civilised world. He sat and wrote the famous letter to all Englishmen. For, say what you will, the Home Government was on the Indian side. Besides, they feared and hated the Boer. They seem to have feared and hated the Boer more than they did the Indian.

The pamphlet was entitled: 'An Appeal To Every Briton in South Africa.'[43]

Gentlemen, Gandhiji seemed to say, let us see point by point what your arguments be. I shall put forward your point of view—sometimes even better than you would. For that is my way. But let me expose before the wide world our point of view as well. And then let you and the world decide together whatever you must do. That is your problem not mine. Let us now see the various items of your argument:

1. Indians do not enjoy the franchise in India.
2. The Indians in South Africa represent the lowest class Indian; in fact, he is the scum of the earth.
3. The Indian does not understand what the franchise is.
4. The Indian should not get the franchise because the Native who is as much a British subject as the Indian has none.
5. The Indians should be disfranchised in the interest of the Native population.

---

[43] 16 December 1895. Pamphlet printed by T.L. Collingsworth, Printer, 401 Field Street, Durban, 1895. C.W., Vol. I, pp. 256-86.

6. The Colony shall be and remain a white man's country and
    not a black man's; and the Indian franchise will simply swamp
    the European vote, and give the Indian political supremacy.

'I shall take the objections seriatim.'[44]

Your argument is, he continued, that unless you have the same
franchise in the land of your origin, you cannot have them here.

'If such a doctrine were to be of universal application it is easy
to see that no one coming from England even could get the
franchise in Natal, for the franchise law there is not the same
as in Natal, much less could a man coming from Germany or
Russia, where a more or less autocratic government prevails.
The only test therefore is not whether the Indians have the
franchise in India but whether they understand the principle
of representative Government.'

The answer is simple:

'But they (the Indians) have the franchise in India, extremely
limited it is true; nevertheless it is there.'

The position of the Legislative Councils in India is not unlike
that of the late Legislative Council of Natal. And the Indians are
not debarred from entering these councils. They compete on
the same terms with the Europeans. Actually the London *Times*
says, talking even of the difficult Province of Bengal, the elective
system 'after a severe trial has proved a success'.

---

[44] C.W., Vol. I, p. 256-57.

And now to your second point. What you say about the class of Indians in Natal is not entirely true. It is certainly not true of the trading classes and even among the indentured Indians there are some of the highest castes in India.

'They are certainly all very poor. Some of them are even vagabonds in India. Many also belong to the lowest class. But I may be permitted to say without giving offence, that if the Indian community in Natal is not, nor is European community here, drawn from the highest class.'

And he now refers the reader to his other 'open letter' wherein he has quoted authorities to prove that the Indian 'is as much civilised as a 'model' European . . . Loved and well treated he is capable of rising higher like any member of every other nationality. He cannot be said to be well treated as long as he is not even given those privileges which he enjoys or would enjoy in India under similar circumstances.'

Your third point that the Indian does not understand franchise is almost to beg the question. India is villages, and the villages are from time immemorial run by the Panchayat, and the Panchayat is elective. So, how could you say we do not understand the significance of franchise?

Your other point says if the Indian gets the franchise, the Natives should have it too. This is, if one may say, beside the point. For what we are stating is that the Indian has already the franchise, and you want to take it away. Further, the Indian has 'his Charter of Liberty, the Proclamation of 1858'.

'One of your points, gentlemen, is that the Indians corrupt the Native by selling the latter liquor. If you examine the point carefully you will see it is not founded on facts. The Indian trader, the one who has the franchise, belongs to a community who are not only teetotallers themselves but would like to see liquor banished altogether from the land.'

And now see what the Indian Immigration Commission (1885-87) has to say on this point.

'We, however, doubt that they (the Indians) are more guilty in this matter than the white people who traffic in liquor . . . It has been shrewdly observed that the people who make the loudest complaints against the Indian immigrants for selling or disposing of liquor to the Natives are the very persons who themselves sell the liquor to the natives. Their trade is interfered with, and their profits are lessened by the competition of Indian liquor traffickers.'

And Superintendent Alexander giving his evidence explicitly says:

'I find that people generally suspect coolies of doing everything wrong, stealing fowls, etc. but I find such is not the case. Out of the last nine cases of fowl-stealing, all of which were laid to my corporation night-soil coolies—I find that two natives and three white men have been convicted of stealing fowl.'

And again, Superintendent Alexander has said:

'In the present condition of Natal, I do not think it is possible to substitute a white for an Indian population. I don't think we can. I can deal with 3,000 Indians with the staff I have, but if there were 3,000 corresponding white British workmen, I could not . . .'

Gandhiji goes on giving further facts:

'In 1893 while there were 28 convictions against Europeans in the borough for supplying liquor there were only three against Indians.'

The sixth point is that it shall be a white man's country and so the Indian should never be given franchise. This is once again a fallacious argument. People in Natal forget that it's not a country of 'one man one vote' but there is a property qualification for voting; an immovable property of £50 or a rented one of £10. And here Gandhiji analyses the electoral districts and the number of voters in each. Though the Indian and the European population is about the same in the Colony, whereas there were 9,309 white voters on the list, there were only 251 Indians as registered voters, that is one Indian vote to every thirty-eight European votes.

'What the Indians do and would protest against is colour distinction-disqualification based upon racial difference. The Indian subjects of Her Majesty have been most solemnly assured over and over again that no disqualifications or restrictions will be placed upon them because of their nationality or religion. And this assurance was given and has been repeated upon no sentimental grounds but on proof of merit.'

The coolie, as any government report would tell you, and as in fact the Indian Immigrant's Commission's report would tell you, has only brought prosperity to the country.

'Indian immigration,' says Mr. Saunders, a member of the Honourable Legislative Council and one of the commissioners, 'brought prosperity, prices rose, people were no longer content to grow or sell produce for a song, they could do better: war, high prices for work, sugar, etc. kept up prosperity and prices of local produce in which the Indians dealt . . . If we look to 1859 we shall find that the assured promise of Indians labour resulted in an immediate rise in revenues which increased four-fold within a few years.' But the natural fear that the Indians would swamp the Colony brought rumours that immigration would be suspended. 'Down went the revenues and wages. But later fresh promise of immigrants immediately sent wages and revenues up. Retrenchment was soon spoken of as a thing of the past. . . .' Records like these ought to tell their own tale and silence childish race sentimentalities and mean jealousies.'

'To separate the two communities,' said Gandhiji 'is easy enough, to unite them by the 'silken cord of love' is equally difficult. But then, everything that is worth having is also worth a great deal of trouble and anxiety.'

Let us work then for this cord of love uniting us all.

And this pamphlet went out into the large and difficult world. The *Natal Mercury* spoke praiseworthily of 'its great merit of moderation'. And now the London *Times* was completely won over by the Gandhian argument. 'We cannot afford,' wrote the *Times*, 'a war of races among our subjects. It would be as wrong for the Government of India to suddenly arrest the development of Natal by shutting off the supply of immigrants as it would be for Natal to deny the rights of citizenship to British Indian subjects who by years of thrift and good work in the Colony have raised themselves to the actual status of citizens. The Indian Government have on occasions found extreme measures the only way of dealing with certain foreign colonies. It is the duty of the Home Government to take care that the necessity shall not arise in regard to any Colony of British men . . .'

With so strong a warning the Government of Natal was shaken. There was nothing to do now but to change—to amend—the Bill.

> 'Tis true that we solemnly promised to take
> The Indian from the roll.
> But the Bill we hadn't the gumption to fake
> To please of Lord Ripon the soul.
> So now we agreed a short measure to try
> Which really poor Sammy protects:
> And if the Assembly will not be too slow
> Gandhi gets all he expects.[45]

Gandhiji of course did not get all he expected. It was not so easy. For immediately a new bill was introduced. And the new bill said not simply Asiatics but anyone whose mother country did not have parliamentary government could not get franchise, except those who were already on the voter's list—thus the 251 Indians could still vote. And any further addition to the list could, of course, be made but by the Governor in Council.

---

[45] *Natal Witness.*

The principle of the colour bar was dropped. Here Gandhism won.

The Natal Government however would not pass this bill without giving Gandhiji a side-kick, as it were. The government at once discovered there was a secret organisation of Indians sitting in Durban and plotting. Plotting against whom? Against the government, of course. The Prime Minister said, 'Members might not be aware that there was in this country a body, a very powerful body in its way, a very united body though, practically a secret body . . . the Indian Congress. That was a body which possessed large funds; it was a body presided by very active and very able men, and it was a body the avowed purpose of which was to exercise strong political power in the affairs of the Colony.'

Gandhiji immediately questioned this irresponsible statement. The Congress was by no means a secret body. It did not often get into press because it believed in action and not in publicity. Actually, when the body was founded it was noticed in the *Natal Witness*. And, again, he wrote to the Prime Minister, Sir John Robinson:

'The Annual Report and the list of members and rules have been supplied to, and have been commented on by the Press, and that these papers have also been supplied to the Government by me in my capacity as Honorary Secretary to the Congress.[46]

'Truly to speak,' he went on to inform the government, 'the Congress meetings are always held with open doors, and they

---

[46] C.W., Vol. I, p. 321.

are open to the press and public. Certain European gentlemen who, the Congress members thought, might be interested in our meetings, were especially invited. One gentleman did accept the invitation and attend a Congress meeting once or twice. One of the Congress rules provides that Europeans may be invited to become Vice-Presidents. According thereto, two gentlemen were asked if they would accept the honour, but they were not disposed to do so. Minutes of the Congress proceedings are regularly kept.'[47]

Sir John Robinson was an honourable man. When he knew the facts he apologised to the House for having expressed opinions based on insufficient information. Had he, however, as some have suggested, used this accusation as a trick to have the bill passed quickly? But Gandhiji accepted the recantation at its face value. 'To put the most favourable construction on the opponent's words and actions consistently with truth, became his second nature.'[48]

The bill was passed. But Sir John and Gandhiji became friends. Thus Gandhism won again.

* * *

The nominal gerund is the bane of history. In the name of the unknown—and often the unknowable—creeds, myths, empires crumble. Yet the domain of reason is, as it were, just round the corner, and the little flowers of faith. The near is overlooked, the far seems clear. And the tempest of purification looks paradigmatic, inevitable. Little murmurs arise in secluded

---

[47] Ibid., p. 322.
[48] E.P., p. 616.

corners, by the side of brooks, among shady circles, among the
famined, the beaten, the brother of the hanged, and the farthest
clarity enflames then succumbs, but arises again and spreads till
all the gigantic landmass is aflame. It's a forest fire in the name
of a new divinity. Like animals, men flee. In the name of reason
men are sent to the guillotine, to be shot. The mouzhik—so
neglected—now loved by the aristocrat, the high-priest, is
forgotten—or just killed—or made a soldier, gets killed—and
the chant of the revolution sings like a new prayer. He would go
and fight the masses. All of Holy Russia will be one some will
argue (from within and without), but the peasant, the humble,
the former serf—he the son of God, he the true man, he the
beloved of Christ. And Tolstoy will say he probably has more of
the Christ than we, the privileged, the corrupt, the truly poor.

Studying his Plekhanov, and now turned to Marx in
Samara, Ulyanov, then still unknown, would be writing his
treatise on *The Rise of Capitalism in Russia*. Without going
through the progress of capitalism (from feudalism) there is no
revolution, Marx had decreed. Thus capitalism became the road
to communism. But if Russia did not have the proletariat, what
do you do? You just hasten the progress of capitalism—then
perform the revolution. For whom? If you asked, the answer
was simple—for man. Meanwhile, Tolstoy was trying to divest
himself of his capitalist (or were they feudalistic?) cloaks. He
wanted to heal the sick, to clothe and educate the mouzhik. He
loved—or tried to love—man because Christ was love. Lenin
(Ulyanov) tried to revolutionise the decayed and decaying
society so that man may live happily ever after. Would happiness
then be the consequence of history? Was love caught up in the
dialectical process? If your brother were hanged—an innocent,
handsome young man, almost a saint—then you would know

better. Power never gives up except with hate. Love only binds the enslaved to the slave-owner. So let revolution be.

The discovery of Christ within one seemed for Tolstoy, the only solution to all ills. History was made by God for His ends. Let us leave Him to perform His deeds according to His designs. (Tolstoy had learnt Hebrew and Greek to read the holy texts. And he knew.) Let us try to understand the Kingdom of God within us. The kingdom outside will only be a pale reflection of that which is within. The Holy Russia is within. There is no Holy Russia, Lenin would retort (but with due respect to the great writer whom he admired for his knowledge of Russia, a true knowledge, and his great power of the word)—but there is a universal Russia if that is what you mean by saying holy—and that Russia works and suffers for all mankind. It believes in a universal revolution. But God, Tolstoy would say, is the only Universal Truth, and the discovery of Him the only Truth. At this Ulyanov could laugh and say, well, well, truth is a question of class belief—you create your own god to be comfortable when you die. Your god did not mind the serfs. We do. Your god did not worry about the corruptions of the Imperial Court. We do. We shall build a state which will not wither away. Holy Russia, your Russia, is not far, don't you see? But the Tsar could not bear this dialogue anymore. Lenin was sent to Siberia and Tolstoy, now officially condemned, waged a holy war of pamphlets. Someday God would hear.

* * *

Gandhiji's house in Durban was called Beach Grove and it overlooked the mighty Indian Ocean. Once this coast too, one must never forget, was a geological part of India—but something happened to the earth, and it wafted away, as it were, and oceans beat between these huge continents. The ocean is a great teacher. It reminds you that there are laws which govern us, however human we may think we are. Birth and death, the pains of human distances, of hatred, of animal passions, of gain and loss, how to integrate these into a knowable human law? Whence did we come? And where are we going? If God is, could he be so exclusive as to have only one son? If so, why? In Durban, too, Gandhiji's best friends were the Christians—missionaries, and honest and true believers. He enjoyed being with them— they loved mankind, it would seem, almost more than we did in India. Could this be true? Was Christianity a superior religion? But then you turn to the Upanishad, the majesty of its thought, the dialectic of subtle argument here is often so convincing— look at *Yoga Vasistha*—and yet where are we today? Remember our temples, the filth there is unspeakable. In comparison how clean and healthy, simple and true the Christian Church was. Gandhiji would attend the Wesleyan Church on Sundays. He read more and more books on Christianity.

About that time he met an excellent Christian family. And he went to dinner with them every Sunday after church. However, he suddenly had to stop going there.

'It happened thus. My hostess was a good and simple woman but somewhat narrow minded. We always discussed religious subjects. I was then reading Arnold's *Light of Asia*. Once we began to compare the life of Jesus with that of Buddha. 'Look at Gautama's compassion!' said I. 'It was not confined to mankind, it was extended to all living beings. Does not one's heart overflow with love to think of the lamb perched on his shoulders? One fails to notice this love for all living beings in the life of Jesus.' The comparison pained the good lady. I cut the matter short and we went to the dining room. Her son, a cherub aged five, was also with us. I am happiest when in the midst of children, and this youngster and I had long been friends. I spoke derisively of the piece of meat on his plate and in high praise of the apple on mine. The innocent boy was carried away and joined in my praise of the fruit.

'But the Mother? She was dismayed.

'I was warned. I checked myself and changed the subject.'[49]

Then he went away and came back, not without trepidation, the Sunday after. But the good mother had prepared her speech.

'Mr. Gandhi, please don't take it ill if I feel obliged to tell you that my boy is none the better for your company. Everyday he hesitates to eat meat and asks for fruit reminding me of your argument.

This is too much. If he gives up meat he is bound to get weak, if not ill. . . .'

Gandhiji understood her position very well indeed. And he suggested that the best thing he could now do was to stop going to them altogether.

'That certainly need not affect our friendship,' he added warmly. 'I thank you,' she said with evident relief.

---

[49] A., p. 199.

Such the way to the City of Truth. Kabir has said one has to tread softly, ever so softly, on this high road.

Gandhiji's honesty and courtesy were ever exquisite. His love seemed to have no form, have no limitations. And yet, and this was the problem, the whiteman wanted to dominate the black and the brown in Africa, and the evil in man, of man, is present everywhere. But he was against the acceptance, for himself, of any theory of original sin.

There's another significant story he tells us of those days. His great friend of their adolescent years, Sheik Mehtab had now come to join Mohandas. He stayed with Gandhiji at Beach Grove. The house was large and as there was a servant too, and a good one, the household ran with joy and harmony. Gandhiji was very happy to have his old friend with him. One day, however, the cook fell ill, and had to go away. A new cook was found. He did not seem the best of fellows but he would do. And one day the new cook, there he came running to his master, and said, 'Come, come, Master and see what is happening at home!' What after all could be happening? And who does not know servants exaggerate in what they see and say. Gandhiji, however, rushed home and opened the door of his friend's room—for that's towards where the servant took his master—and to his horror found Mehtab with a prostitute. Gandhiji always believed in men. But once they cheated him he suffered with them, for them. But he could also be very severe. Mehtab was asked to leave the house. Mehtab said he would not, and threatened to reveal secrets of the household to the public. Gandhiji had no secrets—what secrets could a man of truth have? He asked his servant to fetch the police. At the mention of the police, Sheik Mehtab left the house, and peace and purity settled over Beach Grove again. Why, asked

Gandhi now, why did the old servant have to fall ill? Why did the new one have to be brought in? 'God came to the rescue as before. My intentions were pure, and so I was saved in spite of my mistakes.' Every time a sincere soul is striving to live life according to the dictates of his moral code, he is in the hands of God. Or rather he sees the hands of God visible. And if God alone were to be our guide, then there could be no evil in the world.

How then to throw oneself into the hands of God? Despite the beauty of the Buddha, and his parables of compassion, there seemed something lacking in it all. The splendour of Hindu philosophy was evident to anybody and the story of God's devotees, the Bhaktas, brought one to the verge of tears. Yet, 'Hindu defects,' he wrote, 'were pressingly visible to me. If untouchability could be a part of Hinduism, it could but be a rotten part or an excrescence. What was the meaning of saying that the Vedas were the inspired Word of God? If they were inspired, why not also the Bible and the *Koran?'* But the living God, the total God, how shall one know him, see him, and obey him? Here Tolstoy's sincerity, the contemporary accent of his writings, found an echo in his own heart. Indeed Gandhiji's biographer, Pyarelal, is probably right in saying the very style of expression in young Gandhi was moulded by the style of Tolstoy's *The Kingdom of God Is Within You.*

'I am a horrid creature,' wrote Tolstoy 'and deserve blame and contempt for not fulfilling them (the Commandments). But yet not so much in justification, as in explanation of my inconsistency, I say: Consider my former life and my present one, and you will see I try to fulfil them. I do not fulfil a thousandth part, it is true, and I am to blame for that; but it is not because I do not wish to fulfil them that I fail, but because

I do not know how to. Teach me how to help me from the nets of temptation that have ensnared me, help me, and I will fulfil them; but even without help I desire and hope to do so. Blame me—I do that myself—but blame me, and not the path I tread and show to those who ask me wherein my opinion the road lies. If I know the road home and go along it drunk, staggering from side to side—does that make the road along which I go a wrong one? If it be wrong, show me another; if I have lost my way and stagger, help me, support me in the right path as I am ready to support you, but do not baffle me, do not rejoice that I have gone astray, do not delightedly exclaim: 'Look at him. He says he is going home yet he goes into the bog . . .' See I am alone, and I cannot wish to fall into the bog. Help me!'[50]

This was indeed Gandhi's own inner state. Act he must, but what was the way? Through violence or non-violence, he had not yet known. 'Non-violence is the path,' answered Tolstoy, not only non-violence but the service of the poor and the meek. Gandhiji now decided this was probably the way.

'If I found myself entirely absorbed in the service of the community, the reason behind it was my desire for self-realisation. I had made the religion of service my own, and I realised God could only be realised through service. And service for me was the service of India, because it came to me without searching, because I had an aptitude for it. I had gone to South Africa for travel, for finding an escape from Kathiawari intrigues and for gaining my own livelihood. But . . . I found myself in search of God.'[51]

---

[50] E., p. 703.
[51] A., p. 197.

And service of the poor was certainly the surest way to reach God. To reach God, of course in the Indian sense, meant self-realisation.

Thus, he concluded, service was the only path to self-realisation. One must therefore divest oneself of all that is unnecessary. To serve the poor one must live like them. Barrister Gandhi would now live a simple life. He would accept all work as an honour, as a dedication. There is no work that one man does that would be menial done by another man. The most humiliating of all human jobs is the scavenging of human excreta. Gandhiji would now learn how to clean latrines. Thus non-violence and service of the poor would change the face of mankind. This, if ever there was one, would be the true revolution. Such a revolution anywhere, and for whatever cause, is universal. So stay where you are and do what you have to do truthfully—you will go very far.

With such thoughts in his mind he left for India to bring Kasturba and his children—and to see India again.

Part Two

5

The Great Indian Way

To understand India—the Indian—one must know the *Mahabharata*. The great nativity and life of the Bharatas is called the *Mahabharata*. 'After Bharata is the lineage named Bharata. Through Bharata is the glory of the Bharatas.'[1] It is not only the longest epic in the world, but maybe it is man's highest literary achievement. Written in simple—almost primal—Sanskrit verse, wave after wave of prehistory and proto-history arise, and vastitudes of space and time are absorbed into one running tale—not merely of conquests and expansions but of defeats and disasters, of human meanness, of human indomitableness, of the clever, of the juggleries, of the exalted, of the faddish, the crooked, the brutal—and throughout it all, one discovers, the noblest expressions of philosophy man has ever stated—the *Gita* is from the *Mahabharata* but, remember, it is spoken on the battlefield, before the armies launch violently against one another. The characters are not heroes or fools, there are men and women representing every colour of man's comportment—Dussasana the boaster, Uttara the coward,

---

[1] The official name for India in the Constitution of 1947 is: 'India, called Bharat,' that is the land of the Bharatas.

Karna the bastard and hero, perhaps the greatest hero amongst them all—Arjuna, India's Hamlet, in love with action but afraid of human frailty (it is easier to be killed than to kill) and Dhritarashtra, the blind king (called also Prajnachakksusa, to whom the mind alone is the eye!) who was just but weak, Duryodhana his eldest, so given to gaming that he would win an empire with it, defeating his cousin, Dharmaraja, eldest among Pandavas, the very symbol and gift of Dharma, the law, but he loved dice, and so lost his all, including his kingdom and his wife, while his brother, Bhima the big, the bold, the excitable hero who would smash his enemies with one stroke of his club, yet he will not, for how, says Dharmaraja, could you go against the Dharma, you cannot and must not do so—does the sun rise from the west?[2]—and above all Bhishma the grandsire, the eldest who gave his throne (and thus remained unmarried, a *brahmachari*) so that his blind brother could have the kingdom. Noble, austere and fearless, he fought against those whom he admired with those he condemned—for he was commander-in-chief by right of his evil kinsmen, the Kauravas, and so he would fight, but telling his adversary they should win for wheresoever Krishna, the Guru, the Absolute is, there is victory—victory is always of the Absolute. And Krishna himself, the chief, the best, a military adviser, the charioteer of the Pandavas, a Prince by right and yet a Sage, the Truth, who having lavished every friendly feeling towards the evil Kauravas, offering one compromise after the other but failing to have it accepted, agreed upon, then, because he had given his promise to Draupadi, the Pandava heroine, married to the five brothers but wife only unto one,

---

[2]   'I am not one to go back on a pledge taken, even if the sun were to rise in the West,' wrote Gandhiji. C.W., XII, p. 430.

she, the strong, the fervent, the rich-haired, her shame-makers
will now be corrected—and so to the war.

Who can win such a war? The armies were ranged against
one another, *akshauni* against *akshauni*,[3] chariots, elephants,
horses, infantrymen and 'all round conches, drums, cymbals
and horns were sounded by the Kauravas' and great was the
uproar, 'and the Pandavas now replied with their conches' and
that blare loudly reverberating through the earth and the sky
rent the hearts of the Dhritarashtras (Kauravas) . . .

At first the battle presented a glorious spectacle. Soon,
however, it became fierce. Elephants rushed furiously at
elephants, car-warriors against car-warriors, steed against steed,
and foot-soldier against foot-soldier. And in that awful carnage
the sire slew the son and the son slew the sire; and sister's son
slew the maternal uncle and maternal uncle slew the sister's son;
friend slew friend; and relatives slew kinsmen. 'We then saw
those elephants, huge as hills, running hither and thither with
their forehead split and their limbs bathed in blood . . .'[4]

And such the slaughter now that the poet finds words fail
words, and after the battle is over, the whole lamentation of the
women over which rises that of Gandhari, wife of the blind king.

Stainless Queen and stainless woman, ever righteous,
      ever good,
Stately in her mighty sorrow on the field Gandhari stood!
Strewn with skulls and clotted tresses, darkened by the stream
      of gore,

---

[3] Duryodhana's army was probably 'a hundred thousand strong'—this being
a moderate estimate.
[4] *The Mahabharata*, pt. 3, Translated by C.V. Srinivasa Rao.

With the limbs of countless warriors is the red field
   covered o'er.
Elephants and steeds of battle, car-borne chiefs untimely
   slain,
Headless trunks and heads dissevered fill the red and
   ghastly plain,
And the long-drawn howl of jackals o'er the scene of
   carnage rings,
And the vulture and the raven flap their dark and
   loathsome wings.[5]

And now kinsmen will bury kinsmen; the war is won—but
it is lost before it is won.

Conquered, others conquer;
Conquering, we are conquered.

The noble Bhishma is dead, and so is Karna, the pure, the
exalted, and when the final funeral ceremonies are performed (on
the Ganges) and the victors return home—what is there to rule?
You cannot rule a crematorium. Dharmaraja has no interest in
being a king. He awaits the establishment of order, of Dharma,
and now his task over, he ascends to the heavens, accompanied
by his faithful dog. Dogs are not allowed in heaven but how
could he not take his loyal servant with him? Meanwhile, hardly
has the Bharata war finished than Krishna's own kinsmen go
to fight with one another. They send for Krishna's help. But
Krishna will not come. The Truth obeys no laws—laws obey the
Truth. A hunter taking Krishna's heel to be that of an animal—

---

[5]   *The Mahabharata*, pt. 3, Translated by R.C. Dutt, p. 349.

Krishna was sitting under a tree in deep contemplation—shoots an arrow and kills him. Thus ends the *Mahabharata*.

The people in India always live a *Mahabharata* war. Indians are perhaps the world's most complex people, with layer behind layer of argument and explanation, for every virtue or vice seen from one point of view there's always one seen from another point of view, every opinion is arrogant and another—remember Bhishma on the field of battle, on his bed of arrows, speaking of the greatness of Truth—

> Truthfulness is eternal dharma;
> Truthfulness is the eternal Brahman;
> Truthfulness is the greatest offering to God;
> Everything is based on Truthfulness.

Such, too, Mohandas Karamchand Gandhi, who, on his field of battle, lying on his bed of arrows while his adversaries and kinsmen brought him lime and water to drink, talked of love, and was finally killed by an un-understanding man. Wave after wave of history had passed by, and with each wave his belief in non-violence and love grew and for each event he pleaded differently; no event is similar to another, as no man is like another, so various circumstances need variant solutions. But his movement was like a cosmic wave. Once started, like Sri Krishna had started—with the whirl of his disc—or Bhishma by his vow of celibacy—history seemed repetitious with it, dissolving time. Truth knows no defeat. The little story of the £3 tax and the fight of the Indians against it by Gandhiji, of which each step is like a mathematical statement—its logical position once established, it spread its psychic, its cosmological force to all of Natal, to all of South Africa and later to North India, and then wave after wave to the all of India, and finally when India was free, to the whole round world—colonialism died the day Gandhi stayed back in South Africa to fight his first battle. Victory was sure for Dharmaraja, the Prince of Dharma, because Bhishma, the grand-sire, the adversary, the great *brahmachari*, the celibate, was also a disciple of Sri Krishna—they both fought on the side of Truth. Indian victory was bought at the price of Pakistan. So every worldly victory is truly a defeat, like Dharmaraja's. Who wins or who loses is not the point. Did you fight for the Truth? That is the only proper question. Thus wheresoever Truth is, said Bhishma, is Victory as well. So that when *Gandhi Mahatma ki jai* (Victory to Mahatma Gandhi) became a revolutionary cry in India, it meant victory to the Truth. Truth is victory. Truth needs no victory. But it's only a way of saying the same thing over again. All words, as the Great Sage has said, have only one meaning—the Absolute.

* * *

And thus we now go back to the story. It will not be a tale of rapid conquest or of easy defeat. It will be the story of a slow victory—internal and then external, for the external is only an expression of the internal. Thus Gandhiji's personal story is also the expanded story of a world revolution.

First he returns to India. Something has happened to him already. He is not the Mohandas Gandhi that had left India for six months to be, as it were, a clerk in a court case at Pretoria where he would just give counsel to an attorney. And what a humiliation this for a 'London-returned' barrister! But, as he has said, ambition had driven him to Africa. A little humiliation here or there seemed of so little consequence—the humiliation of being under the British was worse, or so he thought. But once in South Africa it seemed as if being born with a brown skin was the biggest of all humiliations—next to being born black. A proud man, he would find a proud way of getting out of it, an Indian way, a *Mahabharata* way.

Thus when Gandhiji reached the shores of India (meanwhile on board the ship he had worked hard to learn Tamil and Telugu, the languages of most of the coolies) his heart was so happy. He already did not belong to himself. He did not either know to what he belonged. But the sight of the Ganges at Calcutta made him joyous, and he immediately took a train to Rajkot to see Kasturba—his Draupadi. Faithful and proud she waited for him.

Gandhiji however had the plight of the Natal Indians on his heart. Missing his train at Allahabad, he went to see the English editor of the *Pioneer*, an able honest, imperialist paper and on which Kipling had once worked. It spoke for the Empire. The Englishman received him politely and sincerely, receptively— but he could not obviously be on the side of the Indian against the whites in Natal, he had to be on the side of the one and not the other. Catching the next available train, Gandhiji travelled straight to Rajkot (via Bombay) and came back to Kasturba. What happened between them then is a closed story.[6] Nobody knows and perhaps Gandhiji himself did not. He was a changed man inwardly. Yet his masculine passion had such a thrust there—he was only twenty-seven years of age. He probably found not a sister, a wife, but an equal, a woman. He loved her more as himself than as another.

---

6   So far no letters or other documents have revealed the nature of this reunion
    with Kasturba of a changed Mohandas Gandhi.

And to be woman one has to be another's. The body's demands may be met, body to body may speak—but on coming out of it all, there was something strangely unreal about the union. Was she really his wife? Was Draupadi the wife of Bhima? Or Arjuna? Or was she just the wife of one, and the sister-wife to every other brother? There began then in Gandhiji, it would seem, an aversion to it. But who could control the passion he had? He could have married five wives. Such the impression one has on reading his own story. Nothing happened to him except that he never had a wife—though she bore him many sons. Strange, she herself seemed to demand so little. How could she—he seemed a brother. She saw all his follies—she had a compassionate understanding of them. She was first and foremost a sister. She never rebuked him. She understood him. How could not a sister understand a brother? He was dazed, fooled and lost. Was she still his wife?

Gandhiji hid himself from himself. He now sat and wrote a pamphlet. It was on the grievances of Indians in South Africa. He did not say everything—in fact he 'played it down.' After all, from a distance things look so exaggerated. In fairness to the white people of Africa, he would never do that. And he gathered all the children of the neighbourhood and made them fold the pamphlet, paste them and post them—getting outside help would have cost him too much money. These children received used postage stamps for their affectionate services. 'That was my first experiment of having little children as volunteers,' he wrote later in his autobiography. 'Two of those little friends are co-workers today.' And the pamphlet went out to the whole world.

All the important newspapers commented on the 'Green Pamphlet' as it was called, because it had a green cover. The *Pioneer* wrote an editorial, slightly misrepresenting the case, of which Reuter's made a garbled summary and cabled this to London, and Reuter's-London made their own picturesque version of the story and cabled it to Natal, and thus through Reuter's it went round and round the round world. And the world was upset. The storm had arisen and the biggest one was of course in Natal, and Reuter's-Natal sent back the news to Reuter's-India. Everybody was disturbed, compassionate or angry. Never what Gandhiji said or did could leave man indifferent.

And now many British newspapers, like the *Englishman*, the *Statesman* opened their columns to Gandhiji. He had won their instant respect.

Gandhiji went to Bombay, meeting leaders and explaining the facts. Facts always speak better than any impassioned statement. Truth has this infinite power. In Bombay, first of all he met Sir Phirozeshah who said, 'I see that I must help you. I must call a public meeting here.' A date was fixed for the meeting which was to be a few weeks later. He also met Badruddin Tyabji, President of the Indian National Congress, and Justice Ranade. Meanwhile he had to look after a sick brother-in-law—Gandhiji took him back to Rajkot and nursed him there. Despite all the care, night and day that Gandhiji gave the patient, the poor man died in Gandhiji's arms. 'My aptitude, for nursing,' he writes, 'gradually developed into a passion . . . Such service can have no meaning unless one takes pleasure in it . . . All other pleasures and possessions pale into nothingness before service which is rendered in a spirit of joy.'

He returned to Bombay for the meeting, wrote down his speech, but when he rose to read it—'I stand before you, today, as a representative of 1,00,000 British Indians at present residing in South Africa'—the hall was full and Sir Phirozeshah in the chair—Gandhiji's voice would hardly emerge out of the depths. He was so shy he could not make himself heard. It was finally read by the veteran political leader Dinshah Wacha. 'The audience became perfectly quiet, and listened to the speech to the end, punctuating it with applause and cries of 'Shame' where necessary. This gladdened my heart.' Further, wrote Gandhiji, 'Sir Phirozeshah liked the speech. And I was supremely happy.'

From Bombay he went to Poona, that old home of Indian nationalism, and met leaders from both the schools of thought—Tilak, the fiery, the revolutionary figure, the Decembrist, the most popular nationalist of his day, and Gokhale, the liberal, the truthful, the just. 'He listened to me,' says Gandhiji talking of Gokhale, 'like a school master, a pupil.' And, once convinced, Gandhiji spoke nothing but the truth. Gokhale treated him like a son. Gokhale became, says Gandhi, his political guru.

Meanwhile other events were happening in India, in Kathiawar. The government was going to celebrate Queen Victoria's Jubilee. Gandhiji believed in the British Empire. 'Hardly ever have I known anybody to cherish such loyalty to the British Constitution,' he wrote in his autobiography, 'I can see now that my love of truth was at the root of this loyalty.'[7] He even taught school children how to sing: *God Save the Queen.*

Plague having broken out in Bombay, and fearing it might spread to Rajkot, the State appointed a committee to take preventive measures. Gandhiji offered his services to the State, which were gladly accepted, and he was appointed a member of the committee. As usual, he was worried about sanitary conditions.

He even visited untouchable homes—and they were so clean, it made him weep. So these are the so-called despised

---

[7] A., p. 212.

classes. On the other hand he found such dirt in the temple yard—as if it had never been cleaned 'since the temple was built'. He was indeed shocked with what he saw. 'In the upper class quarters,' he relates, 'we came across a latrine which I cannot help describing in some detail. Every room had its gutter which was used both for water and urine, which meant that the whole house would stink. But one of the houses had a storied bedroom with a gutter which had a pipe descending to the ground floor. It was not possible to stand the foul smell in this room. How the occupants could sleep here I leave the readers to imagine.'[8]

From Bombay he went to Madras. In Madras the story of Balasundaram was very well known. Crowds came to greet him, and the eldest among the Bar and the politicians and the press received him and praised his endeavours.

Then he went to Calcutta. A meeting was going to be organised to receive him when suddenly a telegram came from Durban; he was wanted immediately for the Rand of Transvaal was going to pass a law making the position of the Indian untenable. He wired back for cabin accommodation. His client, Dada Abdulla, owned ships of his own. One of them *S.S. Courland* was leaving for Africa soon. Thus with his wife and two sons, and a nephew (whose father was the same who had died in his arms), he now sailed the stormy ocean with excitement. He was taking his family 'home'—he had a house and a good legal practice. He would become his children's sole schoolmaster. He would teach his wife too. She was dressed in Parsi sarees (so as to look chic) and his two sons in pantaloon and long coats. He was Barrister Gandhi returning to his job and he would live as a prosperous lawyer should. Even knife and

---

[8]   A., p. 211.

fork became obligatory—and those wretched shoes that pinched and smelt! But in 'Rome do as the Romans do'.

But 'Rome', by now, was all aflame. Reuter's cables had made Gandhiji the villain—he had gone to India to complain of how badly his countrymen were being treated in Natal. Then let him stay home! But look at him. Not only was he coming back but eight hundred other Indians he is bringing with him. There were two sister ships, the *S.S. Courland* and the *S.S. Naderi* bringing the whole bang lot to this fair and fruitful colony. Even members of government took part in protest meetings. The ship was not allowed to land her passengers[9] but Natal was a British Colony. The Indians were British subjects. Feelings were so aroused against Gandhiji everybody was afraid that something irrevocable might happen. So the best thing, most people felt, was that the ships should return to India. Gandhiji would never accept such a cowardly solution. What could happen worse than death? Well, if it comes . . . let it come. The captain of the ship, an Englishman, could not believe Gandhiji meant what he said. Gandhiji gave an interview to the *Natal Advertiser* on board the ship explaining he had, in a lower key, only repeated what he had so often written and said in Natal, but his reasoned explanations did not stop the agitation against him and the Indians. Come what may, the Indians would not go back. They had right of entry to Natal. Finally, the government allowed the Indians to land. But Gandhiji was advised by the Attorney General, Mr. Escombe, to land only after sunset. And, again, the Port Superintendent would escort him home in safety. But

---

[9]   Officially, under quarantine, for twenty-three days, supposedly because of plague in India. But the real reason was otherwise. The whites of Natal did not want these Indians.

Laughton, the lawyer and friend, disagreed. Send the family to Parsi Rustomji's house, he advised. 'I do not at all like the idea of your entering the city like a thief in the night. I do not think there is any fear of anyone hurting you. Everything is quiet now.' And they would walk home.

No sooner had they landed than some boys discovered his identity and shouted, 'Gandhi, Gandhi!' Now some more joined the youngsters and started shouting too. Of course this was the Gandhi who had slandered us! Go at him! Laughton was now separated from him, and stones were thrown on Gandhiji—rotten eggs and stones, while someone snatched away his turban. And now came kicks and blows—'they came upon me boxing and battering'—and he lost consciousness. On recovering he found Mrs. Alexander, the wife of the Superintendent of Police, her parasol spread in his protection against the crowd. He who would touch Gandhi must first hurt her. Who would? The Police Superintendent, hearing of the incident, rushed policemen for protection. They arrived in time.

'The police station lay on our way. As we reached there, the Superintendent asked me to take refuge in the station, but I gratefully declined the offer. "They are sure to quieten down when they realise their mistake," I said. "I have trust in their fairness."'

Then accompanied by the police he reached in safety Parsi Rustomji's home. Inside, all was peace. But the crowd outside were howling for blood. 'We must have Gandhi!' they shouted.

The Police Superintendent now stood in front of the house chatting away with the crowd, telling them humorous stories. And the crowd half in fun, half-serious sang:

Hang old Gandhi
On the sour apple tree.

Meanwhile, he sent word to Gandhiji. He must (for the sake of his family at least) disguise himself as a policeman and escape through the back door. 'Thus on the same day,' writes Gandhiji, 'I was faced with two contradictory propositions. When danger to life was no more than imaginary Mr. Laughton advised me to launch forth openly. I accepted the advice. When danger was quite real, and other friend gave me contrary advice and I accepted that too. Who can say I did so because I saw that my life was in jeopardy, or because I did not want to put my friend's life and property or the lives of my wife and children in danger? Who can say for certain that I was right both when I faced the crowd in the first instance bravely, as it was said, and when I escaped from the disguise?'

'It is idle to adjudicate,' continued Gandhiji, 'upon the right and wrong of incidents that have already happened. It is useful to understand them and if possible, to learn a lesson from them for the future. It is difficult to say for certain how a particular man should act in a particular set of circumstance. We can also see that judging a man from his outward act is no more than a doubtful inference, inasmuch as it is not based on sufficient data.'

Finally, therefore, he escaped in disguise from the back door to the police station. And when the news came that Gandhiji was safe there, Superintendent Alexander, who had kept the crowd humoured by singing, announced to them that their victim was no more in the house. Some were angry but others laughed. The crowd, angry or amused, dispersed and went home.

The news spread throughout the world. Joseph Chamberlain, Minister for Colonies in London, cabled to the Government of Natal that the assailants must be prosecuted. Mr. Escombe, the Attorney General, said to Gandhiji when they met: 'Believe me, I cannot feel happy over the least little injury done to your person. You had the right to accept Mr. Laughton's advice and to face the worst, but I am sure that if you had considered my suggestion favourably, these sad occurrences would not have happened. If you can identify the assailants, I am prepared to arrest and prosecute them. Mr. Chamberlain desires me to do so.'

'I do not want to prosecute anyone,' replied Gandhiji. 'It is possible that I may be able to identify one or two of them but what is the use of getting them punished? Besides I do not hold the assailants to blame. They were given to understand that I had made exaggerated statements in India about the Whites in Natal and calumniated them. If they believed these reports it is no wonder that they were enraged. The leaders and, if you will permit me to say so, you are to blame. You could have guided the people properly but you also believed Reuters and assumed that I must have indulged in exaggeration. I do not want to bring anyone to book. I am sure when the truth becomes known, they will be sorry for their conduct.'

He gave this in writing, and it was cabled home to London. Also the one interview he had given on ship to the *Natal Advertiser*, and documents to prove on every speech he made in India, showed to everyone 'that in India I had said nothing which I had already not said in South Africa. The press declared me to be innocent and condemned the mob.' This incident brought prestige to the Indian community and to himself as well. He now settled down to his legal practice. But more danger was round the corner again.

The whites of Natal admired Gandhiji and the Indians now—but feared them even more. Bills were immediately introduced to restrict the right of the Indians and to put severe restrictions on immigration. The fight was getting grimmer.

Truth is the real adventure; all others mere reflections of this one theme. Even in a country like Africa, where the mighty Paul Kruger on his endless trek, it is believed, had killed two hundred lions in mortal combat, but sought his answers in the Bible, that is in Truth. And again that extremely delicate son of an English clergyman, Cecil Rhodes, who came to seek health in Natal and found diamond in West Grignaland, yet he was an angel (of sorts, he lived on Plato and Winwood Reade)[10] and had mystical longings for the brotherhood of man. So too was Jan Smuts, of the Cape Colony, who believed in the British, went to Cambridge, and studying the classics was so moved by philosophy—by Plato, of course—Truth again became his search, but he was to end up a general. Even young Churchill had to appear and disappear on his horse in South Africa, sending dispatches to his paper in the British homeland for the glory of the Empire, and be imprisoned by the Boers— yet in such a land (despite Rider Haggard) the greatest of all adventures is still the Truth. Once you taste of its 'honeyness', as the Upanishads say, you, like the bee, will always go seeking it, and all the universe is one great forest for the search of this honey, *madhu*. Gandhiji had just a little taste of this *madhu* and like everyone who had once tasted it he wanted it and nothing else. His politics, his legal activity, his fatherhood—and his duty as husband—everything became desirable only in terms of It. Each experience, therefore, became an experience with Truth, and there was thus not a region of human living with which he was not to experiment—nothing was ever to be taken for

---

[10]   Author of *The Martyrdom of Man*.

granted. If you believed in anything you must act fully in terms of its premises—and this was the only way to live even in the pursuit of 'normal existence'.

The True is the normal. All others are exiguous.

* * *

He now lived in a spacious house, surrounded by his wife and children—his nephew—and innumerable others who helped him with the running of the household, Indians and a few Europeans. Nothing in life was to be done by habit and for the sake of convenience. Everything must yield meaning. For example, there's the education of children. It had to be taken up seriously. How do you bring up a child? This set Gandhiji thinking. To send his children to school—to an ordinary school—created many problems. First, in South Africa all schools were for white children only. Even if, because of his present status (he had become a notable member of the Natal community), his children could be admitted to white schools, there would still be the problem of how the other boys would respond to his children. Besides—(and here Tolstoy was of help)—the type of training one receives at school—was it indeed based on a true perspective of education? Does this education lead one to God? Certainly not—all the textbooks give you 'objective facts', and you use them as you care.

Then how to bring up a modern child? The ancient way—the parents are its true teachers. What happens around a child till he is five years of age will shape the man he is going to be. Hence parents must have a direct link with a child's education. Gandhiji therefore began spending time teaching his own children and talking to them of simple and important things—and the very atmosphere of the household educated the child. His sons, says Gandhiji, had at least as good an education and probably better than an education given by any public school. He even, at the beginning, employed an English governess so that his children should have a good accent. If his sons, he believed, did not know all that others might have learnt at school and university, they at least knew more about the essentials of true living and of service. And this was enough. 'It all shows the length to which a votary of truth is driven by his experiments with the truth, as also the votary of liberty—how many are the sacrifices demanded by that stern goddess.'

And, also, if children have to be brought up rightly they have to be looked after since the moment of their conception. The thoughts and feelings of the parents go into the very make of the child—so says the Indian tradition. If your thoughts are pure and noble, your child too will be pure and noble. Thus parenthood is a period of spiritual discipline. When children are born they need medical help. Medical help is not easy in a new country like Africa—nurses are not many and they are so busy. What if at the moment of birth no nurse were available? Gandhiji therefore procured a book in Gujarati—*Advice to a Mother*—and he would now be the delivery nurse, if necessary. He found later that he was no worse than any other. One day when the pains of birth came somewhat earlier than expected, Gandhiji delivered his wife of one of his own children. And after the event the nurse came to look after the baby. By the way, why should he not also try to look after babies? After some time he learnt the art of looking after babies as well.

Further, there are the sick, the maimed and the helpless. One must help them. He therefore had some money given by one of the Indians—Parsi Rustomji—so as to establish a dispensary for the Indians. Gandhiji would himself be present there two hours a day; he would be the compounder explaining the case of the patients to the doctor—the coolies spoke only Tamil or Telugu—thus he learnt to heal wherever he could.

The worst enemy of all is oneself. How to conquer oneself? How to control one's appetites. Especially his passion for Kasturba. This appetite, people say, is like hunger or sleep. Gandhi decided it is not so. The sexual instinct is something very special. It has somehow connections with God. God created this universe and made it peopled with men and women. It was for the expansion of the universe—for its growth and glory that the instruments of procreation were given to us. One must only have children to play the game of God. To do anything else would be to misuse the instrument, would be dishonest, corrupt. Of course, there are ways of not having children. He had heard, again and again—while in England—of Dr. Allison's ideas on contraception. Even then he had believed in the spiritual precepts of Mr. Hill. The control of the sexual instinct is more important than just the denial of not having children. It must all come from within.

He went into his own depths and tried desperately day after day to control himself. Hard work and the right diet should be the way.

Hard work left him too exhausted for anything else. Yet, when he returned home and to his bed, Kasturba was there—so innocent, so free, so giving. How could one resist the urge for union? So he went to it. Yet it was so humiliating when he had done all the inner work. But God never fails in His gifts—if only we strive.

And proper diet too was of help. Fruits and nuts, he was certain, were the best food in the world—not only vegetarianism was the best way of living but even in vegetarian diet there are variants to be made to improve your moral perspectives. For example, milk certainly produced states of sexual incitement. But if you give up milk, with what would you substitute its essentials? As anybody can see, there is no end to experimenting with one's diet. What he eats makes man.

Further, there was so much to read. All the great wisdom of India and of the world was to be found in a few great and noble books. How to find time to read them? There's the *Gita*. How was Gandhiji to learn it by heart? He stuck verses from it on the walls of the bathroom—thus while shaving he learnt two verses of the *Gita* per day.

All in all, life is never more exciting than when you are earnest. The more you give to life the more it gives back to you.

There are other and more difficult activities for which we depend on outsiders—washing one's clothes and barbering, for example. However much you try the washerman is never on time. You might have three dozen shirts—even they are finally exhausted. Therefore why depend on the washerman? Gandhiji learnt how to launder and how to iron, and use starch for the better showing of shirts. One day—in the beginning—the starch began to come down his clothes while he was at court.

'What Gandhi, what's the matter?'

He was never upset by the mockeries of others. They saw it that way, and they had every right to laugh. He would have himself in their place.

But when—and this was many years later—he began to cut his own hair, people began to mock at him, again.

'What Gandhi have the rats been at you?'

'No. The white barber would not condescend to touch my black hair,' said he, 'So I preferred to cut it myself, no matter how badly.'

'The barber,' continued Gandhiji, 'was not at fault in having refused to cut my hair. There was every chance of his losing his customers if he should serve black men. We do not allow our barbers to serve the untouchable brethren . . . That it was the punishment for our sins saved me from becoming angry.'[11]

However, while you are experimenting with yourself the world does not sit quiet—it goes its own mysterious way. The Boers and the British could not bear the situation any longer. They went to war.

* * *

The Boer War was maybe the meanest war in British history. 'Madam,' Field Marshal Sir Evelyn Wood is reported to have said to Queen Victoria, 'Madam, it's not a gentleman's war. And may it please Her Majesty not to send me to such a battlefield.' Queen Victoria agreed with her Commander-in-Chief. It was after all a war of politicians. Milner, Her Majesty's High Commissioner in Africa, wanted it, and so in a curious way did Chamberlain. But whereas Chamberlain had to show a gentlemanly face—because of Parliament, etc.—Milner could drive his secret wedge wheresoever he wished, and 'crush the dominion of Afrikanerdom'. He and Cecil Rhodes disagreed. For Rhodes, a student of Gibbon, wanted a glorious Empire for the Queen but it had to be won in an imaginative, wise, gentlemanly manner. He himself tried and behaved in as gentlemanly a way as circumstances permitted—'Remember always you are a Roman,' he quoted to himself, again and again, from Marcus Aurelius. First he had fostered the famous Jameson

---

[11] A., p. 263.

Raid (1895)[12] and then he had suddenly withdrawn his support, and so had Mr. Chamberlain. It was certainly not a gentlemanly thing to do—sending an uncertified expedition to Johannesburg from the Cape Colony so as to 'relieve the British' who needed no relief. Even so, Jameson entered the Transvaal on his own but there was no uprising of the Uitlanders, the English, and the whole business was a British disaster. The Boers however forgave this foolish misadventure but they never underestimated it.

And Milner would accept no defeat. The Boers were certainly the biggest obstacle in Africa to the growth and splendour of the British Empire. After all, they are, the Boers are, sort of a pastoral folk who believe in cattle, Kaffirs, and in the Old Testament God. ('Ever since the gold mines of the Rand had brought wealth and power to the Transvaal its leaders seemed to be playing their own separate hand: if ever they thought at all about a united South Africa it was South Africa made in their own image, a domination of old ways over the new ways, of Boers over all the rest.') The Boers had to make way for the civilising influence of British rule and ultimately for the possession of all Africa by Her Majesty's Government! The Transvaal—with that stubborn Kruger, and the Orange Free State in between the two—were the real obstacles. They had to be subdued—if necessary, destroyed and absorbed.

Smuts, the young son of a minor Cape politician, however wanted to remain British and Boer at the same time. He was very much a gentleman—he had, while in Cambridge, come under the influence of G.E. Moore—and he would fight with the British for a Boer South Africa. And he dearly wanted to build a human commonwealth—in this he was inspired by

---

[12] See Glossary.

Walt Whitman and John Bright, and he would therefore fight against any jingoish capitalistic adventure. He often called the existing British territories 'that ramshackle Empire'! He preferred the pure and free colonialism where every part made its simple, independent contribution, but under the august aegis of the Queen. In this adventure Rhodes seemed at first an ally and then an adversary. Finally, they had to choose their own paths. Rhodes had deceived him—so Smuts thought. 'Smuts,' says his biographer Sir John Hancock, 'could never give his loyalty by halves: he must always give it fully or not at all.' Rhodes was, however, finally a weak man—a dreamer to whom fortune had shone almost without effort—the famous 'angel of God', etc. It was not to be thus with Smuts. Calvinistic and Platonist at the same time, he wanted everything straight, good and true. Milner was a politician and not very British at that. The Jameson Raid was a fiasco. The British should by now have learnt their lesson.

But politicians never seem to learn their lessons. They always feel they make history. Armies were gathered. The South African League (a small British fifth column organisation) was asking for a fight. Kruger, and Smuts, now Attorney General of the Transvaal, knew there was no time to lose. The best success in war is always attack. 'The republics must get the better of English troops from the start.' The Boer Republic of Transvaal sent her troops down the mountains to Natal and they were hoping to push on quickly to the sea. This would shake the British, even in India. And once you have a port, supplies could always come. After all, Europe was not going to sleep while Africa was being swallowed by the British. And with such unholy haste. The Afrikaners in the Cape Province, in the Orange Free State would rise in sympathy with their brethren. The great God of

Israel would never allow this mean trick of history. Somewhere Kruger began to feel his people were not only like the lost tribe of Israel but the lost tribe itself.

'Brother Afrikaners!' wrote Smuts in noble patriotic rhetoric, 'once more the day has dawned in our blood-written history when we are compelled to take up arms and renew the struggle for liberty and existence and to entrust our national cause to that Providence which has led our people by miracles through South Africa . . . Afrikaners, I ask you to act as Leonidas with his 300 at Theropylae in the face of the vast hordes of Xerxes, and to ignore men like Milner, Rhodes and Chamberlain, and even the British Empire, and to commit your cause to the God of your fathers and the justice which sometimes acts tardily but never sleeps or forgets . . . Whether we conquer or we die: Freedom shall rise in South Africa as the sun rises from the morning clouds, as Freedom rose in the United States of North America. Then shall it be from Zambesi to Simon's Bay: Africa for the Afrikaner.'

But there was no general Afrikaner uprising. Europe did not come to the rescue and Britain poured in her armies from India, Ceylon and from home. The old Boer General Joubert who had fought successfully and brilliantly against the Zulus could not fight a modern battle. Commandos were driven from mountain to mountain. The war dragged on. It was to be a war of conquest and defeat—of a slow moral decay. And it was under such conditions that Smuts wrote this letter to his wife: 'Should I be seriously wounded or killed you will be officially informed of the fact. So don't worry yourself with groundless fears. I have never been in better health or spirits in my life. Military life agrees wonderfully with me . . . From time to time stray items of news about you have reached me.

Of Kosie's death[13] in August I heard for the first time near the end of last year; of mother's death I heard last March. How deeply I have felt these losses—especially the first, I need not tell you . . . Our future is very dark—God alone knows how dark. Perhaps it is the fate of our little race to be sacrificed on the altar of the world's ideals; perhaps we are destined to be the martyr race . . . In any case there is nothing worse awaiting us than death.'[14]

Gandhiji in Durban was unprepared for such a grim battle. What was he going to do? His heart went out to the Boers— brave and God-abiding people. He respected them. But he had given—pledged—his complete loyalty to the British. His duty lay with the British. They may be wrong. So were the Kauravas, yet Bhishma gave his loyalty to them. You pledge your loyalty to one, and you remain with him, though you may not approve of him. In fact, you might think justice is on the side of the adversaries. But that is another matter. Gandhiji had nothing to choose. He argued:

'Our existence in South Africa is only in our capacity as British subjects. In every memorial we have prescribed, we have asserted our rights as such. We have been proud of our British citizenship. It would be unbecoming of our duty as a nation to look on with folded hands at a time when ruin stared the British in the face as well as ourselves, simply because they ill-treat us here. Our ordinary duty as subjects, therefore, is not to enter into the events of the war, but when war has actually broken out, to render such assistance as we

---

[13] His son, Jacobus.
[14] S., p. 130.

possibly can. The underlying principle in the above argument
is . . . insistence on truth.'

Therefore he now offered his services to the British Colony
of Natal and he was willing to do whatever they wanted of him.
The British found him an irksome friend. How could you pass
laws against the Indian franchise, and hope to drive the Indian
merchant out of the country, and yet have him fight for you,
with you?

Knowing the dilemma Gandhiji offered an Indian
ambulance corps. He knew nursing—he loved it. It was one of
his two passions, he had said—the one was loyalty to the British
and the other his love for nursing. Thus he could combine the
two and wanted very much to go to the front and look after the
wounded, the forlorn. But the British, would they have him and
his crowd?

The British refused this offer. They could get along with
their job without Indians meddling in their affairs. But the
Boer fought so well, it went ill with the soldiers of the Empire.
And Gandhiji went on putting pressure on the British to accept
him and his corps of nearly eleven hundred trained volunteers,
'free' Indians and many from the class of the hated 'indentured
labourers'. Finally the offer was accepted—the help was sorely
needed. And the Indians were in splendid form. They were
happy to serve and sometimes went to the firing line to get the
wounded out. A new spirit of friendship and comradeship was
born.

'The relationship formed with the whites during the war
were of the sweetest,' Gandhiji writes. 'We had come in contact
with thousands of tommies. They were friendly with us and
thankful for being there to serve them.'

'I cannot,' continues Gandhiji, 'forbear from recording a sweet reminiscence of how human nature shows itself as its best in moments of trial. We were marching towards Chievely camp where Lieutenant Roberts, the son of Lord Roberts, had received a mortal wound. Our corps had the honour of carrying the body from the field. It was a sultry day—the day of our march. Everyone was thirsting for water. There was a tiny brook on the way where we could slake our thirst. But who was to drink first? We had proposed to come in after the tommies had finished. But they would not begin first and urged us to do so, and for a moment a pleasant competition went on for giving precedence to one another.'

This humble work of the Indian Ambulance Corps was much applauded and mentioned by General Buller in his dispatches. The leaders were even awarded gold medals. One (coolie) Parbhusingh had shown such heroism that the Viceroy of India, Lord Curzon, sent him a Kashmir robe, and 'wrote to the Natal Government asking them to carry out the presentation ceremony with all possible publicity. This duty was assigned to the Mayor of Durban who held a public meeting in the Town Hall for the purpose.'[15]

The British Empire was now a united entity. The Indians too were part of this great Empire. The press henceforth began to speak of the Indian in a different manner. And the popular refrain sang:

We are sons of Empire after all.

His job was over. The Indian community had won great prestige with their ambulance corps and with the heroism they had shown. It had become a vital part of African life and

---

[15] S.S.A., p. 79.

politics. Henceforward the work started could but go on. The bill against the Indians will certainly be dropped now. Gandhiji must think of going back to India. True, he was earning a very good income, he was respected not only by his own community but also among his adversaries. Nevertheless one must go back to where one belongs. Thus, entrusting his legal work to two Indian colleagues, and his political work to those whom he trusted, he told them of his decision to leave for India. In fact, now there is not much to do. But there is, his colleagues believed, so much that can still happen. They would let him go only in case he would accept one firm condition. If ever they needed him he would come back to them. This was, of course, an understandable demand. Yes, he would return whensoever they wanted his services. This agreed, there were to be festivities to give their leader an appropriate farewell. Not only his clients gave him presents, which was natural, but many other members of the community as well. The more these accumulated, the more anxious he became. But his wife was overjoyed. This is how it has always been in Kathiawar. Presents are offered ever to the Sovereign. And was not young Mohandas a true leader? A king? Look at him, so young and yet so nobly respected. One could be proud of him. His children too looked up to their prestigious father with respect, with love. And they also welcomed these gifts of gold and silver. Gandhiji spent sleepless nights. How could he, who had done everything as an expression of service to the community, accept any gift?

This was not a question of give and take, but of giving alone. No, he could accept no gifts from his fellow-Indians. What would the wife think?

'Oh yes,' she said, 'fine thing to do. You earn a lot of money but there is nothing left in the coffers. What shall happen to us if ever we are in difficulty? And what shall I give my daughter-in-law? It is well to believe in God and all that. But for a woman, gold is her only safety, her protection in need. No I will do nothing of the sort. The jewels are mine.'

'The jewels and presents were given to me,' remarked Gandhiji.

'Why, what do you think I am, not behind you, a part of you, toiling and moiling for everyone? No, I will not let the jewels go.'

Not able to argue any further he set his children to work. Don't you think the jewels should be given back to the community? Remember, we served the Indians in the name of God. Of course! the children agreed. They too could not convince their mother. Finally between the one-pointedness of Kasturba and the sweet stubbornness of Gandhiji, of course Gandhiji won. The jewels were all turned over to a trust for the furthering of the cause. The trust continues to exist to this day in the Republic of South Africa.

To whom does money belong is a most pertinent question to ask. The wealth of man is only the bounty of God. Is that it? Gandhiji was still uncertain. He went on questioning.

Meanwhile, the Indian community gave him a regal send-off. He was unhappy to leave his brethren in the struggle. But he was not going far.

The boat stopped at Mauritius. Gandhiji's name had become so well known in the British Empire that the Governor asked him to spend the day with him. Gandhiji agreed to and also availed himself of the occasion to look into the condition of the Indian indentured labour. Here they did not suffer from the same disabilities as in Natal—nowhere where the Indians had gone were they treated as anything but British subjects—in every way equal to the whites, at least by law. The problem in South Africa, he could see, was a very special one.

* * *

Reaching India was a delight but where was he to settle? Bombay was the proper place for a barrister to practise—but Bombay was frightening after his first experience of it only a few years ago. Gandhiji therefore went straight to Rajkot—his home town, as it were. He had relatives and friends there. He won two or three important cases in that area and immediately the local members of the legal profession said that he could easily settle in Bombay and they would send him enough clients to give him a decent and regular income. With this promise he felt free to uncover his destiny in Bombay. He would soon settle down there as a lawyer—but before then he wanted to inspect the Indian scene.

The Indian National Congress, now grown into an imposing body, was holding its sessions in Calcutta this time. Sir Phirozeshah Mehta was to preside over it. In those days great men travelled in great style. Sir Phirozeshah travelled in a special saloon car. Gandhiji wanted to speak to him about the problem of South African Indians. Gandhiji spent some time with him in his saloon. Yes, the Congress would surely pass a resolution about the wretched conditions of Indians in Natal. But what about the wretchedness of the Indians in India? Unless India is free what can we do in far Africa? Is that not the precise question?

Even so, the Congress sessions were going to be an impressive experience. The great Lokamanya Tilak was there, learned, and dedicated. Gokhale was there too, civilised—almost too highly so—truthful and fearless. And there were others as well, all come to make speeches, pass resolutions, and go back to where they came from having sent petitions to Her Majesty's Government. And as for the organisation itself—it was thin, inadequate. The Indian National Congress worked just for three days in the year; it had no permanent staff. So Gandhiji offered his services. Mr. Ghosh, an elderly, energetic and eccentric man, was in charge of the Congress office. He had somehow never heard of Gandhiji. Therefore Gandhiji did the clerical job badly needed—to go through the correspondence, and answer letters. Gandhiji found this an enriching experience especially as Mr. Ghosh would often talk, and talk much about the Congress from its very beginnings—he was, as it were one of the founding members.

The living conditions for the delegates were inadequate. The sanitary instincts of Gandhiji never left him in peace. The delegates did not seem to mind the smell of human excreta from wheresoever it came. They would use the latrines freely and not worry about the accumulation of human intestinal remains. When the volunteers were asked, they said they knew nothing about it; it was the job of the scavenger, and not theirs. Thus Gandhiji started scavenging his own bathroom but having had to share it with some others, he cleaned the place for himself and his companions as well. But of course he could not do it for the whole camp. And naturally the delegates went on living in their own filth and odours. Who cares? This is India.

Meanwhile, however, the Congress went on with its doings. The Subjects Committee met and debated what they were going to say and discuss in the general assembly. Gandhiji's resolution on South Africa too would come up for discussion, like every other, before the Subjects Committee. But everyone made such long speeches that 'Mine,' says Gandhiji, 'was but a feeble pipe

among the veteran drums'. It was almost eleven o'clock in the
evening. Everybody was by now exhausted and empty.

'So we have done,' said Sir Phirozeshah.

'No, no, there's still the resolution on South Africa. Mr.
Gandhi has been waiting long,' cried out Gokhale.

'Have you seen the resolution?' asked Sir Phirozeshah.

'Of course.'

'Do you like it?'

'It is quite good.'

'Well, then, let us have it, Gandhi.'

He read it trembling.

Gokhale supported it.

'Unanimously passed,' cried out everyone.

'You will have five minutes to speak on it, Gandhi,' said
Dinshah Wacha.

'The procedure was far from pleasing to me.'[16]

The next day he had to make his speech. What could he say
in five minutes? And yet he had spent all night preparing himself
for some sort of explicit statement. 'But the facility of speaking
that I had acquired in South Africa seemed to have left me for
the moment . . . As soon as it was time for my resolution Mr.
Wacha called out my name. I stood up. My head was reeling.
I read the resolution somehow.' Then he read a poem written
by someone for the occasion, praising emigration. The bell was
rung. Hurt, he sat down.

That's how the first Congress resolution on South Africa
was passed. It seemed to convey nothing to anyone—especially
when one remembers in Natal every Indian who signed the
petition to the Governor had to be told what it contained, and

---

[16] A.

only with his full consent would one accept his signature. Here it was a noble formality. But it gave an official status to the meagre demands of the Indians in South Africa. It would still serve.

And after this annual political festivity everyone went back—leaving Gandhiji behind and in holy despair. Be this the politics of India? And everybody making speeches in English. Dressed like Englishmen, most of them behaved like their masters too. Could this ever bring freedom?

Gokhale had decided to stay on in Calcutta. He was staying at the India Club. Would Gandhiji like to join him? And for one whole month this great Indian leader and Gandhiji shared their experiences.

Gokhale treated Gandhiji like a younger brother.

'To see Gokhale at work was as much a joy as an education. He never wasted a minute. His private relations and friendships were all for public good. All his talks had references only to the good of the country and were absolutely free from any trace of untruth or insincerity. India's poverty and subjection were matters of constant and intense concern for him.'

Gokhale too was moved by the unfaltering honesty and noble devotion of his young companion. Gandhiji thus met many of the important leaders, Gokhale himself arranging the introductions. One of them was with Kalicharan Banerji, the first President of the Congress. He was a convert to Christianity. He was a noble and a humble man.

'Do you believe in the doctrine of original sin?' he asked.

'I do,' replied Gandhiji.

'Well, then, Hinduism offers no absolution therefrom; Christianity does. The wages of sin is death,' Kalicharan Banerji continued, 'and the Bible says that the only way of deliverance is surrender unto Jesus.'

Gandhiji answered that the path of devotion—the Bhakti Marga of the *Bhagavad Gita*—was indeed also a path of salvation. But Kalicharan Banerji would not be convinced.

Gandhiji continued his search. He visited ashrams and spiritual centres. He went in search of Swami Vivekananda at Belur Monastery but the Swami was not there. It is intellectually exciting to question and ponder what might have happened to India and to the world had they really met. Would Swami Vivekananda have talked to him of his own Guru, Sri Ramakrishna, and showed that love, knowledge and freedom are one, and the surest path to liberation the lotus feet of the Sat Guru, the true Guru: the search for the Guru, the only path to the truth?

'I believe in the Hindu theory of 'Guru and his importance' in spiritual realisation. I think there is a great deal of truth in the doctrine that true knowledge is impossible without a Guru. There must, therefore, be ceaseless striving after perfection. For one gets the Guru that one deserves. Infinite striving after perfection is one's right. It is its own reward. The rest is in the hands of God.'[17]

Now Gandhiji went visiting temples.

He went to the temple of Kali and was stupefied the way God, or the Goddess, was worshipped. Did God want so much blood? What a tragedy that this great province of Bengal should have such a tradition. And there were many sadhus around the temple too. One of them stopped Gandhiji and asked:

'Whither are you going, my boy?'

---

[17] A.

'Do you regard this sacrifice as religion?' Gandhiji asked.

'Who would regard killing of animals as religion?'

'Then why don't you preach against it?'

'That's not my business,' said the sadhu. 'Our business is to worship God.'

'But why could you not find another place to worship God?' persisted Gandhiji.

'All places are equally good for us,' said the religious mendicant. 'The people are like a flock of sheep, following where leaders lead them. It is no business of us.'

And what he saw that day he could never, never forget.

So Calcutta had both the bloody temple of Kali and the monastery of Sri Ramakrishna.

He met editors of newspapers. He gave them interviews, wrote letters and articles on the condition of Indians in South Africa. And living in Calcutta[18] he also saw the manner the Indian upper classes lived, the Maharaja and the Nawab, and the way they behaved with the Viceroy—like cooks, thought Gandhiji. 'Do you see any difference between us and the cooks?' asked a Maharaja. 'We are Lord Curzon's cooks.'

'How heavy,' Gandhiji reflected, 'is the toll of sins and wrongs that wealth, power and prestige exact from man!'

He would now go to Benares. And he would no more travel first class. To know India, you must travel third class. That is where India is seen best. Gokhale thought the experience would be exhausting, and excruciating. Gandhiji would not change his plans even to satisfy his leader. He bought himself simple Indian clothes and with just a canvas bag (worth twelve annas), and a long coat made of rough wool, a water-jug, a blanket, he

---

[18] Calcutta at that time was the capital of India.

started on his pilgrimage. Gokhale himself came to mark this great event. 'If you had travelled first, I would never have come. But now I will.' And after blessing his disciple, Gokhale went back to his cab while Gandhiji walked on to his awaiting train. But there was no room in any of the third class compartments. 'It was with great difficulty,' he wrote to Gokhale later, 'that I found a seat in one of the intermediate (class) carriages and that (again) after I offered to stand the whole night if necessary. As it was, it was merely a trick on the part of the friends of some of the passengers. The former had occupied all the room with a view to prevent any more passengers from getting in. They got out as soon as the guard blew the whistle for the train to go . . . You cannot adopt gentleman's time and travel 3rd.'

Yet, when the confusions of Calcutta are left behind and the train settles to its own rhythm, there's a feel, a hidden awareness, not only of the rich rice-fields of Bengal and the rapid bridges over canal and bund, but soon, very soon, one would come to the Ganges herself—great mother of mankind, she flowed with the whispers and sorrows of all the dead and washed them clean of their sins again, and again, and took them from world to world of purification. Was not Hinduism right in worshipping this holy river—come from the head of Shiva himself, so the Shastras say? Her very looks (for example, even when one lands in Calcutta) are other and auspicious. How miserable are we living in our filth and discomfort, carrying baggages of sin on our heads, when she flows by us—she who through Bhagiratha's prayers came down to the world and raised the dead from their ashes, hence is she called Bhagirathi. We too are dead, though no heroes of the *Mahabharata*. Life is a cycle of events. Everything happens in circles. We die and we are reborn. Ages pass, the age of virtue and of lesser virtue, of activity and, finally, of darkness.

No doubt this India with its filth and its corruptions proves
Kali-Yuga, the iron age, is with us.

For Benares, holy Benares, seemed the very epitome of
filth. Is this where Shiva is worshipped—in the midst of these
dank and muck-covered lanes, where street curs sat licking
human excreta, cows browsing cast-off eating-leaves,[19] or monks
shouting their holiness for a piece of bread or coin or a puff of
smoke? Yes, splendour and filth and fervour (look at the devout
white-clad pilgrims) was what Benares revealed. But how go
through such foulness to the holy of holies?

Visiting the temple of Lord Vishwanath was an ordeal.
Should man worship God amidst such noise, slush and priestly
greed?

> 'When I reached the temple I was greeted at the entrance by
> a stinking mass of rotten flowers. The floor was paved with
> fine marble, which was however broken by some devotee
> innocent of aesthetic taste who had set it with rupees serving
> as an excellent receptacle for dust. I went near the Jnana-vepi
> (Well of Knowledge). I searched here for God and failed to
> find him.'

And yet, just round the corner on the bank of the vast, shining
river on which barges floated carrying fuel, grain and pilgrims, was
the burning ghat where Harishchandra was once guardian of the
crematorium—he who had given up his kingdom for his word of
truth. India has to rise someday. But who will save her, hé Rama?

Even at the Benares railway station one saw such corruption.
Tickets were so difficult to get, the police had to be bribed.

---

[19] See Glossary.

'Many availed themselves of the offer. Those of us who would not, had to wait nearly an hour after the window was opened before we could get our tickets, and we would be fortunate at that if we did so without being presented with a kick or two from the guardians of law . . . In the carriages we were packed anyhow. There were no restrictions as to numbers . . . I feel all the richer and stronger in spirit for the experience which I would resume at the first opportunity.'

The only happy factor, however, of his pilgrimage to Benares was the visit he made to Mrs. Annie Besant. She was just recovering from a serious illness. The old free-thinker, suffragette, labour leader, friend of Bernard Shaw, and Fabian, had now turned a theosophical saint devoted to the regeneration of India, the hope of mankind. She had built the Hindu College at Benares to train young Indians to see themselves as esoteric wisdom and tradition saw them—fortunate brethren born to this holy land and home of the future Messiah. Was India truly all this, Gandhiji wondered in torment and sorrow? Now, however, he was going back to Bombay. He would settle down there, practise law, look after his family, and think. And pray!

'I have taken up a room,' he wrote a few days later, 'from Payne Gilbert, Sayanai, and Moos, for office, and a part of Keshavji Tulsidas Bungalow in Girgaum Back Road, for residence. This is all the progress I have made so far.[20]
'I . . . am now free to lounge about the High Court, letting the solicitors know of an addition to the ranks of the briefless ones . . . The work is uphill. But I do not despair.

---

[20] 6 Aug. 1902, C.W., III, p. 261.

I rather like the regular life and the struggle that Bombay imposes on me.'

But this time his legal practice began quickly to grow. And he felt he was well on his way to settling down as a Bombay barrister. 'I am not however anxious about the future,' he wrote to another correspondent some weeks afterwards. 'So far the office work has paid my expenses.'[21]

But God has his own programme for every man.

One day Gandhiji's son, Manilal, fell ill. He had typhoid with pneumonia. The Parsi doctor was an able man and he prescribed for the patient chicken-broth. This is what he gave to all such patients. But Gandhiji was a strict vegetarian. Well, well, said the doctor, his other Hindu patients did not mind. So what should one do? Gandhiji would give the boy fruit juice and liquids. Give him hip-baths that Dr. Kuhne had suggested. Perhaps hydrotherapy is a good way of healing a sick person. 'So I began to give Manilal hip-baths according to Kuhne, never keeping him in the tub for more than three minutes, and kept him on orange juice mixed with water for three days.' But, for the rest, God alone could help. The fever raged and rose up to 104°—and often the boy would be in delirium. It was altogether moving, terrifying. With fervent prayer Gandhiji put a wet sheet round his son's body and a wet towel about the head, and exhausted and in great despair, he went out to have a bit of fresh air. What would happen to his son now? Should he have accepted the doctor's suggestions? Was he a good father at all? Of course the son had agreed with the father, he would not touch chicken-broth. Yet, he was so young. Gandhiji took the

---

[21]   3 November 1902, C.W., III, p. 262.

name of Rama, repeating the Ramanama. 'The thread of life was in the hands of God. My honour is in Thy keeping, O Lord.'

After a short time he came back home, anxious, his heart within his breast.

'You have returned, Bapu?' 'Yes, darling.'

'Do please pull me out. I am burning.'

'Are you perspiring, my boy?'

'I am simply soaked. Do please take me out.'

A little later Gandhiji undid the wet pack and dried Manilal's body. The temperature was coming down. He thanked God. 'Father and son fell asleep on the same bed. And each slept like a log.'

Who knows what gave recovery to the boy. 'Let everyone decide according to his own faith. For my part I was sure that God had saved my honour, and that belief remains unaltered to this day in Bombay.'

He now took a spacious well-ventilated house, and at Santa-Cruz as being best in view of sanitation. 'I prospered in my profession,' he wrote in his autobiography, 'better than I had expected.' However, Gokhale had his eyes on Gandhiji and 'had been making his own plans on my behalf . . . But it may be said,' continued Gandhiji, 'that God has never allowed any of my plans to stand. He has disposed them in His own way.' For the call came from South Africa. 'Chamberlain expected here. Please return immediately.' And once again he sailed for Natal.

'The separation from wife and children, the breaking up of a settled establishment and the going from the certain to the uncertain—all this was for a moment painful, but I had inured myself to an uncertain life. I think it is wrong to expect certainties in this world where all else but God that is

Truth is an uncertainty. All that appears and happens about and around us is uncertain, transient. But there is a Supreme Being hidden therein as a Certainty and hitch one's wagon to it. The quest of that Truth is the *summum bonum* of life.'[22]

* * *

God-inspired and God-fearing Paul Kruger was the hero—'the greatest man the Boer race has produced'. Away in Holland, the country of his pious ancestors, he had tried to rouse the Dutch to their moral responsibility towards his people and also the Germans who were now so boastful of their growing imperial power. The Kaiser had made many and large promises but nothing came of these. The Dutch were busy elsewhere—in Indonesia—and again, who could fight the might of the British? Thus no one came to the help of the poor Boers—however brave they be in their struggle. And like two biblical sons were Smuts and Botha, fighting against the British, though they would not make great headway against their adversaries. The British brought reinforcements from India, from Ceylon—the battle would be won by the magnitude of the Empire. It was a pleasant war for nobody. Finally reduced to the smallest little guerrilla units, the Boers sued for an honourable peace. 'The Boer war is a story of disaster. It was a titanic struggle fought, if one may say so, by pygmies and constitutes a dauntless battling against invincible fate . . .,' wrote Smuts.[23] 'It is a question whether in purely human interest it does not transcend all the great struggles of the past. Such for instance the Persian invasion

---

[22] A., p. 308.
[23] Smuts to Emily Hobhouse, S., p. 188.

of Greece or the Eighty Years War in the Netherlands.'[24] The British decided to declare an armistice. The terms were severe but honourable. Whatever might happen in the future the British and the Boer would have to live together. The Boers had to be tamed but not subjugated. 'God save us from our friends and rulers. And He will.' Anyway the war was now over[25] and everybody sat down to work—the young, the far-seeing Smuts, and the hero, Botha. Meanwhile, however, their great leader, their father, Paul Kruger died in Holland.[26] He was not there to guide them anymore. But such the veneration for him that a short time afterwards when a Dutch ship brought the remains back to his own country, the train that carried them across the veld was asked by the government to stop wheresoever anyone stood by the railway line showing a light. Almost every hamlet had its bunch of flowers, almost every isolated cottage its homage to the great leader. The Boers would remain where they were. Nobody would move them from their home. This was their fatherland that they had built, as it were, with their own mighty hands, led by God the Almighty. And, by God, they would remain here.

The British had to deal with this difficult situation. As long as the road to Kimberley and Johannesburg was clear, the rest would be well. For a while the Boers and the British would have to be ruled from London. Humiliating though this was, it was understandable. The adversary nevertheless was Smuts. He

---

[24]   S., p. 120.

[25]   31 May 1902, when the Peace Treaty was signed at Vereeninging.

[26]   'Ex-President Kruger is dead,' wrote Gandhiji in the *Indian Opinion* (23-7-1904), 'and in him one of the most striking personalities of the nineteenth century has passed away, leaving the world poorer for it. His demeanour . . . was worthy of a great and godly man.'

loved Britain too, and so unhappy the country of John Bright had played the game of 'Capitalists'.

'The world is not exactly made after our pattern,' he wrote to Emily Hobhouse, that brave English woman, suffragette, Fabian, and friend of humanity who had come to South Africa to see things for herself and rouse the British to their moral responsibility, and as such became a lifelong friend of Jan Smuts. 'The world is not exactly made after our pattern, and things do not always come in the way we choose—and somehow the world's and nature's way is fundamentally no worse than which we would have chosen. We learn more and more what a Dutch word expresses so aptly—*to berusten,* to rest in world order, to attain the attainable and to pay silent homage to the unattainable.'[27]

One of the pressing problems however was—what shall one do with the Indians here in Transvaal? Not only the older inhabitants of Indian origin were trying to come back to Transvaal, but the soldiers from Ceylon and India were told by the British, once the war was over, they could stay back if they so wished—after all, it was British territory now. But here a new element had crept into the picture. The British civil servant from India had also come in with the invading army. He also liked a nice comfortable job, in a kind salubrious climate. There were of course jobs going—a country desolated by war always needs active men to help in the reconstruction of the land. And now that there were so many 'Asiatics', an Asiatic department was opened to deal with the Indians who wanted to stay in Transvaal, and also for those who wanted permits to come in. During the war money was easy to make, as always, for everyone, soldier

---

[27] S., Vol. I, p. 197.

and civilian. The Indians were not unwilling to stay back if at all they could. Thus a whole system of 'oriental' bribery was set to function and it became the despair of the Indian. 'In South Africa there was a sort of responsible government or democracy, whereas the commodity imported from Asia was autocracy pure and simple.'[28] Meanwhile, suddenly the British Government had decided on sending Joseph Chamberlain to South Africa.

He would go there to assess the situation and advise, and fix a War Debt on the conquered people. But he was however not going there as a conqueror. He was come to tell the Boers, as long as they were faithful to the Queen there would and should never be a problem for the safety and prosperity of their community in the British Empire. They would be a proud part of it. Smuts, however, with its past deceptions did not believe in the ultimate destiny and nobility of the British Empire. But Gandhiji did. 'They (the Indians),' he wrote, 'are proud to be under the British Crown, because they think that England will prove India's deliverer.'[29]

When Gandhiji landed in Durban the city was totally in ruins because of the war, but everybody was in excitement. A minister of the British Queen was coming to settle matters, and the Indian will not be ignored. Not only he would not be ignored but full justice will be done to him as a British subject, for 'Lord Lansdowne and Lord Selborne had declared the treatment accorded to the Indians was one of the causes of the war'.[30] Gandhiji had by now prepared a memorandum giving a brief summary of the disabilities suffered by Indians in Natal. The

---

[28] A., p. 315.
[29] C.W., Vol. I, p. 258.
[30] S.S.A., p. 81.

Minister of Queen Victoria had, however, to be realistic. The whites ultimately would have to rule South Africa. Of course, the Indians too were British. First, let us deal with the Boers; the Indian problem could wait. In fact, it was a small problem. When he received the Indian delegation and Gandhiji's memorandum, Chamberlain plainly told them that they would have to adjust themselves to circumstances. He almost confessed he could do nothing. Gandhiji realised Chamberlain's delicate position.

Chamberlain could do no better. Does that mean the Indians should be thrown back into the sea? No. The fight will have to begin all over again.

For example, Gandhiji wanted to get into Transvaal. He wanted to be present when Chamberlain came to Pretoria. But one needed to have a permit to get there. The British officer in charge of the 'Asiatics' of course would never give this trouble-maker, Gandhi, a permit to create more confusion in confused Transvaal. His clients wanted him to come to Pretoria. That might well be true. But Gandhiji will not enter Transvaal. Further, if he did he would have to give a little bribe. Why not? As an Indian he must be pretty well accustomed to such methods. But Gandhiji went to his friend in Durban, Police Superintendent Alexander, who was always ready to help. He took Gandhiji straight to the officer in charge and had the permit duly given. Who could refuse the security officer a permit?

So Gandhiji arrived in Pretoria. The authorities in Pretoria were unprepared for him. However, they would see to it Chamberlain would not receive the intruder. Who was Gandhi anyway? Gandhiji did not mind being unwanted by the powers that be. The Indians, however, deeply resented this attitude of the British authorities. Yet, persuaded by Gandhiji, a delegation went to see Chamberlain led by George Godfrey, a Natal-born

Indian barrister. 'Mr. Chamberlain was . . . so anxious to humour the Europeans,' wrote Gandhiji, 'that there was no hope of his doing us justice. Still the deputation waited on him only in order that no legitimate step for obtaining redress be omitted, whether by oversight or through a sense of wounded self-respect.'[31] But Gandhiji did not know what we know today (from official records) that Chamberlain was cold and condescending even to the Boers. 'We saw him only once,' wrote Smuts, 'in a joint body as a public deputation. For the rest he saw none of us and preferred to gather his information and advice from quarters the less said the better.'[32]

For the British had their own plans. Milner continued to dream his British dreams. And since there was the painful problem of insufficient labour in the mines and elsewhere— and, anyway, the Indians were such a nuisance—Chinese coolies would now be imported. The Boers who wanted an all-white South Africa found this would create a further problem. Hence, with Emily Hobhouse as their propagandist, the Boers made the British press and governing class know of this proposed introduction of what they called 'Chinese slavery' into South Africa. Meanwhile, Botha and Smuts played for time against the British. The liberals in England will come to power and the whole perspective would change. For, if the present policy were followed, in the ultimate constitution of South Africa the British idea of one man one vote, would, because of the property qualifications, make the future legislature dominated by the English. The Boers were therefore planning representation by population which would divide the country electorally in such

---

[31] S.S.A., p. 81.
[32] S., p. 192.

a way that the English and the Boers would have almost equal number of seats—the countryside and the city would therefore have equal importance. The Boers, thus, had to woo the British. And in the midst of these urgent preoccupations neither the British nor the Boer had any time for the Indian. Thus, Gandhiji decided, at least for some months his work lay in South Africa. 'I thought even if it meant living in South Africa all my life, I must remain there.' He opened a law office in Johannesburg—he got his chambers through a Theosophist, Mr. Ritch—and somehow even the Supreme Court accepted his application to be enrolled a member of the Bar. He took a house and started his legal practice forthwith. His family would join him later.

He soon wrote to Gokhale, from Court Chambers, Rissik Street (P.O. Box 6522), Johannesburg. 'I have settled here under very great difficulties. The question has assumed a very serious aspect and requires very close attention. How long I will have to stop (here) it is difficult to say. I have hardly time to write about myself.'

He sent letters to the press, he saw ministers, he even led a delegation to Lord Milner, the High Commissioner in South Africa. If anyone could influence government policies, it was he. For Milner, as everybody knew, believed that only Britain would bestow 'equal rights for civilised man south of the Zambesi'. But the Asiatic Office in the Transvaal under a British Governor was often behaving with greater ruthlessness. Indeed, the administration under the Boers was so lax the Indian could own land anywhere, or almost anywhere, ply his trade without much interference though legally there were many impracticable restrictions, and he was especially not made to live in his 'locations'. The British now called these the bazaars, and thus it made the ghetto sound respectable. But it was a question of legal segregation—the Indian could neither own land nor buy land anywhere beyond the bazaar, nor ply his trade beyond the limits of this location. Further, the Asiatic passes were re-introduced though these were made temporary. Thus under the British administration the Indian found himself more unhappy than under the Boers. And the £3 tax, as for that, it would go on. Discussion about this matter, declared Lord Milner, was 'a small point among many big ones'. But for the Indians, and for Gandhiji, it was a very important point, indeed, the most important for it meant a poll-tax just because the Indian was not white but brown.

'But,' said Lord Milner, 'there is no choice in the matter. The law at present says you have to pay £3, and that law is going to be enforced.'

The Indians argued: The Greeks and the Armenians and others, do not pay a special tax. They pay eighteen shillings a year, and that is all. But, objected Lord Milner, they pay it every year and you pay it only once. To which the Indians in answer said: We would rather pay the eighteen shillings a year. No, this would not do. The law was the law. And it would be enforced. The British were there to see to it.

The problem was clear now—Gandhiji could not go home at the end of the year. It was going to be a patient and grim fight here. He wrote to Gokhale to arouse the Viceroy against the inhumanities being perpetrated in South Africa against the Indians. 'The curious thing is,' wrote Gandhiji to Gokhale, 'even here Lord Milner seems to be most anxious to do justice . . . but is almost frightened by what passes as public opinion. As a matter of fact, people in South Africa are so much engrossed in making money that they take very little notice of what is going on outside their own sphere.'

He would have to fight in Transvaal as he had in Natal many years ago. Then what about Kasturba and the children? 'It is a time of constant exertion and worry,' he wrote to an old friend, Haridasbhai Vora, in Rajkot, 'and I see no prospect in the near future of public work slackening . . . I think it will be impossible for me to get away for many years. The question then is as to the fulfilment of my promise to Mrs. Gandhi. I told her that either I should return to India at the end of the year or that she should come here by that time. He could not go back in less than three or four years, perhaps maybe not even then. Would she like to wait in Rajkot or come to Johannesburg? If she came he would be 'content to quietly settle down in Johannesburg for ten years'. So he asks his friend to consult Kasturba and let him know her feelings in the matter. He could not, after all, write to her directly for she could not read—what a pity, for if they had used their time better, when they were younger, she would have learned to read and write. Now perhaps it was too late. Was it?

'I do think,' he went on to say to his friend, 'that if she would consent to remain there for the time being, at any rate, it would enable me to give undivided attention to public work . . . However, I wish to be guided entirely by her sentiments and I place myself entirely in her hands.' And Gandhiji continues, speaking of his friend's daughter: 'I am very glad Bali is not to be married this year. The later she is married the better it will undoubtedly be for herself and her future husband.'

Then he writes to his nephew Chhaganlal. 'I enclose a copy of my letter to Haridasbhai. It gives all the news about me. Read it out and explain the situation to your aunt . . . If she remains there, savings made in this place will enable her and children to lead a comparatively easy life in India . . . But if she insists, I shall not retreat from the promise I made her on the eve of my departure.'

So, it was not that he wanted her back. He was happy to work from a quarter-to-nine in the morning till ten o'clock at night with just enough time for a quick lunch and dinner and a short walk. It was, as he says, a time of constant exertion and worry. And with Kasturba and the children, greater time would be demanded for household affairs. Asceticism seemed somehow to suit him. May it not after all be, as our ancestors believed, the right, the only way of the true life?

Again Indians came to his office to tell him of their manifold woes. The British officers (of the Asiatic Department) told him they did not need his help to look after the Indians. They insulted him. They even 'summoned' him and asked him to leave the country; the British agent was there to look after the welfare of the Indians. 'I pocketed the insult like many others,' wrote Gandhiji later. How could you truly insult a seeker after Truth? Who is there to receive it? But the Indians felt the insult deeply. They had fought for him, beside him, when the British were in trouble. But the times had changed. The British were now the conquerors. The British repealed all Boer laws but the anti-Indian acts were left on the statute books. Yet we must, said Gandhiji, believe in God and go on struggling. Life is meaningful only from this high perspective. Otherwise what *rasa* has life?

The most significant aspect of the Gandhian story is again and again this: You always find someone among your adversaries who takes interest in you, sides with you. You never deal with a monolithic enemy. There is always a just Vibhishana in the court of cruel Ravana.

In fact, for Gandhiji there was no enemy—there were only adverse aspects of man which face you against him. But he, in

essence, is the same as yourself . . . 'It is quite proper,' he wrote
in his autobiography, 'to resist and attack a system, but to resist
and attack its author is tantamount to resisting and attacking
oneself. For we are all tarred with the same Creator, and as
such the divine powers within us are infinite. To slight a single
human being is to slight those divine powers, and thus to harm
not only that being but with him the whole world.'[33]

And there was so much corruption to fight against—the
Indian with his sloth and his filth, the white man with his
arrogance and his greed. The Asiatic Department continued
its habits of 'Oriental bribery'. Indians needed more than ever
to have permits to stay on in the Transvaal. A few pieces of
silver and the trick was made. The police official of Pretoria,
however, was a fine man. Gandhiji showed incontrovertible
documents to reveal the Asiatic Department was making money
on the permits. The police officer had secret agents posted to
watch the evil-makers. This the British officers quickly knew.
They absconded. When, later, brought to trial—the white jury
acquitted them. But the bribery disappeared.

Just as in India there were the Brahmin quarter, the
copper-smith quarter, the weaver's quarter, the potter's quarter,
the pariah quarter—so too there were in Johannesburg, the
rich people's villas, the lesser rich and their homes, and then
somewhere far away, and out of any 'human' proximity as it
were, were the coolie locations or the bazaar, where several
hundred Indians (mostly former indentured labourers) lived in a
small area, leasing land from the government and doing menial
jobs, or hawking vegetables and cheap goods, for the blacks and
the whites, to make a living. Gandhiji had arranged lectures

---

[33] A., p. 337.

and even house-to-house visits to explain to these people how wrong it was to live in the poor sanitary conditions they did—but they would not care. They dumped their filth into the streets, and the filth looked after itself. Gandhiji even appealed to the municipality for help but they were not interested. These ghettos needed no whiteman's worry. But the gods have a sharp eye. Somewhere far away the black plague broke out across the veld in the mining area. It started with the Zulus. And quickly it spread—it spread, the fevers rising quickly, the people dying almost without time for help. One day while Gandhiji was working at his office a message arrived: 'Come immediately. You are needed.' He ran to the coolie location and found almost twenty persons stricken with the black plague. Gandhiji forthwith arranged for emergency isolation and treatment—an abandoned garage was cleaned up, beds put in, and volunteers asked to look after the sick. But the volunteer must not be married and should have no responsibility—in case he too gets the plague. Gandhiji as usual was fearless. The municipality suddenly realised the danger. Even a nurse was sent to look after the patients. Then they sent brandy, the only remedy then known against the black plague. Gandhiji however tried curing three patients with his mud packs. Two of them recovered. All the rest however died—including the nurse.

This was to be the end of the coolie location. The government bought back the leases from the Indians. They were so poor they had no place to put their money—so they dug their small riches out, and with the government compensations, the whole amount was given to Gandhi just for safe keeping. He became their accounts keeper, their banker. Finally a bank opened accounts for them. Meanwhile they had been moved over to the open spaces for about three weeks. And a new township was built for them. The government, almost symbolically, set fire to the coolie locations and the whole Indian town burnt to ashes in a day. 'And the city once more breathed freely.'

An eccentric Englishman of the growing Gandhian tribe was Albert West of Louth (Lincolnshire). The son of a simple cobbler, he had come to South Africa to earn an honest living. While there he had found the moral significance of vegetarianism. From vegetarianism interest he had now moved on to Buddhism. And as there was a vegetarian restaurant in Johannesburg, Mr. West went there to eat; so did Gandhiji, the two seeing each other almost every day. But they did not say very much to one another. Gandhiji was always very shy and so was Mr. West. One day, however, Mr. West discovered that Gandhiji seemed to have been absent for too long a time. He wondered why. And he heard that Gandhiji had become a nurse looking after his people stricken with the black plague. Could he not help? Of course he could, on condition he had no commitments elsewhere, that he was not married, etc. All the Indians working at the nursing station were bachelors—all except Gandhiji, of course. Mr. West joined them. And thus Gandhiji and he became true friends.

Now at this time the Indian community had become alive to its position, its problems. They wanted to know what was happening and where, and South Africa is vast—almost as vast as India. It was therefore proposed an Indian paper be started. Gandhiji liked the idea; a journal of Indian affairs in four languages—Gujarati, Tamil, Telugu and English. To be called *Indian Opinion,* it was to appear from Durban. Mr. Naazar, a colleague and a journalist by profession, was to be its editor. Gandhiji gave money to support it and soon it appeared a real success. But the success of a journal has two sides to it—its influence on public affairs, and its own financial stability. Financially the paper was not able to live by its own earnings. Very soon, on ethical grounds, it refused to take on advertisements or job works. Gandhiji did not mind giving it all the money he could—almost a thousand pounds a year—however, was it morally justifiable? The paper, to be sane, had to stand on its own earnings. After some time, however, the *Indian Opinion* seemed to pay its way.

Its printer, Mr. Madanjit, was wanted in Johannesburg to look after the sick. Could Mr. West, professionally a printer, go and look after the paper? Since he wanted to work with Gandhiji here was something he could do that would be of great help. Mr. West thought it over for a moment—he was to be paid the modest sum of £10 a month—all that the publishers could pay. Mr. West accepted. There was also a proposition; if ever profits were made he would have a percentage of that as well. 'The very next day,' says Gandhiji, 'Mr. West left for Durban by the evening mail . . . From that day until the time I left the shores of South Africa he remained a partner of my joys and sorrows.' But soon Mr. West discovered, on arrival at Durban, that not only the paper was not making any money—but it was running at a loss. 'I had simply accepted Mr. Madanjit's estimate without caring to examine it, and told Mr. West to expect a profit . . . I now realised that a public worker should not make statements of which he has not made sure. Above all, a votary of Truth must exercise the greatest caution. To allow a man to believe a thing which one has not fully verified is to compromise truth.'

Now at this time there was another eccentric Englishman—a Jew. Could there be an ideological or anti-ideological movement, anywhere in the world, without the humble Jew ready to help humans bear their heavy, their ancient sorrow, he the eldest of humanity, he himself ever bearing the moral burden before his God. Such was Mr. Polak, gentle, highly civilised, widely-read, and a vegetarian. He and Gandhi had as usual met at the vegetarian restaurant. Mr. Polak worked on the *Critic*. And he began to get interested in this young Indian and his ideas.

On hearing of Mr. West's plight, Gandhi immediately started (once the black plague was over) for Durban. He had to set things right there. When Mr. Polak came to the station to bid goodbye to his new friend, he left a book in Gandhiji's hands. It was Ruskin's *Unto This Last*.

'The book,' says Gandhi 'was impossible to lay aside once I had begun it. It gripped me. Johannesburg to Durban was a twenty-four hour journey. The train reached there in the evening. I could not get any sleep that night. I determined to change my life in accordance with the ideals of the book.'

'I believe that I discovered,' goes on Gandhiji, 'my deepest convictions reflected in this great book of Ruskin and that is why it so captured me and made me transform my life. A poet is one who can call forth the good latent in the human breast . . .'

'The teachings of *Unto This Last* I understood to be:

'1. That the good of the individual is contained in the good of all.
'2   That the lawyer's work has the same value as the barber in as much as all have the same rights of earning their livelihood.
'3   That the life of labour, i.e. life of the tiller of the soil and the handicraftsman is the life worth living.

The first of these I knew. The second I had dimly realised. The third had never occurred to me. *Unto This Last* made it clear to me that the second and the third were contained in the first. I arose with the dawn ready to reduce the principles to practise.'

Thus when he reached Durban, and after due discussions with Mr. West, Gandhiji (with the aid of some friends) bought a farm some fifteen miles away from Durban—a hundred acres of dry land with snakes and shrubs—and this was going to be the colony from where the *Indian Opinion* would henceforth appear. A steam-press was bought too, and a supplementary hand-press in case something went wrong. The Durban office continued for Mr. Madanjit preferred to live there. But the Phoenix Settlement, as it was called, was already active with houses to build and wells to dig, and soon the paper would also be printed from here. On the night, however, when the paper was ready to come out of the press—the machine would not work. People were desperate. It just would not move. Why not wait till the morning and then the mechanical help would be available from Johannesburg and everything will be set right. Why should one wait till the morning? was Gandhiji's question. Let us take the hand wheel and work it. There were the building carpenters asleep nearby. Perhaps they too would be of help. Many of them had been with Gandhiji in the Boer War. They readily agreed.

'West was greatly delighted and started singing a hymn as we set to work. I partnered the carpenters, all the rest joined turn by turn, and thus we went on till 7 a.m.' And then when one went to the machine, it suddenly started working . . .

'For me,' Gandhiji goes on to comment, 'the failure of the engine had come as a test for us all and its working at the nick of time as a fruit of our honest and earnest labours . . . The copies were despatched in time and everyone was happy.'

For years he had contributed articles to the paper and it had virtually become his means of communication with other Indians, with the sympathetic Westerner, and finally with the vast world. 'Indian Opinion in those days,' he writes, 'was a mirror of part of my life. Week after week I poured out my soul in its columns. I cannot recall a word in those articles set out without thought or deliberation, or a word of conscious exaggeration, or anything merely to please. Indeed the journal became for me a training in self-restraint.'[34]

Kasturba had by now joined him. She preferred to be with her husband. Her husband was Lord, whatever his makings, and his home her sanctuary. 'Rama walked in front and Lakshman behind him wearing with dignity their hermit's dress, and between the two came Sita resplendent as Illusion between the Absolute and the Individual Soul.'[35] The children too, Harilal and Manilal, came along with her. And with all the co-workers about one, it was already a large family, whether in Johannesburg or at the Phoenix Colony. And everybody worked, including the children, giving the best of themselves to each other. For what is the world but an enlarged joint-family. Thus wheresoever Gandhiji established himself was ever a new Porbandar, the home town and the family home.

* * *

The Christian God could be his God—no, not the God of the Old Testament. He wanted Truth to be 'tender as a blossom', the simplicity, the love of Jesus, the Christianity of the Sermon on the Mount, and not of Moses speaking to God on Mount

---

[34] A., p. 348.
[35] The *Ramayana* of Tulsidas.

Sinai. Hence what was Gandhiji to do? He wanted a Krishna, a Sri Rama. But you had only to go to a temple like the one at Rajkot—*how* could one accept such a god? At this moment appeared the Theosophists who had discovered Krishna and Christ spoke the same Truth—in fact, the balance of splendours lay on the Krishna incarnation. India, the 'hoary home' of religion, the great receptacle of the spirit, it was she the mother of the world. She knew not of herself what none others knew. She spoke for Jesus and for Mohammed, for Zoroaster, for the prophets of the past and of the future. Glory be to India!

The Theosophists of Johannesburg asked Gandhiji to be their guide, their 'teacher'. How could he who knew so little Sanskrit, and so little of Hindu philosophy? Yes, he could, so they decided. His *samskaras*[36] (of his past life) were in him—otherwise he would not be a Hindu. His blood would understand what his mind might not know. And as he went back to the Indian texts which he thus far knew only in English or Gujarati translations, the Sanskrit seemed, even with the feeble knowledge he had of that language, so precise, so rich. He turned to the *Gita* all the time. 'It became,' he writes in his autobiography, 'my dictionary of daily reference. Just as I turned to the English words that I did not understand, I turned to this dictionary of conduct for a ready solution of all my troubles and trials.' It became, ultimately, '*Gita,* my mother'.

* * *

The Zulus were a direct people, tall, extravagant, cruel and beautiful. They killed without stint, as they gave without

---

[36] See Glossary.

calculation. They bore no grudge against their enemies, they trusted as much as they once deceived but never trusted a second time. When Retief, the Boer leader, and his men came to Dingaan, as fierce and true as his half-brother Cheka—Cheka the hero and nation-builder—Retief wanted from the Zulu chief the whole of Natal. It would be a Boer republic and away from those devilish British. He, Retief, had recovered for Dingaan most of the cattle the chief Sikonyele had stolen from him, and so Natal was but a proper gift to such a courageous ally, indeed a true wizard was he. Retief then went back to the trekkers to tell them of their new dispensation. But by now Dingaan had become suspicious. Even before the treaty was concluded these Retief's people were wandering about as if indeed it was already their territory. After giving his people the good news Retief went back to Dingaan, despite all the warnings of his friends. Meanwhile, when news came to Dingaan that the white 'army' was already on the march—with their 'walking houses' (ox wagons), 'hornless cattle' (horses), and 'shooting sticks' (fire-arms),[37]—though these were only impatient trekkers who'd started moving in while the negotiations were still in progress— Dingaan thought he understood their wizardry. He invited Retief to a party, a great war dance, and when everybody was merry he shouted, 'Kill the wizards' and all the whites were slain. And the men hidden behind mountain and high bush fell on the Boers—wagon loads of a thousand men, women and children, and they were all massacred. But the whites were going to come back. What could assegais do against the gun—nothing. Now the whites had an even more powerful weapon. They had, with great difficulty, pushed up one piece of cannon through the

---

[37] E.P., p. 342.

trails of the trek. Against this monster who could ever fight? Dingaan's men suddenly came towards it, wave after wave of them—'Thirty-six regiments . . . close-packed, with proud-plumes, with shields and assegais, with great roaring'—and they were all slaughtered. Thus the story of Blood River and the celebration of Dingaan's Day by the Boers.[38] The Zulus moved elsewhere, to another Africa; Africa was so large. Yet the whites would follow them. For the gold and diamond rush made every bit and piece of Africa important. Little by little the Zulu had to be subdued and then made to work. He would not work. Why should he? The whites therefore imposed a poll-tax on him. And the Zulus revolted (1906). Called the 'Zulu Rebellion', it was only a skirmish—a police action of the whites against the Zulus. The whites would go hunting the Zulus, hang them, or wound or kill them wherever they could and leave them there. Who was there to look after them?

Loyal to the British as ever, though he did not believe this police action to be just, Gandhiji offered his help. 'I then believed that the British Empire existed for the welfare of the world.' He would organise his stretcher bearers again. The British eagerly accepted the help. Gandhiji sent his family—which had now joined him in Johannesburg—to Natal, to the Phoenix Colony. He became a sergeant major. 'I was,' says Gandhiji, 'delighted on reaching headquarters to hear that our main work was to be nursing the wounded Zulus. The Medical Officer welcomed us. He said the white people were not willing nurses for the wounded Zulus—that their wounds were festering and that he was at his wit's end . . . The Zulus were delighted to see us. The white soldiers used to peer through the railings that separated

---

[38] It is now South Africa's national day.

us from them and tried to dissuade us from attending to the wounds. And as we would not heed them, they became enraged and poured unspeakable abuse on the Zulus . . .Gradually I came into closer touch with these soldiers, and they ceased to interfere. Among the commanding officers were Col. Sparks and Col. Wylie who had bitterly opposed me in 1896.[39] They were surprised at my attitude and specially called and thanked me.'

Most of the wounds were not wounds of battle. They were the result of floggings. And being uncared for, became vicious sores. Besides nursing, Gandhiji also 'had to compound and dispense prescription for white soldiers . . . This work,' he says, 'brought me in close contact with many Europeans.'

Sometimes they had to march thirty or forty miles a day—and the terrain was the harsh veld. 'But,' continues Gandhi, 'wherever we went I am thankful that we had God's work to do, having to carry to the camp those Zulu friendlies who had been inadvertently wounded, and to attend to them as nurses.'

* * *

High on the veld however, as Gandhiji walked, he had time and peace to think of other and more inward growing things. 'Marching with or without the wounded through these solemn solitudes I often fell into deep thought.' He now knew he had to take important decisions. For over ten years his spiritual energies

---

[39] They were civilians having volunteered for military duty because of the Zulu 'rebellion'. Col. Wylie took an important part in the opposition of the white citizens of Durban against the landing of the Indians from the sister ships, the *S.S. Courland* and the *S.S. Naderi*.

had been growing—they sought far and wide for pointedness and guidance. But at some moment in one's existence one must take solemn decisions. His most important problem was not non-possession or even equanimity but the vow of *brahmacharya,* of celibacy. Was it not time, his spirit said, to take the decision now?

'I pondered over *brahmacharya,'* he writes, 'and its implications, and my convictions took deep root. I discussed this with my coworkers. I had not realised then how indispensable it was for self-realisation, but I could see one aspiring to serve humanity with his whole soul could not do without it . . . In a word I could not live both after the flesh and spirit . . . Without the observance of *brahmacharya* service of the family would be inconsistent with service of the community. With *brahmacharya* they would both be perfectly consistent.'

'So thinking,' he continues, 'I became somewhat impatient to take a final vow. The prospect of the vow brought a certain kind of exultation. Imagination also found free play, and opened out limitless vistas of service.'[40]

The Zulu 'war' was over. Returning to Phoenix he discussed the problem with some of his colleagues including his loyal cousin and follower, Maganlal Gandhi. And with West as well. The task was difficult but the decision had to be made.

The primal thrust towards God, the final turning away from body—our first possession—the way. If everything belonged to God and only to God, our first possession must be our supreme gift, back to Him. The body must not only be kept pure and strong—it must also become the true vessel of our being. Hydropathy was not in itself the whole remedy. Of

---

[40] A., p. 386-88.

course, hip-baths and such other cleansing methods (so lauded by Dr. Kuhne) were indeed of very great help. But to this was added mud treatment. A wet pack on the belly gives one relief from most stomach diseases. And after all the stomach is the chief source of malady—and earth, mother of man.

To remove the source of malady is one thing but to give up the feeling of the body is something totally different. If the taste for food is one of our primary attributes—and Gandhiji liked good and tasty food—our desire for sexual intercourse is even more vitally so. You could, little by little, change your diet from spiced foods to boiled vegetables and fruits and nuts. But with his best efforts the desire for his wife's body persisted, almost with intolerable potency. He would still sleep away from her, or exhaust himself altogether so that he should have no vitality left for sexual consummation. But such is bodily passion—and Gandhiji was, as we have seen, a very passionate man—the body would come back to itself, and make its ungovernable demands. What could one do? And here the *Gita* gave him the final help. Brahmacharya is the way, it said—celibacy itself is called The Way to God.[41] Then may it not be the only way to be dedicated totally to God? And he prayed for guidance. The spirit was always there, within, to help. Yes, it would help him. And what about his wife, Kasturba? Her body was never a problem with her. The procreative energy must now and finally be turned away from all 'carnal passions'—it must be burnt at the fire of Truth—therefore he must now take a vow of celibacy. Would he?

Now the power of the vow (*vrata*) is one of the most mysterious attributes a spiritual man possesses. It is not merely a decision to do or not to do a thing. It makes, as it were, for a

---

[41] Literally, Brahmacharya means Way to Brahman.

total transformation—or rather a transfiguration of our spiritual element which establishes one in a different sphere to which one is accustomed to move and have one's being in. It gives one a new perspective on the things one sees—the vow creates, as it were, cosmic reverberations. A vow, any vow, taken by a serious man and in the right spirit has the power, for reasons as yet inexplicable, an alchemic quality of transformation.

Gandhiji, for example, had written to Rajachandra asking him what one should do if a serpent were there, ready to attack him. Rajachandra had replied—you must choose between wanting to preserve your own perishable body and the desire to destroy a life. Which is the better way? Gandhiji then decided he would not inflict *himsa,* or suffering, against any living thing. So, as it should, one day he found himself face-to-face with a serpent. It was inside a lumber room. Its only way out was by passing close to Gandhiji. And by now the situation was such that Gandhiji could not go back on his footsteps. He could go forward or stay where he was. If he stayed where he was the serpent would certainly attack him, afraid for its life. Thereupon Gandhiji sat himself down, stretched his legs across the doorway, and waited, praying to God to give him help. Slowly, very slowly, the serpent unwound itself and moving quietly and carefully, went over Gandhiji's legs like it would over a log, and then it disappeared. This is not the normal behaviour with serpents. How then explain such an experience? The answer is direct; there was an inner transformation—a transfiguration in Gandhi—not a passing one but, as it were, of a primary psycho-biological nature. The serpent had no fear. Gandhiji was saved both in his life and in his desire not to kill.

Such is the power of the vow. He had seen his mother take vows and keep them strictly. And she went about life as if nothing was ever given up. For a vow is not a deprivation—it is consecration.

He would now take the vow of celibacy, of *brahmacharya*.

'I took the plunge—the vow to observe *brahmacharya* for life. I must confess that I had not then fully realised the magnitude of the task I undertook. The difficulties are even today staring in the face. The importance of the vow is being more and more borne in upon me. Life without *brahmacharya* appears to be insipid and animal-like. The brute by nature knows no self-restraint. Man is man because he is capable of, and only in so far as he exercises, self-restraint. What formerly appeared to me to be extravagant praise of *brahmacharya* in our religious books seems now, with increasing clearness every way, to be absolutely proper and founded on experience . . .

'It *(brahmacharya)* begins with bodily restraint but does not end there. The perfection of it precludes even an impure thought . . . Saints and seers have left their experiences for us, but they have given us no infallible and universal prescription. For perfection of freedom from error comes only from grace, and so seekers after God have left us mantras, such as *Ramanama,* hallowed with their own austerities and charged with their purity. Without an unreserved surrender to His grace complete mastery over thought is impossible.'

The second discipline enjoined by the *Gita* is *aparigriha*: Non-possession (of material things, mainly wealth). For Gandhiji this was not such a difficult problem. He earned well but he had no taste for money. Money should belong to nobody. Yet what was the true attitude towards money? He suddenly had light on the problem—money belonged to God, we were only trustees. Every piece of copper coin belonged only to God, and whether you were rich or poor you used it for the service of God, not own it—nobody owns money.

> 'My study of English law came to my help. Snell's discussion of the maxims of equity came to my memory. My regard for jurisprudence increased. I discovered in it religion. I understood the *Gita* teaching of non-possession—that those who desired servants should act like the master . . .'[42]

God seemed, at once, so near and so far. Every act could now become an act of prayer.

Already Gandhiji had in his house his clerks, his relations, and friends (and a number of Europeans amongst these). Everybody shared whatever there was to be shared.

There was no real need to give up anything. But to enlarge this joint family to the whole of the humankind was the next problem.

How to do it with a brother in Kathiawar, so loving, so worthy of reverence, but who, however, depended on Gandhiji's own regular monthly payments for living? That would have to be stopped from now onwards. If the whole world is your family you may of course love your brother. But you cannot give him any special place in your responsibilities.

> 'To my brother . . . I wrote explaining that I had given him all that I had saved up to the moment but that henceforth he should expect nothing from me, for future savings, if any, would be utilised for the benefit of the community.'

---

[42] A., p. 323-29.

The brother was upset. He wrote back an angry letter. What? Had Mohan forgotten it was he, Lakshmidas, that had against hatreds and anxieties, sold land, honour, and jewellery to send the younger brother to London? How could one be so unremembering? What would their revered father and mother have said if they were still in body and breath? What would not happen to the family if no money came from he for whose future they had poured their all, and on whose munificent future depended the material welfare of so many, many? Is this what tradition had taught his younger brother? Let him recognise his duties to the family, as his father and grandfather had ever done. And not show disrespect to your elders, your home, your religion. To this rhodomantade Gandhiji wrote a noble and realistic reply.[43]

'Respected Sir, I have received your letter. I wish to answer it with the utmost calmness and as fully as possible.

'I am afraid our outlooks differ widely and I see no possibility, for the present, of their being reconciled. You seek peace and happiness through money. I don't depend on money for my peace: and for the moment at any rate my mind is quite calm and able to stand any amount of suffering.

'You desire to attain *moksha*, so do I. If you have really got to the stage of striving for *moksha*, you should remain calm and unperturbed, and forget all about me, even if I am extremely sinful and maybe deceiving you. But you are not able to do so because of your excessive attachment. This is

---

[43] Written in Gujarati about 20 April 1907, of which this is a much condensed English version. C.W., Vol. I, pp. 631-35.

what I believe: but if I am wrong in holding this belief, I prostrate myself at your feet and beg to be forgiven.

'I fail to understand what you mean by the word 'family'. To me the family includes not only the two brothers but the sister as well. It also includes our cousins. Indeed, if I could say without arrogance, I would say my family comprises all living beings: the only difference being that those who are more dependent on me because of blood relationship or other circumstances, get more help from me.'

In actual fact when he was looking after the plague-stricken, had not the elder then reproached him saying, what might happen if he, Mohan, died—Kasturba and the children would all have to be dependants on the joint family. It was because of this incident, truly to speak, that Mohan had taken out an insurance policy. 'If by any chance you die before me you may be sure that I shall myself (serve as) an insurance policy for your wife and children. I beseech you to feel sure on this account.'

Further, all these marriages that are taking place, how corrupting? For example, Harilal, Gandhiji's own son, had been married away, and now the nephew was engaged to get married. This was all due to the sensuous atmosphere they lived in back in Kathiawar. Even his son, one could say, Harilal, who had gone home for some time went astray because of this dissipated environment. Fortunately the other three children, Manilal, Ramdas and Devdas, they are all growing up in the healthy atmosphere of Phoenix. It is necessary for Indians to observe *brahmacharya* even if they are married. In fact, even if his three sons should go unmarried, 'I should not be sorry but rejoice instead.'

However, to return to the problem of money.

'As for your demand for a hundred rupees a month, I see neither the means at present nor the need of meeting it. Moreover I may have to go to gaol in the course of the struggle here against the new Ordinance . . . If . . . I am free from trouble I shall try and send you the money you have asked for by money order with the sole intention of pleasing you.

'I am not the master of my earning since I have dedicated my all to the people. I do not suffer from the illusion that it is I who earn; I simply believe that God gives me the money for making good use of it . . .

'I revere you as you are my elder brother. But I have greater regard for truth. Do please believe me when I say I have written all this with the best of intentions. If you do that your displeasure will cease. Wherever you think I am erring, please bear with me.'

Kasturba was upset with the financial situation. What will happen to us now? Son of a prime minister and all that, and henceforth we would have to live like beggars. Fine thing to say 'possess nothing'. How can a woman trained life after life to fend for herself in times of calamities—how could she be without a piece of gold? But the God, Gandhiji argued, who sends you these calamities is also the God who protects you. Every experience is a trial—a loving trial placed by Him for us to get nearer Him. There is nothing to fear. Everything is his doing—his compassion.

Thus all money henceforth was going to belong to anybody that needed it. But there was a small problem. How could a man insure himself when God was there to protect. The small insurance policy he had taken earlier was now given up. From now on Gandhiji had no money of his own.

The *Gita* also gave one more category of spiritual discipline: *samabhava*—equanimity. For a man of passions to have equanimity is difficult. There is that moving story of Kasturba with the untouchable's chamber-pot. Once when they were living in Durban, one of Gandhiji's clerks, a Christian, also lived with them. He was only a recent convert—he was, by birth, an untouchable. To eat with him and stay in the same house with him was itself a great torture for Kasturba. But Gandhiji insisted that among the duties of the household for everybody's performance, was the clearance of the daily chamber-pot as well. But when it came to Kasturba's turn, her ancestral prejudice rose up—she would never touch that chamberpot! A thousand times never. Gandhiji pleaded with her but she would not bend. Finally he became angry—he shouted, 'Get out of the house!' If she could not do what she was expected to do in this house— and a wife obeys her husband—she had just to go back. But go where? Here she was in South Africa, far away from her people and home—where was she to go? He opened the gate and wanted her to leave. She begged him to have a little self-respect. 'I put on a brave face, but was really ashamed and shut the gate. If my wife could not leave me, neither could I leave her.' Yes, he was wrong to be angry. But he would not give up his principles. The chamber-pot of the untouchable had to be cleared. There was no question whatsoever about it. And Kasturba now accepted the rule and followed her husband's 'idiosyncrasies'. 'Willingly or unwillingly, consciously or unconsciously, she has considered herself blessed in following my footsteps.'

'Today I am in a position to narrate,' said Gandhiji almost twenty years later, 'the incident with some detachment as it belongs to a period out of which I have fortunately emerged. I am no longer a blind, infatuated husband. I am no more my wife's teacher. Kasturba can, if she will, be as unpleasant to me today, as I used to be to her before. We are tried friends, and no longer regarding the other as the object of lust . . . Suffice it to say, with the gradual disappearance in me of the carnal appetite, my domestic life became and is becoming more and more peaceful, sweet and happy.'[44] A sister at last!

6

Towards *Ramrajya*

The Kingdom of Sri Rama

The erect, the true, is not easy to reckon with. It creates its own moods, movements, majesty. It will not be subjugated, it plays its own game, as if in solipsist intoxication. Out of the contradictions of the possible it chooses its own mystery—its way of redemption. The true has no barriers and is therefore senseless to time. What comes and goes has to do with the laws of give and take, the mighty and the meek, but this which only gives, what a Ganges!—which Smuts and which Botha could ever stop its flow? Rolling on itself it appears in unexpected corners of space or seasons, monsoons, forever a play of creative revolution—you must be fascinated with the play and not be carried away by its consequences. The consequences are included in the play—they never stay apart. Life must be played. Its rules are simple. To obey not the players but the play.

Now that the Boer War was long over, and the British and the Boers—the two Teutonic peoples—in spite of all their differences, being white in a black land wanted to live together. 'At the southern corner of the vast continent,' Smuts had written earlier, 'peopled by 200,000,000 barbarians, about half-a-million whites have taken up a position with a view not only to working out their destinies—our destiny, but also of using that position as a basis for lifting up and opening up that vast dead weight of immense barbarism and animal savagery to the light and blessing of ordered civilisation.'[1]

They, the whites, had to learn to live together if they were not going to be submerged by this rising tide of prolific barbarism (to which a spot of trouble, some yellow and brown, were also now added) and therefore when a new government came, new laws too had to be enacted. After all, the Boers were very brave and they were willing to play the game. Each of the colonies—the Cape, Natal, the Orange Free State and Transvaal—were to be independent and self-governing colonies, to be sometime later fitted into a federation. For the moment they would claim independence, and they would have it. Jan Smuts rose out of it all the principal, the austere figure, understanding enough to be British and tough enough to be a Boer. Philosophy was his strength (he had stubbornly fought against philosophical dualism of every type) and he had reached a rude but fierce and noble perception of his God. His God played for holism.[2]

'From the Whole you can go down to the parts,' he wrote, 'from the parts as such you can never rise to the Whole; and if you are in search of truth, it is hopeless to begin with partial truths, however important and useful they may in other respects be . . . The Whole is the All, but not in an arithmetical sense.' Yet evolution was a 'cosmic process of individuation.' And in this process man has become a 'legislative being' and thus by degrees

---

[1] S., p. 56.

[2] 'Holism, is the ultimate activity which prompts and pulses through all other activities in the universe.' S., p. 304.

to attain his own wholeness, and finally become united with the Whole. And progress then might be through history, though Evil and Good may both increase with the progress of man. Yet Evil 'in its gross external form may diminish' though the sensitive may feel it with even greater acuity. 'Hence the greatest men are the least happy in the ordinary sense. But here again the Whole exerts its wholesome influence and as a compensation they know a blessedness which is unintelligible and unrealised to smaller natures.'[3] And thus, as Marcus Aurelius has said, we march on, ever and ever to the 'City of God'.

It is, as Smuts' biographer has remarked, the creed of the warrior.

In trying to put order in Transvaal affairs, now that independence was soon coming, new laws were passed—one of them the Immigration Restriction Act. It became Asian for two reasons. The Indian problem had to be removed from the context of the Empire. Therefore, since a few Chinese too were now being recruited, they also became 'coolies'. The new law simply stated that all adult Asians had to register and carry an identity card for fear of illegal immigration into the Republic of Transvaal. This ruling was not, however, legal,[4] for in all other parts of the British Empire any subject could go and come anywhere he liked and, again, wheresoever the indentured Indians had settled, no such law prevailed. If you were a British subject you had to be treated like a British subject. (The Boers were trying hard to be British subjects—they never could, nor

---

[3] S., p. 307.
[4] The London Convention (signed on 27 February 1884) between the Boers and the British, Article XIV, assured persons other than natives, full liberty of entry, travel, residence, ownership of property and trade in the South African Republic. C.W., Vol. I, p. 385.

could the Indians—but they were all making an earnest attempt to be so.) The Boers, however, wanted such a law passed and the British joined with them in this demand, for one could never forget, first of all, one is white in a very black country. But there was also some good reason for the Boer attitude. Indians could cross over the Natal border easily, and how could one know one Indian from the other? And the Indians were ubiquitous and very clever. Thus a certain justification being seen, Indians accepted the law, and registered themselves obediently. But the truth of the truth was, Smuts and Botha ultimately wanted the 'Asiatic cancer' out. This the Indian community at that time did not know. They still basked under the protective glory of the British Empire.

Meanwhile, for no understandable reason the new Asiatic Law Ordinance was published (22 August 1906), the forerunner to the historic Black Act. According to this, Indians above the age of eight had to register themselves, giving their finger and thumb impressions, and carry a pass on them which could be asked for by any policeman. And any policeman could, in fact, even enter an Indian home and demand to see this certificate. 'I have never known,' wrote Gandhiji, 'legislation of this nature being directed against free men in any part of the world.' But the Boers had very good reason to be suspicious of the growing Indian population. 'It is not the vices of the Indians,' wrote Lionel Curties, the Assistant Colonial Secretary of Transvaal, 'that we fear, but their virtues.' Therefore harass them till they leave you bale and bundle. We don't want them. We hardly need them. So they must go. And in actual fact, once these laws were effective in South Africa they could serve as an example for all other 'Dominions of the Empire'.

When the Indians heard of this new ordinance—they were very angry. Gandhiji was in Phoenix when this legislation was formulated and he rushed to Johannesburg to be of help to the community. Polak, who had now become an attorney, was there looking after the law office. And many whites were as enraged as the Indians with the ordinance. A meeting was called at the Empire Theatre, Johannesburg (11 September 1906). Abdul Gani, President of the Transvaal British Indian Association, was in the chair.

There were three thousand Indians in the hall—'from door to ceiling'. The atmosphere was one of war rather than of negotiation: 'Better die than submit to such a law'. The Muslims—and the majority were Muslims—were even more enraged. The ordinance had not only demanded a photograph of themselves—which was forbidden by their religion—but said their women too should go and sign in for such a registration, and this no decent Muslim would allow his woman to do. 'If anyone came forward to demand a certificate from my wife, I would shoot him on the spot and take the consequences.' Such was the mood. Sheth Haji Habib, one of the chief speakers, by the time he came to read the resolution, was already in a highly emotional state. In getting angrier and angrier he cried out that the resolution had to be passed 'with God as our witness'.

This touched Gandhiji to the depth of his awakened being. He had just taken the vow of *brahmacharya*. He now knew the power of taking a vow before God. If the Indian meant what they said they should not simply vote a resolution—but each one, before his God, should take the oath, to himself. 'We all believe in one and the same God, the differences of nomenclature in Hinduism and Islam notwithstanding,' Gandhiji declared.

'To pledge ourselves or to take an oath in name of God or with him as witness is not something to be trifled with. If having taken such an oath we violate our pledge, we are guilty before God and man. Personally I hold that a man who deliberately and knowingly takes a pledge and breaks it forfeits his manhood . . . A man who lightly pledges his word and then breaks it becomes a man of straw and fits himself for punishment here as well as hereafter . . .'

'The Government,' he went on, 'has taken leave of all sense of decency. We would only be betraying our unworthiness and cowardice if we cannot stake our all in the face of the conflagration which envelopes us, and sit watching it with folded hands.

'There is no doubt, therefore, that the present is a proper occasion for taking pledges . . . But every one of us must think out for himself if he has the will and the ability to pledge himself . . . Everyone must search his own heart, and if the inner voice assures him that he has the requisite strength to carry him through, then only should he pledge himself and then only will his pledge bear fruit.

'A few words now as to the consequences. Therefore I would give you an idea of the worst that can happen to us in the present struggle. Imagine that all of us present here, numbering three thousand at the most, pledge ourselves. Imagine that the remaining 10,000 Indians take no such pledge. We will provoke only ridicule in the beginning . . . Some or many of those who pledge themselves may weaken at the very first trial. We may have to go to jail where we may be insulted. We may have to go hungry and suffer extreme heat or cold. Hard labour may be imposed upon us. We may be fined heavily and property may be attached and held up to auction. Opulent today we may be reduced to abject poverty tomorrow. We may be deported. Some of us may fall ill and even die. In short, therefore, it is not at all impossible that we may have to endure every hardship that we can imagine. If someone asks me when and how the struggle may end I may say that if the entire community manfully stands the test, the end will be near. If many of us will fail back under storm and stress, the struggle will be prolonged. But I can boldly declare, and with certainty, that as long as there is even a handful of men true to their pledge, there can only be one end to the struggle—and that is victory.'

He was applauded. But it was not applause he wanted. He now spoke gently, softly, with that clear, halting, musical voice, that became so familiar to us later, and somehow tied us to it. It seemed to draw the breath out of you to yourself. It made you face yourself as if he were indeed you.

'There is only one course open to someone like me to die but not to submit to the law. It is quite unlikely, but even if everyone else flinched leaving me alone to face the music, I am confident that I will never violate my pledge. Please do not misunderstand me. I am not saying this out of vanity, but I wish to put you, especially the leaders on the platform, on your guard. I wish respectfully to answer it to you that if you have not the will and the ability to stand firm even when you are perfectly isolated, you must not only take the pledge but you must declare your opposition before the resolution is put to the meeting . . . Although we are going to take the pledge in a body no one may imagine that default on the part of one or many can absolve the rest from their obligation. Everyone should fully realise his responsibility . . . to be true to his pledge even unto death no matter what others do.'

This was the spirit of creative revolution: '"Not to submit", these words have the ring of the revolution,' wrote Smuts' biographer, Professor Hancock. 'To suffer: these words became a new revolutionary technique.'[5] However, what name to give this new adventure in history? 'I did not understand,' writes Gandhiji, 'the implications of 'passive resistance' as I called it. *I only knew some new principle had come into being.*' Finally it was to be called satyagraha. Truth (*satya*) implies love,' he went on to explain, 'and firmness (*agraha*) engenders and therefore serves as a synonym for force . . . That is to say the Force which is born of Truth, and Love, or nonviolence.'[6] How then could this not lead one to true victory?

Meanwhile, everything must be done to bring harmony between the adversaries. That is what Sri Krishna has taught us in the *Mahabharata*. Remember the way he begged Dhritarashtra, the blind king, and then Duryodhana, the evil one, the heir, for five provinces to be endowed to the five Pandava brothers, then five districts, five villages, if not, at least five houses? To which evil Duryodhana had answered back:

Take my message to my kinsmen, for Duryodhana's words
   are plain,
Portion of the Kuru Empire, sons of Pandu seek in vain,
Town nor village, mart nor hamlet, help us gods in heaven,
Spot that needle's point can cover shall not unto them be given.

---

5   S., p. 329.
6   The italics are mine, R.R. *Ahimsa*, non-violence in the Hindu tradition always meant love.

Gandhiji, then, with H.O. Ali (a member of the Transvaal Indian Association) went on deputation to England. The *S.S. Armadale Castle* on which they sailed had among her passengers Sir Richard Solomon, the acting Lieutenant Governor of the Transvaal, and possible first future prime minister under the new constitution.[7] He was also going to see the colonial secretary. There was further on board the same ship, a Chinese delegation going to London to present the Chinese case before the British Government. Gandhiji talked politics with the Chinese consul and played with his young daughter of nine. The more Gandhiji saw the British, the more he came to respect and admire them. They are so hard-working, united, silent and love to get things done. And finally: 'We cannot,' he wrote in his letter to the *Indian Opinion* from board the ship, 'match their record in public sanitation.'

Gandhiji and Ali took this miraculous opportunity offered them to meet Sir Richard Solomon. The result, however, promised nothing substantial, a commission would eventually be appointed to examine the case of the Indians. Sir Richard was aiming at big things for himself and he could not possibly commit himself to side issues. The battle in London was therefore going to be a hard one. The press was very well-informed of the various delegations coming to meet the British Government. And, in fact, even before Gandhiji had reached London representatives from Reuter's, *The Tribune,* and *The Morning Leader* had come to interview him. Facts always prepare for victory. So he gave them pure facts.

And now London at last, where he was once a shy, diligent student, and such an eager learner of the facts—London

---

7   Sir Richard indeed became the first prime minister.

where he had his old friends, the Fabians, the vegetarians, the esoteric Christians, the Irish, the Theosophists, and those who favoured contraceptives and those deadly against them. The women's movement too had grown in the meanwhile—he saw suffragettes' processions, admired their courage, their one-pointedness, and saw that the 'weaker sex' was not so weak after all. Indians had to learn this courage from the British women resisters, some of whom, like Cobden's granddaughter, preferred going to jail than pay a fine. This was pure satyagraha. He met persons of every party, even extreme conservatives, as long as they believed in the Empire which he still persisted in trusting as an instrument of God. 'Here, as elsewhere, he pursued his usual practice of discovering and concentrating on areas of agreement instead of dwelling on differences.'[8] He also met the Chinese and drew up a petition on their behalf. His colleague, Ali, fell ill, and Gandhiji had the man looked after by his old and trusted friend, Dr. Oldfield. (Gandhiji himself, as a result of his fruit and nut diet, had lost his sense of smell—doctors had called it chronic ozaena. But he had found no time yet to go to Dr. Oldfield for diagnosis and treatment.) A deputation was finally going to be received by the Colonial Secretary, Lord Elgin, formerly Viceroy of India. The deputation consisted of old India hands like Sir George Birdwood, Sir Henry Cotton, and Indians like Dadabhai Naoroji and Sir M. Bhownaggree. Sir Lepel Griffin, chairman of the powerful East India Association, led the delegation.

'My sentiments,' declared Lord Elgin opening the proceedings—and seeing so many familiar faces he had known in India—'would all be in favour of doing anything I could

---

8   Preface to C.W., Vol. IV, p. x.

for the interests of British Indians.' (Hear! Hear!) 'My Lord,' began Sir Lepel Griffin, 'what you have said makes my duty in introducing the delegates more easy. . . . We are very glad without any question of party feeling—because all sides are represented in this deputation—to introduce to you the delegates from South Africa.' And here he recalled the excellent work done by Gandhiji in South Africa during the Boer War and at the time of the Zulu rebellion. 'And you, My Lord,' Sir Lepel went on to say, 'who have been Viceroy of India, and whose sympathy is with the country, must know that legislation of this sort is unheard of under the British flag; indeed today in Europe, I may say without exaggeration that, with the exception of the Russian legislation against the Jews, there is no legislation comparable to this on the continent of Europe; and in England, if we wanted a similar case, we would have to go back to the Plantagenets.

'And against whom is this directed? Against the most orderly honourable, industrious, temperate race in the world, people of our own stock and blood, with whom our own language has as a sister-language been connected.

'And by whom is this legislation instigated? . . . It is the aliens who are opposed to this honourable Indian community.

'My Lord, we ask that the whips which the Boers have inflicted upon us may not be changed into scorpions wielded by the British Government.

'The grievances of the Chinese have received the utmost sympathy at the hands of the Government . . . We ask not for the Chinese but for our own fellow-subjects, and we ask that justice, if not generosity, may be dealt out to them, and that your Lordship will save them from insult and oppression.'

Then a similar deputation, once again led by Sir Lepel Griffin, waited on John Morley, at that time Secretary of State for India. Morley was one of the most enlightened men of his time, a Liberal and a writer of classical width and distinction. And under the circumstances in which he was placed, he tried to do for India the very highest he could. He explained to the deputation that ultimately the India Office had little influence with the Colonial Department, the two rarely coming into contact with one another, and least of all in circumstances of conflict. But the situation in South Africa was totally a different matter. 'If a foreign power,' he stated with obvious conviction, 'were to impose these disabilities upon fellow-subjects of ours, I think the Foreign Office would be set in motion to represent such a proceeding as an unfriendly act. It is a disagreeable truth, but we have to face these things: that there is no doubt we can more effectively remonstrate with foreign powers than in certain circumstances with our own folk.'

He therefore promised all which was within his power to make the Colonial Office realise these 'harsh and humiliating indignities' heaped against the Indians in the Transvaal. 'Nobody occupying my position,' he went on to say, 'can do anything less than promise you not only the sympathy of which someone has spoken today, but as much support as I can find myself able to give.'

Gandhiji and Ali were grateful for the friendly and generous way in which the two deputations were received. The *Times* (London), almost the mouthpiece of the government, supported the Indian case. Even Winston Churchill, then Lord Elgin's Under Secretary, received Gandhiji and Ali and promised to do what he could for them. Finally Gandhiji, with the help of Sir William Wedderburn, one of the founders of the Indian

National Congress, addressed a meeting in the House of Commons where over a hundred members were present. All the parties agreed Transvaal was behaving in an un-English manner. Harold Cox, a Member of Parliament, angrily declared, 'After all, we have got to defend these Colonies. We pay for and provide the soldiers for the defence of Transvaal . . . When Transvaal was a foreign country we claimed a right to interfere on behalf of our subjects; now that it is our own colony defended by our troops, we humbly withdraw and dare not oppose their will. If this is so, we may as well altogether abdicate our position as an Imperial race.'

Such sentiments had to be given a channel for organised expression. Therefore a South Africa British India Committee, with Sir M. Bhownaggree as Chairman, was formed. Mr. Ritch, formerly working with Gandhiji in Johannesburg (but now studying law in London), would be its Secretary. Many distinguished British politicians and former civil servants from India became its founding members. Now the Johannesburg Indians would have a permanent voice in London. Gandhiji had worked very hard—he said he almost never went to bed before one o'clock in the morning. Eventually he and his colleague set sail on *R.M.S. Briton* on 1 December 1906, feeling their visit had borne fruit. And there was expectant joy when at Madeira a cable awaited them to say His Majesty's Government, it was so rumoured, would never give assent to the Black Act. 'But,' writes Gandhi, 'as soon as we landed at Cape Town, and more so when we reached Johannesburg, we saw that we had overrated the Madeira cablegram.' Yes, the Black Act would be disallowed by the present government. But on 1 January 1907, Transvaal was going to have a responsible government. Lord Elgin could not disallow the Act if the Colony passed it after achieving its independence. The Royal Assent would automatically have to be given to it. How could it not be?

There was much disappointment therefore in Johannesburg. The feeling turned into sorrow and indignation. The community became deeply aware that satyagraha was now the only way left to achieve one's self-respect.

> 'We must look for assistance only to our own selves and to God in whose name we had pledged ourselves to resistance. And even a crooked policy would in time turn straight if only we were true to ourselves.'

Responsible government indeed did come to Transvaal, with Botha as Prime Minister and Jan Smuts as Colonial Secretary, and the first measure the new parliament passed was naturally the budget. And immediately after this the Asiatic Registration Act was taken up and passed at a single sitting, on 21 March 1907. 'The disallowance of the Ordinance, therefore, was forgotten as if it was a dream.'[9] The Act became law from 1 July 1907. Indians were given thirty days to register themselves. Otherwise they would have to go to prison or be deported according to the fancy of the Government of Transvaal. Lord, whose game is it all?

* * *

When the drums of dharma beat, say the texts, the very hosts of heaven slip through chinks of space and of time, through crevices of event, to help the righteous in battle.

---

9   'In fairness to Lord Elgin it would perhaps be said that while assuring Botha the Act would not be disallowed, he asked him to look into the question of its operation, with a view of removing some objectionable features.'

On the land of dharma,
On the field O the Kurus,
Tell me, O Sanjaya,
How did they, my sons,
And the sons of Pandu
Act, when gathered
Eager for battle.[10]

On that cold day of 1 July 1907, Kurukshetra was ready for the fray—Smuts on the one side with his Boers and the Britons and Gandhiji on his with a few handful of Indians. No flags flew and no conch shook the air. Leaflets had already been made ready to be distributed to those who came to register. With courtesy and love, where love could come from your heart, you were supposed to tell the Indian who went to register the meaning of the law. Would he accept it? If so, he should go and sign the register or give his thumb impression—if not, he had better go home or join the non-violent resistors. Of the few Indians who came to register, very few went into the registering offices, but those who did were neither abused nor deflected from their decision. It was a question of their own conscience. We may not be able to change men's hearts immediately—but it will come—we may only show the way.

Ninety days—three months—were given to the Indians to register. After the first day very few went to the registry. What was going to be Smuts' next move? The government also, be it said, awaited results. 'I do not know a single Indian,' wrote

---

[10] This is the famous beginning of the *Bhagavad Gita*. Kurukshetra means the field of the Kurus—the Kauravas. It was the battlefield of the *Mahabharata* War, not far from present-day Delhi.

Gandhiji later, 'who held it proper to submit to the Black Act.'
Nevertheless some, afraid of financial loss or fear of jail, gave
in. 'They arranged with the permit office that an officer should
meet them in a private house after nine or ten o'clock at night
and give them permits.' Every move now was to be carefully
made. Three months elapsed without any drama on either side.
The Indian merchant went on with his business, and the coolie
with his labour, except once in a while when a white wholesale
dealer refused to give credit to a coolie hawker who had no cash
to pay. However, this made no great impact on the community
which could always come in to help the coolie in distress. And,
then again, there were so many whites willing to offer means and
services to the Indian cause. Man always stands by man when
men are men of God, and manly.

Outwardly, however, nothing seemed to have changed for
anyone. Then suddenly, one day, an Indian from Germiston,
a man with a certain local popularity—there were only nine
Indians in this suburb of Johannesburg—was arrested. In fact,
he was the first satyagrahi ever to be arrested and fined. His name
was Rama Sundara. He came from North India, and knew his
Tulsidas *Ramayana* well. He also knew a little Sanskrit, so people
addressed him as Pandit. Thus he seemed the proper person to
start civil resistance in a small community on the great velds of
Africa. He let himself be taken to jail. 'The day on which he was
sentenced was celebrated by the Indian community with great
eclat.' But thereafter nothing happened. Gandhiji waited for
the next move. Eight Indians of Germiston now were arrested.
There was an anxious lull. But on Christmas week 1907, several
important Indians were asked to appear before the magistrate,
Gandhiji among them. This was an act of gentlemanliness on
the part of the government for the Indians could easily have

been arrested. Instead, they were invited to appear individually before the magistrate on a fixed day, which they did. Once again the government realised this was going to be an unusual game. They expected a gentlemanly response, which came as expected. They all pleaded guilty, and each one was given a forty-eight-hour delay, or a longer one, to quit Transvaal or be arrested. Having failed to comply with the government's demands, they were asked to reappear before the courts which they did with extreme courtesy. Once again they pleaded guilty. And now it was Gandhiji's turn to explain himself. He asked permission to make a short statement. His compatriots in Pretoria had been lately condemned for the same offence to three months imprisonment with hard labour, and if they did not pay the fine they would have to undergo a further three months of incarceration. 'If these men,' he said to the magistrate, 'had committed an offence, I had committed a greater offence.' Therefore he asked to be given the highest penalty.

As he addressed the court he could see all around him familiar faces. Strange, says Gandhiji, to have stood at the dock of the accused in the same court where he had worked, and for so many years, as counsel. Everyone knew him, including the judges. However, he was prouder now of being the accused than the defender of the accused or the accuser. 'On the sentence being pronounced,'—two months imprisonment was his part this time—'I was at once removed into custody, and was then quite alone. The policeman asked me to sit there on a bench kept for prisoners, shut the door on me and went away.' Gandhiji fell into deep thought. 'Home, the Courts where I practised, the public meeting—all these passed away like a dream . . . I was now a prisoner.' Would he stay the two months? Would the satyagraha go on, and the prisons be filled with all those who had taken pledges, in which case they would all have to be released soon. What a thought, he corrected himself. 'These thoughts passed through my mind in less than one-hundredth of the time it has taken to dictate. And they filled me with shame. How vain I was.' He had called the prisons His Majesty's Hotels, and the suffering perfect bliss 'and the sacrifice of one's all and of life itself in resisting it (the Black Act) as supreme enjoyment. Where had all this knowledge vanished today?' He now began to laugh at his own folly. Now he kept on thinking of the suffering of others. 'But I was disturbed by the police officer who opened the gate and asked me to follow him, which I did.' He was driven straight to Johannesburg jail.

The satyagrahi had, on principle, to obey all jail rules 'as long as they were not inconsistent with our self-respect, or with our religious convictions.' Gandhiji was asked to take off his clothes. Naked, he was given convict clothes, and these again were dirty. He had never worn dirty clothes, but today he would have to. He was then taken to a large cell where other satyagrahis joined him. From them he learnt of the events outside. On receiving news of his sentence the Indians had taken out a procession and the police had pursued them and flogged them, and finally dispersed them. But day after day more prisoners came in—the movement obviously was growing in intensity. Hawkers refused to show licenses, and others their registration cards. The jail was overflowing.

And everybody was now punished with hard labour. The food was intolerable. It would neither suit the Indian palate nor the Indian stomach. That extraordinary Natal-born Indian, Thambi Naidoo, polyglot and Hanuman of all vocations, who could at once preside at a meeting or be a porter carrying 'loads on public roads', to whom the night was the same as the day, and to whom sacrifice came quicker than his temper (of which he had a vicious lot)—but say what you will, he was a born leader and a good cook—he became the chef of the Indian prisoners. The jailed who had been given only simple imprisonment received permission to practise drill in the small yard before their cells, which seemed to be in the nature of a merry-go-round. The Pathan Nawab Khan was sometimes their commandant. He often shouted with all his might, 'Sundlies', but nobody understood what that extraordinarily roar meant. 'We could not for the life of us understand what Hindustani word it was, but afterwards it dawned on us that . . . it was only Nawabkhani English.' He meant only to shout like a good soldier: Stand at ease!

In Phoenix everything was running according to a firm time-table. Everyone performed what he had to do with diligence and devotion. The latrines were cleaned, the vegetables planted, and arithmetic taught as usual. Kasturba and the children were very well. The *Indian Opinion* went on appearing regularly. The government was wholly unprepared for this situation. In jail, too, Gandhiji asked his followers to obey every rule and conduct themselves as model prisoners. Almost all of them did. If something irregular had happened, the government could have dramatically intervened. Lord Selborne confessed he had never anticipated such events. 'It filled him with foreboding.' The coloured people too were watching the events. 'They have an instrument in their hands—that is combination and passive resistance—of which they had not previously thought of.' However grave the situation, Selborne advised Smuts, the Act should not be repealed. 'The Asiatic is a very bad person from whom to run away, and I do not think any repeal would be consistent with self-respect of the Government or of Parliament.'

The South African politician, Merriman, however, warned that liberal opinion in England might be alienated—this persecution of the Indian, does it not, he asked, 'savour of the yellow cap of the Jew or the harrowing of the Moriscoes in Spain'? Public opinion was deeply impressed with the peacefulness of the whole drama. It was the politest, the most courteous revolution history had ever seen.

The government, now finding no way out of the situation, used a liberal newspaperman Cartwright, a member of the Progressive Party, as negotiator. Smuts sent word to Gandhiji: What you call the Black Act will be repealed—on one condition; that you promise to go to registration voluntarily. Gandhiji understood the implications—Smuts and Gandhi had both studied Roman Law at the Inns of Court in London, and almost at the same time. This new procedure meant Indians were not second class citizens with the dog's collar, but true British subjects. Yet, since entry into any colony had to be restricted, Indians had to carry an immigration card. This seemed not unfair. Gandhiji only changed some wordings in the text. He then explained the position to his colleagues. They agreed that the document truly described their considered opinions. And with this agreement in hand, Cartwright went to see Smuts. Smuts was happy the way the game was being played.

Gandhiji was now conducted to see Smuts in Pretoria by the Chief of Police himself. Smuts, too, was a man of principles. 'The encounter between Smuts and Gandhi,' remarks Professor Hancock, 'was an experience of deep significance in both their lives, but was also far more than that; it was an event of world historical significance.'[11] A cabinet meeting was immediately

---

[11] S., p. 321.

called and the Smuts-Gandhi Agreement was approved. Everything seemed to be going right. Smuts seemed pleased as he came out. Yes, between two gentlemen there could never be an insoluble problem. Sitting down, Smuts said to Gandhiji: 'I could never entertain a dislike for your people. You know I too am a barrister. I had some fellow Indian students in my time. But I must do my duty. The Europeans want this law . . . I accept the alterations you have suggested in the draft. I have consulted General Botha also and I assure you that I will repeal the Asiatic Act as soon as most of you have undergone voluntary registration.'

Then Smuts stood up. Gandhiji asked: 'Where am I to go now?'

'You are free this very moment,' said Smuts and laughed.

'And what about the other prisoners?'

'I am phoning to the prison officials to release the other prisoners tomorrow morning.'

How was Gandhiji to go back from Pretoria to Johannesburg? He did not have any money on him. Smuts' secretary gave him the fare and Gandhiji returned to Johannesburg, not victorious but satisfied. Truth's ways were beginning to shine.

'With an even mind face happiness and unhappiness,
gain and loss, victory and defeat, and so join battle,
thou son of Pritha, thou shalt incur no sin there.'[12]

This was how Gandhiji commenced his article 'Triumph of Truth' immediately after his release from jail.

A public meeting was called. Indians were in an angry mood.

---

[12] The *Bhagavad Gita*.

There was no question of voluntary registration until the Black Act is first repealed. We just will not do it. We know the whites. It's their trick. Gandhiji pleaded. One must always trust another till the trust is broken. And what do you do, pray, after that? Trust again, said Gandhiji. And after that, then? Trust again and again, and again, said Gandhiji. 'We are creators of this position of ours, and we alone can change it. We are fearless and free as long as we have the weapon of satyagraha in our hands.' For such is law, the law of humankind.

Was this feasible? May this be true? Are you sure Gandhi is not betraying us to the whites? Who knows what really happened between Smuts and Gandhi? There was a rumour Gandhi had been given a comfortable bribe. And thus, brothers, see all this peace-making! One Pathan asked angrily if finger-printing, that humiliating procedure, was removed. You remember the song we used to sing:

Of fingers ten
Those who give impressions
Forsaking their pledge to God,

—and you told us in India only criminals gave their fingerprints. And so what is this now? How has it changed? Gandhiji explained it would now be purely optional, but to show his good grace he would fingerprint himself first. 'Circumstances have now changed,' pleaded Gandhiji, 'I say with all the force at my command, that what would have been a crime against the people yesterday is in the altered circumstances of today the hallmark of a gentleman. If you require me to salute you by force and I submit to you, I will have demeaned myself in the eyes of the public and in your own eyes as well as in my own. But if I of my own accord salute you as a brother or fellow-man, that evidences my humility and gentlemanliness, and it will be counted to me as righteousness before the great White Throne. That is how I advise the community to give the fingerprints.'[13]

'You are sold to General Smuts for fifteen thousand pounds,' Pathan shouted, 'I swear with Allah as witness that I will kill the man who takes the lead in applying for registration.'

Gandhiji smiled. What could one say to such an innocent accusation. Gandhiji repeated he would be the first to register and also give the finger-prints. 'Death is the appointed end of all life. To die at the hand of a brother, rather than by disease or in such other way, cannot be for me a matter of sorrow. And if even in such a case I am free from the thought of anger or hatred against my assailant, I know it will resound to my eternal welfare, and even the assailant will later on realise my perfect innocence.'

Thus on 10 February, Gandhiji was going to register. He would, as he had promised, be the first to do so. The Pathan, Mir Alam, with some of his friends was waiting at Gandhiji's legal office. Gandhiji coming in as usual greeted them courteously. Mir Alam replied coldly. 'I noticed his angry eyes and took a mental note of the fact. I thought something was going to happen.' But now with a few companions, Gandhiji walked towards the Registration Office.

'Where are you going?' Mir Alam asked.

'I propose,' said Gandhiji, 'to take out a certificate of registration.' And here before he could finish his words 'a heavy cudgel blow' struck Gandhiji, and he fainted crying: Hé Ram,

---

[13] S.S.A., p. 162.

O God!—and the Pathan kicked the victim as he lay on the ground. People came to his rescue. The news soon spread.

Polak and Reverend Doke, who had great admiration for Gandhiji, rushed to the spot. They carried him to an office nearby. And there, as he regained consciousness, he asked:

'Where is Mir Alam?'

'He has been arrested, with the other Pathans.'

'They should be released,' said Gandhiji. 'They certainly thought they were doing the right thing.' He did not want them to be prosecuted.

Gandhiji was then taken to the Doke home. His wounds were a little better, his lips stitched. He asked the Registrar of the Asiatics Bureau to bring the papers if possible so that he could still be the first one to register. The given word should be honoured. The Registrar, Mr. Chamney, who had all along seemed a harsh man now had tears in his eyes. 'I had often to write bitterly against him, but this showed me how man's heart may be softened by events.'

Gandhiji stayed with the Dokes for ten days. Reverend Doke did not care what the consequences may be. The whites may beat him up, burn his house, or boycott his church. 'I claim to be a humble follower of Him,' and whose love was as wide as the world . . . 'My anchor is God.' Night and day dozens of Indians came to visit their leader and the house became a caravanserai as long as Gandhiji stayed there. And often he would ask Doke's daughter, Olive, to sing his favourite Christian hymn, *Lead Kindly Light*:

> Lead kindly light, and amid the encircling gloom,
>   lead thou me on;
> The night is dark, and I am far from home,
>   lead thou me on.

This act of satyagraha, that is, not to prosecute the man of harm, had a profound effect on the European community of South Africa. At home, British papers spoke of it all with respect and fear. What was this going finally to mean?

Smuts had probably gone too far with his promises. Gandhiji and Smuts were hopelessly at cross-purposes with each other, writes Professor Hancock. 'In the art of political negotiation, Smuts was already an old hand, but Gandhi a novice. The two ever were attracted to each other—for example, their basic political loyalties, and their belief in compromise . . . they both set great store upon the virtue of keeping faith, but they would have given different definitions of what constitutes a breach of faith . . . Gandhiji believed when you took a pledge, you had to accept the interpretation given by the person administering it.' And, again, you always honoured the interpretation of the 'weaker party'. Further, Gandhiji's programme in Africa, says Professor Hancock, was dynamic. He wanted 'partnership with the white people of this country'. Smuts tried to hold a static position. White Africa was going to be white—or not at all. There could or would be no compromise on this. And, yet, Smuts could see—for he was himself without any colour prejudice—Indians had every right to be there. What was the solution? Are you going to be a saint willing to lose all for a principle, or a politician who holds to limited but eminent finalities? Smuts declared: What finality could you reach with a man of truth except the truth? For when you have to face a saint, the politician is so overcome that he makes promises—or near-promises he could not possibly keep. This happened again and again with Gandhiji. The Black Act was never repealed. Those who had voluntarily registered, their position was legalised. That was all Smuts did. Was it a breach of faith?

The Indian community was once again irate. This is how the white man always behaves. Whatever you may say, this is ever and ever the story. Then what next? Satyagraha will start again, said Gandhiji. Trust your enemy and start. And this new satyagraha was to be more dramatic than the first one.

For Gandhiji was not only the politician of God but ever the true politician. He knew realities were ever ridden by illuminations. He knew the sense of ritual, hence of the symbol. Thus the dramatic. There are so many ways of being dramatic. The violent is only visible drama. The ritualistic however evokes the subtler, the more inherent forces of man. Once drawn there, all propositions become not utilitarian, but perspectives of the true. This in-drawing answers the deep-most, hence it also becomes most reverberant. But the effective event has to take its own time. Hence the contradiction between the linear act—an act of progression—and the cyclic act. In the one you go, as Smuts would, from act to act, believing in the scheme of God. Time knows no irreversibility. There was a beginning, and so there is to be an end. God had made a plan for man. But Gandhiji's God—his Truth—was a dissolving principle. It had no system, for facts depend on systems. Truth is free. And since it is free, it goes on itself as it were, repeating and repeating itself—from aeon to aeon, from *yuga* to *yuga,* and then the floods, over which reigns the universal quiet, and then the birth of things again. How therefore could one be defeated? What acts on itself—the circle does—ever the same but never at the same point; it changes without changing, as it were. One is ever where one seemed to have moved on. This was, and is, the significance of the Gandhian drama, and the drama of the West. For the one there is tragedy—and so there is the cross. For the other, the unhistorical, there is *lila*, play. Who will ultimately win?

The timeless. For time implies the timeless but the timeless does not imply time.

The straight line may imply the circle, but the circle never implies a straight line. The straight line has an end, the circle never. Hence the mystery, the hypostatis of satyagraha. You do the same ritual over and over again, and what you win you win, and what you lose you will win again, for in the circle there is no loss. Once on the straight line you have moved on, you have left the past behind you. It will never come back. Ever emergent as a person, and brief in life on this earth, the Westerner must act and at once, to achieve, to achieve significance in this earthly drama—that you may have a great hereafter, a perfect one. But not so with the satyagrahi. He has the timeless before him. He will wait. In this life. In the next life. In the life after the next. And he will win. For truth knows only victory. Victory then to the truth!

* * *

The Hamidia Mosque in Johannesburg is a large one. At four o'clock on 16 August 1908, a strange sight was to be seen on its grounds. On a raised platform a huge cauldron was placed, resting on three curved legs. Most Negro families had these cauldrons—for cooking their meals in—and this cauldron came to play its ritual part in a historic drama. The stage was well set.

'On the platform,' wrote the *Transvaal Leader,* 'were the Congress Leaders, various prominent Transvaal Indians: Mr. Leung Quinn, Chairman of the Chinese Association and Mr. Gandhi. Mr. Essop Isamil Mia presided over the vast gathering, beyond that a sea of upturned and expectant faces, with determination and a bitter merriment stamped deep.'

Then Gandhiji addressed the immense and eager gathering, almost religious in its fervour.[14] Of course he realised his responsibility. He knew some of his adversaries ridiculed him and his methods of political fight, but that mattered little. He would still advise his friends: Burn the certificates! He was warmly applauded for this statement. 'My countrymen, . . .' he went on to say, 'have taken a solemn oath not to submit to the Asiatic Act. The solemn oath was taken not merely to be fulfilled by the letter but in spirit as well.'

He had come to an understanding that Smuts would abolish the Black Act the moment every Indian had voluntarily registered. 'I know none to tell of who had not made his application for voluntary registration.' Smuts now seems to have made a breach of faith. So, we have to fight again.

'I would pass the whole of my lifetime in gaol, and I say that in the House of God, in the House of Prayer, and I repeat I would far rather pass the whole of my lifetime in jail and be perfectly happy, than see my fellow-countrymen subjected to indignity and I should come out of the gaol. No, gentlemen, the servant who stands before you is not made of that stuff, and it is because I ask you to suffer everything that may be necessary than break your oath, it is because I expect this of my countrymen, that they will be, above all, true to their God, that I ask you to burn all these certificates. (Cries of 'We are ready to burn them').'

It's not, he went on to explain, that he does not understand the government's point of view. Of course, he did. The

<hr>

14 C.W., Vol. VIII, pp. 456-58.

government does not want unrestricted immigration of Asiatics. He would be willing to abide by the wishes of the majority if the welfare of the country needs a check on Asiatic immigration.

'I should claim that this country is just as much mine as any other Colonist's, and it is in that sense that I put forward that claim on behalf of my countrymen . . . It cannot benefit the colonists to have British Indians in the Transvaal who are not men and who may be treated as cattle, even though it may be show cattle.'

Anyway what are we fighting for?

'Unfranchised though we are, unrepresented though we are in the Transvaal, it is open to clothe ourselves with an undying franchise, and this consists in recognising our humanity, in recognising that we are part and parcel of the great universal whole, that there is the Maker of us all ruling over destinies of mankind, and that our trust should be in Him rather than in earthly kings, and if my countrymen recognise that position I say that no matter what legislation is passed over our heads, if that legislation is in conflict with our ideas of right and wrong, if it is in conflict with our conscience, if it is in conflict with our religion, then we can say we shall not submit to that legislation. We use no physical force, but we accept the sanction that the legislature provides. I refuse to call this defiance, but I consider it a perfectly respectful attitude for a man, for a human being who calls himself man . . . It can do no harm whatsoever to the Government of the Colony, it can do no harm to those who are engaged in the struggle; it simply tests them, and if they are true they can only win: if they are not true then they simply get what they deserve.'

And now the ritual truly began. The registration certificates were, one after the other, solemnly thrown into the cauldron. Paraffin was then poured in and Mr. Essop Mia, in the name of the whole community, set the papers ablaze 'amidst scenes of wildest enthusiasm', wrote the *Transvaal Leader*. 'The crowd hurrahed and shouted themselves hoarse, hats were thrown into the air and whistles blown.' The London *Daily Mail* called this a Second Boston Tea Party.

The Chinese too joined in the performance of this ritual. The Asiatic may be slow or submissive, but once he begins to move, tell me who can stop him? Tradition wins where history fails. And tradition is but ritualistic history. And ritual the link of man with Logos.

> I, Lord Agni, the chosen priest, god, minister of sacrifice,
> the hotar, lavisher of wealth.
> Worthy is Agni to be praised by living as by ancient seers:
> He shall bring hitherward the gods.[15]

And the Indians now waited for Smuts to act.

There was already a Satyagraha Office at Johannesburg. With the picture of Jesus and of Annie Besant on the walls, it was the cell of a new type of revolution. Many Europeans came to sympathise with the Indians in their struggle. For example, a rich businessman in Johannesburg, Kallenbach by name—and

---

[15] From the *Rig Veda*. Agni, the god of fire, is the god who links earth and heaven, and carries our prayers.

now Rev. Doke—joined the Indians in their sure and all-out crusade.

Gandhiji's political activity had a symphonic quality about it. He seemed to hear inaudible melodies, and he picked one of them for theme—for no explicable reason—the £3 tax, and later the salt tax or the Quit-India call, all, all, as if orchestrated by a master artist who knew the score before he started to play and yet he seemed totally innocent, taken as it were by the hand of his God, his famous inner voices and shown what to select and what to keep in innocent abeyance, minor themes that would be of beautiful purpose one day. In this orchestration, the Boer, the Indian, the British, the Chinaman and the Kaffir— indeed, even the Hindu, the Muslim, the Parsi, the Jaina, and the Christian—were not at all either adversaries or friends but modes of a play, as it were, for finally all play is Truth's own game (*lila*). Each time he or his God chose a theme, it would start on a feeble note—a missive to Smuts' secretary, a letter sent to the Viceroy through a Quaker friend, a walk to Jinnah's house for talk, and knocking and knocking at his door and crying: Hé, Jinnah, open the door—and rising, the movement rapidly became pure music of such convolutes and involutes of the mode, that minor modes would join in (tributaries of the stage) for an ultimate orchestration, and a dramatic finale that would end not in applause but in an indrawn void of pure silence. There was sureness of touch about the orchestration, yet over all a gentle accent that seemed cosmic, magical. He seemed to be able to play where he liked and with what he liked, and like Sri Krishna, himself, in not being there. It is this anonymity in satyagraha that gave every man and woman a sense of fervour and of freedom. In satyagraha everybody is the chosen one, for Sri Krishna plays his play with you.

Gandhiji tried to please no man. Therefore he served all living beings.

* * *

In the dim (and confused) past of South Africa, as we have seen, there was the Boer and the Britisher, and then the Britisher and the Boer, and then the Boer and the British again, so that when the London Convention was signed, it had said simply that all 'British subjects' (except the Kaffirs, of course) had the same rights as the Boers. British subjects did not all vote or serve in the commando armies against outside enemies—but otherwise they were treated, whenever white, as one and the same as the Boers themselves. Now, the word British subject meant the Englishman for the Boer, and every citizen of the Empire for the Englishman, especially so in England. The Englishman was busy building the Empire and imbued with such an exalted sentiment he hadn't analysed the consequences of such universality. Under Queen Victoria who could worry? Then the Empire began to grow larger and richer and the subject peoples seemed happy and content under the benign British rule. But as each country or colony under the British began to learn of the British ways (of justice, of administration, of freedom), there arose among the various peoples, especially among the Indians, the feeling that we had just to follow the law and the British would respect them. Indians did not know then that it was not the same with other European nations. Thus when the Boers regained their Transvaal, first as a colony, then a self-governing entity of the British Empire (loosely tied together under the name of South Africa, with the Cape Colony, the Natal, the Orange River Colony), the Boer laws were either abrogated, if found unsatisfactory, or applied with a 'large dose' of common sense. The British believed more in tradition and custom than in statute law as such. This seemed humane and wise. But the Boer was more strict with his law—it was God's own statute, so to say. Sometimes the British tried to modify them, and sometimes too they used these laws for their immediate purposes—perhaps with a bad conscience, but they did it. For the Indian, however, British law was the only law—it was almost *dharmic,* the holy law. How could anyone go against it. No one shall, or will. There was, it would seem, a private commitment between God and the British.

Now under the first Immigration Restriction Act, the Indian was not worthy of much consideration. He was relegated to the outskirts of the City of God where he could live in his filth and with his gods as he liked, as long as he had his passes and he paid the £3 tax. Of course he did not go on the main footpaths in Pretoria, or travel in the cities by tram or go in the first or second class in a train. Now, however, the Indian fought these laws one by one and showed their iniquity. With the British Government behind the Indian, some of the laws were either reduced in stigma or were entirely modified. And English friends, like an Emily Hobhouse, a Lord Ampthill, now here, now there, came in to help. But sometimes—and this is an important point—a British law and a Boer law conflicted, and then who was to say which was the right one? Especially if the Boers were ultimately (God forbid) to become a part of the British Empire?

Under the Immigrants Restriction Act passed by the new legislature, any Indian who had registered had some rights in Transvaal but everybody, including children, had to pay the £3 poll-tax. At the same time, an old British law, called the

Immigration Law, gave every British subject the right to enter Transvaal and become a Colonist if he was sufficiently educated. Since most of the Indians were either indentured labourers or sons of these, there was, it was thought, going to be no problem with the Immigration Law being applied to Indians. If Smuts had removed the Asiatic Registration Act from the statute book as he seemed to have promised Gandhiji, there would have been no problem left between the two statesmen to settle. The Immigration Law would cover all future entry of Indians as of any other immigrants and Gandhiji would have happily gone home (as Gokhale was urging him to), leaving the future of his countrymen in the hands of a man as humane as wise—Jan Smuts. Emily Hobhouse thought so well of him and so many others did too—he seemed almost British in his convictions and ways. But few realised that he was not dealing with the British but with the Boers. He was, after all, Colonial Secretary of the Boer Government and not of the British Government. Gandhiji however treated all governments as if they were British. And if they did not behave the British way, Gandhiji would make them realise their human inadequacy.

The Immigration Act would now be used by the Indians—a minor theme in the orchestration, and one waited to see what the Boers would do.

Now Gandhiji, like all profoundly religious persons, loved his symbols. He would use one satyagrahi as a symbol to see what the Boer Government would do if an Indian tried to enter Transvaal as an immigrant. He had a right. And so now he would use it.

Gandhiji chose Sorabji Shapurji Adajia as his first symbolic satyagrahi. He was a Parsi, and everywhere in the world the Parsis are known for their ethical integrity. Yet, would Sorabji be able 'to stand to his guns in critical times'? Gandhiji wondered. 'But', he went on to argue, 'it was a rule with me not to give any weight to my own doubts where the party concerned himself asserted the contrary. I therefore recommended to the Committee that they should take Sorabji at his word.'

Sorabji now went through the whole ritual of the satyagrahi. He wrote to the Transvaal Government that he was going 'to test his right to remain in the country under the Immigrants Restriction Act'. Then, having satisfied himself that he had given the government enough time to consider the whole matter, and hearing nothing from them in reply, he crossed over the border of Natal, entering the Transvaal. He asked the Immigration Officer to examine him and see if he spoke and wrote English as required by law; if not, to arrest him. The officer had no instructions as to how he should behave in this particular situation. Thus Sorabji was allowed to travel freely into Transvaal territory. He went straight to Johannesburg and the Indians received him with great enthusiasm. 'Very often,' wrote Gandhiji referring to this incident, 'it so happens that when we take our steps deliberately and fearlessly, the Government is not ready to oppose us.' The officer usually has his ideas fixed on a given subject and again he has so many problems to resolve, he cannot look into any one matter too thoroughly, for all rules have their flaws. Further, he 'suffers from the intoxication of power'. On the other hand, the public worker or satyagrahi has thought out all his plans clearly and conscientiously and is prepared for every circumstance. 'If therefore, he takes the right step with decision, he is always in advance of the government.' And if racial and political movements fail, they fail because leaders have not prepared themselves in an appropriate manner for every possible situation, agreeable or disturbing. A man who follows the law strictly carries with him somehow the magic of truth.

Sorabji wrote to the Police Superintendent of Johannesburg that he had arrived in the city and told him he, Sorabji, had a right to remain in the Transvaal in terms of the Immigration Act 'for he knew the English language sufficiently well, and would be ready to take an examination if the government thought it necessary'. There was no reply either to this letter. But the government after anxious deliberation decided something must now be done: Sorabji was summoned to appear before the Court.

He did indeed appear before the court on 8 July 1908. Crowds of Indians had gathered to see this eventful scene. Before he went in, Sorabji had addressed them with a 'fighting speech in which he announced his readiness to go to jail as often as necessary for victory, and to brave all dangers and risks'. In court, Gandhiji defended the accused. Because of a slight mistake in the summons the accused was released. He was, however, summoned again the next day and was asked to leave Transvaal within seven days. But Sorabji duly informed the Police Superintendent that he had no intention to leave the country. He was, therefore, a few days later sentenced to a month's imprisonment with hard labour. And when more Indians were increasingly found not obeying the laws, the judges dismissed the cases, often feeling 'the workers would cool down, finding no outlet for their energies in view of the masterly inactivity of the government'. But the government did not know the Indians or Gandhiji well enough. 'A satyagrahi is never tired so long as he has the capacity to suffer. The Indians were therefore in a position to upset the calculations of the government.' And this is what the Indians did.

There was an Indian merchant, rich and ancient as in a fairy tale, with a pure and beautiful son, and a wife duly pregnant—

patriarchs seem to have this privilege of sowing the seed at any age—and he would be the next satyagrahi. Daud Seth was his noble name. He was not only President of the Natal Indian Congress but was one of the oldest businessmen that had come from India to South Africa. He was full of tact, says Gandhiji, and he could also speak a little English and Dutch. He was as much respected by his British and Dutch colleagues as by the Indian ones. And, above all, he was a man of immense generosity. About fifty guests, wrote Gandhiji, used to dine with him every day. And he also made munificent contributions to the Indian cause. But God has strange ways of dealing with man, like in the story of Abraham and Isaac. Daud Seth's son Husen was, according to Gandhiji, even nobler than his father, and was duly sent to England to become the perfect gentleman. But he caught tuberculosis soon thereafter and died very young. Daud Seth never recovered from this shock. Humiliation and even death are as nothing when Husen is no more. Daud Seth became a satyagrahi.

Daud Seth was joined by a few others: there were Parsi Rustomjee, another staunch follower of Gandhiji's, and Gandhiji's own son Harilal who had at last returned from India. They could all speak English, and as British subjects they had a perfect right to enter Transvaal. Thus the 'satyagraha army' was going to invade Transvaal. And they did. And they were duly arrested (otherwise, what a humiliation for the government) on 18 August 1908. They were asked by the magistrate to leave the country in seven days. They disobeyed and were arrested again and deported back to Natal. They re-entered the Transvaal. The satyagrahis were now sentenced to a fine of fifty pounds or three months jail with hard labour. As satyagrahis, of course they preferred hard labour. In Volksrust jail they received the following telegram from Osman Ahmed, a colleague of theirs from Natal: 'Congratulate you all. Trust in God. Pray to Him. Obey him who saved Noah from deluge, Moosa from the Pharaoh, Abraham from fire, Joseph from the well, Ayoob from sickness, Enoos inside a whale, and our Prophet when he was in the Cave. He is with us and He is ever just.' This was the mood of the first satyagrahis and of their supporters.

Immediately after the judgement was pronounced, the following cable was sent by Gandhiji to London to the South African British India Committee: 'Fifteen deported Indians on re-entering heavily sentenced. All claim right to enter Transvaal either as pre-war residents or educational qualifications. Prisoners include three sergeants recent Zulu campaign, seven Mohammedans, two Parsis, six Hindus. Profound sensation. Since renewal of struggle 175 imprisoned, all classes, all parts.' He concluded the cable by saying it seemed all so needless and un-British. 'Indians should not be allowed to despair simple justice.' And when news came that these prisoners were breaking stones on public streets, he thought such work was indeed a great honour. He was proud of his countrymen.

The enthusiasm of the Indians from Natal, especially because of the rich businessmen who went to jail, was infectious. Would the Transvaal Indians lag behind their brothers? Of course not. Those who had burnt their registration cards and licenses now started hawking again without permits or entering the Transvaal from Natal, thus breaking the law. You just cross over and return, and if at the frontier station they ask you for a pass, laugh and say you haven't got one. Then you're arrested and sent to prison. Finally you will join those who break stones on the highways. Such the circle around the circle again.

There was one Imam Saheb, a delicate and aristocratic man who always went about in a carriage, wore the finest of muslins, and loved excellent food. But once in jail he accepted all the jail rules. He was made a sweeper, a job he accepted with alacrity, and functioned with efficiency. There was again Barrister Royappen. A graduate from Cambridge, he lived and worked as an Englishman would. He was, what the British used to call, a Pukka Sahib. Royappen, one fine morning, took a basket, put vegetables into it, and started hawking carrots, eggplants, lettuces and lemons on the goodly streets of Johannesburg. He was, of course, arrested and sent to jail as everyone else. Finally it was to be Gandhiji's own turn. He went to Durban, addressed huge meetings there, asked Indians to protest against 'this method of exploiting human labour under a system of indenture which should rightly be prohibited by law'. The movement would now grow wider. The Natal Indians should therefore start satyagraha and 'bring the system of indenture to an end'. For satyagraha never knows any frustration or failure. 'Indeed satyagraha is a form of true education . . . and our grievances will disappear in the measure in which we cultivate truthfulness.' Remember, too, he told them, we fight because we are Indians, for India, in true fact we fight for all humanity. That is the reason why, he explained, so many whites are with us. And after explaining all points in great precision, and giving final advice to the Congress and to the family in Phoenix, with fifteen Indians he took the train to Volksrust (for now the train went straight from Durban to Pretoria!). He was arrested at the border for not giving his thumb and finger impressions according to the new Act. And at his trial in Volksrust, he said he had advised his countrymen to resist the application of the new Act because 'it offends our conscience'. 'I am now before Court,' he went on to say, 'ready to accept the penalties that may be awarded to me. I wish to thank the prosecution and the public for having extended to me ordinary courtesies.' The prosecution pleaded that as he admitted his sin to be greater than that of others, he should be fined a hundred pounds and be given three months hard labour. The Judge, on the other hand, declared how very sorry he was to have to judge Mr. Gandhi and argued a difference must be made in his case, whatever the prosecution may say. Gandhiji was therefore sentenced to pay twenty-five pounds or undergo imprisonment with hard labour for two months. Gandhiji happily agreed to go to jail. His last message to the Indians was: 'Keep absolutely firm to the end. Suffering is our only remedy. Victory is certain.' And as soon as he was taken to jail, he was given a uniform—short breeches, a shirt of coarse cloth, a jumper, a cap, a towel, a pair of socks and sandals. 'I think,' he remarked, 'this is a very convenient dress for work. It is simple and wears well.'

But there's a game of life, a pattern that seems imbued with intelligence which seems to encourage you, to test you, even to defeat you, as if everybody had a law of his own dharma and one's faiths and failures, one's fears and successes, are but movements in a cosmological system. And the satyagrahi having taken truth as his essence in action and in inaction, truth played back tricks with him. It is, as Gandhiji said, like a rope-dancer's drama. He cannot look left or right, up or down, he has to look at the rope and at the rope alone. (The Upanishads called it the razor's edge.[16])

---

[16] 'Arise, ye! Awake, ye!! obtain your books (from your teachers) and understand them! A sharpened edge of a razor hard to traverse, A difficult path is this—Poet-sages (Kavis) declare.' *Katha Upanishad*. 4.3.14.

And this supreme rope-dancer, Gandhi, was now faced with an important problem. His wife, Kasturba, was dangerously ill. She had a ghastly haemorrhage. A telegram from West said so. What was he going to do? How should a man of truth act? 'It is impossible for me,' he wrote to West, '(to) leave here unless I pay the fine, which I will not. When I embarked upon the struggle I counted the cost . . . I am writing to her. I hope she will be alive and conscious to receive and understand the letter . . . Let Manilal read it to her.'

And here is the letter, perhaps the only letter he ever wrote to Kasturba:

(Volksrust Gaol)
9 November, 1908
Beloved Kastur,

I have received Mr. West's telegram today about your illness. It cuts my heart. I am very much grieved but I am not in a position to go there to nurse you. I have offered my all to the satyagraha struggle.

My coming there is out of the question. I can come only if I pay the fine which I must not. If you keep courage and take the necessary nutrition you will recover. If, however, my ill luck so has it that you pass away I should only say that there would be nothing wrong in your doing so, in your separation from me while I am still alive. I love you so dearly that even if you were dead you will be alive to me. Your soul is deathless. I repeat what I have frequently told you and assure you that if you succumb to your illness, I will not marry again. Time and again I have told you that you may quietly breathe your last with faith in God. If you die even that death of yours

will be a sacrifice to the cause of satyagraha. My struggle is
not merely political. It is religious and so quite pure. It does
not matter much whether one dies in it or lives. I hope and
expect that you will also think likewise and not be unhappy.
I ask this of you.

Mohandas

Meanwhile, once again truth played a trick on Gandhiji. He
was suddenly whisked off to Johannesburg to give evidence for
Dahya, the tailor who was under arrest. A special warder came
to fetch him and a special compartment kept at his disposal,
yet he was in the jail uniform and had, when he came down,
to carry the luggage like any other prisoner. Naidoo and Polak
having somehow heard of Gandhiji's coming, they were at the
station. Naidoo was moved to tears on seeing his great leader.
Gandhiji had no food, and no money either. The stationmaster
at Volksrust had voluntarily offered him money. Gandhiji,
however, had thanked him and then borrowed ten shillings from
Kazi, an Indian who was present at the station. With this money
Gandhiji had bought food for himself and for the warder. Finally
they reached the Johannesburg jail. Gandhiji was taken to a cell
filled with Kaffir and Chinese prisoners convicted of murder
and larceny. They mocked at Gandhi, laughing and showing
each other their genitals. Gandhiji opened his *Bhagavad Gita*
and began to read it, meditating on some of the verses, and
exhausted fell soon asleep.

The next morning, though, he was removed to another
cell. There were troubles again. The latrines were few, and
the Kaffirs also used them. Once, while sitting there, a Kaffir
threw him out, so that he could use it himself. 'I was not in the

least frightened by this,' wrote Gandhiji. 'I smiled and walked away.' But the Indian prisoners looking at the scene wept. Soon, however, Indians were to have their own lavatories.

While in jail he learnt to sew—stitching caps with a sewing machine. But in a few days he was taken back to the Volksrust prison. And Indians at every station, when they saw him, were moved to tears seeing their leader in convict's clothes. And at the Volksrust station once again he had to carry his own luggage. But he realised they were not prisoners, but soldiers of satyagraha. 'What then did it matter whether we were treated well or ill by the warders?'

And in its own way the time spent in prison was a fruitful one. One could think on God. And one could read. This time Gandhiji read Ruskin again, Thoreau, and the Bible, a life of Garibaldi and essays of Bacon (both in Gujarati) and of course the *Gita*. 'I can say today,' he wrote in *Satyagraha in South Africa*, 'that life in gaol is not in the least boring.'

On the very first day Gandhiji was taken with about thirty other Indians to dig up the soil somewhere near a main road. The day was very hot and the work strenuous. But since the majority of these Indians had never done any hard work, being generally business or professional men, most of them were exhausted. And the warder shouted the louder. Some Indians became nervous. And one was in tears. But Gandhiji encouraged every one to do all he could. Gandhiji too was exhausted, there were large blisters on his palms, and lymph oozing out of them. 'Placing my trust in Him, I went on with the work.' But the warder went on shouting at the prisoners. One of them fainted. Water was sprinkled on the victim's face and he woke up. And Gandhiji started thinking. 'A great many Indians have been going to gaol at my word. What a sinner I would be if I had been giving wrong advice. Am I the cause of all this suffering on the part of the Indians? I considered the matter afresh with God as witness . . . I felt I had given the right advice. If to bear suffering is in itself a kind of happiness, there is no need to be worried by it.'

Sometimes, too, they were allowed to cultivate their own garden, to sow maize seeds and clear the potato beds. Also, everybody had to do scavenging. Gandhiji did not mind this in the least, but others did, and one even vomited while doing his duty. How could a satyagrahi object to the work he is given? Then it will no more be satyagraha.

And now he turned to his chief duty, as cook to the Indian community at the Volksrust jail. There were some seventy-five Indian prisoners, they had petty jealousies, mainly about the rations. 'I became the cook as only I could adjudicate on the conflicting claims to the rations supplied. Thanks to the love for me, my companions took without a murmur the half-cooked porridge I prepared without sugar.'

The government however thought it was all going too well. Gandhiji was therefore taken away and sent to the prison in Pretoria and given solitary confinement 'reserved for dangerous prisoners'.

On 12 December, however, Gandhiji was suddenly released from the Volksrust jail, and was received by the Indian community in reverence and tears. Yes, he had led them rightly, he, this thin and deep-eyed man, soft-voiced and silent, and he would take us where we have to go, to that *Ramrajya,* the Kingdom of Rama, which is ours. And like Sri Rama he only speaks of the truth and of love; and the Muslims among the followers, thought he was of the same stuff of which their saints were made, those who were buried on hill-tops or under ancient trees, a pink shroud on their tombs, like Sheikh Chishti or Sheikh Nizamuddin, and who would cure the world of its ills. Look, even the whites were so full of praise of him, and the government may try as it would, more and more whites were on his side, even Hosken and Campbell, members of the Legislature, and then again, in London the great ones, the King and his ministers. How could truth not win?

'My experience has taught me,' Gandhiji wrote later, 'that the law of progression applies to every righteous struggle. But in the case of satyagraha the law amounts to an axiom. As the Ganga advances other streams flow into it, and hence at the mouth it grows so wide that neither bank is to be seen and a person sailing on the river cannot make out where the river ends and the sea begins. So also as a satyagraha struggle progresses onward, many another elements help to swell its current, and there is a constant growth in the result to which it leads. This is really inevitable, and is bound up with the first principles of satyagraha. For in satyagraha the minimum is also the maximum, and as it is the irreducible minimum, there is no action of retreat, and the only possible movement is an advance . . . The Ganga does not leave its course in search of tributaries. Even so does the satyagrahi not leave his path which is sharp as the sword's edge. But the tributaries spontaneously join the Ganga as it advances, so it is with the river that is satyagraha.'[17]

And now to the fight.

The next day at the Hamidia Mosque (for the majority of the merchants were Muslims) there was a big meeting held, and Gandhiji was garlanded and applauded and praised. 'I

---

[17] S.S.A., pp. 208-209.

said yesterday,' he told them, 'that we had won. We have won because of the sufferings of our people . . . That of our population of 7,000, as many as 1,500 have gone to jail must surely, I think, be counted as victory.' And he asked the crowd to say, was it not decided and the pledge taken, that until justice was done, the satyagraha movement will never, never stop. Are we not bound by the same pledge? And all the crowd raised their hands. Yes, of course, a pledge is a pledge. 'Please remember that you have raised your hands in such a place (the sacred premises of a mosque) in the name of God.' And did not all scriptures say: I give unto those that are with Me all that they ask for. The struggle will, therefore, go on. And then, as a final exhortation, he said: 'If both the eyes, of the Hindus and Muslims, remain unharmed, you will prosper. If the . . . Indians continue to fight in the name of God, and if the two communities remain united, you will also be the masters of India.'

For his eyes were, finally, on India. It was for India's freedom that they were fighting here, far away, in, as it were, a land on the frontiers of man. He now realised that this was a demoniac struggle. The struggle was not for permits ('of no value in themselves'), nor for the entry of a handful of Indians, but it was, he declared, 'a battle of principles'. Sri Krishna was asking not five provinces for the Pandavas, nor five districts nor indeed for five villages. He was asking for just five houses. Yes, even only for five cottages. Do you hear me, Duryodhana? Duryodhana was too drunk with power to see.

> Silent sat the proud Duryodhana wrathful in the Council hall
> Spake to mighty-armed Krishna, and to Kuru warriors all.
> Ill becomes thee, Dwaraka's chieftain, in the paths of sin to move

Kuru Dwaraka's chieftain
Bears for me a secret hatred, for the Pandavas secret love.[18]

He had won in his chess game, had Duryodhana, and so
had acquired a kingdom. And the fit place for the defeated
Pandavas is the forest—the exile! The forests of Dandaka are
large, so go there and seek ye, the livelihood. You have no place
here. Indians indeed had no place in Transvaal now except as
helots. What Indians asked for now was merely equality, like the
Pandavas did—a symbolic one. A new theme was introduced;
the right of entry of six educated Indians each year to Transvaal.
That was all. Not to treat the brown skin as not human because
it was different from the white. The Pandavas, after all, were not
different from the Kauravas, of the same blood and bone; the
Pandava exile an anointment. 'Hundreds of Indians have been,
as it were, sanctified through anointment in prisons.' He declared
mighty is the battle to come. The Transvaal Indians must 'win
immortal fame for themselves—for India—throughout the
world'. And this would be the final struggle.

Ushas with her crimson fingers opened the portals of the day,
Nations armed for mortal combat in the field of battle lay.

Now, however, Gandhiji had to turn to his family. His wife
had to be operated upon at Durban. He went there not only for
her sake but to see what the Natal Indians were doing. Were they
prepared for the bigger fight which was coming? In Transvaal,
the government was arresting people indiscriminately. This did
make a certain impression. And some Indians, at Potchefstroom

---

[18] *The Mahabharata* (Udyoga Parva).

and Kleksdrop, were beginning to yield to government pressure. If only they admitted openly they were human and were weak, even this would bring strength to the movement. The campaign would be shorter for that.

And now he must go back to his Kurukshetra. He was going to Johannesburg. He was arrested at Volksrust again because he refused to show his registration card. He was taken to the Natal border and released. He took the first train back, and was once more arrested. This time released on bail, he finally returned to Johannesburg.

In the meantime, the whites decided on attacking the Indians on another and (so they thought) vulnerable point. Rich Indian merchants who had enjoyed credit with the white wholesale dealers, banks, agencies, and with whom they were on the friendliest of terms, had now come to the conclusion that these Indians should be ruined. Indian businessmen— Kachhalia among them, a rich and generous merchant, who was also the President of the Transvaal Indian Association, a devout Muslim and man of firm principles—and others like him—asked the white creditors for delay in payment (because of the Indian struggle) and as their account books showed, they could, if necessary, give back twenty shillings to the pound if demanded. This is exactly what the white merchants desired. So the creditors of Kachhalia were called at a meeting at Gandhiji's offices (Court Chambers, Corner of Resik and Anderson Streets). Kachhalia declared himself insolvent. Every debtor was finally paid his last penny. Kachhalia embraced poverty. And other Indian merchants followed his example.

He went back to Durban this time for the operation of Kasturba. Kasturba was too weak to have anaesthesia. She had such courage, she decided to have surgery performed on her

without chloroform. Gandhiji stood beside her all the time.
Then he helped her to convalesce.

Meanwhile, Parsis, Hindus, Muslims, young and old,
including Harilal Gandhi, came out of jail only to go back to
jail. They were arrested and deported, released and rearrested,
while some brave Britishers in London, important politicians
in India, were deeply aroused by what was happening to the
Indian community in South Africa. It had now reached beyond
a local or national event—it was becoming a historic fight.
Gandhiji took Kasturba from Durban to the Phoenix Colony,
nursed her devoutly, and when she was well enough he took her
permission and left for Johannesburg. He was arrested again at
Volksrust along with Polak, and once again sentenced to three
months imprisonment with hard labour for refusing to show his
registration card. He was however not going to be left there any
longer. There were too many (seventy-seven) Indian prisoners
at Volksrust, including his son Harilal. Gandhiji needed a stiffer
treatment. He was made to carry stones for road-making. Then
they sent him to Pretoria and to solitary confinement. His cell
measured ten feet long and seven feet broad. The floor was
covered with black pitch. He had to go naked to his bath, some
one hundred and twenty-five feet away. He had to be quick.
'Are you ready, Gandhi?' the warder would soon ask. And the
same thing at the lavatory: 'Sam, come out now.' He had to lie
on a coir-mat with neither pillow nor bed-board. And the work
he had to do was to polish doors and floors, which of course was
not the worst of all jobs.

There were some Kaffirs too in the jail, and they asked if he
had committed theft or was caught in selling illicit liquor. His
neighbour was a man condemned for attempted murder. Often
Gandhiji ate only one meal a day. He would not accept food

that other Indian prisoners could not have. After some time he was given blankets or purses to stitch or sweaters to knit. The warder himself soon realised he had to deal with a different type of prisoner this time. His difficulties about lavatory and bath vanished as if by magic. And when a new warder came in, he was even warmer. He admired, he said, people who fought for their country. 'I am myself something of a fighter,' he added. 'I do not regard you as a prisoner.'

But, try as he might he could not communicate with his ailing wife. They would not permit him to write to her in Gujarati. The prison rules did not permit this (he could only write in English or in African-Dutch.) So Gandhiji wrote no letters to her at all. Yet Smuts had not forgotten him. He sent his prisoner two books on religion.

Suddenly Gandhiji was summoned as witness in a case. 'I was,' he writes, 'accordingly taken to the court. I was handcuffed on the occasion. Moreover the warder locked up the handcuffs rather tight. I think he did this unintentionally. The Chief Warder saw this. I had obtained his permission to carry a book with me to read (on the way). He asked me to hold the book with both hands so that the handcuffs might not be seen. I was rather amused at this. To me the handcuffs were a matter of honour. It happened by chance that the book I was carrying, if rendered in Gujarati would be: *Khuda-no Darbar Tara Antar-man Chhe.* (*The Kingdom of God is Within You* by Leo Tolstoy). I regard this as a wonderful coincidence. Whatever the difficulties that pressed me from outside, so long as I kept my heart worthy of God's presence, what need had I to mind anything else?' But his being handcuffed and taken to court thus, on the main road of Johannesburg, raised storms of protest both in the local and the imperial press. Questions were asked in the British House of

Commons. Was this British rule? The Reverend Doke has left
us an impression of what he saw on those trying days.

> 'He looked thin and unkempt . . . His face was 'steadfastly set
> to go to Jerusalem' and he saw nothing but that.
>   'I wonder what he saw in that long march. Not the
> immediate Jerusalem I imagine—the place of crucifixion . . .
> The Fort with its cells and its hateful associations. Those
> long files of prisoners. The white-clad brutal native warders
> swaggering along with their naked assegais. The lash for the
> obdurate and the criminal taint for all. A city whose secrets
> may not be told . . .
>   'No not that: it is another Jerusalem which he faces
> steadfastly . . . a new Jerusalem whose beautiful gates are
> open to all nations.'

Being in solitary confinement, he had much time to read.
He says he read some thirty books during that period—books
in English, Hindi, Sanskrit, Gujarati and Tamil—the books in
English were mainly those of Tolstoy, Emerson and Carlyle.
'Tolstoy's writings are good,' he writes, 'and simple that a man
belonging to any religion can profit by them.' He also read
Carlyle's book on the French Revolution. 'I realised after reading
it,' Gandhiji remarks, 'that it is not from the white nations
that India can learn the way out of her present degradation.'
He agreed with Mazzini that the French did not gain anything
of value by the revolution. But even in the French Revolution
he came across incidents reminding one of satyagraha. For
satyagraha is not of today or of tomorrow—it has always been
there. We have only to recognise its worth and make use of it
wheresoever we can.

The books he read in Sanskrit and Hindi and Gujarati were on different topics of philosophy: he read a book on the understanding of the Vedas, and again he read the Upanishads which made a deep impression on him. He also read the *Ramayana* of Tulsidas, now printed at the Phoenix Press itself in Durban, that great book of books, the basic book of all North India, the common man's *Gita* as it were, and of course he read the *Gita* itself. He also read the writings of Rajachandra, who as we have seen, came closest to being Gandhi's Guru. 'It was the writings of the poet Rajachandra which proved the most satisfying. His way of life was noble like Tolstoy's. Good books are like meeting good men,' he remanded. 'Every Indians who wants to be happy in gaol must form the habit of reading good books.'

In a famous letter to his son Gandhiji wrote:

'All confirm the view that education does not mean knowledge of letters but it means character building. It means knowledge of duty. Our own (Gujarati) word literally means 'training.' If this be the true view, and it is, to my mind the only true view, you are receiving the best education training possible . . .

'I was much struck by one passage in Nathuramji's introduction to the Upanishads. He says the *brahmacharya* state, i.e. the first state is like the last, i.e. the *sanyasin*[19] stage. This is true. Amusement only continues through the age of innocence, i.e. up to twelve years only . . .

Everybody from such an age should practise continence in thought and deed, truth likewise, and not taking of any life . . . It should be natural to him. It should be his

---

[19] The monk.

enjoyment . . . Armed with them, believe me, you will earn your bread in any part of the world, and you will have paved the way to acquire a true knowledge of the soul, yourself and God . . .

'Remember please that henceforth our lot is poverty. The more I think of it the more I feel that it is more blessed to be poor than to be rich. The uses of poverty are far sweeter than those of riches.

'In your lessons you should give a great deal of attention to mathematics and Sanskrit. The latter is absolutely necessary for you.

'Please tell Maganlal Bhai that I should advise him to read Emerson's essays. They can be had for nine pence in Durban. The essays to my mind contain the teaching of Indian wisdom in a western guru. It is interesting to see our own sometimes thus differently fashioned. He should also try to read Tolstoy's *Kingdom of God is Within You*. It is a most logical book. The English of the translation is very simple. What is more, Tolstoy practises what he preaches . . .

With love to all and kisses . . . from Father.'

Yes, like Tolstoy, you could live in the world, yet renounce the world. For this you have only to seek God. And how does one find Him? 'The poet says,' writes Gandhiji:

'When smiling and playing my way through life
I see (Him) revealed to me, a visible presence,
Then shall I consider my life to have attained its true end.'

He was duly released on 24 May, but he was not so happy. He wanted to suffer with the other Indians who were still in prison.

But this was not to be. These are all God's ways. And when he reached Johannesburg nearly a thousand people, Indians, Chinese, and some Europeans greeted him. He was heralded with the cry: Salute the King of the Hindus and the Muslims. This was not the right way to welcome him. After all, he was a servant of the community, not its king. 'My aspiration,' he continued and with deep emotion, 'will only be fulfilled if I have to lay down my life in the very act of serving the community.' And he added prophetically, 'It is indeed my duty so to die.'

By now big events were happening in South Africa. The Boer and the Briton would work closer together. There will be a Union of South Africa, and the country would become a Dominion like Canada, like New Zealand. Gandhiji, as soon as he was free from prison, intended to go to London and plead for an honourable position for the Indians in a united South Africa. At home, here in the Transvaal, the satyagraha movement was continuing—'his diminished band of satyagrahis carried on the fight with undiminished fortitude, year in, year out. Life for them had lost almost all regularity except the movement in and out of gaol.'[20] Some died. Others were ill; some stayed back in their homes yet others took to their vocations, and plied their various trades. There was a certain war-weariness among the Indians, and a sense of indifference on the part of the government. Smuts had by now learnt how to deal with the situation. If the satyagrahis wanted to go on thus forever, he too could put people to prison, and send them out and bring them in again, forever and ever.

However Smuts and Botha had now to go to London (July 1909) for political discussions with the British Cabinet. Once

---

[20] S., p. 340.

the Union was achieved and the Boers and the Britons would
be masters together, the Indian question would never be a big
problem. The Asiatic cancer had to be out anyway—the stranger
within the gates must go or serve the purposes of the white man.
What had the British to win or lose in this matter? Nothing
except some vague adherence to a principle. The Empire
was a growing and practical entity—the future will achieve a
solution to all problems. Meanwhile the Transvaal was hurriedly
deporting coolies back to India.

This may take some time. But that too may be a suitable, a
legitimate, answer. Let the Indian go back from where he came.
Public opinion in India was strongly disturbed by this new move.
The courts, however, found deportation illegal. (People who had
given their very best had now to go back poor to where they
had no one and where they were unremembered. The recruiting
will have to stop now). But other laws could always be passed,
especially later, under the aegis of the Union. For the moment
the urgent problem was to convince the British that Botha and
Smuts were willing to work for a dominion of South Africa. The
Boers had been somewhat tamed by experience, and the British
more tolerant of the Boer. 'In the creative Spirit of History,'
wrote Smuts, 'the blunders of men are often more valuable
than their profoundest wisdom . . . From the blood and tears
of nations which human passions have ceased she proceeds
calmly and dispassionately to build up new nations and to lead
them among new undiscovered paths of progress. And when the
darkness of the night has passed at last and the light of a new
consciousness dawns, the scale falls from men's eyes, they perceive
that they have been led, that they have been brought forward in
the darkness by deeper forces than they ever apprehended to a
larger goal than they ever conceived, and they stand silent in the

presence of that greatest mystery in the world, the birth of the soul of a new nation.'[21] Gandhiji would have agreed with this statement. For India herself arising, she great and glorious, one of the most ancient among the nations of the world, and she again would affirm her right to exist and to be respected, nay revered, such the message of history. The Indian franchise then was not a question of some small gift to be begged for, but the right of a great nation. This would not be a political decision but a historic, a metaphysical one. Indeed, the politicians of South Africa, like Merriman and Schreiner, were deeply concerned, not only with the Indian problem but with the problem of native franchise. What was the use of having a nation where the majority have no real voice? Not that the Zulu and the white, in the eyes of these politicians, were equal in competence, but the Zulus also had a legitimate place under the South African sun.[22] The Boers, however, were unwilling to listen to the advice of these wise men. The Boers wanted a Boer nation, with, if necessary, the Englishman who would have the same rights as themselves, why even the German and the Jew, as long as they were white—and as for the rest, the future would look after itself. And in all this passionate debate the Indian problem seemed a minor one— from Johannesburg. London would not however accept this point of view. What then would the British Cabinet do?

Gandhiji took the Union Castle *S.S. Kenilworth Castle* and set sail (23 June 1909) with Haji Habib, an Indian merchant from Transvaal, for London. Two others who were coming

---

[21] Quoted in S., p. 269.
[22] 'I do not like the natives at all,' wrote Merriman, 'and I wish we had no black man in Africa. But they are there . . . and the only question is how shape our course so as to maintain the supremacy of the race and at the same time to do our duty'. Quoted in S., p. 220.

with them had been arrested by Smuts; and Haji Habib was not a convinced satyagrahi. It did not however matter, for he was a sincere man, and an Indian. Merriman also was on the same boat, going to join his colleagues. Merriman was friendly to the Indian point of view as he was to the Coloureds and the Native points of view. But he was no match to Botha and Smuts. The British were impressed with Boer statesmen, and London wanted peace on this continent. She had other and more pressing problems to think of, the growth of the Prussian army and of the Russian ambitions towards India.

Gandhiji saw Lord Crew, Secretary of State for the Colonies, who expressed sympathy for the Indian cause. Gandhiji also saw Lord Morley, Secretary of State for India, who was always friendly to India. All that Gandhiji asked for was that the Black Act be repealed and six educated Indians be admitted annually, like any other immigrant, to the Transvaal. This would remove, at least in the eyes of law, the colour bar, and that was all Gandhiji ultimately aimed at. Lord Ampthill, as Chairman of the South Africa British India Committee, met both Smuts and Botha to see what could still be done. But the Boers would not give in. 'General Botha,' said Ampthill to Gandhiji, 'appreciates your feelings in the matter and is willing to grant your minor demands. But he is not ready to repeal the Asiatic Act or to amend the Immigrants Restriction Bill. He also refuses to remove the colour bar which has been set up in the law of the land . . . General Smuts is of the same mind as General Botha.'[23]

---

[23] Haji Habib was willing to accept these minor concessions but not so Gandhiji. The situation had a humorous side for Haji Habib did not understand English very well, and Gandhiji had to translate the questions of his colleague into plain English, Gandhiji of course, faithfully translating the reply of Haji Habib.

So there it was, there was nothing further to be done. He had seen almost every important member of Parliament or newspaper editor it was possible to meet. 'I realise,' he wrote in the *Indian Opinion,* 'that deputations, petitions, etc. are all in vain . . . It is better to be in gaol than to have to seek interviews.' And he was reminded of Mirabai's[24] famous song:

> Prepare not your draught from the twice-bitter *neem*
> Shunning the sweetness of the sugar and the sugarcane.
> Give not your love to the glow-worm
> Turning away from the light of sun and moon.

On the other hand, this visit to London was a most fruitful one. He met the new generation of Indian politicians, including extremists and anarchists. After the defeat of Russia by Japan, Asia was suddenly awake to the realisation; the white man was not so powerful after all. The first glimmers too of the Russian Revolution (1905) caught the imagination of the intellectual and the young. 'I have noticed,' wrote Gandhiji to Lord Ampthill, 'that some of the members of the party are earnest spirits, possessing a high degree of morality, great intellectual ability and lofty self sacrifice. They wield an undoubted influence on the young Indians here . . . An awakening of national consciousness is unmistakable.'[25] The young were seething with hatred against the British, and eager to spill British blood. Madan Lal Dhingra, an Indian student and belonging to an excellent family, decided with some others

---

[24] The famous princess who became a mystic (seventeenth century) and whose songs are popular all over North India.

[25] C.W., Vol. X., p. 508.

that apart from killing Englishmen in India (and this had been going on for some time) Englishmen in England, too, had to be shot, to make the British at home realise the amplitude of the tragedy. So one day Dhingra went to a reception and deliberately shot Sir William Curzon-Wyllie (Political A.D.C. to the Secretary of State for India), a man who had done no harm to any Indian. It was just as a symbol of the British Empire that Curzon-Wyllie had to be killed. Only the letting of blood, one's own and that of others, would satisfy the Goddess of Liberty. India has to be freed with the sword. 'Even if India could be free that way, what would it do with that freedom?' asked Gandhiji. But to these young revolutionaries it was the sure way to independence. There was even a Lotus and Dagger Club working in secret in England. Aurobindo Ghose, who was once at Cambridge, also belonged to it. Back in India, Aurobindo was preparing a revolution in the name of the Goddess, in the name of the Mother. We worship Thee O Mother . . .

> Rich with thy hurrying streams
> Bright with thy orchard gleams
> Cool with thy winds of delight
> Dark fields waving, Mother of might
> Mother free . . .
> Who hath said thou art weak in thy lands,
> When swords flash out in seventy million hands,
> And seventy million voices roar
> Thy dreadful name from shore to shore.[26]

---

[26] This is the famous National Hymnody, *Vande Mataram,* the translation being Sri Aurobindo's.

The partition of Bengal—that fair and noble province, so as to divide the Hindus and the Muslims—was an act of British treachery.

And who could not see it, so plain and clear it all was.[27] Rich young men became ascetics and revolutionaries in the name of the Great Goddess, our Motherland. Practising yoga in forests and temples, they vowed vengeance to British rule. And in the name of the Goddess they learned the art of the sword and the bomb. Like the Rajputs that went to battle leaving their women reading the *Mahabharata* in the palace, the flaming fire in front of them—if the men returned from battle the Goddess would be celebrated with the pomp of blood and worship, but if the Turk won, the sound of the bugle of defeat would make the women put on *kumkum* on each other's foreheads, and saluting Mother Earth, jump into the fire while the men would lie dead, brilliant on the battlefield. That is the spirit of India. 'Arise, awake and stop not till the goal is reached,' Vivekananda had shouted to the Indians. This was not rhetoric. This was the spirit of the Upanishads and the revolutionaries. And many never returned from their missions. They cried, 'Victory to the Mother' and died on the gallows.

Others there were too, who'd hit and fled to Afghanistan, to China, to Russia, and finally to Europe or the Americas, where they learnt to make bombs or earn on farm and field (growing oranges in California, hewing wood in Canada) to buy ammunition and send it to the fighters in unhappy India. Hindu or Muslim, it did not matter; the Britisher must go, and only the gun will make him go. Gandhiji did not think this was the way of great India. Fight one must through *ahimsa*, through

---

[27] Here was the seed of Pakistan ahead and irrevocably sown.

love. 'The sword of satyagraha,' he wrote, 'is far superior to the steel sword. Truth and justice provide its point. Divine help is the hilt that adorns it. Therefore brave Indians arise and without ado, draw the sword of satyagraha and fight unto victory!' Only thus the true kingdom of God can be established on earth. Independence of India was not to mean more Bombays and Calcuttas, and more brown sahibs instead of the white ('I should be uninterested in the fact as to who rules') but it should be the Kingdom of Love, *Ramrajya*. In Sri Rama's Ayodhya there were no poor nor meek. Everyone was happy for everyone did his acts of life in terms of the truth. He performed his dharma. Lord, what more powerful weapon than the name of Sri Rama.

Gandhi's mind now turned to India. On the boat back from London to South Africa he wrote *Hind Swaraj,* the first book of Gandhian doctrine. It was his picture of *Ramrajya,* the India of his dreams.

The Kingdom of Rama has been the dream of the Indian mind. The tiger will, according to the tradition, drink water at the same stream as the deer, and the elephant will never dream of the lion (for that would announce his death.) The widow will never lament in that kingdom, the husband will never die before the woman for that would be inauspicious—Sri Rama protects dharma. And of course no child would ever cry, for its mother's breast would ever be full. The low will never know poverty, and the humble will be protected. For Hanuman, the great and generous disciple of the Lord, will peep through hut-holes, and lay his ear against thatched roofs, to hear the way the husband treats the wife or the brother the sister. And Lady Sita, the spouse of the Lord, awaits the news of the world that Hanuman will bring, and in her love of her Lord that he be not disturbed in his many great tasks, she would, would Sita Devi, send her brother-in-law, the faithful Lakshmana, for the right ordering of human condition; for wheresoever sorrow is or want, there's the dharma's burn in Sri Rama's heart. All sorrow he owns as his own, the Lord does, and Sita Devi his expression of Love for the suffering mankind. Mankind shall not suffer for Sri Rama rules from Ayodhya. Sing the praise of Ayodhya's Lord:

> *Rama nama santanako sarabasa*
> *Janama Suphalata Karanai.*[28]

And even from afar, any visitor to the Kingdom of Rama can see smokes from sacrificial fires. Wheresoever the ascetic creates his hearth of sacrifice, and the curling smoke goes up into heaven, there does dharma flourish, and every one gets his reward of dharma. And sages go from hermitage to hermitage asking the anchorites their conditions and purposes and when Sri Rama himself knows they are coming, there he is awaiting the Guru, with pots of warm and cold water, and the stand-stool of honour, and when the Guru appears, Sri Rama will lave the Feet of Truth. Can Truth wash Truth's feet? you might ask. But it's like asking can play play. Truth truths Truth, such the game of the Lord. When Sri Rama washes the feet of the Guru, the whole Kingdom is purified. And then does Sri Rama take the holy visitor inside and with Sita Devi beside him, Sri Rama will ask questions of his Guru and thus the *samvāda,* the dialogue continues.

For Truth can only be stated by inference, never by statement. Truth is not a thing. Just as you can indicate the

---

[28] The name of Sri Rama brings all of life's demands to final fulfilment—Tulsidas.

many roads that lead to Ayodhya, but never could say, here is
Ayodhya, for who has ever seen all of Ayodhya at one moment—
such the nature of the Truth. Standing in it you cannot say,
look here it is. For that which says and that which sees and that
which has heard and the silence before and after—are all Truth.
So Truth cannot say Truth to Truth. But you can say, brother,
if you take this road you will not reach Ayodhya, you may
reach Lanka, the Lanka of the monster Ravana. Go, instead,
by this avenue of trees, cool with their evening breezes, rich
in its multiple hospices, and the water-offerers at every other
milestone who stand there night and day for the betterment of
their dharma to offer this cooling element to tired pilgrims—
the water is of the Ganges, for all good water is the Ganges.
You will smell the perfume of jasmine round the waterpots,
while birds come to drink of the gifts, sputtering and chattering
above you. Remember, the Kingdom of Rama is based on love.
Take this road, dear wanderer, and turn right by the well, and
go straight up the rising mounds and hills, and as morning
breaks you stand by the Saraju River and on the other side is
the Thrice Holy city of Sri Rama, Ayodhya, the beautiful. Will
you not come with me, traveller?

This was, in many ways, the tone and argument of *Hind
Swaraj* or Indian Self-rule. For he who rules himself alone can be
free—he who seeks the truth alone the true Indian. We want no
other India. You young men, Gandhiji says to his interlocutor, a
revolutionary, you want Indian independence. So do I. But you
want, if I may so tell you, not your India or my India, but an
India of British manufacture, as it were. You are so corrupted by
this English education that you cannot (nor for that matter can
I, authentically) speak of the Indian whose India it is. We want
another England in India—we want every shape and purpose

of an alien culture and civilisation, for in fact we are envious of them. You think if you can chop off a few British heads, and you know it is at once easy and difficult; easy because killing is not so complicated a business, yet by nature conspiracy is a much entwined endeavour, whereas non-killing is an arduous job. But again killing is difficult for you face the gallows as many, too many young and brave men have, or the Andaman Islands where you will wither and die—but there's another road, a sweeter road, maybe a longer road (I do not believe this to be true, but I will say it for argument's sake), and at the end of it you come to the perfumed city of Sri Rama.

Interlocutor. What sir are the characteristics of this city?[29]

Gandhi. First let us talk of the road to the City. Then we can prophesy what the City might be like. The road to that City is all green with cultivation. The peasants till the earth and grow their crop and the seasons are regular, and when they are not the government has granaries filled with rice for the poor and the famined.

Interlocutor. When you talk of the City you never seem to remember that a City today is a centre for production and distribution. Where will your factories be then?

Gandhi. That's just my point. In Sri Rama's Kingdom or in an Independent India there will be no factories. Of course I know even this body is a factory. I know all nature is a factory. But nature goes towards the Truth, towards liberation. But factories belittle man, make him mean by

---

[29] I have tried to summarise here the *Hind Swaraj*. All quotes are from this book. The book is conceived, as many books of Indian philosophical doctrine are, as questions and answers.

tricking wants and no satisfactions. I do not mean by that people will be lazy. I simply mean that only such work will each man perform that his dharma demands. Now what do I mean by that? I mean that each man will do such jobs as will lead him to salvation.

Interlocutor. You mean everyone wants salvation.

Gandhi. I affirm that man seeks only and only salvation. Truth as God is what man wants. And the jobs we do must be pathways to that Truth.

Interlocutor. You mean there are people like that.

Gandhi. That shows, my dear friend, despite your willingness to be shot or hanged by the British for India's freedom, you have no idea of what an Indian is. Our whole culture from the most ancient times has only talked of this. Man seeks the Truth. That rule is good for man which leads him to the Truth. Our *Ramayana* and our *Mahabharata* say it, our very folksongs speak of it. We must all be humble as Hanumans in the Kingdom of Sri Rama.

Interlocutor. Go on, sir, I would like to hear.

Gandhi. In the past there have been great civilisations. Egypt and Sumeria, Greece and Rome. Look what has happened to them. You know them only through history books. Ours is perhaps the oldest human civilisation in existence.

Interlocutor. You mean it's greater than Greece and Rome?

Gandhi. All I say is, Greece and Rome have passed away. India remains, even if what she covers herself with are only threadiest shroud of her past splendours. We are alive. And we shall not be another England, however grand England may seem to you.

Interlocutor. I am not enamoured of England. I am enamoured of Freedom.

Gandhi. So am I. But what is freedom?

Interlocutor. Well, freedom is to be rid of the British and have our own people rule us. Like Italy was freed by Garibaldi and Mazzini and Cavour.

Gandhi. That's just it. I'm glad you've brought up the names of Garibaldi and Mazzini. May I ask of you, is Italy today a better place because the Austrians have been driven out and you have Italians ruling Italians? Do you think Mazzini was happy with the way Italian freedom was conquered? A few guns and many people willing to die for the revolution. Of course Garibaldi was a courageous man. But who won? Cavour won. The astute politician won, and Victor Emmanuel. What did the Italian man get? He lives in the same poverty and the working class men live under the same slavery. Mazzini saw this. He talked of the duties of man. He alone is free—that is full of love—who performs his dharma. Duty is the foundation of a free state.

Interlocutor. What about the British parliament?

Gandhi. If it were not such a serious discussion I would laugh. That vote-catching machinery by which the most astute talks people into his party is hardly worthy of being called the home of freedom. Freedom and love are the same. You can only be free because you love. To hate even one man is to hate all men.

Interlocutor. You mean it?

Gandhi. Yes, sir, I mean it. I mean every word I say. I would rather India were never free than we give it over to brown Englishmen. We want an Indian India—Hind Swaraj.

Interlocutor. Sir, I do not understand you.

Gandhi. Listen, I want the music of the spinning wheel instead of the machine exuding its smoke and eating up the soul of man. I want men to walk and to ride horses or camels, for this way they know the country, they know and love the Indians. The way we travel today by trains is a travesty of travel. We rush through hundreds of miles in a day and we do not know the India we are traversing. Softened by these western means of comfort we have become emasculated. We have lost our manhood. We have become cowardly. Railways, lawyers and doctors have impoverished the country so much that if we do not wake up we will be ruined. Doctors assure us that a consumptive clings to life even when he is about to die. Consumption does not produce apparent hurt—it even produces a seductive colour about a patient's face so as to induce belief that all is well. Civilisation is such a disease and we have to be wary. And you were talking of the railways. The holy places of India have become unholy. Formerly people went to these places with very great difficulty. Generally therefore only the devotees visited such places. Nowadays rogues visit them in order to practise their roguery.

Interlocutor. Then what about the Muslims and Christians?

Gandhi. To me all are Indians. A man's religion is his relation to his God. The Hindus have no quarrel with any other religion. To me all men are children of God.

Interlocutor. Even the Englishman?

Gandhi. Yes, of course, the Englishman as well. If Englishmen gave up avarice and violence—it's on this that imperialism is based—and if they be full of non-violence, and seek the Truth they are better in my mind than the

Indians who would be small Englishmen. I would rather be ruled by the truth-seeking Englishman than by the power-seeking Indian. My Indian is not an Indian because he's born in India. My Indian is an Indian because he loves the Truth.

Interlocutor. I think I am beginning to see something of what you say. Please sir, enlighten me on how one could get there.

Gandhiji. If you agree that we want an Indian India, that is based on love and truth, then the only way to get there is through non-violence. Passive resistance is a method of securing rights by personal suffering; it is the reverse of resistance by arms. When I refuse to do a thing that is repugnant to my conscience, I use soul-force. For instance, the government of the day has passed a law which is applicable to me. I do not like it. If by using violence I force the government to repeal the law I am employing what may be termed body-force. If I do not obey the law and accept the penalty for its breach, I use soul-force. It involves sacrifice of self.

Everybody admits that sacrifice of self is infinitely superior to sacrifice of others. Moreover if this kind of force is used in a cause that is unjust, only the person using it suffers. He does not make others suffer for his mistakes. Men have before now done many things which were subsequently found to be wrong. No man can claim he is absolutely in the right or that a particular thing is wrong because he thinks so, but it is wrong for him so long as that is his deliberate judgement. It is therefore meet that he should not do that which he knows to be wrong and suffer the consequence thereof whatever it be. This is the key to the use of soul-force.

It is contrary to our manhood if we obey laws repugnant to our conscience . . . A man who has realised his manhood, who fears only God will fear no one else . . . If man will only realise that it is unmanly to obey laws that are unjust, no man's tyranny will enslave him. This is the key to self-rule or home rule.

Interlocutor. Perhaps you are right, sir. But may I ask: Is not non-violence a form of cowardice?

Gandhi. What do you think? Wherein is courage required—in blowing others to pieces from behind a cannon or with a smiling face to approach a cannon and be blown to pieces? Who is the true warrior—he who keeps death always as a bosom friend or he who controls the death of others? Believe me, that a man devoid of courage and manhood can never be a passive-resister.

That nation is great which rests its head upon death as a pillow. Real Home Rule is possible only where passive resistance is the guiding force of the people. Any other rule is foreign rule.

Passive resistance has been described as truth-force. Truth therefore has to be followed and that at any cost. One who is free from hatred requires no sword.

* * *

Now, far away in the heart of Russia, a great voice had arisen. It was willing to soothe the ills of all mankind. Stumpy in frame, aristocratic and fearless, Tolstoy spoke with fire against the injustices man did to man—he addressed himself mainly to the Christian nations. He had gone to the roots of Christianity and he had found love there. He had gone to the sources of

'Brahmanism, Judaism, Mazdaism, Buddhism, Taoism, Confucianism' and he found love there. For love is the very essence of man.

> 'In every individual a spiritual element is manifested that gives life to all that exists, and that spiritual element strives to unite with everything of a like nature to itself, and attains this aim through love.'[30]

Why then this horror of war and tyranny, and often in the name of religion? He abhorred riches, he abhorred killing—even of animals. He became a vegetarian. He tried so hard to find the Kingdom of God within himself. God was very near and yet far, it seemed to a man of passion like Tolstoy. Of Tartar blood he would always be close to the mouzhiks, would always fight with passion in whatever he did. He sent the Doukhobors to Canada, he condemned the atrocities of the Russian regime, and as with Gandhiji the government of the day could neither condemn him openly—for fear of his becoming too important—nor leave him free, so that he was perpetually at war with the powers up high. And one day a strange letter came to him from London. He had never heard the man's name. 'Received a letter,' wrote Tolstoy in his diary, 'from a Hindu of the Transvaal.' Tolstoy replied to this unknown Hindu.'[31]

'I have just received,' he wrote, 'your most interesting letter which has given me great pleasure. God help our dear brothers and co-workers in the Transvaal. The same struggle of the soft against the harsh, of meekness and love against pride and

---

[30] *Tolstoy and Gandhi*, p. 89.
[31] Louis Fischer. *Life of Mahatma Gandhi*.

violence, is making itself felt every year more and more among us here . . . I greet you fraternally and am happy to have contact with you. Tolstoy.'[32]

Gandhiji, however, was not the first Indian to have communicated with Tolstoy. The Russian sage had been in correspondence with Indian revolutionaries, now actively working from London or elsewhere—and among them was the slender young Bengali, Chittaranjan Das, who was ultimately to become one of the closest associates of Mahatma Gandhi in India. Chittaranjan Das, like the other young Indian revolutionaries, refused to believe in non-violence. For them the main road to success was to overthrow the British in a pure and holy revolution. They also published a paper, *Free Hindusthan* from Vancouver. In reply to these young Indians Tolstoy wrote a long letter, a typewritten copy of which, auspiciously, fell into Gandhiji's hands and immediately he wrote to Tolstoy asking permission to print it. It was soon published as 'A Letter to a Hindu' in *Indian Opinion*[33] with a brief introduction. Gandhiji said: 'To me, as a humble follower of the great teacher whom I have looked upon as one of my guides, it is a matter of honour to be connected with the publication of his letter, such especially as the one which is now being given to the world.[34] True we all want freedom,' wrote Gandhiji, but he added, and how properly, 'there are as many opinions as there are Indian nationalists.' Yet what is the right way to achieve it—freedom? Violence of course is one of the ways: 'The assassination of Sir Curzon Wyllie was an illustration of that method in its worst and most detestable

---

[32] *Tolstoy and Gandhi*, p. 98.
[33] 25-12-1909, 1-1-1910, 8-1-1910.
[34] C.W., Vol. X, p. 3-4.

form. If we do not want the English we must pay the price. Tolstoy indicates it. Do not resist evil, also do not yourselves participate in evil. He is sincere and is earnest. He commands attention.'

What indeed did Tolstoy have to say to the Indians, in this long, over long letter? Quoting the Vedas and Sri Krishna— Vivekananda to begin with—Tolstoy asks the reason for the astonishing fact that a majority of working people submit to a handful of idlers, who control their labour and their very lives, and this is always and everywhere the same—whether the oppressor and the oppressed are of one race or, as in India and elsewhere, the oppressors are of a different nation. This phenomenon, Tolstoy went on to point out, seems particularly strange in India, for there more than two hundred million people, highly gifted, both physically and mentally, find themselves in the power of a small group of men quite alien to them in thought, and immeasurably inferior to them in religious morality. And yet the chief, if not the sole, cause of the enslavement of the Indian peoples by the English lies in this very absence of a religious consciousness, and of the true guidance for conduct which should flow from it—a lack common in our day to all nations East and West, from Japan to England and America alike. He quotes the *Kural*[35] as saying: 'The aim of the sinless One consists in acting without causing sorrow to others.' Love indeed represents the highest morality, a truth which was 'neither denied nor contradicted by anyone, anywhere', but 'falsehoods and superstitions were woven with it. And yet the great religious teachers of the world of Brahmanism, Buddhism and above all of Christianity, foreseeing such a perversion of the

---

[35] An ancient Indian text in Tamil.

law of love, have constantly drawn attention to the one invariable condition of love, namely, the enduring of injuries, insults and violence of all kinds without resisting evil by evil.' Yet the same people have often accepted 'as lawful . . . an order of life based on violence and allowing men not merely to torture but even to kill one another'. But has not Krishna said: 'Children, do you want to know by what your hearts should be guided? Throw aside your longings and strivings after that which is null and void: get rid of your erroneous thoughts about happiness and wisdom and your empty and insincere desires. Dispense with these and you will know love.' Nevertheless we must pause and consider here the arguments of those who throw at us the so-called science to prove that violence is part of human nature, it has all along been there, and that 'among plants and beasts there is a constant struggle for existence which always results in the survival of the fittest'. And as such the coercion of the majority. All this is not science but pseudo-science.

You say, dear Hindu friends, Tolstoy goes on to argue, that the English have enslaved India, and that you should fight. But is it not laughable that 'a commercial company enslaved a nation comprising two hundred millions? Is it not clear therefore it's the Indians who have enslaved themselves . . . When the Indians complain that the English have enslaved them it is as if drunkards complained that the spirit dealers who have settled amongst them have enslaved them.' Why, do you forget your Rajas and Maharajas who have oppressed you, like the Sultans and the Tsars, all in the name of the divine right of kings? The truth is if the Indians are enslaved 'it is only because they themselves live and have lived by violence and do not recognise the eternal law of love inherent in humanity'. Finally what does the Indian want, the Englishman or the German want, not constitutions and revolutions, nor new universities nor 'an augmentation of papers and books, nor gramophones nor cinematographer—nor those childish and for the most part corrupt stupidities termed art'—no, what humanity needs, what every individual needs, is to accept the validity of the one and only true law: the law of love, which brings happiness to every individual and as well to all mankind. And once again has not Krishna said:

> 'Children, look upwards with your beclouded eyes, a world full of joy and love will disclose itself to you . . . Then you will know what love has done with you, what love has bestowed upon you, what love demands of you.'

Indeed, Tolstoy was only speaking of *Ramrajya,* the Kingdom of Sri Rama.

7

The Mountain and the Stream

Kallenbach, the rich and idealist Jew, and ever a great admirer of Gandhiji's, offered his farm, some twenty miles from Johannesburg, and here therefore would start the first experiment in *Ramrajya*. For the wives of those who went to jail, and their children as well, had to live somewhere, and one could not, after all, go on giving maintenance allowance to each of these families—first of all it would create confusions of many kinds, and again where was one going to find the money? True, on landing at Cape Town, Gandhiji had just received a cable from Jamshedji Tata (the leading Indian industrialist) saying he had sent twenty-five thousand rupees towards the satyagraha fund. Important though the sum was, it could not feed and clothe and pay the rent of every family whose men were fighting the battle. Thus a 'cooperative commonwealth' was to be founded and naturally Kallenbach came in to help. It was aptly to be called the Tolstoy Farm. 'He has,' wrote Gandhiji, 'great faith in Count Tolstoy's teachings and tries to live up to it. He himself wants to live on the farm and follow a simple mode of life. It appears Mr. Kallenbach will gradually give up his work as architect and live in complete poverty.'[1]

---

[1] *Indian Opinion*, 18 June 1910.

Over eleven hundred acres large, the farm possessed fruit trees of all types—oranges, apricots and plums—a small stream to have permanent and fresh water from, two wells and many snakes of all castes and colours, and a railway station just a few walkable miles away. There was even a small house to begin with at the foot of the hill, but to accommodate all the members of his new household, fresh structures had to be quickly built, mainly from corrugated iron sheets, Kallenbach, himself a professional architect, directing the works. For the doors and windows there was enough available timber; and anybody who applied himself of course becomes a good carpenter. Even so, Indian carpenters came from Johannesburg to make a gift of their services, and some who could not, sent money to hire other carpenters. This, if anything, was the true spirit of 'community service'.

Sometimes even the weak and the meek among the members of the Farm tried to do work, any work, and one here, one there, fell ill or fainted. But a little bit of fresh water or a mud-pack did the trick and they were eagerly back at work. Barrister Royappen was a finicky young man. Yet he too would take down loads from railway trucks, and haul them into the waiting carts. 'There has been feverish activity on the farm,' Gandhiji wrote in the *Indian Opinion*, 'to complete the arrangement for (housing) women. Mr. Gandhi has been working at stone rolling, side by side with the Kaffirs. Stones are available on the farm itself, but they have to be carried from the hill to the building site. Mr. Gopal Naidoo attends to cooking . . . I am both surprised and glad that Mr. Kallenbach lives amidst this group like a member of the family.'

Other interesting news in the same paper reported: 'Mr. David Andrew, Mr. Samuel Joseph[2] and Mr. Dhobi Narayana

---

[2] Obviously Indian converts to Christianity.

will be free for eight days. They will be deported next Friday.' Under the heading, Thambi Naidoo: 'It is not yet known where he is to be taken. There are four other satyagrahis with him.' *Indian Opinion* also contained news about the great big activity of the whites, the building of the South African Union[3]. So far there were the Het Volk, the Union, and Bond Parties, in the Transvaal, the Orange Colony and the Cape Colony, respectively. 'Efforts are being made by Mr. Botha and friends to amalgamate the three under the name of the South Africa Party.' Mr. Botha's programme seemed simple; the Native policy was to be fair and sympathetic, European immigration to be encouraged, and the prevention of Asiatic immigrants from entering South Africa. The Indians therefore knew clearly and inexorably where they stood.

In the meantime, however, the work on the Tolstoy Farm continued, 'the weak became strong and labour proved a tonic for all'. 'A school has now been opened,' reported the *Indian Opinion.*

'Mr. Gandhi teaches every day between two and five, except on Mondays and Thursdays. The (only) pupils at present are: Mr. Gopal, Mr. Chinan, Mr. Kuppuswami, and his two sons.' Thus Gandhiji was busy teaching the adults as well, and soon, very soon, the Farm buildings would be completed, but what about the community's other needs? The *Indian Opinion,* therefore, asked contributions of the following articles:

blankets or cotton mattresses
wooden planks

---

[3] South African Union came into being on 1 June 1910. And the Tolstoy Farm, significantly enough, was offered by Kallenbach and accepted by Gandhiji on 30 May 1910.

empty kerosene tins

clean gunny bags or gunny-bag cloth or hessian

implements, such as hoes and spades, needles

sewing thread, etc.

coarse cloth of any kind

books for use in school

fruits and vegetables

cooking utensils

food grains of any kind

And all these had to be addressed to: Mr. Gandhi, Tolstoy Farm, Lawley, Transvaal.

During the time the Farm was getting ready to house the inmates Gandhiji was invited to address the Socialist Society of Johannesburg. After offering an apology for differing from them but then he was an ardent searcher of truth. He asked, was not modern civilisation too busy, too preoccupied with bread and butter and the complexities that arose out of a materialistic way of life? Was not simple life better than a complex one? The flesh is not the be-all and end-all of life. After extolling the qualities of ancient civilisations which were kind, God-fearing and simple, and looked upon the body as a means of spiritual uplift, he declared, for that purpose one should adopt simplicity and rural life. The public was mostly white and a vigorous discussion followed.

However, now Gandhiji was to go back to the Farm. The buildings were completed and the inmates were coming. Soon the Farm was busy settling down the families to an established pattern of accommodation and a clear programme of activity.

The women were housed on one side, and at some distance from them were the men. And children met at the school, a

heterogeneous group of them, from any age to any age, and
since everybody worked in the mornings, the teachers and the
pupils went to school in the afternoons. The teachers and the
taught sometimes would be so exhausted, sweet sleep would
steal on their eyes, but a little bit of cold water did the trick,
and the pupil would wake up to an eager class. There was one
further difficulty. In what language was one going to teach? The
majority of course were Gujaratis, but there were also Tamils,
and some who spoke Telugu. What would become of these
children? Gandhiji taught his pupils first in Gujarati and as he
knew a little Tamil, he coached the 'Madrasis' in Tamil as well.
Of course, Kallenbach also taught. He would teach English and
the cobblering of slippers. (Thus almost everybody wore self-
made shoes.) There were other teachers too, but they were not
very exciting. The main burden once again fell on Gandhiji.
And again, what was one to teach?

The basis of education, after all, is one, Gandhiji believed,
of giving the pupils a deep and true perspective on life—that
is, a spiritual one. But since the pupils belonged to so many
faiths and philosophies, what was the proper way to give them
religious instruction? Each one was therefore encouraged to read
books on his or her own religion, the Parsi the *Zendavesta*, the
Muslim the *Koran*, and since the Hindu has no such central
book—unless it be the *Gita*, and the *Gita* is a difficult book
for children—Gandhiji wrote a treatise on Hinduism. 'If this
document was in my possession,' confessed Gandhiji almost
twenty years later, 'I should have inserted it here as a landmark
in my spiritual progress.' Not to be burdened with too many
objects, he destroyed his papers as he moved along from place,
from stage to stage of his wandering life. Life was more urgent
than any history.

Since so many religions were thus represented, it taught pupils tolerance and they learnt, says Gandhiji, to view one another's religions and customs with a large-hearted charity. For example, when the Muslim boys went on a Ramzan fast, some Hindu children also went on fast. Further, the Hindus practised *ekadashi* and some even kept the *chaturmas* like Gandhiji's mother used to; they would fast the whole day and not eat till the sun was seen again. And at prayers, hymns were sung in English, Hindi, and Gujarati, and sometimes the *Ramayana* was read, or some text of Islam.

The food was very simple. Wheaten 'coffee' and home-made bread for breakfast, rice and lentils and vegetables for lunch, and wheat and milk or bread and 'coffee' towards the evening. The meat-eaters were offered their own food, lamb or even beef, but one and all preferred to be vegetarians. But Gandhiji himself suddenly turned from a vegetarian to a fruitarian diet. This was because he couldn't bear the thought of the way cows were milked. Further, for spiritual reasons, sometimes it is better, he felt, not to drink milk. Kallenbach had joined Gandhiji in these dietetic experiments—and they finally gave up cooked food altogether. And during that period Gandhiji could sometimes walk forty to fifty-five miles a day and not be too exhausted.

For there were other rules too that made walking a necessity. Since one lived on public money, one could not and should not spend on unessentials. Why take a train to Johannesburg at all, why not walk the twenty-one miles back and forth and a small sandwich, taken from the farm, would do excellently for lunch? Except the old and the maimed, everybody did it, and with joy, and the most joyous of all was of course, Kallenbach. For anyone's trip to Johannesburg, and at any time, he would be the ever ready and happy companion.

Of course one did not care that one had to wake up at two o'clock in the night, especially if one had to be at Johannesburg in good time for the opening of the shops or the offices. After one has finished one's job, one can return home safely for one's evening bath and dinner. The normal time to go and come would be between twelve and fourteen hours. But some could do each way in four hours and eighteen minutes. These were not indeed hard demands. Everybody did these jobs cheerfully, and the young especially enjoyed themselves in whatever they were doing. Sometimes too they would play clever pranks, but that was natural, after all.

One day, however, Gandhiji, who had made a bold experiment in co-education, heard of an improper act. Two boys had (sort of) teased a girl. 'The news made me tremble,' says Gandhiji. He argued with the two young men, but what was he to do for the girl, so that this misdemeanour will never occur again? 'The passionate Ravana,' he said to himself, 'could not so much as touch Sita with evil intent while Rama was thousands of miles away. What mark should the girls have to bear so as to give them a sense of security and at the same time sterilise the sinner's eye? The question kept me awake all night.' Finally he decided he should perhaps suggest to the girls that he might cut off their fine, long hair. They weren't easy to convince. Nevertheless, once they understood the motive behind his suggestion 'they came around after all, and at once the very hand that is narrating this incident set to cut off their hair'. Afterwards he explained what he had done and why to his whole class. 'I never heard of a joke again.'

In fact, boys and girls went to the stream to bathe, all together, and never an accident occurred. 'I knew, and so did the children, that I loved them with a mother's love.'

And satyagrahis who left their gaols continued to come straight to the Tolstoy Farm. They did not care what happened to them later—their only aim was to have the Black Act removed from the Statute Book, till which time the pledge—their pledge taken in the name of God—had to be kept alive. They came here for repose, and to make preparations for their next move. 'And as it rests with him (the satyagrahi) to prosecute the fight, he believes that victory or defeat, pleasure or pain, depends upon himself.' As the *Gita* says, the fruits of action should never be important; the fight alone matters. And the means employed for the fight. For the right means alone lead to the right end.

There is a beautiful story, like a parable, of two satyagrahis who, released by the Magistrate on personal recognisance, now came to spend a few days on the Tolstoy Farm. They were to be convicted the next day. They were however so engrossed in their talk that when it came to catching the last train, this seemed almost an impossible task. Being athletes they both ran towards the station but the train had already steamed up. In a moment it started. The station master however, seeing them, waved the flag, stopped the train, and they finally jumped in. The station master, like most local officials, though white, was full of respect and consideration for the satyagrahis. The magistrates also by now trusted them enough to let them go home and return on the appointed day for the conviction. Had they missed the train, what a slur on the fair name of the movement it might have been.

Gandhiji also, in those days (apart from fasts and changes of diet), continued his experiments on earth and water treatment, and there was never a single case of illness on the Tolstoy Farm. And again there was his constant concern for safe sanitation. Indians never seemed to worry enough about it. So new rules had to be framed. 'All rubbish was buried in the trenches sunk for the purpose . . . All waste water was collected in buckets and used to water trees.' And what about the night soil, that most offensive item of human sanitation? A deep square pit received these remains, and fresh earth was thrown over it all to keep one away from smells and flies. Besides, it also gave very rich manure to the farm. 'A man who does not cover his waste,' concluded Gandhiji, 'deserves a heavy penalty even if he lives in a forest.' For Gandhiji could never forget the Indian riverside performances in mornings, or on the streets of Benares. After all, this noble earth is God's own mantle. And the water ever holy, every bit a Ganga.

But there were other and more difficult problems to resolve. One remembers he had asked Rajachandra, the great teacher, what should be done if a snake came to attack you? Rajachandra had said you must choose between the two lives. Gandhiji's higher self was willing to give up his own life for the snake's. And this, he had, we know, proved to himself. However, what about the others? Even if you meant no harm your fear is communicated to the other, and fear creates fear. So Kallenbach had an enchanting idea. He would buy all the books he could on snakes, study these and teach people about them, and make people accept snakes in a friendly, almost domestic way. He even brought the hunch-back Albrecht, a German, poor and disabled, who seemed to enjoy playing with snakes. 'He would bring snakes in his hand and let them play on his palm. If our stay on Tolstoy Farm had been prolonged, goodness knows what would have been the upshot of Albrecht's adventures.'[4] And again to show how kind and friendly the snakes were, nothing could be more magical than direct demonstration. Kallenbach thereupon caught hold of a

---

[4] S.S.A., p.252.

king cobra on the Farm, tamed him, and fed the tangled creature with his own hands. And children enjoyed the pleasure of this new inmate immeasurably. One day, however, the cobra slipped away, and Kallenbach lost a very good friend.

* * *

During this time, Gandhiji was reading a great deal. And the correspondence with Tolstoy continued. 'As your devoted follower I send you herewith,' wrote Gandhiji, 'a brief booklet (*Hind Swaraj*) which I have written. It is my own translation of a Gujarati writing. Curiously enough the original writing has been confiscated by the Government of India. I therefore hastened the above publication of the translation. I am most anxious not to worry you, but if your health permits it and if you can find time to go through the booklet, needless to say I shall value very highly your criticism of the writing.'

Tolstoy wrote (8 May 1910).

'I read your book *Hind Swaraj* with great interest because I think the question you have dealt with is important not only for the Indians but for the whole of mankind.

'I cannot find your first letter but by discovering your biography by Doke I happen to know you through that biography which gripped me and it gave me a chance to know and understand you better.

'Your friend and brother Leo Tolstoy.'

For Tolstoy was already not very well, and was preparing to make his final flight from home and family. He therefore sent a last message to Gandhiji (7 September 1910).

'The more I live—and specially now that I am approaching death, the more I feel inclined to express to others the feelings which so strongly move my being, and which, according to my opinion, are of great importance. That is, what one calls non-resistance is in reality nothing else but the discipline of love undeformed by false interpretation. Love is the aspiration for communion and solidarity with other souls and that aspiration always liberates the source of noble activities. That love is the supreme and unique law of human life . . . That law of love has been promulgated by all the philosophies—Indian, Chinese, Hebrew, Greek and Roman. I think it had been most clearly expressed by Christ . . . He knew that once violence is admitted, doesn't matter even in a single case, the law of love is thereby rendered futile. That is to say that law of love ceases to exist. The whole Christian civilisation, so brilliant in the exterior, has grown up on this misunderstanding and this flagrant and strange contradiction, sometimes conscious but mostly unconscious . . .

'Consequently your work in Transvaal, which seems to be far away from the centre of our world, is yet the most fundamental and the most important to us—supplying the most weighty practical proof in which the world can now share and with which must participate not only the Christians but all the peoples of the world.'[5]

A few weeks later (5 November 1910) Tolstoy was dead. His last words, almost whispered, were: '. . . the Truth . . . I love much'.

'The great Tolstoy,' wrote Gandhiji in the *Indian Opinion*, 'has quit this corporeal frame at the ripe old age of 83. It is truer

---

[5]   *Tolstoy and Gandhi*, p. 71-76. The English version had Tolstoy's approval.

to say that "he has quit this corporeal frame" than that he has died. There can be no death for Tolstoy's soul. . . . Only his body, which was of dust, has returned to dust.

'Tolstoy is known to the entire world: but not as soldier though once he was reputed to be an expert soldier; not as a great writer, though indeed he enjoys a great reputation as a writer; nor as a nobleman, though he owned immense wealth. It was as a good man that the world knew him. In India we would have described him as a maharishi (Great Seer). . . .

'It is no small encouragement to us that we have the blessings of a great man like Tolstoy in our task. We publish his photograph in today's issue.'[6]

The satyagraha movement was at this time perhaps at its lowest ebb. 'The time came,' writes Professor Hancock, 'when his force of satyagrahis fluctuated between a higher limit of sixty-six and a lower one of sixteen. He needed some new and exciting issue to arouse enthusiasm among the masses but his principle forbade him to manufacture one: in satyagraha the minimum must also be the maximum; a deliberate extension of conflict beyond the objectives professed at the beginning would be a violation of truth.'[7] And truth alone knew the game it was playing.

His Royal Highness, the Duke of Connaught and uncle to King George V, was going to inaugurate the birth of the Union of South Africa. *Indian Opinion* was always a royalist paper, and for every birth and bereavement in the imperial household, it

---

[6]   *Indian Opinion*, Gujarati edition 26-11-1910. C.W., X, p. 369-70.
[7]   S., p. 340.

sent respectful and warm telegrams, whether it be anxiety over the illness of Princess Alexander, the sudden death of King Edward or the succession of King George V. Long Live the King, it stated. The paper constantly reminded its readers, the good Queen Victoria, the Crown of England, was *Kaiser-i-Hind*, the Ruler of India. And as loyal British subjects, of course when the Duke came, it was but right for the Indian community to offer its respects to the representative of His Imperial Majesty, and to welcome him as everyone else. However, whereas every one had something important to rejoice about, what did the Indians get? And the Chinese? And the Coloureds? The satyagrahis were still going to prison despite the important promises made in London by responsible ministers of South Africa. Nothing had changed. The Indians, therefore, with the Coloureds, decided to boycott the celebrations of welcome to the Duke. Indian leaders informed him respectfully why they could not be present for the 'Ceremony of Presentation'. The Duke later expressed, more or less publicly, his hopes for an early settlement of the problems and said how impressed he was with the way the Indians had behaved as satyagrahis. The difficulty, one must admit, was real for Smuts. It was not the liberal Merriman who was to preside over the destinies of the new Dominion, but Botha—a Boer general like Smuts himself, but more Boer than British. Besides, the Orange Free State—always the most Boer of Boer republics, suspicious, withdrawn, and somehow unwilling to participate in any event except that which took the Boer back to the days of the great trek—was an unwilling partner. Even so, the Union made the four colonies an important and an international entity. Those most fitted to lead were the British-dominated Provinces of the Cape and Natal, but they were out-numbered, even out-manoeuvred by the Boer elements. Smuts was in the middle of these passions and contradictions, unable to know which way to turn. But as for the Indian question, of course, he wanted an honourable settlement. He took the whole responsibility on himself and started to work on it with real fervour. There was thus great optimism in the air. Gandhiji sent telegrams to Gokhale, to Ritch in London—yes, one was perhaps round the corner for a settlement. How could South Africa start her entry into the world with such an acute and internationally sensitive problem, as the position of the Indians, unresolved. But try as he would, Smuts could not convince his Boer colleagues. Especially the Free State leaders (who were, one must remember, the first to prohibit Indians from settling in their territory, and preventing Indians from taking any jobs except the most menial ones)—Free Staters were totally opposed to any concessions being made. Their laws would prevail in their own province. Thus each province will have its own laws about Indian immigration and rights of citizenship, and there could be no one statute for the whole of South Africa. In which case the Transvaal law, against which, mainly, the Indians were fighting and offering satyagraha, would simply have to be modified. This should not hurt the feelings of the Transvaal Boers. Even the British agreed to this. And one must not forget it was, after all, Jan Smuts who had made and worded the law in the Transvaal. Obviously he could not go against himself. Caught in these dilemmas Smuts saw no solution. But the public knew nothing of the inner political struggle. And it was under these circumstances that the new Bill was drafted. How could one satisfy everybody, anyway? Finally, when the Bill was listed in the Gazette Extraordinary[8] (the Immigrants Restriction Bill)

---

[8] *The Union of South Africa Government Gazette*, February 1911.

the Indian community felt a restrained joy. 'The long expected
Immigration Bill has now been received,' wrote Gandhiji in
Indian Opinion. 'It is very complicated and comprehensive.'
And he went on to explain specific implications of the Bill. Yes,
the Black Act seems to definitely disappear from the statute
book, the Black Act against which for these four years so many
hundreds of Indians had gone to jail and come out only to go
in again, and so many merchants had become bankrupt. But
they had gained so many friends, not only in South Africa but
from all over the world. One had to be careful, however, for
there was a rumour Smuts had said: 'I will see every Asiatic out
of the country'. That might well be true. But Gandhism was
in principle against any beliefs in rumours. One must test the
sincerity of the man at each instant. Immediately, therefore,
telegrams were sent to Smuts for clarifications on many points.
The Bill was also given to a special legal adviser to find out
if, in fact, some of the points that Gandhiji had found to be
unclear would not eventually be confusing if and when it
became law. The legal advisers agreed with Gandhiji, and for
every explanation Gandhiji asked of Smuts, the answer was
ever more confusing. Yes, the new Bill was for the whole of the
Union—as Lord Crew had declared. Only, it wouldn't apply in
the Orange Free State. And there was also the question of the
wives and minors of those who were registered in Transvaal, a
small point in itself, but of great importance to the Indians. As
the correspondence prolonged itself, the prevarication became
greater. So Gandhiji would now go to Cape Town and see
Smuts—meanwhile the good Ritch, now back in South Africa,
would look after the Johannesburg office, and Polak the British
Indian Association of Natal. Thus coordinated there could
never be any confusion. And in Cape Town the Coloureds

and the Chinese were already not too satisfied. Gandhiji would not rush into conclusions. Smuts alone could explain the real purport of the Bill. Here is a dialogue among the confidential papers of Gandhiji[9] noted immediately after his meeting with Smuts which is moving because of the desperate position in which Smuts found himself.

Cape Town
27 March 1911

Smuts: You see Gandhi, I am giving you everything. I do not know why, but everybody suspects me. I could have done so by regulation *but* now I am protecting wives and children in the Bill . . . I am also recognising domicile, but you are very unreasonable. Your point is absolutely new.

Gandhiji: How can you say so General Smuts? Are you not creating a racial bar?

Smuts: No, I am not. Can you show it to me?

G.: Certainly. Will you admit that throughout the four years we have been simply fighting against the racial or colour bar?

S. (startled and said after some hesitation): Yes.

G.: You know that in the Transvaal Immigration Law there is no colour bar but you read sub-section 4 of the Asiatic Act and you have the bar.

S.: You are not stating it fairly.

G. Then you shall state it in your own words.

S.: In the Transvaal we wanted total exclusion and that is brought about by the effect of the two laws.

---

[9] C.W., Vol 10., p. 494-496.

G.: And now you want the same thing for the Free State. The combined effect of the Free State Law and the new Bill will be (to) shut out the Nizam of Hyderabad,[10] and I assure you the passive resisters will fight against it.

S.: You do not know my difficulties.

G.: I do. And because I do I suggest that only so much of the Free State Law should be a basis for exemption as will enable a highly educated Indian to enter the Free State. If you send for the Law I will show you what I mean.

S. (sends for the law): But the Free Staters will never consent.

G.: Then why did General Botha write to Lord Crew that educated immigrants will be able to enter any province?

S.: You do not know all the dispatches . . . Lord Crew knows that we never wanted to give the rights as to the Free State.

G.: But you repeated the same thing at the second reading.

S.: Yes, I was simply sounding the Free Staters; and I noticed they were very much opposed.

G.: If they are, it is your duty to persuade them, and if they cannot be, you may simply amend the Transvaal legislation.

S.: But I am bound to the Imperial Government to pass this Bill.

(Reads the law and asks G. to go over to his side. G. points out the section from which the exemption is to be granted.) Yes, I now see what you mean.

---

[10] The most senior ruler of a state in India, being the head of a territory as large as France, called the Dominion of His Exalted Highness the Nizam of Hyderabad.

G.: Yes, the educated Asiatics will still be prohibited from owning fixed property and from trading. I am not raising that issue at all . . . I for one do not wish to offer passive resistance for material gains, but the racial bar we can never accept.

S.: But you have no idea of my difficulties.

G.: I know that you are quite able to overcome greater difficulties.

S.: What are you doing in Jo'burg?

G.: Looking after the families of passive resisters, etc.

S.: It has hurt me more than you to imprison these people. It has been an unpleasant episode in my life to imprison men who suffer for their conscience. I should do the same thing for conscience's sake.

Smuts' holistic perspective was never in true contradiction with the Gandhian argument. But in politics Smuts was essentially a Boer (and an ambitious one at that)—the Boers whose sole aim had once been, as we have seen, to build an Afrikaner state with the Dutch Reformed Church its religion, Afrikans as the language, its lingua, and live the peaceful lives of an agricultural and moral community its Jerusalem, but even with the Anglo-Boer War, there could now at least be a white Dominion where they would build a new, rich and powerful state.[11] Smuts had, as he said to Gandhi, nothing against the Indians. If anything, he respected them—though the petty Indian shopkeeper might have exasperated him, the hawker with his sloth and his economy, and his extra-legal

---

[11] The famous Native question—'the apple of discord'—was left out of discussion. The future alone could resolve it.

business continuance. And Smuts too respected the Empire though perhaps less than Gandhiji did, but he did, and wanted to make this country a noble element in the future commonwealth—and might it not be the beginning of a secret achievement of history. The coronation of George V was soon coming and the whole Empire was to celebrate it—so should South Africa.

However, if only the Indian question were settled, so important in the eyes of Whitehall, and settled once and for all. Already the British Government took its first step. The Government of India, seeing the intensity of the agitation in the country, decreed that immigration of indentured labour would stop from 1 July 1911, a very great achievement in itself. Thus an African settlement of the Indian question was imperative. But the South African Parliament was soon to be prorogued. While considerations were still taking place as to how to accommodate both the Boer point of view and the Indian, something had to be done immediately. And Smuts and Gandhi must meet again for a frank discussion. Could there not be a provisional settlement?

'I am sincerely anxious to help you,' wrote Gandhiji,[12] 'but I do not know how I could promise inactivity (for twelve months) on the part of the passive resisters. What you, the Imperial Government and I want to avoid is the ferment.' Yet, he goes on to say, 'it would be churlish of me not to appreciate your own difficulty . . . You have many difficult questions to solve. Indians know at present only one.' Perhaps Smuts could do something immediately so that the Indians could take part in the coronation festivities. Once again therefore Gandhi and Smuts met. And

---

[12] Cape Town, 19 April 1911.

here is the dialogue as preserved in the Gandhian archives. It reads as follows.[13]

Cape Town
(19 April 1911)

Unrevised
Nothing to be published
To be kept in the safe aft(er) perusal

Abstract of an interview Bet[ween] J.C.S. and G. at 11-30 P.M.[14] 19-IV-11

The general extracordial, S. (and G) are such friends they have left off shaking hands. But at this interview there was a hearty handshake.

'Well, Gandhi, I am sorry for you. You have been long delayed, but what can I do? You will insist on enjoying yourself in Cape Town,' commenced J.S. 'You, as a lawyer, will understand that it is difficult to carry out your alternative suggestion.'[15]

S. turns away from G. appears to be looking at something in his basket and continues: 'Gandhi, my boy, I am sorry for you. You know I want peace.'

(I suppose he is having a quiet laugh when he is saying this.)

'But,' looking now towards G., 'my adversaries consider your suggestion cannot be carried out . . . Parliament will

---

[13] C.W., Vol. XI, p. 31-34.

[14] Should be A.M.

[15] That it should not be a Bill covering the whole of the Union, but just that the Transvaal Act of 1907 be repealed.

never pass such a Bill. I therefore want to pass my Bill which I like and which I consider fair. I shall try but I may fail to pass it during this session. All the members want to go away. And the Free State Members are still opp[osed] to admitting any Asiatic. I think I can beat them in the Assembly but the Senate will throw out the Bill. I want therefore to pass the measure during the next session . . . But meanwhile I want peace. I do not want to harass your people. You know that . . . I want to help the Imperial Government and they want to help me. I want to help you and you want to help me. Will you not see our point of view?' J.S. continues.

'I emphatically do,' interposed G.

S. continued, 'I know you have many leaders. I know you to be high-minded and honest. I have told the Imperial Government so. You have a right to fight in your own way. But this country is the Kaffir's. We whites are a handful. We do not want Asia to come in . . . But how can we hold out against you? I have read your pamphlet.[16] You are a simple living and frugal race. In many respects more intelligent than we are. You belong to a civilisation that is thousands of years old. Ours, as you say, is but an experiment. Who knows but that the wh[ole] damned thing will perish before long . . . But you see why we do not want Asia here. I want time. I shall yet beat the Free Staters . . . You should therefore wait. Now just think it over and let me know . . .' After changing the subject S. said: 'Gandhi what are you doing for a living?'

G.: I am not practising at pr[esent].

S.: But how then are you living? Have you plenty of money?

---

16 *Hind Swaraj.*

G.: No. I am living . . . like a paup[er] the same as the other passive resisters on Tolstoy Farm.

S.: Whose is it?

G.: It is Mr. Kallenbach's. He is a German.

S. (Laughing): Oh, old Kallenbach! He is your admirer eh? I know.

G.: I do not know he is my admirer. We are certainly very great friends.

S.: I must come and see the Farm—where is it?

G.: Near Lawley.

S.: I know—on the Vereeniging line. What is the distance from the station?

G.: Ab[out] 20 minutes. We shall be pleased to see you there.

S.: Yes, I must come one day.

So saying, he got to say goodbye. G. did likewise and said: You say, you cannot amend the Transvaal Immigration Act. I must confess, I do not see any difficulty.

S.: Yes, there is. The whites won't have it unless you adopt my suggestion.

G.: And that is?

S.: To give the Government power to make regulations setting a different test for different people. The regulation must only refer to Indians. And this I know you won't like. But you think the whole thing over and let me know what you think. You know I want to help you.

During the conversation he said the Free State matter was confidential. The interview lasted nearly 40 minutes.

Now there could only be a provisional settlement, as between two gentlemen. The coronation was soon coming and everything should appear neat and prosperous. Gandhiji drew up such a document containing his conditions. Smuts studied it and wrote back accepting most of them, but the problem for Gandhiji was how to convince his colleagues, this time Smuts was really meaning what he said. There was a violent outburst from the members of the British India Committee of Transvaal. 'The discussion was at times heated if not stormy,' the *Indian Opinion* reported, 'and throughout there was intense distrust as to intentions of the Government.' 'At Last' was the significant title of an article by Gandhiji published in the *Indian Opinion* a few weeks later.

> 'A provisional settlement of the Asiatic trouble in the Transvaal has at last been reached, and the Indian and the Chinese of Transvaal are free to resume their ordinary occupations at least for eight months. The correspondence between the Minister of the Interior[17] and Mr. Gandhi shows that every precaution has been taken to see that the parties understand each other and to leave no room for misunderstanding.'

And he quoted:

> 'Seek ye first the Kingdom of God and His righteousness and all else will be added unto you.'

King George V by the Grace of God, Defender of Faith, King of Great Britain and Ireland, and the Dominions beyond the Seas, Emperor of India, etc., etc. was going to be crowned at Westminster Abbey on 22 June 1911. The whole Empire

---

[17] Smuts.

was going to celebrate this magic ritual. Later, King George V was to travel to that ancient city of India, Delhi, which would once again to become the capital of the great sub-continent, this city of Delhi, since the time of the *Mahabharata* ever the true capital of India. Who does not know every King that is king of India has to be crowned in Delhi; King George (with Queen Mary) will go there. There will be a resplendent Durbar, where he would receive the homage of Indian kings representing some of the most ancient dynasties on earth—the Rajput princes of Udaipur (who have ruled India, at least, since the first century after Christ), and those like the Maharaja of Mysore whose throne is supposed to be older even than that of Sri Rama of Ayodhya, and of all the princes of Kathiawar, most of whom had direct ancestral connections with Sri Krishna himself. What greater honour could the British King have than accept fealty from such a glittering assemblage of noble princes. Further, there would be festivities all over the land, and every one will feel pride in the truly mighty achievements of British rule in India.

At Westminster Abbey, the great of Europe and of the whole world had come to pay him homage, and notice the magnificence with which the British invoke God that His benignance be upon this new and able ruler, grandson of the gracious Queen Victoria and son to the kind King Edward. The princes of Germany and of Russia, cousins of King George, those of Sweden and Greece, many Maharajas, the King of Siam, representatives of the Emperor of Japan, they were all there with their tiaras, turbans and gartered splendours. And in the new Dominion of South Africa, too, there would be rejoicings, even among the Boers—after all the British are a decent people, and they will allow us to live and let live! The Kaffirs were still too uneducated to perform any special ceremonies—they would be given sweets and medals. The Coloureds, though dissatisfied, had still some white blood in them, and to that extent they too could, as it were, in private, celebrate, this important occasion. But what had the Indians to celebrate? The Empire was the empire because of them. Delhi would crown George V Emperor. But here, in Durban and in Johannesburg, the Indians had only, as an Englishman had remarked, their dog-collars. True because of the Provisional Settlement these dog-collars were removed and put on the rack for further use, only when necessary. Yet, we must trust our adversaries, argued Gandhiji. Maybe the dog-collars will one day go and go forever.

'South Africa,' wrote Gandhiji, 'will be celebrating on the 22nd instant, the coronation of King George V. What part are we going to play in the celebrations? The Provisional Settlement removes the cause of mourning . . . If Europeans cannot see their way to accord and forget their prejudice at such a time, we consider that it is the duty of the Indian community to refrain from taking part in the local official celebrations, to refuse to accept any grant that may be made for a separate celebration for us . . . The community will express its loyalty to the throne by sending an appropriate message . . . But let the 22nd of June be held as a sacred day on which, at any rate, we may practise Imperial ideals . . .

> 'At the time of the late war, on the battlefield, all distinctions disappeared as if by magic. Tommy drank from the same cup—or rather—tin as the Indian stretcher-bearer . . . The lesson of the war remained and was repeated at the time of the Zulu revolt . . . Is it possible to repeat the two experiences on the Coronation Day? We appeal to South Africa for an answer.'

And again he reminds the Indians that if we suffer it is because we are not truthful enough, and if we rebel against ourselves, 'thus exorcising the devil' we could shout: 'Oh, how happy we are under George V!' The British constitution offers equality of rights for every subject. Should we not therefore honour the King who is the symbol of that constitution? But, remember, the British have fought for this constitution 'with rivers of blood. We on the other hand have shed no blood, endured nothing, for the sake of freedom, real or imaginary.' True, the satyagrahis have suffered—but it's only a drop in the ocean. 'The British constitution permits one to seek freedom . . . We can therefore and ought to, remain loyal to the British Emperor, our grievances not withstanding.'

After all this, may it not still be said, though the British people themselves feel that they have reached freedom, yet they are strangers to real freedom—the freedom of Self. 'For if *Ramrajya* meant anything, it is where everyone tried to enjoy the freedom of Self.' Otherwise what use was there of politics, and of equal rights, and of even our fight against the dog-collar: Even so let us all join together and joyously shout:

Long Live the King,
Long Live King George V, Emperor.

But, soon, South African Indians were going to welcome their own 'King'.

* * *

Gopal Krishna Gokhale, 'the coolie King', was coming. And who did not know he lived on frail food and cool water, and though he sat amongst the high of the high in his own land, India, and would be received by His Britannic Majesty when he went to London—who did not know he was a saint, who spoke no word of untruth, and never said a harsh sentence to anyone, and all in all, he was going to come, and bring freedom to the indentured labourer among the plantations of Natal—those who lived amidst the rows on rows of silver-edged sugar cane fields on the ridges or among the tea plantations in the hills—or maybe he would even visit the mines of Dundee or of Newcastle and smile at the coolie children, and perhaps gift them gold and bless them, and after that, Shiva! Shiva!, who cares if death came or dire poverty—the kindly look of a saint could take one straight to the only true world. He was like sage Vishwamitra, who could bless any assembly, or like sage Vasistha who taught Sri Rama the meaning of Truth. Such, I tell you, was Gopal Krishna Gokhale, and if you would know, you have only to hear of the arches the whites be putting up for him, in all the big capitals of the land.

And mayors and mining-kings would receive him—as equal to equal, in fact, as superior, because he was a Brahmin—and maybe thus the widow will find back her registration card, the orphan his inheritance papers and the coolie would lose his £3 tax—that evil smelling thing which seems to hang round our necks. And the satyagrahis too, would they not, then, come out of prison and the husband will find his wife, the father his children, the businessman his shop, and Gandhiji would now lead us all into a white, clear world where we can breathe as in India—indeed better for we are rich here and we can worship and chant and sing like one does at the harvest festival:

Sapphire is the meadow, mother,
And the white cow has Yellow dew milk,

The father will come back to his abandoned son,
The potter round his rounding twist of clay.
For the Goddess is the Goddess of all the lands,
And she has given us water and shine.
And happen what might, the coolie would not forget his God.

Such the fervour among the Indians. Even the Coloureds thought this brought them some truth of hope—yes, they would not be lost between the black and the white, participating as they did in both. Dr. Abdurahiman, their leader, had Malay blood in him and Dutch, and he too had gone on deputation to England (before the Union was declared) and he also sat with the Indians, in his hopes for a better world. For if the Indians were going to get something, so, too, at least should the Coloureds. And the Chinese as well.

The harbour of Cape Town is among the most majestic harbours in the world. With the Table Mountain at the back, of elaborate-hewn crags and sheer precipices, and the rich golden earth that tumbles in folds from cloud-lost heights and descends down to the deep wine-dark sea—that is when the waters are quiet—Cape Town is no whit inferior to Bombay or Naples or Gibraltar, and yet she is very different. Here is a new nation, with, as it were, a new legislative capital, and whatever she did the other towns in the Colony naturally followed. In fact, even if the Boers felt they led the nation, indeed the English-speaking and English influenced city of Cape Town, formulated the stable policy of the Union. True, Xavier Merriman, the well-known Cape leader, was not the prime minister of the Union of South Africa, but he was ever consulted by Smuts on almost all questions of policy, and the young politician listened to Merriman with respect. Merriman had asked Smuts in one of his letters what was

he going to do with 'that worthy and inconvenient Brahmin?'—
by which he meant of course, Gokhale. This was just the hint to
say he realised how important, if indelicate, Gokhale's visit was
going to be.

Indeed, as everybody knew, Gokhale's proposed visit had put
both the South African Government and the British Government
in an awkward position. If the British had said no it would have
shaken the moral fibre of the Empire, especially as Gokhale was
a name to contend with, even in the British Parliament. If the
South African Government had said no, it would have revealed
its racial schemes too openly—and Whitehall was always awake
to put the Dominions in their place. After all, each important
legislative act of any Dominion of His Majesty had to be finally
signed by the King himself. And thus one could not say no to
Whitehall. Therefore the 'coolie King' had to be received, and
received rightly, The Union Government deputed a high official,
Mr. Runciman (of the Immigration Department), to greet the
Indian leader on board ship and accompany him wheresoever
he cared to travel.

During his very first speech in Cape Town, Gokhale made
his position unmistakably clear. He said:

> 'I shall go through South Africa in three weeks at my disposal
> with every real desire to understand the European standpoint,
> and whatever conclusions I arrive at, I will endeavour to state
> them with due restraint, and with such regard as may be
> expected from one in my position in India, to the interests of
> the Empire of which we are all members. I have not come to
> light a flame: flames have often a knack of burning those who
> light them; I have come to find out how my countrymen in
> this land are doing.'

There was an impressive reception at the City Hall with the Mayor, Harry Hands, in the chair. Schreiner, the Liberal politician of the Cape, Dr. Abdurahiman, and many leaders of the Asiatic community, sat on the platform.

'The Mayor, in opening the proceedings,' reported the *Indian Opinion,* 'said they were met together to welcome a very distinguished Indian subject of His Majesty the King: a gentleman who was a member of the Council of the Viceroy of India, and who had come to the Union of South Africa with, he believed, the full consent of the Union Government, to inquire at first hand into an economic difficulty which had arisen in their midst, and which their fellow-Indian subjects were feeling for some time. He had pleasure in extending to him a warm welcome to the Mother City of South Africa, and ventured to express the hope that the result of his mission would be the solution of the difficulty in a manner satisfactory to all concerned.'

It was an excellent beginning for a white representative to speak as he did. But when it came to Gandhiji, he was all confused and moved. This Gopal Krishna Gokhale was no ordinary man. The name of Gokhale was sacred to him, he said. He was, Gokhale was, Gandhiji's political Guru, 'and whatever he (Gandhiji) had been able to do in the service of his countrymen in South Africa—of which he claimed to be a citizen—was due to Mr. Gokhale' (Cheers). The South African question was not new to him, Gandhiji went on to observe, but they loved him not only for what he, this great man, had done for us in South Africa. It was also because his very life was an example to us all. 'Although he (Gokhale) was a candid critic of the Indian Government he was also a friend to it.' (Applause). That the Mayor of the City of Cape Town presided over the meeting showed, that though there were historic struggles between the Indians and the European communities, there was no bitterness. Of course, Gokhale was going to do all he could to help us, but we have to remember there was nothing as valuable as self-help. They could get nothing they did not deserve. Time alone would show the true fruits of action.

Gokhale himself was brief. He was very happy, he said, at last the system of indentured labour was abandoned. He had come here only to study the problems of Indians in South Africa and listen to every point of view that would be placed before him before giving his own opinion on the subject. Gandhiji was happy with this short speech—'concise, full of sound judgement,' he wrote many years later, 'firm but courteous, which pleased the Indians and fascinated the Europeans.'

By now word had spread that Gokhale was an interesting and kind man and even whites were eager to meet him. 'Dear Smuts,' wrote Merriman to his friend in Pretoria, 'You may perhaps like to hear my impressions of Gokhale . . . Gokhale was good enough to call on me at the Club, and I had three quarter hours conversation with him: he impressed me very favourably— an educated gentleman, who speaks English as well as we do, is not a Baboo, but a High Caste Mahratta, who were, as you know, a fighting race who gave us many a twister. We did not,' Merriman went on to explain, 'discuss the question here beyond generalities, but drifted off into the relation of our question to India, upon which he was very interesting—the new spirit that has arisen in East of disgust at Western domination and the curious stirrings in that stagnant pool . . . Of course the Greeks and the Asiatics always felt in the same way to the Romans who were nearly as brutal and unsympathetic as we are but without the additional arrogance of Christianity and Colour.'

'What this exordium means,' continues Merriman, 'leads up to an expression of a hope that you will be able to arrive at some real solution that may do away with all the onerous and illiberal machinery of repression.' Then he reminded Smuts that history had shown such repression was fatal to the very 'race' that used it. 'Recollect, I implore you, that there are other and surely greater interests at stake than the convenience of traders and prejudices of the community . . . Bring your philosophy to bear.'[18]

This is, in many ways, a historic letter. Here was an elder statesman of South Africa and an old friend of Smuts, a former prime minister of the Cape Colony, giving the government an advice that was valuable, for Merriman knew the strength and frailties of Smuts and of the country itself. Later he was to call his friend 'a philosopher, ruthless and cultivated'. There was no question whatsoever that Smuts was a man of real intellectual gifts, but, he repeated, 'ruthless and determined, a charming companion, and perhaps a better friend than a counsellor'.

Gandhiji would never formulate such judgements on any man. He would have liked to think that Smuts had made a mistake, perhaps ten, maybe even a hundred—but the person beneath it all was ever honourable. And Gandhiji must have said kind things about Smuts to Gokhale himself. They two were to meet soon, meanwhile there would be the long journey from Cape Town to the far north, via Kimberley, Johannesburg and Durban, to the Portuguese port of Telia Bay—where Gokhale would take a steamer and go back to India. The government gave Gokhale their special saloon car—so that not only would he be able to travel in comfort, as so distinguished a guest

---

[18] S.S.P., Vol. III, p. 119.

should, but he could also stop at cities where Indians lived in great numbers, like Klerksdorp, Potchefstroom or Isipingo, and be feted and honoured by them. At Kimberley he visited the mines, and Gandhiji himself was immensely impressed with the technological achievements he saw. If only, he thought, men could work with the same harmony as machines seem to, what a world we could build. Gokhale had indeed come to bring this harmony between the Indians and the Europeans. His mission was therefore a holy one. The very fact that for the first time Indians and Europeans met the way they had showed:

We shall know each other better
When the mists have rolled away.

But it was Johannesburg, naturally, that was to give the Mahratta Brahmin the most august reception of all. The holy one was coming.

The golden city, with its immense ridge, underneath which the chimneys spat and the trolleys threw out dunes of dust, and the narrow streets gorged with coaches, rickshaws, and even cars, with offices that connected the city with every part of the world, for what would the world be without gold— the Witwatersrand gave to the world almost half the gold the world needed[19]—and there were buyers and sellers, prospectors and fakes, or sons of fakes and impostors, who had come rushing in to make gold when gold lay, almost in the streets of the township—this golden city to which people came from all the parts of the world to make money or sometimes hang

---

[19] 'Right through Johannesburg City runs the gold reef on whose product is largely based the economic system of the world.' P.S.A., p. 75.

themselves if they made it not—this city, which had Americans, Australians, German Jews, Russian Jews, Armenians, Greeks, the British, the Hollander, the Indians of course, and the Chinese, and amidst them all walked the gaunt Kaffir—the city of silence, they said, for from the Karoo the winds blew and took away every sound so far away that the only sound one heard at night was the pounding of the batteries, like the arteries of the heart—batteries that pumped out earth from which through other and subtler instruments, mere earth was taken up and gold dust was spewed out and then came the nuggets—the streets themselves had such significant names as Nugget Street, Bank Street, or Claim Street,[20] and every day the city was getting, as it were, richer and grander, so that a magnificent town hall was built and a railway station worthy of this new metropolis—for though Pretoria was the administrative capital of the country and Cape Town its legislative capital—Johannesburg indeed was the capital of the Union, whether you wanted it or not, and one of the great capitals of the world, and the Indians were going to welcome their 'King' as befits the representative of so great a country, and a very friendly one at that. The railway station was sumptuous with the decorations. Kallenbach had designed the arch of welcome—he had spent fifteen days on it—and there were rich carpets spread everywhere, and a dais raised for Gokhale to make a speech from. The special train carrying five hundred Indians—for their 'King' was travelling in great state, so to say—when it drew up at Park Station at four p.m. exactly, on the 22nd of October, 1912, the Mayor Ellis and the Mayoress were there to receive him, and many other dignitaries of Johannesburg. For though the visit of Gokhale

---

[20] Ibid., p.79.

was private it was as if he were still the guest of the State, and he had to be accorded the highest honours of the city. The Mayor even left his official car for Gokhale's use during the week the Indian leader was to spend in Johannesburg.

As the train stopped and the Mayor and Mayoress received Gokhale, a rain of rose petals fell on him from the Indians, and he walked amidst 'oriental warmth and magnificence' to the platform where, once he was seated, Gandhiji stood up to welcome the guest on behalf of the Indians. The address was presented befittingly on a 'solid gold plate representing a map of India and Ceylon', and it read as it should, expressing their gratitude for what he had done during the passive resistance when Indians were undergoing imprisonment for conscience's sake. And may God give him long life, etc., etc.

Kallenbach had given his villa on the top of the beautiful hills for Gokhale to stay at during his visit to the city. From there the air was so pure, one could see up to the blue of the Magdelienburg mountains, and fresh breezes blew all the time, giving breath and strength to man. And maybe even the gods of Africa floated among these, telling man, the tragedy and the splendours of this great continent.

There were chambers hired too during that week for Gokhale to receive anyone he cared to in the city. But the most impressive gathering of the whole visit was at the Masonic Hall, where with the Mayor in the Chair, there was a regal Indian banquet with some five hundred guests, and at least a third among them being Europeans of the city. The food, fifteen dishes in all, was cooked by volunteers and served also by them. The whole feel of the evening, friendly and exalted. 'It was a novel and wonderful experience,' wrote Gandhiji, 'for the Europeans of South Africa to sit at dinner with so many Indians at the same table, to have a purely vegetarian menu, and to do without wines altogether. For many of them all the three features were new, while two features were new to all.' And it is to this gathering that Gokhale 'addressed his longest and most important speech in South Africa . . . The clearness, firmness and urbanity of Gokhale's utterances flowed from his indefatigable labour and unswerving devotion to truth.'[21]

And how could the great leader come to South Africa and not visit the Tolstoy Farm, the only (Indian) sanctuary, as it were, in the country. So he had to be taken there, for which all the arrangements had been made—a bed was specially brought for him, for everyone here slept on the floor; a lavatory commode was also placed for him to use that he might not be forced, like everybody else, to 'go into the country' for such purposes; only he would have to walk the one-and-a-half mile from Lawley Station to the Farm. But as it would happen, it rained on that very important day, and Gokhale with so delicate a health and with so long a programme of activity still before him, was forced to walk in the rain to the Farm and, what was more unbearable to think of, says Gandhiji, the food that was brought to him from the kitchen was cold, but Gokhale bore it all without the least sign of disappointment or of discomfort. When night came, and Gokhale heard everybody slept on the floor, of course, he too would sleep on the floor. Further, as 'to going out into the country', did they think he was so spoilt as all that. Gandhiji, seeing how misguided he had been, wanted at least to massage his master. No, Gokhale would not hear of it. He became angry. 'You all seem to think,' he said finally, 'that you had been born to suffer hardships and discomforts and people like myself have been born to be pampered by you. You must suffer today the punishment for this extremism of yours. I will not even allow you to touch me . . . I will bear any amount of hardship, but I will humble your pride.' It was like Arjuna, Gandhi felt he was, forgetful of Sri Krishna's majesty and 'careless in the fondness of love'.

From Johannesburg Gokhale went to Pretoria where he was the guest of the Union Government. Gokhale was, of course, received both by Botha and Smuts. Gandhiji had prepared a memorandum and Gokhale had gone through it carefully, not so much to have an opinion but rather to possess the facts and be ready, if necessary, to use them effectively. The conversation between the ministers of the Union and the Indian leader was most friendly. Indeed, some important promises seemed to have been made to Gokhale. But Gandhiji had his doubts. 'What I have told you is bound to come to pass,' assured Gokhale. 'General Botha assured me the Black Act will be repealed and the £3 tax abolished. You must return to India within twelve months, and I will not have any of your excuses.'

And from Johannesburg they went to Durban, where, again after the various receptions and interviews, there was the official visit to the Town Hall, and to the gathered Indians and the Europeans, Gandhiji spoke once again, of the greatness of Gokhale. 'Had he been born in England,' he told his audience, 'he would, like Asquith, be her Prime Minister. Had he been born in America he would probably be occupying the position to which Mr. Woodrow Wilson has been elected, and if he had been born in the Transvaal, he would be occupying General Botha's position.'[22] His visit here therefore is very important.

---

[22] C.W., Vol. XI, p. 367.

But let us not build high hopes on it. They may still have to agitate, they might yet have to go to jail. But as Mr. Gokhale is here in our midst let us pay 'tribute to the great character of the man who stands before us . . .'

Soon Gokhale was to leave the country. It was a painful prospect for Gandhiji. Why not accompany him up to Zanzibar where Gokhale was finally to embark on a boat that would take him back to India? But Kallenbach too wanted to come. So the three went by boat to Zanzibar, and after Gandhiji and Kallenbach had seen Mr. Gokhale safely on his ship, and while returning, there was, as it were, a dramatic anti-climax. At the Portuguese port of Telia Bay, whereas Kallenbach as a whiteman could pass the police authorities, the Indian barrister could not.

'Where are your papers?'

'I have none,' said Gandhiji, 'I am a barrister practising in Johannesburg.'

'Wait here,' said the official rudely.

'Rage flared up in my heart,' wrote Gandhiji. But slowly he argued himself out of it.

He had travelled by deck on the returning ship. He had to be economical, it was public money he was spending. The Indians on board the ship were filthy and lacked dignity.

'We are ants, 'said one of them. 'We must endure this suffering somehow and have done with it.' While another said: 'Once I get my wages, the whites may call me a coolie, a deck-hand might kick me. I might be obliged to live in a Location . . . Mine might be a dog's plight. But I don't care.' Gandhiji reflected that the Indians alone were responsible for the sorry conditions they were in. We have to get rid of our deficiencies of character, on the one side, and fight against the oppression of the whites on the other. Such our real problem.[23] And such the problem that awaited him on his return to Johannesburg.

Soon after he left Gokhale, Gandhiji wrote a letter of adieu to Gokhale from Dar-es-Salam. 'And now,' he said in it, 'will you forgive me for all my imperfections. This is not mock humility but Indian seriousness. I want to realise in myself the conception I have of an Eastern pupil. We may have many differences of opinion, but you shall still be my pattern in political life.'

With the saint and poet, Rajachandra, also Gandhiji had his differences, but he would treat the saint as if he was his spiritual Guru. And now whatever differences of opinion there might still be between Gokhale and himself, Gandhiji would treat him as his political Guru. And shaping a creative purpose of these two forces, he would make Satyagraha the pure weapon of truth.

There's in the Gandhi Archives a small note-book (crown sexton-decimo size)[24] which goes from 15 January 1912 to 6 January 1913, the period which one might call his 'waiting on God'. It covers the period roughly between the provisional settlement with Smuts—and the happy interlude of Gokhale's visit and finally the time he returned from Zanzibar, expectant to see how General Botha and Smuts were going now to act. This little diary is precious because it's full of brief notations of the people he wrote letters to, or his visit to Johannesburg (J.B.) or to the farm at Phoenix, near Durban, the money he spent here and there on his trips or little monies he paid to Kallenbach (K), or to his own Secretary, Miss Schlesin—or prices of railway tickets or of stamps.

---

[23]   C.W., Vol. XI, pp, 357-60.

[24]   The *Indian Opinion Pocket Diary* published by International Printing Press, Phoenix, Natal.

15 Jan. 1912
Medh, Manilal Pragji returned
Trip ticket book 1.6.3.
Stamps 0.2.0. Bal(ance) 3.3.10.

26 Jan.
Mohi and Soni came and left. Two whites came for sandals.

29 Jan.
Lutvan left. I went to town and returned. Velshi and his son
Rajbali came. Hoosen and his uncle came to J.B. Wrote to
Lane about New Bill. Wrote . . . Alexander, Schlesin, etc.

5 Feb.
Drafted telegram Smuts.

8 Feb.
Telegram from Smuts, drafted reply. Pragji came. Wrote
Schlesin.
Paid Wire Kallenbach 0.1.6.
Freight balance yesterday 0.0.9.
Stamps 0.2.6.

25 March
Sorabji left—I went to town on foot. Started at 3 and reached
J.B. at 9-15.

1 April
Letters. Winterbottom, Maud, Mr. MacDonald, West,
Langston, Halim—K. arrived—A boy—Feda came for the
night. Ratanshi and Rajabali left.

4 April
Went to Johannesburg on foot and returned, K and I with
Sorabji . . . Reached office at 8-50.

7 April
Mr. Phillip's choir came. Ritch, Gordon and many others
came . . . About 200 persons came etc. etc.

11 April
Both went to town on foot—West etc. came yesterday
accompanied to Farm today.

18 April
Jamnadas and I left at six o'clock on foot. K. took 4-45 hours
to reach J. and I six hours. etc. etc.

29 April
. . . Arrived at Farm at 6-20 a.m. along with the boys. K met us
with the boys and turned back. Albert broke fifteen days old fast.

1 May
K and I went to J.B. on foot, starting at 1-40 a.m. and from
there to Germiston. K went to Pretoria. Krishnaswamy came.
Ba ill.

2 May
Went to town with K in the morning on foot. Took 5
hours—40 minutes.

28 June
Ba and I left for Durban.

Tickets to Dur(ban) 6.6.8.
Schlesin 0.3.0.

29 June
Arrived in Durban. Considerable inconvenience on the way.
A good many people had come to the station. Meeting of
Ottoman Cricket Club in the evening. Jamnadas and the two
of us went to Phoenix by train.

30 June
Jamnadas and I left Phoenix on foot . . . Congress meeting in
the evening . . . Problem of Colonial born (Indians). Night
at Omar Sheth's.

5 July
I and Purushothamdas left for Durban by the afternoon
train. Left for J.B. in the evening.
Rail, phone, cycle 0.6.0

19 July
Three persons came and went back. Cold continues. Sorabji
came in the evening. Telegram from the Interior that
settlement stood.[25]

And so on. Then Gokhale comes, receptions are held in
Cape Town, Maritzburg and New Castle. Gokhale is to sail
back and Gandhiji and Kallenbach accompany him as far as
Zanzibar. One item simply says: '24 November At sea.' Then
they reach Mozambique, from Dar-es-salaam—and there's

---

[25] The Settlement is the Provisional Settlement with Smuts.

the unhappy experience at Telia Bay ('Interrogation by the police.'); and Gandhiji arrives back at the Tolstoy Farm for the baptism of Burnett's son. And finally the important entry on 1 December—Wore Indian Dress'—for till now in South Africa he wore only western clothes.

It was all a quiet patient awaiting, the moving here and there and all about and around, only necessitated by urgent demands from one member, then the other, Johannesburg and Durban, Tolstoy Farm or Phoenix. During these days Gandhiji prepared himself for what he knew was coming, sent those away to their homes who were uncertain, or tired, and knew that this time if and when he would strike, it would be an all-out war, although it would still be a pilgrim's war.[26]

* * *

Returning from Zanzibar, Gandhiji had to rush to Phoenix where an inmate was ill. Whenever anyone was ill, Gandhiji enjoyed the privilege of nursing. Was it because for him death and life were so close and in the mystery of death, he saw the prognosis of life ('There is no life except through death.')—the ultimate meaning of truth. Or was it his great need for giving tenderness—he received so little of it himself. Frail and so sensitive that speech came with difficulty, he had to live and move with a humanity in hurry, living in confusion and mythical values, and never caring for the other except in an instinctive, an awkward, way. Indians, of course, had love in them, but

---

[26] 'As one studies the unfolding conflict from 1908 until 1914, one has the feeling that Gandhi could see in advance what course it would follow, where Smuts again and again, was taken by surprise.' S., p. 338.

how undependable they were. What foul food they usually ate, how callous where they lived or how. And it was during this recess between the passing of the Provisional Settlement and the opening of the new Parliament (while 'waiting on God') that Gandhiji sorted out his problems, planned for the future, and wrote on how to keep well. He wrote a series of articles for *Indian Opinion* (which later became the book *Guide to Health*) where he meditates on the human body and its needs. He tells his readers that the universe is made of the five elements—earth, water, sky, fire and air, and says how the body, an image of the universe, has all of them and in the right proportions. A regulated diet would in fact keep the body as fit as a machine— the body, for example, has 238 bones, etc., etc. Indeed, if he admired the machine this was because it appeared to be such a symbolic replica of the human body—but without a soul. So what could you not do if only you could add a soul to it. You can attain the quietude of mind, which finally is what we all seek.

For Gandhiji illness seemed almost always mental. He could quote authorities from the West to show this was a scientific fact. Therefore to keep your mind fair is to keep your body strong. But since it's the body that seems to house the mind (at least so it seems) why not give the body just what it wants, and the mind thus made free for whatever it may have to perform?

What then are the requisites of such an attitude towards good health? First of all, remember, what you eat makes your mind think what it thinks. Has not Milton said heaven and hell are but shades in the mind of man? And the Indians have said: The mind is the cause of bondage (hell) and liberation. Thus if you follow this argument you will realise 'whether a person is ill or well, he is himself for the most part responsible'. One falls ill owing to one's thoughts as well as to one's deeds. And is it not a shame we reflect so little upon the relationship between the body and the mind? And whenever anything bodily happens we rush to a doctor—whether I am hurt by a thorn or bitten by a snake. To say man cannot understand these matters by himself, for himself, is 'fraud' pure and simple. Just as we accumulate filth outside our houses, we pile filth on filth inside us, fall desperately ill, and medicine only consolidates this filth, giving you mere appearance of well-being.

The first problem of health is one of having good, clean air. 'Bad air is the cause of ninety per cent of the diseases.' And air is not only inhaled through the nose but taken in through the skin as well. The pores are made just for that purpose. 'Latrines, open spaces, narrow lanes (dirtied through misuse) and urinals, where these are separate, are the principal agencies for the defilement of air.' Then again—we Indians do not care where we spit—we should, if need be, keep a spittoon. Further, our people do not mind throwing refuse anywhere—if only this could be thrown into the earth, the garbage becomes pure rich manure; it also keeps us away from every disease.

Further, one must not only learn to breathe fresh air but not to breathe through the mouth. This is not good for one's health. The rooms where we sleep must also be full of fresh air— if possible, one should sleep in the open. 'It is imperative that we inhale pure air for as long as possible, especially while sleeping.' And light, remember, is just as important as air—hence hell is called dark.

If air is food, water is food as well. One can, as everyone knows, live on water for a long time and without food. In actual fact, water is seventy per cent of our body—and if we had no water in us we would weigh only ten or twelve pounds. But what is good water? Rain water alone is pure water—all the rest are more or less defective but in degrees. Hard water should be boiled before drinking. Also, most water contains salts, and vegetable matter, etc. Finally, one could go as far as to say, water is unnecessary for drinking—for most vegetables contain water anyway. Also, if anybody is inordinately thirsty one could be sure something is wrong with him.

Now let us come to food. Let us best get over the idea of what we should not eat before we decide what we should eat. Of course, nobody needs to be told that alcohol is bad and smoking as well.

Tolstoy has shown, in one of his stories, how a man wanted to kill his beloved (so jealous he was of her) but couldn't decide on it, so he went to have a smoke, came back, and finally killed her. Apart from these evil effects on the mind, smoking weakens your lungs, corrupts your digestive system. Even tea and coffee are to be avoided—they also are poisons—which explains why in one of his letters Gandhiji notes with joy: 'Ba has given up tea today.' If you are so keen on coffee, you could make wheaten coffee drunk by all with such eagerness at the Tolstoy Farm—and if you are too lazy to roast and grind your own wheat, you have just to write to the manager of the Tolstoy Farm, and he will send it straight to you for just 9d.[27]

As to what we can eat—it may be said in general that humanity on the whole is vegetarian, not because it is convinced of its virtue but because of necessity; not only people in India, but in China and Japan, Ireland and Italy too, they mostly practise vegetarian diet. And again: 'The structure of the body would

---

[27] Later this became the basis for the famous 'Gandhi-tea'.

seem to indicate that Nature intended man to be a vegetarian.' If we resemble the apes, we must also eat like them. And they live on fresh and dry fruit. Whereas the very stomach of the lion and the tiger is made differently to ours and that of the ape.

Now chemists have found that the fruit contains 'all the elements necessary for human life'. Fruits such as bananas, oranges, dates, figs, pineapples, almonds, walnuts, peanuts, and coconut. Just as animals, say the scientists, can live on sun-ripened food, so could man. Cooking is totally unnecessary. Suppose we accept this to be true, how much of our time would be saved, and how wonderful it would be for our women not to blow the pipe and wash the sink, but to read and cultivate themselves.[28] Does it all look like a dream? Perhaps it does. But then one can and should live one's dreams. That is what man is made for.

There was a very wise German called Just. He had written a book *(Return to Nature)* which showed fruit to be the natural diet of man. And, further, all you need is grown about and around you. And if you cannot eat only vegetables, you could of course eat cereals, pulses, beans, milk, etc. Wheat is the best grain of all. 'It contains all the nutritive elements in good proportions.' But the flour must be ground at home, of course. Then come the vegetables—they are really like grass and should be eaten with care. And pulses, though as good as meat, no doubt, are difficult to digest. 'Those however, who cannot master their palate may eat them but with care.'

It goes without saying that chillies and spices of all sorts should be avoided. True they give taste to your food but they also vitiate your well-being. And so does, believe me, salt. There

---

[28] And Kasturba would at least have learnt Gujarati alphabets by now.

are even doctors who say salt is a poison, and if you do not eat salt even a snake bite has no effect on you, such medical testimony. Having given up salt himself, Gandhiji says he felt less lethargic. Kasturba who was ill and gave up salt for sometime felt so much better. 'I am confident too that had the patient been able to give up salt completely, her malady would have been entirely eradicated.'

Some people think milk is good. This is dire superstition. For what the cow eats is as important as what she makes of it. Further, even a calf gives up milk when it has grown into a heifer, why not we? Olive oil, for example, could be a magnificent substitute for milk.

And now let us consider that important question: how much one should eat? People most often eat three or four times a day. This is unnecessary and makes the stomach into a refuse pit. When one has grown up, two meals a day suffice.

Not only food is important for health but also exercise. If possible everyone should be a farmer. And if you cannot, you should take to long walks—ten to twelve miles a day—so that you exert every day as much as a farmer does. Has not Thoreau, the American writer, said that 'the writings of one who refuses to leave his house on the excuse of lack of time', are bound to be anaemic. Speaking of his own experiences, he (Thoreau) says that when he wrote his best books, he was doing his longest walking. 'Unless one exercises one's body, one's intellect will be dull. And walks are also good because we see the beauty of Nature.'

What should one wear? The simplest of clothes, the barest possible, for the body needs air. The body also is beautiful.

There should be very little hair on the head: 'Dust, dirt and lice collect in long hair.' And as for the feet, use not shoes if possible; they smell bad. Sandals are best for outside use; they are also cheap. If you want sandals, write to us at Phocnix; we make them and we will send them to you.

And in a letter written to Gokhale (immediately after these articles were completed), Gandhiji is solicitous of the great leader's health. Gokhale was in England at that time. Had he found time to visit Just's dietetic institute at Jungbor, he asks, or Dr. Kuhne's nature cure centre? 'I should,' writes Gandhiji, 'much appreciate a line about your health and the treatment you may be undergoing.' If only the master could eat fruit, he would live long, and give India the leadership she needs.

* * *

Sure as Gandhiji's instinct was—after all God had written the score as it were—and while his 'inner voice' felt what the next ordained movement was to be, General Smuts (as in the Boer War) made simple, heroic and ambivalent gestures, led as much by reason as by his puritanical instinct, so that he went from one dud act to the other, saved only by his patriotism, his moral courage, and, finally, his vast humanity. He was indeed never to be a great statesman, but a divided and a noble figure, the politician becoming stage by stage an elder, and a philosopher. With Gandhiji it was otherwise. Politics was only one mode in his diverse making—in actual fact he would have liked to give himself wholly to God, but the world too, he slowly realised, was made by God and meant to be the play of God. If we listened to Him carefully as we would a tree, a mountain, a man, we would play only His game, and He surely knows where He is leading us. But Smuts dealt with men when he dealt with politics, and with God when he spoke of the Deity—he had no intermediary instincts linking one with the other. Whereas with Gandhiji, layer behind layer of philosophical, nay metaphysical, solutions to a moral problem, or a moral escape from a metaphysical dilemma, had built itself up through millennia of tradition, and even when he did not know he felt and acted with his total being, and thus led his people to final victory. The dualism in Smuts created, so to say, its own complex universes, its focal contradictions, reminding one of his compatriot Van der Post and his *Venture to the Interior*.

Here was a silent young Colonel who was none other than Van der Post himself—and this (soon after the Second World War, that is after Abbyssinia and Burma, and the Japanese prisoner of war camp in Java) who was asked by Whitehall to go on a secret mission to Southern Africa—his home which he knows as himself. As he leaves London, a dualism appeared, a contradiction between what he was and what he had to perform. He went through flag-flying British outposts of deputy commissioners and commissioners, isolated, efficient, imperial—slipping through dawn and dusk to higher and yet higher reaches of the land ('The physical fact of Africa is by far the most exciting and interesting thing about it. The tragedy is that it has not as yet produced the people and the towns worthy of its greatness.')—jeeping through uneven and endurant roads, streets, footpaths, circling and marching through mists, rocks, dark silent cedars, finally reaching the heights of the Mlanje, dipped in wetness and wizardry. There he discovers a young, a happy couple, Vel and Dick Vance, living in perfect bliss if ever there was bliss ('I had never seen two human beings more complementary, more sufficient unto themselves than these two.') perched in a cabin with their new-born, Penelope, 'crystal clear streams' flowing about and around them. But the mountain should have been left alone. Man should never have interfered with these mountains. No, not for his own material betterment.[29] The mountain, the couple knew, was alive with breath and magic and myth; it was, as it were, a god who spoke, the tutelary deity of the English couple, and high protector of their child. No sickness or leopard would touch them. The Vances wanted no human being there either.

But when the mystery was being penetrated into, through pick-axe and jeep and camp and compass, the spirits were awakened: a fight among the gods *(devas)* and the anti-gods *(asuras)* took place. It was a frightful battle and dreadful to feel, under one's feet, in the air, so to say—to feel beyond coming knowledge. After nine days of living in derelict cabins and tents, and probing the depths of nature, the vastness and intents of the mountain and the trees, Dick Vance, trying to take Van der Post and his companions across an easy and seemingly crossable stream, simply, inevitably Dick slipped from his roped vines, and was carried away into the eddyings of waterfall sounds and spirits of unsteady silences, his body never to be found again. The young Colonel Van der Post had to convey the message of this mysterious and tragic happening to the wife, who knowing as she did the mountain, also knew the mountain's laws. The mountain had taken Dick to itself. And she had to go back to London with her child, Penelope. Who created the tragedy? asks Van der Post. He did it himself; his duality did it. Everywhere he stepped was a duality, a contradiction and thus the Garden of Eden—the 'Whole' of Smuts—was not destroyed, but Smuts' politics was carried away. Who remained: the hill.

---

[29] This mission was sent so as to see if Britain could grow more food here for her own needs—the war had ruined her economy.

Such the dream that unfolds itself again and again in South Africa—not only with the Indian but with the Boer, the Coloured, the Kaffir. Africa would accept nothing less than its total self, the African Self. There's an African way as there's an Indian way, a great, young African way. Who dare disturb the growing mountain, the unique man and woman and holy child, the thumping and as yet unhumanised waterfall, the smell of rising cedar, itself covered with mist and total sleep? The African knows his earth, the Indian worships his, while the Westerner turns on himself unable to move or stay his humanity having no choice but separate the Greek from the Christian, the sage-hero from the sainted-worker, dividing singleness from the crowd. He alone could be (one day) the all, but the all-seeker—the fervent failure of dualised man. Do you seek wholeness of man or wholeness of Truth? such the question of history. He who knows the proper answer has to play his game outside of time. Hence satyagraha. Or, there's the apartheid.[30] The answer is always a return of the forest echo. One goes nowhere when one knows the hill. One could of course go about the hill, but do not delve into her mysteries: you'll be carried away by the arcane stream, and be made into the roots of cedar. Penelope now goes to London. The cedars will continue to stand swathed in garlands of vine and moss.

* * *

---

[30] Laurens Van der Post's father was one of the elders among the Boers with Smuts and Botha. A Free-Stater, he was later to become a faithful British subject. Van der Post himself seems so Gandhian in his understanding compassion, as prisoner of war of the Japanese, or as visitor to 'All the Russians' under the Soviet Rule.

The world of Smuts seemed to be cracking all around him. The Free Staters had never really accepted the British flag—Hertzog, a member of the cabinet, had been restless and, finally, was left out of the government. The working classes, as yet not very clearly organised—nearly two-thirds of them were from the United Kingdom—had brought to this wild and incoherent landscape their own ideas of syndicalism. They did not, of course, worry about the Kaffir miners—these belonged to a different species, as it were, of breathing and of living. Therefore, workers of the world unite, was to mean, workers of the white world unite, etc. The country, not a nation as yet, was desperately trying to become one, and Botha, the chief, was still unused to the vitiating manoeuvrings of a new state—his nerves were rapidly giving way. Smuts was in fact the real prime minister. He often acted for Botha, and took most of the important decisions. Xavier Merriman, on the other hand (prodded by Emily Hobhouse and other English friends), kept saying the problem of the Natives has to be seriously considered from now on if one has to have a civilised and just government. And in the whirling middle of these complexities, this Gandhi was threatening passive resistance again. Young as Smuts was, and largely inexperienced in the arts of government, he still managed to carry out his responsibilities with great courage and foresight, and even of moderation. But history does not wait on reason. Somewhere the forces were gathering to thrust rudely forth. One felt this, as it were, in the air. And the Union was young.

Some new workers—white workers of course, and about forty in all—were asked by the manager of a mine to give a quarter of an hour more, every Saturday, for the better efficiency of output. For no understandable reason the workers refused.

Their leader argued with the manager, and came out of the dialogue dissatisfied. The manager insisted on his decision. The workers felt this was an insult to their leader and finally to themselves. They struck work.[31] The strike caught on in other mines. At one time there were almost 40,000 miners who had downed tools. A certain picturesque figure called Mrs. Fitzerald, Gandhiji says, 'accompanied by a gang of fifty people . . . threatened the shopkeepers and made them close the shops. Trade,' continued Gandhiji, 'came to a standstill. People were in panic and began to store foodgrains, etc. The cost of a bag of coal went up to ten shillings.'

Then the same Mrs. Fitzerald went to the railway station and reduced parts of it to ashes. The office of the *Star* was burnt down too in a fury—the paper was not liked for its clearly conservative ideas. When the fire-brigade came, they were driven away by the gathering crowds. Then they looted arms and ammunition from shops 'and taking possession of guns and powder' prepared themselves for a true big fight. The rabble now entered the scene, and other shops were plundered. 'When there is chaos,' wrote Gandhiji, 'who will listen to whom?'

Suddenly the government realised the gravity of the situation. The police came quickly on to the scene. But the infuriated crowd attacked the Rand Club. The police threatened fire. The crowd did not care. But losing patience, the police fired and killed a few of the strikers. 'Bullets descended in a shower, killing the guilty and innocent. Blood flowed in streams.'[32] And soon it was the reign of terror. The city for several days was entirely in the hands of rioters. Botha and Smuts called in the

---

[31] C.W., Vol. XII, p. 132-35.
[32] C.W., Vol. XII, p. 133.

Imperial Troops, that is to say British troops. 'Rioting broke out more violently than ever . . . The mob remained master of Johannesburg. Botha and Smuts entered the city and parleyed with the miner's leaders . . . The strikers had won.'[33] Some eighteen persons were killed and about four hundred wounded. Nine strike leaders were deported to England, in secrecy and haste, and against all legality. The nation had to survive. Smuts did it all. Now the white workers too understood Smuts. He had made grand promises to the Asiatics but had never kept his word. Somewhere the pattern was exactly the same. A commission of inquiry was appointed, and a pained and sorrowful peace came back to the city.

During all this while Hertzog was neither mute nor inactive. He was establishing the Nationalist Party, and the fight would now move on to its historic end.

Even so, the country seemed to be settling down. Law and order appeared to reign everywhere. The commission of inquiry was listening to the workers' grievances. It was the proper time, Smuts must have decided, to publish his new Immigration Regulation Act. The vine ropes were ready for crossing the gurgling stream. Penelope cried but the mountain escaped the imagination of Smuts.

Gandhiji sat to study the gazette. There were so many admirable points one could agree with, and yet some nefarious ones undid all the good intended. The main points of the Provisional Settlement, that is all existing rights of the Indians remain on the statute books, and only such new ones be introduced as would remove the taint of racial bar—these assumptions were lost sight of. Gandhiji once again wrote to the

---

[33] S., p. 366.

government for clarifications—specifically about the removal
of the £3 tax, the main theme of contention. Smuts, however,
concentrated on the crossing of the stream. He was ready to leap
over the waves. The mountain did the rest.

The Gandhian dialectic demands an imperative and an
imaginative honesty. Once the objective is fixed—say to fight
against the £3 tax or the new Immigration Act of Transvaal,
no further accommodation between heaven and earth may be
permitted, however noble your cause. The adversary must know
what you are precisely fighting for. For example, when you're
struggling against the £3 tax that the 'free Indians' of Natal have
to pay, there could be no admission of indentured labourers
into the fight—though the 'free Indians' were but indentured
labourers of yesterday. This change of definition would be
but an act of adultery. Further, if the Transvaal Immigration
Bill has to be fought against, one should never permit anyone
but Transvaaler Indians to join the fight, or those that have a
right as a free citizen of the British Empire to enter into the
Transvaal, like Sorabji Shapurji Adajania. Hence therefore of
the four colonies three had their own branch of the British
India Association (in the Cape, and in Natal, apart from the
Transvaal where Gandhiji worked—the Orange Free State
needed no such association for there were almost no Indians
there). So that when the Transvaal fight was at its height, and
hundreds of Transvaaler Indians went to jail, the Natal Indians
looked after their own affairs—hawking their own wares, plying
their own trades—except where they could legitimately come
into the drama. 'In the early stages,' explains Gandhiji, 'the
Indians were every now and then asking for other grievances
besides the Black Act to be covered by the struggle. I patiently
explained to them that such an extension would be a violation

of the truth, which could not be so much as thought of in a movement professing to abide by truth and truth alone.' And again whether you are many or everybody had dropped out of the fight but yourself, you go on fighting because (to repeat, and it bears repetition) satyagraha knows no defeat, even in death. 'For death alone can raise us . . . It is the great secret by which one can gain true life. Those alone who join satyagraha in this spirit will win in this great fight that is beginning.'[34] Suppose, however, something dramatic, something totally unexpected, brings in new reinforcements. One should never yield to such temptations. One should fearlessly refuse all improper help. 'I have often said,' continues Gandhiji, 'that a satyagrahi has a single objective from which he cannot recede and beyond which he cannot advance. For one must remember the world learns to apply to a man the standards which he applies to himself.' Thus the Smuts government learnt what to expect from the satyagrahis and what the satyagrahis would do or never do. The principles of non-violent war thus established, as on the field of Kurukshetra, one could now launch out, and give final battle.

'When the battle is fought and finished, there shall be mutual friendship between us. Those who have gone out of the ranks shall never be killed. One mounted on a chariot shall be fought by one on a chariot, one on an elephant with an elephant, one on a horse with a horse, and a footsoldier only by a footsoldier. One engaged with another, one inattentive, or disinclined to fight or one who was turned away from the field, one who has lost his weapons and without armour shall never be killed.'[35]

---

[34] C.W., Vol. XII, p. 187-188.
[35] *Mahabharata*, Bhishma Parva.

But Arjuna and Bhima, and Dharmaraja himself, will, before making this first move, lay down their arms and go through enemy lines to fall at the feet of Bhishma, the grandsire, the chief of the opponent's forces, asking for his blessings. Would Smuts bless?

Smuts (and Botha) had declared to Gokhale that the £3 tax might definitely be removed within a year, and after proper consultations appropriate legislation would be introduced when the Parliament met again.[36] Smuts however explained that as the Natal authorities had refused to abrogate the £3 tax (the dog-collar tax), he could not remove it either from the statute book. But anybody could see now that the Union was there, and Natal only one part of it; the laws of Smuts ruled the whole territory. If Smuts was even somewhat a Bhishma—and he should have been one by temperament and training—he would have kept to his word and would have lost his job fighting, even unto death.

'A king should build up his victory by means other than war; victory through war is said to be the worst. Death through dharma is better than victory through a sinful act . . . Truthfulness is the eternal dharma; truthfulness is the eternal Brahman; truthfulness is the greatest offering to God; everything is based on truthfulness'[37]—said Bhishma on his death bed of arrows. But Smuts would not lose his job. So the fight there shall be, for this failure on the part of the government, to honour its words, was not only a personal insult to Gokhale, Gandhiji's Sri Krishna, but to the whole of India.

---

[36] 'It is quite clear . . . that Smuts and his colleagues in their interview with Gokhale, aroused expectations which they failed subsequently to fulfil.' S., p. 342.

[37] *Mahabharata,* Santi Parva.

Now that the fight was the fight against national insult, indentured labourers, thus far strictly kept away from the struggle, would come in too, and therefore it would hence forth be the might of all the Pandavas against the untrustworthy Kauravas. We might have lost our throne and country because we lost our game of chess, but we can always win it back for where Sri Krishna is Truth is, and where Truth is Victory is: *Yathah Krishna tatho jayah.*

Gokhale, truthful man that he was, felt sorrowful and hurt that Smuts and Botha had not honoured their friendly commitments.

Despite his poor health and his continuous travelling, whether in India or sailing to England and back, he was not going to lose his interest in the South African struggle. He will perform what he has to. Had he not on reaching Bombay from South Africa declared at the Town Hall, not only to the citizens of Bombay, but to all India: 'Gandhi has in him the marvellous spiritual power to turn ordinary men around him into heroes and martyrs . . . In all my life,' he went on to declare, 'I have known only two men who have affected me spiritually in the manner Mr. Gandhi does, our great patriarch, Mr. Dadabhai Naoroji, and my late master, Mr. Ranade—men before whom not only are we ashamed of doing anything unworthy, but in whose presence our very minds are afraid of thinking anything that is unworthy.'[38]

But Gandhiji, considering the condition of Gokhale's health, pleaded he should not worry himself about their needs, but just give his blessings. 'We in India,' wrote back Gokhale, 'have some idea of our duty even as you understand your

---

[38] *Speeches and Writings of Gopal Krishna Gokhale,* Vol. II, pp. 444-45.

obligations in South Africa.' And Gokhale asked how many were the fighters he had in mind, and after careful calculation Gandhiji replied, 65 or 66 at the highest, and 16 at the lowest. Gandhiji warned his followers that it would be a prolonged struggle. And maybe this time they would have to undergo long terms of imprisonment. The Tolstoy Farm would have to be more or less closed now, and one would have to function from Phoenix. Some of the women from the Tolstoy Farm were therefore sent back when their husbands returned from incarcerations. Some of the women, however, protested and wanted to fight as their husbands did. 'But we did not,' remarks Gandhiji, 'think it proper to send women to jail in a foreign land.' And again the £3 tax was only against men, therefore men alone should participate in the satyagraha. Thus, the men would fight, and from Phoenix as the base, against the inhuman £3 tax, the dog-collar tax.

God is the Truth, Gandhiji declared. So God is on the side of the satyagrahis, they who believed in the absolute power of truth. And God would show himself in many ways when the auspicious time came. Having waited on God for so long, as if in mortification and prayer, God now showed his gentle hand, his compassion, to his devotees. For suddenly a new event broke asunder not only every hope of government understanding, but seemed to dramatically open new avenues of fight. The secret thought, consciously spoken or unconsciously felt, of Botha and Smuts seemed always to have been—the Asiatic cancer must be out.

This time they touched on the most sensitive side of the Indian temperament. For Mr. Justice Searle of the Cape Supreme Court gave a judgement on 14 March 1913 which implied that all Hindu, Muslim, and Zoroastrian marriages were illegal, not having been consecrated according to the Christian rites and before the Registrar of Marriages. Hence all Indian women overnight became concubines. The women too were enraged. And the women of India from Draupadi onwards have the vow-power of wifehood *(pativratya)* in them. Thus, then, wifehood their religion, and anyone who touches that unwittingly touches fire.

Gandhiji again wrote to the government. Was this an authoritative statement of policy? Did the government agree with this judgement? For so far, and in all these years, the government had never raised the question. Why suddenly this bug-bear now? And would the government assure the Indians that in their new Immigration Bill clauses would be added validating Indian marriages and the heirs of such marriages allowed the inheritance they have a right to, etc. The government gave a vague, soothing but unsatisfactory reply. They were certainly not in a mood for compromise. They were building up a nation, and they had so much to fight against. And they would fight.

'Patience was impossible,' wrote Gandhiji, 'in the face of this insult offered to our womanhood.' There would be stubborn satyagraha this time, and women too could now join the movement. Of course, the first ones to be asked were the women of the Tolstoy Farm: 'I warned them that they might be given hard work in jail, made to wash clothes and even subjected to insult by the warders. But these sisters were all brave and feared none of these things. One of them was pregnant, while six of them had young babies in arms. But one and all were eager to join and I could not come in their way.' They were from the South, all from Tamilnad. And the first move in this satyagraha movement was to enter the Transvaal from the border at Vereenging, and without permits, and see how the government would react. The government did nothing—the women were not arrested.

They cried to the heavens that something should happen—anything might happen—the buzzard pursue the eagle.

'The buzzard was the first to reach the height it sought. Suddenly it shot up, did a loop and came down on the eagle once again, beak, talons, wings and all . . . There was another burst of feathers as the birds fell. They shot up at us at a tremendous speed, then far below us the eagle broke free and fled. The buzzard made no effort to pursue it but rose impressively to a tremendous height on one of the great currents from the plain, then on calm impressive wings floated away over the grey peaks behind us.'[39]

So Gandhiji decided the supreme moment had come: 'I had contemplated sacrificing all the settlers in Phoenix at a critical period. This was to be my final offering to the God of Truth.' Except those who would run the *Indian Opinion* (and thus give the news to all concerned regarding what was happening to the Indian community in South Africa), everyone else would join the movement. These were the sixteen that Gandhiji had in mind when he wrote to Gokhale about the minimum satyagrahis he could think of. And this time a novel idea would be used by the satyagrahis: When asked by the police their name and address, they should refuse to give it. And these men and women from Phoenix were to enter the Transvaal from Natal, and those from Tolstoy Farm who if they had not been arrested should now proceed to Natal. If they were arrested, so much the

---

[39] Laurens Van der Post, *Venture to the Interior*.

better. But better still, if they were not taken into custody, the women of the Tolstoy Farm should go straight to Newcastle and ask the indentured labourers in the mines to down tools. 'If the labourers struck in response to the sister's appeal, government was bound to arrest them along with the labourers, who would thereby probably be fired with still greater enthusiasm.' This was the strategy of Sri Krishna.

'The kings have (already) started for Kurukshetra for their own ruin.'

Now, Gandhiji rushed to Phoenix and started talking to the women there. The difficulty here was they were mostly his cousin's wives or his nephew's wives or his nieces. If they agreed to satyagraha because of him, what if they could not stand the ordeal when the actual moment came? This would cause a deep shock to the movement, especially as most of them bore his family name. And above all he did not want to speak of these to his wife. 'If she said yes, I would not know what value to attach to her assent . . . In a serious matter like this the husband should leave the wife to take what step she liked on her own initiative, and should not be offended at all if she did not take any step whatever.' The other women readily agreed to join the fight, come what may. But Kasturba overheard the conversation, and said to Gandhiji: 'I am sorry you are not telling me about this. What defect is there in me which disqualifies me?' To which Gandhiji replied, 'You know I am the last person to cause you pain. There is no question of distrust in you. I would be only too glad if you went to jail, but it should not appear at all you went at my insistence. In matters like this everyone should act relying upon one's own strength and courage.' What if brought before the courts she should tremble or flinch? Would it not affect the movement, she the wife of the leader. Kasturba replied: 'I am bound to join the struggle.'

'Then I am bound to admit you,' replied Gandhiji. But she should think it over again, take her own time to come to her decision. And if she changed her decision there was nothing to be ashamed of. But the whole of the *Ramayana* was behind Kasturba.

'I have nothing to think about. I am fully determined,' she said, and thus stopped any further discussion. She would do what everybody else did. Pray, why not?

He came back to the point again with the settlers: Do not hesitate to say no if you do not wish to join the movement. There is still time. The struggle is going to be fierce and long. And again, not only humiliation of all sorts but even ill-health might pursue you. Take good care and think. But no, they were all ready. The invading party, crossing over from Natal to Transvaal had sixteen members, and the first on the list was Mrs. Kasturba Gandhi.

Draupadi's humiliation would now be avenged.

Call to mind that coward insult and the outrage foul and keen,
Flung on Drupad's saintly daughter and our noble spotless queen![40]

'What's your name?' No answer. Just a nodding of the woman's head.

'Address?' No answer. The nodding continues with a smile. 'Can you read and write?' No answer again. This was at the Volksrust frontier between Natal and Transvaal.

Then the police go to another Indian, this time a man. 'What's your name?' No answer again.

---

[40] *The Mahabharata.*

'Address?' No answer again, and a nodding of the head and a smile.

'Can you read or write?' Nodding of the head again, and this went on with each man and woman that was questioned at the frontier. They smiled or they were quiet and silent, as if they were all dumb, and made no gesture. Gandhiji was waiting at the other end for news.

'Ba and others,' he wrote to his son Manilal on 17 September 1913, 'boarded the train with great courage on Monday.' And again the next day he wrote to his eldest son Harilal who was still in India:

'Ba, Ramdas, Kashi, Chaganlal, Kuppoo, Govindoo, Revashankar, Shivapujan, Raojibhai, Maganbhai, Sam, Rustomjee Sheth, Solomon and others have set out to get imprisoned. They were arrested at Volksrust on Tuesday. There has been no telegram yet as to what happened yesterday.'

Finally he got news of the Phoenix party—those who were stopped at Volksrust. They would neither be arrested nor allowed to go on to Johannesburg. The police not knowing what to do, deported them back to the Natal frontier, that is, left them in the middle of 'a shallow stream'. The satyagrahis came back, but this time they were arrested and taken to jail.

'I shall leave for Johannesburg on Saturday,' he wrote to his son. 'People at Johannesburg will then try to get arrested, one which requires a little especial courage. I am constantly praying to God to grant me that.' And now he talks of Manilal, his other son. 'He has subjected himself to strict vows and is going through a vow of penitence . . . Jamnadas is impatient to be in gaol.' Then after giving his blessings to his son, he adds a P.S.:

'My wish is that whatever you take should be without reference to me or to my views.'

But by now Reuter's had cabled the news of this non-violent war to the whole world. 'The irrevocable step has been taken,' said Mr. Kachhalia, but the letter was actually written by Gandhiji.

'The British world knows . . . that the handful of Indians in South Africa have declared passive resistance—that this microscopic minority of men have pitted themselves against a mighty government. This was a notice not only to the South African Government but to the Imperial Government as well. What then are our specific demands:

Removal of the racial bar from the Immigration Act. Restoration of rights that existed prior to the new legislation.

Generous and just administration of the existing laws throughout the Union affecting the Indians.

Removal of the £3 tax.

A spirit of friendliness instead of one of hostility towards the Indian community.

We stand by what we say. If the white community does not understand us, we shall proceed by our own methods: we are capable of dying for our honour, and we shall fight the adversary 'by a process of voluntary suffering which at once purifies and dignifies'.

The buzzard now pursued the eagle with greater insistence. The mountains loom behind, the Mlanje does, and the cut rocks shape the ever rising silence into sheer commitments. Man's folly is to think his law the law of reciprocity. Would it not be true to say silence speaks the law—to those who would hear? The buzzard will unfeather the eagle, sail up and perch on the crag. History then subsumes the meaning of Truth.

8

The Processional

High on the wild veld a new spirit seemed to be stalking
the wide, wind-broken earth. Isolated rings of silence,
arisen from the earth-navel, self-created, so to say, whirled into
concrete distances, and shaping into a Mariamma, Badakamma,
Brihadnayaki, Bhadra-Kali, as if indeed it were the harvest
festival in the far Dravidian lands, and the African gods, Bantu,
Shono, Zimbabwe too had been invited—come divinity on
this palanquin with the curled silver trumpet shouting your
glory, and you, with a thousand arms and a million teeth,
blood pouring from your nostrils and tense-pitched mouth, you
too, on this maned lion, you ride him as to a celestial party.
You know in the wild hills of the Tamil land where there are
festivals that rotate according to zodiac stars, the gods visit one
another, and you are so welcome to us thither. Remember once
we had ridden to you too, and you had welcomed us there in
those stately nilotic gorges, and the sacrifices of the buffalo, the
elephant, the rhino were so huge and high, you built us a temple
there by the Zambesi, and we were enshrined amidst you, for
many a century to come. But slowly the wild forests, the super-
populated animals, now bereft of consideration, demolished us.
And the earth in shame took us back slowly into herself, leaving

only a few cones and specks of temple slabs. But now our people have come to you again. They walk the African earth singing our Tamil or Telugu songs, and they are so happy they go where they like, and do whatever they do. And sing:

> We have bowed three times at your feet,
> We have bowed our heads.

And the sisters, the women who walk there far, singing our songs, bearing our talismans, and speaking our sweet Tamil tongue, they're bidden to your august company—receive them, please Goddess, as you would us, for their prayers are ours, their gifts of gold and silver hang on our necks and feet. The cocks and goats that betimes are sacrificed with their coins—with your gold—fertilise the hearts and roots of our fruits here. Remember you were once one of us, cousins of a distant epoch, Goddess, of renewed time-cycles. We are ever here. But you are there. Let us play the ancient game, however. The pilgrims will come to you.

> The clouds feed earth with rain,
> The earth makes no return.

From the Drakenburg to the Zambesi, indeed, there seemed the flutter of heavenly hosts, the earth moving backwards underneath as it were, while the Indians had started their great new pilgrimage. The continents would be connected again.

First, the Tamil women who entered Transvaal, the goddess on their neck, forehead, heart, would not be arrested. What could you after all do? They had their mantras, they had their vow-armlets. If you asked them for their passes, they nodded their heads. Did they understand anything? If you stopped them they smiled. If you got angry they laughed as if they understood not this sputter-spitter language. And they were, as it were, drunk with some new waters, had washed themselves in the river with many unguents, and had garlanded themselves with fresh flowers, and with *kumkum* and turmeric on their faces, they were going to the festival of the Goddess. You can almost hear the pipes blow and the trumpets keen across the valley, stand still over the width of rivers, fall and rise again towards the Goddess as of the mountain, they the sister goddesses of the seven hills; and with garland and musk, and dripping wet clothes, children in their arms, they, the pilgrims, will walk any festival fire—yes, let us see what any fire will do—it will not scorch us for we've seen the face of the hill Goddess, she who's vanquished a demon for our benefit, that our children could be fed on our breasts, and that neither pox nor poverty touch us again—we the pilgrims are bent on the visit to the high, mountain festival, don't you see?

We cross frontiers and Smuts' sentries do not arrest us. The Goddess is with us. We get into trains and the white ticket collectors do not so much as ask us our tickets—for they be seeming to look far into the hills and see the heavenly hosts with winged chariots and gold palanquins that wander with us. We, the women of the Tolstoy Farm, you know Sir, where we are going? We are going to the Newcastle Collieries. There, said our saint, our father, are Tamils like us, men who should honour us for we be women in a foreign land and we are going to the Goddess festival. Won't you protect us from the wild beasts of the forest—from the hyena and the bear and the leaping leopard of the Drakenburg? Oh, ye Tamilmen, and lead us to the festival of the Goddess. Come, the train whistles and we go.

There is no life like in the high wilds,
And wilderness has five black eyes.

Our saint's wife too, so we hear, Kasturba has been bidden
by the gods and she too takes her train—she comes towards the
Transvaal veld, and we go, where the mountains meet and the
passes are cut, and soon thence and down to the coal mines of
Newcastle in Natal.

And when we come there, and one here, and one there, we
meet, brother, father, brother-in-law, grandfather, and we say to
them: Father, would you not protect us, our honour? You know
we are women, and we know not the wrought knots of men. We
came here bidden by the saint.—And the father, or the brother,
sits awhile on the road-stone, smiles awhile and thinks.—What
bids you come here, sisters? he asks of us.—And we say to him:
The saint has said, have you not heard the saint, our father? We
are like dogs with a dog-collar, and we pay the £3 tax. So do we,
said the brother, the father.—And your sons too will pay, say
we.—And he does say: And so it is.

—And so you mean you will go on paying the £3 tax,
and that you will carry this collar as long as the sun and moon
shine? We never thought of it, says the father, the brother, the
husband-looking man.

—And then: Brother and man, you see these beads on our
necks—Yes, so we do, say they.—And we have husbands, and
they are in prison. Oh, our husbands have gone in prison for
the saint has said, our father has said, as long as the wife who
bears the black-beads of marriage is not a wife, on earth as in
the upper regions, we would rather go to prison.—How so? asks
the miner, the father, the brother.—Father, brother, say we:
How so? Why the government of the whitemen have said us

so: they've passed the laws that say: Marry the Christian way or it's no marriage.—Yet we are not Christians, says the father, the brother. But this is a Christian country, say the whites, and this be the new law.—But why not come with me, says the father, the brother, and takes us home to his hut and hearth, and feeds us, talks to us and we talk to them, the menfolk, and then to the women.

And we tell them what the saint, the father, he Gandhi-swami, had told us on Tolstoy Farm. Sons, and fathers of sons, must fight, fight that the marriage necklace be kept holy. That we be married as Parvati to Shiva, and to Shiva we're wed. And we have offered Him our beads at festivals, and our fineries, and have fasted for Him and walked a month that we see Him in his high, cold wintry hills surrounded by the silence of the mountain, the year and the dew; and when the moon has come to the eleventh day of the seventh month, we honour Him with our shivering shining prayers and count our beads and fall flat at His feet, that women and fields be well-cultivated, and that our hearts ringing as at harvest time. And the flower falls on us from the gods. Such our promises to Shiva.—Then keep your promises, say the brothers from the Newcastle Mines. Keep them, and we protect you.—And we all sit as if it were our marriage day, and the Brahmins were chanting hymns. One could almost hear the trumpet sound. And the camphor lit.

> Oh you, wealthy of virtue,
> Beloved of my living breath.

And other brothers and fathers gather about us, and yet others. What shall we do, say the elders among them. What's to be done but strike. Strike work, and then the whites would know

we, too, have an honour to save. Look at these, our sisters—
and we shall not house them roofless, unwalled. And yet other
brothers join the gathering, and fathers talk to sons, and uncles
to nephews, and women talk to daughters, and the gathering
grows as on the dawn of the first-sowing festival. Indeed, the air
was all so deep, auspicious. One could almost hear the drums
throb betwixt silences. The procession was coming. Shall we go
to meet it? Shall we?

> Oh the Goddess is coming.,
> The Goddess is coming,
> She with the metal-mirror before Her,
> And the umbrella above,
> Her feet made of jasper,
> Her chest shine of the five precious stones,
> Her smile the silence that sounds.
> O, fill the valley with Her benediction,
> Sing the song of the swing-swinging soar,
> Soar, soar, soar higher, sisters, soar.

And one here, and one there, they joined together and rolled
over to the elder—the elder hardly an elder, for he was less than
thirty, and caught by a tout and bought over, as it were, for he
was young and perhaps had quarreled with his step-mother, or
was it with his uncle, and had left home and fields and run away,
and hearing of this far and rich country where gold and diamond
lay there, just for you to pick up, and you would be paid fifteen
rupees a month to begin with, and after three years you could go
back home and cultivate your own fields on the holy Cauvery
bend, but if you so bethought yourself and had godly ambitions,
you had to contract for a further three years, just go down the

mine and come up, and that paid you over twenty-five rupees a month now, and you could have a bungalow to live in, or you could settle on the rich African land and cultivate it, the government gave it to you, like a present, for your endeavours, as if with a coconut, *tulasi* leaves and coin of silver as present settled down,—and you sold vegetables to the whites above and to the Kaffirs below—thus the tout, and the schoolboy, for he'd been to school once, but for a year or more and could read and write and he said, 'Yea uncle, I'll come,' and thus came, but such the strain in his lungs (he coughed all the time) that wisdom came to him little by little, and he went to no women, and he read and read all the time, the *Ramayana* and the newspapers, and he told everyone about the Gandhi struggles and of Smuts and of Botha and of the King in England who was still interested in us, in our round of life, and that shows why at all the big meetings in the city when Gandhi-swami came, the leader, he sings that strange song to the King—and everybody stands up—thus brothers that we gathered too under the elder, and we listened to him, and when he spoke it was always as if you spoke to yourself, for he spoke to you your own thoughts, so to say, and said the things the texts would say, or told a story, and that is what happened that evening at the Newcastle mines. For by now a large body of men and women had gathered, the Transvaal-sisters in front (and their babies—there were two of them there, one young and one old slept on the floor) while the elder spoke thus and thus again, and told everyone the story of Draupadi, daughter of King Drupada, the wife unto five Pandava brothers, 'How so?' you may ask.

That is simple. The brothers five were like one, and one day-when they still in exile and hiding as Brahmins—heard of a *swayamvara* ceremony. They would go there and show their prowess and beautiful Draupadi was thus won, but she would be wife not to Dharmaraja or to Bhima but to Arjuna the brave, for it's he who shot the first arrow, and thus she became his wife. Even so when they came home and knocked at the door they cried out like happy home-coming children do: Mother, Mother, a present for you, we've a present for you—and without as much opening the door, the mother in all motherliness says: And may ye share it all between ye—but when the door opened and there she was, fair Draupadi, what were they going to do? She would, before the gods, be the wife of every one of the five, but to man, only to one, and that would be to Arjuna who'd won her. Yet, you remember, when the Pandavas grew up and Dharmaraja, the truthful Dharmaraja, so loved his dice he staked his all to his uncle's son Duryodhana, the wicked, and lost his kingdom and his wife Draupadi was thus became his slave, Duryodhana's slave. And do not the texts say: 'For the Panchala's princess lost all and vile Duryodhana deemed her slave.' And when Duryodhana the wicked-one taunted her, did not Bhima lose his temper, but truth is truth to Dharmaraja—he had given his word and the word would be honoured. Bhima could do nothing. But when Draupadi said: How could she, a Panchala princess, be thus treated, did not the wicked Dushasana in front of the whole assembly of kings and kinsmen, pull her by the hair and she would from then on—'wear her hair in clots and strings', added some women, as if in chorus from the assembly—'and not till this humiliation be avenged would she braid it'. And since she thought on Krishna, with this thought, Krishna knew this, he, the Lord knows all, and thus brothers, when Krishna had offered the Kauravas, everything but five provinces, five districts, five villages, five homes, and the wicked Duryodhana would say nay and nay and nay, then did the battle be assembled ready, and the men were going to smash one another. For wheresoever the truth there be victory, say the texts.

So brothers, said the elder, and now we've got to fight. These sisters of Transvaal have come to us and say: How long shall we be slaves? The battle of Kurukshetra is ready, brothers, Gandhi-swami, the father calls us. Shall we fight?

'Yes yes,' said one here and one there.

'And the dog-collar tax must go!'

'The dog-collar tax must go,' said many young men.

'And we don't want to be like the whites,' continued the elder who read the Gandhi newspaper. 'And we don't want to build palaces for ourselves—we want to worship our gods, and keep the marriage-necklace of our women tight.'

'Yes,' said some here and some there, for the assembly had grown with the growth of night, and the home-going miners stood on with their dirt-dark clothes and coal-coloured faces, to listen to this assembly.

'Yes, and till this government honours our marriages, like Dharmaraja, with Krishna on our side, we will fight. What do you say to that, brothers?'

'Good, good,' said they all and they looked at the Transvaal-sisters with affection, with gratitude, for it's they who'd brought them this new eye-view.

'And promise,' said the Transvaal-sisters, 'And promise that come jail, come death, we shall not flinch.' At this they were all silent. Is that what it all means? And the Transvaal-sisters spoke to the men of the Tolstoy Farm, and the fruits and the vegetables that they grew, and the sandals they stitched and how men went to jail and came back, for so truthful were they, even the government honoured them. And there were whites too at the Tolstoy Farm.

'Whites with you?' asked some young people, unbelieving.

'Why, yes so,' said the learned elder. 'The Gandhi papers say so. There's Kallenbach, the German, and Polak, the Jew, and Schlesin, the woman, and West the Englishman, and so many many and they are all with us.'

'And the King of England too,' said someone half in jest and half in seriousness.

'Where Truth is kingship is,' quoted the elder, again from the texts, and thus when the night rolled into itself and the assembly was getting thinner, the women asked each sister from Transvaal, 'Come to my house, sister.' And another, 'Come to my home, auntie,' and another, 'Come to my hut, little mother.' But Lazarus said, 'Stay here with us, sisters.' And they stayed with Lazarus, his wife and his wife's sister, and all night they told such wondrous tales of Gandhi-swami and his doings. He washes his own clothes, said one Transvaal-sister to the wife of Lazarus—and eats only fruits like the sages did in the sacred books. And another said: When we're ill he takes the good mother earth and pours water on it, and flattens it and puts a poultice of it on our heads, our stomachs, and then we are cured. Oh really! say the Newcastle sisters. And a third one talks of the whites that come and go, and of the ministers who send him telegrams, and he sends back to the white ministers, and even to the King of England and to the great men in India—like Gokhale you know, the Coolie King, who came to us.

'Yes, and a Brahmin too, and what kindness in his face and what shine of wisdom on his forehead.'

'And the whiteman's government gave him their own train to travel in.'

'And banquets were held in his honour.' 'And Smuts had said: The dog-collar tax will go.' 'And he never took it away,' said the Transvaal-sisters. For they knew it all.

And thus when the night was over and night miners went down to their shifts and came back, others heard of the Transvaal-sisters, and the Transvaal-sisters, with the two babies in their arms, went here, went there, and news spread from colliery to colliery, the dog-collar tax must go, what do you say to that, brothers? Look, they say the Gandhi-swami's wife, like a true Draupadi, has gone to jail. Come let us fight. Enough of this black-slavery.—And again: What do you say to that? Yes, yes, and everybody is talking, the Kaffir and the Coloured, that the Gandhi-swami's fight is getting bigger and bigger, and the Swami himself is now going to Johannesburg, but he too will be arrested. What then?—The Gandhi-swami says as long as one speaks the truth no man can do anything to you.

'It's all a Brahmin's talk. The whiteman does not care,' said a young fellow.

'The whiteman is also a man,' says Lazarus. 'And he does care. That is why there are so many whites with the Gandhi-swami.'

'Then what shall we do?'

'Fight,' says the elder and there is unanimous silence.

The silence staggers, as it were, slips out of the window towards the grasses outside, and the hills beyond, and comes back as if it could not possibly stay out. Something has to be said, something has to be done.

'Fight,' then says a young man.

'Let us fight,' says another man.

'Why not fight? Now or tomorrow we've to die. And the Gandhi-swami's wife in jail, and he himself will go to jail, let's all fight. The whites have their strike, let's strike.'

'Yes,' said a worker. It carried a magic meaning.

'Strike, and strike all.' Everybody seemed to understand. This was a holy war. This was not for better wages or for better houses. This was for the Gandhi-swami. Shiva, Shiva, let's take Thy name and go on strike. And women suddenly lit lamps at the sanctuaries, and others recited mantras, and yet others remembered their holy namings as they went on pilgrimage: Ayyappa-Samy, Ayyappa-Samy. The God lay in the Malabar mountain heights and through the travails of darkness, of jungle darkness and of elephant and tiger terrors, we'll go and pay homage to him—we the pilgrims, Lord, we come to you with long beards and without having touched our women for three fortnights, thus we come pure and gold-giving. Lord, open the doors of your sanctuary and let us see You face to face. There He stands, can you not see the great God, in his snake-crowned splendour, the Ganges coming down His head and Parvati by his side? Lord, we burn camphor and incense and we'll shave away our beards that your blessing be upon us.—And the bell rings and priests offer us worship, and when our eyes are lit with her splendour, we close them long, long, that we carry his shine for all the year to come. Come Gandhi-swami, we're your pilgrims, We'll strike. And we join you on your pilgrimage.

The next day a hundred, two hundred, went not to work, and by the evening they had swollen to a thousand, and the papers that came the next morning spoke of it, and the manager's agents were here and there asking questions. The miners, you know, can have their electricity cut, their water cut, and the rations cut. Let them, said Lazarus the wise, the God that saved the elephant from the crocodile would know how to save us too—said the women. Hold fast to His name and He will look after us. One thousand persons became two thousand and then men came from Dundee and Glencoe and soon, so people said, the Gandhi-swami himself was coming. And there was such a wide clap of joy in the sky, yes, when the Gandhi-swami came we'd all know what to do. We'll follow him, yes, now we'll know where to go and he'll take us beyond the forest paths to that long sanctuary. Can you not hear the stout temple bell ringing?

> Tongue the gong, tongue the gong
> Of the Pillar of Fire, of the Mount of Dawn.
> The sky-born orders, winged and vehicled,
> Go round and round Him to flaming camphor-worship,
> In melted butter sacrifice,
> In the adoration of *bilva* leaf and of Shiva-lip,
> And to her the bride,
> We'll offer *parijata* flower.

So then there was this other elder, and Lazarus his auspicious name. Of the family of indentured labourers, he himself was one, and had bought himself afterward a plot of land, and built himself a little house with three rooms and a garden, and he lived here, with his family, happily, in the outskirts of Newcastle. The mines were not far away, and men came and men went, and women as well, and though his parents (or he himself) had converted to Christianity, he was like every other Indian, and spoke Tamil, and was brother to one and all. And the eleven sisters of Transvaal, therefore, with their babies and themselves, settled into this household, and the workers and the elders came here, or the sisters went from house to house to spread the gospel of satyagraha: Gandhi-swami says this, and this and this again— that one should speak the truth and seek the truth, and wrest the dog-collar tax, and the deportations will disappear as wet wood before a mighty fire. For Truth burns when it touches and purifies and frees love. Yes, love we should—even the whiteman says he, for the whites are not bad. Only there's a shadow over them like a mist over the Zambesi mountains, and which will go when the fair winds blow. And after that the true rains come, and the harvest beautiful for the Goddess to see.

How do you like that, brothers?

They were silent. Maybe it's true. Maybe it's not true. Of course, we too have heard of the Transvaal happenings. Be they proper? That men went to prison again and again, and big merchants lost all, for they followed the great Gandhi-swami. Yes, so it is, the Transvaal-sisters assured them, and more, it shall be greater this time—for, from the Cape to the open end of Transvaal and Natal, every Indian will fight—he'll fight that you, the Natal Indians, bear not the dog-collar, and our women keep their marriage necklace firm and sound. And they said yea, yea, and rose and went thinking on these happenings.

* * *

And now he was come, the Gandhi-swami himself had arrived. And where would he stay, sister? For when he came here to Newcastle he ever stayed in those villas up the hills amidst sweet smelling avenues, where the big live, for some Indians too have their habitations there. And thither amidst the lawns and the playful fountains would he live, and move about in those excellent horse-carriages, and talk to the whites as a white man. But now—but now he would not live in those villas—this time he came for the labourers, he would fight with them, and so would live like them, with them. They say too he's changed from the costume of silk pants and black lawyer-coat to those of cotton and jute like that of an indentured labourer, a girmico. They say he looks like us. Does he, sisters?

So that when he did come, Gandhi-swami, he went straight to Lazarus and said: Lazarus, may I stay with you? For you know perhaps there's going to be a big big fight, and from London and Bombay people are looking at us, and we shall not fail them this time. Now, I would not want to worry the merchants on the top of the hill who live in their villas. The whites would ruin them. Here I can sleep on the floor with you, and cook with you, and work in your garden, you know, I am now a good gardener, I, your brother, Lazarus.—And nobody had come to Lazarus thus—and so big. And Lazarus said: Of course, Gandhi-swami Avargal,[1] and the women in the household broomed again the floor that not a speck of dust lie there, and he and his handbag, he laid against the wall, did Gandhi-swami, and spoke to the Transvaal-sisters and then to the others, and played with the babies a while, and said: And now to work.—And he went to see the miners, the miners that had laid their tools aside.

And the miners welcomed him and gave him a loud ovation, but when they saw him in his new clothes, they had tears to their eyes. He was like them; he would fight for them. And staff in hand he looked the pure pilgrim. Brothers, shall we go up the hills and behold the God face to face? And from the silence one knew the workers were ready, and one here and one there, the educated amongst them, learnt this Gandhi speech too, and went behind him from compound to compound to know whether the young and the elders too were ready or were not. 'But look the women are in prison, and his own wife, like Sita, is in jail. And how shall we rest when the women have gone to jail?'

---

[1]   An honorific in the Tamil country.

'Of course not,' replied the elder. And meetings were held and vast gatherings took place in the open and in houses, and the movement leapt forth like a temple chariot on the festival day. 'Shiva, Shiva, Hara, Hara,' and you give a giant pull: the chariot moves now—look. People struck work in this mine and that, and the white managers, they cut off electricity or water, but the Indians did not care. They could do without these lights, God had given them eyes—oil lamps would do, and as for water, they could go to any well, and carry water on their hips and heads as in India. What will you do then? And the whites sent fierce men, Kaffirs and whites, to flog our workmen, but the Gandhi-word had spread: Hurt not even were you hurt.

There's that story of the fierce Pathan who while being flogged shouted: Thank your stars, our leader has asked us not to use whip against whip, or you'd not have gone back alive.— But others bled too and the whites did not know which way to turn. And then he came again, did Gandhi-swami, and told them: It's no use striking work and living in the mine-owner's quarters, eating their rations. If you would be true to truth, you should leave the mine-owner's compounds—sell your things or give them away, or leave them in the huts, but leave the compound. And touch not the food they give you, for that would be eating morsels of untruth. And the workers obeyed, a hundred of them, then five hundred and a thousand and then two thousand, but where now, pray, would they live? And good Lazarus, said to them: Come brothers, come sisters, camp on my land—and the chariot festival continued.

They were so happy, and the young leaders who read gave them the news the papers gave, and the old looked after the babies while the others went from home to home preaching the doctrine of satyagraha. And the Indian merchants high on the hills took compassion and gave vessels and rice and dal and oil—bag after bag came to the house of Lazarus and his garden looked like one big temple yard, and the women cooked, the young volunteers carried bags now, and the Hindus and the Muslims, Christians and the Zoroastrians, the Tamils, the Hindustanis, the Telugus, the Gujaratis lived like brothers. Were they not all brothers, say?

Two thousand workers had struck work and the whites in Durban now said: Gandhi, we would parley with you. Gandhi-swami now, dressed in his indentured-labourer's habits, went to parley with the whites at the big Mansion of the Mines. And so the papers said, and the whites said: What is it you want, Gandhi? And he answered with the courtesy that he showed to the poor or the rich: Sirs, the £3 tax must go. The government promised our reverend leader Gokhale, yes, this tax would go. We are not dogs to have this collar around our necks—no sooner we are born. True the government has now said after all the struggles, that the women and the children will not pay the tax henceforth. But we say no man that's man should pay a poll-tax for being a man. And Indians are men like you. And if to be born brown instead of being born white is sin, then must most mankind perish for the whites are so small in this vast round world.—Nay, nay, said some of the mine-owners, we have no quarrel with you.—Then said Gandhi-swami to them: Now tell the government you're not interested in the dog-collar tax. And the workers will go back to the mines and work.—But we have been so nice to them, protested some white mine-owners. Look, we've built houses for them, given them doctors and good food and electricity and what more do you want?—Sirs, said Gandhi-swami, would you be just satisfied with water and electricity . . .?—Of this they were all unsure and divided.—Let the government stop the tax, and we'll all live together in peace, and the workers will go down the mines. If not, I've told the workers to leave the compounds and go on a long pilgrimage. Yes, man is ever a pilgrim, I tell you that He has the sky above, the earth below, the sun that gives him warmth, and the rains that give him water—fruits bear on the trees. Yes, we will go on a grand pilgrimage to God, and get the dog-collar decimated and forever.

The white mine-owners would say neither ye nor nay, but sent telegrams to the government. And the government said, of course not, Gokhale had never received such a promise. So, whereas the mines were slowing down in work, the workers had gathered in the garden of Lazarus and they bethought themselves: We have never been so happy since we left our country. God seems to shine somewhere between us, and there's such a look of holiness on our women's faces. Even our children seem so playful and peacesome. There's sainthood in this Gandhi-swami that we should all be so—the good and the murderer, the rich and the clever thief, the wise wife and the concubine, we seem all so united. And there was as it were on the heights of the African mountains, far and clear, some light of a temple epiphany. What was it that was coming?

And now the government decided; they've played enough. And one day the police came and took away the eleven sisters of Transvaal, and men and women cheered them as they went; people came out with garlands and *kumkum,* and they were sent away on their forest exiles. After all, Queen Sita went on a forest exile and come back; and Draupadi too, that the humiliation be avenged. The marriage necklace is stronger than any Smuts law, for Truth is stronger than power. When will the whites learn this? Remember, it's said in our *bhajans*:

He who changed (the cup of) poison into ambrosia,
And shames us into holiness, He, our Krishna,
He knows, for he protects.

And when the Gandhi-swami had come back and with a
no, no, from the white masters (and from Durban) and the
ticket-collectors, whites all, that came into the train, said:
And what may have happened, Sir? and he said to them, did
Gandhi-swami, a compassionate smile on his face, Why, they
would want their pound of flesh.—Of course they do. Don't
we know them, said the ticket-collectors, as they too had gone
through their own sorrowings, for the powered man only yields
when he cannot but give. There was all pain in the train, but
when he reached Newcastle and the camp of Lazarus, such
was the joy among the pilgrims. Father, said they, what would
you have us do now?—and he said to them: Why, the whites
will not give in till their hearts are melted. Let us pray and
melt their hearts, said he, clapping hands and smiling. And
one said here and one said there: And they have taken away
our Transvaal-sisters, with babes in their arms—and Gandhi-
swami said: And the paper says they too are lodged with the
Natal-sisters at Volksrust Jail—and the people were happy, for
they knew, she, Kasturba Gandhi too was in Volksrust Jail, but
yet they all wondered what would happen the morrow arriving
when the papers said—the white papers—that the women with
babes in their arms, they were given three months rigorous
imprisonment, and ordered to cut the stones and hew the
wood, make dresses, and water the garden, people said and the
warder might spit at them, and the white sahib, the jailer, and
threaten them (and would some be molested too? a few asked
and asked themselves) and when the evening came and all the

pilgrims gathered for prayers, there came others, hundreds, the hundreds behind hundreds, of the miners and they said: Now that the women are in jail, we shall not touch the tools till the whites learn the lesson, and how can we, when the women are so brave? And Gandhi-swami said to them: Brothers, the power of India, Bharata-Shakti, is in the way Draupadi or Savitri or Sita or Damayanti loved her God. Women are not feeble, they indeed the stronger of us both; I have learned this from my own wife said he and smiled, and the miners said: And now what Gandhi-swami? And he said: Lay down your tools and take bag and blanket, and come. God will feed us. I have no money. I have no promises from any. But God knows what to do with us—and he told them the story of Mirabai who left her King and wandered away to the temple, for God indeed was her true husband, and she sang songs to her God, but the King would not have it that way. He threatened her with this and that, with the cup of poison which finally came and when she drank it, was it not become celestial honey—and at this, remembering it all, the women in the assembly wept. And he told them too about Sudhama who had only a handful of rice, and when he went to the palace of Sri Krishna, did not the Lord himself come and wash the feet of the poor man, and feed him in vessels of silver and gold, and when he left and the royal carriage took him to his home, had not white marble walls risen where his thatch had stood, and had not his wife in silken raiments stood at the door awaiting the royal coach—such the ways of God when man waits on Truth, and the people were right heartened by these tales, Hindus, Muslims and Christians, indeed all, all, they all said: Come, we come with you. And he said, wait for the night and we shall know what God would want. And he waited on God for his answer.

And God never abandons you when you do not abandon Him.

For with the morning came the answer: Take the pilgrims straight to the Transvaal—make them march all on foot, and if they could pass through the gate of the frontier, take them on to the great Tolstoy Farm. Yes, that indeed seemed the voice of God speaking. And meanwhile Gandhi-swami sent away telegrams to his Guru, Gokhale, in India: Eleven women sent to jail. Sentenced to three months rigorous imprisonment. The movement gathering strength. Do not worry. We will manage our needs.—And he sent also to the Lords in London his telegram about the women and the miners and the pilgrim march that was to be. Hé Rama, how glorious the world shines when Truth is on our forehead. 'There's brother, I tell you, never a defeat for Truth,' said Gandhi-swami.

And when evening came and Gandhi-swami made his speech, his final one, he said: True you are with me, rather you are all with God. But remember, we are all of us filled with guts and bones, humours and filth, and a mind that never knows itself. We have our weaknesses. We need, remember, a comfortable bed, or when our stomach is hungry, a good meal. As I have told you, I can only give you one and half pounds of bread per man, per woman, and an ounce of sugar. And not a mustard-seed more. And on that hungry and drum-beating stomach must you walk, walk, walk, perhaps two hundred miles—unless the whites arrest us, and then we know not what might be. They may beat us. They may spit on us. They may even shoot us. Death after all is the end of life. Are you ready to die?—Yea, yea, shouted most of them. But some thought within themselves: This is going to be no easy pilgrimage. We had come for other things—for better salaries, perhaps for no dog-collar tax. But death? Did we come for that? And then when they came back to themselves, they heard Gandhi-swami saying: The old and the maimed, the lame, the sick, the babies, they can travel by train. But, the rest, with God in your hearts and the bundle on your heads, will you march up to the temple-peak, high up there from where surrounded by the seven seas you see nothing but the big face of the shivering, heightening, morning God? Will you then, once on the top, pull the festival-chariot of God with me?

There was a shiver of straight silence. Nobody knew the answer. But suddenly as if from nowhere the answer came. Yes, Swami, yes, said the crowd here, and the crowd there, and yes spoke the whole assembly, and when the night was not gone far deep, bundle on their heads, they came one, two, three, one hundred, three hundred—and when the dawn broke and the bath was over, the prayers were said, then Gandhi-swami said to some, the young: You take these, the maimed and the sick to the oncoming trains, join us at Volksrust—and now, turning to the assembled crowd, he said: And even now those who would stay back, kindly stay behind, for there is no shame in being afraid of cold and tyrannous hunger. But murmurs rose saying: No, no, we're coming, and when all was ready and the dawn not yet red round on the mountain passes, he turned, did Gandhi-swami, towards the smoking and lit city of Newcastle, as if in prayer and in blessing to those he'd left behind, and turning to Lazarus and to the women of his household, he said unto them: Noble your name, Lazarus, and you've won the heart of God Himself, I am sure,—and turning towards the road, as Lazarus fell at the great man's feet, Gandhi-swami struck his staff to the ground, and cried, Ram Ram, and the pilgrims marched forth shouting Rama Rama, Haré Haré, Krishna, Krishna, Haré Haré. One never, brother, turns back from a pilgrimage. One goes to the nether world if having turned to the face of God, we turned back to the maw of the city. We can only go forward, brothers. And men sang hymns and women sang popular songs of marriage and of harvest, and the holy army marched forward, the first three hundred in all, and all the hearts seemed richly happy. Even the hearts of the whites: For the black plague was coming and with such a crowd and of Indians who know no dirt or drainage, what would happen to us, of the City of Newcastle? God give them peace too. For God, brother, is undivided. He knows neither the white nor the black nor the brown: He does truly affection them all.

This and this alone
is true religion—
To serve thy brethren.
This is sin above other sin,
To harm thy brethren.

As the road leapt and sizzled before us, there was a sense of pious joy in the air. All roads lead to God, one might say, as the twist and twang of the highway, going up and back into itself, and merging again into newer and clearer heights, and yet bend back behind and going up around a shady rock or a clump of trees. There was in us, as it were, an inner touching of outer depths and a river's slow flow, for the buffalo was, you know, over the ridges, and with bundles on our heads, as the vessels clanged or the sacks slipped, or the children cried, or here and there the stragglers sat for their 'early morning needs', or the women sat behind a stone, and another woman kept watch that no eye fall on the squat self—and high up there on the hills was there not such a drum and drone that the gods

seemed to be in conference? Here were we singing of Vishnu
or Shiva or Rama, or Sri Krishna, or the Devi with the fierce
teeth and a garland of skulls—she who'd slaughtered the mighty
demon for our safety, and brought harvest and gold to autumnal
eyes—were our goddesses at fight in the air with the African
divinities, Brihad-Aranyaki against the Milungo or Sada Shiva
against Culkulukulu, and did the mountain leopard and the
elephant somewhere far take part in this battle, and was Allah,
that the Kaffir sometime took the name of, the same as the Allah
of the Indians?—the Muslims as they kneel there, look, look, on
grass or sward, bent knee on carpet—and when the Christian
crosses came, everybody felt here we are and we know this is
the sign of peace, for so the Gandhi-swami said. The Christians
amongst us, crossed themselves, and we too might have had we
known their God. And sometimes a padre would jump out of
his pointed church and give us a wave of hand, in affection and
in blessing, his eye-glasses shining on his red, swelling nose, or a
Kaffir from the valley below wave at us from his dark egg-shapen
hut. For everybody knew this was indeed a procession to God,
and it was as though we were in the high Himalaya where Shiva
sat with Parvati, his left hand on her breast and his head high
in the clouds, to hear of our grievances. Did he, our great God,
with trident in his hand and moon on forehead, did he hear of
the dog-collar tax and the laws of this desertic land? Shiva, did
you send us here? Parvati Devi, did you hear us? Do you?

But one here, one there, we came across the tombs of the
dead—the whites had made big battle between themselves
among the hills here, and there were many dead hereabouts, so
the people said, though that battle was long, long ago. There,
said someone, that's called the Majuba Hill, high like a rising
divinity, and here the Boer just ran up and ran down like a lion

grunting and smashing the English Tommy, and then, when the Boers were hit back against those hills—one after the other killed and buried there, amidst other hills, and Smuts too, so people said, ran for his life, Smuts and Botha, and they said there was at that time a great and good Queen in London, and she was most remorseful and wept like Gandhi-swami himself, for all the dead of everyone. She did not like that man kill man. And so she wept. And she ordered the whites make peace, and they made peace, and became brothers, the Boer the British.

Now the British said the Indian and whites are the same, all children of the same Queen—and so we march, do we, Gandhi-swami, we know, to redeem the vows of this Queen that the coolie and the whites are the same, and that before God, as before that sky, there may be mountain and plain, the mimosa tree and high eucalyptus—why even the monkey, the ostrich and the big elephant—but before the sky we're all the same. And that's what Gandhi-swami said we be battling for; that is, man must be seen as man. But, brother, I want to tell you something, one thing, that like a kernel in the betel nut in the depths of our hearts there's a great true sorrow and we chew it and we chew it again. We know not whence it came and where it goes—but whether you've babies born or a mother dead, there's a twist in the navel, as it were, and you want to weep. Why, why, we ask ourselves. But we know not. The dog-collar tax or no whiteman's slavery, it's all the same, I tell you. What we seek be that going round and round and back again up like these mountain roads, the wife behind us and the children behind the wife, some kids that hold our arms and some that hang to the wife's breast, or is carried in a sling on the back—there's sorrow, and that's why we move forward. We go to God. The road is hard, brother, and even our toes weep tears. We wipe our tears on our shirt edge, for it's cold here up in the mountains, and we sit a while on a rock. The women leave the kids with us and go gathering lilies in the field. Red some are and some be white, and the women put them in their hair. And some will gather a few pebbles and stones on the roadside, make their temple of the deity and place their flowers before the goddess, *kumkum* on their forehead and clap hands and lowly whispering, sing. What, Lord, would we do without our women, their quietude talisman, and prayers? And Gandhi-swami marches on.

And down the valley as you look behind there are others and yet others coming, and we know from Newcastle and then from Dundee, and then from beyond that, the coolies are still coming, coolie after coolie will trudge to the Transvaal frontier that the uprightness of man before God be held forth as a mirror, and the whites give us our right to breathe, to wed, to worship. The nostril widens in strength and fingers back to a spot, where, breathless we merge into that shimmer and silence, we know not what. Be that God?

He breathes, does the Lord,
Through the pores of existence,
His shine is speech, His silence ornament.

You can see the procession move higher and yet higher, countable but all far, each man and woman so small, so peculiar, so intense, as if they knew where they were going—turban or crooked cap on their heads, pantaloon or *dhoti* hanging from their waists, bent or straight, limping, slobbering, sneezing, chattering, lecher-looking, murdersome, fevered, tuberculous, mud like, how curious to see them against the mountain rising up one after one. The mountain air gives you a puff of strength, and you wonder that man should be so immoderate, lost amidst all this stone. Where are we going, brother, and where, mother? Do you know? Do you know the name of the high sanctuary, and what God performed what miracle thither, and for which sainted devotee's illumination we go to commemorate? Did he or she see God? Did they get married, the god and the goddess? Else did she, the goddess, like Goddess Parvati refuse the marriage? And what river, what Ganges, brother, what Cauvery flows besides the temple, or bathe we in what goddess-water tank and laying our burdens on the ghats, dipping and rising from the holy waters, wet in clothes, singing His name, we'll ring the bell, see Him open-eyed? Shiva, Shiva, Hara, Hara, we beat our cheeks and ask you our pardon.

Ignorant and lost in the Maya of this world we have wandered from life to life, and yet here we are, in the sorrow of our portent Africa. We're meek and we're poor, great God, with the Ganges in your tight hair, burn us this world (with that your third eye) and turn it into all beaten silver.

The women join us again, and with the kids on our shoulders or holding to our hands, baggages perched on our heads, we're sad, but we're true to you, we go, God!

And as night came, we slept, and we sat up, and we lay again and slumbered, and rose for the bugs were about and the bonfires stared into our eyes, or the whites that had battled here still seemed battling and breathing, shouting volleys of vengeance, some spittle, or agonising on bed, for people say, so they say, many a white Tommy lay night after night in wound-anguish, and the Boer came and cut his throat or shot him with gun and pistol while horses ran wild. Do the horses still run wild hereabouts? And sometimes too amidst us the kids kicked or the old ones snored, and this one said, I have an ache, and another,

Oh I've my mother's disease, it never stops once it starts and goes on for many a day and the people sometimes woke to go to the rock-side or the ridge-side, and others and yet others would go behind them, as it were, in fear, need or protection, and the bonfires leapt like eyes into the night—were there shadows, shadows of dead horses? The young volunteers kept guard, and suddenly one hears a cry and a shout, and an angry spit of abuse, and the other says one thing, and this one says another thing, and then Gandhi-swami himself comes over and as everybody wakes the volunteers cry: Oh, stop rising and go to sleep, the night will be over quick. And when the sleep comes and goes and everybody wakes and washes in the stream below as on a pilgrimage, and we open our bundles and baskets, and one eats one's puffed rice or bread and pickle, there's still much dark in the air—and the whisper goes here and goes there that a woman from this man went to that man in the dark of night, or a young son went to that mother of three children—and did it all behind the ridges and between the tombs of the fallen whites, horses leaping above them, and the husbands when they found whatever did happen thereabouts, would they not flay their wives like a banana trunk? But Gandhi-swami came, and he said: remember you not we go on a pilgrimage, and he that goes on pilgrimage takes a vow of *brahmacharya* and grows the beard of dedication and the men said: Yes, father, so it is, yes swami, so it be—and they all vowed then and thus never to touch woman or girl again. When morning came we were all so fresh, and we knew once that bend and that rock and the pass would come, it would suddenly take us down to where we shall rest and masticate puffed rice again—but the bend came and the rock, and another bend and many rocks again, and no pass ever arose till the sun stood high on men's heads and cool breezes came rushing at them as if in playfulness, and Gandhi-swami suddenly sat on a rock—and down below spread valley after valley of the Transvaal, gentle and kind like a well-shapen turban, and so lovely, I tell you, as if carved and clayed by God, river and hill, and rock and river again. Far off rose a smoke here and a smoke there, smokes of the white-townships, of the black locations, and somewhere thereabouts would be Charlestown too. And Charlestown that's where the pilgrims would go, and word came, the word of Smuts Sahib awaits us there. And we knew when we had bathed in the river below and eaten our puffed rice or bread and sugar again, we would rise and march and nobody would stop us till we came to the gates of Charlestown—you could almost see the curling of the railway line that suddenly went under the mountain and came out and slipped from moment to moment into the wide-curving uplands, and then on to the flat plains below—and the river shone as of mercury and we hungered for a dip and mouthwash and for the sweetness of the mountain stream to drink in. Some here and some there, many the people that had bandages on their feet—their feet were sore, and they had no song in them, but the women were gay and they did not stop singing marriage songs.

Oh Rama why have you taken so long a time to come?
Don't you see my father is preparing the winning-of-the-bride-ceremony?
And all the princes will soon be here Oh Rama

or

And the swan went and told Damayanti,
Nala indeed the name of the prince,
He the Horse-Lord,

And he is flowering as an aloe
At the thought of you, O petal-skinned one

and thus on and on, as if indeed we were going on a perennial
marriage procession. The trouble is, brother, for the woman
it always seems a marriage procession and for men journey to
death or pilgrimage to God.

One had hardly washed at the river and had eaten and
snoozed and belched than the time was for one to go down thither
to Charlestown—and often the whites passed by in carriages up
the hills and to the road beyond, and they sometimes waved
hats and handkerchiefs at us, and talked to Gandhi-swami. Soon
however messengers came from Charlestown, and everybody
knew once in Charlestown we will stay for many a day, and we
shall eat and wash and sing *bhajans* till we finally march across to
the Transvaal frontiers. The men of Smuts, so people rumoured,
were waiting for us there, with stick and gun, but others said, oh
no, it's all a washerwoman's tale—no guns and no pistols against
Gandhi-swami—and one did not know whether to think right
or to think left, everything seemed to go round and round in our
heads. As we neared Charlestown the whites were all at the door,
silent and glum a few, but smiling and open-hearted many,
many others, and one came to Gandhi-swami and shook hands
and said: Here, sir, may you stay with me—and another, a white
woman spoke and said: Here, sir, is where the woman can sleep
in my house and cook, and Gandhi-swami said: Why, sisters,
what a miracle of God for here was I be thinking to myself,
where will the kids sleep and the mothers stay? And many a
white woman took our women in and the kids, and at the edge
of town, as we all arrived, there were two whites, one man and
one woman, and they smiled at us and had garlands ready for

Gandhi-swami, and we knew we had come to friends. And the Indian merchants were behind these whites, and they said: Why you want vessels, we have vessels for you, and you want rice, and we have rice and flour and *ghee,* and all you need—and thus we camped on the swards of Charlestown, first seven hundred, then fifteen hundred and then two thousand three hundred in all, with cooks and kitchen-helpers and bread-kneading-planks, and jars of salt and jugs of sugar. Tea and coffee too we had, and we drank to our fill. And when dinner time came one was so right happy one knew the heart of Smuts would melt, and we would go back home.

Kallenbach, for that was the name of the friend, the white man, was like Hanuman to Sri Rama, big and smiling and ever ready to curl at the feet of Gandhi-swami, to fly anywhere, to any Lanka, and Schlesin, the white woman, she was in charge of the ladies of the camp, the one daily helper of Gandhi-swami, so people rumoured. But men did see armies on the other side of the frontier gates, and so Smuts was not going to let us in. Some of us had, be it said, fear big as a pumpkin within our bellies, and our heads swirled in anguish. What if the troops fire? And the police arrest us all? But Kallenbach, our Hanuman, he smiled to us as if we need have no frights, for they said he had once been a boxer and he could lay any ten-headed stalwart on the ground. And Gandhi-swami seemed all so gentle and peace-giving. He came to ask of the wounds and the stomach pains, and whether we had eaten enough—and he smiled for he knew we did not have that much to eat. But we all said, oh, yes, father. We've eaten as at a festival, and he smiled and he said: the festival, the real one, is still to come, and he was meaning the fight with the white army. And there was even a whisper the whites had said to Kallenbach, the brave, at Volksrust: We'll

shoot every coolie that comes in into our land of Transvaal, and
Kallenbach had told them: Oh wait ye, white brothers, you can
kick them and shoot them, but I know my coolies. They will
neither kick nor strike—they'll die with God in their eyes. Try
and you will see—and, you know, he had said to them too, and
you see me here. I was once a wrestler, trained by Sandow in
Germany. And Sandow, as you know, was big and great. And
I could down a man in the wink of an eye. This man Gandhi,
he is so good. He says, if I hit and you hit me back, where is
the good? I'll march to the shooting guns with him. And here
the whiteman, Kallenbach, laughed. And we smiled back. It
gladdened our being that one like him, and a white, was with
us. We had no fear now and we would face the whites—come
what might.

And then he, Kallenbach, told us all a story. Listen.

Once upon a time in olden olden times, when the world
was still young and bright-lit, there was born a Prince in India,
and he was so kind and so good never a shadow moved where he
stood, nor a cry of an injustice from a woman heard or a father
complain against a son. And every subject of the kingdom was
good, wise and true. And so he said to himself: This be not true,
this cannot be true. I must go other where to a farther spot and
situation where I could find that from which I know the virtue
of true virtue. And he said to his charioteer: Charioteer, put
my horses to yoke—and so through the clear star night did he
excursion through his kingdom while all nature slept—through
plains, foothills and mountains, and narrow passes (and here
Kallenbach showed the Drakenburg behind us)—up he came,
the king, to the top, say, of Laird's Neck. And on the other side
of the mountain ruled another king who had made all virtue his
palace; his breath was sweet, his works pure and his subjects,

even in their dreams, lived in proper morality. But he rolled and
rolled in his bed in dire anxiousness: You miserable king, said
he to himself, how could virtue be so easy and truth so simple?
There must be plains and principalities where virtue is more
ashine. And he also said to his charioteer: 'Charioteer, put my
horses to yoke.' And he too went, say, from Natal towards the
Transvaal. And on the top of the mountain, the passes were so
narrow, finally they both came to a spot where only one chariot
could pass. Now the fine problem was, who should pass whom
first, who by prerogative, by propriety, thus one charioteer asked
of the other. The two kings were in such sorrow they heard not
the dialogue of the charioteers. The night was now deep and
cold, but all nature seemed suddenly awake as if to watch this
contest of truth. 'My king,' said the Charioteer of Transvaal,
'My king is good to the good. He is true with the true. He's kind
to the weak. But with the wicked he's strong,' said he.

    And the other to him made reply:

> 'And my King
> He's good to the good.
> He's kindliness even to the weak,
> And to the wicked all compassionate is he.'

And the first to the second, unharnessing his horses, moving
the chariot to a side, said: 'And now pass, brother, my brother,
for your king is more virtued than mine,' and thus the Natal
King, so to say, entered the kingdom of Transvaal and found
his, indeed, be the virtue of high virtue. And the Transvaal King
went to Natal and found his be the virtue of ignorance. Virtue is
not born on eucalyptus trees, is it? And thus he, our Hanuman,
made us all laugh, and we laughed and we laughed so, sisters,

till the very rocks on which we sat grew hot, they burnt our backsides, and tears fell from our eyes.

All along the way, however, the whiteman's policeman had taken a pilgrim, one here, one there they had arrested him and had torn him away, and to stop our breath and dry our tears and turn our dread to laughter, we sang, and we sang hoarse:

> Why dost thou go to search for him
> In lonely forest glades?
> Forever God abideth in thee
> And yet above, beyond thee.
> As in the fragrance in the flower,
> As is the likeness in the mirror,
> So is God everywhere at all times.
> Search for him, friend, within thyself.[2]

And sister, Gandhi-swami said, and our Hanuman said, an hundred and fifty again were thus arrested, one after the other, and we prayed for their safety and their good acts withal. Then we put our heads against our bundles and stone-props, and went to deeper sleep.

* * *

With kitchen cauldrons around him, ladle in hand, Gandhi-swami stood. Straight he looked as if into the morning hills, but he looked so deep into you, deep as if he was where you were, deep in the valley, then he looked at the child in arms, and he said: O Ponnamma or O Chinnamma, there's not much gruel

---

[2] *Songs from Prison,* p. 95.

left as you know—and this is all we have, as gruel, as rice, as dal—
and we've still a long way to go, and we're almost a thousand
in all, and Ponnamma and Chinnamma just smiled back, for
sometimes there was anger in us, we thought of the children in
our arms. What should one do when they cry and cry again? But
we remembered Shankaramma who had that look on her face,
she cried not nor did she smile any more: she looked at water
and thought it water, and she looked at you and she thought it
was a woman, a man and thus from cow or cart, she just looked,
and we who've borne babies we know what that is; her heart
knew no tears but her belly did. You see, while she was crossing
a spruit, her child slipped from her hands and fell into the water,
and men sprang behind the child and the women raised up a
cry, but the spruit was deep and before one knew where one was,
there was the child pulled out, and she was dead. Yes, her tubby
face stared at us, and she had been playing with our children but
yesterday. Yet we knew when death comes, it just comes. It does
not ask for your name or age. And Shankaramma and her man,
they buried the baby in the sands, picked some wild grass from
the shrubs around and putting stone after stone covered it all
up with the child's clothes. Then she rose and as if she were in
front of Goddess Satyammal at Sattannur, she tore her marriage
necklace, yes, she did, laid it on the baby's jacket and pants, and
without a cry, spoke: O Goddess, if this be life, let life not be.
Her eyes were red and she never spoke a word after that. Such
our Shankaramma.

And there was again that another young woman, with
mango-cheeks and a beguiling smile. And we never liked her
for she seemed so all-assuming. And we never looked at her.
But when death came to her child—he shivered and spoke in
his fevers, and they'd tied many a talisman to his arm but he

died in his shivers, and it happens like this, people said, when children and men have these ancient kickings, and they bite their tongue, and their eyes stick to their sockets—and they go. And being still in the mountains they laid him under the rocks, and Gandhi-swami himself stood and said a prayer to him in solemn Sanskrit, and then we all walked down, knowing twist behind twist, we knew our lives were entwined like the betel-creeper to the areca nut palm, we were going to no town or place but to some new kingdom, to Sri Rama's bright state in which parrots spoke wisdom from windows and men talked but of truth, and gold shone on palace gates and happiness poured like rain upon us. Yes, we were going to the Kingdom of Sri Rama, come brother, come sister, and that was when we saw Kallenbach the white, and we named him Hanuman.

And later he too stood beside Gandhi-swami dispensing the ladles, giving the child a little pinch here and a smile there, and we knew if he had a treasury full of gold and diamonds he would give it to all of us, to every one of us. And people said this indeed is the truth, for he had said to everyone: Come to me and to the Tolstoy Farm and we'll build you a home with a verandah, a well at the back, a *tulasi* plant podium in the backyard, and the house beaming with nine round pillars. He's like a man of gold, we said, and when we knew not what to say to Gandhi-swami, we'd go to our Hanuman, and strange to say, sisters, he understood did he our sweet Tamil speech. And Gandhi-swami too spoke our Tamil and we all felt in Ayodhya and King Rama that sat on the Throne of Dharma was very happy. But he gave away his kingdom for the truth, and Sita Devi was imprisoned by Ravana and she wept year after year under the Ashoka tree, thinking on her Lord. Yes, our Sita Devi was in prison, so it was rumoured. We had never seen her but people said Kasturba was

her name, and Ba people called her. And one here and there
and these volunteers from Gujarat called Gandhi-swami, Bapu,
which in their tongue means Father, and as our Hanuman too
called him Bapu, we also shyly said Bapu, as though we spoke his
speech, and he gently gave us a broad smile, his mouth touching
his ears. Such, sisters, our Bapu, who seemed to dispense gold
and goodness around one, and we were so happy singing and
sleeping, eating and walking, we wanted the pilgrimage to never,
never end. And why should it? Has not the saint said:

From where have you come and what do you do, son?
Like towns our bodies change
Like rivers our breath flows
Like rain our tears drop
Like forest fire our body's burnt—
We go brother from sanctuary to sanctuary
In one pilgrimage.
Shiva, Shiva, the wild bear does not frighten us
Nor the big elephant deafen us with his roar;
The tiger cubs play in the foreground
While the milkman takes his rounds around
Sri Rama dispenses justice for His heart is Grace.

Meanwhile others and yet others came down the mountains
to Charlestown from Dundee (with Naidoo, the good Naidoo)
and Newcastle (with Mathur) and they said the indentured
labourers further down in the plantations too, near Ingogo, have
struck work and will face the police if need be. And people said,
and hill top after hill top there looked like roving animals—
bison, nilgai, panther, porcupine, elk, monkey, the great tiger
himself—army after army which the forest fire has driven

towards the river—men behind men and women, bundles
and babies on their heads and shoulders and children between
them, they were marching towards Charlestown, and some said
twenty thousand, and another a thirty thousand, and we then
heard a hundred thousand in all had left the estates and would
walk behind Bapu. Yes, Bapu, we'll walk behind you. And take
us where you will, and you'll free Sita Devi who now sits in
Volksrust prison, and we'll come back all of us to Ayodhya, and
you will fly with Hanuman behind you, in a chariot of all noble
flowers. Sister, brother, you think we're singing a song. No,
that's how we were in Charlestown, awaiting the burning of the
city of Lanka, and the gracious Sita Devi be freed for us. You
remember that song:

Sita Devi sat under the Ashoka tree
And Ravana would not know what to make.
For when he thought of her he thought of Sri Rama
And he that thinketh on Sri Rama,
He be ever a devotee,
Then how touch Sita Devi, tell me, sister?
But She, She weeps under the tree.

And Smuts like Ravana sat in Pretoria. Gandhi-swami, I
mean Bapu, sent wire after wire to Smuts, so the men said. Bapu
said: I have no hatred against you, Ravana. I know you grew
ten heads because you're a devotee of Shiva, of Truth, and that
you wanted a quick end to the cycle of birth and death, and
death and birth again, and thus Shiva gave you the blessing:
Be born a monster and I'll be born in Ayodhya to Dasaratha,
the pure, and I'll kill you myself. Such the joy of Ravana.
Shiva himself would give him liberation. I ask of you, who else

would give us liberation if it be not Shiva? And Bapu always told us, in every speech he made: Brother, sister, you think we are fighting against the dog-collar tax or that the Hindu and Muslim law be reckoned with for our marriages. But I tell you, I want Truth. I want Swaraj, that is the freedom that comes of Truth. India will be free only when we seek that. Freedom that comes from Truth. That's my India. The dog-collar tax and the marriage laws against which we fight are like Kaikeyi's demands on Dasaratha. Send Rama to exile and make Bharata king. For Dasaratha had made a promise in his past life, as the Viceroy had made a promise to the government of Natal: Yes, yes, we shall send indentured labourers to you. Dasaratha had made a promise to his very wife, and he kept to it. And Sri Rama kept his father's words. The Viceroy has kept his words with Smuts. And Bharata ruled in the name of Sri Rama the city of Ayodhya, the sandals of the elder brother on the throne. Such the glory of Sri Rama.

Like Bharata, I tell you, was another white, and Polak his name. And he looked after us when Bapu was no more amidst us. However that was long, long later. But let me come back to Charlestown and to Ravana who would not understand this army of Sri Rama, of monkeys and squirrels, of the boar and of birds, and Sri Rama will take your kingdom, you know, ten-headed Ravana, thus our folk spoke and breathed and walked. Shall we conquer Lanka, Bapu? Wait, he said, let these tingling wires bring me back a message. I've told him, Smuts Sahib, remove our dog-collar tax and we'll stop from entering into the kingdom of Transvaal. And we want to come to you, Ravana Smuts, not to settle amidst you and become one of you. No, we come to beg of you, Lord of the Four Kingdoms, Lord of the Cape Province and of Natal and of Transvaal, the Orange

State, Lord, free us from this our slavery. We may be brown, but we believe in Shiva, the Lord, with Ganges in His hair, He who wedded Parvati, daughter of the Himalayas. Smuts Lord, give us back our freedom, for we know you too are a worshipper of Shiva, of Truth, and we will go back to the mines and the plantations and never shall you hear a cry from us again.

Gandhi-swami, or rather Bapu, waited and waited long, but no answer came. Then said he one day: Wait here, all of you. Before we enter the Kingdom of Transvaal I will telephone to Smuts Sahib once more. And he said to Smuts' minion this time: Tell your Lord and King, we will enter Transvaal now. But before we enter we want your Lord and King to tell us if he will not remove the £3 tax. If not our peace-army will invade your kingdom. And then they say the Whites in Volksrust have pistols and guns ready to shoot us. If true, and if we die, you, Smuts Sahib, you will be cause and curse of it all. Remember we have no violence in us, and no hate. We pray for your soul. Be good Smuts Sahib, and do not bring ill-omens to your crown.

The telephone rang. And Ravana's minions said: Do what you care and I'll do what I have to perform.

Say, brother, 'Rama, Rama, Sita's Rama'
Beloved of Janaki
Victorious, O Victorious Rama.

And so the pilgrim army was all ready now. We prayed all night, then we bathed and prayed again, and when Gandhi-swami said, 'Come'—we all marched behind him: 2,037 men were there and 127 women and 57 children, and like in the story when the sage counted his disciples before they crossed the river, we were all counted, and with the name of Sri Rama on our lips and Sri Rama before us we would march thus into the kingdom of Ravana.

Ram Ram, Sita Ram
Janaki, Vallabha
Jaya Jaya Ram.

And, sister, Charlestown had become such a sanctuary-yard and inn for us, it was all sorrow leaving the town, and the whites looked behind the doors and some waved at us too, again and again, some threw biscuits and peppermints to us, and a few of us plucked flowers from our hair and threw these back at them, the friendly whites, and then, at the right final moment that came, the good doctor Briscoe arrived too—good doctor Briscoe, so they told us, who was so a feared of our poxes and our fevers, he came and asked this of us, and held his machine to our hearts and to our backs and gave us powders and lotions, and for our children he gave us cough-powders and eye-fluids so that the sun might not hurt them, and he gave to Bapu a big box filled with pills and trichurations for snake bites and pneumonia and bandages many and many and as we marched on, some of the whites stopped their horses and the carriages stood as we passed by; and some waved their whips at us, yet others stood dumb-eyed and we knew not which way to turn, for these seemed so right compassionate. And Bapu went through the main street and the square, and we were moving towards the spruit that, so they said, was where the white army was waiting to stop us, and Smuts stood somewhere far behind.

Ravana, he Ravana, we said to ourselves, know you not, the more you fight with Rama the more you will twist your bowels in pain, for you know he's in your heart, and he it is that makes you go where you go, and makes you stop where you stop, for just the tail of our Hanuman could twist your trunk of a body like a mere twig and throw it into the high-up air for he, remember, has been trained by Sandow himself of Germany— so we spoke to one another. But I tell you in our hearts we had such blocked fear we would rather run back, back to Newcastle or to Dundee, and never more go on such an itinerary. Lord, what's all this of, and to what end Lord, my Lord? No answer came as our hearts beat fast for there far away we could see the mounted men in uniform, black horses and bright shining swords and heavy big boots: Yes they'll beat us and shoot us and our children will they kill. Shiva, Shiva, what's there to be done? Once you start on a pilgrimage you never go back, do you? Bapu is with us. That is true. That is the only truth. Maybe like in some *Ramayana*, Ravana's shots will turn flowers as they fall on us. Take the name of Rama, Rama, Sri Rama, Bapu has told us, and it has the power that no gun has, and we knotted our fears in our sari-fringes, tied our bodices tighter, hid our children's eyes from gun ghost or man, and we twisted, and came suddenly to the spruit.

Bapu, staff in hand like a Shankaracharya, clear in his eyes and spotless in forehead, as if in trembling prayer said: Stay a while here brothers and sisters, let me go across the spruit and parley with the policeman. And I tell you, sister, it was a dire moment, our hearts cried in fear if they'd shoot him, our father, our saint, and what might happen then. But from the vast sky some great large god seemed to speak, and Kallenbach was with us, and his being there gave us breath and firmness of foot. And we stayed.

Across the spruit that was like the very bridge that the monkeys and the squirrels built to Lanka was the Kingdom

of Transvaal—hills behind hills with roads that twisted and
went up like running children into the skies and roundabout
into the valleys and rose again while the sun just rising gave
us the clarity of individual trees. The holy mimosa was yellow
in flower and all about the spruit were lilies and down below
ran the stream—a thin soundless stream as if where kingdoms
frontiers meet fear makes them creep and slip into mother
earth, leaving the pebbles dry. The police horses too seemed to
champ and kick and wave their tails in restlessnesses. There was
a curve of a high long silence in the air, and we shuddered and
closed our eyes. Fear, sister, brings man back to himself. We
shuddered and some had tears in their eyes as Bapu stood before
the commandant of the horse-police, and we wondered what
next. Perspiration trickled down our cheeks and foreheads, and
even the children did not as much as whimper. Then suddenly
someone cried, Hé Ram, and rushed across the spruit, and we all
rushed behind him like maddened elephants and we rushed to
the left among thorns and briars, and to the right to rocks and
boulders, and 'Hé Ram' came back the cry across the valley and
Hé Ram, Hé Ram, we shouted back giving courage to ourselves
and we felt the horses would run and trample on us or the guns
would shoot, and blind and helpless we ran behind the men,
children in our arms, and bundles and baskets on our heads, old
men, young women, and the males, strong and fiery before us,
and Hé Ram, *Ramachandra Maharaj ki jai*—we said and ran up
the bank of the spruit, and I tell you, the world seemed broad
and bright and every sound was like horse-breath, and children
cried but we did not care, we muffled them with our hands,
and pressed them against our breasts and now we go forward—
forward, we've entered the kingdom of Ravana, and we'll see
what the Smuts will say unto us. The police were behind us, and

Bapu still talking to them and the man who'd said Hé Ram and had rushed over the spruit, he marched on—Hé Ram, he cried again and we broke into a *bhajan*:

> I chant only the name of Rama
> It's the joy of flame,

and singing we marched into the new world, and the world seemed all fresh and of goodly shape—the hills seemed kind, the trees shady and broad and to tell you the truth, in the kingdom of Ravana the world seemed altogether noble. Was it this way, we wondered, for every stone and bush looked so eye-full—they seemed awake as if to a new make of man. For remember, sister, when love enters the world, even the tree and the sky shine it, and we walk on grass where only briars break. And now the horses galloped in front of us, going around us as if indeed we were a king's procession, and a king was walking forward to receive us. Was Smuts Sahib there, and was he awaiting with fruit and gold coin to receive Bapu? Was it Lord, the Dussehra festival? Where then, Lord, the Royal Elephant, the camels with drums and pipe, the prancing white steeds? Shall we then procession to the Banyan tree and the Maharaja be received by the populace? The music will strike at any moment—look, look, the Maharaja is on the *howdah*, and flowers fall on him, from the windows and welcoming-platforms. Bapu is our king, and he will go to meet Smuts at the Royal Banyan Tree. And because of it all, out on the arc of the earth, there was such a beat of strictest silence. Only the birds cawed.

And now as the police neither barred us nor kicked us, for they were so few of them, and holding to our marriage beads and breath, we rushed through briar and gulley towards the

Volksrust road, and I tell you even the children did not seem full afeared—and when we'd come to the road, such the freedom of breath and speech, we began to laugh and sing and somebody sang again:

And there's only one naming of the name,
And that be Sri Rama's

And we sang it all together:

And there's only one naming of the name,
And that be Sri Rama's,

and as we neared Volksrust-town our men became dire silent for suddenly one remembered the guns and the pistols, but no man ever came before us, and those that rode past us seemed intent on their noses or on their horse's manes. Meanwhile the white women, some of them, opened their doors and smiled and we smiled back, and a few even threw chocolates at us and we threw our flowers back at them, and when we stopped a while at the village-end (and the shops and the offices were still unopened, for it was so early of day) we camped briefly on the sward beyond the village and soon, very soon, Bapu joined us, and sister, when we saw him it was like when the chariot of the gods is ready, and the God seated in the chariot, and the pilgrims at the rope, at Thirukavallur temple, and suddenly there he comes, the sacred eagle from the nowhere of sky—does he be coming from Vishnu's own home?—and we say: Krishna, Krishna, and he circles once, twice, and thrice over the chariot, and we say: Hé Krishna, Hé Rama, and we pull the chariot and the chariot at last shakes and moves straight towards the temple—thus our move now, for we stood up, and Bapu walked in front of us and we walked behind him, and he seemed lost in thought. But our Hanuman, Kallenbach, had stayed behind—had he gone back to the whites of Volksrust? Had the police stopped him—no, he was a white. Then it was someone said here and someone said there: Oh, he's gone back to receive the new pilgrims, for more and more were going up the passes from Newcastle and coming down to Charlestown, hundreds and hundreds of them, each army led by P.K. Naidoo or Beharilal Maharaj, Ramnarayan, Raghu Narsu or Rahim Khan, and someone had to receive them and give them bread to eat and sugar and jam, maybe, and we felt sad too that he, our Hanuman, not be with us. To tell you the truth, sister, even Bapu felt as if he'd forgotten his younger-brother at home, for he looked back, quick and deep often and often and there was nothing but the empty morning road that now went through the high grasslands through the village and back again up the hills to the passes on which clouds sat as a baby-bun on a child's head. There's play, sister, between mountain and cloud, between river and road, between bird and flower, as if there's a text written of them and God speaks to us if we could listen between the silences of heart. Krishna, Sri Krishna, is always playing somewhere, and as the song goes:

> When the nostrils are full
> and the sacred breath wafts,
> We know it's he playing,
> He's playing hide and seek with Yasodhra.

Why is it, we sometimes wondered as we walked, such thoughts never do visit us when we're before our kitchen blow-pipes or cleaning the backyard of dung or banana leaf—why is it God does not speak to us when our child cries, or when the nine months are over and we await the day—the day looks so long, long? And one of us said to the other—for it's not always a pilgrimage, sister, and that's why we cry and we fight, and we tear each other's hair if we could, and some even slip out and sleep with other men when our men are out sometimes, for the body begs for a big blurt of juice. And when our men come back from the mines, how sad the world seems as if the earth had eaten itself out and of it only dung-beetles came—a procession of them, and we would tie knots in our bodices, and vow to Mother Durgamma or Badakamma: 'Goddess we shall be true to the man,' and we cook, and let the child go to sleep, and when the night has gone deep, we slip into our husband's beds, and holy seems the nuptial. All, Lord, all is the play. But make us pure, make us Bapu's men and women, make us the crown of Truth.

> Let the murderer be pure,
> The thief simple,
> The prostitute turn a pumpkin
> And vowed to God at temple festival.
> Such thoughts I tell you only come when Bapu is in front of us.

The grasslands wave with fresh breezes, as though they too were enjoying our company, and we walk and we thirst, we drink and we slip behind stones to lay our excreta, we stand behind trees and sit that the kidney give us no further woe, and some that are seven months pregnant that say: sister, look here, here I have the pain, and another says to her, I am a midwife and don't you fear, and be afraid, for what would the whites do, a woman rolling on the earth and thrusting a child out of her womb—and nothing indeed did happen to us that day. But no sooner we came to Palmsford and we all stretched out to munch our bread and sugar—'one-and-a-half pounds of bread and an ounce of sugar'—it ran in our minds like a mantra—and we made little holes in the bread and poured the sugar in, while others sang *bhajans* and the young men went from one edge to the other asking: Sister, brother, did you have your ration, did you?—and tired and rich, we lay our heads against our bundles, the kids pressed against their mothers, sleep came to us as on the top of the chariot festival night and all the dreams were full of torches and of wheeling birds, and of pipe music and in dream we bore silver bodikins and walked by God's palanquins. We could almost feel the waving of the white-yak whisks and Hanuman stand behind the Lord, the guardian of the city gates. He loves us, does Hanuman, in the name of Sri Rama.

O, where, O where are you, O Father Hanuman,
For wheresoever I see be your curve of fame.

But now one here and one there, we saw a strange sight, brother, that night. A lantern came dangling across the swards from far, far, as though it were the taluk-collector's cart coming, or some night-cremation that the brahmins were preparing and the logs would go towards the river and the fire-wood piles one over the other, thus the lantern that moved. It went this way and that and some of us woke from our sleep and walked towards it. The more it shone the nearer it went to Bapu's rock. He'd left the tired women and the ailing men at Volksrust, so this would be no doctoring. But when we came nearer we saw a white man, and another white man behind this white man, and they were policemen no doubt. They smiled to us and we smiled to them.

And we followed them. Bapu knew. He stood up with the smile of a brother and said in English something, and they showed him a paper and said something other to him. He smiled and turned to his Hanuman; this new Hanuman whose name was Naidoo, and Bapu said in Tamil, and that we could all understand: The marriage *muhurtham*[3] is come and you should now take care of the procession. Tell no one where I be gone unless someone asks, and questions and says: Tell me true where is Bapu gone?—And you say, he's gone to his father-in-law. He rode away during the night on his white steed.—And Bapu smiled.—Only when the day is high up and you rest for your breakfast and you give away your rations, then may you give them the news; the police came to arrest Bapu, and he went away smiling with them.—You must always smile whenever the police arrest you. And tell the pilgrims their *yatra-sthala*[4] is called the Tolstoy Farm, and that is another eight days journey. At every stop of day or night the train will deliver you the bread rations. The Volksrust baker has promised us that, though he is white. You know how good the whites have been. God is with us. If you, young Hanuman, if you be arrested, then appoint another Hanuman to take your spot. Understand. And thus on till you reach the holy city of Johannesburg and the beloved Tolstoy Farm. And that my friend be our Ayodhya.

Taking a book or two and his sheer bundle of clothes, Bapu asked us to walk in peace and joy, while the whiteman took him away. We neither cried nor did we sputter our tongues in anger. We felt he was going home. For once had he said to us: And prison is my home now.

---

[3]   The auspicious moment, according to astrological calculations, for any religious ceremony.

[4]   The end of their pilgrimage.

Remember where Krishna was born. He was born in Kamsa's prison cell—What is good for Him, brothers and sisters, must at least be good for us!

And now silence and sleep swept over the sward of Palmsford and except for a quail here and there, and the sharp cry of a coughing child, we went into a united sleep.

And the next day, when the day was round again, and we lay among the veld grasses for our morning bread—and the young who served were so courteous, so quick,—no, no one amongst the people heard or asked what happened to Bapu. Then all of a sudden someone asked us here and someone questioned them there, the word went from mouth to mouth, and then came back in diligent answer: Ravana's henchmen have taken him away, to prison, and it was as if a mountain had suddenly risen before one and one was breathless, and one knew not how to go up. But Naidoo, our new Hanuman, was sharp in limb as quick in intellect, and he went running towards them, and gathered them all, and spoke and said: The Saint, our Bapu has been taken to prison by the whites. He said before he left: Everyman who's a satyagrahi is his own general. So be not of fear. Nothing will happen to you. If we reach the Tolstoy Farm that would be great, beautiful. I hope however— he went on to say—women won't go on having babies on the way.—And we all laughed. And one woman said: Perhaps the one within us too wants to see the big procession. And Naidoo said in reply: That day will come too, sister. Ravana is not going to give us freedom with garland and gold plate in a day, would he? And so laughing and joking, we started again, but the women suddenly sang such long keens as if it would bring Bapu back.

He rode his white horse (they sang)
And he turned round and said he was coming,

His aura fell from his neck, a scarf,
His horse's mane held up like flame,
But we asked him, when brother,
For the cut of blood is on our forehead—[5]
And he said, when the star *margashira* is in
The seventh house of moon.
And so he'll come, sister,
And so he will, he will.

Thus they sang, but our thoughts were not too bright. We felt it was like a house without a sanctuary corner, a courtyard with no *tulasi* podium, a hall with no pillars. An empty granary invites no mice, and the widow never has bangles.

But when we'd rested and spat, and had risen and walked, and been given rations and we were munching our food there it came, a car, a sputtering plug-ploughing car, and the nearer it came the more afeared were we, for we thought it was a white who'd suddenly remembered his gun and his pistol or the police back to take away our Naidoo—but no, there was a white in the car, and that was Kallenbach, and there was another with this Hanuman, and that was Sri Rama himself. Yes! Bapu had returned! I tell you, he looked brighter than he did yesterday. And he gathered us and told us how sad, sad, he was to have left us. But he had to go because Smuts' policemen came to take him. And they took him to the courthouse.—And in the courthouse of Volksrust, Smuts' lawyer said he would not let me go. And I said to them, the law says this and this. And since I have done no murder, you understand—and we all laughed—

---

[5]   When the brothers and husbands went to war, they cut their fingers a little
      and put the blood as *kumkum* on the forehead of their women.

and since I have such a big family of children, and I am taking them on pilgrimage, let me go, and I promise you I will return. A man of truth always comes back.—And the judge said that my law was the right law, and I left fifty pounds with the judge in security, and our friend Kallenbach had this chariot-of-oil ready for me, and here I am back at the festival. 'Say *Ramachandraji ki jai*. Say Victory to Sri Rama,' shouted someone and we shouted unanimously, *Ramachandra ki jai*. And with the blue of sky under our shut eyes, when we rested our heads on bundle or stone, it seemed as if the procession was soon reaching the hill top, and the big temple with the eagle tower, the sacrificial slab, and the hanging hundred-lamps of the sanctuary, would all be there. So that sleep came that night as never it had before. One woman gave birth to a baby too, and the child was washed and his placenta cord cut, and his belly bundled into a flat belt, and since it was a boy someone said call him Satya, the truth, for he was born on this march, and the mother and child, Kallenbach housed them in an Indian house nearby, and they would be sent to the Tolstoy Farm when the ten-day-time be gone, and it was all as if something auspicious had happened to us. One more man had joined our army of God.

And now, said Bapu, and now we're off to Standerton, and I tell you, Standerton seemed an implausible place. Standerton and Standerton, we said to one another, while the women wailed some song or the other, and the men smoked and gossiped and walked, bundle on head, or bag in arm, with shoe or slipper, pantaloon or *dhoti* or knickers, turban, cap or coat, some with glasses and some with God-given eyes, some that limped and were bandaged, and some that seemed rushing to the afternoon market, the heifer before them that they'd not sell but argue and spit and be silent, and again argue one price up and half a price down till the looks spoke, and they said. 'And now for eighty rupees, the heifer is mine,' and the heifer is his—and before the sun be set we buy ropes for our carts or oil for the wheels or a trinket for the daughter-in-law, for she be seven months gone in child-carrying, and she needs the worships to be made—and thus on returning home there's silence in the house, and only the wall-lizards cluck or the river sounds rise from the Mari-temple corner, as she purrs through the sluices. God made humans for marriage and baby-carrying, for the plough to be yoked to the bulls, and the wife sow paddy behind you as you push the blade into the earth—man never was made to be out of home and God. And here in the darks of Africa there's a fright in our limbs for we cannot know where God is. Bapu before us is all we ken of, and we know he'll not make the child eat grass or the woman sell herself for a ladle of gruel. There was, I tell you, much sorrow in the pure air again.

But at Standerton the good Indian merchants gave us a thousand tins of marmalade, so someone said, and the volunteers boiled a broth of tea and we were so gay, and we smiled, and Bapu came and said: Remember this is no common day, and you will not have tea always, and we said, God will give tea to us when we need, but he, Bapu smiled and said: God will give us better condiments than tea—he could with a stroke remove the dog-collar from our necks, and we all were awed. Yes, it's for that were we on pilgrimage, and we'd forgotten the vow. Such is man, brother. He's like a village pond that shows cloud or bright sky to your face when you dip your pot in and you wonder and say how can this pond go on reflecting sky and cloud, and cloud and sky again. And then if I look in and see my face and run home, the water spirits would curse me. For evening water is good or bad according to the position of stars. Was this evening water good or was it bad, brother? How would I know? Tell me.

We had no time to think it all when they were already there, Yama's henchmen with their nooses, and he would take away our Bapu again. To tell you the truth, we were so happy with marmalade and tea and felt all was well again when the whiteman's magistrate came and stood by Bapu, for we all saw it. And they took him away quick as a corpse, but Bapu had told us, go on, go on, on this road and on, and after twist and rise and rise and twist again, you'll come one morning to the Tolstoy Farm. But such Bapu's wits, we'd hardly spat and shat and laid ourselves down, and had risen and started again on our march singing, singing loud across the vast spacious verberant grasslands, for they had no evil with us and we had no evil with them—did we?—then suddenly a cart came behind us rushing and we look, and we see Bapu in it, and with some Indian merchants as well. And up went our hearts with joy and we shouted, *Ramachandra Maharaj ki jai, Bolo Ramachandra Maharaj ki jai,* and it was sweet to shout it again. But he told us, his many Hanumans had been arrested too, Naidoo and Behari Maharaj, Ramanarayan Sinha and Raghu Narsu and Rahim Khan. And they would not be let out. Yet Bapu smiled and said: And this time, brothers and sisters, we'll perhaps reach the Tolstoy Farm in peace. The government wants no war with us, and we're only pilgrims. Holy our hearts seemed again, and we felt the round look of pilgrims on our faces. Why is it god seems to sit on our foreheads only when the pilgrimage be right remembered?

That night as we were fed again, and we would be going to our slumber, Bapu talked to us and said: Now brothers and sisters, Johannesburg will soon come. Only four days remain—

we've come four stages of our God's march and four more stages there be still to do. Smuts and Botha sit on their high seats, and are watching us. Let us never forget anything might happen to me, to you. If you'd thrown a stone at the white man that came to arrest me or spat at the policeman at the Volksrust spruit, I tell you, bullets would have poured on us. But Smuts knows, and so do you, that death does not have fear for us. Truth knows no death. And if you're already dead, how can they kill you again? You don't kill a dead mouse. Do you? The cat only runs after a live mouse. But if the mouse were to say, eat me, brother cat, what would the cat do? He may try to eat you once, twice, or thrice, and at the fourth trial he would say, nay, nay, this be not God's law. And he would run towards the kitchen for butter or milk, will he not? So it would be if the lamb said to the lion: May I live with you, do you think the noble lion will fall upon a poor lamb? Suppose people who hunt lions suddenly find the lion that says: Kill me, brother, kill me if you will, and be happy in whatever you do. Do you then think the lion will be killed, no. No one kills a kind lion. Such God's ways.

Now, brothers and sisters, let me tell you about God. And what Bapu told us of God. For when I say God, said our Bapu, remember it is not an idol in a temple, though the idol in a temple be also the shadow of God. The idol tells you I am not God, but if you think deeply of me, then will you go to God, and then there will be neither temple nor gong. God is not anywhere outside of you. He is your *Atman,* your being, your soul. For this, as the *Gita* says, and as the *Koran* says, and as the Christian Bible says, there is no death. How can soul have death? How can day know night? And finally what is it you and I want? We don't want money. That comes and that goes. We don't want palaces and palanquins, for kingdoms have come and gone, and great cities like Hastinapur are now in ruins. Men die and they are burnt and they are born again. This world of *samsara*, of birth and death and birth again, what sorrow be it that it goes on and on like a well's pulley. The water is pulled, it creaks hard. The water is emptied, and the bucket goes down, it slips quick. But for the pulley itself there is no water. It rotates and rotates and that is all its life. Suppose all were water, and there was nothing but water—that is God. And you need no pulley to bring that water up. And that water our ancestors have called Brahman—the Truth. So we, today, going to the Tolstoy Farm, are satyagrahis—marchers to the City of Truth. March, march on, for there's nothing you will lose. All is yours because Truth is yours.

And we sat down and we sang that *bhajan* again:

The Road to the City of Love is hard, brother,
Is hard,
Take care, take goodly care, as you walk along it.

Such has been our pilgrimage, my brother, my sister. Were we not going to Sri Rama's coronation? The city of Ayodhya is all lit with brilliant arches of banana leaves, and mango-twigs, coconuts hang from bamboo poles, and Sri Rama's name be drawn in ochre before every courtyard and the five-wicked lamp lit in the mid middle of rice-powder mandalas. Rama, Sri Rama, Lord of the Raghu Race. Your feet our safety, your compassion our warmth, Your presence our breath. We breathe because Sri Rama of Ayodhya is.

Rama is going to be crowned. Can you not feel it in the air? And as if to announce the coronation, Brother Polak himself comes to announce all is ready for the festival. But it will not be this way. Kaikeyi's promise to another life has to be kept. Smuts' promises to the Natal Government have to be kept. No, Smuts will not let us go to Tolstoy Farm, for he knows we have no hatred in our hearts, and his God is our God.

But, brother, Bapu had not known the stars of Smuts right. He must have a Saturn and Mercury facing each other somewhere. If not why would he, I ask of you, send another white man, and a big, big official, Mr. Chamney, and this one came in a Cape-cart and he said: 'I arrest you.' And we all saw this and heard this.

'And what about our pilgrims?'

'We shall see to that,' said the big officer.

And Bapu turned to Polak, as to Brother Bharata, and said: And now you be in charge of the pilgrimage—and then did Bapu turn to us and say in Tamil, in Hindi. Be ye peaceful, my brothers, my sisters, for I go now where Smuts takes me. And the bold officer said to Bapu: You cannot talk, you are under arrest—and Bapu smiling said,—And the officer says I may not talk,—and the officer and the carriage pulled quickly away and so fast it went, we had hunger in our hearts, for where be they taking him to, where, O where, Brother Polak? And this time we had so much sorrow in our eyes, no tears would come. But the women unable to bear it all sang:

And when they led him to the forest edge
He turned, did Sri Rama, with Lakshmana his brother
And mother Sita,
And said: City may you be happy.
But the fishermen and the potters cried:
Lord, Lord, stay, for how will the fishes swim now or the
     pot turn?

And Sri Rama said: Truth feeds the fish and turns the pot.
The road of Truth is long brother,
Is very long,
But fresh winds blow.

Then, suddenly, we held our bellies, and we sobbed. And
Brother Polak said, like Bharata, where can they take him away
when all is His play? And now we marched behind Brother
Polak. Be it the Lord's play always, I ask you? Is this it then?

Bapu being taken away was like a slab of sun fallen or a
mountain hollowed, nothing grew and nothing sang, and there
was neither shine nor rain nor sound nor silence except the soft-
touch steps of the pilgrims and the cracked whine of a child here
or there, or a cur that had slipped itself amidst us on our roads
that gave a moon-cry to the day, for there was so much misery
you might have heard jackals moan or vultures grunt—yet there
was peace in our hearts, Bharata walked in front of us, and
wheresoever he took us, Sri Rama would be. And when we came
to Greylingstad, and Kachhalia Seth from Johannesburg met us,
it was as if the whole of Bapu's family was there too, and we
thought we'd have no fears for all the revolving time to come.

Whispers went from here to there among the learned
volunteers, they seemed very grim, and would not say anything.
'Eat well and sleep,' is all they said, and there was a dull pain in
our hearts. We knew all would not be well by morning, but soon
we hoped we would be at the sanctuary, and Bharata looking
after us, we should all settle into our huts and hearths and we
would wait till Ravana come down his fortress and give battle to
Sri Rama himself. But the dawn came too soon at Greylingstad,
and we rose and we washed, we marched again and we rested
amidst the rocks and shrubs, and we munched our sugar and

bread, when suddenly from afar like monster-hosts of Ravana, they appeared from afar, and they were bunches and bunches of them, and as we came nearer the nearer came they, and before we could come too near, Bharata stopped us, and went forward and parleyed with the soldiers, and they said something to him and he said something to them that the winds did not carry, but soon we knew, we would not go straight along the pilgrim road, but left and into Balfour town. Why, why, we asked and people whispered. Well, we may all become guests of Ravana— who knows and they gave a wry, dry laugh. And we understood not and as we passed by the town, the padres still came to greet us and smile to us, and some even threw cakes and flowers from the churches at us, and we sent the flowers back, and a white here and white there smiled at us, but many that seemed sullen, and strong, and evil-looking. But nothing came to be. Through shop-laden streets and white, high houses we were huddled into the railway station yard and one train stood and two and three, and we asked of the volunteers. Brothers, my brothers, what may this be?—but they would neither look nor answer and our heart beat so big, big, some of us looked from door to gate and from gate to door, and we said to our women: Something is amiss here, and we may not be safe—but the white soldiers guarded the doors now and the women began a song of lament; they sang thus:

> When the night was dark and the blue god was born,
> Kamsa sat in his seat of satisfaction
> And counted every child-cry of the night.
> For he that would down him,
> He be born too that night
> Under the Rohini Star,
> And fear ran through the street like hyena.

As if this would drive the trains away—thus we sang.

Then came a white officer—Chamney again was his name—they said, the same who had come to take Bapu away at Standerton, and this Chamney said: Get into the train, and it was translated into us by Kachhalia Seth or by a volunteer, while Bharata stood amidst the whites talking away. And we said, nay, nay, our Bapu is not here to tell us—and we were bent on the sanctuary near Johannesburg, the Tolstoy Farm, and we will walk and we will fight if need be, and we will get there. But an elder volunteer stood up and said: Bapu has told you to follow the leader whoever that may be, and be non-violent. You remember in the *Ramayana* too it is thus spoke: Follow Bharata, said Sri Rama, for he rules in my name, and by now Brother Polak himself came to us, and he spoke and said: Remember you are satyagrahis. You will never harm anyone. You will obey the truth. Bapu told you to obey your leader. We understood not his speech, but a volunteer told us what was said and Brother Polak nodded and nodded away as though he understood Tamil and Hindusthani and this was indeed what was told but, I tell you, the women would not let the men in. The women sat at the train doors and said: Until Bapu comes we shall not go.—And others, the men that were already in the train, they jumped over the women and came out on the platform and cried: Brothers, we will not go, and all the men then shouted, *Sri Ramachandra ki jai*, and the whiteman must have thought we were going to run, for he held his gun tighter, but such the noble heart of God, brother, neither the gun was shot nor did we run, for Kachhalia Seth and Polak Brother, they both stood up on a table and made more speeches. The children cried and the women were all a-chatter. But soon silence came, and Brother Bharata said: Obey Bapu. He said never to resist the police. And with hunger roaming our bellies, our turbans twisted in hand, the women wiping their tears, we entered the long awaiting trains. One after the other she whistled, did the wretch, and the guard gave a signal and in the first train travelled Brother Bharata himself. Where were we going, my brother, my sister? Were we going to the City of Lanka?

No, for at Volksrust station the police hurriedly came and took away Brother Polak, and as if to submerge our sorrow, the train whistled and entered tunnels and it was all dark, stomach-heaving, distressful, and suddenly we emerged on the other side of the mountain wherefrom through twists and roads that we could overlook, and that we'd walked but yesterday, we came down quickly and hungrily (for they gave us neither food nor water on the train)—till we reached Newcastle, where was again an army, and the army marched us, man, woman and babies in their mothers' arms, and walking, limping, crawling into the mining compounds, and the chief of army said (through a volunteer): 'The government has declared all of you prisoners. Stay in your compounds', and we saw the thorny-wire all around us, and men with guns at the four corners, and when we had found our homes and had descended our heads on our pillows, the siren howled as never it had. And the next morning, we were driven, brother, like bullocks into the mines. We had to work, for the whites had decided so. We were coolies-on-contract; were we free?

* * *

Just then, O just then, when all was dun dark, like elephants, who, when the heats of summer have heavied, hobble squabble in puddles and mud-pools of the lower hills, where the waters are still a little wide, and there's still a crop or grove to plunder, but when monsoon silences start, and the winds suddenly begin to howl through the forests and whistling through the valley, the elephants rise and move towards the summits for breath and bath, and trumpeting through the upper forests they rush, quelling the trees, and the rains coming dash and churn on their foreheads—like Vishnu's discs the waters churn, quibble and pour down the long, silent trunks—and the elephants more higher and yet higher, washed and blue and reaching the cloud-heights, walk on the ridges one, two, three . . . a countable hundred, trumpeting and lifting the branches, and beating their backs with these, or rushing through the open as if in open combat with the little ones—Come let us play, they seem to say, and now that we're fresh and free, let's combat before the goddesses of the forests (for here and there on hill tops you can still see a temple spire, and somewhere even a bell is rung and the camphor burnt and all through the night you hear a verberant drone as if a mantra repeated day and night and night again ancient but alive)—and people looking from the plains say, there, there, the mountains move, the elephants have found their native clouds, and there will be such auspicious rains for the *margashira* crops—likewise the movement on the southern hills of Natal where coolie after coolie, heaving his breath ran towards the north, towards Newcastle—one thousand, four thousand, nine thousand, seventeen thousand, twenty-five and forty thousand, in all, and as the moving mountains they edged the hills, uncaring for policeman or planter—all they knew was in some prison lay their Sri Rama, and he should be freed now, now that the rains have auspiciously come. Holy and bright as the monsoon mornings seem the day, and all night one heard the rain patter on the tiles and by morning the procession of elephants will reach the summit—and see the white curled sea. But the volunteers said: Bapu has told the plantation men they were not to strike, the citymen, Bapu's men, rushed to the southern mountains to tell them, No brothers, no, Bapu has only told the miners of Newcastle to strike, not you, not you, for there would be a war thus—but who would listen to whom when Sri Rama is not in the war-camp—the plantation coolies were angry and would strike back, thirty thousand of them, forty thousand of them, if the whiteman struck but one (and the whiteman with us, he took out his whips and he lashed and blood broke out from their veins, our men's, but one rushed not at him)—and now it was we heard that on the estates of tea and sugar cane there were shootings—coolie after coolie, his turban on his head and his hand lifted in anger or prayer had died one, two, then ten. And it was then the news came that our Bapu was taken to Dundee (so the papers said) for having driven us into the march, and they gave him nine months hard-labour (that's what the whiteman's papers said, so spoke the volunteers), and afterward he was, was Bapu, taken again to Volksrust jail where he met his Hanuman and his Bharata, and it was as if the holy family had come together again (only Sita Devi was still in prison)—but the whiteman's court could find nobody to bear witness to the evil deeds of Sri Rama or of Hanuman or of Bharata, so like a true Rama, our Sri Rama chose his accuser, and his accuser—disciple Polak—said: I saw Sri Rama, the Lord, say this to us and that, so that we would all march into Transvaal (for that was the evil our Sri Rama had done, to make us march into Transvaal) and yet when it came to Hanuman who was there to say what Hanuman had done, for he had done nothing, he had burnt no Lanka. So, laughing, Bapu said: I will bear witness and say: Hanuman, I saw you help the marchers to enter Transvaal, and the white judges gave him, Kallenbach, three months of prison too, and when it came to Brother Polak, not only had he done nothing, but he had helped the police to send us into the trains and then send us to the mines again, and pray what evil could he have done? But in Ravana's kingdom, you know, all that which is white in Ayodhya is black in Lanka, the lotus smelleth the putrid humours of the backyard or inauspicious jackals cry during the day, and sleep at nightfall. Such Ravana's kingdom. So Brother Bharata was given three months prison and lest there should be mischief between them, they were all taken to different districts of the kingdom, and then the police opened fire anywhere they liked, in the total vastitude of the land, and killed as many as they relished. For the trouble is, brother, the whites don't have so many prisons. Yet when you kill, others will see a man killed and will see it's like felling a tree—it just drops and falls and lies as if awake in sleep. That's death. Then the coolies fell one after the other, a hundred of them, so people talked, and the killed were burned or buried according to scripture.

But the whiteman's papers told us of many things happening far and wonderful—that in all India there were meetings and processions and that Sir Phirozeshah Mehta struck his trident against the white government of South Africa, and Gokhale his mace against the mines monster of Newcastle and the Coolie masters of sugar cane estates—and then, be it known, the viceroy himself, King George's own cousin and Minister, he said to the whites, how accursed they were to shoot and imprison us, and in King George's own kingdom—such the commotion in court and durbar hall, there was no question; the coolies have to be freed. And Bapu, he be taken out of prison and set on his lotus throne, that man knows, that all men know, for Bapu there is no war: he is one to black and white, to brown and yellow, to Hindu or Muslim or Christian or Parsi, Bapu is the same for all. So said the papers, so people told everyone in London and in India. Brother, I tell you, we saw the face of Truth in those mountain mornings as if it were a fruit hanging from a tall tree. When ripe it falls, and you eat it, and you know such a fruit will bring the very death of death. God makes no separation between man and man, and Bapu showed us that. Lord, may Sri Rama's reign come and Truth prevail over all the round world, such our true prayer was, brother, believe it, for we know not how it came and when it came, but it came as if to wake us up. And never shall we be the same again.

* * *

Now, I tell you, my brother, my sister, Ayodhya seemed not far, the smell of incense wafted in the autumnal air. And the white papers said the Viceroy had spoken straight to our Ravana and King George's minister had twisted his ear, and now, Smuts Sahib, what are you going to do? And Smuts Sahib looked right and looked left, and suddenly he'd a bright star in his brain— he'd appoint a group of whitemen who'd tell him what to do. And so the papers said (and Bapu was not in prison but ten days)—the commission wrote, let Gandhi-swami be free, and he was freed. But there was, I tell you, no joy on his face. He knew the tricks and pricks of his Ravana. What would Sri Rama do now? He said to Smuts: You want to hear our wails and our prayers, but there must be a wise man or many wise men to listen to us. And you appoint one white man who's good, and two whites who'd said the Indians should be drowned in the ocean (and that was when Gandhi-swami had come from India, and there were eight hundred men and women and children in the two Indian ships and the whites in Durban had gathered and swore that they would give a prize for he who would kill the first Indian that came down the ships, and it was then, too, the whites almost killed him, our Bapu, you remember, in Durban—and it's two of the same whites that were there to listen to us. It's like asking the serpent to listen to the frog or the vulture to the sparrow—there can be no justice from this whiteman's court.) But the Viceroy from India sent wires and said: I am sending my own man, a whiteman though but a good man, and he'll defend ye all, and Gokhale sent two Englishmen, two padres, one that had given up all his money and sent it to Bapu for the satyagrahis and refused to convert a Hindu and make him Christian, and another one, too, who said: We're Christians and by our works shall Christ shine. And they came to Cape Town, and so it's said, brother, for we've not seen it nor heard it straight, but the papers have spoken and said: When the white Padre, Andrews,[6] was his name, saw Bapu clad all in white, the staff of pilgrim in his hand, like a devotee did the white man touch our Sri Rama's feet, and all the Indians and the whites wondered what the world be becoming. And the two white padres, Pearson the other padre's name,[7] took the train and went to see Smuts here and Botha there, and they spoke to one another, and somehow Bapu said well, this time we'll not quarrel, though we will not come before the white court and speak to them all our sorrows. Our sorrows are known not only to the whites and the Indians, even the hills and squirrels will tell you our tale. But the whites you know, they always want

---

[6] C.F. Andrews.
[7] W.W. Pearson.

something on paper. Lots and lots of words were going to be put on paper. But Bapu said, if this time ye still speak in one voice at home and another in the Durbar Hall, we will not hear of it, and the whole of the Indian community, one hundred and fifty thousand in all will bear witness to this evil £3 tax, and the concubinage you've lawed our women into, and we all said: Let's go on pilgrimage again, brother, if that come. It was better than this slavery with the whites—guards at the four corners and the trolleys that take us down the mines, and we sweat and we spit, we crack our bones and we go up to food and woman and babies altogether, and sleep, which wakes us swoon into the trolley again. We don't want this, Bapu, we don't want these white soldiers in directions eight.

And our women too said: Is it for this we've lost our dead ones, for we heard of the many dead in prisons, and many dead by the shootings on plantations, and we are sore angry with the whiteman.—And just then, brother, when the whites were beginning to feel secure, and they thought they could do what they liked of us of India, and our Bapu was already speaking of a new procession to the sacred hills, up the passes and round and down to wheresoever it would lead us, may be even to the sea, the whites themselves rose against the whites—white workers in mines and trains, in mills and offices—they said: And this time we will have what we want—and having learnt from us Indians, they too gathered together and marched into Johannesburg, and Bapu told the government: Since you, Ravana, are in trouble, we'll neither march nor abandon the mines. Your sorrow should be our sorrow. Otherwise, where is Truth? But we, I tell you, were big sorry for all this, as already we had begun hearing the songs on the high roads and smelling of the tea and the one-and-a-half pounds of bread and the four ounces of sugar and Bapu ladling out the one, two, three courses of gruel to us—'And, mother, I am sorry we have so little'—and he gives us a smile that touches his ears. Where love is, brother, I tell you, one can walk a thousand leagues and sing Mirabai:

> I will never forget my God,
> For he is in my heart.
> Beautiful he is and very joyful.
> I have given my all to him
> Who is Master and Lord.

And now, the white workers unions had all gathered in Johannesburg and there would be neither train at work anymore, and all the world's workers were so happy. Yes, even the whites will now have their need, and we were so pleased. But such are Ravana's ways, he'd his troops all ready and in hiding, sixty thousand of them, you understand, sixty, fifty plus ten, I say unto you, and when the workers were all in deliberation, the troops came round and round the building—for Ravana is such a good commander, you know, a general as you will remember—and the white workers who knew not the power of Truth said, nay, nay, but when they saw the troops said, yes, yes, and the workingman went back to his home, by train and tram, and their leaders, eight in all, were put on sailing ship, and sent quick, quick, home to their kingdom, London. And the workers came back so sorrowful, I tell you, it made our hearts sick. For man is man, brother, white or black, and where there's sorrow or death, it asketh for no colour. Our women too were grieved to see their women. And we cheered each other. This was only for a few days though. For then the whiteman became the whiteman, the brown remained brown, and as for the dark man

nobody worried, one would think, not even the Kaffir himself.
How could this be, brother? And in our hearts we prayed: Kaffir
brother, why not you also own temples and shrines? We have
heard of your heroes too, of Dongaan and Cheka, why won't you
go to their tombs, and laying a copper and burning a camphor
say: King, our King of Kings, He who rides the flaming lion and
hears the royal drum beckon at his door, when will you lead
us into our own land? For, brother, each man has his land, his
sacred tree. And we all know Africa is the blackman's land, and
his gods, the Milango, live up those dark mountains.

> And his God be He called Unkulunkulu
> Or Mtang,
> He is the Bantu God, and they His people.

The whiteman is here because he be so powerful and well-
knit, and we are here because we'd famine and plagues and
so many deaths, but our gods are not here, they are there on
Shabari Malai in Malaya mountains and we'll still go up there,
ring the gong and open our eyes and see the morning God face
to face. For he who has not seen God has no place to live on our
kind earth. So we think, and so we sing and live.

Bapu, however, was dire distressed that the whiteman's
rebellion be thus disastrous, and he said to us; You see, the power
of Truth. Since not one of you threw a stone at the whiteman
even when he hit you and even killed our men, and yet never did
we hurt a whiteman. And so, brothers, Smuts can send the white
leaders away to their country, but he cannot send me away. And
that's the meaning of it all, said he, Bapu. Anyway, he wrote,
we seek not for wealth or success here—we seek only for the
face of God. And that brought peace to our hearts, and we slept

knowing some day, guardians at the door of the temple will open the gates—and we would rush into the inner courtyard, and be received with music and camphor smells. To be born a man is great, say the texts, do they not, brother, my brother? But to be born a man and seek God—that's the greatest treasure of all. House and jewellery, wife and child can go or come, but he that faces the road to God, how could he not see the sunrise over the sea? The first ray of that sun will fall on the head of Shiva in the high forest temple, the Ganges flowing on his head, and beating our cheeks, we shall close our eyes and know that we know, if you understand what I mean. Like sleep is that kingdom, and all is awake as at a festival.

Had we reached the temple already, brother? Perhaps we had. For the Padre Andrews went to see Smuts Sahib and came back and Bapu saw Andrews and came back too, and then finally Smuts Sahib said: Gandhi come to me and let us talk as brothers.—And they talked as brothers. And like in a sacred text, every word and breath of argument was writ in clear (whiteman's) language and every word talked and understood. And Smuts Sahib said to Bapu: And now be you well satisfied. It will now be like a holy text. I will read it to the Parliament, and there they will say, Yes, indeed this is right or this is not right. Bapu returned smiling. Yes, the words were noble and true, as in a sacred book. We all saw the gazette though we understood it not. The volunteers read it all to us. And now even Draupadi was free. Here and there, Indian men and women were coming out of their jails. Processions wound round the roads and the railway stations, and each one was now going to his home. Botha and Smuts, they were like Ravana and Kumbhakarna, they both said to the Parliament: This Gandhi is a good man. He has never broken his word, never. And if you will not vote for us, we give up our high ministership. Vote for us or we will go. And here be our new law. Now this is what we shall give the Indians: First, the dog-collar tax will go; the £3 tax will be abolished forever and ever. Second, the women married to men in India or here, Hindus or Muslims, their marriage will be like our marriage, sacred, and one before law. But every man will have but one wife. (After all it is thus with us Hindus.) Third, that every thumb-impression card of the Natal Indian would be considered true for all the long times to come. That is to say the Natal Indians are Natalese from today, from tomorrow and for always.

And the white Parliament clapped hands and passed one law on one single day—yes, on one single day.

And suddenly now we were all free—there were no white soldiers guarding our gates nor thorny wires all around our houses, our women walked in freedom to the bazaars and the whiteman, I tell you, he did not give us more food or money, but he spoke to us differently—like the village elders when they sit at the Common's tree, and they say: Hé, there, you Shivan, Hé there, you Raman, how is your child today? The fever has gone down, has it? And we all went, that is, those who could, to Durban to see Bapu, for he was now going away—going away home to India, so people said. Who, brother, would defend us now, Father, who, we asked. But he made such a noble speech, brother, one can never forget as long as one breathes life on earth. We had the paper framed, and have hung it on our walls, glass above it, garlands around. Read and listen slowly.

'Brothers and sisters:

'When I agreed to come over to Verulam I had no idea in my mind that I would receive an address. I came only to pay homage to my indentured brothers and to explain to them the facts under the new law. Moreover, a visit to this place is for me like going on a pilgrimage for the Indian friends here played a great part in the recent strike; and in what a wonderful manner! When all the so-called leaders were resting in their private rooms or were busy making money, the indentured brethren of this place, the moment they happened to hear that a strike was on in Charlestown and elsewhere about the £3 tax, struck work too. They looked for no leaders. The leaders at Verulam, Tongaat and Isipingo, were busy going round collecting money. But spontaneously the friends here struck work. This proves that poverty is real wealth. The poor are like kings. They will have their way. Be it here or in India or elsewhere, our salvation lies through poverty. The poor are the soul of a great movement like this.

'As I accept the address that you have presented to me, I remember an injunction in our scriptures: "Man, flee from the place where you find yourself being praised or at least plug your ears with cotton-wool." I keep turning over this injunction in my mind whenever I hear myself praised. But, on this occasion I have not been able to act as enjoined. When one can do neither the injunction says: "Jiva,[8] if you cannot act as enjoined here, offer all praise you receive to Lord Krishna." And this is what I do. Obedience to such religious injunctions and the path of uprightness will ensure success in every undertaking. What I mean to say is that you are not right when you attribute our success to me. It was the strength of our indentured brothers that brought us success. It is they who have done something great.

8   ¹The Ego—Soul.

'On the expiry of your contract you can stay as free Indians.

'Your feeling unhappy, as you say, on my going away binds me all the firmer to you in love. But I am leaving Phoenix behind me . . . You are under indenture with one person for five years but I am under indenture with three hundred millions for a lifetime. I shall go with that memory of service before me and never displace you from my heart.

'It made me very unhappy to know that during the recent strike, provoked no doubt by excessive cruelty or some other cause, you raised your hand in retaliation. Had I been with you I would have had my head broken rather than allowed you to do what you did. For the future however I wish to put before you one important suggestion. If it should ever happen that the Government is harsh with you or that your employers ill-treat you, you should fearlessly strike work; sit yourselves down at one place, go hungry if they do not give you food, suffer yourself to be abused and kicked and finally, if such be your lot, submit even to hanging or being shot dead, but do not waver in your faith in God. If you act thus even the stoniest heart will melt. Such is the power of satyagraha. Have trust, in it. This alone is pure satyagraha. It is a weapon which surpasses all weapons, all your clubs and other weapons. Cling to it—therefore: it will never fail you in times of need. Good-bye to you.'

Such, brother my brother, our Bapu. How shall we ever, say, honour his eyes and truth?

* * *

When Sri Rama, Lord Sri Rama, was returning from Lanka to Ayodhya and the chariot of flowers flew high, high, and with Sita Devi beside Him and brave Hanuman, his tail arched over the back, standing tall and low behind his Lord, all the demons and demi-demons of Lanka, those whose hearts were right but whose minds were wrong and had fought against him—their minds and hearts today were turned towards the sky, for not only perfume and incense seemed to fill the mighty air of the up surging earth, but the very rivers seemed to stand still, lifting their heads like seven-hooded serpents, to gaze at this great and heavenly happening, and the nearer he came, did our Sri Rama, journeying towards India, the bigger the arches to welcome him, and Bharata himself would one day go carrying the sandals of the Lord to the banana-leaf-arching and begarlanded doors of the City—such, my brothers, my sisters, the procession that ran through the streets of Durban and Tongaat and Newcastle and Kimberley and Johannesburg, and mayors and white citizens that came to honour him, they who'd feared him and betimes hated him, Chamney or Campbell, Smuts or Botha, they all made bold and noble speeches, for indeed Smuts Sahib again said to his people, 'Say what you like about Gandhi but he has never spoken of violence or revolution against Government'— and arch after arch bore inscription from the hearts of the Indian people, and addresses offered: Father, our Bapu, forget us not, for not only have you given us eyes to see but hearts to understand, and we shall live with the whites and never hate them, no we will not; if they were to beat us, we will not bite them, were they to throw us out of the compounds, we shall chant the name of Sri Rama, whether we cry, fast, fret or pray, we know that like our procession through Charlestown and Volksrust there's only one road, then the spruit and after that the twist and now the grand upward road to truth. Is that not what you've told us Bapu? And we know too, if we have trouble we can always go to Mr. West in Phoenix or to one of your sons or nephews, to Chhaganlal, Maganlal or Sunderbhai, and we know too if we wanted the help of law, Mr. Langston or Mr. Polak would always be there to help, and never a shilling need be spent on court cases or cards. So you have told us. And we vow never to forget the many dead, the martyrs, our Father, neither Valiamma the young, or Gurbaksinh the patriarch, Nagappen nor Narayanswamy the brave, the bold—and all those others whose names nobody knows, how many that the whites shot one after the other on the plantations. We now know you ate for long only one meal a day as if to make your offerings to the dead. And you wear those simple and sad garments in memory of the dead. What greater offerings to the manes can there be, Bapu, than that you should fast and pray for them. And because of it all they will be reborn to an upper existence. And we have just now heard, Bapu, that your spouse Kasturba had been gravely ill. The papers said, and those who can read the papers told us, she'd been between this life and the next, and that you had been bending over night after night to help her vomit or to go to the latrine, that you had fed her with spoon and cooked her food and squeezed the juice of orange, and yet you went on talking to Smuts Sahib and Botha and to the many mayors and mine-kings. Such your truth, Bapu.

And now you are going. What shall we tell you that you do not have knowledge of; we are weak and we are frail and how many among us can live up to your truth, Father, how many, Bapu? Man is a beast of prey—he eats and he fornicates and he spits and he passes excreta in his backyard, and when he is angry he kills and gets killed. Forgive us if sometimes in our anger we argumentate hot with the whites, but we shall remember that such is not our way, such is not the way of our country, India—India of the sages, of Vishwamitra and Vasistha, of Sri Krishna and Sri Rama. We shall not forget what you told us, Bapu.

And how glad our hearts are that the City of Cape Town took you out in procession, yea, even here in Lanka, and that they spoke to you and swore to you, the white and the Coloured, the Chinese and the Indian, that they will work for the truth, and that they shall keep the tree of satyagraha growing like a large pipal tree. The larger it becomes the holier the shade, and mankind will build a platform around it, hang garlands to its trunk, put sandal and *kumkum* on its big face, and going round and round, worship the pipal tree with sacred thread, incense, *tulasi*-leaves and Ganges water. We shall worship the tree of satyagraha and it shall grow till its branches touch not only India and London, but all the wide, white world. Such your prayer, Bapu, and we shall honour it. And now as the ship that takes you away from us will shout and leave the African shores we prostrate before you and sing: *Jaya Jaya Rama Rama,* Victory to Sri Rama.

Auspicious the waters of the ocean will feel, father, and holy the earth wheresoever she will see you. May you live amongst us a hundred years.

Part Three

The Epilogue

The mohowa flower is red, rich and pulpy, loved by birds. And men. When the young monsoon rains swirl the forests into one active ocean of sounds, and the very trees begin, as it were, to cry and the animals run, turn and hide, as though the Goddess of the Hill were in commotion giving birth to a new calendar, a new kingdom, and suddenly, just as after prayers and worship, quietude settles into the sanctuary, the forest settles into a rain-pouring silence as if you could count the drops. Each flower of mohowa that's fallen has, so to say, found its own place on the head or by the feet-jewels of the Goddess, for all the hill is the goddess herself, and little by little as streams form and run through the narrow lanes amidst trees, the flowers seek their own coincidences and rest. They rest thus, but the trees still drip rain, the animals slither through the trees leading their young, and sometimes even an old Santhal[1] will walk on some mission to another hamlet, sheltered under his palm hat, going maybe towards his widowed sister-in-law or to the naming ceremony of his grandnephew. The Goddess is generous in her gifts, and the birds sometime slip between showers, and seek a flower for

---

[1] An Indian tribe, probably the original inhabitants of India.

their young ones. It's bad time for the young. Here and there an animal would have crushed a flower—a panther, a boar, a deer—and the flower yields blood-red juice. The deer will come and drink of it, for it intoxicates so—and the whole forest seems to be full of sound. Somewhere far away the drums beat and maybe worship is being done to the village divinity for it's she who gave to us pouring rain.

Little groups of men and women, meanwhile, go from village to forest frontiers to seek the fallen flowers. They will gather it all, all, and when the time comes and it's brewed, it yields a liquor that will shew the Goddess brighter. But while the rains stop, of course, the Santhal will go and gather the flowers, and bring them to you. For the tiger is friend to him and not to you. Sometimes on a quiet day when the mohowa is being gathered and nobody hears a sound, an old tiger will slip in and carry away a woman (but never a Santhal) and no shrieks and shouts will ever stop him from his prey. He has been hungry too long. And maybe it's about here that in some past life, as the text says, the Buddha himself (still a Bodhisattva) gave himself to be eaten up by an old and tired tigress. 'Wait,' he said, did the Bodhisattva, 'wait, and let me slip just a little higher, there, so that when your old teeth cut into the veins of my neck, blood will run straight down your gullet.' Yes, it's hereabouts too that among the Bihar hills the Buddha, later, had walked carrying his message of liberation from the bonds of the psycho-chemical components which we are, and once you are freed of those collocations, of course you are in Nirvana. Nirvana is where nothing is attained, for there is no one there to attain anything.

It's hereabouts, once again, that Emperor Ashoka, after having conquered the confines of the Pathan-lands and even beyond up to Parthia and to the south and down as far as Mysore, he, the Emperor, having seen that horrible carnage—*a hundred thousand killed* in one battle, the battle of Kalinga—sick in sorrow, he, there and then stopped all war, and turned his total army into pilgrims of peace, forbade by edict the killing not only of men but even peacocks and deer, and sent emissaries of the good word to the fartherest Hellenic kings, to wit, to Ptolemy, Antigonus and Cyrus, so that soon Buddhists walked the streets of Alexandria, and the Buddha's word honoured by the Mediterranean and on the other side through Persia it would reach China itself.

It's also in this same Bihar that almost twenty-four centuries later the Mahatma came to talk of love to the indigo workers, who like the indentured workers in Africa, had become bond-slaves, so to say, of the white planters. It's here in Champaran that he showed how the satyagraha he'd practised in Africa could be worked, and victory won through *yagnya*, sacrifice. It's here again that he showed to the incredulous Indian that you must love the white rulers before you can fight them, and Gandhiji would go from officer to officer, test personally the verity of each particular incident, scrupulous as ever to every detail, and when the government saw the truth of this man, as in South Africa, the government had two views on the matter. The bureaucrat thought him a danger, the honest administrator took sides with him. But would the salvation of India be won this way? Many laughed and plotted and killed an Englishman in the Punjab, a police officer at Bombay, but Gandhiji would, with folded hands, say, brother, my brother this is not the great Indian way.—Pray, sir, what other way would be Indian?—To which the Mahatma would make answer: Do you want the true independence of the Indian people or do you want just a change of masters? Let us have swaraj—the rule of the Self and not self-rule. For the one leads to love and other to mighty greed. Either Indian independence is won through the way of love, or not at all.

In the middle of this forest of Ramgarh, then, came the Congress (1940). Every year the Indian National Congress built a temporary city for itself, just so as to take the congressmen straight to the people—and thus with festoons and fresh-cut roads, and bamboo huts, and elephants to draw the Congress President from wherever he or she alighted by train or car, a procession of almost a hundred thousand people would lead each year its new president to his august vocation. He would for that year be the voice of India; Nehru or Subhas Bose or Abul Kalam Azad, they were all the same—the Congress President would rule the politics of the country, but like the *purohita* to the king, Gandhiji would always be the high-priest. It was his voice that made India. 'He is India.'[2] It was his voice that people came to hear, his *darshan*, people in tens of thousands came for—by bullock cart and on foot, by train and bus and car and horse-carriage, they came, the peasant, the shop-keeper, the retired civil servant (when he was not afraid of the wrath of the masters), the industrialist, the intellectual, the barber, the Brahmin, and there were women and men volunteers too, who kept the whole town clean (sanitation was still one of the principal tenets of Gandhism) and Hindus and Muslims, and journalists from all over the world too, came to these annual sessions—and of course, spies. But what was there that the Congress could hide? Everything they said and did was known to the whole of Indian mankind. Gandhiji insisted on truth and Jawaharlal on gentlemanliness, that the British did not always

---

[2]   A famous statement by Jawaharlal Nehru.

understand—but they will. Give them time. They were now in a bad posture—the Second World War had come. In fact, even from the First World War they had understood little. They had promised Indian independence (in 1917) when they were in dire need of peace and help. And when the war was happily won by the allies, not self-rule but the massacre of innocents took its place. A British officer, Dyer, put his gun against a gunless crowd that had gathered in the name of Gandhiji, at Amritsar, and shot 377 men and woman and children and maybe more, but the records do not say it. He had just come back from the war, had General Dyer, and this was another aspect of the show, that was all. Many Britishers congratulated him on his quick suppression of sedition, but a few and some very important voices rose against this very un-English behaviour of his. (But the truth of the truth was, and never even whispered about, during this war Indian revolutionaries in California and Japan, in Afghanistan and in Mexico, had gathered tons on tons of gun and powder to blow up the British in India. But such the great secret of the Indians, the British knew it all—of the boat *Kamagata Maru* that was sailing down the Pacific from the shores of Ontario, and midway somewhere, the boat and its ammunition were seized—Britannia ruled the waves—and Britain would rule India come what may. Dyer's massacre came as a reply to the hot-heads of the *Kamagata Maru*, and of such likes.) The supreme truth is that the might of the cannon can blow anything to pieces. Do you understand?

It was time therefore to start a satyagraha in India. The experiment in South Africa should prove even better here, this 'the holy land where all acts work for good', as the Puranas say. And wave after wave of satyagraha started, first the Swadeshi Movement, 1921-22, then the no-tax campaign of 1928, and finally the revolution of 1931-34 which almost brought the British Empire to a collapse. Yet Britain was not only able but noble and astute. Not only were the British imperialists but they tried hard to be gentlemen. Caught thus in their own dilemma, they were now fierce, now friendly, now calculating and now (at least in words) generous. The Labour Party in England was on the side of India, or so we thought. But when Hitler's war came, India was declared a belligerent country, and no Indian consulted—India belonged to the British; they could do what they liked with her. British will rule, and the Labour Party will, now, rule India, with the others. Hitler was there, and later the Japanese—Hitlerism our principal enemy, so they argued, the British did. And Indian armies (mercenaries) went to fight with the British in Egypt, in the Middle-East. Whatever happens the road to India has to be kept free, otherwise there would be no empire. And like Napoleon, Hitler too wanted his route to India. Hitler believed Indians were not quite Aryans although, the swastika he wore came from the Indians, however he wore it the wrong side round—but he was not to be worried about such trifling historical inaccuracies. For him the Indians were to be pullers of water and hewers of wood (just as Kruger had thought) but the great Aryans, yellow this time, were to be the Japanese. Nehru was caught in a desperate dilemma—for he hated Hitler and the Japanese more than most of the upper-class British did, because of his Fabian views perhaps, but the British were now behaving here, in India, in their pure Teutonic manner. In fact, Smuts this time (as in the First World War, he was a member of the British Cabinet) sided with the Indians, not so Churchill. Roosevelt greatly admired the Indian nationalists, but war is war the British argued, there's no morality about it. The Indian army was needed. Thus India had to be held slave.

High on the flag-flying platform, gaunt in his solitude, on this rain-washed morning, he stood, Gandhiji did, still in his girmico dress (but now stylised to a symbol, his knee-touching dhoti, his white and hard-wool shawl, his steel-rimmed glasses, his folded hands in worshipful obeisance to every man) and Nehru stood behind Gandhiji, and Khan Abdul Ghaffar Khan, the fiery and not violent Pathan chief, yet behind him, holding Nehru as an elder would a younger brother, and Sardar Patel, Gandhiji's lieutenant, the man who did what he said and would not say what he did not mean, and Sarojini Naidu the poetess, who had left her gulmohurs and her maina birds for this extravaganza in political adventure—sharp in tongue and tender in action, and withal very intellectual—and the twenty thousand or thirty thousand or the fifty thousand men and women and children, hidden behind tree trunks, sheltered under arched branches, wet in clothes and dirty in their muddied looks and hair, the children held in arms or the young ones on men's shoulders—the intellectuals with their glued-eyes and sharp fibered fingers, the communists, at that time still very angry with the British,[3] the terrorists with side-looks and sharp quick gestures, short-haired, and all the whiteclad Congressmen, to whom this was at once a festival and a durbar—the annual *tamasha*—and a pilgrimage, where they saw their master and heard him, and he spoke to them and sometimes they made themselves heard (so that they could go back to their town, village, or city, in Mysore, in the Punjab, in Madras or Kumbakonam, and say, 'I said this to Gandhiji, and this to the whole Congress in assembly!') till sometimes

---

[3]   For soon, be it remembered when Stalin entered the War, they too, the communists upheld Churchill!

Nehru pulled them with their shirt-tails or their stretched back and, fierce in his non-violent but dictatorial temper, yet before his master and himself, as a child, a prince, who'd be free till the father was there, and he could thus play all of his pranks till the day come when he too would have to stand up and affirm his truths, his biases and his diktats. To all there he turned in deep salutation, did Gandhiji, and then did he speak: Brothers, he seemed to say, this is an ancient land, and we walk today where the Buddha might have walked. Up there is the Ganges to whom the Saraju, Sri Rama's Saraju, throws in her waters. And yet higher up is the Jumna where and on whose bank Sri Krishna, yes, the Yadava, from Dwaraka, he did come and give advice to Arjuna: Fight, for action is natural to man. Fight, but without your ego. The ego is made of the three modes of the self—the *gunas*—one essential, one active and one indolent, and beyond it the Self. Such his message, and such is what I have tried to live. Remember what Dharmaraja, that prince among the Pandavas did: He would never tell a lie even when he lost a kingdom. And Bhishma, who on his bed of arrows dying, spoke of the nobility of Truth. Yes, the Britishers have no understanding of us. As you know, the British and I have had a pact of friendship. I have loved in my time the British Empire and served it the best way I could. Now it's all different, yet their distress must not be our opportunity. They are at war with Hitler. I say Hitler made this war. I also would like in my manner to help the British. But the British are so proud of themselves and of their possession, India, that we were all mortgaged to this war before we knew where we were. I say unto you, let us not harm them, yet let us not accept their arrogance. We must always be ready to be manly. Only the coward can be truly defeated. The courageous even in his death is a hero. And how much more so if one is non-violent, he the truest of true hero, the Mahavira.

I would have liked to have met Hitler personally. I wrote to him a long letter. The British would not forward it to him, but had I met him, I would have begged him on bended knees, Brother, don't you see every man you kill is of divine essence? And what, in your short passage on this earth, would you get of all this carnage? Nothing but blood and cries of revenge—yet the British too, in their own way, talk the same Teutonic language when it suits them. Chamberlain will talk to Hitler because Hitler shows them his armaments. Chamberlain will not talk to us the same way—we have no cannons, machine guns, tanks. But we have, we in India, the best army in the world—the non-violent army. Nobody can defeat us even when they kill us. In satyagraha, I repeat, death is no defeat, Truth ever the victor. And with Truth is love. Not only should we practise love with the British, but also each one of us with his neighbour, whether he be a Hindu, a Muslim, a Christian, a Parsi or a Jew, and of course were the Japanese or French, Italian or American. And, we should not forget the Chinese, our neighbours, either.

Japan too has learnt all the evil methods of the West. She has now begun to conquer the Chinese whose culture had once conquered them. I would plead with the Japanese, as with the British. I would have written a letter to the Emperor Hirohito of Japan, but who will take it to him? Who will listen to me? I am a spent force, says Mr. Churchill. Perhaps I am. But India is not. So brothers, I say unto you all, let us spin that love between us, let us spin and weave such love that humanity be as of one substance made, one carpet for the tread of God. Perhaps, as some among you, the young, think I am a madman. But even the mad can sometimes speak the truth, you know. Maybe you will hear me, some of you will know, even one amongst you must know, what I say is true. I have always said, was there but one pure satyagrahi, victory is certain. After all, Sri Rama conquered Lanka and Sri Krishna the Kaurava hordes of hate. Brothers and sisters, let us worship the Truth. Shall we?

And yet, brother, as he began to talk, it was as if he were not speaking to you or to me or to anyone, or maybe to himself, and not even to himself but to his truth, to his God, and we who had been talking to one another, and each to the other, and each with himself to himself, our minds still caught in the memory of incident, in the memory of words (and looking at Jawaharlal and seeing his smile of comradeship and of spoilt child, and Abdul Ghaffar Khan who looked solemnly as if promising to the world, he it was the elder brother, and he would protect and subsume the whole world in good and bad for his younger brother, his Jawahar, and Patel standing still at a distance, solitary, with a look of one amused, as if to say: so you all think this is simple and it is not simple—and Rajagopalachari, wise, shrewd, cynical and sure, stood too white and unconvincing but there—and the communists in front crying gently to whisper, to heckle, Oh, never so loud, but just a cough or a slogan here and there, and yet now here, now there again saying, Oh, let's get the British out and so on, and the Congressmen so filled with their pure-white innocence and importance, they felt they each knew and possessed their Gandhiji)—and amidst all these like the first notes of a raga, like the *alaap*, it began, the talk of Gandhiji, almost inaudible because of the screech of parrots and jays and the variegated cry of children, and even with the sound of women talking somewhere far away, and the sound of cooking vessels ever farther and beyond under the trees—but as the music moved from note to deeper note there was, as it were, a seeping of a drip-drop silence into the atmosphere—did anyone speak, if not who heard it all? Nobody heard it, so Nobody spoke, the air and the world seemed to say, and yet there was just this voice, one melody that without rising or falling, went on playing to itself, and we too, each of us, yes, even the communists, felt there was something happening to oneself, one was not listening to a speech or even to any sound, one was listening to sound itself, so to say thus, there was no listener—who was where, and what did we hear, and did we hear anything at all?—Yes, the British are there and they are in difficulty—one seemed to hear, and then a great white blank that seemed to hear and yet not hear. All was, as it were, set to one single note and each one heard his Gandhiji, and there was no one else than oneself, except for that high flag-staff and the spinning wheel, and then as time went and the sun came hot and even Nehru stood as though he too could neither stand nor think, but stare into himself—we were all staring into ourself—and when Gandhiji stopped it was as if we were suddenly awakened to a collateral world, and the bells (of the bulls) began to ring, and the children cried, and the men shouted to women, and Patel said something, and Nehru waved his hand at someone, and the Congress flag flew high, high, and the important people began to feel important (that is, those who stayed in the leader's quarters) and Rajagopalachari and Patel all came down the dais, and walked back through the woods and passed the handicraft exhibits, and by bookshop displays, cottages, worshipping crowds, and round and around the Ashoka Pillar, to the Congress meetings where, of course, they all spoke in Hindi, chaste, hesitant or bastard, and some even in English, and Gandhiji listened to it all, spinning and spinning away. It was as though he were saying: Don't you see action is more important than brave words? And they who thought they'd get the British out of the country the most vociferous. Gandhiji hardly ever spoke, but Nehru dramatised himself to extravagant idioms and positions, using high-flown Urdu, then elementary Hindi, and altogether mingled with many well-spoken English words like democracy, fascism, British Empire, cannons, tanks, aeroplanes, Viceroy: no, he would not hurt the English, of course, but he would not want the British to be British, and so on—Nehru never talked straight, it was as though he wanted you and he to think together on anything, and so often he never finished a sentence, but when the time came and he did give a smile, it was as though India could be adorned with just such a princely look—he would never let us down, whatever came, and he would fight the British. And that night, and the night after, when the voices of the speakers and the volunteers had become hoarse with misuse, the rains had been swept away by fierce kind winds, and each one was thinking of his train and his family, while Subhas Bose on the other side of this Congress ground, held his own angry Congress, and there they made mighty brave speeches about driving the British out and so on till finally they all went, too, went back to Calcutta, and thence in the middle of the night, of one night, did Subhas leave India, a Muslim fakir on pilgrimage and he reached, did he, through Afghanistan and other friendly countries like Russia to Hitler's Germany, where indeed Hitler promised him many great things, and Subhas' voice could now be heard from Berlin, on the radio, and then came the Japanese, and Subhas went to the Japanese, and he would build up a whole army to liberate India.

The British, meanwhile, plodded along their tired routes, administering the country through civil servants and stooges, but Gandhiji could not bear this humiliation any longer. Why, the whole world is involved in a monstrous, in a metaphysical fight, and we, the Indians, perhaps the eldest among mankind—eldest not in means but maybe in our search for truth—we were to be treated as kept and willing slaves. And he slept, woke and he slept and rose on his hard ashram bed at Sevagram, under the open stars, wondering and wondering as to the what next. Lord, what next? Would not the *Ramayana* help, his *Gita?* The inner voice somehow seemed silent. So he spun and prayed, discussed with the Congress committees when they met at Wardha or Sevagram, and many there were that wanted that India enter the war and fight and kill, and be like every other nation or country—thus would India find her own liberty. But would that be Indian? Would it be true? And to calm the restlessness of the young and the men of action, Gandhiji planned protests against the British—he would make a well-chosen man make an anti-war speech. This satyagrahi would tell the government at the appointed time and place: 'Brothers and Sisters, do not help the British war effort.'

England had lost Singapore and Burma, but England would hold on to India. Yet, even in their distress, the British would be British. For when the disaster came to Burma, the British chalked a white way for the whites and a black way for the Indians—the white way would be by plane, truck or bus, and the black way would be on foot and through the footpaths of the Assam jungles, infested with tiger and panther, wild boar, hyena and elephant, and as the thousands of Indians, men and women and children, marched, the rain constantly pouring on them from on high, and the cold of mountain air biting them, and hearing the tiger cry or the hyena growl, the women could do it no more, and some just lay down and wept, and the husbands and the brothers said, Come when you can and join us, and the child would cry and to the crying child the women would shout, 'And now can you not shut up,' and one here and one there, the women unable to bear the children on their arms, heads or slinged backs, and the men unable to bear their bundles and bags, babies were left behind, and bags sometimes too, and motherhoodless mothers would pick up a baby and say: Oh, you do look so beautiful and why did they leave you there, son, why did they leave you among the grasses, my daughter, and thus the baby would be taken till other mountains came and cold and churning streams—and by a river side, and with a warm covering, would they sometimes leave the babies asleep, thus the adopted mothers, and who could bear to see the big butterflies of Assam settle swiftly and sedately on the babies, face and eyes and penis and feet—so many, many beautiful butterflies—and by evening there would only be the bones—such the stories that the men and the women brought to Gandhiji in Sevagram, and the soldiers too brought stories of how the British had run away from the Japanese with ammunition and guns heaped up and all left behind, and no orders given to the sepoy even to blow them up, the British just fled, *bhago*—they fled to India, and for those Sepoys that could not escape the Japanese there would be the concentration camps, and one day, and a proud day, some thought, but not so proud a day for Gandhiji, did the Japanese radio announce the great Indian leader Subhas Bose had formed with remnants of the Indian army of Burma and Singapore from the young Indians of all Asia, the Indian army of liberation. Gandhiji sat in his gloom in Sevagram, spinning and praying. Time had come for a stout stand. This symbolic satyagraha would not do. Yet after Narvik and Egypt, would it be fair to embarrass the British? But now a decision had to be made. Azad was for a fight, but not so Nehru—he wanted the allies to win, yet in a way so did Azad. But, said Gandhiji, what would happen to India with the Japanese marching in? We would be slaves, again. So, one day, he called his ashramites to a small meeting. Vinoba Bhave, the eldest among the satyagrahis who lived some distance away, was late in coming. But Vinoba finally arrived, wiped his perspiration, and sat with us.[4] This time there's no way out. Caught between the Japanese and the Germans we have to fend for ourselves. I will tell the British, 'Come chaos, come bloodshed: Quit India'. It was not as if a contemporary was speaking. Against the high midsummer heat of India, the dizzy silence of the countryside, it was as if some Bhishma was talking to the Pandavas. The battle has to be for nothing in particular, but the battle will decide our destiny.

He now called a meeting in Bombay—in the middle of the big monsoon was this Congress meeting held—and the tired Congress, powerless without him and afraid with him, agreed that he be the sole spokesman with the British, and he would talk straight and firm to the Viceroy. But poor Linlithgow, he knew more about accounts (he was a banker by profession) than of human understanding. And Churchill was now supreme in London—he'd refused to talk to Roosevelt about India, he said he would rather resign as Prime Minister of war-time England than talk of India to the American President. For, you see, Churchill was once a cavalry officer on the North-Western Frontier some forty years ago, and he loved so his king, his pathan and his Empire. Then half-heartedly, in deep distress of Europe and of Asia, some months earlier he had sent Sir Stafford Cripps, his representative and friend of Nehru's, to get something out of the Indians, yet Churchill was willing to give nothing in return. What then to do now? Churchill had Nehru and Gandhi, Azad

---

[4]   The author was present at this meeting.

and Patel all arrested overnight after the Congress session (9 August 1942), and taken to different prisons of the land, and all in mighty secret lest there be a rebellion. But the biggest rebellion in the history of India since 1857 (when British power there was almost torn and cremated) happened—'Do or Die' were Gandhiji's last words to the Indians—and rails were lifted and telegraph wires cut, and peasants refused to pay taxes and women would go singing from home to home, chanting, lamps and *kumkum* water-plates in hand:

> Wake up, wake, my brother, my sister,
> Our Bapu is in prison,
> The horse does not stay in his stable
> Or the tiger in his lair
> When Ayodhya is weeping—

and people fasted every Thursday, the day the Mahatma was arrested, but people did not then know that Churchill had motived sending all the leadership far away to Africa, to Kenya. There they would be safe and protected from playing high tricks with the British, but the Indian councillors of the Viceroy begged the government not to make such disastrous moves, for were it true and known, not a white man would be left in the country, no not one, as everybody knew, this would be thousand-fold 1857 again, and the Viceroy at least could see the fact of this, and so the leaders were left in Indian prisons and concentration camps. However, the Americans were not too happy; they could not move from place to place, neither they nor their armaments assembled to fight the Japanese, and Stillwell, the commander, told Churchill they were not going, for the sake of the British, to have one American soldier killed here, thus the stalemate. But in secret be it now known, an American soldier here and an American soldier there, gave ammunition to Indian revolutionaries, guns to kill, powder to blow up bridges, and some of the Tommies too, when asked to shoot the Indian crowd, would not. They said, the Tommy said: We've come to fight the Japs and we've no quarrel with the Indians. Thus Churchill lost India.

For I tell you, my brother, my sister, what the 1942 revolution did could never, never be undone. The Indian faced death without fear. For example, there's that story of a Canadian regiment against sixty thousand gunless Indians in Bihar, and wave after wave of them went to dislodge the soldiers, and so many were killed that no ammunition was left and of the Indians and the Canadians that remained, they did lustily cry there and all together, *Mahatma Gandhi ki Jai*, and Victory to the Mahatma became the most potent revolutionary cry of the country, but the Mahatma meanwhile in his isolation sat in deep distress. For stories of atrocities that the British committed came to him, but more stories and more painful were those where an Indian here or there had killed a European. And Gandhiji in the Agha Khan Palace, his place of incarceration, sought his peace in prayer and in reading. But, then, God would not leave him alone. For suddenly his wife Kasturba fell ill. She became desperately ill. And if she died in prison there would be tension and rioting again. So the British were willing to let Gandhiji and she go out. But he would not. No, not till every Indian is out of jail would he accept his own liberty. And Kasturba's condition grew evil. Their children came to her bedside. Nothing seemed to cure her. And one afternoon, calling her husband, and laying her head against his chest, she died, brother, in his arms, a true Hindu wife. The cremation took place in the garden of the Agha

Khan Palace—an open space was cleared, some sandalwood heaped together and she, Kasturba, was laid on it. Gandhiji saw the first fires of the pyre being lit. Yes, sixty-two years had they been married, sixty-two active, tenuous and wholesome years. And little by little as if in gentleness and sorrow and tender care, the fire consumed her pure body. She had indeed been a *pativrata*, a holy wife, and she had taught him more than any other human being—she had been his silent teacher, though she seemed his pupil. That's the Indian way. And he had understood India and her womanhood through Kasturba.

Uneducated, she was wise. Stubborn, she was obedient. Severe in manner, she was loving to all. Such had been her life. Be it not right she should have died thus, in jail, and in his arms? What better end for a Hindu wife and a devotee of her land? How could he forget the way she had begged him on Phoenix Farm, on that historic day, begged that she be allowed to join the others and enter the Transvaal and thus be proud of Indian womanhood like the Rajputs had been, like the Kathiawaris had been through tradition and history. And because of her, all Indian womanhood had been awakened. She had indeed been a true Draupadi. Krishna one day, when he decides, will redeem his promise. The British would be defeated. And India will again become the land of dharma, the *Punya-Bhumi*,[5] and the Indian woman queen again of her household.

* * *

Meanwhile the British with the mighty American help, had been winning war after war—first in Libya, then in Italy, and

---

[5]　The Land of Righteousness.

finally they crossed the Channel and attacked Hitler face to face. Millions died during those battles, millions too on the battlefields of Russia, and Stalingrad had become the most famous epic of all the war. Yet, here in India, the British still ruled. But the spirit of the Empire had already left them. So that when Churchill had almost won the war, and he thought he would win his peace as well and keep His Majesty's India still for Britain to be Great, he was defeated in the votings, and the Labour Party came to power. They had always promised freedom to India. But India now had two voices. For Churchill and his party had built up the Muslim separatists—had fed them with money and encouraged them with tides and favours. Jinnah had told them if Hitler could win, he too could win. And he hated all this smelly Hindu business—the spinning and the half-naked Mahatma. Jinnah wanted to be a gentleman, rule a stout-hearted people. He was astute, was Jinnah, and he understood politics. If you go on saying no and no, one day someone will get exhausted, like the French and British did with Hitler. So Hitler got his Czechoslovakia. Thus Jinnah would have his Pakistan.

The British Government, now the Labour Government, were loathful to perform this division of India. Whatever their opinion of Empire, they did feel pride in the great achievements of their race. So how could they divide the country, the country they had so lovingly built up with some of Britain's best hearts, best of intellects, and furnished since a hundred years with structure, with unity, and an army firm and loyal, a country that they had created and led in war after war, and won victories that all history would speak of—no they would not divide India; the Indian Army is one, India is one. But Jinnah had his own S.S. men. Troubles started here and there and Hindus started being killed in tens and twenties and then in hundreds. No, said Jinnah, we the Muslims do not want to be a minority under the Hindus. We have nothing in common with them. Yet that great Muslim scholar Azad was the President of the Congress, and it was with him the British had to deal. Even the Muslim theologians were with the Congress. And Jinnah knew no theology. All he knew was politics. And politics can inflame a people, specially a fanatical community. But brother, when the rabble get their say there is always joy in the heart of the crowd. It seems easier to hate than to love. It was now that Mountbatten—cousin to the Queen and Admiral of the British Fleet, tall, gentlemanly, courageous and British withal (accompanied by his slim, beautiful and democratic wife who would heal the wounds and elevate the spirit)—was sent, the last Viceroy of India. He pleaded with Jinnah to be fair, to be just. Gandhiji, finally freed with the rest of the leaders, was willing to go far to propitiate the needs of Jinnah. At one moment Gandhiji even said: Give India to Jinnah, I do not mind. We will know how to deal with him, after all, he is one of us. Abdul Ghaffar Khan, that man of violence turned non-violent, and a Muslim as pure as any, he wanted no partitioning of the country, either. He and his people were happy with Gandhi and Nehru. But, brother, what can you do where there's a Duryodhana? You can plead with him and beg him to be reasonable. Like Krishna, Gandhiji begged his old friend to be reasonable. He begged in humility and love: Jinnah, be reasonable with India, have most of what you want. Jinnah wanted nothing else than his kingdom. And he would have it. The Kauravas must rule from Indraprastha.

> Indraprastha which my father weakly to Yudhishthira gave
> Never more shall go unto him while I live and brothers brave.

The killings continued, for once the Muslims had started the Hindus and the Sikhs lost patience. Shiva danced his terrifying Tandava in the crematoria. They killed back, and with glee. And whole villages were blood-spattered, the houses gutted into ash. And now that freedom was soon coming anyhow, Nehru was asked by the British to be Prime Minister of a Provisional Government, and Gandhiji was then given a special train to Calcutta that would stop wheresoever people wanted it to (just like Kruger's train, the train containing his ashes that Smuts decreed would stop wheresoever anyone stood on the railway line with flower or lantern) and Gandhiji would make earnest speeches for brotherhood, for harmony, and beg the Hindus and the Muslims stop this unnameable horror. For months there was bloodshed as never India had seen since the Muslim conquest of the country, six centuries earlier. For at that time the Muslims were better armed than the Hindus, and had an altogether better feel of strategy, But today the Hindus were proud and powerful again. When it comes to killing, people forget they ever were men. And, the more civilised, the more fearsome the killing seems to be. Men and women, even pregnant women, were killed by the Hindus, and the babies in the womb taken out so that no Muslim child would remain behind to infect Hindu India. And the Muslims in Pakistan, they took the Hindu women to their harems and converted them to Islam, or simply converted whole villages to their religion—or the men would be slaughtered. Temples were desecrated. There was safety for no one in Bengal or the Punjab and no safety for the Muslim in Bihar or the Hindu in Sindh or the North-Western Frontier. This was truly not the freedom that Gandhiji wanted. He pleaded with the Hindus, being an austere, an ascetic Hindu himself.

And in the middle of these orgiastic killings a drama within drama was happening—Gandhiji began to ask himself whether he had, in truth, achieved *brahmacharya*. Had he? To achieve Indian freedom was one thing. To achieve true freedom, the sway over self, Swaraj, the highest freedom. Had he achieved celibacy? No. It was time to test. And with his usual experimental temper and his scrupulous adherence to truth, he asked one of the young married women among his followers whether she would sleep, in the same bed, with him. Yes, she would. And day after day he slept in the same bed with her, she, young, desirable and submissive. And he discovered much to his astonishment and joy, he had no inkling whatsoever to possess this bounty beside him. *Brahmacharya* was at last achieved. Truly it had been. And so should freedom be. India could now be free. He wanted immediately to tell the whole world about it. He, the great Mahatma, who was quelling those gigantic massacres of India, he who was worshipped a saint—and indeed often as an *avatara,* an incarnation of God—by many millions of Indians, in fact by hundreds of millions of Indians, was going to tell the whole round world, *brahmacharya* indeed is real and achievable. It is absolute. One can therefore conquer one's senses. Thus one could wholly be true. He wrote an article on this subject for *Harijan*—his weekly paper. But when the government of Nehru heard of it all, they begged him not to publish the article—for said they this would damage his figure in the eyes of India, and especially now in an India torn asunder by such deadly conflict. He did not care. A satyagrahi always stands by his truth. Truth was more important to Gandhiji than accommodation with contingent realities. Truth alone conquers.

However he agreed to keep silent for the moment. But one of his fervent followers took it on his conscience to read the manuscript, and then saintly and horrified, he threw it into the fire. Thus Gandhism was saved from Gandhi. The inquisitor wins—or thinks he does. And Gandhiji continued his march of love.

* * *

Over bamboo bridges and on boats he went along the estuary of the Ganges, alone amongst the Muslims, to give courage to the Hindus—he would chant his Hindu mantras and listen to the Muslim prayers,

> *Ishwara Allah Tere Nam*
> *Ishwara Allah Thy name*

and it worked miracles in the rich and once fair land of Bengal. Peace began to come, yes it came slowly. Then Delhi wanted him, for the seven million Hindu refugees pouring into India from Pakistan brought nothing but stories of dire disaster. One could bear this killing no more. Muslims were baited and killed, their mosques occupied and their houses filled with pouring refugees. He preached, did Gandhiji, love and love again to the Hindus. But they seemed not to listen. Now there was only one thing to do. He would fast unto death. Yes, death were better than this spectacle of desecration. And he started to fast. The Hindus of Delhi began to give back the mosques and the houses to the Muslims. Azad and Nehru, Mountbatten and Lady Mountbatten, Sardar Patel and Rajagopalachari, ran from one area of disaster to the other to protect human lives in thousands, by train, jeep or helicopter. Finally when the Hindus began to quieten down and listen, the Hindus and Muslims signed a pact of friendship with one another, and the Indian Government that had refused to give to Pakistan the money she owed her, that she would now, angry Nehru would now, give back that money come what may, a promise made is to be reverenced if you are a satyagrahi—thus when truth seemed to prevail, Gandhiji took, amidst prayers and tears, his first glass of orange juice. Azad, the Muslim scholar and Congress President, gave it to him. But a fanatic Hindu, proud of his heritage, was waiting beneath the wall. He could not bear this love-love business any longer. A bomb was thrown at Gandhiji. He would not care. He had said death was sweet. He wanted no protection from the police. He had God's protection.

One day, however, on 30 January 1948, when he was walking down, still weak from his fast, to the prayer garden, Godse, a young Indian, knelt in worship to this great man, and shot him dead. Gandhiji's face seemed sweet and holy at death. And three million people accompanied him to his pyre. The last British Viceroy squatted on the ground with his spouse, Nehru beside them, looking at the playfulness of this all-consuming pyre. Death is beautiful when the body is become ash. A palmful of this ash was given in ceremony and chant to each of the Indian rivers, and they took his remains down to the open sea. The oceans touch the round rounding of this revolving earth.

People all over the world broke down when they heard of this—peasants and workers who'd never known who he was but only what he was, so said Léon Blum. Einstein remarked he could not believe that such a one had ever walked on this, our earth. And Smuts, his old friend, said a prince among men had passed away. Satyagraha had indeed won.

Chronology

1757	Battle of Plassey. Beginning of the establishment of British rule in the subcontinent of India.
1795	Cape (South Africa) occupied by the British because of its strategic position, being on the route to India.
1806	Cape taken over by the British, completely.
1847	Karamchand Gandhi becomes Prime Minister of Porbandar.
1869	(2 October) Mohandas Karamchand Gandhi born in Porbandar.
1874	Karamchand Gandhi appointed Karbari of Rajkot with limited powers.
1876	Karamchand Gandhi becomes Dewan of Rajkot, with full powers.
1879	Mohandas Gandhi enters Taluk School, Rajkot.
1880	Becomes a student at Alfred High School.
1882	Marries Kasturba Makanji, daughter of Gokaldas Makanji of Porbandar.
1885	Death of Karamchand Gandhi.
1888	Birth of Gandhiji's eldest son, Harilal. Gandhiji sails for London. Is admitted to the Inner Temple.
1889	Meets Madame Blavatsky and Annie Besant.
1890	Member of the Executive Society of the London Vegetarian Society. Starts living on £1 a week.

1891   Called to the Bar.

Leaves for India.

(12 June) Meets Rajachandra in Bombay.

1892   Starts working as a barrister in Kathiawar.

Birth of Manilal, the second son.

1893   Sails for South Africa.

The dramatic experience of Pietermaritzburg.

Experiments on Vital Foods.

Writes to Rajachandra.

1894   Decides to stay back in South Africa, and to fight for the cause of the Indians settled there.

Founds the Natal Indian Congress.

1895   Argues in the press, and in public, on behalf of the Indians in South Africa.

1896   Returns to India.

Publishes the 'Green Pamphlet'.

Addresses meetings all over India.

Called back to South Africa. The family accompanies him.

1897   Landing in Durban. A mob attacks him.

Presents Petition to the Natal Legislature against anti-Indian Bills.

Birth of his third son, Ramdas.

1898   Fights against Indians being confined to 'Locations'.

1899   The Boer War breaks out.

Organises the Indian Ambulance Corps.

1900   Indian Ambulance Corps on the battlefield.

Devadas Gandhi, the fourth son, born.

1901   Death of Queen Victoria. Gandhiji addresses a Memorial meeting. Congratulates the British Government on its victory in the Boer War.

Felicitates the Sultan of Turkey on the Silver Jubilee of his reign. Attends Indian National Congress Session in Calcutta.

1902   Practices law in Rajkot.

Moves on to Bombay to set up practice there.

Returns to South Africa, without his family.

1903 Settles in Johannesburg, opening a law office.
Indian Opinion founded.

1904 Plague in Johannesburg.
Reads Ruskin, *Unto This Last*.
Presents Address to Lord Roberts.
Phoenix Settlement founded.

1905 Lectures on Hindu religion.
Tries to learn Tamil.
Sails for England on Deputation. Meets the Prime Minister.
Talks with Winston Churchill.

1907 Asiatic Registration Bill passed by the Transvaal Parliament.
Mass meetings held against the Bill.
Voluntary Registration offered.

1908 Sentenced to two months' imprisonment.
Released on coming to an understanding with Smuts about voluntary registration.
Wounded by Mir Alam.
Burning of Registration Cards.
Arrested and sentenced to two months' hard labour.

1909 Arrested and sentenced to three months' imprisonment.
Released.

1909 Sails for England.
Meets ministers in London.
Returns to South Africa and writes *Hind Swaraj* on board the ship.

1910 Death of Edward VII.
Tolstoy declares the importance of passive resistance for all humanity.
Kallenbach offers his farm near Lawley, which becomes the Tolstoy Farm.
Passive resisters deported back to India.
Smuts promises a liberal immigration policy for the Indians in the whole of South Africa.

1911   Smuts talks of Indian civilisation to the Parliament.

New Immigration Bill presented.

Government of India prohibits further recruitment of indentured labour for South Africa.

Provisional Settlement arrived at between Smuts and Gandhiji.

Coronation of King George V at Westminster Abbey.

1912   Gokhale in South Africa.

1913   Supreme Court decision against the validity of Indian marriages.

Immigration Restrictions Bill published in *Gazette Extraordinary.*

Kasturba decides to join the struggle.

Immigration Regulation Bill passed.

Railway strike in South Africa. 'In accordance with Smuts' wish refrained from taking action because of the unexpected troubles of the Government.'

Decision finally to resume passive resistance.

Women join the movement. Workers strike in Natal coalfields.

Gandhiji leads the Pilgrims on the Great March, from Natal to the Transvaal.

General uprising of workers all over Transvaal and Natal.

Government of India intervenes. Sends negotiator.

Andrews and Pearson arrive.

1914   Passive resistance suspended.

Kasturba ill.

Passing of Indian Relief Bill.

Leaves South Africa for England.

1915   Returns to India.

1917   Champaran Inquiry.

1919   Amritsar Massacre at Jallianwala Bagh.

1921   Visit of the Prince of Wales to India.

1922   Chauri Chaura.

1922	Arrested and given six years' imprisonment.

1922   Arrested and given six years' imprisonment.

1924   Released and fasts for Hindu-Muslim unity.

1928   Bardoli no-tax campaign.

1930   (26 January) Declaration of Indian Independence.
        The Salt March to Dandi.
        Arrested and jailed.

1931   Released.

1932   Arrested. Fasts unto death if untouchables given separate electorates by the British Government.

1933   Self-purification fast.

1937   Congress accepts office under the system of Dyarchy.

1939   Gandhiji writes to Hitler. Letter not delivered.

1940   Personal Disobedience campaign.

1942   'Quit India' resolution passed by the Congress.
        Arrested and imprisoned.

1943   Twenty-one-day fast.

1944   Death of Kasturba.
        Released from jail.

1945   British willingness to talk.
        The Simla Conference.

1946   Calcutta riots.

1947   Mountbatten appointed Viceroy of India.
        (15 August) India and Pakistan declared independent Dominions.
        Fasts to stop riots.

1948   Fast for communal unity.
        (30 January) Shot and killed by Godse.

Glossary and Notes

A

Ahuramazda. The Illuminated One or the Principle of Light in (Parsi) Zoroastrian religion.

anekatwa. A Jaina philosophic concept which believes that manynesses of an object that is seen from many points of view, and at least six according to some texts, does not prove the existence of an object.

arathi. The sacred adoration of a god or of a sanctified person or persons—the ritual consisting of offering *kumkum*-water, flowers, and a sacred lamp.

B

Banias, Modhi. A community of Gujarat belonging to the merchant (or business) caste.

bhajans. Devotional songs.

Bhakthi Marga. The way of devotion through the worship of a personal God.

Bharata. The founder of one of the first Aryan tribes settled in India. India in the ancient texts is called Bharata Varsha or the Land of Bharata.

Birdwood, Sir George (1832-1917). Served first in the Indian Medical Service. Later worked in the India Office in London and published various works of historical importance, like The Miscellaneous Records of the India Office. He also published the famous, almost encyclopaedic, work, *The Industrial Arts of India.*

Bose, Subhas Chandra. The most famous Indian leader after Gandhi and Nehru. More traditional in his perspective than Nehru—he was more a nationalist than a socialist—he was also more revolutionary, in the sense that he did not accept either the philosophy or the technique of nonviolence. He left India during the early years of the Second World War, for Germany first and then to Japan, so as to be able to organise a National Liberation Army of Indians to conquer India. He died in a plane crash towards the end of the hostilities.

brahmacharya. The vow of celibacy. It is also the name given to the first stage among the four stages of human existence—it being the stage of the adolescent. Literally, *brahmacharya,* the path to Brahman.

C

chaturmas. Literally 'Four Months'. A sort of Lent which might include one day—or several days—fasting.

D

dasyus. Men of the darker inhabitants of India before the Aryan invasion. Perhaps the Dasyus were the Dravidians. This was anywhere before 1200 BC and 4500 BC.

dharma-patni. Wife; sharer of the dharma with her husband.

darshan. Vision of a holy or dear one. The look of a holy one (or looking at a holy being) is supposed to have the power to transform the life of ordinary men radically.

Devaki. Mother of Sri Krishna. She is the wife of Vasudeva and daughter of Devaka.

Dharma. The Law or the Principle that upholds, sustains, the universe—hence applies universally to each class of its constituents.

Doukhobors. A Christian sect in Russia which believed in non-violence. They were persecuted by the Tzars and Tolstoy took their defence. They finally migrated to Canada.

E

ekadashi. The eleventh day of the lunar fortnight on which Hindus usually fast.

F

fakir. A Muslim mendicant.

G

Gandhi, Chhaganlal. A nephew of Mahatma Gandhi.
Gandhi, Jamnalal. A nephew of Mahatma Gandhi.

H

Hunter, Sir William (1840-1900). A very distinguished member of the British Civil Service in India for almost twenty-five years. He is famous for editing *The Imperial Gazetteer of India,* an incomparable encyclopaedia of information on the country from geology and fauna and flora to history, and then the various castes and communities, their peculiar traditions etc., etc. He also wrote a standard book of history: *Indian Empire.* He influenced Indian policy by writing on Indian affairs for the *Times* (London).

J

Jameson Raid. An abortive attempt, in December 1895, led from the Cape Colony by Dr. Jameson, Administrator of British South Africa company, to annex the Transvaal by taking advantage of a projected Uitlander uprising which did not materialise. Jameson was captured, tried and convicted. The Raid, and the failure of the British Government to repudiate it unequivocally, were among the causes that led to the Boer War.

Joshiji. Usually a family chaplain and astrologer who fixes the horoscope of important events as births, initiation-ceremonies, death, and anniversaries. He often gives advice to people on what line of action has to be in a certain situation from the point of view of the stars or of the dharma shastras, the laws that bind the community according to a particular text.

jowar. A form of Indian corn.

K

Kaffirs. A generic name given to the native population of South Africa. In Arabic it means the unbelievers, the heathens.

katha. The story of some god or goddess told in extempore composition, often in verse form, with prose explanations. Generally it may go on for several hours in the evening, and often late into the night.

M

Mahabharata.

The great epic consisting of over 90,000 verses thus making it perhaps the longest poem of the world. Like the *Ramayana*, it also is of unknown date and is believed to have been composed by the sage, Vyasa.

The *Mahabharata*, like all Indian epics, is a story within a story, and this story again placed in another tale, so that they go from one episode to the other, containing not only descriptions of births, initiation ceremonies, family quarrels, marriages, battles, and the peace after war, but also great expositions of philosophy which explain each episode, its origins and ends, and its ultimate meaning. The great Indian scripture, the *Bhagavad Gita*, is one of the famous chapters of the *Mahabharata*, where Sri Krishna, the Guru, the Prince, gives metaphysical and moral advice to his friend and cousin Arjuna about the ways of liberation *(moksha)*.

The main theme of the *Mahabharata*, as of the *Ramayana*, is to tell people how each one should perform his dharma, his vocation. Action is natural to man, and the dharma of each caste is according to its own place in a composite society. Thus a warrior has to make war and kill if necessary, after having tried every other means of achieving peace without violence, but if violence is the only way, the violence must be. A war thus fought could not be for the ego but rather for the performance of one's dharma. One who is established in the Truth—and here Sri Krishna, the Guru, gave Arjuna an exposition of, and initiation to, the Truth—well, one who knows there is no ego can kill and be killed knowing the ego is only *Maya,* a phantasmagoria. Thus the *Mahabharata* describes a battle where in fact there was no battle—who can go to war against whom[6] when there is no one, for all is the Truth. Action is a means to actionlessness. Rather to see 'action in inaction and inaction in action' is the true meaning of the *Bhagavad Gita,* and so of the *Mahabharata.*

Specifically, the *Mahabharata* talks of the quarrel between the cousins, the Pandavas and the Kauravas. The fact of the fact was, the right heir to the throne Bhishma, when he realised he had half-brothers who being born of non-royal mothers could never become kings and princess, took a vow of *brahmacharya* (celibacy). First Chitrangada became king, then his brother Vichitravirya. But he, too, died soon. Now Dhritarashtra became the eldest heir to the kingdom but he was blind and so his younger brother Pandu became king. (Hence, the Pandavas, the sons of Pandu.) The father of the Pandavas, on his turn dying, Dhritarashtra was made king, with half the kingdom; the other half going to the Pandava brothers. Dhritarashtra's sons, the Kauravas, however, with Duryodhana the eldest-born as leader, plotted against their cousins, the Pandavas, so that the whole

---

6 Mahatma Gandhi read the *Gita* as a symbolic poem, and said the war spoken of here, is a war within oneself only. There is also such a tradition, one among other traditions.

kingdom could be theirs. Dharmaraja (Prince of Dharma), the eldest among the Pandavas, though he was a man of great virtue, had one weakness, he loved dice.

In a tricky game that his cousins played with him he lost his kingdom and finally he was so enticed into staking everything to gain all, he lost even his wife, Draupadi. So what now remained was only exile: twelve years anywhere and a thirteenth where nobody will know them, recognise them. The thirteen years were soon over (filled with many adventures of wisdom and irrationality) and ultimately when they returned to ask back their kingdom, Duryodhana would not hear of parting with what was not his. Krishna, their close kinsman, pleaded with the sons of Dhritarashtra, the Kauravas, but who was there to listen? So the war had to be.

Krishna was Arjuna's charioteer and counsellor and Bhishma the grandsire, the terrible, the celibate, on the opposite side, the commander-in-chief of the Kauravas armies. And Bhishma reminded the Kauravas, 'Know where Krishna is, Victory is'. But who would listen to whom in the heat of passion?

Thus the great eighteen-day war in which mighty armies were assembled on either side, but as in all wars there was an absurd situation, for, Bhishma, the grandsire of the Kauravas and the Pandavas, was not only the head of the Kaurava armies, but was a devotee of Krishna, and Krishna was Arjuna's charioteer. So that when the battle was on the point of beginning, the Pandavas suddenly stayed it for a while that they could go and seek the benediction of their elder, the grandsire, Bhishma, and Bhishma on the field of battle blessed the adversaries that they should win the battle; he would not fight for them, for he was by right and duty the commander-in-chief of the Kauravas. And again what could be more glorious than that he should be killed before the eyes of Krishna, perhaps by Krishna himself? It would indeed be the most beautiful of deaths and the means of his true liberation.

There was further another drama within this drama. Karna, the next great hero of the Kauravas, unknown to anyone except to his mother, of course, was half-brother of the Pandavas. Thus indeed brothers faced brothers, the elders faced elders, and behind it all the wives and mothers of the heroes lamenting the tragedy that they could not prevent happening. Ultimately Bhishma is deeply wounded and lies on the field of battle, thirsty and unable to move. The Pandava heroes stop the war and bring him water to drink, after which the battle is as fierce as ever, and when all the Kauravas are dead on the field of battle (the Kurukshetra) there rises the lamentation of Queen Gandhari, Mother of the Kaurava heroes.

Dharmaraja is finally crowned king. He had no heart to rule so desolate a state. However, Krishna himself would crown him king. But as the coronation is just finished, one knows Bhishma the great hero is still lying on the field of battles, on his bed of arrows, contemplating his Krishna. The Pandavas rush with Krishna to the revered elder. There, Bhishma declares: 'Obeisance to the great dharma . . . Death through dharma is better than victory through a sinful act. Truth is the Godhead, Truth is penance . . . The secret of the Veda is Truth; of Truth self-control, release from bondage: this is the all-comprehensive gospel.' And after giving this advice to Dharmaraja, he added: 'King, go to your city, let your mind be set on dharma.' And when the time came for Bhishma to leave his body, surrounded by all his kinsmen he declared: 'I desire to give up my life now. You will give me leave. You must strive for Truth; Truth is the greatest strength.' Thus passed away the great hero, the celibate, the compassionate, the Krishna-devoted Bhishma.

Dharmaraja ruled his kingdom for the time it was strictly necessary to put the country in order. Then he retired to the

Himalaya and gave up his life. 'Bathing then in the sacred and the sanctifying celestial river, the Ganges, that is lauded by the sages, Dharmaraja cast off his mortal frame.'

And Sri Krishna went back to where he came from—but of course there is neither coming nor going for him. Where can the Truth go when there is nowhere?

Pandavas. Sons of King Pandu; Dharmaraja (Yudhishthira), Bhima, Arjuna, Nakula and Sahadeva.

Kauravas. Sons of King Dhritarashtra, legendarily one hundred, with Duryodhana, the eldest, and his evil counsellor and younger brother, Dushasana.

Duryodhana. The eldest son of Dhritarashtra, the evil genius of the Kauravas. Jealous and fierce, he wanted everything and was willing to fight for everything. He was the main figure urging everyone towards the war—the Mahabharata war.

Dharmaraja. Also called Yudhishthira, the eldest son of Pandu. He was just and true, unwilling to commit the smallest non-dharmic act. He resembles in many ways Sri Rama of the *Ramayana*.

Arjuna. The third son of Pandu—he the natural man with all his contradictions—heroic and confused, compassionate and sensuous, unable to make up his mind as to what course of action to take in any given predicament. For example, should one fight against cousins and kinsmen, is war worth all this massacre? But Krishna knows Arjuna's weakness. And to give him (and the world) a guide to pure action, Krishna gives him the gift of the *Bhagavad Gita* (the Holy Song), perhaps the greatest guide to metaphysical living.

Sri Krishna. The Guru, the visible embodiment of Truth. The Principle that awaits to help the sincere creature, wheresoever he might be, who in his helplessness seeks the ultimate light. And as it happens, again and again in life, and is the main theme of most Indian texts, the Guru being the Principle, knows suffering everywhere and his 'birth' (Truth has no birth, but this is only a way of saying it) is set in such a manner that all event and history seem to be patterned for a metaphysical drama. Hence Krishna the prince, and cousin to the Pandavas, who after having conquered, while still young, many evil forces, monsters and giant men, and having dallied and danced with young maids on the banks of the River Jumna, finally becomes the king of the Vrishnis, with Dwaraka as the capital, Dwaraka on the Cambay Sea. He, later, comes to the aid of the Pandavas when he saw there was going to be confusion and war. He established dharma, and when the time came, just disappeared. (He had himself killed, in a seeming accident by a hunter taking him to be a deer.) The beauty of Krishna is the play of Truth, the *Krishna-lila*. What is obstacle to the ego, is just the thin thread by which you escape from the mesh of life—to Truth.

Bhima. Second son of Pandu, Bhima, the angry prince, mighty in power, and ever ready for a good fight. He is constantly controlled by his eldest brother Dharmaraja, for without this moral intervention Bhima would have destroyed anyone he disapproved of. And he disapproved of many. He was simple, fierce and true.

Bhishma. Son of King Santanu and Ganga, perhaps the most beautiful figure, after Sri Krishna, in the whole of the *Mahabharata*. Bhishma's vow of celibacy seems to have given him inner power, both of vision and of surrender, so that he is not concerned with himself but with what is right, right in terms of dharma. Again and again he moves us by his loyalty to dharma, by his clear relationship with the others, and dies on the field of battle perhaps the most compassionate hero of any epic in the world.

Dhritarashtra. The poor blind king, elder brother of Pandu, Dhritarashtra the weak, the confused, who could not rule his kingdom, not his kinsmen, nor give up his human vanities. A pathetic prince led by his evil son Duryodhana, to immoral adventures, and yet he had nothing but affection towards the Pandavas, the sons of his brother. Gandhari, Dhritarashtra's obstinate wife did not help him either— often she seemed to waver, like him, between duty and attachments. After defeat they went into a forest-retirement, and died there consumed by a jungle-conflagration.

Pandu. Son of King Vichitravirya. Pandu marries Kunti, aunt of Sri Krishna. It is through Kunti's yogic power that she gave her husband three sons—Dharmaraja the eldest, Bhima the second, and finally Arjuna—'equal to Shiva in valour'. Through his second wife, Madri, Pandu had two sons, Nakula the beautiful and Sahadeva, the scholar. 'Once in springtime when forests were in full bloom and (all) beings were entranced, King Pandu wandered in the forest with his wife (Madri). Wearing bright attire, Madri, herself alone, was following him. The king then seized her forcibly . . . Uniting with her, Pandu died,' Soon after which, mounting her husband's pyre, Madri burnt herself alive.

Karna. Son of Kunti. Before being married to Pandu, the Sun-god gave Kunti the gift of Karna, so he was virgin-born. Abandoned by her on a river he was brought up by a charioteer, and ultimately became king of Anga, helped by Duryodhana. An excellent archer, he was Arjuna's (his half-brother) natural rival. Karna was generous and very brave, but he suffered from a curious divine malediction. So that when after the defeat of Bhishma and Drona he became

the commander-in-chief of the Kauravas, his chariot got
stuck in thick mud, and so could not move, and died thus.
'When Karna son of the Sun-god had been killed, the fear-
stricken Kauravas, turned to all the quarters and fled in
their thousands.'

Draupadi. Daughter of Drupada, King of the Panchalas, and
later queen of the Pandava brothers, though true wife only
to one. She was won-by Arjuna at her *svayamvara* (a women
selecting a husband of her own choice) ceremony, and when
he and his brother returned home, they told their mother
that they had that day made a great acquisition. Wherefore
the mother said, Children divide it among yourselves. As
the words once uttered could not be changed, she became
the common wife of the five brothers. She was however
true wife to Arjuna, who had won her. She was a dutiful
and understanding wife, and later a noble widow. She is to
this day considered among the five holy-wives, worshipped
by women that they too may thus be made devoted, and
true wives to their lords. Sri Krishna himself had promised
to avenge the humiliation she had undergone soon after
the dice game was lost by the Pandavas. Hence Krishna,
who after trying every peaceful method of resolving the
differences, had to advise war till the wrongs inflicted on
Draupadi be avenged, and she would not do her hair till
victory was won.

Dushasana. The evil brother of Duryodhana.

Drona. The great teacher of archery, and a sage. He fought, like
Bhishma—and for the same reasons—with the Kauravas,
and when Bhishma fell, Drona succeeded him as chief of
the Kaurava forces, and died fighting valiantly. Now it was
Karna who succeeded him as head of the Kaurava army.
Drona himself was the son of Bharadwaja, the great sage.

Manes. The psychic remains of a dead person, sometimes also the soul of the dead.

Megasthenes. Ambassador of the Greek King Seleucas Nikator to the court of Chandragupta Maurya. He has left one of the first documents we have on the conditions of government and of society in Ancient India.

P

Pan. The betel leaf which is eaten with the areca-nut—a mouth perfumer and digestive.

Parsis. A community that escaped from Iran and came to India because of the persecution they suffered from the Arab and Islamic invaders. They were welcomed to India, and permitted to practise their religion as they wished.

prasada. The fruit, flower, or any food, that is first offered to the Gods or the Guru, and then sanctified thus is distributed to worshippers or disciples as adornment if flower, or to be eaten if food.

Prahlada. A legendary boy-hero whose faith in his god was such that it created the intense jealousy, and then hatred, of his self-opinionated father. The father made the boy drink poison which had no effect on Prahlada—the father had him thrown down the mountain and he stood up unhurt, and the elephant sent to kill him bent low in homage to this god-intoxicated boy. Finally challenged by the father who said, 'If your god is everywhere, is he then in this palace pillar?' when out of the pillar came God (in his Lion-incarnation, Narasimha) and tore the bowels of the torturer father.

R

Ramachandra Maharaj ki jai. Ramachandra or the Moon-Rama, the beautiful Rama, a familiar name with which Sri Rama is called. Maharaj means king, a shortened form of Maharaja. *Jai* means victorious. The whole cry means. Victory to the King, the Moon Rama.

Ramakrishna (1836-86). The great Indian saint, who had his ashram
(monastery) near Calcutta. He was perhaps the greatest of the
nineteenth-century saints, and without his influence there would
be no modern India.

Rana. A minor king or nobleman.

Ramayana

The famous Indian epic of unknown date composed by the
great sage Valmiki. The epic tells the story of Rama, son of King
Dasaratha of Kosala (and whose capital was Ayodhya)—Rama
while even a boy having shown unusual prowess was sent by his
father on a royal expedition to kill monsters that were worrying
ascetics and sages (living in the forests and merged in deep
meditation). After the destruction of the monsters Sri Rama
was taken by his preceptor to a bride-winning competition
(*swayamvara*) where he broke the bow, and won Sita, daughter
of the wise king Janaka of Videha. Sita and Rama came back
to Ayodhya, and while Dasaratha was contemplating having Sri
Rama crowned king, one of Dasaratha's wives, Kaikeyi, wanted
her own son Bharata on the throne. And because the king had
given her a promise in another life that whatsoever she asked for
she would be given, Bharatha had now to be crowned king, and
so Sri Rama and his half-brother Lakshmana, and the Princess
Sita, had to go on an extended exile of fourteen years. Dasaratha,
soon after, however, died broken-hearted. (This was as we now
know, because of the curse of Sravana.) And while Sri Rama
lived in exile Bharata ruled the country in the name of Sri Rama,
the sandals of the brother upon the throne.

Sri Rama, Sita Devi and Lakshmana wandered from the
plains again, living on roots and shrubs, visiting the hermitages
of ascetics and the wise, befriended by animals, tribal chiefs and
kings, till they came to the great forests of Dandaka where they
settled for a long, long while. Ravana, the king of Lanka (Ceylon),

however, was deeply in love with Sita, and while Sri Rama and Lakshmana were away hunting, Ravana abducted Sita, and took her away to his island kingdom of Lanka in an aerial chariot. Sita was Ravana's prisoner but he could never touch her, such the fire of her devotion to her Lord, Sri Rama. When Ravana thought of Sri Rama, he himself became a devotee. And pray how could he think of Sita without thinking of Sri Rama?

Meanwhile, Sri Rama and Lakshmana, helped by the monkeys and the animals of the wild, and even by the birds and squirrels, built a bridge across the waters to the island of Lanka, killed Ravana, giving him liberation from birth and death (*samsara*), after which Sri Rama with Sita Devi and brother Lakshmana, accompanied by the monkey devotee Hanuman, flew back to Ayodhya in an aerial chariot of flowers. And the holy couple ruled Ayodhya for many happy decades and the world shone with their unearthly glory. Thus, *Rama Rajya*, the happy kingdom of Sri Rama.

Bharata. Devoted half-brother of Sri Rama, born to the same father but to different mother. The devotion of Bharata to Sri Rama is one of the most moving aspects of the *Ramayana*.

Lakshmana. Faithful half-brother of Sri Rama who accompanied his elder brother and sister-in-law in exile.

Sita. The wife of Sri Rama who preferred to follow her husband in exile through forest and desert wilds than live behind in the comforts of her father-in-law's (or father's) court. Later, according to another version of the *Ramayana*, Sita herself (after their return from Lanka) was sent away on exile by her loving husband, because his subjects were suspicious that she, their Queen, having been a prisoner of Ravana might have been unable to keep her virtue straight. Rama loved her deeply and knew the gossip was baseless, but obeying his dharma, and knowing the welfare of his subjects was the most sacred aspect of his kingship, had to send his wife away on cruel exile. Yet she felt he must have done it in the fullness of his love, and indeed this was so, for while Sri Rama ruled the kingdom a gold image of Sita stood beside him, anointing the acts of his kingship with her presence. Remember, it's she the queen who hears the plaints and sorrows of her people, and it's because she pleads that the king rules not only with justice but with compassion. If woman were not would man know the sorrows of others? Later, so the story goes, Rama and Sita were reunited.

Hanuman. The gods and demigods thus consorted that finally when the battle came, Rama would have the necessary army to conquer Lanka, kill Ravana and free Sita. Hanuman was one of those monkey-gods born specifically for this historic achievement. Hanuman himself was the son of the God of the Winds, hence called Maruti, and could take great leaps into the air. He finally visited Sita in exile with a message from Sri Rama, and set fire to the city of Lanka with his flaming tail. On return to Ayodhya he remained the faithful servant of Sri Rama, and consoled the poor and lowly with care and love. And it's said wheresoever the *Ramayana* is recited he, the eternal devotee of Rama, Hanuman, is present.

Ravana. The monster king of Lanka. In a previous life he had performed great austerities to have the benediction of Shiva and won such powers that he almost toppled the earth, but Shiva stabilised it with just the tip of his toe. Ravana, however, only wanted liberation (*moksha*) and as quickly as possible. But Shiva begged him to be patient, and promised that in ten lives he would attain liberation. Ravana preferred to have one terrible life and be done with the cycle of birth and death, forever. Thus was Ravana born a monster with ten heads (and according to certain traditions), Shiva himself was born to destroy Ravana—hence the incarnation of Sri Rama. (According to another tradition, it was Vishnu who was born at the request of Shiva, as Sri Rama.) All this, as one sees, is a grand game of the gods, for the liberation of the ego from its illusions (Maya). The sages and the gods use every means to help man attain liberation, the true aim of man.

S

samsara. The cycle of birth and death, or just the human condition through birth and rebirth.

samskaras. Tendencies of another life, which condition our way of acting and reacting to the various aspects of our existence today.

shamiana. A large tent meant to shelter people attending a civil or religious ceremony.

T

Thakore Sahib. The great Lord, meaning, sometimes, Sri Krishna.

Thakur. A nobleman, and sometimes, a Prince.

Talukdar (**Collector**). The Administrator of a Borough (Taluk), a small but powerful official. Talukdars usually rode horses or travelled by box-carriages, a two-wheeled closed-vehicle with colourful windows and drawn by one or two horses.

tamasha. An assembly, gathered for a show.

U

Ujjain. The legendary political and cultural capital of India (in Central India) associated in tradition with the great Emperor Vikramaditya and his celebrated court, to which belonged Kalidasa, India's greatest poet.

V

Vasistha. One of the seven sages, and Guru of Sri Rama, hence the famous text, the *Yoga Vasistha*, being the philosophical discourses given by Vasistha to Sri Rama on the Nature of Truth.

Vishwamitra. One of the great sages of the Indian tradition, being already a famous seer in the *Rig Veda*, many of the hymns in that text being attributed to him. A Kshatriya (or of the warrior caste) but because of his spiritual austerities he becomes a Brahmin. He is the rival of Vasistha, a rivalry which is never serious, for both being sages, they play a game for the sake of uplifting humanity from level to level of spiritual awareness.

Vaishnava. Of the religion of Vishnu, one of the aspects of the Trinity: Brahma, Vishnu, Shiva. Vishnu is the enjoyer and preserver (Brahma and Shiva being, respectively, the Creator and Destroyer). Vishnu had many incarnations. Nine so far, the tenth is the one to be. The last incarnation being that as Gautama, the Buddha.

vakil. A minor country-lawyer who can only plead in borough or district courts but never at the level of the High Court because he has only a diploma in law and not a degree from a university.

Y

Yama. The God of Death, but also a wise God, for in the Upanishads it's he who gives Nachiketas a famous and long discourse on the nature of Truth.

yogic. From Yoga, which through subtle gesture and sound symbols and various controls of body and breath takes you to subtler forms of mental, and then psychic experiences, preparing one for initiation into *Jnana* or Knowledge which dissolves all illusion.